Here's what reviewers are saying about *Inside ASP.NET*:

"*Inside ASP.NET* provides readers with an in-depth look at building ASP.NET applications using pratical examples and 'real world' analogies. Scott has a way of breaking down complex technical ideas so that experts don't feel like they are being talked down to, but beginners can grasp them too."

—**Alex Lowe,** *Technical Director Analysts International (Sequoia Services Group), AspFriends.com Moderator/Contributor*

"This book is easily the peer of any currently available books on ASP.NET, and superior to most in scope, organization, detail and practical examples. It does an excellent job of answering questions that smart developers need to know in order to become quickly productive in the ASP.NET environment."

—**Joel Mueller,** *author, Senior Engineer, DeLani Technologies, LLC*

"This is the best book that I've seen on ASP.NET. It is perfectly organized and written very clearly...It contains real world samples and real world solutions for some of the most common problems."

—**Andrey Kruchkov,** *Quarta Technologies—Microsoft Gold Certified Partner in E-Commerce*

Inside ASP.NET

Contents at a Glance

Inside ASP.NET

Scott Worley

New Riders

www.newriders.com

201 West 103rd Street, Indianapolis, Indiana 46290
An Imprint of Pearson Education
Boston • Indianapolis • London • Munich • New York • San Francisco

Inside ASP.NET

International Standard Book Number: 0-7357-1135-6

Library of Congress Catalog Card Number: 2001087699

06 05 04 03 02   7 6 5 4 3 2 1

Interpretation of the printing code: The rightmost double-digit number is the year of the book's printing; the rightmost single-digit number is the number of the book's printing. For example, the printing code 02-1 shows that the first printing of the book occurred in 2002.

Composed in Bembo and MCPdigital by New Riders Publishing.

Printed in the United States of America.

Trademarks

Warning and Disclaimer

Publisher
David Dwyer

Associate Publisher
Stephanie Wall

Production Manager
Gina Kanouse

Managing Editor
Kristy Knoop

Product Marketing Manager
Stephanie Layton

Publicity Manager
Susan Nixon

Acquisitions Editor
Deborah Hittel-Shoaf

Senior Development Editor
Lisa Thibault

Project Editor
Suzanne Pettypiece

Copy Editors
Jill Batistick
Sarah Cisco
Anne McGrath

Indexer
Brad Herriman

Manufacturing Coordinator
Jim Conway

Book Designer
Louisa Klucznik

Cover Designer
Aren Howell

Proofreader
Debbie Williams

Composition
Gina Rexrode

I would like to dedicate this book to my wife, who some how managed to put up with my cursing, yelling, screaming, and acting like a child at the most inopportune times.

This book is dedicated to a man, without whom I would not be writing this book. It is only because Peter Raistrick (Managing Director of Competec [South Yorkshire] Ltd, England), my first mentor in IT, who took a chance on an arrogant, cheeky, and somewhat ambitious youth some 11 years ago by giving me the opportunity to get somewhere in the IT industry. So thank you Peter, for all you did, and still do.

Scott Worley, still arrogant, cheeky, and ambitious, but somewhat older.

❖

TABLE OF CONTENTS

About the Author

Scott Worley is a freelance IT consultant specializing in Microsoft-based technologies and SDLC project management. During the past 10 years, he has worked on many leading-edge development projects, utilizing the latest technologies. Scott is currently focusing all of his attention on the .NET framework and associated technologies, paying specific attention to ASP.NET and distributed web development.

Contributing Authors

Ron Buckton has been an information technology professional for five years, working as both a network operations resource and a web application developer. For the last two years, he has been involved with numerous web projects using Microsoft Active Server Pages (ASP) and Microsoft Visual Studio. Most recently, he has been involved with research and development using the Microsoft ASP.NET framework. Ron currently lives in Southwestern, Pennsylvania with his wife Lindsey.

Ken Cox is a technical writer and web applications programmer in Toronto. After receiving his bachelor's degree in radio and television arts from Ryerson Polytechnical University, he started work in radio. He was a journalist for 20 years for top-rated radio stations and news networks in Toronto and Montreal. During that time, he spent seven years as a correspondent in Quebec City. Computers were only his hobby when Microsoft invited Ken into the beta test for a new product code-named "Denali"——later known as Active Server Pages (ASP). To pursue his passion for things hi-tech, Ken earned a college certificate in Technical Communications and began a second career as a technical writer for Toronto-area companies that included Nortel Networks. Thanks to his grounding in Internet technologies, Ken found himself in demand as a writer and technical reviewer of books and magazine articles on ASP and related technologies, such as Internet Information Server, ActiveX Data Objects, VBScript, Visual InterDev, XML, and HTML. Microsoft has recognized Ken's volunteer contribution to online newsgroups by making him a Microsoft Most Valuable Professional (MVP). When not at the keyboard, Ken can be found riding his moped around Toronto or listening to '60s rock 'n' roll.

Amit Kalani has been programming with ASP.NET since its introduction. He works as a consultant in Michigan where he lives with his wife Priti. When not exploring .NET, he spends his time exploring beautiful Michigan. Amit can be reached at amitkalani@yahoo.com.

Budi Kurniawan is an independent consultant based in Sydney, Australia. He is the author of *Internet Programming with Visual Basic* published by Apress Books (ISBN: 1893115755, August 2000) and has published articles for more than 10 print and online magazines. He is also the developer of the popular File Upload Component for Java from BrainySoftware. He can be contacted at budi@brainysoftware.com.

Roberto G. A. Veiga, MCSE, is a young, yet experienced, IT professional who studied Business Administration for two years until realizing that he prefers to read about atoms rather than marketing and finances, so he currently is pursuing a degree in physics. He works at Serpro, a Brazilian state-owned company of data processing linked to the Brazilian Treasury Department, where he currently develops solutions for web-based distance learning using ASP and SQL Server (and Zope, unofficially). He also provides technical support in Microsoft BackOffice products to Serpro's clients. When not involved with the work at Serpro, he works as a freelance programmer and technical reviewer of computing books (including for New Riders books). He can be contacted by email at raveiga@yahoo.com.

About the Technical Reviewers

These reviewers contributed their considerable hands-on expertise to the entire development process for *Inside ASP.NET*. As the book was written, these dedicated professionals reviewed all the material for technical content, organization, and flow. Their feedback was critical to ensuring that *Inside ASP.NET* fits our readers' need for the highest quality technical information.

Robert L. Bogue has contributed to more than 100 book projects and numerous magazine articles and reviews. His broad experience has lead him to networking and integration topics as well as software development. He is currently doing strategic IT consulting. He is MCSE, CNA, A+, Network+, I-Net+, and Server+ certified. When not killing trees or getting certified, he enjoys flying planes and working to advance his pilot's license ratings. Robert can be reached at `Rob.Bogue@ThorProjects.com`.

Ajoy Krishnamoorthy is a consultant with more than five years of experience working in Microsoft technologies, such as ASP, Visual Basic, IIS, MTS, and most recently, .NET. He writes regularly for leading online publications. He received a bachelor's degree in electronics and communication and a master's degree in systems and information. He is currently working for his master's in business administration at Fisher College of Business, Ohio State University. His interests include writing, hanging out with friends, and travel. He is originally from Chennai, India and currently lives in Columbus, Ohio with his wife Vidhya. He and his wife are excited to have their first child in October 2001. He can be reached at `ajoykrishnamoorthy@hotmail.com`.

In addition to Rob and Ajoy's technical editing, contribution authors **Rob Buckton** and **Ken Cox** also shared their techical expertise in reviewing the original manuscripts.

Acknowledgments

At many times during the process, I have called on numerous people for their assistance. I never would have imagined that writing a book would be so difficult. I certainly have no trouble boring my peers with long conversations on the subject.

To begin, I'd like to thank Deborah Hittle-Shoaf, my acquisitions editor, for taking me on as a prospective author and for all the help and insight she has provided me.

Also thanks to Lisa Thibault, my development editor, who was lenient with me when my deadlines slid, and who somehow worked my drafts into order.

Additional thanks goes to the technical reviewers for their assistance and understanding over the past few months.

A special thanks goes to Ken Cox, one of my technical reviewers and co-author, for the gracious amount of time and effort he put into completing this book. Without a doubt, he has been the most valuable asset. Ken, thanks for everything; you have taught me a hell of a lot in a short amount of time.

Thank you to all the other people who helped me complete this book—a list of people too numerous to mention.

Finally, I'd like to acknowledge orcsweb for hosting the www.project-inspiration.com web site, which holds the source examples for this book, and acts as a modest ASP.NET and commerce server information site.

Sincerely,
Scott Worely

Tell Us What You Think!

As the reader of this book, you are the most important critic and commentator. We value your opinion and want to know what we're doing right, what we could do better, what areas you'd like to see us publish in, and any other words of wisdom you're willing to pass our way.

As the Associate Publisher for New Riders Publishing, I welcome your comments. You can fax, email, or write me directly to let me know what you did or didn't like about this book—as well as what we can do to make our books stronger.

Please note that I cannot help you with technical problems related to the topic of this book, and that due to the high volume of mail I receive, I might not be able to reply to every message.

When you write, please be sure to include this book's title and author as well as your name and phone or fax number. I will carefully review your comments and share them with the author and editors who worked on the book.

Fax: 317-581-4663
Email: stephanie.wall@newriders.com
Mail: Stephanie Wall
          Associate Publisher
          New Riders Publishing
          201 West 103rd Street
          Indianapolis, IN 46290 USA

Introduction

Over the past few years or so, there has been a great deal of movement in the Internet development market and we have seen the arrival of new languages, development tools, methodologies, and standards. Microsoft entered the Internet development market late; you could say they missed the boat, as it were, or you could say they made a savvy decision by waiting.

At first, Microsoft provided a limited set of web development tools. The most popular and notable of these tools was Active Server Pages (ASP).

ASP made the development of database-enabled web sites easy. However, it lacked advanced development features, such as Object Oriented Programming (OOP), compiled code, portability, XML Web Services, and a specifically-architectured language/class library for Internet development. Most people wanting to do serious web application development started to turn to other tools, such as Java, or they learned to live with the limitations of ASP web development and created code-based workarounds at the expense of much needed performance.

So why the brief recap? Well, Microsoft has been developing a new language platform/system architecture that is Internet-based web application development. This new platform is called *.NET*, and it is a radical departure from previous Microsoft development products. No longer is Microsoft focusing on independent languages that are deeply entwined with Microsoft operating systems.

You might think from the previous paragraph, or indeed from the product name, that .NET has its focus set primarily on Internet development; however, this is not exactly true. Although it is true that Internet-related technologies are indeed at the core of .NET, and some of its most appealing features are those that deal with the issues of web application development, .NET also has features that greatly aid distributed development across multiple languages and platforms. In essence, the .NET framework allows for the development of fully-distributed enterprise applications that can run on the desktop. These applications also can be Internet-hosted across multiple platforms. All this can happen in an environment that still provides scalability, performance, and robustness.

Who Is This Book For?

This book covers the development technologies of Microsoft's .NET development framework in relation to ASP.NET web development, and as such, it is targeted at both new and experienced web developers, although developers with ASP experience will benefit the most.

The aim of this book is to enable web developers to gain quick and efficient understanding and experience of the ASP.NET development framework, so they can become productive ASP.NET developers.

This book also covers some enterprise development topics, such as Messaging Services and Directory Services, so it will be of interest to enterprise developers.

And finally, anyone who is migrating from ASP to ASP.NET will find this book an invaluable source of information, on both migration and ASP.NET development in general.

Contents of the Book

This book consists of the following chapters, which are discussed in the next few sections.

Part I: Introducing ASP.NET

Chapter 1, "An Overview of ASP.NET," introduces ASP.NET as a technology, and it explains what ASP.NET is and what it can do.

Chapter 2, "Developing Applications with ASP.NET," takes the knowledge gained in Chapter 1 and looks at developing ASP.NET-enabled applications. Chapter 2 provides information on the structure of an ASP.NET application, migration issues, and an introduction to some programming techniques and technologies related to the ASP.NET framework.

Chapter 3, "Configuring ASP.NET Applications," explains and demonstrates the application configuration aspects of ASP.NET. In Chapter 3 are details of the web.config file, and the file's supporting objects are discussed and demonstrated. By the end of this chapter, you will have a firm understanding of configuration files and their use in ASP.NET applications.

Part II: Core ASP.NET

Chapter 4, "Web Form-Based Development," deals with the core of ASP.NET—the Web Form. Chapter 4 introduces the ASP.NET Web Form from an overview of the technology to examples of the Web Form syntax and controls. Finally it concludes with an explanation of validation controls and their uses. By the end of this chapter, you should have a good understanding of the use and architecture of Web Form development with ASP.NET.

Chapter 5, "State Management in ASP.NET," explains state management concepts and their uses, starting with an overview of the technology and then looking at the two main types of cache control support—page caching and request caching. This chapter also looks at the issues with web farms and web gardens in relation to cached data. By the end of this chapter, you should understand the concepts behind cache management in ASP.NET and know what type of caching to use and where it will benefit the performance and scalability of your web applications.

Part III: ASP.NET and Data Access

Chapter 6, "Using ADO.NET in ASP.NET Applications," introduces the reader to the data access techniques and technology used by ASP.NET. By the end of this chapter, you will be able to interface to multiple data sources, use the two supplied data providers for ASP.NET (OleDB and SQLClient), and you will also understand where and how to bind retrieved data to data-aware web controls.

Chapter 7, "Using XML in ASP.NET Applications," explains the .NET XML API. Topics covered include a basic introduction to XML, including details on how integral XML is to the .NET framework, and reading, writing, and manipulating XML data in your web applications.

Part IV: Advanced Technologies

Chapter 8, "XML Web Service Development in ASP.NET," introduces another core technology in the ASP.NET development framework—the XML Web Service. Here you will learn what exactly an XML Web Service is, where you use them, and most importantly, why you use them.

Chapter 9, "Securing ASP.NET Applications," introduces the security aspects of an ASP.NET application and covers form and Windows-based authentication and authorization, as well as a brief look at the passport authentication system. By the end of this chapter, you will understand the concepts behind authentication and authorization, and also how to implement and secure a web application using these technologies.

Chapter 10, "Using Component Services with ASP.NET," looks at Component Services—the .NET versions of COM+. Also covered in this chapter are issues involving COM/COM+ interoperability. By the end of this chapter, you will be able to understand, create, and use a component service. You will also learn how to use existing COM/COM+ objects in your web applications.

Chapter 11, "Using Messaging Services with ASP.NET," introduces the messaging services provided by the .NET framework. In this chapter, you will learn the basic concepts of message queue development and how to use these services in ASP.NET. By the end of this chapter, you will understand how to use messaging services in your web applications.

Chapter 12, "Using Directory Services with ASP.NET," introduces the .NET directory services. This is a set of objects that enables your web application to use Windows 2000 Active Directory technology in your applications. By the end of this chapter, you will have a good understanding of directory services and how they can be used in your applications.

Chapter 13, "Localizing and Globalizing ASP.NET Applications." Most web sites can be accessed globally from various differing countries, and in this chapter, we look at how to support multiple languages and culture-specific information in your web applications. By the end of this chapter, you will understand the concepts and issues behind globalizing and localizing a web application, and also how to implement a multi-cultural web site.

Part V: Advanced Web Forms

Chapter 14, "Cache Control in ASP.NET," introduces the cache control capabilities of ASP.NET. By the end of this chapter, you will understand the two main types of caching—page output and page data caching—and you will also understand when and where it should be used.

Chapter 15, "Creating User and Custom Controls for ASP.NET." One of the more powerful features of the ASP.NET Web Form is user and custom controls. These controls enable developers to create new Web Form controls for use in their applications. These controls are generally used to encapsulate specific functionality on a Web Form or in a web application. By the end of this chapter, you will understand the difference between custom and user controls, be able create and use your own controls, and understand where these controls can be best used in an application.

Chapter 16, "Mobile Device Development with ASP.NET," introduces the Mobile Internet Toolkit. This is a set of objects that enable the developer to produce web applications for mobile devices. In this chapter, you will learn about mobile device development and the issues involved, and get a brief overview of Wireless Application Protocol (WAP). You will also see examples of mobile device web controls using ASP.NET. By the end of this chapter, you will understand issues related to mobile device development and be able to make your web applications mobile-device aware.

Part VI: Putting It All Together

Chapter 17, "Putting It All Together," makes use of the various technologies presented in the book to produce an online project management web application known as Project Pal.

Project Pal provides the following features:

- Project managers can create and maintain projects, tasks, and teams from a single web-based interface.
- Project team members can view the status of a project and their task lists.

Part VII: Appendixes

The final section of this book is made up of various appendixes, which are listed as follows:

- **Appendix A, "An Overview of .NET"**—A brief overview of the .NET framework.
- **Appendix B, "ASP Common Object Reference"**—A brief list of common ASP.NET objects and syntax.
- **Appendix C, "ADO Common Object Reference"**—A brief list of common ADO.NET objects and syntax.
- **Appendix D, "HTML Server Control Reference"**—A brief list of HTML server controls supported by ASP.NET.
- **Appendix E, "ASP Server Control Reference"**—A brief list of ASP server controls supported by ASP.NET.
- **Appendix F, "Microsoft Mobile Internet Toolkit"**—A brief list of mobile device controls supported by ASP.NET when using the mobile Internet toolkit.
- **Appendix G, ".NET Resource List"**—A list of web-based information resources for the .NET platform.

I

Introducing ASP.NET

1

An Overview of ASP.NET

THIS CHAPTER PROVIDES A BRIEF OVERVIEW of ASP.NET, including the technologies and features that make it such a powerful and flexible web development environment. At various points, I make references to other chapters in the book where more detailed exposures of the technologies and features reside.

ASP.NET

ASP.NET is the next generation version of ASP (now referred to as *Classic ASP*). Like its predecessor ASP, ASP.NET is a web development platform that provides the services required to build web applications. Although ASP.NET can be syntax-compatible with ASP, it also provides a lot of new features and technologies.

ASP.NET is a web application development framework that provides the functionality and tools required to build enterprise web applications. ASP.NET is syntax-compatible with Classic ASP, however it also supports a new development architecture that enables you to create very powerful and flexible web applications. ASP.NET is fully integrated into the .NET framework, which enables the developer to take advantage of the *Common Language Runtime* (CLR), type safety, inheritance, and all the other features of that platform. (For more information on the .NET framework, see Appendix A, "An Overview of .NET.")

ASP.NET has a lot of new concepts and technologies, such as enhancements to the session and state management, ADO.NET, Messaging, and Directory Services to name a few. Table 1.1 outlines some of the new technologies introduced to ASP.NET. As you can see, there are quite a few differences between Classic ASP and ASP.NET. New features have been introduced in ASP.NET since Classic ASP.

Table 1.1   **New Technologies in ASP.NET**

Technology	Description
Multiple Programming Language Support	A Web Form can now have its scripting done in .NET-supported development languages. We no longer have to use a limited scripting language with which to program because we now have the full power of a complete development language to use. Languages supported at the time of this book's publication are C#, Managed C++, Visual Basic. NET, and JSCRIPT.NET.
Compiled Code	ASP web pages are now compiled on the server, which means that the pages generally perform more efficiently.
.NET Base Class Libraries	The real power and flexibility of ASP.NET comes from the .NET *Base Class Libraries* (BCL). These libraries cover a very diverse range of functionality from user interface classes to security and general language support functions.
Advanced Configuration	ASP.NET has a configuration file that is used to hold and maintain configuration information about the environment, and it can also be used to hold any application-specific configuration data for a web application.
Web Forms	Web Forms are basically a web page with a lot of new additions. The main additions are event management/trapping, a set of server controls, user control creation, custom control creation, and full programming language support for all .NET-compatible development languages.
XML Web Services	XML Web Services are basically objects that can be used through the web. They use SOAP (Simple Object Access Protocol) as their main transport layer and are unhindered by firewalls. An XML Web Service generally performs a task or returns data—it is not normal for a Web Service to maintain state—in fact, the development model is pretty similar to Distributed Component Object Model (DCOM), except without the deployment and security issues.

Technology	Description
ADO.NET	ADO.NET is the next generation version of ADO, and like ASP.NET, it has been completely reengineered/designed by Microsoft for use on the web. It uses XML internally as its main storage format and also for transporting data.
Native XML Support	XML is deeply entrenched inside the whole .NET development framework—it is used as the main transport format for ADO.NET and the Messaging Services. The .NET base class libraries have complete support for XML, and XML-driven application development.
Enhanced Cache Control	ASP.NET has two main ways of caching data for performance, including request caching, which is used for developed web pages to improve code efficiency and to share common data across pages, and page caching, which is used to improve rendering performance of web pages to the client based on various criteria.
Enhanced State Management	State management has been enhanced in lot of ways. The most notable of these is the use of an external "State Store" to store state information. This enables the easy use of session variable data across web farms or web gardens, and it also enables the use of cookieless state management, which gets past the issues that occur when a client's browser does not support cookies.
Enhanced Security	The .NET security system gives the developer the ability to authenticate and authorize users who want their applications to use various technologies and techniques.
Mobile Device Development	ASP.NET has a Mobile Device Development Software Development Kit (SDK), which allows the programmer to write web applications that run on Wireless Application Protocol (WAP)/Wireless Markup Language (WML) and HDML-compliant devices.
Messaging Services	The Messaging Services class libraries are a wrapper for Microsoft Message Queue (MSMQ) Messaging Services, and they enable you to support this technology in your .NET applications.
Directory Services	The Directory Services class libraries are a wrapper for Active Directory and enable the developer to access Active Directory Services Interfaces (ADSI), Lightweight Directory Access Protocol (LDAP), and other directory services through ASP.NET applications.

continues ▶

Table 1.1 **Continued**

Technology	Description
Migration	One of the biggest issues ASP.NET developers face is migration; however, when designing ASP.NET, Microsoft took this into account, so you can run Classic ASP and ASP.NET applications side by side without issue. Ranging from ASP.NET to COM interoperability, you can use ActiveX Data Objects (ADO) and other third-party COM functionality, thus allowing staged migration to ASP.NET. (Note that you cannot share state information between an ASP.NET application and Classic ASP.)
XCOPY Deployment	Deployment has always been a major issue for ASP-based applications, which utilized COM and DCOM objects because of registration. However, the components used in .NET do not require registration because they are registered automatically when they are first called.

The .NET Base Class Libraries

As mentioned previously, one of the most powerful features of ASP.NET is its complete access to the .NET Framework Base class libraries. These libraries contain classes, interfaces, and data types that optimize the development process and provide access to system functionality. To aid the interoperability between multiple languages, the .NET framework types are CLS-compliant and can, therefore be used from any programming language whose compiler conforms to the *Common Language Specification* (CLS). You can find more on this in Appendix A.

The .NET framework data types are the basis for which .NET applications, components, and controls are built. The .NET framework includes data types for the following areas:

- Represent base data types and exceptions
- Encapsulate data structures
- Perform I/O
- Provide data access, rich client-side GUI, and server-controlled, client-side GUI

This framework provides a comprehensive set of interfaces as well as abstract and concrete classes. You can use the concrete classes as they are without modification or your own classes on them. This is the most likely case when developing ASP.NET applications.

Table 1.2 outlines the Base Class Library functionality provided by the .NET framework, which is fully available to any ASP.NET web application.

Table 1.2 **Base Class Library Functionality**

Model	Description
COMPONENT MODEL	
System.CodeDom	Representation of the elements and structure of a source code document and compilation and handling of such code.
System.ComponentModel	Implementation of components, including licensing and design-time adaptation.
CONFIGURATION	
System.Configuration	Retrieval of application configuration data.
DATA	
System.Data	Access and management of data and data sources.
System.XML	Standards-based support for processing XML.
System.XML.Serialization	Bi-directional object–to-XML mapping.
FRAMEWORK SERVICES	
System.Diagnostics	Application instrumentation and diagnostics.
System.DirectoryServices	Access to the Active Directory of an Active Directory service provider, such as *Internet Information Services* (IIS).
System.Management	Services and application management tools that work with the *Web-Based Enterprise Management* (WBEM) standards.
System.Messaging	MSMQ access and management, and the sending and receiving of messages.
System.ServiceProcess	Installation and execution of Windows-based service applications. Does not access specific services, such as Active Directory or XML Web Services.
System.Timers	Event raising on an interval or more complex schedule.
GLOBALIZATION AND LOCALIZATION	
System.Globalization	Support for internationalization and globalization of code and resources.
System.Resources	Resource management and access, including support for localization.

continues ▶

Table 1.2 **Continued**

Model	Description
NET	
System.Net	Support for sending and receiving data over a network, including simple programming interfaces for common network protocols.
COMMON TASKS	
System.Collections	Collections of objects, such as lists, queues, arrays, hash tables, and dictionaries.
System.IO	Basic data stream access and management, including file I/O, memory I/O, and isolated storage.
System.Text	Character encoding, character conversion, and string manipulation.
System.Text.RegularExpressions	Full regular expression support.
System.Threading	Multithreaded programming support, including locking and synchronization.
REFLECTION	
System.Reflection	Access to type metadata and dynamic creation and invocation of types.
RICH, CLIENT-SIDE GUI	
System.Drawing	Rich 2D graphics functionality, and access to GDI+.
System.Windows.Forms	Rich user interface features for Windows-based applications.
RUNTIME INFRASTRUCTURE SERVICES	
System.Runtime.CompilerServices	Support for compilers that target the runtime.
System.Runtime.InteropServices	Support for interoperability with COM and other unmanaged code.
System.Runtime.Remoting	Support for creating tightly or loosely coupled distributed applications.
System.Runtime.Serialization	Object serialization and deserialization, including binary and SOAP encoding support.
.NET FRAMEWORK SECURITY	
System.Security	Access to the underlying mechanisms of the .NET framework security system, including policy resolution, stack walks, and permissions.
System.Security.Cryptography	Cryptographic Services, including encoding and decoding of data, hashing, random number generation, message authentication, and formation of digital signatures.

Model	Description
XML WEB SERVICES	
`System.Web`	Support for web server and client management, communication, and design. Provides core infrastructure for ASP.NET, including Web Forms support.
`System.Web.Services`	Client- and server-side support for SOAP-based Web Services.

As you can see, ASP.NET developers have a much-improved development from which to build enterprise level/quality applications.

ASP.NET Web Application Configuration

In ASP.NET, configuration information is stored in an XML-based configuration file. This means it can be viewed and edited by the user. Because of this, administrators and developers can update web application and site configuration settings with ease—no longer do developers have to wait for an administrator to change IIS settings and reboot the web server for the settings to take effect. Understandably, this improves a developer's productivity.

The configuration system is fully-extensible because you can store your own configuration settings in the Web.config file for a specific web application.

When an ASP.NET application is run, the configuration information provided by Web.config is used to configure the applications runtime environment and the configuration settings are then cached for all subsequent requests of any resource that is part of an ASP.NET application.

These configuration files can be changed at runtime either through the application itself or by user intervention. When this happens, ASP.NET automatically applies the revised/changer configuration settings to the application resources affected by the changes.

Where is the configuration information?

Configuration information is stored in XML-based text files. Any standard text editor or XML parser can be used to create and edit ASP.NET configuration files.

The server does not have to be rebooted to enforce changes to a web application's configuration.

Session and State Management

State is any piece of information or data that alters or affects the behavior of a web application. ASP.NET provides easy-to-use application and session state facilities that are familiar to existing Classic ASP developers.

The state management support offered by ASP.NET has better support for web farm server deployments because it uses an external state management service that runs in a separate process on a server. It is accessible by all web servers in a web farm because the session state is not stored on the web server dealing with the web requests. It is stored in a fixed location.

More information on state management can be found in Chapter 5, "State Management in ASP.NET."

Cache Management

One of the more important issues in creating high-performance, scalable web applications is the capability to store items in memory after they are requested.

These items can be stored on a web server. This enables you to avoid re-creating information that has already been created by a previous request. This is especially important with complex data that takes a significant amount of processing time and resources. This technique is referred to as caching, and it can be used to store web page output or application data across HTTP requests.

ASP.NET provides two types of caching:

- **Page Output Caching**—The capability to store dynamic page and user control responses that are generated by a user request.

- **Request Caching**—The capability to programmatically store objects and data to server memory, so your application can save the time and resources it takes to recreate them.

ASP.NET Web Application Development Layers

When developing an ASP.NET application, there are various layers of functionality and technology available. In Figure 1.1, you can see a typical ASP.NET application architecture. For more details on ASP.NET application architecture, see Chapter 2, "Developing Applications with ASP.NET."

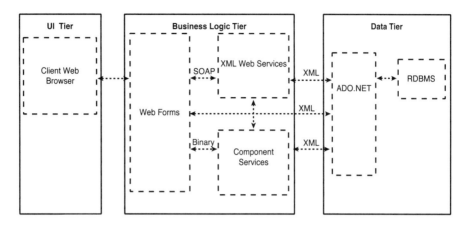

Figure 1.1   Simple ASP.NET Application Architecture.

As you can see, the ASP.NET application architecture is quite similar to the DNA structure. You still have your three tier system split between the three main tier types: UI tier, Business Logic tier, and Data tier. The next sections introduce the tiers, and also explain the technologies ASP.NET brings to bear for each tier.

The UI Tier

The UI tier, as its name suggests, is used to present data to a client. There are two main types of clients in ASP.NET. The first is a standard web browser that supports HTML 3.2 or better. Mobile devices, such as mobile phones and personal digital assistants (PDAs) are the second type.

The presentation data/information is sent to the client from an ASP.NET Web Form in both of these clients. The only difference is that as a developer, you will use different controls on the Web Forms.

The Business Logic Tier

This is where ASP.NET does most of its magic. As you can see in Figure 1.1, the Business Logic tier is made up of ASP.NET Web Forms, .NET XML Web Services, and .NET Component Services.

Web Forms

ASP.NET Web Forms are the core of any ASP.NET web application development effort. The Web Form is fundamental to presenting information and data to the user and also for responding and processing information and data from the client's interactions with the displayed Web Form.

A *Web Form* is like a traditional ASP page, with a few notable exceptions. The following sections briefly outline these exceptions.

Flexible/Powerful User Interface

It is possible to create complex interfaces that can interact with users in a more controlled and flexible way using *Web Form server controls*. These are a set of controls provided by the ASP.NET framework for interface development. Without these controls, complex user interfaces are generally difficult and tedious to create using HTML/DHTML and VBScript/Jscript. These controls also provide the capability to generate web browser–specific code for rendering and managing the controls. It is especially hard to create a rich user interface for applications that are likely to run on many different browsers.

Client Browser Capabilities

Short of forcing your users to use a single browser, your application will have to support many browsers, and this provides the developers with many challenges to overcome—the biggest one being browser compatibility.

It is difficult, if not impossible, to have a web application support all web browsers—it certainly takes far too much time and resources. Thankfully, ASP.NET has a solution to this scenario, which uses ASP.NET server controls. So you can let the ASP.NET environment deal with browser compatibility issues for you. Depending on an internal setting, you can tell ASP.NET to generate run-of-the-mill HTML3.2 code for the browser with very limited scripting, or you can tell it to produce browser-specific code, which checks the capabilities of the browser and then sends code to the browser optimized for it. It also takes advantage of any advanced browser features available. This process is referred to as "browser down-leveling" and "browser up-leveling".

As you can see, Web Forms provide a solution for web browser compatibility, so the developer does not have to explicitly code for differences in browsers.

Event-Based Programming

Another exciting feature of Web Forms is the capability to write event-handling methods for events that occur on a Web Form at either the client or server.

Intuitive Development

A Web Form can be programmed in a much more intuitive way than traditional web applications, including the capability to set properties for form elements and to respond to events. Web Form controls are abstracted from the physical contents of an HTML page and from interaction between the browser and server.

This means you can use Web Form controls the way you might use controls in a regular client application, and you do not have to worry about how to create the HTML to present and process the controls and their contents.

In short, Web Forms are an ASP.NET technology that you use to create programmable web pages. They can present information, using various markup languages, to the user in any browser and use code on the server to implement application logic. Web Forms also run on any browser to automatically render the correct, browser-compliant HTML for features such as styles, layout, and so on.

Web Forms support a rich set of controls that enable developers to cleanly encapsulate page logic into reusable components and can handle web page-level events.

For more information on Web Forms, see Chapter 4, "Web Form-Based Development."

XML Web Services

An *XML Web Service* is a routine procedure that can provide a particular piece of functionality, such as application logic.

An XML Web Service is generally accessible to any number of potentially-distributed systems through the use of Internet protocol standards, such as HTTP.

An XML Web Services depend on the acceptance of XML and other Internet standards to create an architecture that enables application interoperability.

Developers can create applications that use an XML Web Services from different sources in much the same way that developers traditionally use components when creating a distributed application.

A key characteristic of an XML Web Service is the high degree of abstraction that can exist between the implementation and use of a service. Because it uses an XML-based messaging system as the method by which the service is created and used, the XML Web Service client and the XML Web Service provider are not required to know anything about each others environments apart from the location and the inputs/outputs of the service; so the technology and the platform become less relevant.

You can use an XML Web Service to access server functionality remotely in pretty much the same way you would if you were using COM/DCOM. By using XML Web Services, businesses can expose application interfaces to their business logic, which can be manipulated by client and server applications.

XML Web Services enable the exchange of data in client-server or server-server scenarios; XML Web Services are not tied to a particular component technology or object-calling convention. As a result, programs written in any language, using any component model, and running on any operating system can access web services. For more information on ASP.NET XML web services, see Chapter 8, "XML Web Service Development in ASP.NET."

COM/COM+ Interoperability and Component Services

The .NET framework encourages and supports interaction with existing COM components, COM+ services, and Operating System Services.

.NET Component Services are comprised of transaction processing, queued components, and object pooling.

For more information on this, see Chapter 10, "Using Component Services with ASP.NET."

ADO.NET

Accessing database information is one of the most common uses for an ASP.NET application, which often manipulates and displays data to web site users. ASP.NET makes this easier than ever with ADO.NET.

ADO.NET is an improvement on Microsoft ADO. It is a standards-based programming model for creating distributed, data-sharing applications. ADO.NET offers several advantages over previous versions of ADO. The following are some of the benefits:

- Increased interoperability (internal use of XML)
- Maintainability (simpler object model, more intuitive)
- Programmability (simpler object model, more intuitive)
- Performance (optimized for distributed data management)

For more information on ADO.NET, see Chapter 6, "Using ADO.NET in ASP.NET Applications."

Migration from Classic ASP to ASP.NET

One of the design goals for ASP.NET was to make the new platform backward-compatible with previous versions of ASP. However, due to the architectural differences between Classic ASP and ASP.NET, complete backward compatibility is impossible. Fortunately, the migration issue is not as bad as it could be because you can run Classic ASP applications and web pages on the same server with ASP.NET; however, you should note that you cannot share information between the two different technologies.

You can, however, seamlessly upgrade your system from Classic ASP to ASP.NET because of the following reasons:

- You can run both Classic ASP and ASP.NET applications on the same server and ASP.NET runtime will process only those files with an .aspx file name extension. Files with the extension .asp will continue to be processed by the existing, unchanged ASP engine. session state and application state are not shared between ASP and ASP.NET pages.

- ASP.NET offers full syntax and processing compatibility with Classic ASP applications. Developers just need to change file extensions from .asp to .aspx to migrate their files to the ASP.NET framework. They also must make some minor changes to any VBScript code. Developers can also add ASP.NET functionality to their applications with ease—sometimes by simply adding just a few lines of code to their ASP files.

- ASP.NET can use Classic ADO for data access through COM Interoperability.

It is possible through Web Services to share data between independent Classic ASP and ASP.NET applications, although this is not recommended.

Existing Classic ASP skills are not obsolete. The ASP.NET programming model will seem very familiar to those who have used Classic ASP. Unfortunately, almost all existing ASP pages will have to be modified to some extent to run under ASP.NET. The reason for this is because the ASP.NET object model has undergone significant changes to be much more structured and object-oriented. In most cases, the code changes will be very minor and will only involve a few lines of changed code.

It should be noted that it is more likely that developers will redesign and recreate existing applications to take advantage of the ASP.NET technologies to gain performance, readability, and maintainability.

Chapter 2 provides more detail about migration issues.

Globalization and Localization

The .NET framework has support for the development of international applications. International application development requires two separate processes: globalization and localization. Globalization is the process of creating a core application that supports localized user interfaces and regional data for all users. Localization is the process of translating an application's user interface into a specific language. Truly, global applications should be culture and language neutral.

Further information on this can be found in Chapter 13, "Localizing and Globalizing ASP.NET Applications."

Enhanced Security

ASP.NET Web Application Security provides a way to control access to a site by comparing authenticated credentials (or representations of them) to Microsoft Windows NT file system permissions or to an XML file that lists authorized users, authorized roles, or authorized HTTP verbs.

Most web sites need to restrict access to some portions of the site. ASP.NET, in conjunction with IIS, can authenticate user credentials, such as names and passwords, using any of the following authentication methods:

- Windows: Basic, digest, or Integrated Windows Authentication (NTLM or Kerberos)
- Microsoft Passport Authentication
- Forms
- Client Certificates

The .NET framework and ASP.NET provide default authorization and authentication schemes for web applications. You can easily remove, add to, or replace these schemes depending on the needs of your application. More information on security can be found in Chapter 9, "Securing ASP.NET Applications."

2

Developing Applications with ASP.NET

THIS CHAPTER INTRODUCES VARIOUS TOPICS involved in creating applications using ASP.NET. The topics covered are

- Application settings files
- Web page syntax
- Commonly used objects and classes in ASP.NET
- Trace functionality
- ASP.NET migration issues

Application Settings Files

ASP.NET applications can be configured through two different file-based mechanisms:

- **global.asax**—Global application setting file.
- **web.config**—XML-based application configuration file.

The global.asax File

The global.asax file has two main purposes:

- To enable you to define application- and session-wide variables, objects, and data.

- To enable you to define event handlers for application- and session-based events that happen in the scope of the application.

Directives Used in the global.asax File

The global.asax file can include the following possible elements:

- **The `@Assembly` directive**—Is used to register a compiled assembly with the web application; another way to register assemblies is to use the web.config file, which is discussed later in this chapter in the section "web.config Configuration File."

```
<%@ Assembly Name="MyAssembly.dll" %>
```

- **The `@Import` directive**—Explicitly imports a namespace into an application, making all classes and interfaces of the imported namespace available to the application.

```
01 <%@ Import Namespace="System.IO" %>
02 <%@ Import Namespace="System.Collections" %>
```

- **The `@Application` directive**—Defines application-specific information used by the ASP.NET web application; its only function is to inherit its properties from another object. It takes two attributes: the first is `INHERITS`, which is the name of a class from which to extend, and the second is `DESCRIPTION`, which is a text description of the application. (This is ignored by the parser and compiler and is only there for the developer's benefit.)

```
<%@ APPLICATION INHERITS="myClass" DESCRIPTION="Description" %>
```

Application- or Session-Scoped Variables

You can create application-scope variables using the `Application` object, and you can create session-scope variables using the `Session` object. Later in this chapter, we will take a more detailed look at these objects and their other uses.

To set a variable:

```
01 Application("myApplicationScopeVar") = "MyValue")
02 Session("mySessionScopeVar") = "MyValue")
```

To get a variable:

```
01 MyValue = Application("myApplicationScopeVar")
02 MyValue = Session("mySessionScopeVar")
```

Static objects or COM/COM+ components can be declared in the global.asax file through the `Object` tag. The scope of these objects or components can be session- or application-wide.

The `pipeline` scope specifies that the object or component is for the current instance of `HttpApplication` and is not shared.

```
01 <Object id="id" runat="server" class="myClassName" scope="pipeline">
02 <Object id="id" runat="server" progid="MyCOM-ProgID" scope="session"/>
03 <Object id="id" runat="server" classid="MyCOM-ClassID" scope="application"/>
```

Session Events

The following session-based events can be trapped in the global.asax file:

- **Session_OnStart**—This event is fired when a client first starts a session.
- **Session_OnEnd**—This event is fired when a client completes a session.

Script Blocks

Script blocks also can be used in the global.asax file. Generally, however, you would just use a script block in the global.asax file to declare your application and session variables and also to declare your event handlers for the .NET framework. See the global.asax example in Listing 2.1.

> **Making Changes to the global.asax File**
>
> When you change an active global.asax file, ASP.NET detects the file change, completes all current requests for the application, fires the `Application_OnEnd` event to all listeners, and then restarts the application.
>
> In effect, this resets the web application or site, closing down all sessions and clearing all stored state information.
>
> When a new request arrives, ASP.NET recompiles the global.asax file and fires the `Application_OnStart` event.
>
> You only make changes to the global.asax file when the web application is in a period of no traffic or low traffic, for obvious reasons.

The following sample global.asax file is displayed, as shown in Listing 2.1.

Listing 2.1 **Sample global.asax File**

```
01 <Script language="VB" runat="server">
02
03
04  'Application start up code goes here
05  Sub Application_OnStart()
06    Application("MyApplicationScopeVar") = "MyValue"
07    Session("MyApplicationScopeVar") = "MyValue"
08  End Sub
09
10  'Application clean up code goes here
11  Sub Application_OnEnd()
```

continues ▶

Listing 2.1 **Continued**

```
12  End Sub
13
14  'Session start up code goes here
15  Sub Session_OnStart()
16  End Sub
17
18  'Session clean up code goes here
19  Sub Session_OnEnd()
20  End Sub
21
22
23  </script>
```

Some Key Points About global.asax

The global.asax file must reside in the root directory of your web application or site.

You can only have one global.asax file per web application or site.

The global.asax file is compiled by ASP.NET into a class (derived from the `HttpApplication` class) the first time any resource or URL within its application is activated or requested.

The global.asax file itself is configured, so that any direct URL request for it is automatically rejected; this is done to stop unauthorized access to the global.asax file.

web.config Configuration File

In ASP.NET, configuration information is stored in an XML-based configuration file. This means that it is user-viewable and editable. Because of this, administrators and developers can update web application or site configuration settings with ease; no longer do developers have to wait for an administrator to change Internet Information Server (IIS) settings and reboot the web server for the settings to take effect. Obviously, this improves a developer's productivity.

The configuration system is fully extensible because you can store your own configuration settings in the web.config file for the web application or site for which it is designed. The configuration system is fully extensible because of a hierarchical configuration infrastructure that enables extensible configuration data to be defined and used throughout ASP.NET applications. At the same time, ASP.NET provides a rich set of initial configuration settings.

A detailed look at the web.config file can be found in Chapter 3, "Configuring ASP.NET Applications."

Changing the global.asax File
Changes to ASP.NET configuration files are automatically detected by the system and are applied immediately.

The Page Syntax

When programming Web Forms, it is important to know the page syntax of an ASP.NET file. There are ten distinct syntax elements in ASP.NET. Each is explained below.

Page Directives

Page directives specify optional settings used by the page compiler when processing ASP.NET files. They can be located anywhere within an .aspx file. Each directive can contain one or more attribute or value pairs specific to that directive.

The general syntax of a page directive is as follows:

```
<%@ directive attribute=value [attribute=value … ]%>
```

The Web Forms page framework supports the following directives:

- @ Page
- @ Control
- @ Import
- @ Register
- @ Assembly
- @ OutputCache

The *@ Page* Directive

The @ Page directive defines page-specific attributes used by the ASP.NET page parser and compiler. It has the following syntax:

```
<%@ Page attribute=value [attribute=value … ]%>
```

You can only include one @ Page directive per .aspx file. To define multiple attributes, use a space-separated list, with no space around the equals sign, as in TRACE="True".

The @ `Page` directive has the following attributes:

- **AspCompat**—Determines whether the page is backward-compatible with ASP. If this is not set to `true`, ActiveX DLLs written for ASP applications does not work. In particular, set to `true` if either the page needs to be executed on an STA thread, or the page calls a COM+ 1.0 component that requires access to unmanaged ASP intrinsics through the object context or `OnStartPage`. The default is `false`.

- **Buffer**—Defines HTTP response buffering semantics. `true` if page buffering is enabled; otherwise `false`. `true` is the default.

- **CodePage**—Indicates the culture code page value for the ASP.NET page. Supports any valid code page value.

- **ContentType**—Defines the HTTP content type of the response as a standard Multipurpose Internet Mail Extension (MIME) type. Supports any valid HTTP content type string.

- **Culture**—Indicates the culture setting for the page. Supports any valid culture string.

- **Description**—Provides a text description of the page. Supports any string description.

- **EnableViewState**—Indicates whether view state is maintained across page requests. `true` if view state is maintained; otherwise, `false`. The default is `true`.

- **EnableSessionState**—Defines session state requirements for the page. `true` if session state is enabled; `ReadOnly` if session state can be read but not changed; otherwise `false`. The default is `true`.

- **ErrorPage**—Defines target URL for redirection if an unhandled page exception occurs.

- **Inherits**—Code behind class for page to inherit. Can be any class derived from the `Page` class.

- **Language**—Language used when compiling all `<% %>` and `<%= %>` blocks within the page. Can be Visual Basic, C#, or JScript.

- **Local Identifier (LCID)**—Defines the locale identifier for code in the page.

- **ResponseEncoding**—Response encoding of page content. Supports values from `Encoding.GetEncoding`.

- **SRC**—Code-behind class to compile. (source file name).

- **Trace**—Indicates whether tracing is enabled. `true` if trace is enabled; otherwise `false`. The default is `false`.

- **Transaction**—Indicates whether transactions are supported on the page. Possible values are: `NotSupported`, `Supported`, `Required`, and `RequiresNew`.

- **WarningLevel**—Indicates the compiler warning level at which you want the compiler to abort compilation for the page. Possible values are `0` through `4`.

The @ *Control* Directive

In addition to HTML and Web server controls, you also can create your own custom, reusable controls by using the same techniques you have learned to develop Web Forms pages. These controls are called *user controls*.

User controls offer you an easy way to partition and reuse common UI functionality across your ASP.NET web applications. Like a Web Forms page, you can author these controls with any text editor, or develop them using code-behind classes. Also, like a Web Forms page, user controls are compiled when first requested and stored in server memory to reduce the response time for subsequent requests. Unlike pages, however, user controls cannot be requested independently; they must be included in a Web Forms page to work.

User controls are explained in length in Chapter 15, "Creating User and Custom Controls for ASP.NET."

The @ `Control` directive defines user control-specific attributes used by the ASP.NET page parser and compiler. This directive can only be used with user controls. The syntax for this directive is as follows:

```
<%@ Control attribute=value [attribute=value … ]%>
```

The @ `Control` directive supports the same attributes as the @ `Page` directive, except the `AspCompat` and `Trace` attributes. To enable tracing, you must add the `Trace` attribute to an @ `Page` directive in the Web Forms page that contains the user control. You can include only one @ `Control` directive per .ascx file.

The @ `Control` directive has the following attributes:

- **AutoEventWireup**—Indicates whether the page's events are autowired. `true` if event auto wiring is enabled; otherwise false. The default is `true`.

- **ClassName**—Specifies the class name for the page that automatically compiles dynamically when the page is requested. This value can be any valid class name.

- **CompilerOptions**—Any compiler string that indicates compilation options for the page.

- **Debug**—Indicates whether the page should be compiled with debug symbols. `true` if the page should be compiled with debug symbols; otherwise `false`.

- **Description**—Provides a text description of the page. Supports any string description.

- **EnableSessionState**—Defines session state requirements for the page. `true` if session state is enabled; `ReadOnly` if session state can be read but not changed; otherwise `false`. The default is `true`.

- **Explicit**—Indicates that the page should be compiled using the Visual Basic Option Explicit mode. `true` if option explicit enabled; otherwise `false`. The default is `false`.

- **Inherits**—Code-behind class for page to inherit. Can be any class derived from the `Page` class.

- **Language**—Language used when compiling all `<% %>` and `<%= %>` blocks within the page. Can be Visual Basic, C#, or JScript.NET.

- **Strict**—Indicates that the page should be compiled using the Visual Basic Option Strict mode. `true` if option strict is enabled; otherwise `false`. The default is `false`.

- **SRC**—Indicates the path to the code-behind class to compile.

- **WarningLevel**—Indicates the compiler warning level at which you want the compiler to abort compilation for the user control. Possible values are `0` through `4`.

The @ *Import* Directive

The @ `Import` directive explicitly imports a namespace into a page, making all classes and interfaces of the imported namespace available to the page. The imported namespace can be either part of the .NET Framework class library or a user-defined namespace.

The @ `Import` directive has the following syntax:

```
<%@ Import namespace="the namespace to be imported" %>
```

The @ `Import` directive has only one attribute, `value`, which is the namespace to import for the page.

Note that the @ `Import` directive cannot have more than one namespace attribute. To import multiple namespaces, use multiple @ `Import` directives.

The following namespaces are automatically imported into all pages:

- `System`
- `System.Collections`
- `System.Collections.Specialized`
- `System.Configuration`
- `System.IO`
- `System.Text`
- `System.Text.RegularExpressions`
- `System.Web`
- `System.Web.Caching`
- `System.Web.Security`
- `System.Web.SessionState`
- `System.Web.UI`
- `System.Web.UI.HtmlControls`
- `System.Web.UI.WebControls`

As an example, the following code imports the .NET Framework base class namespace `System.Net` and the user-defined namespace `WebTools`:

```
01 <%@ Import Namespace="System.Net" %>
02 <%@ Import Namespace="WebTools" %>
```

The @ *Register* Directive

The @ `Register` directive associates aliases with namespaces and class names for concise notation in custom server control syntax. It has the following syntax:

```
01 <%@ Register Tagprefix="tagprefix" Namespace="namespace" %>
02
03 <%@ Register Tagprefix="tagprefix" Tagname="tagname" Src-"pathname" %>
```

The @ `Register` directive has the following attributes:

- **`Tagprefix`**—An alias to associate with a namespace.
- **`Tagname`**—An alias to associate with a class.
- **`Namespace`**—The namespace to associate with `tagprefix`.
- **`Src`**—The location (relative or absolute) of the user control associated with `tagprefix:tagname`. For example, the following code fragment uses `<% Register %>` directives to declare `tagprefix` and `tagname` aliases for a server control and a user control. The first directive declares the `MyTag` alias

as a tag prefix for all controls residing in the `MyCompany:MyNameSpace` namespace. The second directive declares `Acme:AdRotator` as a `tagprefix:tagname` pair for the user control in the file adrotator.ascx. The aliases are then used in custom server control syntax within the form to insert an instance of each server control.

```
01 <%@ Register Tagprefix="MyTag" Namespace="MyCompany:MyNameSpace" %>
02 <%@ Register Tagprefix="Acme"
03   Tagname="AdRotator" Src="AdRotator.ascx" %>
04 <HTML>
05  ...
06    <form runat="server">
07        <MyTag:MyControl id="Control1" runat="server" /><BR>
08        <Acme:AdRotator file="myads.xml" runat="server" />
09    </form>
10
11  ...
12 </HTML>
```

The @*Assembly* Directive

The `@ Assembly` directive declaratively links an assembly to the current page, making all of the assembly's classes and interfaces available for use on the page. You can also use this directive to register assemblies in the configuration file to link assemblies across the entire application.

It has the following syntax:

```
<%@ Assembly Name="assemblyname" %>
```

or

```
<%@ Assembly Src="pathname" %>
```

This directive has either the `Name` attribute or the `Src` attribute. `Name` is a string that represents the name of the assembly to link to the page.

`Src` is the path to a source file to dynamically compile and link against.

Assemblies that reside in an application's \bin directory are automatically linked to pages within that application. Such assemblies do not require the `@ Assembly` directive.

The automatic linking is disabled by removing the following line from the `<assembly>` section of the web.config file:

```
<add assembly="*"/>
```

As an alternative to using the `<%@ Assembly %>` directive, you can register such assemblies within the web.config file to link assemblies across an entire application.

As an example, the following code fragment uses the `<%@ Assembly %>` directive to link against MyAssembly.dll:

```
<%@ Assembly Name="myassembly.dll" %>
```

The @ *OutputCache* Directive

The `@ OutputCache` directive declaratively controls the output caching policies of a page. The syntax is as follows:

```
01 <%@ OutputCache Duration="#ofseconds"
02 Location="Any | Client | Downstream | Server | None" VaryByControl="controlname"
03 VaryByCustom="browser | customstring" VaryByHeader="headers"
04 VaryByParam="parametername" %>
```

This directive has the following attributes:

- **Duration**—The time, in seconds, that the page or user control is cached. Setting this attribute on a page or user control establishes an expiration policy for HTTP responses from the object and automatically caches the page or user control output.

  Note that this attribute is required. If you do not include it, a parser error occurs.

- **Location**—One of the `OutputCacheLocation` enumeration values. The default is `Any`.

  Important: This attribute is required when you output cache ASP.NET pages and user controls. A parser error occurs if you fail to include it.

- **VaryByCustom**—Any text that represents custom output caching requirements. If this attribute is given a value of browser, the cache is varied by browser name and major version information. If a custom string is entered, you must override the `HttpApplication.GetVaryByCustomString` method in your application's global.asax file.

- **VaryByHeader**—A semicolon-separated list of HTTP headers used to vary the output cache. When this attribute is set to multiple headers, the output cache contains a different version of the requested document for each specified header.

  Note that setting the `VaryByHeader` attribute enables caching items in all HTTP/1.1 caches, not just the ASP.NET cache. This attribute is not supported for `@ OutputCache` directives in user controls.

- **VaryByParam**—A semicolon-separated list of strings used to vary the output cache. By default, these strings correspond to a query string value sent with `GET` method attributes, or a parameter sent using the `POST` method. When this attribute is set to multiple parameters, the output cache contains a different version of the requested document for each specified parameter. Possible values include none, *, and any valid query string or POST parameter name.

Important: This attribute is required when you output cache ASP.NET pages and user controls. A parser error occurs if you fail to include it. If you do not want to specify a parameter to vary cached content, set the value to none. If you want to vary the ouput cache by all parameter values, set the attribute to *.

- **VaryByControl**—A semicolon-separated list of strings used to vary the output cache. These strings represent fully qualified names of properties on a user control. When this attribute is used for a user control, the user control output is varied to the cache for each specified user control property.

```
<%@ OutputCache Duration="10" %>
```

Code Declaration Blocks

The page syntax that you almost always use is the code declaration blocks. The *code declaration blocks* define member variables and methods to be compiled in the dynamically generated Page class that represents the ASP.NET page.

```
01 <script runat="server" language="codelanguage" Src="pathname" >
02    Code goes here….
03 </script>
```

The code declaration blocks have the following attributes:

- **language**—Specifies the language used in this code declaration block. This value can represent any .NET-compatible language, such as Visual Basic, C#, or JScript.NET. If no language is specified, this value defaults to that specified in the @ Page directive. If no language is specified in the directive, the default is Visual Basic.

- **src**—Specifies the path and file name of a script file to load. When this attribute is used, any other code in the declaration block is ignored.

Code Render Blocks

Code render blocks define inline code or inline expressions that execute when the page is rendered. There are two styles: inline code and inline expressions. You can use the former style to define either self-contained code blocks or control flow blocks. You can use the latter as a shortcut for calling `Response.Write`.

Inline code has the following syntax:

```
<% Inline code or expression %>
```

Note that you can't directly include the character sequence `%>` anywhere inside a code render block. That sequence can only be used to close the code render block. For example, the following code fragment will cause an error:

```
01 <%
02   Response.Write(" %>")
03 %>
```

To work around this, you can build a string containing the offending sequence:

```
01 <%
02   Dim s As String = "%" + ">"
03   Response.Write(s)
04 %>
```

Server-Side Comments

Server-side comments enable you to include code comments in the body of an .aspx file. Any content between opening and closing tags of server-side comment elements, whether ASP.NET code or literal text, are not be processed on the server or rendered to the resulting page.

```
<%-- Commented out code or content --%>
```

ASP.NET server-side comment blocks have the same uses as traditional language-specific comment blocks, including documentation and testing.

Within `<script runat="server"> </script>` and `<% %>` blocks, you can use comment syntax in the language in which you are coding.

A compilation error occurs if you use server-side comment blocks within `<% %>` blocks.

The opening and closing comment tags can appear on the same line of code or can be separated by commented-out lines.

Server-side comment blocks cannot be nested.

The following example demonstrates an HTML `Button` control that is commented out.

```
01  <%--
02 <button runat="server" id="MyButton" OnServerClick="MyButton_Click">
03 Click here for enlightenment!
04 </button>
05  --%>
```

Custom Server Control Syntax

Custom server controls are used best to encapsulate common programmatic functionality. You can create your own custom server controls, or use the controls shipped with the .NET frameworks at runtime.

The following details the syntax used with custom server controls.

Custom Web Forms Control Declaration Syntax

You can declaratively instantiate a Web Forms control by specifying elements in an .aspx file. The opening tags of these elements must include a `runat="server"` attribute or value pair. If you want to enable programmatic referencing on the control, specify a unique value with the `id` attribute.

Use this syntax to insert custom Web Forms server controls (including user-authored controls and all web controls):

```
<tagprefix:tagname id="OptionalID" attributename="value" attributename-propertyname="value"
↪eventname="eventhandlermethod" runat="server" />
```

> or

```
<tagprefix:tagname id="OptionalID" runat="server > </tagprefix:tagname>
```

The syntax has the following attributes:

- **tagprefix** —An alias for the fully qualified namespace of the control. Aliases for user-authored controls are declared with the `@ Register` directive.
- **tagname**—The name of the class that encapsulates the control.
- **id**—A unique identifier that enables programmatic reference to the control.
- **attributename**—The name of the attribute.
- **propertyvalue**—The value to assign to `attributename`.
- **propertyname**—The name of the property being defined.
- **supropertyvalue**—The value to assign to `propertyname`.
- **eventname**—The event name of the control.
- **eventhandlermethod**—The name of the event handler method defined in the code for the Web Forms page.

For example, the following code inserts a TextBox web control:

```
<ASP:TextBox id="MyTextBox" runat="server" />
```

Data Binding Expressions

Data binding expressions declaratively create bindings between server control properties and data sources. Data binding expressions can be written either on the value side of an attribute or value pair in opening tag of a Web Forms control, or anywhere in the page.

The syntax of data binding expression syntax is as follows:

```
<tagprefix:tagname property="<%# databinding expression %> runat="server" />
```

or

```
literal text <%# databinding expresion %>
```

The parameters are as follows:

- **tagprefix**—An alias for the fully qualified namespace of the control. The alias for web controls is ASP. Aliases for user-authored controls and are declared with the @ Register directive.
- **tagname**—The name of the .NET class that encapsulates the control.
- **property**—The control property for which this databinding is declared.
- **expression**—Any expression that conforms to the requirements below.

All data binding expression, regardless of where you place them, must be contained in <%# and %> characters.

ASP.NET supports a hierarchical data binding model that supports associative bindings between server control properties and parent data sources. Any server control property can be data bound. Control properties can data bind against any public field or property on either the containing page or their immediate naming container.

Using *DataBinder.Eval*

The Web Forms framework also supplies a static method that evaluates late-bound data binding expressions and optionally formats the result as a string. The DataBinder.Eval method is convenient because it eliminates the explicit casting you must do to coerce values to the desired data type. It is particularly useful when data binding controls within a templated list because often both the data row and the data field must be cast.

Consider the following example: An integer is displayed as a currency string. With the standard ASP.NET data binding syntax, you must first cast the type of the data to retrieve the data field, IntegerValue. Next, this is passed as an argument to the String.Format method:

```
<%# String.Format("{0:c}",
➥((DataRowView)Container.DataItem)["IntegerValue"]) %>
```

This syntax can be complex and difficult to remember. In contrast, `DataBinder.Eval` is simply a method with three arguments: the naming container for the data item, the data field name, and the format string. In a templated list like `DataList` class, `DataGrid` class, or `Repeater` class, the naming container is always `Container.DataItem`. `Page` is another naming container that can be used with `DataBinder.Eval`.

```
<%# DataBinder.Eval(Container.DataItem, "IntegerValue", "{0:c}") %>
```

The format string argument is optional. If it is omitted, `DataBinder.Eval` returns a value of type `object`. For example:

```
<%# (bool)DataBinder.Eval(Container.DataItem, "BoolValue") %>
```

Server-Side Object Tag Syntax

Server-side object tags declare and instantiate COM and .NET objects.
The syntaxes are as follows:

```
<object id="id" runat=server class=".NET Framework Class Name">
<object id="id" runat=server class="COM ProgID"/>
<object id="id" runat=server class="COM ClassID"/>
```

The parameters are:

- `Id. Unique name`—References the object in subsequent code.
- `NET Framework` **class name**—Identifies the .NET Framework class to instantiate.
- `COM ProgID`—Identifies COM component to instantiate.
- `COM ClassID`—Identifies COM component to instantiate.

When the page parser or compiler encounters a server-side object tag in an ASP.NET file, it generates a read or write property on the page, using the `id` attribute of the tag as the property name. The `read` property is configured to create an instance of the object on first use. The resulting instance is not added as an object within the page's hierarchical server control tree; it is instead treated as a non-UI variable declaration.

The `classid`, `progid`, and `class` attributes are mutually exclusive. It is an error to use more than one of these attributes within a single server-side object tag.

The following code presents an example of server side object tag syntax:

```
01 <html>
02 <object id="MyDatabase" class="Microsoft.OLEDBAdaptor" runat="server"/>
03 <script language="VB" runat=server>
04 Sub Page_Load(Sender as Object, e as EventArgs)
05   Dim StockDetails as Recordset
06   Set StockDetails = MyDatabase.Execute("DSN:money", "select * from stocks")
07 End Sub
08 </script>
09 </html>
```

Server-Side Include Directive Syntax

Server-side include directives insert the raw contents of a specified file anywhere within an ASP.NET page.

```
<!— #include pathtype = filename —>
```

The *pathtype* parameter specifies the type of the path to *filename*. The *pathtype* parameter can be File or Virtual.

If *pathtype* is File, the file name is a relative path from the directory containing the document with the #include directive. The included file can be in the same directory or in a subdirectory; it cannot be in a directory above the page with the #include directive.

If *pathtype* is Virtual, the file name is a full virtual path from a virtual directory in your web site.

The *filename* parameter specifies the name of the file to be included. *filename* must contain the file name extension, and you must enclose the file name in quotation marks (").

Note that the included file tag is processed before any dynamic code is executed (much like a C pre-processor).

The #include tag must be enclosed within HTML or XML comment delimiters to avoid being interpreted as static text.

The following code gives an example of the use of a server-side include directive:

```
01 <html>
02    <body>
03        <!— #Include file="header.inc" —>
04        Here is the main body of my file:
05        <% For I=0 to 10 %>
06            <!— #Include virtual="/Includes/Foobar.inc" —>
07        <% Next %>
08        <!— #Include virtual="footer.inc" —>
09    </body>
10 </html>
```

Commonly Used Objects and Classes in ASP.NET

Now that you have an idea of what files are used in an ASP.NET application and you have been introduced to VisualBasic. NET, Web Forms, and pages, it is time to look at some essential objects that are used by ASP.NET applications.

The *Application Intrinsic* Object (*HttpApplication* Class)

The HttpApplication class defines the methods, properties, and events common to all HttpApplication objects within the ASP.NET Framework.

The HttpApplication class contains many other classes as properties that users of Classic ASP will recognize, but others that they will not. Because the application object is integral to the development of a web application or site, it covers a lot of ground.

Application Object Properties

The Application object has a few properties that are used by the system:

- **Application**—Returns a reference to an HttpApplicationState bag instance. This is the object that is used in the global.asax file and, indeed, any ASP.NET Web Form, and it is this collection that holds the Application-scoped variables, objects, and components.

  The HttpApplicationState class enables developers to share global information across multiple requests, sessions, and pipelines within an ASP.NET application. (An *ASP.NET application* is the sum of all files, pages, handlers, modules, and code within the scope of a virtual directory and its subdirectories on a single web server.)

- **Context**—Provides access to an HTTPContext object for the current application instance.

- **Request**—Provides access to the HttpRequest Intrinsic object that provides access to incoming HTTP request data.

- **Response**—Provides access to the HttpResponse Intrinsic object that enables transmission of HTTP response data to a client.

- **Server**—Provides access to a Server Intrinsic object (HttpServerUtility class).

- **Session**—Provides access to the Session Intrinsic object.

Application Events

The Application events used by the system include the following:

- `Application.OnStart()`—This event is fired when the application is first started or run on a web server.
- `Application.OnEnd()`—This event is fired when the application has stopped running or processing on a web server.
- `Application.OnError()`—This event is fired when the application encounters an error; it can be used to create or re-assign a new error handler for the web application.
- `Application.BeginRequest()`—This event is fired when the application receives a new request.
- `Application.EndRequest()`—This event is fired when the application completes a new request.
- `AuthenticateRequest()`—This event is fired when the application receives a new request and it is ready for authentication.

The *Request Intrinsic* Object (*HttpRequest* Class)

When a client navigates to a web page on a web server, it is called a *request* because the user is technically requesting that the web server send the page to his browser for consumption. The `Request` object is used to get information from the web server and the client browser.

Request Object Properties

An overview of the `Request` object properties follows:

- `AcceptTypes`—Returns a string array of client-supported MIME accept types. This property is read-only.
- `ApplicationPath`—Returns the root path of the virtual application.
- `Browser`—Provides information about the incoming client's browser capabilities.
- `ClientCertificate`—Gets information on the current request's client security certificate.
- `ContentEncoding`—Indicates the character set of data supplied by the client. This property is read-only.
- `ContentType`—Indicates the MIME content type of incoming request. This property is read-only.
- `Cookies`—Gets a collection of the client's cookie variables.

- **FilePath**—Indicates the virtual path of the current request. This property is read-only.
- **Files**—Gets the collection of client-uploaded files (multipart MIME format).
- **Form**—Gets a collection of Form variables.
- **HttpMethod**—Indicates the HTTP data transfer method used by the client (GET, POST).
- **InputStream**—Provides access to the raw contents of the incoming HTTP entity body.
- **IsAuthenticated**—Indicates whether the HTTP connection is authenticated.
- **IsSecureConnection**—Indicates whether the HTTP connection is secure (HTTPS).
- **Path**—Indicates the virtual path of the current request. This property is read-only.
- **QueryString**—Gets the collection of QueryString variables.
- **RequestType**—Indicates the HTTP data transfer method used by the client (GET, POST).
- **ServerVariables**—Gets a collection web server variable. (Used for compatibility; it is generally better to use the defined properties of the Request object instead.)
- **TotalBytes**—Gets the number of bytes in the current input stream.
- **Url**—Gets information regarding the URL of the current request.
- **UrlReferrer**—Gets information regarding the URL of the client's previous request that linked to the current URL.
- **UserAgent**—Gets the client browser's raw User Agent String.
- **UserHostAddress**—Gets the IP host address of the remote client.
- **UserHostName**—Gets the DNS name of the remote client.
- **UserLanguages**—Gets a sorted array of client language preferences.

Request Object Methods

The Request object methods include the following:

- **BinaryRead(int32 numBytes)**—Performs a binary read of a specified number of bytes from the current input stream.

- **MapPath(String VirtualPath)**—Maps the virtual path (in the requested URL) to the physical path on the server for the current request.
- **SaveAs(String filename, Boolean incHeaders)**—Saves an HTTP request to disk.

The *Response Intrinsic* Object (*HttpResponse* Class)

The Request object is used to send information from the web server to the client browser.

Response Object Properties

An overview of the Response object properties is as follows:

- **Buffer**—Provides access to the HttpResponse buffer, allowing the assembly of complete page on the server and then sending the complete page as a whole to the client rather than in processed sections.
- **BufferOutput**—Sets a value indicating whether HTTP output is buffered.
- **Cache**—Returns the caching semantics of the web page (expiration time, privacy, vary clauses).
- **Charset**—Sets the HTTP charset of output.
- **ContentEncoder**—Provides access to the current content encoder.
- **ContentEncoding**—Sets the HTTP character set of output.
- **ContentType**—Sets the HTTP MIME type of output.
- **Cookies**—Gets the HttpCookie collection sent by the current response.
- **Expires**—Sets the Expires setting on the client.
- **IsClientConnected**—Gets a value indicating whether the client is still connected to the server.
- **StatusCode**—Sets the HTTP status code of output returned to the client.
- **StatusDescription**—Sets the HTTP status string of output returned to the client.

Response Object Methods

An overview of the HttpResponse object methods is as follows:

- **AppendToLog(String logEntry)**—Adds custom log information to the IIS log file.
- **Pics(String PicsValue)**—Appends a *Platform for Internet Content Selection* (PICS) label HTTP header to the output stream.

- **Redirect(String newUrl)**—Redirects a client browser to a new URL.
- **Write(String outputString)**—Writes values to an HTTP output content stream.
- **WriteFile(Filename)**—Writes a file directly to an HTTP content output stream.

The *Server* Class (*HttpServerUtility* Class)

The ServerUtility object is pretty much the same as the Classic ASP Server object. It provides access to useful server-side tools for use in an ASP.NET application.

Server Object Properties

A brief class overview of the Server object properties follows:

- **MachineName**—Gets the web server's name.
- **ScriptTimeout**—Requests a timeout for server-side scripts in seconds.

HttpServerUtility Class Methods

The following is a brief class overview of the HttpServerUtility class methods:

- **CreateObject(String progid)**—Instantiates a COM object identified through a progid.
- **Execute**—Executes another web page on the server, holding the execution of the current page until the server has finished processing the new page on the server.
- **GetLastError**—Returns the last recorded exception in the current web application or site.
- **HtmlEncode**—Encodes a string and returns the encoded string.
- **HtmlDecode**—Decodes a string and returns the decoded string.
- **Mappath**—Maps a virtual path to a physical path.
- **Transfer**—Terminates the execution of the current page and begins execution of a new request using the supplied URL path.
- **UrlEncode**—Encodes a string.
- **UrlDecode**—Decodes a string.
- **UrlPathEncode**—Encodes a path portion of a URL string and returns the encoded string.

Tracing ASP.NET Applications

When you are developing ASP.NET applications, you have the ability to *trace* (or track) the state or progress of your application in real time. This is done through the Trace functionality of ASP.NET.

The usual way of doing this in Classic ASP applications was to include `response.write()` statements everywhere in your code. However, this technique has the following issues:

- **Performance impact**—Due to more code in the web page, this means that the page takes longer to download.

- **Maintainability/Readability of code**—Heavy use of the `response.write()` function in a web page's code, which is not specific to the output of the application (debug stuff), can make the code very confusing to read initially and also to maintain.

- **Ability to be disabled**—Probably the most important capability lacking in the `Response write` method is the capability to enable and disable output to the browser.

ASP.NET provides a way to trace the state of your web applications dynamically through its tracing system. The tracing system supplied by ASP.NET has two types of operations:

- **Page-Level Tracing**—This provides web page-level tracing on a page-by-page basis.

- **Application-Level Tracing**—This provides web application-wide tracing.

Both of these tracing types are configured from the web.config configuration file.

The Trace Information

So far, I have only talked about tracing in an abstract manner. ASP.NET automatically traces the state of your application and web pages on a web server, and when tracing is enabled, ASP.NET makes most of this information available to the developer. The information available from a trace operation is shown in the following paragraphs.

Before detailing each section of the trace results, it is best that you create a simple web page with tracing enabled to do this simply put the following directive at the top of an .aspx web page:

```
%@page Trace="true" %
```

When the page is processed, a trace listing is rendered at the end of the web page, and is made up of the following sections.

The Request Details section is as follows:

Session ID	The session ID for the specified request.
Time of Request	The time the request was made.
Request Encoding	The character encoding for the request.
Request Type	GET | POST
Status Code	The status code value associated with the response. For more information, see http://www.w3c.org, RFC 2616 for HTTP 1.1.
Response Encoding	The character encoding for the response.

The Trace Information section is as follows:

Category	The trace category that you specified in the Trace.Warn or Trace.Write method.
Message	The trace message that you specified using the Trace.Warn or Trace.Write method.
From First(s)	The time, in seconds, since the first message was displayed.
From Last(s)	The time, in seconds, since the most recent message was displayed.

The Control Tree section is as follows:

Control ID	The ID for the control. If you have not specified an ID property for the control, ASP.NET generates an ID using the ClientID property.
Type	The fully qualified type of the control.
Render Size Bytes	The size, in bytes, of the rendered control (including child controls).
ViewState Size Bytes	The size, in bytes, of the control's view state (excluding child controls).

The Session State section is as follows:

Session Key	Session State key.
Type	Data type of object stored.
Value	Actual object stored.

The Application State section is as follows:

Application Key	Application State key.
Type	Data type of object stored.
Value	Actual object stored.

The Cookies Collection section is as follows:

Name	Name of the cookie.
Value	Data stored in cookie.
Size	Size of cookie in bytes.

The Headers Collection section is as follows:

Name	The name of an element in the header.
Value	The data in the header element.

The Form Collection section is as follows:

Name	The name of the form variable.
Value	The value of the form variable.

The Server Variables section is as follows:

Name	The name of the server variable.
Value	The value of the server variable.

The *Trace Intrinsic* Object (*TraceContext* Class)

The Trace object is a new intrinsic control in ASP.NET and is used to alter the trace settings of a web page or to send trace information from your web application to the trace system.

TraceContext Class Properties

The Trace object properties are outlined in the following:

- **IsEnabled**—Indicates whether tracing is enabled for the current web request.
- **TraceMode**—Sets the sorted order in which trace messages should be output to a requesting browser.

Trace Object Methods

The `Trace` object methods are outlined in the following:

- **Write**—Writes trace information to the trace log.
- **Warn**—Writes trace information to the trace log. Unlike `Write`, all warnings appear in the log as red text.

Using the *Trace* Object

The `Trace` object is used in a Web Form for one of the following four tasks only:

- **Change the sort order of rendered trace information**—This is done by using the `trace.TraceMode` property. An example where the rendered trace information is sorted by category is shown in the following:

```
Trace.TraceMode="sortByCategory"
```

- **Check to see if tracing is enabled for the current page**—This is done by using the `trace.isEnabled` property of the `Trace` object. An example of its use would be if the `trace` flag were to act as a custom switch for your own debug code:

```
01 If trace.enabled then
02   'do some debug specific code
03 End if
```

- **Send a Trace Information string to the trace system**—You can send a Trace Information string to the trace system by using the `trace.write()` method; this method enables you to specify both the string and the category it falls under. The following example adds a string to the `"USER DEFINED"` category:

```
Trace.write("USER DEFINED", "this is a user defined trace string")
```

- **Send a Warning Trace Information string to the trace system**—This is exactly the same as the `Write` method with one exception: the string sent will show up as red on the rendered trace information. An example is shown in the following:

```
Trace.warn("USER DEFINED", "this is a user defined trace string")
```

Using Page-Level Tracing

To use page-level tracing, you have to include the `Trace` attribute in a `@ Page` directive. The following is an example:

```
<%@ Page Trace="true" %>
```

After this has been done, your web page renders all trace information at the end of the directive when it is run.

When you set the `Trace` attribute to `true`, the `TraceContext.IsEnabled` property is also set to `true`.

The `@ Page` directive also supports one other attribute for use with the Trace system and that is the `TraceMode` attribute. This attribute is used to set the sort order of information displayed by the trace system. There are only two possible values for this:

- `SortByTime`

- `SortByCategory`

The following example is of the `@Page` directive using the `TraceMode` attribute:

```
<%@ Page Language="VB" Trace="True" TraceMode="SortByCategory" %>
```

When tracing has been enabled for a page, trace information is displayed on any browser that makes requests for the page from the server.

An example of page-level tracing is shown in Listing 2.2.

Listing 2.2   **Page Tracing Example (trace01.aspx)**

```
01 <%@ Page Trace="True" TraceMode="SortbyTime"%>
02
03 <Script runat="Server">
04
05 Sub Page_Load( s As Object, e As EventArgs )
06 trace.warn( "USER DEFINED TRACE WARN", "Page loaded!" )
07 trace.write( "USER DEFINED TRACE WRITE", "Page loaded!" )
08 End Sub
09
10
11 </Script>
12
13 <html>
14 <body>
15 <b>Enter Your Name:</b>
16 <br>
17 <form runt=server>
18   <asp:textbox id="myname" runat="Server" />
19   <asp:button id ="mybutton" text="Submit" runat="server" />
20   <br>
21 </form>
22 </body>
23 </html>
```

In Listing 2.2, we enable the tracing system and set its sorting order to that of Time. Next, we have a page_load event handler, which creates both a Warning trace message and a Normal trace message. The output of this code can be seen in Figure 2.1.

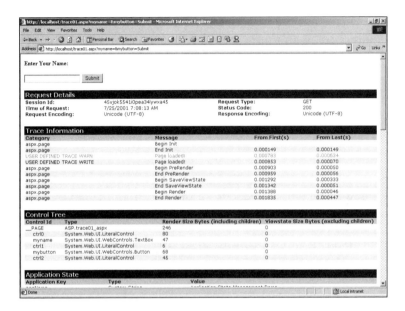

Figure 2.1 Example of page-level tracing.

Application-Level Tracing

To enable application-level tracing, you have to add the Trace section to the web.config file, which is used to configure the tracing system of ASP.NET:

```
01 <configuration>
02     <system.web>
03         <customErrors mode="Off"/>
04         <trace
05          enabled="true"
06          requestLimit="10"
07          pageOutput="true"
08          traceMode="SortByTime"
09          localOnly="true"
10         />
11     </system.web>
12 </configuration>
```

The following is the trace section syntax:

- **enabled**—Set to true if tracing is enabled for the application; otherwise false. The default setting is false.

- **requestLimit**—Number of trace requests to store on the server. The default is 10.

- **pageOutput**—Set to true if trace information should be displayed both on an application's pages and in the .axd trace utility; otherwise set to false. Pages that have tracing enabled on them are not affected by this setting.

- **traceMode**—Indicates whether trace information should be displayed in the order it was processed, SortByTime, or alphabetically by the user-defined category, SortByCategory.

- **localOnly**—Set to true if the trace viewer (trace.axd) is only available on the host web server; otherwise, set to false.

Using the Trace Log Viewer (trace.axd)

After you have enabled tracing for your web application, each page processes all page requests as though tracing has been enabled. These requests are stored on the server and can be viewed using the trace trace viewer application (trace.axd). This file is stored in your web application's root directory and only is created after you have added the web.config trace section defined previously. See figures 2.2 and 2.3.

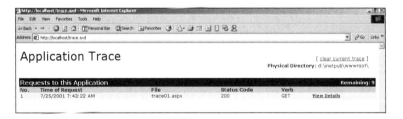

Figure 2.2   Application Trace page.

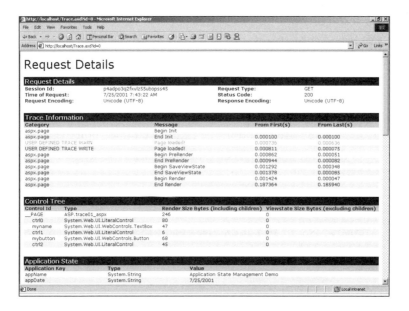

Figure 2.3   Request Details page.

ASP.NET Migration Issues

One of the issues that will be faced by most users of ASP.NET is the migration from Classic ASP to ASP.NET. This section outlines areas of possible incompatibility between Classic ASP and ASP.NET web pages.

ASP and ASP.NET can run side by side on an IIS web server without interference; there is no chance of corrupting an existing ASP application simply by installing ASP.NET.

This side-by-side interoperability is done by using separate filename extensions for ASP and ASP.NET web pages. This means that migration will typically entail copying an .asp file to an .aspx file, testing it, fixing the problems, and then deploying it.

A list of possible problems due to incompatibility between Classic ASP and ASP.NET follows.

<script> and *<% %>* Changes

All ASP.NET subs and global variables must now be declared within <script runat=server> blocks and not between ASP <% %> rendering blocks.

A page can contain more than one <script> block, but the programming language must be the same in all blocks on a page.

All code that is included within the <script> </script> tags, except global variables, must be encapsulated within sub-procedures.

In Classic ASP, code was enclosed between <% %> tags and any page processing that followed the very first <% tag got processed as soon as the page loaded. In ASP.NET, however, if you need to have code processed as soon as the page is loaded, you now have a page_load event for this purpose.

Script Rendering Functionality

Render functions are not supported in ASP.NET. By using Classic versions of ASP, it was possible to insert literal HTML within the body of a function as shown in the following:

```
01 <%
02 Function myRenderFunction()
03 %>
04 <table>
05  <tr>
06   <td>
07     <% Response.Write "Render function sample text" %>
08   </td>
09                    </tr>
10 </table>
11 <%
12 End Function
13 %>
```

This code will cause an error in an ASP.NET page. To fix this, rewrite the code as follows:

```
01 <SCRIPT LANGUAGE="VB" runat=server>
02 Function myRenderFunction()
03  Response.Write ("<table><tr><td>")
04  Response.Write ("Render function sample text")
05  Response.Write ("</td></tr></table>")
06 End Function
07 </SCRIPT>
```

Be able to call this render function from wherever you want this HTML to be rendered.

Supported Web Page Languages

An ASP.NET page is restricted to code written in a single programming language. Currently, ASP.NET supports Visual Basic, C#, and JScript. An example follows:

```
<%@Language="Jscript"%>
```

The language element can also be declared in the <script> attribute if required, but it must be the same language as the rest of the code on the page.

If different languages are declared in separate script blocks on the same page, an error will occur because only one language can be used on a single web page. However, you can use user controls written in any of the ASP.NET-compliant languages.

No More VBScript

VBScript is no longer supported, but VBScript syntax is very similar to Visual Basic. NET syntax. A brief overview of some key differences follow:

- The data type Variant no longer exists. It has been replaced with the type object. Object types must be explicitly cast to any other primitive data type.

- Parentheses are now required around the parameter list in all method calls, even for methods that don't take parameters.

- Arguments are passed by value by default, not by reference as in previous versions of Visual Basic.

- Objects no longer have default properties. All properties must be spelled out. For instance, the text values of text boxes must now be referenced as:

```
Dim str As String = TextBox1.Text
```

- The Integer data type is now 32 bits; the Long data type is 64 bits.

- Data types should always be explicitly cast to other data types. Implicit type casting is risky. For instance, always cast numerical values to String if a String is expected:

```
Response.Write("Number Entered is: " + Ctype(count, string))
```

- Variables dimensioned within the same Dim statement will be of the same type. For example, in the Dim statement Dim i, j, k As Integer, i, j, and k will be dimensioned as Integers. Previous versions of Visual Basic would dimension i and j as Variants and k as an Integer.

- Set and Let are no longer supported. Objects can be assigned by a simple assignment operation:

```
myObject1 = myObject2
```

- Class property syntax has changed. There is no longer Property Let, Property Get, and Property Set.

```
01 Public Property myProperty As String
02
03     Get
04         myProperty = _Value
05     End Get
06
07     Set
08         _Value = myProperty
09     End Set
10
11   End Property
```

- Spaces must always be included around the & operator when concatenating strings. VBScript enabled you to write `a&b&c`; this must now be written as `a & b & c` to avoid a syntax error.

- All `If` statements must be constructed on multiple lines. With VBScript, it was possible to write a single-line `If` statement.

Web Page Directives

Previous versions of ASP required that a page directive, if used, be placed on the first line of a page and that all directives be placed within the same delimiting block. For example:

```
<%@LANGUAGE="VBScript" CODEPAGE="932"%>
```

Several new directives have been added to ASP.NET. The `Language` attribute must now be placed within a `Page` directive, as shown in the following example:

```
01 <%@Page Language="VB" Codepage="932"%>
02 <%@OutputCache Duration="10 VaryByParam="location"%>
```

Directives can be located anywhere in an .aspx file, but standard practice is to place them at the beginning of the file. Case is not important in ASP.NET directive statements, and quotes are not required around the attribute values.

COM+ Interoperability

Most COM components work with ASP.NET, and you can still implement late binding using `Server.CreateObject` as with previous versions of ASP.

Summary

This chapter has briefly covered information on the some of the fundamental objects used in ASP.NET applications. All of the information is enhanced throughout the rest of the book. More detailed information on each of the objects and their use can be found in the online documentation which comes with ASP.NET or on the MSDN web site (`msdn.Microsoft.com/net`).

3

Configuring ASP.NET Applications

IN ASP.NET, CONFIGURATION INFORMATION is stored in an XML-based configuration file. This means that it is user-viewable and editable. Because of this, administrators and developers can update web application and site configuration settings with ease. It is no longer necessary for developers to wait for an administrator to change Internet Information Services (IIS) settings and reboot the web server for the settings to take effect. This understandably improves a developer's productivity.

The configuration system is fully extensible because you can store your own custom configuration settings for a web application. This is achieved through a hierarchical configuration infrastructure that enables extensible configuration data to be defined and used throughout ASP.NET applications. At the same time, ASP.NET provides a rich set of system-provided configuration settings.

Updating the web.config File

Changes to ASP.NET configuration files are automatically detected by the system and are applied immediately.

The configuration system is designed to give your web application or site configuration information easily and efficiently, so you don't have to worry about the details of the storage media and location of the configuration information.

Deploying the web.config Configuration File

The web.config usually resides in the root directory of your web application, and its settings are applied to all child subdirectories therein; however, each subdirectory can also have its own web.config file. Take a look at the following directory structure shown in Figure 3.1, and I will explain why.

```
\WebRoot
        web.config
        \Images
        \Application
                web.config
                \Public
                \Secure
                        web.config
```

Figure 3.1   Example of a web directory structure.

In Figure 3.1 a web.config file is placed in the \WebRoot directory. Any ASP.NET code processed in that directory or any subdirectories therein use the settings in the web.config file.

Also, a web.config file is in the \Application subdirectory, which means that all the web.config settings in the \WebRoot directory and all the settings in the \Application directory's web.config file are combined and applied to the contents of the \Application directory.

The duplicate settings in the \WebRoot web.config file are overridden by those of the web.config in the \Application directory.

As a final illustration, any files in the \Secure subdirectory inherit all the settings of the \WebRoot web.config directory. The \Application web.config directory, and also those of the \Secure web.config directory (the \Secure web settings takes precedence over the \Application web.config settings) take precedence over the initial \WebRoot web.config file.

The web.config File Format

Now that you know where the web.config file is deployed, look at the structure of the web.config file. As previously mentioned, the web.config configuration file is a standard XML format text-based file. All of the settings inside the configuration file are in pure XML. See Listing 3.1 for a sample web.config file.

Listing 3.1   **A Sample web.config File**

```
01 <configuration>
02
03 <system.web>
04 <compilation defaultLanguage="vb" debug="true" />
05
06 <customErrors mode="RemoteOnly" />
07
08 <trace enabled="false"
09 requestLimit="10"
10 pageOutput="false"
11 traceMode="SortByTime"
12 localOnly="true" />
13
14 <sessionState mode="InProc"
15          cookieless="false"
16 timeout="20" />
17
18 <globalization requestEncoding="utf-8"
19   responseEncoding="utf-8" />
20
21 </system.web>
22
23 </configuration>
```

The Structure of the web.config File

Now that you have seen a sample web.config file, it is time to explain its structure. The web.config file is made up of four main sections. These are described in the next sections.

<configSections> Section

This section of the web.config file is used to specify <configSections> handlers, which are functions used to interpret the XML used in a web.config section and to return information to the user of the section.

This section should only be used if you are adding your own custom configuration file handlers.

<appSettings> Section

The <appSettings> configuration section is used to hold any system-wide custom application settings. These settings are user-defined and return a string-based value. This is covered later in the chapter in the "Using the appSettings Configurations" section.

<system.web> Section

The <system.web> configuration section is the main area of the web.config file. This is where you can configure almost any aspect of an ASP.NET application's environment. Many configuration subsections exist inside the system.web section. The most common are:

- Development Configuration
  - <compilation>
  - <customErrors>
  - <trace>
- Environment Configuration
  - <browserCaps>
  - <globalization>
  - <pages>
- IIS Configuration
  - <processModel>
- Security Configuration
  - <authentication>
  - <authorization>
  - <identity>
- State Management Configuration
  - <sessionState>

Each of these sections is discussed in more detail later in this chapter in the section, "Analyzing the system.web Configuration Sections."

<location> Section

The <location> configuration section is used to apply a set of configuration settings to a specific web application directory; this is an alternative to using multiple web.config files as mentioned previously. Using it is fairly simple; basically, all you do to apply a new collection of settings is create a system.web section inside a <location> section, as demonstrated in Listing 3.2.

Listing 3.2 Example of the <location> Configuration Section

```
01 <configuration>
02
03   <system.web>
04 <compilation defaultLanguage="vb" />
05   </system.web>
06
07   <location path="c#code">
08     <system.web>
09 <compilation defaultLanguage="cs" />
10     </system.web>
11   </location>
12
13 </configuration>
```

In Listing 3.2, the configuration file is set up to use a default language "vb" (Visual Basic. NET) for all ASP.NET web pages except for those in the "c#code" subdirectory, which will use "cs" (C#) as the language for all its stored web pages.

Using the <appSettings> Configuration Section

The appSettings section, as mentioned previously, is used to hold developer-defined configuration values. These values are stored as text strings in the configuration file. An example of the appSettings configuration section is shown in Listing 3.3.

Listing 3.3 Example of the <appSettings> Section of the web.config File

```
01 <configuration>
02   <appSettings>
03     <add key="appName" value="ProjectPal" />
04     <add key="appAuthor" value="Scott Worley, et al" />
05   </appSettings>
06
07 </configuration>
```

In Listing 3.3, are two appSettings entries; these are

- **appName**—Name of the application.
- **appAuthor**—Author of the application.

These settings are added by using the <add /> element of the appSettings configuration section. The <add /> element has the following two attributes:

- **key**—The key by which you reference the application setting.
- **value**—The actual settings value.

So, now that we have created a couple of appSettings, we need a way of retrieving them. Again, as usual, ASP.NET makes this process easy, as shown in Listing 3.4.

Listing 3.4   **Example of a Web Page Retrieving Settings from an <appSettings> Configuration Section**

```
01 <html>
02 <head></head>
03 <body>
04 <b>Application Name:</b>
05 <%= ConfigurationSettings.appSettings("appName") %><br>
06 <br>
07 <b>Application Author:</b>
08 <%=  ConfigurationSettings.appSettings("appAuthor") %><br>
09 </body>
10 </html>
```

On lines 5 and 8 notice the following method call in the script render block:

ConfigurationSettings.appSettings

This method call is what is used to access the appSettings configuration section and the application settings therein. It is pretty simple to use; all you do is provide it with the key of the setting value you want to retrieve, which has been demonstrated in the code, and that is all there is to it.

At this point, it is worthwhile to note that one of the most common uses for the appSettings section is to store a database connection string for use with ADO.NET. (ADO.NET is covered in detail in Chapter 6, "Using ADO.NET in ASP.NET Applications." The appSettings section is used extensively by the sample application presented at the end of this book in Chapter 17, "Putting It All Together.")

Analyzing the system.web Configuration Sections

Now it's time to look at the system.web configuration sections in a little more detail. I'm not covering all the sections or all the attributes of the sections shown here because there are far too many to cover and space is limited. However, in most cases, each of these sections have more detailed coverage elsewhere in this book, and a reference to the specific chapter is provided with the section's overview.

I have also split the configuration sections into logical groupings for ease of reference.

Development Configuration

The sections outlined here control settings, which alter the development environment of ASP.NET when a page is compiled. The sections covered here are

- <compilation>
- <customErrors>
- <trace>

The <compilation> Section

This section is used to define the language in which to compile a web page and whether or not a page should be compiled with debug information included.

The <compilation> section attributes are as follows:

- **debug**—This attribute, if set to `true`, tells ASP.NET to include debug information in a compiled web page.

- **defaultLanguage**—This attribute sets the default language to be used in a web page's script blocks by default. A few of the languages supported are the following:

  - **vb** (Visual Basic. NET)

  - **c#** (C#)

  - **jscript** (JScript)

You can also specify multiple default languages by using a semicolon-separated list of language names, as shown:

```
vb;jscript
```

- **explicit**—If this attribute's value is set to true, the Visual Basic explicit compile option is enabled; if not, it is disabled.

- **strict**—If this attribute's value is set to true, the Visual Basic strict compile option is enabled; if not, it is disabled.

An example of the <compilation> section is shown in Listing 3.5.

Listing 3.5 **An Example of the <compilation> Section**

```
01 <configuration>
02
03   <system.web>
04     <compilation  debug="true"
05                   defaultLanguage="vb"
06                   explicit="true"
07                   strict="true" />
08   </system.web>
09
10 </configuration>
```

The <customErrors> Configuration Section

The <customErrors> configuration section is used to do one of two things—the first is enabling or disabling custom errors and the second is re-directing a URL to a user if a specific error occurs.

The <customErrors> section has the following two attributes:

- **defaultRedirect**—This is the default URL used to redirect the user if an error occurs.

- **mode**—The mode attribute, when set to On, means that the custom errors are enabled; when it is set to Off, they are disabled.

There is one other setting for the mode and that is RemoteOnly. When RemoteOnly is used, the custom errors are shown only to remote users.

The <customErrors> section also contains a subelement, which is used to define custom error pages for specific HTTP status codes. This element is the <error /> element, and it has the following two attributes:

- **StatusCode**—This is the HTTP error status code to trap for a custom error handler page.

- **redirect**—This is the URL that redirects the user when the defined error occurs.

An example of the <customErrors> section is shown in Listing 3.6.

Listing 3.6   **An Example of the <customErrors> Section**

```
01 <configuration>
02    <system.web>
03 <customErrors defaultRedirect="defaultError.aspx" mode="RemoteOnly">
04        <error statusCode="500" redirect="Error500.aspx"/>
05        <error statusCode="504" redirect="Error504.aspx"/>
06       </customErrors>
07     </system.web>
08 </configuration>
```

The <trace> Configuration Section

This section is used to enable or disable the application trace functionality in ASP.NET.

The <trace> section attributes are shown in Table 3.1. Listing 3.7 shows an example.

Table 3.1   **<trace> Section Attributes**

Attribute	Description
enabled	This attribute, if set to true, will enable application-level trace functionality; otherwise, it will be disabled.
requestLimit	Used to specify the total number of trace requests to store on the server.
pageOutput	This defines whether or not trace information will be displayed at the end of each web page; if set to true, the trace information for that web page will be displayed; if set to false, it will not be displayed.
traceMode	This attribute defines the sort order of the trace information when it is displayed. Possible values are • SortByTime • SortByCategory
localOnly	This attribute is used to set the application trace viewer to work only on the web server (local only) if its value is set to true; otherwise, the trace viewer can be used by any client. Listing 3.7 shows an example of the <trace> section.

Listing 3.7   **An Example of the <trace> Section**

```
01 <configuration>
02   <system.web>
03     <trace enabled="true"
04         requestLimit="50"
05         pageOutput="true"
06           traceMode="SortByCategory"
07         localOnly="false"  />
08   </system.web>
09 </configuration>
```

The <pages> Configuration Section

The <pages> configuration section is used to set the default properties for any ASP.NET web page that is part of a web application.

The attributes of the <pages> section mirror the attributes of the @ Page directive in ASP.NET web pages. Table 3.2 describes the attributes of the <pages> section. Listing 3.8 shows an example.

Table 3.2   **Attributes of the <pages> Section**

Attribute	Description
buffer	This attribute is used to define whether or not web pages in ASP.NET use response buffering. If set to true, response buffering is enabled; if set to false, it is not.
enableSessionState	This attribute is used to define whether Session state management is enabled by default for web pages. If set to true, Session state management is enabled for the page; if set to false, it is not.
	One other setting for this attribute is ReadOnly. This value enables read-only access for session state variables only.
enableViewState	This attribute is used to define whether View state management is enabled by default for web pages; if set to true, View state management is enabled for the page; if it is set to false, it is not.
pageBaseType	This attribute is used to specify a .NET class (normally in a code-behind format) from which ASP.NET Web Forms will inherit.
userControlBaseType	This attribute is used to specify a .NET class (normally in a code-behind format) from which ASP.NET user control pages are inherited.
autoEventWireup	This attribute is used to define whether page events are automatically configured and set up by ASP.NET (wiring up the events). If set to true, page events are automatically set up; if set to false, they are not.

Listing 3.8 **An Example of the <pages> Section**

```
01 <configuration>
02    <system.web>
03       <pages
04          buffer="true"
05          enableSessionState="true"
06          autoEventWireup="false"/>
07    </system.web>
08 </configuration>
```

Environment Configuration

The environment configuration sections of the system.web configuration section are used to define the environment in which the web application runs. It can be used to define the level of browser support with which system-generated code needs to comply or the language-specific character encoding used in multi-lingual web sites. The sections covered here are

- <browserCaps>
- <globalization>

The <globalization> Configuration Section

The <globalization> section is used to define locale- and culture-specific settings for ASP.NET web pages and controls. This section is covered in more detail in Chapter 13, "Localizing and Globalizing ASP.NET Applications."

The <globalization> section has five attributes, shown in Table 3.3. Listing 3.9 shows an example.

Table 3.3 **<globalization> Section Attributes**

Attribute	Description
requestEncoding	This attribute is used to specify the encoding of each incoming request. If request encoding is not specified, the server's locale is used.
responseEncoding	This attribute is used to specify the encoding of each outgoing response. If response encoding is not specified, the server's locale is used.
fileEncoding	This attribute is used to specify the default file encoding for .aspx, .asmx, .ascx, and .asax file parsing.
culture	This attribute is used to specify the default culture for processing incoming web requests.
uiCulture	This attribute is used to specify the default culture for processing locale-dependent resource searches.

Listing 3.9 **An Example of the <globalization> Section**

```
01 <configuration>
02   <system.web>
03     <globalization
04         requestEncoding="us-ascii"
05         responseEncoding="iso-8859-1" />
06   </system.web>
07 </configuration>
```

IIS Configuration

This section is used to configure the ASP.NET process model settings on an IIS web server.

The <processModel> Configuration Section

The <processModel> is used to configure the IIS process model settings for ASP.NET web applications. Listing 3.10 shows an example.

The <processModel> section has a total of 11 attributes. These are shown in Table 3.4.

Table 3.4 **<processModel> Section Attributes**

Attribute	Description
enable	This attribute is used to specify whether or not the process model is enabled. If set to true, it is enabled; if not, it is disabled.
timeout	This attribute is used to specify the number of minutes until ASP.NET launches a new worker process.
idleTimeout	This attribute is used to specify the number of minutes of inactivity until ASP.NET automatically shuts down a worker process.
shutdownTimeout	This attribute is used to specify the number of minutes allowed for the worker process to shut itself down. The time is used in the format of hr:min:sec (00:01:00 – 1 minute).
requestLimit	This attribute is used to specify the number of requests allowed before ASP.NET automatically launches a new worker process to take the place of the previous worker process.
requestQueueLimit	This attribute is used to specify the number of requests allowed in a request queue before ASP.NET returns a "503 - Server Too Busy" error to new requests.
memoryLimit	This attribute is used to specify the maximum allowed memory size that the worker process can consume before ASP.NET launches a new process and reassigns existing requests. This value is entered as a %age of the server memory.

Attribute	Description
cpuMask	This attribute is used to specify which processors on a multiprocessor server are being used to run ASP.NET processes.
	The cpuMask attribute value is specified as a bit pattern that indicates the CPUs eligible to run ASP.NET threads.
	For example:
	0011 – CPUs one and two are used by ASP.NET only on a 4 CPU system.
webGarden	This attribute is used to control CPU affinity when used with the cpuMask attribute. (A multiprocessor web server is referred to as a *web garden.*) If the attribute's value is true, the CPU resource usage is controlled by ASP.NET; if false, the cpuMask attribute is used to allocate CPU resources.
userName	This attribute is used to run an IIS worker process with a different Windows identity from the default process (system).
password	This attribute is used with the username attribute to run an IIS worker process with a different Windows identity from the system default (system).

Listing 3.10 **An Example of the \<processModel\> Section**

```
01 <configuration>
02    <system.web>
03       <processModel
04          enable="true"
05          timeout="15"
06          idleTimeout="25"
07          shutdownTimeout="5"
08          requestLimit="1000"
09          requestQueueLimit="500"
10          memoryLimit="40"
11          webGarden="true"
12    cpuMask="1100"        />
13    </system.web>
14 </configuration>
```

Security Configuration

ASP.NET has a very comprehensive security system, which is used to authenticate and authorize access to web resources. This configuration section has three main sections, which are

- <authentication>
- <authorization>
- <identity>

Further information on these attributes can also be found in Chapter 9, "Securing ASP.NET Applications."

The <authentication> Section Attributes

The <authentication> section has one attribute and two subsections. Listing 3.11 shows an example of the <authentication> section.

The mode attribute is used to control the authentication mode for an ASP.NET web application and supports the following values:

- **Windows**—Used to specify Windows authentication as the authentication mode. This is used when using any form of IIS authentication, such as Basic, Digest, Integrated Windows Authentication (NTLM/Kerberos), or certificates.
- **Forms**—Used to specify ASP.NET forms-based authentication as the authentication mode.
- **Passport**—Used to specify Microsoft Passport as the authentication mode.
- **None**—Used to specify no authentication support.

The <forms> section is a subsection of the <authentication> configuration section and is used when forms-based authentication is being used. This tag has five attributes and one subsection tag. These are shown in Table 3.5.

Table 3.5 **<forms> Section Attributes**

Attribute	Description
name	This attribute is used to specify the HTTP cookie used for authentication.
loginUrl	This attribute is used to specify a URL to redirect the user when an invalid authentication cookie is found.
Protection	This attribute is used to specify that the web application uses both data validation and encryption to protect the authentication cookie. Possible values for this attribute are ■ **None**—Used to specify that both encryption and validation are disabled for sites that are using cookies only for personalization and have weaker security requirements. ■ **Encryption**—Used to specify that the cookie is encrypted using Triple-DES or DES, but data validation is not performed on the cookie.

Attribute	Description
	▪ **Validation**—Used to specify a validation scheme, which verifies that the contents of an encrypted cookie have not been altered in transit.
	▪ **All**—This setting enables both encryption- and validation-based protection.
timeout	This attribute is used to specify the time (in minutes) when the authentication cookie expires.
path	This attribute is used to specify the path for cookies created by the web application.

The <credentials> section is a subsection of the <authentication> configuration section, and it is used to define name and password credentials. This section has one attribute, passwordFormat, and also one subsection, <user>.

The passwordFormat attribute is used to specify the encryption format used when storing passwords; it can have any of the following values:

- **Clear**—Used to specify that passwords are not encrypted and are stored in a clear-text format.

- **MD5**—Used to specify that passwords are encrypted using the MD5 hash algorithm.

- **SHA1**—Used to specify that passwords are encrypted using the SHA1 hash algorithm.

The <user> section is a subsection of the <credentials> section and is used to define name and password credentials for each user. This section has two attributes, and these are

- **name**—This attribute is used to hold a user's login name.

- **Password**—This attribute is used to hold a user's password.

Listing 3.11   An Example of the <authentication> Section

```
01 <configuration>
02     <system.web>
03         <authentication mode="Forms">
04             <forms name="projectpal" loginUrl="/login.aspx" />
05         </authentication>
06     </system.web>
07 </configuration>
```

The <authorization> Configuration Section

The <authorization> section is used to define authorization settings for ASP.NET web applications; it is generally used in conjunction with the <authentication> configuration section. Listing 3.12 shows an example of this section.

The <authorization> section has two subsections; these are

- <allow>
- <deny>

The <allow> subsection is used to enable access to a resource; the three attributes for this section are

- **users**—Used to grant users access to resources. This attribute's value is a comma-separated list of users. A question mark (?) allows anonymous users and an asterisk (★) allows all users.
- **roles**—A comma-separated list of roles that are granted access to the resource.
- **verbs**—A comma-separated list of HTTP transmission methods that are granted access to the resource. Verbs registered to ASP.NET are GET, HEAD, POST, and DEBUG.

The <deny> subsection is used to deny access to a resource. The three attributes for this section are

- **users**—Used to deny user access to resources. This attribute's value is a comma-separated list of users. A question mark (?) denies anonymous users and an asterisk (★) denies all users.
- **roles**—A comma-separated list of roles that are denied access to the resource
- **verbs**—A comma-separated list of HTTP transmission methods that are denied access to the resource. Verbs registered to ASP.NET are GET, HEAD, POST, and DEBUG.

Listing 3.12 **An Example of the <authorization> Section**

```
01 <configuration>
02    <system.web>
03       <authorization>
04          <allow roles="Guests" />
05          <deny users="*" />
06       </authorization>
07    </system.web>
08 </configuration>
```

The <identity> Configuration Section

The <identity> section is used to set the identity of a web application through a technique called *impersonation* (this is covered in Chapter 8, "XML Web Service Development in ASP.NET"). See Listing 3.13 for an example of the <identity> section.

The <identity> section has three attributes; these are

- **impersonate**—This attribute specifies whether or not client impersonation is used on each web request. If the attribute's value is `true`, client impersonation is used; otherwise, it is not.

- **userName**—This attribute specifies the user name to use if impersonation is set to `false`.

- **password**—This attribute specifies the password to use if impersonation is set to `false`.

Listing 3.13 **An Example of the <identity> Section**

```
01 <configuration>
02    <system.web>
03       <identity impersonate="true" />
04    </system.web>
05 </configuration>
```

State Management Configuration

ASP.NET has a very flexible and powerful state management system, which can be configured through the web.config file.

The <sessionState> Configuration Section

The <sessionState> section is used to configure the state management features of ASP.NET applications. The <sessionState> section has the following attributes, shown in Table 3.6. Listing 3.14 shows an example of the <sessionState> section.

Table 3.6 **<sessionState>** Section Attributes

Attribute	Description
mode	This attribute is used to specify where the session state is stored; it has the following possible values:
	• **Off**—Used to disable session state management.
	• **Inproc**—Used to enable in-process session state management.
	• **StateServer**—Used to enable the state server-based state management. (State is stored on a remote server.)
	• **SqlServer**—Used to enable SQL Server-based state management.
cookieless	This attribute is used to specify whether or not cookieless sessions should be used to identify client sessions. If the attribute value is true, then cookieless sessions are enabled.
timeout	This attribute is used to specify the total number of minutes a session can be idle before it is abandoned.
connectionString	This attribute is used to specify the server name and port where session state is stored remotely.
	This is used in conjunction with the "StateServer" mode; otherwise, it is not required.
sqlConnectionString	This attribute is used to specify the connection string for SQL Server-based state management.
	This is used in conjunction with the "SQLServer" mode; otherwise, it is not required.

Listing 3.14   **An Example of the <sessionState> Section**

```
01 <configuration>
02    <system.web>
03      <sessionState
04        mode="SQLState"
05        sqlConnectionString="data source=localhost;user id=sa; password="
06        cookieless="true"
07        timeout="25" />
08      </sessionState>
09    </system.web>
10 </configuration>
```

Summary

This chapter introduced the application configuration system of ASP.NET. You have seen how easy it is to create and use your own configuration settings as well as get information on the majority of configuration settings for web applications provided by ASP.NET.

The web.config configuration file is mentioned in various places throughout the rest of this book, and the settings are revisited and are explained in more detail. Also, the application in Chapter 17 uses a couple of web.config files in its operation.

II

Core ASP.NET

4

Web Form-Based Development

THIS CHAPTER INTRODUCES WEB FORMS as the new programming model in ASP.NET. The chapter begins by comparing Web Forms with Classic ASP and takes a brief look at some code and architecture. It also details the page processing stage and object-oriented analysis of the Page class in addition to the separation of user interface and code. It discusses the two types of server controls: HTML controls and Web controls.

This chapter concludes with the discussion of ASP.NET page syntax—the syntax you should know for developing ASP.NET applications.

Introduction to Web Forms

Web Forms are a new ASP.NET programming model that you can use to create programmable web pages. Web Forms are a server-side programming technology. They use code on the server to implement application logic and send HTML tags as the output. If the user of your Web Form's application uses a specific browser, such as Microsoft Internet Explorer 5.5, you can send rich format HTML with features for style, layout, and so forth. On the other hand, if you can't control the type of browser the user will be using, you can output HTML 3.2 tags that can be rendered by all browsers.

Web Forms are built on *Common Language Runtime* (CLR) and provide all the benefits of those technologies, including a managed execution environment, type safety, inheritance, and dynamic compilation for improved performance. By being part of the .NET framework, Web Forms can use the .NET framework base class libraries to ensure optimum code reuse.

You can build a Web Form using a simple text editor. However, if you have installed Microsoft Visual Studio .NET, you can use the WYSIWYG development tool to rapidly design and develop a Web Form's application.

Comparison with ASP

The first difference between ASP and ASP.NET is the page extension. ASP pages have an .asp extension and ASP.NET pages have an .aspx extension. For backwards compatibility, however, ASP.NET still supports the programming model of ASP. Therefore, even though your pages now have an .aspx extension, you can still use the old ASP style to build spaghetti-like code, interweaving code, and HTML tags, which is exemplified by the code in Listing 4.1.

Listing 4.1 **Using ASP Programming Style**

```
01 <html>
02 <head>
03 <title>Using ASP programming style</title>
04 </head>
05 <body>
06
07 <%
08  Response.Write("Hello from ASP.NET")
09 %>
10
11 </body>
12 </html>
```

Note that the Write method of the Response object requires brackets for the argument.

ASP.NET introduces a new programming model—Web Forms. The most important difference from ASP is that in ASP.NET Web Forms you always separate the business layer and the presentation layer and the code from the user interface. If you are an ASP programmer and ASP is the only program that you do, the new programming model is probably not familiar to you. In ASP, you normally have multiple pages for one application, and each page only handles a part of one particular task; it is normal to make your user jump agilely from one page to another. Web Forms, on the other hand, have only one page to process a particular task. So, imagine something like a self-referencing page in Classic ASP. Web Forms are like windows forms, but for the Internet. If you have been programming with Visual Basic or Visual C++, you will find Web Forms very familiar.

To illustrate this point, consider an ASP login page that checks the user name and password. In the old ASP you would have two pages: LoginForm.html and VerifyLogin.asp, which are given in Listings 4.2 and 4.3, respectively.

Listing 4.2 **LoginForm.html**

```
01 <html>
02 <head>
03 <title>Login Page</title>
04 </head>
05 <body>
06 <form action=VerifyLogin.asp method=post>
07 <table>
08 <tr>
09  <td>Login Name:</td>
10  <td><input type=text name=LoginName>
11 </tr>
12 <tr>
13  <td>Password:</td>
14  <td><input type=password name=Password>
15 </tr>
16 <tr>
17  <td><input type=reset></td>
18  <td><input type=submit value="Login"></td>
19 </tr>
20 </table>
21 </form>
22 </body>
23 </html>
```

Listing 4.3 **VerifyLogin.asp**

```
01 <%
02  Option Explicit
03 %>
04 <html>
05 <head>
06 <title>Verify Login Name and Password</title>
07 </head>
08 <body>
09
10 <%
11  Dim LoginName
12  Dim Password
```

continues ▶

Listing 4.3 **Continued**

```
13
14 LoginName = Request.Form("LoginName")
15 Password = Request.Form("Password")
16 If LoginName = "jamesb" AND Password = "takashi" Then
17   Response.Write "Welcome To BrainySoftware Web site"
18 Else
19   Response.Write "Login failed"
20 End If
21
22 %>
23 </body>
24 </html>
```

Note how you need two pages for checking a user's credentials.

With Web Forms, you only have one page. The code for the Web Form's login page is given in Listing 4.4.

Listing 4.4 **A Web Form's Login Page**

```
01 <html>
02 <head>
03 <title>Web Forms Login Page</title>
04 <script language="vb" runat="Server">
05
06 Sub Button1_Click(source as Object, e As EventArgs)
07  If LoginName.value.Equals("jamesb") And _
08    Password.value.Equals("takashi") Then
09    message.InnerHtml="Welcome to BrainySoftware Web site."
10  Else
11    message.InnerHtml="Login failed. Please try again."
12  End If
13 End Sub
14 </script>
15 </head>
16
17 <body>
18 <center>
19 <form runat=server>
20 <table>
21 <tr>
22  <td>Login Name:</td>
23  <td><input id="LoginName" runat=server></td>
24 </tr>
25 <tr>
26  <td>Password:</td>
27  <td><input id="Password" type=password runat=server></td>
28 </tr>
29 <tr>
```

```
30  <td><input type=reset></td>
31  <td><input type=submit OnServerClick="Button1_Click"
32       value="Login" runat=server></td>
33  </tr>
34  </table>
35  </form>
36
37  <p><span id="message" runat=server/>
38  </center>
39  </body>
40  </html>
```

There are a few striking differences between the Web Form's code in Listing 4.4 and the ASP application in Listings 4.2 and 4.3. First, the form in Listing 4.3 does not need to have an action attribute, which means that when the form is submitted, the HTTP request goes to the same page, which is a self-referencing page. Instead of the NAME attribute in every element, you have the id attribute. If your form does not have a method attribute, the ASP.NET server uses POST by default. This is in contrast to Classic ASP, which uses GET as the default method for forms.

Secondly, you may notice in the Web Form's code that there are runat attributes in the form tag, the input tags, and the span tag. All the attributes have the "=server" values. Each element with a runat=server attribute/value pair is processed by the server prior to being sent to the browser. The result of this server processing is shown in the HTML code sent when the page is requested for the first time, which is shown in the following:

```
01 <html>
02 <head>
03 <title>Web Forms Login Page</title>
04
05 </head>
06
07 <body>
08 <center>
09 <form name="ctrl2" method="post" action="LoginPage.aspx" id="ctrl2">
10 <input type="hidden" name="__VIEWSTATE" value="dDwtOTIzMjY0MTA3OZs+" />
11
12 <table>
13 <tr>
14   <td>Login Name:</td>
15   <td><input name="LoginName" id="LoginName" type="text" /></td>
16 </tr>
17 <tr>
18   <td>Password:</td>
19   <td><input name="Password" id="Password" type="password" /></td>
20 </tr>
```

```
21 <tr>
22   <td><input type=reset></td>
23   <td><input name="ctrl8" type="submit" value="Login" /></td>
24 </tr>
25 </table>
26 </form>
27
28 <p><span id="message">Welcome to BrainySoftware Web site.</span>
29 </center>
30 </body>
31 </html>
```

Note how the server supplies the action and method attributes for the form. Also, each HTML object has a name as well as an id. The exception to this is the hidden input element called __VIEWSTATE, which is generated by the server. This hidden field is a container for a collection of information about the properties of a Web Form's page.

When the user submits the form, the HTTP request will be sent to the server just like in the Classic ASP. However, on the server, the submit button has the following tag:

```
<input type=submit OnServerClick="Button1_Click" runat=server>
```

In the previous code, the OnServerClick attribute tells the server what it has to do when the submit button is clicked, which is run the Button1_Click event procedure. For reading convenience, the Button1_Click event procedure is rewritten in the following:

```
01 Sub Button1_Click(source as Object, e As EventArgs)
02   If LoginName.value.Equals("jamesb") And _
03     Password.value.Equals("takashi") Then
04     message.InnerHtml="Welcome to BrainySoftware Web site."
05   Else
06     message.InnerHtml="Login failed. Please try again."
07   End If
08 End Sub
```

What it does is very simple. It compares the value of the text box called LoginName and the value of the password. If the values are "jamesb" and "takashi", respectively, it sets the value of message.InnerHtml to "Welcome to BrainySoftware Web site". Otherwise, it will set it to "Login failed. Please try again.". A successful login is shown in Figure 4.1.

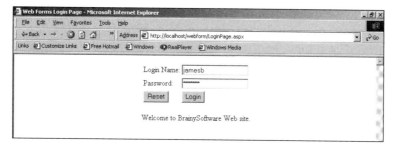

Figure 4.1   A Web Form's login page after a successful logon.

Web Form Architecture

Web Forms divide web applications into two parts:

- The visual component.
- The user interface logic.

The user interface for Web Form pages consists of a file containing markup and Web Form–specific elements. This file has an .aspx extension and is referred to as the *page*. The page works as a container for the text and controls what you want to display.

The user interface logic for the Web Form consists of the code you create to interact with the form. You can choose to have the programming logic reside in the .aspx file or in a separate file (referred to as the "code-behind" file) and written in Visual Basic or C#. When you run the form, the code-behind class file runs and dynamically produces the output for your page.

A Web Form's page is compiled on the first request for the .aspx file.

Web Forms Processing Stages

During a Web Form's processing, the Web Form's page goes through a number of distinct stages. At each stage, the Web Form's processor calls a corresponding page processing method and runs any code in that method. These page processing methods provide entry points for working with the contents of the form.

Table 4.1 lists the most commonly used stages of page processing, when these stages occur, and what you can do at each stage. These stages are repeated each time the page is requested or a form in the page is posted. The IsPostBack property enables you to test whether the page is being processed for the first time.

Note that there are several more stages of page processing than are listed in the following table. However, they are not used for ordinary page processing. Instead, they are primarily used by server controls on the page to initialize themselves, render themselves, and so on. If you are intending to write your own Web Form's server controls, you will need to understand more about these additional stages.

Table 4.1 **Page Processing Stages**

Stage	**Meaning**	**Typical Uses**
Configuration	Page and control view state is restored and then the page's `Page_Load` event is raised.	Checks (using the IsPostBack page property) whether this is the first time the page is being processed. Performs data binding the first time the page is processed or re-evaluates data binding expressions on subsequent round trips.
		Reads and updates control properties.
		Restores the state saved from a previous client request during the Save stage.
Event handling	If the page was called in response to a form event, the corresponding event-handling method in the page is called during this stage.	Handles the specific event.
		Note: Events are not raised in a particular order, except that cached control events (as specified by the control's AutoPostBack property) are always processed before the posting event.
		If the page contains validation controls, it checks the IsValid property for the page or for individual validation controls.

Stage	Meaning	Typical Uses
		It manually saves the state of the global page variables you are maintaining yourself and saves controls you dynamically added to the page.
Cleanup	The page has finished rendering and is ready to be discarded.	Closing files. Closing database connections. Discarding objects.
		Note: It is important that expensive resources (such as database connections) are explicitly closed. Otherwise, they will remain open until the next garbage collection occurs. On a heavily loaded server, too many open resources can exhaust memory.

The *Page* Class

This section looks at what happens in the background when your .aspx file is called. We will also learn the object-oriented analysis of ASP.NET.

By default, every ASP.NET page inherits the `Page` class from the `System.Web.UI` namespace. If you don't supply the Inherits attribute in your page, which is shown in the following page directive, the compiler will assume it.

```
<%@ Page language="VB" Inherits="System.Web.UI.Page" %>
```

Because the class is derived from the `System.Web.UI.Page` class, the new class inherits the properties, methods, and events of the `Page` class. The `Page` class has events that become the processing stages of a Web Form page. If you want to understand ASP.NET thoroughly, you should study the `Page` class.

The `Page` class extends the `System.Web.UI.TemplateControl` class and implements the `System.Web.IHttpHandler` interface. This interface defines the interface inheritence contract that developers must implement to synchronously process HTTP web requests.

The `Page` class defines the properties, methods, and events common to all pages that are processed on the server by the Web Form's page framework.

The *Page* Class' Properties

Among the properties of the Page class are the Request, Response, Server, Application, and Session properties that enable you to retrieve the Request, Response, Server, Application, and Session objects, respectively, from the HTTP Runtime. If you are an ASP programmer, you should be familiar with these five ASP built-in objects. For instance, the Response object enables you to output a string to the browser.

Also important is the IsPostBack property. This property returns false if the current request is the first request from the user. Otherwise, it returns true. You can query the value of this property and do a one-time initialization if the property returns false.

```
01 Function ispostback()
02   If request.servervariables.content_length > 0 then
03     Ispostback = true
04   Else
05     Ispostback = false
06   End if
07 End function
```

Another property is the IsUplevel property, which returns true if the request comes from a fourth generation browser, that is Internet Explorer 4.0 or above and Netscape Navigator 4.0 or above. By utilizing this property, you can have two sets of HTML pages—standard pages and browser-specific pages. If you know for sure that the user is using IE 5.0, for example, you might want to send dynamic HTML to make your site more attractive.

The *Page* Class' Methods

The Page class provides useful methods to perform tasks that are done using methods of the built-in objects in Classic ASP. The MapPath method replaces the same method in the Server object. You can use the MapPath method to assign a virtual path, either relative or absolute, to a physical path.

Another method, Validate, instructs any validation controls included on the page to validate their assigned information for the incoming page request.

The *Page* Class' Events

The Page class inherits events from the Control class, such as Init. The most frequently used events are as follows.

Page_Load Event

The Page_Load event is raised when the page loads. Use this event to read and restore the previously stored values. Also, you can use the IsPostBack property to do one-time initialization for every user. The `IsPostBack` property is `false` if this is the first time a user requests this page. Other uses of this event include the following:

- Performing data binding the first time the page is processed or reevaluating data binding expressions on subsequent round trips.

- Reading and updating control properties.

- Restoring the state saved from a previous client request during the Save stage.

If the page was called in response to a `form` event, the corresponding event-handling method in the page is called during this stage. For example, the code in Listing 4.4 runs the `Button1_Click` event procedure during this stage.

The example in Listing 4.5 demonstrates the use of the `Page_Load` event and the `IsPostBack` property. When the page first loads, it calls the `Page_Load` event procedure, which checks whether this is the first request by the user. If it is, the message `"Welcome. Please enter your user name and password"` is displayed.

Listing 4.5   **Using the *Page_Load* Event**

```
01 <html>
02 <head>
03 <title>Web Forms Login Application</title>
04 <script language="VB" runat="Server">
05
06 Sub Page_Load()
07  If Not IsPostBack Then
08    message.InnerHtml="Welcome. " & _
09    "Please enter your user name and password."
10  End If
11 End Sub
12
13 Sub Button1_Click(source As Object, e As EventArgs)
14  If userName.Value.Equals("merino") And _
15    password.Value.Equals("fragile") Then
16    message.InnerHtml="Welcome."
17  Else
18    message.InnerHtml="Login failed. Please try again."
19  End If
20 End Sub
21 </script>
22 </head>
23
24 <body>
25 <form runat=server>
26 UserName: <input id="userName" runat=server>
```

continues ▶

Listing 4.5   **Continued**

```
27 <BR>Password: <input id="password" type=password runat=server>
28 <BR><input type=submit OnServerClick="Button1_Click" runat=server>
29
30 </form>
31 <p><span id="message" runat=server/>
32 </body>
33 </html>
```

Page_Unload **Event**

The Page_Unload event is used to cleanup, such as closing files, closing database connections, or discarding objects. It is important that resource-hungry objects, such as database connections, are explicitly closed. This way, the objects do not remain in memory until the next garbage collection cycle.

Separating Code from the User Interface

When your application gets more complex, it is recommended to store your code in a separate file from the user interface. If you are using Visual Studio .NET to develop your Web Forms, the code is always saved as a different file.

If you do this, the class in the code file will extend the Page class. In turn, your .aspx file, which is the page where you put your user interface controls, will extend the class in the code file. Web Forms enable you to do this by providing the Codebehind and Src attributes of the Page directive. These two attributes act as the glue between your .aspx file and your code file. You use Codebehind if your code has already been compiled and Src if your code exists as source code.

To illustrate the separation of the user interface and code, consider the following example, whose code is given in Listing 4.6 and 4.7. The code in Listing 4.6 (Testing.aspx) is an .aspx file that uses the code in the file MyCode.vb, which is shown in Listing 4.7. Note the use of the Src attribute in Listing 4.6.

Listing 4.6   **Testing.aspx**

```
01 <%@ Page language="vb" Src="MyCode.vb" AutoEventWireup="false" Inherits="MyCode" %>
02 <html>
03 <head>
04 <title>Code separation</title>
05 </head>
06 <body>
```

```
07 <form runat="server">
08 <asp:Label id=Label1 runat="server" Width="186" Height="19">Label</asp:Label>
09 <br>
10 <asp:TextBox id=TextBox1 runat="server"></asp:TextBox>
11 <asp:Button id=Button1 runat="server" Text="Button"
12 OnClick="Button1_Click"></asp:Button>
13 </form>
14 </body>
15 </html>
```

Listing 4.7   **MyCode.vb**

```
01 Imports System
02 Imports System.Web.UI.WebControls
03
04 Public Class MyCode
05  Inherits System.Web.UI.Page
06  Protected Label1 As Label
07  Protected WithEvents Button1 As Button
08  Protected TextBox1 As TextBox
09
10  Public Sub Button1_Click (Sender As Object, E As System.EventArgs)
11     Label1.Text = TextBox1.Text
12  End Sub
13 End Class
```

Listing 4.6 presents an .aspx file that contains some user interface controls: a Label, a TextBox, and a Button. No code is present, however, the first line of the page is the Page directive with the Codebehind attribute and the Inherits attribute. The Inherits attribute has the value "MyCode", which tells the compiler that the .aspx page should be compiled as a new class that extends a class named MyCode. This class is found in the file given by the Src attribute.

The code in Listing 4.7 contains the class MyCode. Note that the class MyCode extends System.Web.UI.Page. This class contains all the needed code to run the application.

If you pre-compile the source code, it has to be compiled into a .dll file, and this .dll file should be deployed to the bin subdirectory of the virtual directory. You then use the CodeBehind attribute to replace the Src attribute.

Server Controls

Server controls are specifically designed to work with Web Forms. There are two types of server controls: HTML controls and Web controls. We review them in the following sections.

HTML Controls

The first set of server controls is HTML controls. Each HTML control has a one-to-one mapping with an HTML tag and, therefore, represents an HTML control you've probably been using.

These controls reside in the `System.Web.UI.HtmlControls` namespace and derive either directly or indirectly from the `HtmlControl` base class. The controls and their corresponding HTML tags are given in Table 4.2.

Table 4.2 **HTML Controls and Their Tags**

Control	HTML Tag
HtmlAnchor	`<a>`
HtmlButton	`<button>`
HtmlSelect	`<select>`
HtmlTextArea	`<textarea>`
HtmlInputButton	`<input type="button">`
HtmlInputCheckBox	`<input type="checkbox">`
HtmlInputRadioButton	`<input type="radio">`
HtmlInputText	`<input type="text">` and `<input type="password">`
HtmlInputHidden	`<input type="hidden">`
HtmlInputImage	`<input type="image">`
HtmlInputFile	`<input type="file">`
HtmlForm	`<form>`
HtmlImage	`<img>`
HtmlTable	`<table>`
HtmlTableRow	`<tr>`
HtmlTableCell	`<td>`
HtmlGenericControl	Any other unmapped tag, such as `<span>` and `<div>`

To use an HTML control in a Web Form, you declare it using the standard HTML tag that represents the control in HTML. However, to get instantiated on the server, the HTML tag must have the `runat="server"` attribute. For example, the following will create an instance of `HtmlInputText` named `"UserName"`.

```
<input type="text" id="UserName" runat="server">
```

And the following to instantiate an `HtmlForm`:

```
01 <form runat=server>
02 </form>
```

HTML controls are divided into three groups:

- **Input controls**—All input controls are derived from the abstract class `HtmlInputControl`, which itself is an extension of `HtmlControl`. Child classes of `HtmlInputControl` include `HtmlInputButton`, `HtmlInputCheckBox`, `HtmlInputFile`, `HtmlInputHidden`, `HtmlInputImage`, `HtmlInputRadioButton`, and `HtmlInputText`.

- **Container controls**—These controls are extended from the `HtmlContainerControl` class. Container controls derived from `HtmlContainerControl` include `HtmlAnchor`, `HtmlButton`, `HtmlForm`, `HtmlGenericControl`, `HtmlSelect`, `HtmlTable`, `HtmlTableCell`, `HtmlTableRow`, and `HtmlTextArea`.

- **Image control**—There is only one class in this category: `HtmlImage`.

Web Controls

Web controls are the second set of server controls. These controls exist within the `System.Web.UI.WebControls` namespace and derive directly or indirectly from the `WebControl` base class. Some of the controls are very simple controls that are identical with HTML controls. Some others, however, provide higher level abstractions.

Web controls are declared using the .asp prefix. For example, the following is a TextBox Web control declaration:

```
<asp:TextBox id="userName" type="text" runat="server">
```

The previous Web control is rendered as the following:

```
<input name="userName" type="text" id="userName" type="text" />
```

This is the same as the HTML tag sent by the following HTML input text control:

```
<input type=text id="userName" runat="server">
```

Note that a Web control must be written using XML syntax whereas an HTML control can use either HTML or XML syntax.

However, you can't interchange a Web control with its HTML control equivalent without changing the code because a Web control in an ASP.NET page will be translated into a different object. For example, to retrieve the value entered by the user to a TextBox Web control, you would use the `Text` property of the `TextBox` object; however, to do the same task with an HtmlInputText control, you use the Value property.

Even though HTML controls are similar in nature, which makes code migration from ASP to ASP.NET easier, Web controls have some superior features that don't exist in HTML controls. These features include the following:

- Web controls provide a rich object model. The richness is attributed to the parent base class, WebControl. This class includes properties such as ForeColor, Font, Enabled, BackColor, BorderColor, Height, and so on. Because all Web controls are child classes of WebControl, all Web controls inherit these properties as well, making programming easier.

- Web controls automatically detect the capabilities of the client browser and customize their rendering to make better use of these capabilities. For example, the following Label control is rendered differently in Navigator 3.0 and Internet Explorer 4.0 and above.

```
<asp:Label runat="server" Text="Label Control" Font-Italic="true" />
```

Using IE 5.5, the Label control is rendered as the following HTML code:

```
<span style="font-style:italic;">Label Control</span>
```

Using Navigator 3.0, on the other hand, gives you the following HTML code:

```
<span><i>Label Control</i></span>
```

- Any property of a Web control can be data bound. In addition, there are several Web controls that can be used to render the contents of a data source.

Most Web control's classes are child classes of the WebControl class. Therefore, these classes inherit the properties of the WebControl class. The following are some of the properties:

- **BackColor**—Sets the background color of the Web control.
- **BorderColor**—Sets the border color of the Web control.
- **Enabled**—Sets a value indicating whether the Web control is enabled.
- **Font**—Gets the font information of the Web control.
- **Height**—Sets the height of the Web control.
- **Width**—Sets the width of the Web control.

Each of the Web controls is explained in the following sections. An example is also given to illustrate the use of the control.

Button

You use the Button control when you want a push button control that posts the page back to the server. The Button class can be used to create a submit button that submits the contents of a form. The Button control has the OnClick event that is triggered when the user clicks the button. The OnClick event is connected to the SubmitBtn_Click event procedure, which in turn will display "ooow…you just clicked me :-).".

The code in Listing 4.8 illustrates the use of the Button control and the OnClick event.

Listing 4.8   **Using the Button Control**

```
01 <html>
02 <head>
03 <title>The Button Control</title>
04 </head>
05
06 <script language="VB" runat=server>
07
08 Sub SubmitBtn_Click(Sender As Object, e As EventArgs)
09   Message.InnerHtml="Ooow... you just clicked me :-)."
10 End Sub
11
12 </script>
13
14 <body>
15 <center>
16 <form method="post" runat="server">
17
18  <asp:Button id="Button1" runat="server" Text="Click Me"
19    OnClick="SubmitBtn_Click" runat="server"/>
20
21   <p>
22
23   <span id="Message" runat="server" />
24
25 </form>
26 </center>
27 </body>
28 </html>
```

CheckBox

The CheckBox control is a control that displays a checkbox that enables users to select a true or false condition. This control has the CheckedChanged event that is triggered when the user changes the checked property, that is from false to true or from true to false. You can use this event to run a function that will be run when the user clicks the CheckBox control.

The CheckBox control has a property called AutoPostBack property. When the property is set to true, the CheckBox posts its state back to the server. In addition, there is also the Text property that you can set with a string displayed with the CheckBox.

The code in Listing 4.9 presents the code that uses a CheckBox control.

Listing 4.9 **Using a CheckBox Control**

```
01 <html>
02 <head>
03 <title>The Button Control</title>
04 </head>
05
06 <script language="VB" runat=server>
07
08 Sub Check_Clicked(Sender As Object, e As EventArgs)
09  If checkbox1.Checked Then
10    Message.InnerHtml="Checked"
11  Else
12    Message.InnerHtml="Not Checked"
13  End If
14 End Sub
15
16 </script>
17
18 <body>
19 <center>
20 <form method="post" runat="server">
21
22  <asp:CheckBox id="checkbox1" runat="server"
23    AutoPostBack="True"
24    Text="Would you like to receive advisory emails?"
25    TextAlign="Right"
26    OnCheckedChanged="Check_Clicked"/>
27  <br>
28  <span id="Message" runat="server" />
29
30 </form>
31 </center>
32 </body>
33 </html>
```

RadioButton

This control represents a radio button control. You always use a group of radio buttons together to represent options that the user can select. The RadioButton class extends the CheckBox class. It has a property named GroupName to indicate the name of the group to which the radio button belongs.

The following example illustrates the use of RadioButton controls to select a type of music that is the user's favorite. When the user clicks the

Button control, the radio buttons' states are sent to the server. The SubmitBtn_Clicked event procedure is executed when the button is clicked. The code given in Listing 4.10 displays the Text property of the selected radio button.

Listing 4.10   **Using RadioButton Controls**

```
01 <html>
02 <head>
03 <title>The RadioButton Controls</title>
04 </head>
05
06 <script language="VB" runat=server>
07
08 Sub SubmitBtn_Clicked(Sender As Object, e As EventArgs)
09  If Radio1.Checked Then
10    Message.InnerHtml = "You selected " + Radio1.Text
11  ElseIf Radio2.Checked
12    Message.InnerHtml = "You selected " + Radio2.Text
13  ElseIf Radio3.Checked
14    Message.InnerHtml = "You selected " + Radio3.Text
15  End If
16 End Sub
17
18 </script>
19
20 <body>
21 <center>
22 <form method="post" runat="server">
23
24  <h4>Select your favorite music:</h4>
25  <asp:RadioButton id=Radio1 Text="Pop" Checked="True"
26    GroupName="RadioGroup1" runat="server"/>
27  <br>
28  <asp:RadioButton id=Radio2 Text="Jazz"
29    GroupName="RadioGroup1" runat="server"/>
30  <br>
31  <asp:RadioButton id=Radio3 Text="Classic"
32    GroupName="RadioGroup1" runat="server"/>
33  <br>
34  <asp:button text="Select" OnClick="SubmitBtn_Clicked" runat=server/>
35  <br><br>
36  <span id="Message" runat="server" />
37
38 </form>
39 </center>
40 </body>
41 </html>
```

Figure 4.2 shows three radio buttons and a Button control.

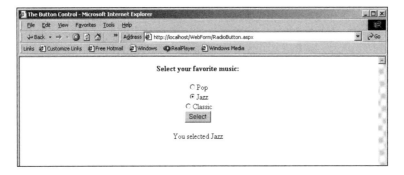

Figure 4.2   The RadioButton controls.

Hyperlink

Hyperlink is a control that displays a link for the browser to navigate to another page. The control can appear as a normal hyperlink, that is under-lined text by default, or an image. If you choose to use an image hyperlink, you need to use the `ImageUrl` property and assign it to the URL of the image. Absence of the `ImageUrl` property will make your hyperlink look like a normal hyperlink.

The `NavigateUrl` property specifies the destination URL that the browser will go to when the hyperlink is clicked. The `Text` property displays the text for the hyperlink. The `Target` property specifies the target window or frame in which the contents of the Hyperlink will be displayed when the hyperlink is clicked.

Listing 4.11 presents code that uses an image Hyperlink control. When it is clicked, the new URL will be displayed in a new browser window.

Listing 4.11   **An Image Hyperlink Control**

```
01 <html>
02 <head>
03 <title>Image Hyperlink</title>
04 </head>
05
06 <body>
07 <center>
08 <asp:HyperLink id="hyperlink1" runat="server"
09    ImageUrl="image1.gif"
10    NavigateUrl="http://www.oracle.com"
11    Text="Oracle Site"
12    Target="_blank"/>
13 </center>
14 </body>
15 </html>
```

Listing 4.12 offers code that displays a normal hyperlink.

Listing 4.12   **A Normal Hyperlink**

```
01 <html>
02 <head>
03 <title>Normal Hyperlink</title>
04 </head>
05
06 <body>
07 <center>
08
09   <asp:HyperLink id="hyperlink1" runat="server"
10    NavigateUrl="http://www.oracle.com"
11    Text="Oracle Site" />
12
13 </center>
14 </body>
15 </html>
```

Image

Image is a control that displays an image on the page. To use an Image control, you must set the `ImageUrl` property to the URL of the image file. The Image control also has the `AlternateText` and `ImageAlign` properties. The `AlternateText` property specifies the alternate text when the image fails to load. The `ImageAlign` property specifies the alignment of the image within the text flow.

Listing 4.13 provides code that displays an Image control.

Listing 4.13   **The Image Control**

```
01 <html>
02 <head>
03 <title>Image</title>
04 </head>
05
06 <body>
07 <asp:Image id="Image1" runat="server"
08  AlternateText="Logo"
09  ImageAlign="left"
10  ImageUrl="image1.gif"/>
11 </body>
12 </html>
```

ImageButton

The ImageButton extends the Image class. The ImageButton control is used to display an image, respond to mouse clicks, and record the mouse pointer position. The ImageButton class has the Click event that is triggered when the control is clicked. The coordinates of the mouse pointer are recorded when the control is clicked.

Listing 4.14 lists the code that responds to a mouse click on an ImageButton control. When clicked, the coordinate of the mouse pointer is displayed relative to the upper-left corner of the control.

Listing 4.14   **An ImageButton Control**

```
01 <html>
02 <head>
03 <title>Using ImageButton</title>
04
05 <script language="VB" runat="server">
06 Sub ImageButton_Click(Source As object, e As ImageClickEventArgs)
07  Message.InnerHtml="The ImageButton control was clicked " & _
08    "at the coordinates: (" & e.X.ToString() & ", " & _
08    e.Y.ToString() & ")"
10 End Sub
11 </script>
12
13 </head>
14 <body>
15 <form runat="server">
16  <asp:ImageButton id="imagebutton1" runat="server"
17    AlternateText="ImageButton 1"
18    ImageAlign="right"
19    ImageUrl="image1.gif"
20    OnClick="ImageButton_Click"/>
21  <br><br>
22
23  <span id="Message" runat="server"/>
24
25 </form>
26 </body>
27 </html>
```

Label

This control represents a Label control for displaying text on a page. Unlike static text, the Text property of a label may be set programmatically. To display the text in the style that you want, you can set the many properties that the Label class inherits from the WebControl class.

The code in Listing 4.15 displays a Label control and a Button control. When the Button is clicked, the Text property of the Label changes to different text. This example is visually shown in Figure 4.3.

Listing 4.15   **Using Label**

```
01 <html>
02 <head>
03 <title>Using Label</title>
04
05 <script language="VB" runat="server">
06 Sub Button1_Click(Sender As Object, e As EventArgs)
07  Label1.Text = "New Text on Label"
08 End Sub
09 </script>
10
11 </head>
12 <body>
13 <center>
14  <h3><font face="Verdana">Label Example</font></h3>
15  <form runat="server">
16
17    <asp:Label id="Label1" Text="Original Text on Label"
18      Font-Name="Verdana" Font-Size="10pt"
19      Width="200px" BorderStyle="solid"
20      BorderColor="#cccccc" runat="server"/>
21    <p>
22    <asp:Button id="Button1" Text="Change Text"
23      OnClick="Button1_Click" Runat="server"/>
24 </form>
25 </center>
26 </body>
27 </html>
```

Figure 4.3   The Label control.

LinkButton

This control represents a LinkButton control that is used for posting a Web Form back to the server. The LinkButton control has the same function as a Button control, however instead of a button you have a link. Like the Button control, the LinkButton control has the `OnClick` event that is triggered when the user clicks the LinkButton control. The LinkButton control has a property named Text that is used to display the text of the LinkButton.

The following example displays a LinkButton control that is used to submit a form. When the user clicks the LinkButton, the `LinkButton1_Click` event procedure is executed on the server. The code is given in Listing 4.16

Listing 4.16 **Using a LinkButton Control**

```
01 <html>
02 <head>
03 <title>LinkButton Example</title>
04 <script language="VB" runat="server">
05
06 Sub LinkButton1_Click(sender As Object, e As EventArgs)
07  Label1.Text="You just clicked the link button"
08 End Sub
09
10 </script>
11 </head>
12 <body>
13
14 <h3><font face="Verdana">LinkButton Example</font></h3>
15 <form runat=server>
16  <asp:LinkButton Text="Click to display a Label"
17    Font-Name="Verdana" Font-Size="18pt"
18    onclick="LinkButton1_Click" runat="server"/>
19
20  <br>
21  <asp:Label id=Label1 runat=server />
22 </form>
23 </body>
24 </html>
```

Panel

A Panel control is a layout region on a page for other controls. The Panel control serves as a container for those other controls. It is especially useful if you want to generate controls programmatically or hide or show a group of controls.

You define a Panel just like any other Web control. The Panel control has a Visible property whose value is `true` by default. To hide the Panel when the page first loads, you set the Visible property to `false`, as shown in the code in Listing 4.17.

Listing 4.17   **The Panel Control**

```
01 <asp:Panel id="Panel1" runat="server"
02    BackColor="yellow"
03    Height="200px"
04    Width="300px"
05    Visible=false>
06    Panel1
07    <p>
08 </asp:Panel>
```

To programmatically add controls to a Panel, use the Panel control's `Add` method. For example, the code in Listing 4.18 adds a Label control to a Panel.

Listing 4.18   **Programmatically Adding Controls to a Panel**

```
01 Dim label As Label
02 label = new Label()
03 label.Text = "Label"
04 label.ID = "Label1"
05 Panel1.Controls.Add(label)
```

Listing 4.19 shows the code that hides a Panel when the page first loads. When the user clicks the button, a Label control is added to the Panel, and the Panel is shown.

Listing 4.19   **Using a Panel**

```
01 <html>
02 <head>
03 <title>Using Panel</title>
04 <script language-"VB" runat-"server">
05
06 Sub Button1_Click(sender As Object, e As EventArgs)
07
08  ' Generate a label control
09  Dim label As Label
10  label = new Label()
11  label.Text = "Label"
12  label.ID = "Label1"
13  Panel1.Controls.Add(label)
14  Panel1.Visible = true
15 End Sub
16 </script>
```

continues ▶

Listing 4.19   **Continued**

```
17 </head>
18 <body>
19
20 <h3><font face="Verdana">A Panel Example</font></h3>
21 <form runat=server>
22  <asp:Panel id="Panel1" runat="server"
23    BackColor="yellow"
24    Height="200px"
25    Width="300px"
26    Visible=false>
27    Panel1
28    <p>
29  </asp:Panel>
30
31  <asp:Button id="Button1" onClick="Button1_Click"
32    Text="Show Panel" runat="server"/>
33
34 </form>
35 </body>
36 </html>
```

The form that shows the Panel when it is visible is shown in Figure 4.4.

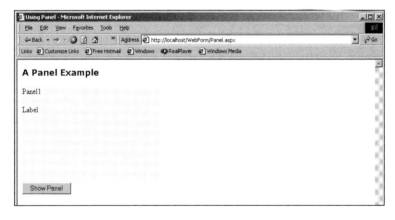

Figure 4.4   The Panel with a Label control on it.

You can also use the Panel control's `BackImageUrl` property to cover the Panel with a background image. If you want to do this, set the `BackImageUrl` to the URL of the image file.

Listing 4.20 presents code that displays a Panel, a CheckBox, and a Button. Initially, the Panel is not visible. The user can check the CheckBox and click the button to display the Panel. The Panel has its `BackImageUrl` property set to the URL of an image file.

Listing 4.20 **A Panel with a Background Image**

```
01 <html>
02 <head>
03 <title>Using Panel</title>
04 <script language="VB" runat="server">
05
06 Sub Button1_Click(sender As Object, e As EventArgs)
07
08  ' show/hide the Panel
09  If Check1.Checked Then
10    Panel1.Visible = true
11  Else
12    Panel1.Visible = false
13  End If
14 End Sub
15 </script>
16 </head>
17 <body>
18
19 <center>
20 <h3><font face="Verdana">A Panel with an Background Image</font></h3>
21 <form runat=server>
22  <asp:Panel id="Panel1" runat="server"
23    BackColor="white"
24    Height="200px"
25    Width="300px"
26    BackImageUrl="image2.gif"
27    Visible=false>
28    Panel1
29  <p>
30  </asp:Panel>
31
32  <asp:CheckBox id="Check1" Text="Show Panel" runat="server"/>
33  <br>
34  <asp:Button id="Button1" onClick="Button1_Click"
35    Text="Show/Hide Panel" runat="server"/>
36
37 </form>
38 </center>
39 </body>
40 </html>
```

The form is shown in Figure 4.5.

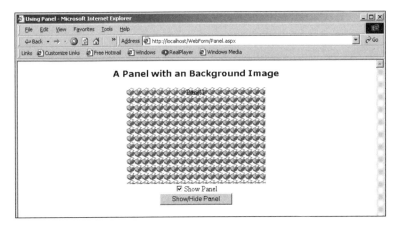

Figure 4.5 A Panel with a background image.

Table

You use the Table control to build an HTML table and specify its characteristics in a straightforward manner using the same abstract object model used for building any other Web control. A table can be built at design time and given some static contents, but the power of a Table control comes when you build the table programmatically with dynamic contents. As for other Web controls, the same code for rendering a table yields appropriate output, accordingly, for both downleveling and upleveling browsers.

Listing 4.21 presents the code that creates a table at design time. The `TableRow` and `TableCell` are also used. The table contains two rows of two cells each with both horizontal and vertical gridlines, and the table is aligned to the center of the page. Figure 4.6 shows such a table.

Listing 4.21 **Using a Table Control**

```
01 <html>
02 <body>
03
04 <center>
05 <h3>Table Control, constructed at design time</h3>
06 <form runat="server">
07
08 <asp:Table id="Table1"
09   CellPadding=10
10   GridLines="Both"
11   HorizontalAlign="Center"
12   runat="server">
13
```

```
14  <asp:TableRow>
15    <asp:TableCell>
16       Row 0, Col 0
17    </asp:TableCell>
18
19    <asp:TableCell>
20       Row 0, Col 1
21    </asp:TableCell>
22  </asp:TableRow>
23
24  <asp:TableRow>
25    <asp:TableCell>
26      Row 1, Col 0
27    </asp:TableCell>
28
29    <asp:TableCell>
30      Row 1, Col 1
31    </asp:TableCell>
32   </asp:TableRow>
33
34 </asp:Table>
35
36 </form>
37 </center>
38 </body>
39 </html>
```

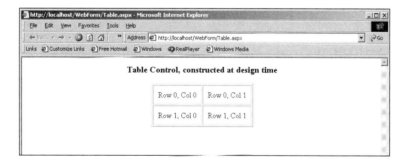

Figure 4.6   A Table control that is constructed at design time.

A Table control can also be created programmatically. To do this, you first add contents to a table cell by adding controls to the table's `Controls` collection. Then, you add `TableCell` objects to the table row's `Cells` collection. After that, you add the `TableRow` objects to the table's `Rows` collection. For this example, we have assigned constants to the number of rows and columns, but often they come from user input controls, such as a ListBox.

Adding or Modifying Table Rows

It is important to remember that any programmatic addition or modification of table rows or cells will not persist across postbacks. This is because table rows and cells are controls of their own and not properties of controls. Therefore, any changes to table rows or cells should be reconstructed after each postback. In fact, if substantial modifications are expected, it is recommended that DataList or DataGrid controls be used instead of Table controls. As a result, this Table class is primarily used by control developers.

Listing 4.22 lists the code that constructs a table programmatically.

Listing 4.22   **Constructing a Table Programmatically**

```
01 <html>
02 <head>
03 <title>Constructing a Table programmatically</title>
04
05 <script language="VB" runat="server">
06 Sub Page_Load(Sender As Object, e As EventArgs)
07 ' Generate rows and cells
08  Dim numrows As Integer
09  numrows = 3
10  Dim numcells As Integer
11  numcells = 2
12 Dim i As Integer
13  Dim j As Integer
14  For j = 0 To numrows - 1
15   Dim r As TableRow
16   r = new TableRow()
17   For i = 1 To numcells
18    Dim c As TableCell
19    c = new TableCell()
20    c.Controls.Add(new LiteralControl("row " & _
21      j.ToString() & ", cell " & i.ToString()))
22    r.Cells.Add(c)
23   Next i
24   Table1.Rows.Add(r)
25  Next j
26 End Sub
27 </script>
28 </head>
29 <body>
30 <h3><font face="Verdana">Table Example, constructed programmatically</font></h3>
31 <form runat=server>
32  <asp:Table id="Table1" GridLines="Both" HorizontalAlign="Center" Font-Name="Verdana"
33    Font-Size="8pt" CellPadding=15 CellSpacing=0 Runat="server"/>
34 </form>
35 </body>
36 </html>
```

TableCell

This control represents a cell within a table. It has a number of properties that control its appearance. For example, the `ColumnSpan` property sets the number of columns the table cell stretches horizontally; and the `RowSpan` property sets the number of rows this table cell stretches vertically. To get the text contained in the cell, you use the `Text` property. The `HorizontalAlign` property gets the horizontal alignment of the content within the cell, and the `VerticalAlign` property gets the vertical alignment of the content within the cell. See Listing 4.21 for an example.

TableRow

This control represents a row within a table. TableRow has the following properties:

- `Cells`
- `HorizontalAlign`
- `VerticalAlign`

The `Cells` property is read-only and indicates the table cell collection of the table row. The `HorizontalAlign` and VerticalAlign properties, respectively, indicate the horizontal and vertical alignments of the content within the table cells. For an example, see Listing 4.21.

TextBox

The TextBox control is an input control that enables the user to enter text. The TextBox control has a very important property called TextMode, which defines the type of TextBox when rendered in the browser. By default, the `TextMode` property has the value `SingleLine`, which renders the TextBox as an HTML input text box. The other possible values for this property are `MultiLine` and `Password`. The value `Password` renders the TextBox as an HTML Password input box and the `MultiLine` value renders the TextBox as an HTML TextArea control.

The display width of the text box is determined by its `Columns` property. If it is a multiline text box, its display height is determined by the Rows property. The persistence of the Text property can be done as an attribute or as the inner contents of the tag, regardless of the TextMode setting.

Listing 4.23 lists the code for displaying various modes of the TextBox control. Figure 4.7 shows the TextBox controls in a browser.

Figure 4.7 TextBox examples.

Listing 4.23 **The TextBox Example**

```
01 <html>
02 <head>
03 <title>Various TextBoxes</title>
04
05 <script language="VB" runat="server">
06
07 Sub Button1_Click(Sender As Object, e As EventArgs)
08  message.Text = "UserName=" & TextBox1.Text.ToString() & _
09    "<BR>Password=" & TextBox2.Text.ToString()
10 End Sub
11
12 </script>
13 </head>
14 <body>
15
16 <h3><font face="Verdana">TextBox Sample</font></h3>
17 <form runat="server">
18 User Name:
19  <asp:TextBox id="TextBox1"
20    TextMode="SingleLine"
21    Columns=50 MaxLength=35 runat="server"/>
22 <br>
23 Password:
24  <asp:TextBox id="TextBox2"
25    TextMode="Password"
26    Columns=50 MaxLength=35 runat="server"/>
27
28 <br>
29 Description:
30  <asp:TextBox id="TextBox3"
```

```
31    TextMode="MultiLine"
32    Columns=50 Rows=4 MaxLength=35 runat="server"/>

33 <br>
34 <asp:Button id="Button1" Text="Submit" OnClick="Button1_Click" Runat="server"/>
35         <p>
36 <br><br>
37 <asp:Label id="message" Runat="server"/>
38 </form>
39 </body>
40 </html>
```

AdRotator

The AdRotator control can be used to display a randomly selected ad banner on a page. To use this control, you need a companion file called the *advertisement file*. The advertisement file is a well-formed XML file that contains the list of advertisements. The root node is <Advertisements> and only the first <Advertisements> will be parsed. Inside the <Advertisements> node, there can be multiple <Ad> nodes. Each <Ad> node is an individual advertisement. The <Ad> node can have attributes as listed in Table 4.3. Only the ImageUrl attribute is required.

Table 4.3 *<Ad>* Node Attributes

Attribute	Description
ImageUrl	The URL of the image to display. This attribute contains an absolute or relative URL to an image file.
NavigateUrl	The URL of the page to navigate to when the AdRotator control is clicked. If the NavigateUrl attribute is not set, the HREF property is not rendered on the anchor tag.
AlternateText	The text displayed if the image is not available. This attribute renders as the ALT attribute of the image. Some browsers display this text as a tool tip for the advertisement.
Keyword	The category for the ad that can be filtered.
Impressions	A value that indicates the bias of how often the ad gets displayed. This value indicates the weight of the advertisement in the rotation schedule in relation to other advertisements in the file. The larger the number, the more often the advertisement will be displayed. If the sum of all impressions in the file exceeds 2,048,000,000 – 1, the AdRotator will raise a runtime exception.

The advertisement file in Listing 4.24 is named Ads.xml and contains two advertisements. The first one has an image file, image1.gif, and its NavigateUrl attribute is set to http://www.brainysoftware.com. Both advertisements have an Impressions value of 80. This means the first advertisement is displayed as often as the second one.

Listing 4.24 **The Ads.xml file**

```
01 <Advertisements>
02  <Ad>
03    <ImageUrl>image1.gif</ImageUrl>
04    <NavigateUrl>http://www.brainysoftware.com</NavigateUrl>
05    <AlternateText>File Upload Tool</AlternateText>
06    <Impressions>80</Impressions>
07    <Keyword>software</Keyword>
08  </Ad>
09  <Ad>
10    <ImageUrl>image2.gif</ImageUrl>
11    <NavigateUrl>http://www.microsoft.com</NavigateUrl>
12    <AlternateText>Microsoft Site</AlternateText>
13    <Impressions>80</Impressions>
14    <Keyword>microsoft</Keyword>
15  </Ad>
16 </Advertisements>
```

Listing 4.25 offers code that uses the AdRotator control. The AdvertisementFile property is set to Ads.xml. The code also provides the AdCreated event procedure that will be executed when the advertisement is created. When the AdCreated event is triggered, it passes an AdCreatedEventArgs object, which provides data for the AdCreated event.

Listing 4.25 **The Code That Uses an AdRotator Control**

```
01 <html>
02 <head>
03  <title>Using AdRotator Control</title>
04</head>
05
06 <script language="VB" runat="server">
07  Sub AdCreated_Event(sender As Object, e As AdCreatedEventArgs)
08    Message.Text="The " & e.AlternateText & " advertisement was selected."
08  End Sub
10 </script>
11
12 <body>
13 <center>
14
15 <form runat="server">
16  <asp:AdRotator id="AdRotator1" runat="server"
17    AdvertisementFile = "Ads.xml"
```

```
18    Borderwidth="0"
19    Target="_self"
20    Width="728"
21    Height="76"
22    OnAdCreated="AdCreated_Event"/>
23  <br>
24  <asp:label id="Message" runat="server"/>
25
26  </form>
27  </center>
28  </body>
29  </html>
```

When run, the preceding code will look like Figure 4.8.

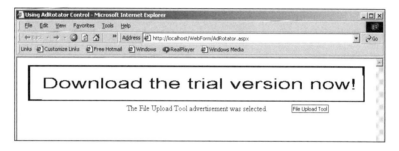

Figure 4.8   The AdRotator control.

Calendar

The Calendar control displays a one-month calendar and enables the user to view and select a specific day, week, or month.

The Calendar control has a large number of properties that enable you to change its look. For instance, the control has the ShowTitle property, which you can set to indicate whether or not the calendar title will be displayed. Also, it has the SelectedDateStyle property, which you can use to change the control's appearance. For example, the following code displays a calendar whose selected date is drawn with a red color as the background.

```
01  <asp:Calendar id="calendar1" runat="server"
02    SelectedDayStyle-BackColor="red"/>
```

One of the control's useful events is the SelectionChanged event that is triggered when the user selects a different date.

The code in Listing 4.26 displays a Calendar control and the date selected by the user.

Listing 4.26   **Using the Calendar Control**

```
01 <html>
02 <head>
03 <title>Using the Calendar control</title>
04 </head>
05 <body>
06
07 <script language="VB" runat="Server">
08 Public Sub SelectChange(Source As Object, e As EventArgs)
09  message.InnerHtml = "Date selected: " & _
10    MyCalendar.SelectedDate.ToLongDateString()
11 End Sub
12 </script>
13
14 <center>
15 <form action="calendarControl.aspx" method="post" runat="server">
16  <asp:Calendar id="MyCalendar" runat="server"
17    OnSelectionChanged="SelectChange"
18    CellPadding="5"
19    CellSpacing="5"
20    DayNameFormat="Short"
21    FirstDayOfWeek="Default"
22    NextMonthText=">"
23    NextPrevFormat="FullMonth"
24    PrevMonthText="<"
25    SelectionMode="DayWeekMonth"
26    SelectMonthText=">>"
27    SelectWeekText=">"
28    ShowDayHeader="True"
29    ShowGridLines="True"
30    ShowNextPrevMonth="True"
31    ShowTitle="True"
32    TitleFormat="MonthYear"
33    TodayDayStyle-Font-Bold="True"
34    DayHeaderStyle-Font-Bold="True"
35    OtherMonthDayStyle-ForeColor="gray"
36    TitleStyle-BackColor="white"
37    TitleStyle-ForeColor="black"
38    TitleStyle-Font-Bold="True"
39    SelectedDayStyle-BackColor="black"
40    SelectedDayStyle-Font-Bold="True"
41  />
42 </form>
43 <br>
44 <span id="message" runat="server"/>
45 </center>
46 </body>
47 </html>
```

When run on the browser, the Calendar control is displayed like the one in Figure 4.9. Note that you can change the title background and font colors, the selected date background color, and so on.

Figure 4.9 The Calendar control in action.

CheckBoxList

CheckBoxList is a control that contains a group of CheckBox controls. You use CheckBoxList when you need the user to be able to select one or more related options or items. For each item in a CheckBoxList control, you use a ListItem control. The syntax of a CheckBoxList with n items is as follows:

```
01 <asp:CheckBoxList id="…" runat="server" [list of attributes]>
02   <asp:ListItem>item 1</asp:ListItem>
03   <asp:ListItem>item 2</asp:ListItem>
04   .
05   .
06   .
07   <asp:ListItem>item n</asp:ListItem>
08 </asp:CheckBoxList>
```

All items in the CheckBoxList control are members of the Items collection. The number of items can be obtained from the Count property of the Items collection, CheckBoxList.Items.Count, and each item can be referred to using an indexing number that starts from 0. Therefore, the first item is CheckBoxList.Items(0), and the nth item is CheckBoxList.Item(n-1).

- The CheckBoxList control has a number of properties that affect its appearance. These include the following properties:
  - **CellPadding**—Determines the padding (in pixels) between items.
  - **CellSpacing**—Determines spacing between items.
  - **RepeatColumns**—Determines the number of columns to repeat.
  - **RepeatDirection**—Indicates whether the control is displayed horizontally or vertically.
  - **RepeatLayout**—Indicates whether the control is displayed in table or flow layout.
  - **TextAlign**—Sets the alignment of the text label associated with each checkbox.

When using CheckBoxList, you can use the SelectedIndexChanged event that is inherited from the ListControl class. This event is raised when one of the items is selected or deselected.

The following example in Listing 4.27 offers code that uses a CheckBoxList control with six items. The control overrides the OnSelectedIndexChanged event that is bound to the Check_Clicked event handler, which loops through the Items collection and appends the Text property of each selected item to the Message label's Text. The output is shown in Figure 4.10.

Listing 4.27 **Using the CheckBoxList Control**

```
01 <html>
02 <head>
03 <title>Using CheckBoxList Control</title>
04 </head>
05 <body>
06 <script language="VB" runat="server">
07 Sub Check_Clicked(sender As Object, e As EventArgs)
08  Message.Text="<b>Selected programming language(s):</b><br><br>"
09  Dim i As Integer
10  For i = 1 To checkboxlist1.Items.Count
11    If checkboxlist1.Items(i-1).Selected Then
12      Message.Text = Message.Text & checkboxlist1.Items(i-1).Text & "<br>"
13    End If
14  Next i
15 End Sub
16 </script>
17
18 Select your programming languages
19 <br>
20 <form action="checkboxlist.aspx" method="post" runat="server">
```

```
21
22  <asp:CheckBoxList id="checkboxlist1" runat="server"
23    AutoPostBack="True"
24    CellPadding="3"
25    CellSpacing="5"
26    RepeatColumns="2"
27    RepeatDirection="Horizontal"
28    RepeatLayout="Flow"
29    TextAlign="Right"
30    OnSelectedIndexChanged="Check_Clicked">
31
31    <asp:ListItem>VB.NET</asp:ListItem>
32
33    <asp:ListItem>C#</asp:ListItem>
34    <asp:ListItem>Java</asp:ListItem>
35    <asp:ListItem>Delphi</asp:ListItem>
36    <asp:ListItem>C++</asp:ListItem>
37    <asp:ListItem>Assembly</asp:ListItem>
38
39  </asp:CheckBoxList>
40  <hr>
41  <br><br>
42  <asp:label id="Message" runat="server"/>
43  </form>
44  </body>
45  </html>
```

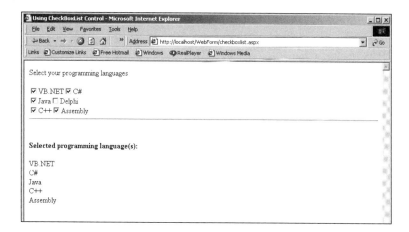

Figure 4.10 The CheckBoxList control.

DropDownList

The DropDownList control is a control that enables the user to select a single item from a drop-down list. All items in the DropDownList control are members of the Items collection. The number of items can be obtained from the Count property of the Items collection, DropDownList.Items.Count, and each item can be referred to using an indexing number that starts from 0. Therefore, the first item is DropDownList.Items(0), and the nth item is DropDownList.Item(n-1).

The code in Listing 4.28 demonstrates the use of the DropDownList control to offer four options from which the user can choose. The selected item is displayed in a Label control called Label1. The output is shown in Figure 4.11.

Listing 4.28 **Using the DropDownList Control**

```
01 <html>
02 <head>
03 <title>Using DropDownList</title>
04 <script language="VB" runat="server">
05 Sub Button_Click(sender As Object, e As EventArgs)
06   Label1.Text = "Your programming language is " & dropdownlist1.SelectedItem.Text & "."
07 End Sub
08
09 </script>
10 </head>
11 <body>
12 <form runat="server">
13   <asp:DropDownList id="dropdownlist1" runat="server">
14     <asp:ListItem>Assembly</asp:ListItem>
15     <asp:ListItem>Delphi</asp:ListItem>
16     <asp:ListItem>Java</asp:ListItem>
17     <asp:ListItem>Visual Basic</asp:ListItem>
18   </asp:DropDownList>
19   <asp:Button id="Button1" Text="Submit" OnClick="Button_Click" runat="server"/>
20   <br><br>
21   <asp:label id="Label1" runat="server"/>
22 </form>
23 </body>
24 </html>
```

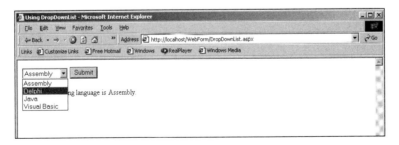

Figure 4.11   Using the DropDownList control.

ListBox

The ListBox control represents a control that enables single- or multiple-item selection. Important properties inherited from the `ListControl` class are SelectedIndex and SelectedIndices. The SelectedIndex property indicates the ordinal index of the first selected item within the list. The SelectedIndices property returns an array of selected indexes within the list.

The code in Listing 4.29 uses a ListBox control to offer a set of items from which the user can select. Only the first selected item will be acknowledged by the server. The text of the first selected item is displayed in a Label called Message. The output is shown in Figure 4.12.

Listing 4.29 **Using a ListBox Control**

```
01 <html>
02 <head>
03 <title>Using the ListBox Control</title>
04 <script language="VB" runat="server">
05 Sub SubmitBtn_Click(sender As Object, e As EventArgs)
06  If ListBox1.SelectedIndex > -1 Then
07    Message.Text="Your first programming language is " & ListBox1.SelectedItem.Text
08  End If
09 End Sub
10 </script>
11 </head>
12 <body>
13 <h3>Your first Programming Language</h3>
14 <p>
15 <form runat=server>
16 <asp:ListBox id=ListBox1
17  Rows=4
18  SelectionMode="Multiple"
19  Width="100px"
20  runat="server">
21  <asp:ListItem>VB.NET</asp:ListItem>
22  <asp:ListItem>C#</asp:ListItem>
23  <asp:ListItem>C++</asp:ListItem>
24  <asp:ListItem>Delphi</asp:ListItem>
25  <asp:ListItem>Assembly</asp:ListItem>
26 </asp:ListBox>
27 <br>
28 <asp:button Text="Submit" OnClick="SubmitBtn_Click"
29  runat="server" />
30
31 <br>
32 <asp:Label id="Message" runat="server"/>
33 </form>
34 </body>
35 </html>
```

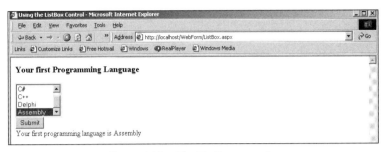

Figure 4.12   The ListBox control.

RadioButtonList

This control represents a list control that encapsulates a group of radio button controls. The RadioButtonList control provides developers with a single-selection radio button group that can be dynamically generated through databinding. It has an Items collection with members that correspond to individual items on the list. To determine which item is selected, test the SelectedItem property of the list.

You can specify the rendering of the list with the RepeatLayout and RepeatDirection properties. If RepeatLayout is set to Table (the default setting), the list will be rendered within a table. If it is set to Flow, the list will be rendered without any tabular structure. By default, RepeatDirection is Vertical. Setting this property to Horizontal will cause the list to render horizontally.

The code in Listing 4.30 is an example of how to use the RadioButtonList. The code uses a RadioButtonList control with four items. The appearance of the RadioButtonList control can be changed by using the two CheckBox controls: chkLayout and chkDirection. The selected item is displayed in the Label control called Label1. The output is shown in Figure 4.13.

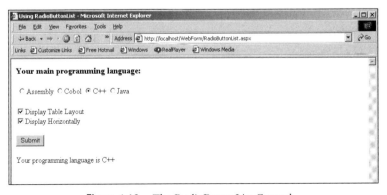

Figure 4.13   The RadioButtonList Control

Listing 4.30 **The RadioButtonList Control**

```
01 <html>
02 <head>
03 <title>Using RadioButtonList</title>
04 <script language="VB" runat="server">
05 Sub Button1_Click(source As Object, e As EventArgs)
06  If RadioButtonList1.SelectedIndex > -1 Then
07    Label1.Text = "Your programming language is " & RadioButtonList1.SelectedItem.Text
08  End If
09 End Sub
10
11 Sub chkLayout_CheckedChanged(sender As Object, e As EventArgs)
12  If chkLayout.Checked Then
13    RadioButtonList1.RepeatLayout = RepeatLayout.Table
14  Else
15    RadioButtonList1.RepeatLayout = RepeatLayout.Flow
16  End If
17 End Sub
18
19 Sub chkDirection_CheckedChanged(sender As Object, e As EventArgs)
20  If chkDirection.Checked Then
21    RadioButtonList1.RepeatDirection = RepeatDirection.Horizontal
22  Else
23    RadioButtonList1.RepeatDirection = RepeatDirection.Vertical
24  End If
25 End Sub
26 </script>
27 </head>
28 <body>
29
30 <h3>Your main programming language:</h3>
31 <form runat=server method=post>
32  <asp:RadioButtonList id=RadioButtonList1 runat="server">
33    <asp:ListItem>Assembly</asp:ListItem>
34    <asp:ListItem>Cobol</asp:ListItem>
35    <asp:ListItem>C++</asp:ListItem>
36    <asp:ListItem>Java</asp:ListItem>
37  </asp:RadioButtonList>
38 <p>
39 <asp:CheckBox id=chkLayout
40  OnCheckedChanged="chkLayout_CheckedChanged"
41  Text="Display Table Layout"
42  Checked=true
43  AutoPostBack="true"
44  runat="server" />
45
46 <br>
47 <asp:CheckBox id=chkDirection
48  OnCheckedChanged="chkDirection_CheckedChanged"
49  Text="Display Horizontally"
50  AutoPostBack="true"
51  runat="server" />
```

continues ▶

Listing 4.30   **Continued**

```
52 <p>
53 <asp:Button id=Button1
54  Text="Submit"
55  onclick="Button1_Click"
56  runat="server"/>
57
58 <p>
59
60 <asp:Label id=Label1 runat="server"/>
61 </form>
62 </body>
63 </html>
```

Repeater

The Repeater control is used to format data from a data source. To format the data, you define a number of templates. For example, if you have a table as your data source, you can display the data in a tabular format using the HTML `<table>` tag, or you can display the data in a comma-separated format.

To use a Repeater control with a data source, you first need to bind the data source with the DataSource property and the `DataBind` method. The following code, for example, binds a data source called `MyDataSource` to a Repeater named `Repeater1`.

```
01 Repeater1.DataSource = CreateDataSource()
02 Repeater1.DataBind()
```

A Repeater control must have an ItemTemplate template. Other templates are optional and include AlternatingItemTemplate, SeparatorTemplate, HeaderTemplate, and FooterTemplate.

ItemTemplate defines how an item is rendered, and AlternatingItemTemplate defines how an alternating item is rendered. SeparatorTemplate defines how separators between two items are rendered. HeaderTemplate and FooterTemplate define how the control header and footer are rendered.

If the data source of the Repeater is set but no data is returned, the Repeater control renders the HeaderTemplate and FooterTemplate with no items. If the data source is null (not set), the Repeater is not rendered.

Listing 4.31 illustrates the use of two Repeater controls and all possible templates. First, we define a `DataView` as a data source that will be bound to both controls. The first Repeater defines its ItemTemplate, HeaderTemplate, and FooterTemplate. The second Repeater defines its ItemTemplate, AlternatingItemTemplate, and SeparatorTemplate. The complete code is listed in Listing 4.31, and the output is shown in Figure 4.14.

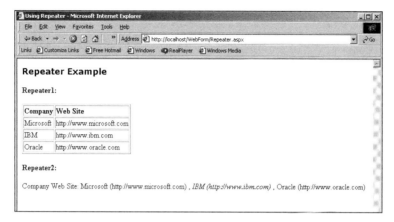

Figure 4.14   The Repeater control.

Listing 4.31   **Using the Repeater Control**

```
01 <%@ Import Namespace="System.Data" %>
02 <html>
03 <head>
04 <title>Using Repeater</title>
05 <script language="VB" runat="server">
06 Sub Page_Load(sender As Object, e As EventArgs)
07  If Not IsPostBack Then
08    Repeater1.DataSource = CreateDataSource()
09    Repeater1.DataBind()
10
11    Repeater2.DataSource = CreateDataSource()
12    Repeater2.DataBind()
13  End If
14 End Sub
15
16
17 Function CreateDataSource() As ICollection
18  Dim dt As DataTable
19  dt = new DataTable()
20  Dim dr As DataRow
21
22  dt.Columns.Add(new DataColumn("Company", Type.GetType("System.String")))
23  dt.Columns.Add(new DataColumn("Web Site", Type.GetType("System.String")))
24
25  dr = dt.NewRow()
26  dr(0) = "Microsoft"
27  dr(1) = "http://www.microsoft.com"
28  dt.Rows.Add(dr)
29  dr = dt.NewRow()
30  dr(0) = "IBM"
31  dr(1) = "http://www.ibm.com"
```

continues ▶

Listing 4.31 **Continued**

```
32  dt.Rows.Add(dr)
33  dr = dt.NewRow()
34  dr(0) = "Oracle"
35  dr(1) = "http://www.oracle.com"
36  dt.Rows.Add(dr)
37  Dim dv As DataView
38  dv = new DataView(dt)
39  CreateDataSource = dv
40 End Function
41
42 </script>
43 </head>
44 <body>
45
46 <h3><font face="Verdana">Repeater Example</font></h3>
47 <form runat=server>
48 <b>Repeater1:</b>
49 <p>
50  <asp:Repeater id=Repeater1 runat="server">
51    <HeaderTemplate>
52      <table border=1>
53        <tr>
54          <td><b>Company</b></td>
55          <td><b>Web Site</b></td>
56        </tr>
57    </HeaderTemplate>

58    <ItemTemplate>
59      <tr>
60        <td> <%# DataBinder.Eval(Container.DataItem, "Company") %> </td>
61        <td> <%# DataBinder.Eval(Container.DataItem, "Web Site") %> </td>
62      </tr>
63    </ItemTemplate>
64
65    <FooterTemplate>
66      </table>
67    </FooterTemplate>
68
69  </asp:Repeater>
70 <p>
71
72 <b>Repeater2:</b>
73 <p>
74  <asp:Repeater id=Repeater2 runat="server">
75    <HeaderTemplate>
76      Company Web Site:
77    </HeaderTemplate>
78
79    <ItemTemplate>
80      <%# DataBinder.Eval(Container.DataItem, "Company") %>
81      (<%# DataBinder.Eval(Container.DataItem, "Web Site") %>)
82    </ItemTemplate>
83
```

```
84    <SeparatorTemplate>
85      ,
86    </SeparatorTemplate>
87    <AlternatingItemTemplate>
88     <i><%# DataBinder.Eval(Container.DataItem, "Company") %>
89     (<%# DataBinder.Eval(Container.DataItem, "Web Site") %>)</i>
90    </AlternatingItemTemplate>
91
92  </asp:Repeater>
93 </form>
94 </body>
95 </html>
```

DataGrid

The DataGrid control is derived from `BaseDataList`, which serves as the abstract base class for the DataList and DataGrid controls and implements the selection semantics common to both controls. An abstract class is a class that has to be inherited from.

DataGrid is a control that you can use to display data in a table. Unlike the Table control, however, DataGrid is bound to a data source using the DataSource property and the `DataBind` method to display whatever data is in the data source. The DataSource property sets the data-binding expression that references any object supporting the System.Collections.ICollection interface. The `DataBind` method is inherited from the `BaseDataList` class and is used to actually bind the data source to the datalist.

For example, the following code can be used to bind the DataGrid control called `MyDataGrid` to a `DataView` object called `MyDataView`.

```
01   MyDataGrid.DataSource = MyDataView
02   MyDataGrid.DataBind()
```

Another important property of DataGrid is the Columns property, which represents the collection of Column controls in the DataGrid. The `Column` class represents a column in a DataGrid and is the base class for all DataGrid column types. `Column` is the parent class for the following classes: `BoundColumn`, `ButtonColumn`, `EditCommandColumn`, `HyperLinkColumn`, and `TemplateColumn`. These child classes are often added to the Columns collection.

Of the classes derived from the `Column` class, the `BoundColumn` class is the most important because it represents a column in the DataGrid's data source. The first BoundColumn control added to the DataGrid's Columns collection represents the first column of the data source, the second

BoundColumn control represents the second column of the data source, and so forth. If the number of BoundColumn controls in the DataGrid's Column collection is less than the number of columns in the data source, then only the first n^{th} columns will be displayed. However, the number of BoundColumn controls in the DataGrid's Column collection should not be greater than the number of columns in the data source because this could lead to an unpredictable result.

The other child classes of the Column class can be used when you expect a user response for the data. For example, you can use a ButtonColumn to create a button that the user can click. Each ButtonColumn represents the data in the same row as the ButtonColumn.

When using a DataGrid control in your Web Form's page, you can define its Columns property using the <property> node. For example, the code in Listing 4.32 adds one EditCommandColumn, one ButtonColumn, and two BoundColumn controls to the Columns collection.

Listing 4.32 **DataGrid Control**

```
01 <property name="Columns">
02  <asp:EditCommandColumn EditText="Edit"
03    CancelText="Cancel"
04    UpdateText="Update"
05    ItemStyle-Wrap="false"
06    HeaderText="Edit Command Column"
07    HeaderStyle-Wrap="false"/>
08  <asp:ButtonColumn HeaderText="Select"
09    ButtonType="PushButton"
10    Text="Select" CommandName="Select" />
11  <asp:BoundColumn HeaderText="Item"
12    DataField="StringValue"/>
13  <asp:BoundColumn HeaderText="Price"
14    DataField="CurrencyValue"
15    DataFormatString="{0:c}"
16    ItemStyle-HorizontalAlign="right" />
17 </property>
```

The DataGrid class has a number of events that can be raised. For example, the CancelCommand event occurs when a button for an item is clicked with a CommandName property of "cancel". Another event, ItemCommand, is triggered when any button for an item in a DataGrid is clicked.

The code in Listing 4.33 illustrates the use of the DataGrid control called ItemsGrid along with its Columns collection and the ItemCommand event. The code first creates a data source using the CreateDataSource function, which returns a DataView containing three columns and ten rows. The three columns are Integer, String, and Currency, respectively.

The data is simply a counter from 1 to 10 for the first column, a string derived from the first column, and a simple mathematical function that multiplies the counter with 1.323, as shown in the following code:

```
01 For i = 1 To 10
02   dr = dt.NewRow()
03   dr(0) = i
04   dr(1) = "Item " & i
05   dr(2) = 1.323 * i
06   dt.Rows.Add(dr)
07 Next i
```

The DataGrid is bound to the new DataView object when the page loads, but only when the page is first requested:

```
01 Sub Page_Load(sender As Object, e As EventArgs)
02  If Not IsPostBack
03    ' need to load this data only once
04    ItemsGrid.DataSource= CreateDataSource()
05    ItemsGrid.DataBind()
06  End If
07 End Sub
```

The Label control and the DataGrid control are defined in the visual interface part of the page.

```
01 <form runat=server>
02 <asp:Label id="Message" runat="server"/>
03 <br>
04 <table cellpadding="5">
05 <tr valign="top">
06   <td>
07     <b>Product List</b>
08     <asp:DataGrid id="ItemsGrid" runat="server"
09       BorderColor="black"
10       BorderWidth="1"
11       CellPadding="3"
12       HeaderStyle-BackColor="#F6F6F6"
13       AutoGenerateColumns="false"
14       OnItemCommand="Grid_CartCommand">
15
16       < Columns>
17         <asp:ButtonColumn HeaderText="Select"
18           ButtonType="PushButton"
19           Text="Select" CommandName="Select" />
20         <asp:BoundColumn HeaderText="Item"
21           DataField="IntegerValue"/>
22         <asp:BoundColumn HeaderText="Item"
23           DataField="StringValue"/>
24         <asp:BoundColumn HeaderText="Price"
25           DataField="CurrencyValue"
26           DataFormatString="{0:c}"
27           ItemStyle-HorizontalAlign="right" />
28       </Columns>
```

```
29      </asp:DataGrid>
30   </td>
31 </tr>
32 </table>
33 </form>
```

Note how four Column controls are added to the Columns collection. Also notice that the OnItemCommand is given the value Grid_CartCommand. When one of the ButtonColumn controls is clicked, it triggers the following Grid_CardCommand sub:

```
01  Sub Grid_CartCommand(sender As Object, e As DataGridCommandEventArgs)
02      Message.Text = "You selected " + e.Item.Cells(1).Text
03  End Sub
```

The sub simply gets the first cell of the row that was clicked from the DataGridCommandEventArgs object and displays it in the Label called Message.

Listing 4.33 lists the complete source code for the example. The output is displayed in Figure 4.15.

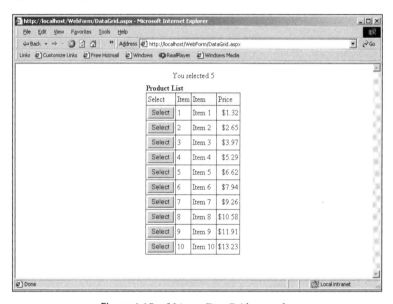

Figure 4.15   Using a DataGrid control.

Listing 4.33   **Using a DataGrid Control**

```
01 <%@ Import Namespace="System.Data" %>
02 <html>
03 <script language="VB" runat="server">
04
05  Dim Cart As DataTable
06
07  Function CreateDataSource() As ICollection
```

```
08    Dim dt As DataTable
09    Dim dr As DataRow
10    dt = new DataTable()
11
12    dt.Columns.Add(new DataColumn("IntegerValue", System.Type.GetType("System.Int32") ))
13    dt.Columns.Add(new DataColumn("StringValue", System.Type.GetType("System.String") ))
14    dt.Columns.Add(new DataColumn("CurrencyValue", System.Type.GetType("System.Double") ))
15
16    Dim i As Integer
17    For i = 1 To 10
18      dr = dt.NewRow()
19      dr(0) = i
20      dr(1) = "Item " & i
21      dr(2) = 1.323 * i
22      dt.Rows.Add(dr)
23    Next i
24
25    Dim dv As DataView
26    dv = new DataView(dt)
27    CreateDataSource = dv
28  End Function
29
30  Sub Page_Load(sender As Object, e As EventArgs)
31    If Not IsPostBack
32      ' need to load this data only once
33      ItemsGrid.DataSource= CreateDataSource()
34      ItemsGrid.DataBind()
35    End If
36  End Sub
37
38  Sub Grid_CartCommand(sender As Object, e As DataGridCommandEventArgs)
39      Message.Text = "You selected " + e.Item.Cclls(1).Text
40  End Sub
41  </script>
42
43  <body>
44  <center>
45
46  <form runat=server>
47  <asp:Label id="Message" runat="server"/>
48  <br>
49  <table cellpadding="5">
50  <tr valign="top">
51   <td>
52     <b>Product List</b>
53     <asp:DataGrid id="ItemsGrid" runat="server"
54       BorderColor="black"
55       BorderWidth="1"
56       CellPadding="3"
57       HeaderStyle-BackColor="#F6F6F6"
58       AutoGenerateColumns="false"
59       OnItemCommand="Grid_CartCommand">
```

continues ▶

Listing 4.33 **Continued**

```
60
61     <Columns>
62       <asp:ButtonColumn HeaderText="Select" ButtonType="PushButton"
63         Text="Select" CommandName="Select" />
64       <asp:BoundColumn HeaderText="Item" DataField="IntegerValue"/>
64       <asp:BoundColumn HeaderText="Item" DataField="StringValue"/>
66       <asp:BoundColumn HeaderText="Price" DataField="CurrencyValue"
➥DataFormatString="{0:c}"
67          ItemStyle-HorizontalAlign="right" />
68     </Columns>
69   </asp:DataGrid>
70   </td>
71 </tr>
72 </table>
73 </form>
74 </center>
75 </body>
76 </html>
```

DataList

The DataList is a control to display a data-bound list. To bind a DataList to a data source, you use the DataSource property and the `DataBind` method. The DataSource property sets the data-binding expression that references any object supporting the System.Collections.ICollection interface. The `DataBind` method is inherited from the `BaseDataList` class and is used to actually bind the data source to the datalist.

For example, the following code can be used to bind a DataList control, called `DataList1`, to a `DataView` object called `myDataView`.

```
01 DataList1.DataSource = myDataView
02 DataList1.DataBind()
```

The following properties of the DataList control enable you to change the DataList controls appearance:

- **RepeatColumns**—Indicates the number of columns to repeat.
- **RepeatLayout**—Sets a value that indicates whether the control is displayed in table or flow layout.
- **RepeatDirection**—Indicates whether the control is displayed vertically or horizontally.

When using a DataList control, you must also set its HeaderTemplate and ItemTemplate properties. The HeaderTemplate property indicates the template to use for the header in the DataList. The ItemTemplate property indicates the template to use for each item in the DataList.

The following example illustrates the use of the DataList control. First, the code creates a one-column data source that is bound to the DataList. This is accomplished using the `CreateDataSource` function, which returns an `ICollection` object:

```
01 Function CreateDataSource() As ICollection
02   Dim dt As DataTable
03   dt = new DataTable()
04   Dim dr As DataRow
05
06   dt.Columns.Add(new DataColumn("StringValue", _
07     System.Type.GetType("String")))
08
09 Dim i As Integer
10   For i = 0 To 9
11     dr = dt.NewRow()
12     dr(0) = "Item " & Int32.ToString(i)
13     dt.Rows.Add(dr)
14   Next i
15
16   Dim dv As DataView
17   dv = new DataView(dt)
18   CreateDataSource = dv
19 End Function
```

The DataTable, `dt`, only has one column of the type `String`. This column contains ten rows—Item 0 through Item 9. This control is used with a few other controls, including a Button, a CheckBox, and three DropDownList controls. The user can select a value for the `RepeatColumns`, `RepeatLayout`, and `RepeatDirection` properties using the DropDownList controls, and the user can indicate whether or not the DataList should be drawn with a border using the CheckBox control. The user can then click the Button control linked to the `Button1_Click` sub. This sub determines the `DataList` properties for the next display:

```
01 Sub Button1_Click(Sender As Object, e As EventArgs)
02
03   If DropDown1.SelectedIndex = 0 Then
04     DataList1.RepeatDirection = RepeatDirection.Horizontal
05   Else
06     DataList1.RepeatDirection = RepeatDirection.Vertical
07   End If
08   If DropDown2.SelectedIndex = 0 Then
09     DataList1.RepeatLayout = RepeatLayout.Table
10   Else
11     DataList1.RepeatLayout = RepeatLayout.Flow
12   End If
13
14   DataList1.RepeatColumns=DropDown3.SelectedIndex+1
```

```
15
16   If Check1.Checked And _
17     DataList1.RepeatLayout = RepeatLayout.Table Then
18     DataList1.BorderWidth = Unit.Pixel(1)
19     DataList1.GridLines = GridLines.Both
20   Else
21     DataList1.BorderWidth = Unit.Pixel(0)
22     DataList1.GridLines = GridLines.None
23   End If
24 End Sub
```

Listing 4.34 lists the complete code for this example. The output is shown in Figure 4.16.

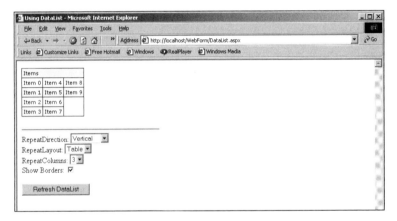

Figure 4.16   The DataList control.

Listing 4.34   **Using the DataList Control**

```
001 <%@ Import Namespace="System.Data" %>
002 <html>
003 <head>
004 <title>Using DataList</title>
005
006 <script language="VB" runat="server">
007
008 Function CreateDataSource() As ICollection
009   Dim dt As DataTable
010   dt = new DataTable()
011   Dim dr As DataRow
012
013   dt.Columns.Add(new DataColumn("StringValue1", _
014     System.Type.GetType("System.String")))
015
```

```
016
017  Dim i As Integer
018  For i = 0 To 9
019     dr = dt.NewRow()
020     dr(0) = "Item " & i
021     dt.Rows.Add(dr)
022  Next i
023
024  Dim dv As DataView
025  dv = new DataView(dt)
026  CreateDataSource = dv
027 End Function
028
029 Sub Page_Load(sender As Object, e As EventArgs)
030  If Not IsPostBack
031     DataList1.DataSource = CreateDataSource()
032     DataList1.DataBind()
033  End If
034 End Sub
035
036 Sub Button1_Click(Sender As Object, e As EventArgs)
037
038  If DropDown1.SelectedIndex = 0 Then
039     DataList1.RepeatDirection = RepeatDirection.Horizontal
040  Else
041     DataList1.RepeatDirection = RepeatDirection.Vertical
042  End If
043  If DropDown2.SelectedIndex = 0 Then
044     DataList1.RepeatLayout = RepeatLayout.Table
045  Else
046     DataList1.RepeatLayout = RepeatLayout.Flow
047  End If
048
049  DataList1.RepeatColumns=DropDown3.SelectedIndex+1
050
051  If Check1.Checked And _
052     DataList1.RepeatLayout = RepeatLayout.Table Then
053     DataList1.BorderWidth = Unit.Pixel(1)
054     DataList1.GridLines = GridLines.Both
055  Else
056     DataList1.BorderWidth = Unit.Pixel(0)
057     DataList1.GridLines = GridLines.None
058  End If
059 End Sub
060
061 </script>
062 </head>
063
064 <body>
```

continues ▶

Listing 4.34 **Continued**

```
065 <form runat=server>
066  <asp:DataList id="DataList1" runat="server"
067    BorderColor="black"
068    CellPadding="3"
069    Font-Name="Verdana"
070    Font-Size="8pt"
071    HeaderStyle-BackColor="#F6F6F6"
072    AlternatingItemStyle-BackColor="#F6F6F6">
073
074    <HeaderTemplate>
075      Items
076    </HeaderTemplate>
077
078    <ItemTemplate>
079      <%# DataBinder.Eval(Container.DataItem, "StringValue1") %>
080    </ItemTemplate>
081
082  </asp:DataList>
083
084  <p>
085  <hr noshade align="left" width="300px">
086  RepeatDirection:
087  <asp:DropDownList id=DropDown1 runat="server">
088    <asp:ListItem>Horizontal</asp:ListItem>
089    <asp:ListItem>Vertical</asp:ListItem>
090  </asp:DropDownList><br>
091
092  RepeatLayout:
093  <asp:DropDownList id=DropDown2 runat="server">
094    <asp:ListItem>Table</asp:ListItem>
095    <asp:ListItem>Flow</asp:ListItem>
096  </asp:DropDownList><br>
097
098  RepeatColumns:
099  <asp:DropDownList id=DropDown3 runat="server">
100    <asp:ListItem>1</asp:ListItem>
101    <asp:ListItem>2</asp:ListItem>
102    <asp:ListItem>3</asp:ListItem>
103    <asp:ListItem>4</asp:ListItem>
104    <asp:ListItem>5</asp:ListItem>
105  </asp:DropDownList><br>
106
107  Show Borders:
108    <asp:CheckBox id=Check1 runat="server" /><p>
109
110  <asp:Button id=Button1 runat="server"
111    Text="Refresh DataList"
112    OnClick="Button1_Click" />
113
114 </form>
115 </body>
116 </html>
```

Validation Controls

One area of Web Forms that has not been covered yet are Validation Controls. These web controls are used to perform validation against any other control in a Web Form. In total, there are six validation controls:

- `RequiredFieldValidator`—Used to ensure that a specified control has been filled out.
- `CompareValidator`—Used to compare the value of a control against another value.
- `RangeValidator`—Used to ensure that data entered into the control falls between a range of values.
- `RegularExpressionValidator`—Used to check the formatting of a control's value against a regular expression string.
- `CustomValidator`—Used to validate the value of a control against a custom validation routine or logic.
- `ValidationSummary`—Used to display a list of validation errors should any occur on a web page.

Issues of Validating Web Pages

When developing web applications, one of the most time consuming and difficult tasks is adding validation logic and code to your web pages. Traditionally, this is done through client-side script. Issues concerning browser script support exist, which normally results in web pages containing validation script for various browsers. This makes maintaining the web page somewhat of a chore and prone to error.

This also leads to another issue, which is what to do when the client browser does not support scripting at all. When this is the case, you have to rely on server-side validation, which again is more code for the web author to maintain and support.

The end result of these two main issues brings up a third, which is the sheer amount of code that needs to be embedded in the web page for all types of validation, both client-side (a version for each browser) and server-side (for those browsers that do not support script features). This makes reading the code of the web page and adding or removing features troublesome at best and a nightmare at worst.

Benefits of ASP.NET Validation Controls

Fortunately for us, ASP.NET provides a rich collection of Validation controls that have been designed to simplify the validation process, both on the client side of things and on the server side.

Each of these controls is placed on a Web Form much like a regular web control. The following code illustrates the use of a basic Validation control with a TextBox control:

```
01 <asp:textbox id="Name" runat="server" />
02 <asp:RequiredFieldValidator
03     id="reqName"
04     ControlToValidate="Name"
05     runat="server"
06     errorMessage="Name can not be blank" />
```

Using Validation Controls

Before I start to explain each of the validation controls available, it is best to explain the common attributes used in all the Validation controls:

- `Id`—User-defined ID for the control.
- `ControlToValidate`—ID of the Web control whose value you want to validate.
- `Display`—Sets the display mode for the Validation control. Possible values are
  - `None`—The Validation ErrorMessage value is never displayed.
  - `Static`—Space for the validation message is added to the web page.
  - `Dynamic`—Space for the validation message is dynamically added to the web page if validation fails.
- `Font-Name`—Font to use for validation error message text.
- `Font-Size`—Size of font to use for validation error message text.
- `ErrorMessage`—Text message to display on the screen if a control's validation fails.

Of these attributes, only the `ControlToValidate` and the `runat` attributes are essential. All the others are optional, but it is best to include the `Id` and `ErrorMessage` attributes.

Using the RequiredFieldValidator Control

The RequiredFieldValidator control is used to ensure that the user does not leave a specified field empty; this is generally used where you need to retrieve a value from a user.

The syntax for this control is

```
01 <asp:RequiredFieldValidator
02 ControlToValidate="Name"
03 Display="dynamic"
04 Font-Name="verdana"
05 Font-Size="9pt"
06 ErrorMessage=""
07 runat=server />
```

An example of using a RequiredFieldValidator control is shown in
Listing 4.35.

Listing 4.35   **(435.aspx) RequiredFieldValidator Example**

```
01 <html>
02 <head><title>Login</title></head>
03 <body>
04 <form runat="server">
05 Please enter you name:
06 <asp:textbox id="Name" runat="server" />
07 <asp:RequiredFieldValidator id="reqName" ControlToValidate="Name" runat="server"
➥text="Name can not be blank" />
08 <br><br>
09 <asp:button id="btnDone" text="Done" runat="server" />
10 </form>
11 </body>
12 </html>
```

The code in Listing 4.35 is pretty straightforward. However, if you look at
the bold-faced code (line 7), you can see that a RequiredFieldValidator has
been used to validate the `"Name"` text control. When the code is run and the
user clicks the `"Done"` button on the form, he will get the screen shown
in Figure 4.17, which tells him that he must enter a value for the Name
control.

Figure 4.17   Simple Web Form validation.

Using the CompareValidator Control

This control is used to compare the value of a control with that of another value; this value can be one of four possible types:

- A static value
- Variable
- A return value from a function
- Another control's value

A common use for this control is when a user is asked to change his password. For example, once the user has entered his password incorrectly, he is asked to enter a new password twice—this is where you would use a CompareValidator control—to ensure that both versions of the control match.

The syntax for this control is

```
01 <asp:CompareValidator
02    ControlToValidate="newPassword2"
03    ControlToCompare="newPassword1"
04    ValueToCompare ="value to comapare against"
05    Display="Dynamic"
06    Font-Name="verdana"
07    Font-Size="9pt"
08    ErrorMessage="New Password fields do not match, please re-enter."
09    runat=server>
10 </asp:CompareValidator>
```

CompareValidator's specific attributes are as follows:

- **ControlToCompare**   Holds the ID of a web control to compare against.
- **ValueToCompare**   Holds a static value to compare the validated control against.

In Listing 4.36, you can see the CompareValidator control in action. This example displays a simple Web Form asking the user to enter a new password and then to re-enter the password a second time to confirm it. If the passwords entered do not match when the done button is clicked, an error message will be shown:

Listing 4.36   (436.aspx) CompareValidator Control Example

```
01 <html>
02 <body>
03 <form id="form1" runat="server">
04 Enter new password:
05 <asp:textbox id="newPassword1" textmode="password" runat="server" />
06 <br>
```

```
07 Re-enter new password:
08 <asp:textbox id="newPassword2" textmode="password" runat="server" />
09 <asp:comparevalidator id="valid1" runat="server" controltovalidate= "newPassword2"
➥controltocompare="newPassword1" errormessage="Both Passwords do not match, please re-
➥enter"
/>
10 <br><br>
11 <asp:button id="btnDone" text="Done" runat="server" />
12 </form>
13 </body>
14 </html>
```

On line 9, you can see that a CompareValidator control is being used to compare the value entered in the textbox "newPassword2" with the value entered in the textbox "newPassword1", so when the user clicks the "Done" button, the "newPassword2" control will be validated. If both textbox controls do not have the same value, an error message will be displayed, as shown in Figure 4.18.

Figure 4.18 CompareValidator control example.

Using the RangeValidator Control

The RangeValidator control is used to ensure that a validated control's value lies between a range of values. It can validate ranges of text, numbers, and dates.

The syntax for this control is

```
01 <asp:RangeValidator
02    Type="Date"
03    ControlToValidate="DateRange"
04    Display="dynamic"
05    Font-Name="verdana"
06    Font-Size="9pt"
07    MinimumValue="1/1/2001"
08    MaximumValue="12/31/2001"
```

```
09   ErrorMessage="Value must be between 1/1/2001 and 12/31/2001, Please enter again."
10   runat="server">
11 </asp:RangeValidator>
12 The RangeValidator specific attributes are as follows:
```

Before going further, let's look at these attributes in more detail:

- **Type**—Defines the data type of the control to validate. The control's value is converted to this data type prior to checking its range. The possible values are

  - String

  - Integer

  - Double

  - Date

  - Currency

- **MaximumValue**—Used to specify the maximum value of a range.

- **MinimumValue**—Used to specify the minimum value of a range.

Range Validation Issue

Be warned that a range validation on a blank control is always validated as though the control were in range. To get around this, you must also use a RequiredFieldValidator as well as a RangeValidator for the control you want to validate.

In Listing 4.37, you can see the RangeValidator control in action. This example displays a simple Web Form asking the user to enter a date between the range of "01/01/2001" and "31/12/2001". If the date entered does not lie within this range, an error message will be shown when the done button is clicked:

Listing 4.37 **(437.aspx) RangeValidator Control Example**

```
01 <html>
02 <head></head>
03 <body>
04 <form id="form1" runat="server">
05 Please enter a date in the range of: 01/01/2001 and 12/31/2001.
06 <br>
07 <asp:textbox id="dateRange" runat="server"  />
08 <asp:rangevalidator id="rangeDateRange" runat="server" type="date" controltovalidate=
➥"dateRange" minimumvalue="01/01/2001" maximumvalue="12/31/2001" errormessage= "Date is not
➥in the required range, please re-enter." />
09 <br><br>
10 <asp:button id="btnDone" text="Done" runat="server" />
```

```
11  </form>
12  </body>
13  </html>
```

On line 8, a RangeValidator control is used to compare the value entered in the textbox `"dateRange"` to ensure that it is within the date range of `"01/01/2001"` and `"12/31/2001"`. When the user clicks the `"Done"` button, the `"dateRange"` control is validated, and if its value does not reside in the specified range, an error message is displayed, as shown in Figure 4.19.

Figure 4.19   RangeValidator control example.

Using the RegularExpressionValidator Control

The RegularExpressionValidator control is used to validate the value of a control against a regular expression. (Regular expressions are explained in Chapter 2, "Developing Applications with ASP.NET.")

This form of validation enables data entered by a user to be validated against a predictable sequence of characters in a string; for example, a social security number, an email address, a telephone number, and so on.

The syntax for this control is

```
01  <asp:RegularExpressionValidator
02     ControlToValidate="zipCode"
03     ValidationExpression="\d{5}"
04     Display="Dynamic"
05     Font-Name="verdana"
06     Font-Size="9pt"
07     ErrorMessage="Enter a zip code in the correct format."
08     runat=server>
09  </asp:RegularExpressionValidator>
```

The RegularExpressionValidator-specific attribute is ValidationExpression, which holds the regular expression that you want to validate a control against.

In Listing 4.38, you can see the RegularExpressionValidator control in action. This example displays a simple Web Form that asks the user to enter a zip code. If the zip code entered is not in the right format (5 digits), an error message will be shown when the Done button is clicked:

Listing 4.38 (438.aspx) RegularExpressionValidator Control Example

```
01 <html>
02 <head></head>
03 <body>
04 <form id="form1" runat="server">
05 Please enter a zip code:
06 <asp:textbox id="zipCode" runat="server"  />
07<asp:RegularExpressionValidator
   ControlToValidate="zipCode"
   ValidationExpression="\d{5}"
   Display="Dynamic"
   Font-Name="verdana"
   Font-Size="9pt"
   ErrorMessage="Enter a zip code in the correct format."
   runat=server />
08 <br><br>
09 <asp:button id="btnDone" text="Done" runat="server" />
10 </form>
11 </body>
12 </html>
```

On line 7, a RegularExpressionValidator control has been used to compare the value entered in the `"zipCode"` textbox against a regular expression, which requires the value entered to be five digits in length. When the user clicks the `"Done"` button, the `"zipCode"` control will be validated, and if its value does not match the regular expression, an error message will be displayed, as shown in Figure 4.20.

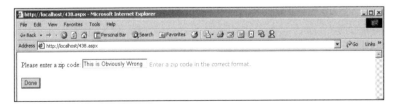

Figure 4.20 RegularExpressionValidator control example.

Using the CustomValidator Control

The CustomValidator control is used when you need to perform some specific validation that the standard validation controls cannot deal with.

This validation control enables you to call your own validation code for client- and server-side validation.

The syntax for this control is

```
01 <asp:CustomValidator id="myCustomValidator" runat="server"
02     ControlToValidate="Key"
03     ClientValidationFunction="ClientSideValidate"
04     OnServerValidate="ServerSideValidate"
05     Display="Dynamic"
06     Font-Name="verdana"
07     Font-Size="9pt"
08     ErrorMessage="You must enter one of the specified values, please re-enter." />
```

The CustomValidator-specific attributes are

- **ClientValidationFunction**—Holds the name of a client-side function used to validate the control.

- **OnServerValidate**—Holds the name of a server-side function used to validate a control.

In Listing 4.39, you can see the CustomValidator control in action. This example displays a simple Web Form that asks the user to enter one of three values (1, 5, and 9 respectively). If the value entered does not match any of these values, an error message will be shown when the Done button is clicked:

Listing 4.39   **(439.aspx) CustomValidator Control Example**

```
01 <html>
02 <head></head>
03 <body>
04 <script language="vbscript">
05 Sub ClientSideValidator(source, arguments)
06 If (arguments.Value = 1 or arguments.Value = 5 or arguments.Value = 9) Then
07        arguments.IsValid = true
08 Else
09     arguments.IsValid = false
10 End If
11 End Sub
12 </script>
13 <form id="form1" runat="server">
14 Please enter one of the following values: 1, 5 or 9
15 <asp:textbox id="myValue" runat="server" />
16 <br>
17 <asp:CustomValidator id="myCustomValidator" runat="server"
```

continues ▶

Listing 4.39 **Continued**

```
    ControlToValidate="myValue"
    ClientValidationFunction="ClientSideValidator"
    Display="Dynamic"
    Font-Name="verdana"
    Font-Size="9pt"
    ErrorMessage="You must enter one of the specified values, please re-enter." />
18 <br><br>
19 <asp:button id="btnDone" text="Done" runat="server" />
20 </form>
21 </body>
22 </html>
```

On line 5, I have created a script block that defines a vbscript sub called "ClientSideValidator". This sub is called by the CustomValidator control to validate the "myValue" textbox. This sub basically tests to see if the value passed is equal to 1, 5, or 9. When the user clicks the Done button, the "myValue" control is validated, and if the return value for "ClientSideValidator" is false (the value was not valid), an error message will be displayed, as shown in Figure 4.21.

Figure 4.21 CustomValidator control example.

Using the ValidationSummary Control

The ValidationSummary control is used to display a list of validation control errors that have occurred on a web page.

The syntax for this control is

```
01 <asp:ValidationSummary
02      id="myValidationSummary"
03      runat="server"
04      DisplayMode="List"
05      EnableClientScript="true"
06      ShowSummary="true"
07      ShowMessageBox="false"
08      HeaderText="A Summary List Header" />
```

The ValidationSummary-specific attributes are

- **DisplayMode**—The display mode defines the format of the summary list. Possible values are

  - **List**   Displays the items of the validation summary on separate lines in a list.

  - **BulletList**—Displays the items of the validation summary on separate lines in a bulleted list.

  - **SingleParagraph**—Displays the items of the validation summary in a single paragraph.

- **EnableClientScript**—This is used to turn client-side code generation on or off for the validation errors summary. The default value is true.

- **ShowSummary**—If true, it displays the summary list on the Web Form.

- **ShowMessageBox**—If true, it displays a popup message box on the client with the validation error summary.

- **HeaderText**—Text displayed as the header of the validation error summary.

In Listing 4.40, you can see the ValidationSummary control in action. This example displays a simple Web Form that asks the user to enter his username (required validation), his password (no validation), his new password (no validation), and then the user is asked to confirm the new password (compare validation). Should any of the validations fail, a validation summary will appear in a summary list alerting the user to the errors (see Figure 4.22).

Listing 4.40   **(440.aspx) ValidationSummary Control Example**

```
01 <html>
02 <head><title>Login</title></head>
03 <body>
04 <form runat="server">
05 <table>
06 <tr>
07 <td>User Name:</td>
08 <td><asp:textbox id="Name" runat="server" /> </td>
09 <td><asp:RequiredFieldValidator id="reqName" ControlToValidate="Name" runat="server"
➡text="Name can not be blank" /> </td>
11 </tr>
12 <tr>
13 <td>Password: </td>
14 <td><asp:textbox id="Password" textmode="password" runat="server" /></td>
15 <td><asp:RequiredFieldValidator id="reqPassword" ControlToValidate="Password"
➡runat="server" text="Password can not be blank" /> </td>
16 </tr>
17 <tr>
18 <td>Enter new password:</td>
```

continues ▶

Listing 4.40   **Continued**

```
19 <td><asp:textbox id="newPassword1" textmode="password" runat="server" /></td>
20 <td><asp:RequiredFieldValidator id="reqnewPassword1" ControlToValidate="newPassword1"
➥runat="server" text="Password can not be blank" /> </td>
21 </tr>
22 <td>Confirm new password:</td>
23 <td><asp:textbox id="newPassword2" textmode="password" runat="server" /></td>
24 <td><asp:comparevalidator id="valid1" runat="server" controltovalidate= "newPassword2"
➥controltocompare="newPassword1" errormessage="Both Passwords do not match, please re-
➥enter" /></td>
25 </tr>
26 </table>
27 <br><br>
28 <asp:button id="btnDone" text="Done" autopostback="true" runat="server" />
29 <br><br>
30 <asp:validationsummary id="mySummary" runat="server" headertext="Following errors
➥occured" displaymode="bulletlist" />
31 </form>
32 </body>
33 </html>
```

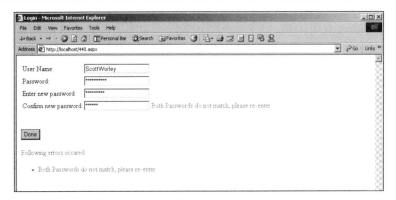

Figure 4.22   CustomValidator control example.

Summary

This chapter introduced Web Forms, the new programming model in ASP.NET. As you have seen, the Web Form's programming model is very familiar to Visual Basic or Visual C++ users. In ASP.NET, every page is compiled as a new `System.Web.UI.Page` object. The compiled version is cached in memory, resulting in a faster response after the first request.

When programming with Web Forms, you have HTML and web controls at your disposal. This chapter has shown you how to use each individual control for rapid development.

5

State Management in ASP.NET

THIS CHAPTER INTRODUCES THE STATE management capabilities of ASP.NET. It describes what state management is and what it can be used for. It also details the types of state management: Application, Session, and Web Page. This chapter also explains how and where the web.config and global.asax files are used with the state management system. Finally, it shows you how to use the various forms of state management.

What Is State Management?

State management refers to the capability to store information. In the case of web applications, state management has the capability to persist and retrieve information from web page to web page because a web page has no state. (A web page is simply a set of rendering instructions for a browser. After the browser has the page's data, it is rendered. The browser does not keep the page or any data in it.)

There are three main ways of doing this in ASP.NET:

- Use *Application state management* to store data for reuse across the whole application (giving the data application wide scope). This data is also available to any user who is using the web application.

- Use *Session state management* to store data. This provides a way to persist and retrieve data based on a user session (giving the session wide scope). The data persisted is only available to a single user or session.

- Use a *Statebag* to store data. A Statebag only has a web page-level scope and is used to persist information on a web page between postback events.

Before this chapter goes into any more detail about the types of state management available to ASP.NET, Table 5.1 lists a few features of ASP.NET state management.

Table 5.1   **Features of State Management**

Option	Feature
For all state management	Easy-to-use dictionary-based storage and retrieval-based interface.
Application state	Able to be accessed by any web page or component being processed within the context of the originating web application.
Session state	Enables ASP.NET to maintain and manage state information in a separate process to Internet Information Services (IIS), which means that if the IIS server should go down, all state information remains unaffected. You can also have the State Store Service running on an external machine from the web server or servers, which means that session management can be used in a web farm scenario.
	With *relational database management (RDBMS)-based state management*, you can configure ASP.NET to use a SQL server to persist state data.
	Session state management gives you the ability to use *cookieless state management*. This feature enables you to use state management on a browser that does not support cookies or a browser that has cookie support disabled.
Web Page state	Gives you the ability to persist additional data with web-page only scope. This means that you no longer have to create hidden textbox fields to store data, so data can be persisted between web page postbacks.

Although ASP.NET provides many powerful state management features, there are some drawbacks developers should be aware of (see Table 5.2).

Table 5.2 **Drawbacks to Using State Management**

Option	Issue
Application state	When using Application state, you are using up memory resources on the web server. Because of this, you should only use Application state if there is a good reason to do so.
	Because Application state data is available to all users of a web application, you have to avoid changing application-wide variables. There are mechanisms available for locking and unlocking Application State variables.
Session state	Depending on which type of Session state management is used, the application's performance can be impacted.

Using Application State Management

Application state management, as mentioned in the preceding section, is used to store application-wide data; it is best used to store data for quick access rather than for storing data that will be edited frequently.

The Application state is accessed and maintained through the `HttpApplicationState` object. This object is instantiated when a web application is first ran; this instance is accessed through the `Application` property.

Abusing Application State Management

When using Application state management, it can be tempting to use it for storing large amounts of static data. This, however, is generally a bad idea because the Application state manager stores the state data in memory on the web server, and this can lead to the possibility of running out of resources on the server side.

If you need to store large amounts of data with an application-wide scope, you should use the ASP.NET Cache Management system; this is explained in Chapter 14, "Cache Control in ASP.NET."

The most common properties, methods, and events for the `HttpApplicationState` class are in the following bulleted list. This section includes code snippets from a simple example web page, which demonstrates the `Application Intrinsic` object.

Common Properties of *HttpApplicationState*

The properties for `HttpApplicationState` class methods are as follows:

- **AllKeys**—Returns a string-based array containing all the Application state keys values.
  `Application.AllKeys`

- **Contents**—Provided for classic ASP compatibility.

```
Application.Contents("myaAppVar") = "A new Application State Variable"
```

- **StaticObjects**—Provides access to all objects declared in a web application by an <object runat=server></object> tag within the ASP.NET web application or site through a HttpStaticObjectsCollection collection.

```
AppStaticObjects = Application.StaticObjects
```

- **Count**—Gets the number of data items in the Application state collection.

```
Application.Count
```

- **Item**—Enables a user to retrieve Application state data. The method is overloaded to enable reference either by name or index number. This property also is the default property for the object.

```
01 Application.item(0)
02 Application.item("appName")
```

The common methods of the HttpApplicationState class properties are as follows:

- **GetKey**—Enables the user to retrieve an Application state object name by index.

```
Application.GetKey(0)
```

- **Remove**—Removes an object from the Application state collection by name.

```
Application.Remove("myAppVar")
```

- **RemoveAll**—Removes all objects from the Application state collection.

```
Application.RemoveAll()
```

- **Lock**—Locks access to all Application state variables.

- **UnLock**—Unlocks access to all Application state variables and facilitates access synchronization.

Events of the *HttpApplicationState* Class

The HttpApplicationState class various events can be intercepted and handled by your web application. You define event handlers for these in the global.asax file. The following lists the most common:

- **AuthenticateRequest**—Event fired when a web application attempts to authenticate an HTTP request.

- **AuthorizeRequest**—Event fired when a web application attempts to authorize an HTTP request.

- **BeginRequest**—Event fired when an HTTP request starts.

- **EndRequest**—Event fired when an HTTP request has completed.

- **Error**—Event fired when the application encounters an error. It can be used to create or reassign a new error handler for the web application.

- **OnStart**—Event fired when the application is first started on a web server.

- **OnEnd**—Event fired when the application shuts down.

Using ASP.NET Application State Management

Listings 5.1 and 5.2 show a global.asax and a web page that demonstrates some of the properties, methods, and events of the HttpApplicationState class, as explained previously. Figure 5.1 shows the Application State demo program.

Listing 5.1 **(global.asax) The Application Intrinsic Object in Action**

```
01 <Script language="vb" runat="Server">
02
03 Sub Application_OnStart(ByVal sender As Object, ByVal e As EventArgs)
04    Application("appName") = "Application State Management Demo"
05    Application("appDate") = DateTime.Now.ToShortDateString
06 End Sub
07
08
09 </SCRIPT>
```

Listing 5.2 **501.aspx**

```
01 <%@ Page Language="vb" AutoEventWireup="false" %>
02
03 <script language="vb" runat="server">
04
05 sub showAppVars()
06
07 Response.write("<b>Application State Demo.</b><br><br>")
08 Response.Write("<b>All items stored using Application State</b><br><br>")
09
10 Dim iCounter As Integer
11
12   response.write("<table
➥border=1><tr><td><b>Key</b></td><td></td><td><b>Value</b></td></tr>")
13
14   For iCounter = 0 To (Application.Count - 1)
15      Response.Write("<tr><td>"+ Application.GetKey(iCounter) +
➥"</td><td> = </td><td>" + Application(iCounter) + "</td></tr>")
16   Next
```

continues ▶

Listing 5.2 **Continued**

```
17   response.write("</table>")
18
19   end sub
20
21
22   Sub addAppVar_Click(ByVal sender As System.Object, ByVal e As System.EventArgs)
23       application.lock()
24       application(txtAppVarName.text) = txtAppVarValue.text
25       application.unlock()
26
27   end sub
28
29   Sub RemoveAppVar_Click(ByVal sender As System.Object, ByVal e As System.EventArgs)
30       application.Remove(txtRemove.text)
31
32   end sub
33
34
35   Sub RemoveAllAppVar_Click(ByVal sender As System.Object, ByVal e As System.EventArgs)
36       application.RemoveAll()
37
38   end sub
39
40
41   </script>
42
43   <HTML>
44   <body>
45
46   <% showAppVars() %>
47
48   <form id="Form1" method="post" runat="server">
49    <br>
50    <table>
51     <tr>
52      <td><b>Key Name</b></td>
53        <td></td>
54      <td><b>Value</b></td>
55        <td></td>
56    </tr>
57    <tr>
58      <td><asp:TextBox id=txtAppVarName runat="server"></asp:TextBox></td>
59        <td> = </td>
60      <td><asp:TextBox id=txtAppVarValue runat="server"></asp:TextBox></td>
61        <td><asp:Button id="btnAddAppVar" runat="server" Text="Add/Edit Application State
    ➥Variable" OnClick="addAppVar_Click"></asp:Button><br></td>
62    </tr>
63    </table>
64    <br>
```

```
65   <table>
66   <tr>
67    <td><b>Key</b></td>
68    <td> </td>
69   </tr>
70   <tr>
71    <td><asp:TextBox id=txtRemove runat="server"></asp:TextBox></td>
72    <td><asp:Button id="btnRemove" runat="server" Text="Remove Application State
➥Variable" OnClick="RemoveAppVar_Click"></asp:Button><br></td>
73   </tr>
74   </table>
75
76   <br>
77   <br>
78
79   <asp:Button id="btnRemoveAll" runat="server" Text="Remove All Application State
➥Variables" OnClick="RemoveAllAppVar_Click"></asp:Button>
80
81   </form>
82
83   </body>
84   </HTML>
```

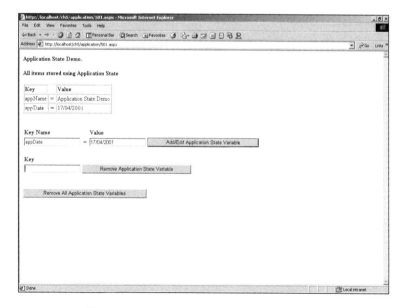

Figure 5.1   The Application State demo program.

Session State

A single instance of an `HttpSessionState` class is created the first time a client requests a URL from within an ASP.NET web application or site. This instance is accessed through the intrinsic object session in ASP.NET applications.

The common `HttpSessionState` class properties are as follows:

- **CodePage**—Returns the code page of the current session. (Fine more details on this in Chapter 13, "Localizing and Globalizing ASP.NET Applications.")

```
Session.CodePage
```

- **Contents**—Provided for Classic ASP compatibility.

```
Session.Contents("mySessionVar") = "A Session State Variable"
```

- **Count**—Returns the total number of session variables in existence for the client's current session.

```
Session.Count
```

- **IsCookieless**—Returns `true` if Session state management is cookieless or `false` if cookie-based.

```
Session.IsCookieless
```

- **IsNewSession**—Returns `true` if this is a new session, `false` if it is an instance of an existing session.

```
Session.IsNewSession
```

- **Item**—Enables a user to retrieve Session state data items by name or index.

```
Session.Item(0)
Session.Item("mySessionVariable")
```

- **Keys**—Returns a `NameObjectCollectionBase` object containing all the key's Session state keys.

```
Session.Keys
```

- **LCID**—Returns the Location ID for the session. For example, `"4105"` for English language settings. (Find more details on this in Chapter 13.)

```
Session.LCID
```

- **Mode**— Returns the current Session state mode. The Session mode can be one of the following:
  - `0`—`Off`
  - `1`—`InProc`
  - `2`—`StateServer`
  - `3`—`SQLServer`

```
01 if Session.Mode = 0 then
02     response.write("Session State Management is disabled!<br>")
03 end if
```

- **SessionID**—Returns the unique session ID for the client's current session.

```
Session.SessionID
```

- **StaticObjects**—Provides access to all objects declared in a session by an `<object runat=server></object>` tag within the ASP.NET web application or site through the `HttpStaticObjectsCollection` collection.

```
Session.StaticObects("myObject")
```

- **Timeout**—Sets the session timeout value.

```
Session.Timeout = 30
```

The `SessionState` class methods are as follows:

- **Abandon**—Forces the session to be abandoned. This happens automatically after a session times out.

```
Session.abandon()
```

- **Remove**—Removes an object from the session state collection by name.

```
Session.Remove("mySessionVar")
```

- **RemoveAll()**—Removes all objects from the Application state collection.

```
Session.RemoveAll()
```

Listing 5.3 demonstrates the usage of the *Session* object in ASP.NET by allowing you to view, add, and remove session variables dynamically. Figure 5.2 shows the Session State demo program.

Listing 5.3   **Example Demonstrating the *Session* Object in Action**

```
01 <%@ Page Language="vb" AutoEventWireup="false" %>
02
03 <script language="vb" runat="server">
04
05 sub showVars()
06
07   Dim SessionKeys as NameObjectCollectionBase.KeysCollection
08   SessionKeys = Session.Keys
09
10   Response.write("<b>Session State Demo.</b><br><br>")
11
12   Response.Write("<b>Codepage:</b> "+ctype(session.codepage, string)+"<br>")
13   Response.Write("<b>LCID:</b> "+ctype(session.LCID, string)+"<br><br>")
14   Response.Write("<b>IsCookieless:</b> "+ctype(session.iscookieless, string)+"<br>")
15   Response.Write("<b>IsNewSession:</b> "+ctype(session.isnewsession, string)+"<br><br>")
16   Response.Write("<b>Mode:</b> "+ctype(session.mode, string)+"<br><br>")
17   Response.Write("<b>SessionID:</b> "+ctype(session.sessionid, string)+"<br>")
18   Response.Write("<b>Timeout:</b> "+ctype(session.timeout, string)+"<br><br>")
```

continues ▶

Listing 5.3 **Continued**

```
19  Response.Write("<b>All items stored using Session State</b><br><br>")
20
21  response.write("<table
➥border=1><tr><td><b>Key</b></td><td></td><td><b>Value</b></td></tr>")
22
23  Dim iCounter As Integer
24  For iCounter = 0 To (Session.Count - 1)
25    Response.Write("<tr><td>"+ sessionkeys(iCounter) + "</td><td> = </td><td>" +
➥session(iCounter) + "</td></tr>")
26  Next
27
28  response.write("</table>")
29
30 end sub
31
32 Sub addVar_Click(ByVal sender As System.Object, ByVal e As System.EventArgs)
33    session(txtVarName.text) = txtVarValue.text
34 end sub
35
36 Sub RemoveVar_Click(ByVal sender As System.Object, ByVal e As System.EventArgs)
37    session.Remove(txtRemove.text)
38 end sub
39
40 Sub RemoveAllVar_Click(ByVal sender As System.Object, ByVal e As System.EventArgs)
41    session.RemoveAll()
42 end sub
43
44 </script>
45
46 <HTML>
47 <body>
48
49 <% showVars() %>
50
51 <form id="Form1" method="post" runat="server">
52   <br>
53   <table>
54   <tr>
55     <td><b>Key Name</b></td>
56       <td></td>
57     <td><b>Value</b></td>
58       <td></td>
59   </tr>
60   <tr>
61     <td><asp:TextBox id=txtVarName runat="server"></asp:TextBox></td>
62       <td> = </td>
63     <td><asp:TextBox id=txtVarValue runat="server"></asp:TextBox></td>
64       <td><asp:Button id="btnAddVar" runat="server" Text="Add/Edit Session State
➥Variable" OnClick="addVar_Click"></asp:Button><br></td>
```

```
65   </tr>
66   </table>
67
68   <br>
69
70   <table>
71   <tr>
72     <td><b>Key</b></td>
73     <td> </td>
74   </tr>
75   <tr>
76     <td><asp:TextBox id=txtRemove runat="server"></asp:TextBox></td>
77     <td><asp:Button id="btnRemove" runat="server" Text="Remove Session State Variable"
➥OnClick="RemoveVar_Click"></asp:Button><br></td>
78   </tr>
79   </table>
80
81   <br>
82   <br>
83
84   <asp:Button id="btnRemoveAll" runat="server" Text="Remove All Session State Variables"
➥OnClick="RemoveAllVar_Click"></asp:Button>
85
86   </form>
87
88   </body>
89   </HTML>
```

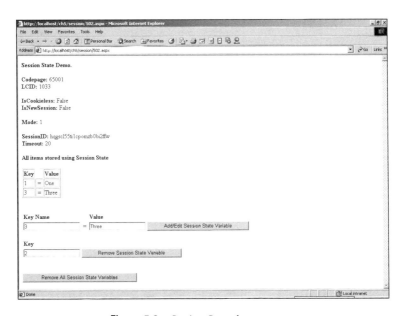

Figure 5.2 Session State demo program.

web.config and State Management

The web.config file has a section in it for configuring the way the Session state manager operates. This section is the `<sessionState>` section of the web.config file, and it configures the Session state `HttpModule`.

The `sessionState` section has five attributes, which are used to configure how state management is used by ASP.NET applications:

- **Mode**—Indicates whether Session state should be stored in process with ASP.NET or in an external state store process, which is either managed by a Windows 2000 service or an external SQL Server database. The values for each of these settings are:

  - **Off**—Turns off all Session state management. This frees up all state management processing resources, if you are not using session state management, and it has performance benefits.

  - **InProc**—This setting lets IIS manage the Session state in its own process space, thus using web server resources. This is the highest performing of the session management options, but if overused, it can end up running out of memory resources in the web server, and it also has the issue of whether IIS should shut down all session data goes as well.

- **StateServer**—The StateServer is an out-of-process Windows 2000 state management service, which can reside on any server. This means that due to communication between server and ASP.NET, there is a small performance hit. However, you do not suffer the same resource issues as you do in InProc mode. It still can drain the resources of the server on which it is installed, though.

- **SQLServer**—Finally, we have the most scalable and flexible solution, using a SQL database to store the session state information. This is the lowest performing option; however, it is very scalable, and it does not suffer from any resource issues, apart from those normally associated with databases.

The following are the remaining attributes of the `sessionState` section:

- **cookieless**—Indicates whether cookieless sessions should be used to identify client sessions or whether cookie-enabled sessions should be used.

- **timeout**—Number of minutes a session can be idle. After this limit has passed, the session will be abandoned.

- **connectionString**—IP or DNS of the server where the State service is being hosted.

- **sqlConnectionString**—Connection string of the SQL Server database where the SQL State service is being hosted.

Listing 5.4 shows a web.config file with a setting for state management.

Listing 5.4 **web.config File with Setting for Session State Management**

```
01 <?xml version="1.0" encoding="utf-8" ?>
02 <configuration>
03
04 <system.web>
05
06 <sessionState mode="InProc"
07
08                 cookieless="false"
09                 timeout="20" />
10
11
12 </system.web>
13
14 </configuration>
```

Cookieless State Management

ASP.NET now has the ability to provide Session state management facilities without the need of cookie support from a web browser. This is achieved by changing a setting in the Session state section of the web.config file, as shown:

```
01 <sessionState mode="InProc"
02             cookieless="true"
03             timeout="20" />
```

When ASP.NET Session management is set up this way, it encodes the sessionid, and sends it to the web server as part of the web request's URL.

The *sessionState* Store

One of the most powerful features of ASP.NET session management is that you can now configure the session manager to manage state in three main ways:

- Using in-process state management
- Using the ASP.NET State Service for Session management
- Using SQLState-Based Session state management

Using In-Process State Management

To configure ASP.NET state management to use in-process state management, use the following web.config sessionState section:

```
01 <sessionState mode="InProc"
02              cookieless="false"
03              timeout="20" />
```

In the web.config sessionState section, I have set the desired state management mode to in-process, meaning that I am letting IIS manage the state in the same way it was managed in Classic ASP. I have also set the Session state manager to use cookies to persist session IDs and to set a session timeout of 20 seconds.

To configure ASP.NET state management to use out-of-process state management, use the following web.config sessionState section:

```
01 <sessionState mode="StateServer"
02              cookieless="false"
03              timeout="20"
04              stateConnectionString="localhost" />
```

Note that the sessionState section now has a new attribute—the connectionString attribute. This is used to tell the state manager where to locate the out-of-process state manager. This attribute can be localhost, DNS, or the IP address of a remote server where the services are being hosted. In the previous example, it is set to use the localhost server.

Using the ASP.NET State Service for Session Management

You will have to start the Windows 2000 ASPState service. This is started from the Windows 2000 Services Manager, which can be accessed by going to the Start menu, Settings, Control Panel, Administrative Tools, and then clicking the Component Services icon. After the Component Services window is displayed, click the Services (Local) branch of the console root, and all the services available on your server are shown. You are then presented with the screen shown in Figure 5.3.

Find the ASP.NET state service and right-click; you will be presented with the following menu, shown in Figure 5.4.

Select Start from the menu, and the ASP.NET state service will start. Any web applications configured to use out-of-process state will now use this service to manage all session state management.

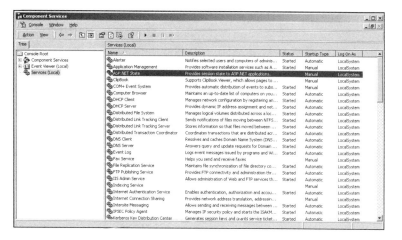

Figure 5.3   Starting the ASP State service.

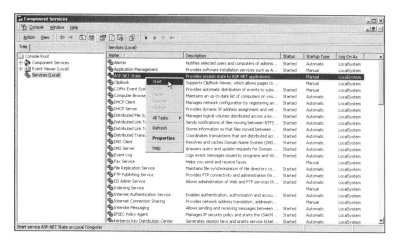

Figure 5.4   Starting the State service through the Services menu.

Using SQLState-Based Session State Management

To configure ASP.NET state management to use SQL hosted state management, use the following web.config sessionState section:

```
01 <sessionState mode="StateServer"
02          cookieless="false"
03          timeout="20"
04          sqlConnectionString="data source=localhost;
05                          user id=sa;password=" />
```

You will also have to run a SQL script, which comes with ASP.NET, to create the tables and stored procedures used by the SQLState Session state management system. To do this, open up the Query Analyzer application, which comes with SQL Server, and connect to your database server. After you are connected, open the InstallSqlState.sql file, which is located in the /windows/Microsoft.NET\Framework\v1.0.3215\installsqlsate.sql (note that the final subdirectory might be slightly different).

After you have opened the script file, you should run it by pressing F5. After this is done, you should end up with a screen similar to Figure 5.5.

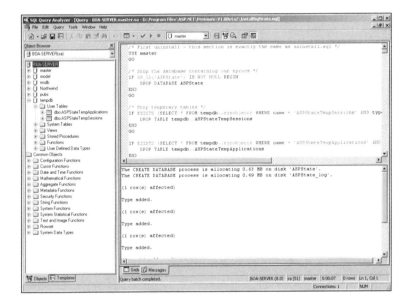

Figure 5.5 Running the InstallSqlState script file.

After this has been done, your web application will use the SQL databases created for Session state management.

Summary

As you can see, ASP.NET now has a very powerful and flexible system for managing both Application and Session state data. With the ability to use Session state on browsers with or without cookie support, you have an easy-to-use external state management system, which is very scalable, that offers a way of working with Session state in a web farm environment. In Chapter 17, "Putting It All Together," the ProjectPal application makes use of both the Session and Application state managers for its operation, and it also uses the external state management store.

ASP.NET and Data Access

6

Using ADO.NET in ASP.NET Applications

THIS CHAPTER DISCUSSES ONE OF THE most important resources that comes with the .NET framework—the data access objects that constitute the ADO.NET technology.

The beginning of this chapter contains an overview of ADO.NET—focusing on how it is related to its predecessor, ADO—and examines its underlying architecture. The goal is to gain an understanding of the importance of data access for web applications. Other sections cover the main data access objects that are at your disposal, data-oriented Web Forms development using the Repeater, the DataList, and the DataGrid ASP.NET web controls. Finally, in the last part of this chapter, is an introduction to the transaction-enabled ASP.NET applications.

Data Access from a Web-Based Perspective

For the past four decades, database systems have occupied the most strategic position inside the software environment of organizations. Because the main role of a database system is to provide permanent storage for all information that is essential to a business, it is perfectly comprehensible that it has held such a strategic position. Nowadays, even with the growing importance of the Internet, this has not changed. After all, even if database systems actually are the most efficient way for storing information, the web has proved to be the most efficient way for sharing it on a wide scale. In other words, the web and database systems can be considered complementary technologies.

As proof of such an affinity, most sites on the web—at least most sites of professional quality—use data access intensively. Primarily, this is done to offer a dynamic experience to visitors by allowing them to interact with the information (data) stored on remote data sources (generally, databases) through Web Forms instead of just viewing it, which is what commonly happens in the pure HTML static sites.

If a site can access remote data, the visitor can store personal data that will enable this site to treat him in a customized manner in subsequent visits. A simple, concrete example is a Human Resources site in a corporate intranet. As soon as an employee identifies himself to the application behind the site, usually through a login, he can view only (or sometimes modify) the stored data that is related to him, such as current address, salary, or benefits.

Of course, there are many more advanced examples that I can give, such as banking web sites, which, among other things, enable customers to transfer funds from one account to another requiring only a few mouse clicks and the transferred amount. Such simplicity is possible thanks to a behind-the-scenes database. E-commerce sites are probably the most well-known example of web applications that need to have access to a database; after all, where would the customers get updated information, such as the current prices of the products offered by these sites, except from a database?

It's evident that this level of interaction would not be possible in today's web sites without the presence of a backend database system—that is, a database server (see Figure 6.1). In fact, a powerful relational database system is recognized as indispensable to most web applications, such as those mentioned previously.

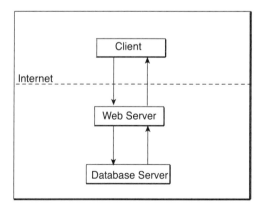

Figure 6.1 A typical client/server architecture on the web that includes a database server.

The scenario described in Figure 6.1 is quite common. The client (generally a PC using a browser) connects to a web server and requests a file, usually—but not limited to—an HTML page. As you probably know, if the requested page is a static HTML page, the web server simply sends it to the client where the page is parsed and displayed. However, if the page is dynamic, like an ASP page, then the web server will process it before sending the resulting HTML to the client. If a dynamic page contains some kind of database query, the query is performed on the database referenced by a corresponding connection. (Database connection will be discussed later in this chapter.) Only the query results will be returned to the web server which, in turn, will send the appropriate HTML code to the client in the opposite corner.

Note
Commonly, the database server and the web server are physically located in the same computer.

A number of actions can be performed on a database, that fall under the generic term "query" such as selection, insertion, updating, and exclusion of data. These actions are usually executed through SQL statements.

What About SQL?

In the early 1980s, IBM developed *Structured Query Language* (SQL) as part of its project called "System R." Ever since, SQL has been the language of choice for all the subsequent implementations of relational database systems. SQL is a non-procedural language that aims to work with groups of rows rather than a single row, which explains why it is the appropriate language for working with databases.

In SQL, it is possible to return, insert, update, or delete data from a specific database as well as create, alter, and exclude common database objects, such as tables, columns, constraints. If you intend to implement data access in your web applications, it is a good idea to achieve some knowledge of SQL.

Note
This book will not get into details about the SQL language, although most of the examples in this chapter demonstrate the use of some SQL statements.

Some Words on SQL Server 2000

By releasing SQL Server 2000, Microsoft brought to the web development arena a product capable of satisfying the performance, ease of use, and standard compliance requirements that are expected from a database system for use on the web. Additionally, SQL Server 2000 is tightly integrated with Windows 2000, which has enabled it to reach outstanding performance levels in tests accomplished by several independent organizations.

As if this were not enough, SQL Server 2000 has an exclusive and optimized ADO.NET provider called SqlClient in addition to the OLE DB provider, which fits into Microsoft's strategy to encourage the use of its corporate relational database system by web developers. OLE DB provider is discussed later in this chapter.

> **Note**
>
> It is possible (and hopeful) that providers for other database systems, such as Oracle, Sybase, Informix, and so on, will be developed. However, for the time being, there are only two available providers: OLE DB and SqlClient. Both of these providers will be discussed in this chapter with an emphasis on SqlClient.

For all the reasons previously explained, developers who plan to build data-oriented ASP.NET applications should certainly think about SQL Server 2000 as their database system of choice. (By the way, all the examples in this chapter will use SQL Server 2000.)

ADO and ADO.NET

ADO.NET, as well as its predecessor *ActiveX Data Objects* (ADO), aims to simplify data access by providing a concise set of .NET classes. ADO, on the other hand, is a COM-based technology that provides a simple, single, and coherent way to manipulate data from a number of data sources, and, along with ASP.NET, intends to be the engine behind a new generation of web applications.

In this section, we are going to look at ADO and ADO.NET, examine their architectures, and then compare the two.

Where Is ADO?

One of the reasons that explains the quick adoption of ASP—and consequently of Microsoft's web server, *Internet Information Services* (IIS)—by the web developer's community is the simplified access to several data sources provided by ADO.

Although ADO has not been developed for exclusive use with ASP applications, it is in this arena that this fantastic data access technology stands out. Together with the scripting languages Visual Basic .NET and JScript, which are known for their ease of use, ADO enables the development of data-driven web applications in a fast and easy way, increasing developer productivity by offering a simple, yet powerful, object model. (The ADO object model is described in Figure 6.2.)

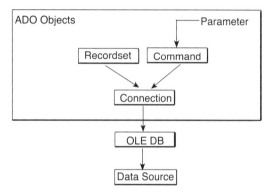

Figure 6.2   The ADO object model.

The two main objects that constitute ADO are the Connection and the Recordset objects. The Connection object is responsible for establishing the connectivity between the application and the data source. A Recordset object behaves like a single in-memory table and is usually populated by a SELECT query performed on the database specified by the Connection object.

The Recordset object primarily enables the navigation along a group of rows. Although it is possible to insert, update, or delete rows using appropriate methods of the Recordset object, most ASP programmers prefer to use the corresponding SQL statements with the Execute() method of the Connection object to do this.

ADO currently is on version 2.6.

ADO.NET: .NET and Data Access

ADO is easy, offers a powerful programming model, fits like a glove into data-oriented web applications, and has been successful among web developers for years. Perhaps you are asking yourself: "Why should anybody learn a new data access technology, taking into account that the current one is so good?"

The answer is simple: With the .NET release, the application development paradigm on the Windows platform probably will change soon. In other words, COM will have to leave the scene, so that .NET and its classes, interfaces, and structures assume the leading role. This implies that even though ADO has been the dominant data access technology in the COM world, ADO.NET will naturally assume this role in the .NET world.

On the other hand, if you do not intend to invest time and money to replace your COM-based environment with a .NET-based environment for the time being (and the previous argument is not enough for you), you surely are convinced of the advantages of adopting ASP.NET for developing your web applications. If this is true, then adopting ADO.NET as your data access technology of choice is the next step precisely because both ADO and ADO.NET are subsets of the .NET framework and share the same development philosophy.

What's more, I hope that the rest of this chapter manages to convince you that although ADO might be a great technology, ADO.NET is better.

The ADO.NET Architecture

At a glance, ADO.NET might look like just an ADO evolution. However, by performing an in-depth analysis, you'll notice that ADO.NET is wholly different from ADO internally in the same way ASP.NET is different from ASP. Indeed, ADO.NET is a revolutionary data access technology concept just as the entire .NET framework is a revolutionary application development platform.

Setting aside the formal ADO.NET architecture for a moment—It's best to explain, empirically, how ADO.NET is structured (see Figure 6.3 and compare it with Figure 6.2).

Two important ADO.NET objects are `Connection` and `Command`. The `Connection` object, like its equivalent in ADO, provides the connectivity between an application and a data source, and takes into account the data source type. To perform actions on a database, ADO.NET uses the `Command` object.

However, the core component that constitutes ADO.NET is the `DataSet` object. A dataset, similar to a recordset, is an in-memory representation of data obtained from a data source (often, but not limited to, a database). A dataset could be a part of a database or even the entire database insofar as a real database is constituted by tables and relations among tables.

Tables in a dataset are represented by `DataTable` objects. A `DataTable` object contains a number of collections of other objects, such as `DataRow` and `DataColumn`.

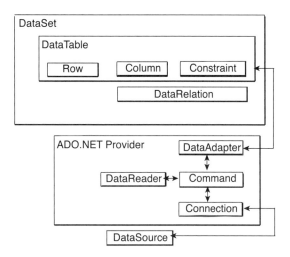

Figure 6.3 Schematic description of ADO.NET operation.

In the middle of the road between a DataSet object and the target data source, you will find a DataAdapter object. This object, along with the Connection and the Command objects, is used to fill the dataset and update the data source.

Finally, the ADO.NET data access providers offer a simple way to navigate along the rows in a set of selected data. This simple way is the DataReader object.

ADO.NET Namespaces

The secret behind the ADO.NET programming model is a set of interrelated .NET classes that enable applications to perform all the tasks related to data access. Those classes are logically placed into namespaces, which are briefly described in the next few sections.

System.Data Namespace

To sum it up in a sentence, the System.Data namespace is the heart of the ADO.NET technology. This namespace supplies the basic functionality for accessing data inside of the ADO.NET programming model.

The main ADO.NET class, DataSet, belongs to this namespace, as well as to the DataTable class, the DataRow class, the DataView class, and so on. This chapter discusses all of these classes.

The System.Data namespace also contains an important enumeration called SqlDbType, whose members represent the SQL Server intrinsic data types (see Table 6.1).

Table 6.1 **The *SqlDbType* Enumeration Members**

SqlDbType Member	Description
BigInt	64-bit signed integer.
Binary	Fixed-length stream of binary data with up to 8,000 bytes.
Bit	A boolean value (1 or 0).
Char	Fixed-length stream of ASCII characters with up to 8,000 characters.
DateTime	Date and time that are contained between January 1, 1753 and December 31, 9999.
Decimal	Fixed scale and precision numeric value between -10^{38}-1 and 10^{38}1.
Float	Floating point number between -1.79E +308 and 1.79E +308.
Image	Variable-length stream of binary data with up to 2 GB.
Int	32-bit signed integer.
Money	Currency values between -2^{63} and 2^{63}-1.
NChar	Fixed-length of Unicode characters with up to 4,000 characters.
NText	Variable-length stream of Unicode characters with up to 2^{30}-1 characters.
NVarChar	Variable-length stream of Unicode characters with up to 4,000 characters.
Real	Floating point number between -3.40E +38 and 3.40E +38.
SmallDateTime	Date and time that are contained between January 1, 1900 and June 6, 2079.
SmallInt	16-bit signed integer.
SmallMoney	Currency value between -214,748.3648 and 214,748.3647.
Text	Variable-length stream of ASCII characters with up to 2^{31}-1 characters.
Timestamp	Date and time in the format yyyymmddhhmmss.
TinyInt	8-bit unsigned integer.
VarBinary	Variable-length stream of binary data with up to 8,000 bytes.
VarChar	Variable-length stream of ASCII characters with up to 8,000 characters.
UniqueIdentifier	Globally unique identifier (GUID), a number that identifies each row in a table in an exclusive manner.
Variant	sql_varient can contain almost any type, except for the following: sql_varient, text, ntext, image, or timestamp.

System.Data.Common Namespace

As its name implies, this is a namespace that contains classes whose functionalities are shared, by inheritance, by the .NET data access providers.

The more important class inside the System.Data.Common namespace is the DataAdapter class, which is an abstract class that works like a bridge between the DataSet object and the data source. DataAdapter is inherited by another System.Data.Common abstract class called DbDataAdapter. This class, in turn, is the base for implementing the specific-provider adapter classes (currently, the OleDbDataAdapter and SqlDataAdapter classes).

System.Data.OleDb Namespace

The first data access provider that is bundled with the .NET framework is the generic OLE DB provider.

The more important classes inside the System.Data.OleDb namespace are OleDbDataAdapter, OleDbCommand, OleDbDataReader, and OleDbConnection. These four classes, along with the DataSet class, offer practically all the necessary functionality for working with a number of OLE DB-supported data sources.

You can use the OLE DB provider to work with SQL Server 7 and 2000 databases; however, for better performance, using the SQL Server-specific provider (SqlClient) is recommended.

System.Data.SqlClient Namespace

The SqlClient provider is the exclusive SQL Server data access provider. Similar to the System.Data.OleDb namespace, the main classes inside the System.Data.SqlClient namespace are SqlDataAdapter, SqlCommand, SqlDataReader, and SqlConnection. Along with the DataSet class, these four main classes of the System.Data.SqlClient namespace enable you to perform every kind of action on a SQL Server database.

System.Data.SqlTypes Namespace

The System.Data.SqlTypes namespace primarily contains structures that map to the intrinsic SQL Server data types. (Table 6.2 shows the existing relationship among the intrinsic SQL Server data types and their corresponding types in this namespace.)

Explicitly declaring objects as an instance of a SqlTypes structure when you work with SQL Server data inside ASP.NET applications results in faster code and avoids conversion mistakes. Anyway, all the data obtained from a SQL Server that you intend to use will be implicitly converted to SqlTypes.

Table 6.2 *System.Data.SqlTypes* **Mappings**

Native SQL Server Data Type	*System.Data.SqlTypes* Structure
bigint	SqlInt64
binary	SqlBinary
bit	SqlBit
char	SqlString
datetime	SqlDateTime
decimal	SqlNumeric
float	SqlDouble
image	SqlBinary
int	SqlInt32
money	SqlMoney
nchar	SqlString
ntext	SqlString
nvarchar	SqlString
numeric	SqlNumeric
real	SqlSingle
smalldatetime	SqlDatetime
smallint	SqlInt16
smallmoney	SqlMoney
sql_variant	Object (found in System namespace)
sysname	SqlString
text	SqlString
timestamp	SqlBinary
tinyint	SqlByte
uniqueidentifier	SqlGuid
varbinary	SqlBinary
varchar	SqlString

Main Differences Between ADO and ADO.NET

As stated in the beginning of this section, ADO.NET shares the same fundamental goal as ADO. The main difference between these two data access
technologies was also determined.

ADO.NET is a set of .NET classes; that is, it uses all the features of Common Language Runtime and the .NET framework, such as managed code. Conversely, ADO is based on Microsoft COM and is, therefore, by definition, unsafe code.

However, there are a lot of additional differences between ADO.NET and ADO, some of which are listed:

- ADO uses the `Recordset` object to represent a set of selected data in memory. ADO.NET uses the `DataSet` object to do this. Although the `Recordset` object looks like a single table, the `DataSet` object, on the other hand, behaves like an entire database with one or more tables.

- ADO is used primarily by scripting languages in ASP applications. Its standard data type is `Variant`, which is the only data type directly supported by scripting languages. The `Variant` data type accepts all types of values, such as integers, floats, strings, and so on. As we know, it has a series of inconveniences, from slow code execution to wasted memory. ADO.NET also can use variables with variant values by declaring them as instances of the `System.Object` class; however, ADO.NET uses strongly typed variables. A consequence of this means that several aspects of ASP.NET application development are improved, mainly those related to performance and best programming techniques.

- XML support in ADO is very restricted. On the other hand, ADO.NET uses XML for almost every task that involves data formatting, such as transmitting data to other applications or components, whether or not it is based on a Windows platform. (By the way, the fact that ADO.NET is fully XML compliant is emphasized as an open door for interoperability with several platforms that also are XML compliant.)

- The connected nature of ADO demands more system resources than disconnected ADO.NET. As a result of its disconnected nature and of saving system resources, ADO.NET is more scaleable than ADO. (ADO also supports disconnected data access, but not by default.)

Working with the Main ADO.NET Objects

The previous section discussed the ADO.NET architecture and the main objects that build the ADO.NET programming. This section gets into more detail on these objects, so that you understand both the role of each in the construction of a data-driven ASP.NET application and how each object is linked to the others.

Connecting to a Data Source Using the *Connection* Object

The first ADO.NET object that we will analyze is the `Connection` object. The function of this object is to make way for data, so it can flow from a data source to an application and vice versa. (No other ADO.NET object can work with data from a remote data source except through a `Connection` object.)

There are two different versions of the `Connection` object—the `OleDbConnection` class, which must be used to connect to any OLE DB-supported data source, and the `SqlConnection` class, which must be used to connect to SQL Server 7 and 2000 databases.

> **Note**
>
> As stated previously in this chapter, the SqlClient provider and its resources will be emphasized; therefore, all the following examples use SqlClient (and its objects) instead of the OleDb provider.
>
> To illustrate how you can use the **SqlConnection** object (the **OleDbConnection** object can be used similarly), Listing 6.1 tries to establish a connection with the Pubs database, which comes with SQL Server 2000. If such an attempt is successful, the browser will display the message **Connection was successful!**. Otherwise, it will display the corresponding SQL Server error message.

Listing 6.1 Establishing a Connection with the Pubs Database (601.aspx)

```
01 <%@ Import Namespace = "System.Data.SqlClient" %>
02
03 <html>
04 <title>Sample ASP.NET Page</title>
05 <body>
06
07 <script language = "VB" runat = "server">
08
09 Sub Page_Load(sender As Object, e As EventArgs)
10
11     Dim ConnStr as String
12
13     ConnStr = "Data Source=localhost;Integrated Security=SSPI;"
14     ConnStr = ConnStr + "Initial Catalog=pubs"
15
16     Dim conn As SqlConnection = New SqlConnection(ConnStr)
17
18     Try
19         conn.Open()
20
21         Status.Text = "Connection was successful!"
22
23     Catch ex As SqlException
24         Status.Text = ex.Message
```

```
25
26      Finally
27          conn.Close()
28
29      End Try
30
31  End Sub
32
33  </script>
34
35  <h1>Connecting to a data source using the Connection object</h1>
36
37  <asp:label id="Status" runat="server"/>
38  </body>
39  </html>
40
```

Let's analyze some pieces of this sample code. First, the directive in line 01 of the previous code:

```
<%@ Import Namespace = "System.Data.SqlClient" %>
```

This directive imports the System.Data.SqlClient namespace, which contains the SqlConnection class. (If you wanted to use the OleDbConnection class and its resources, you would need to import the System.Data.OleDb namespace.)

ConnStr is a String data type variable that contains a connection string. (A *connection string* provides the connection information, such as user name, password, data source name, and so on, which ADO.NET needs to access a specific data source. In general, each kind of data source has its own format for connection strings.) In this case, the value of ConnStr is a connection string that only is valid for the SqlClient provider. On the other hand, a valid connection string that could be used with the OleDbConnection object would look like the following:

```
Provider=SQLOLEDB;Data Source=localhost;Integrated Security=SSPI;Initial Catalog=pubs
```

This OLE DB connection string is specific to accessing the SQL Server database called Pubs, which is being specified as the initial catalog. (You know that this connection string refers to a SQL Server database because the value SQLOLEDB was set to the Provider variable. When you are using the SqlClient provider, it is not necessary to set the value to the Provider variable because you already know beforehand that you are working with a SQL Server database.)

conn is an instance of the SqlConnection class. To declare a SqlConnection object, you need to supply a connection string for the class constructor, which, in this case, is contained within the ConnStr variable. (If you do not supply a connection string for the constructor, then you will need to set the connection string to the value of the SqlConnection's ConnectionString property.)

Finally, it is necessary to call the Open() method to open the connection to the specified data source. After using the connection, it is recommended that you close it by calling the Close() method.

Performing ADO.NET Commands

After connecting to a data source through a Connection object, you can perform actions (that is, commands) on the data source using the Command object. Such actions would be as follows:

- Retrieving data
- Inserting a new row into a database
- Updating existing rows into a database
- Deleting existing rows from a database
- Executing stored procedures
- Building both a DataReader or an XMLReader

> **Note**
> Just like the Connection object, the Command object also comes in two flavors (one for each available ADO.NET provider): the OleDbCommand class, which you will find inside the System.Data.OleDb namespace, and the SqlCommand class, which belongs to the System.Data.SqlClient namespace. Both of these classes can be used in a similar way because you import the appropriate namespace to each one.

Elaborating on the previous example of the Connection object, I will demonstrate how to use the Command object to insert a new row into the Author's table of the Pubs database. (See Listing 6.2.)

Listing 6.2 **Inserting a New Row into the Author's Table (602.aspx)**

```
01 <%@ Import Namespace = "System.Data.SqlClient" %>
02
03 <html>
04 <title>Sample ASP.NET Page</title>
05 <body>
06
07 <script language = "VB" runat = "server">
08
09 Sub Page_Load(sender As Object, e As EventArgs)
10
```

```
11      Dim ConnStr as String
12
13      ConnStr = "Data Source=localhost; Integrated Security=SSPI;"
14      ConnStr = ConnStr + "Initial Catalog=pubs"
15
16      Dim conn As SqlConnection = New SqlConnection(ConnStr)
17
18      Try
19          conn.Open()
20
21          Dim CmdStr As String
22
23          CmdStr = "INSERT INTO Authors VALUES('999-19-4465',"
24          CmdStr = CmdStr + "'Johnson','Brian',"
25          CmdStr = CmdStr + "'607 223-4119',NULL,NULL,NULL,NULL,1)"
26
27          Dim cmd as SqlCommand = New SqlCommand(CmdStr,conn)
28
29          cmd.ExecuteNonQuery()
30
31          Status.Text = "Command performed successfully!"
32
33      Catch ex As SqlException
34          Status.Text = ex.Message
35
36      Finally
37          conn.Close()
38
39      End Try
40
41 End Sub
42
43 </script>
44
45 <h1>Performing ADO.NET commands</h1>
46
47 <asp:label id="Status" runat="server"/>
48 </body>
49 </html>
```

Pay attention to the highlighted code. First, I declared a CmdStr variable of the String data type. This variable contains the SQL statement—in this case, an INSERT statement, which will be used by the Command object to perform an action on the database specified by the Connection object. Subsequently, I created a SqlCommand object supplying two arguments to the class constructor: the CmdStr variable (you could pass the INSERT SQL statement to the constructor directly; however, I used a string variable for convenience) and a Connection object. Finally, the ExecuteNonQuery() method was called; this method executes every kind of action, such as insert, update, exclusion, and so on, on the specified database. In a few words, to perform an action using the Command object, just pass a string representing the appropriate SQL statement (INSERT, UPDATE, DELETE, and so on) plus a Connection object to the SqlCommand (or OleDbCommand) class constructor, and then call the ExecuteNonQuery() method.

> **Note**
> The ExecuteNonQuery() method does not return rows, so it should not be used with a SELECT statement.

An important feature of the Command object is its ability to execute SQL Server's stored procedures, once again using the ExecuteNonQuery() method. This is done by passing the stored procedure name together with a Connection object to the SqlCommand class constructor. Next, you must set the value of the CommandType property of the Command object to CommandType.StoredProcedure (keep in mind that CommandType, in this case, is an enumeration that belongs to the System.Data namespace). The following code demonstrates this:

```
01 Dim cmd As SqlCommand = New SqlCommand("UpdateCity",conn)
02 cmd.CommandType = CommandType.StoredProcedure
03 Dim param1 As SqlParameter = cmd.Parameters.Add _
04          ("@city1",SqlDbType.Char,20)
05 param1.Value = "Menlo Park"
06 Dim param2 As SqlParameter = cmd.Parameters.Add _
07          ("@city2",SqlDbType.Char,20)
08 param2.Value = "San Diego"
09 cmd.ExecuteNonQuery()
```

The previous code executes a stored procedure, called UpdateCity, which takes two parameters (@city1 and @city2). Such parameters are represented by two SqlParameter objects, which were added to the Parameters collection of the SqlCommand object by the Add() method. (The Add() method requires three arguments: the parameter name, its data type (represented by a member of the previously mentioned SqlDbType enumeration) and its length.)

This chapter does not intend to get into detail about stored procedures, but in any event, here is the code of the UpdateCity stored procedure:

```
01 CREATE PROCEDURE UpdateCity (@city1 CHAR(20), @city2 CHAR(20))
02 AS
03 UPDATE authors SET city=@city2 WHERE city=@city1
```

The UpdateCity stored procedure updates each row in the Author's table by setting the value of the city column to @city2 where city is equal to @city1. By executing the previous code, set the value of the city column to San Diego so it is equal to Menlo Park (notice the Value property of the two SqlParameter objects).

Using a *DataReader* Object to Retrieve Data

In a case where you just need to retrieve data from a data source, so that such data is displayed in your ASP.NET page, you would use the `DataReader` object. This object provides a read-only, forward-only way for accessing data.

> **Note**
>
> You cannot modify data in the `DataReader` object. If you want to modify data, then you should use the `DataSet` object.

Just like the `Connection` and `Command` objects, there are also two different versions of the `DataReader` object: `OleDbDataReader` and `SqlDataReader`. In Listing 6.3, I will use the `SqlDataReader` class; however, the `OleDbDataReader` class can be used similarly.

Listing 6.3   *SqlDataReader* **Class (603.aspx)**

```
01 <%@ Import Namespace = "System.Data.SqlClient" %>
02
03 <html>
04 <title>Sample ASP.NET Page</title>
04 <body>
06
07 <script language = "VB" runat = "server">
08
09 Sub Page_Load(sender As Object, e As EventArgs)
10
11     Dim ConnStr as String
12
13     ConnStr = "Data Source=localhost; Integrated Security=SSPI;"
14     ConnStr = ConnStr + "Initial Catalog=pubs"
15
16     Dim conn As SqlConnection = New SqlConnection(ConnStr)
17
18     Try
19         conn.Open()
20
21         Dim CmdStr As String
22
23         CmdStr = "SELECT au_id,au_lname,au_fname FROM Authors"
24
25         Dim cmd as SqlCommand = New SqlCommand(CmdStr,conn)
26
27         Dim reader As SqlDataReader = cmd.ExecuteReader()
28
29         Do While reader.Read()
30             Authors.Items.Add(New ListItem(reader.Item("au_fname") _
31                 + " " + reader.Item("au_lname"),reader.Item("au_id")))
32         Loop
```

continues ▶

Listing 6.3 **Continued**

```
33
34    If Page.IsPostBack Then
35        SelectedAuthor.Text=Authors.SelectedItem.Text
36    End if
37
38    Catch ex As SqlException
39        Status.Text = ex.Message
40
41    Finally
42        conn.Close()
43
44    End Try
45
46 End Sub
47
48 </script>
49
50 <h1>Using a DataReader object to retrieve data</h1>
51
52 <form runat="server">
53    <asp:label id="Status" runat="server"/><br />
54    <asp:listbox id="Authors" rows=10 autopostback="true" runat="server"/><br /><br />
55    Selected author: <asp:label id="SelectedAuthor" runat="server"/>
56 </form>
57 </body>
58 </html>
```

This ASP.NET page will display a ListBox in the browser called Authors, which contains the full name of all the authors who are stored on the Authors table of the Pubs database (see Figure 6.4).

Note

If the AutoPostBack property of the Authors ListBox was set to true, when a visitor clicks one of the listed names, the form will be submitted, and the selected name will be displayed under the Authors ListBox.

The function of the DataReader object here is to supply these values (author names and IDs) to the ListBox. Notice that I used the ExecuteReader() method of the Command object to instantiate the DataReader object. Going to the next line, I used a Do While loop along with the DataReader's Read() method for navigating along and retrieving the requested values from each row that is part of the group of data in the DataReader. Such a group of data is constituted by all the data returned by the SELECT SQL statement passed as an argument to the SqlCommand class constructor.

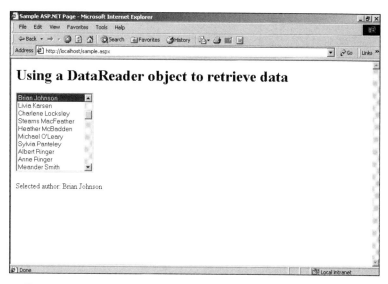

Figure 6.4 Sample page that demonstrates use of the DataReader object.

Taking a Look at the *DataSet* Object

A *dataset* is by definition an in-memory representation of selected data that, as well as in a database, is organized as rows into tables. Within an ASP.NET application, the DataSet object can be used to manipulate data in a disconnected manner, which saves system resources and improves scalability of such an application.

Creating a dataset in an ASP.NET page is easy; see Listing 6.4.

Listing 6.4 **ASP.NET dataset (604.aspx)**

```
01 <%@ Import Namespace = "System.Data" %>
02 <%@ Import Namespace = "System.Data.SqlClient" %>
03
04 <html>
05 <title>Sample ASP.NET Page</title>
06 <body>
07
08 <script language = "VB" runat = "server">
09
10 Sub Page_Load(sender As Object, e As EventArgs)
11
12     Dim ConnStr as String
13
14     ConnStr = "Data Source=localhost;Integrated Security=SSPI;"
```

continues ▶

Listing 6.4   Continued

```
15      ConnStr = ConnStr + "Initial Catalog=pubs"
16
17      Dim conn As SqlConnection = New SqlConnection(ConnStr)
18
19      Try
20          conn.Open()
21
22          Dim da As SqlDataAdapter = New SqlDataAdapter _
23              ("SELECT * FROM Authors",conn)
24
25          Dim ds As New DataSet
26
27          da.Fill(ds,"authors")
28
29          DataGrid1.DataSource=ds.Tables("authors").DefaultView
30          DataGrid1.DataBind()
31
32      Catch ex As SqlException
33          Status.Text = ex.Message
34
35      Finally
36          conn.Close()
37
38      End Try
39
40 End Sub
41
42 </script>
43
44 <h1>Creating a dataset</h1>
45
46 <asp:label id="Status" runat="server"/>
47 <asp:datagrid id="DataGrid1" runat="server" />
48 </body>
49 </html>
```

The preceding code declares both a DataAdapter object called da (in this case, an instance of the SqlDataAdapter class) and, subsequently, a DataSet object called ds. (To use the DataSet object in this page, we imported the System.Data namespace.)

You will use a DataAdapter object and its Fill() method to obtain data from a remote data source to be stored on a dataset. The first argument passed to the Fill() method is the dataset name, and the second argument passed is the name of the DataTable object being added to the dataset, which is filled with data returned by the SELECT query and passed as argument to the SqlDataAdapter class constructor. (Notice that a Connection object also is passed to the Fill() method.)

Note

A DataGrid control is used to display the data of the specified `DataTable` object (see Figure 6.5). The DataGrid control will be analyzed in more detail later in this chapter in the section, "The DataGrid Control."

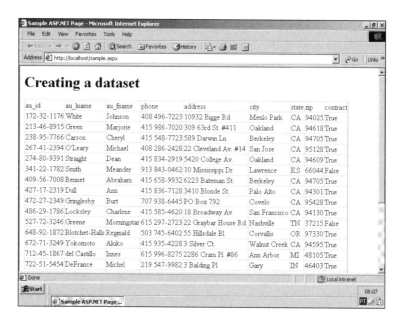

Figure 6.5   A sample ASP.NET page that exhibits data contained within the Authors `DataTable` object.

The `DataSet` object provides several properties and methods you can use in your ASP.NET applications. The most important properties are the `Tables` and `Relations` properties, which enable you to access the dataset's `DataTable` and `DataRelation` collections. Among the methods that are at your service are the `AcceptChanges()` and `RejectChanges()` methods, which you can use to effect or discard all changes made on subordinate objects (that is, `DataTable` object, `DataRow` object, `DataRelation` object, and so on). You can also use the `Clear()` method to remove all rows from the `DataTable` objects within the dataset or the `Copy()` method to make a copy of the dataset. The methods related to XML are discussed in the section, "XML and Datasets."

Using the *DataTable* Object

Refer back to Figure 6.3; note specifically the box that represents the `DataSet` object. Within a dataset, there is a collection of `DataTable` objects and, within a datatable, there is a number of collections of other objects, such as `DataRow`,

DataColumn, and so on. The DataTable object and the other objects that it contains provide all the necessary resources for manipulating data into a dataset.

To use a DataTable object, you need to create an instance of the DataTable class, which belongs to the System.Data namespace (as well as create an instance for all the classes representing the objects that a DataTable object contains). Therefore, the first thing that you need to do is import the System.Data namespace to your ASP.NET page.

There are two ways to create a DataTable object: declaring it explicitly, and adding it to a dataset or populating a dataset with the Fill() method of the DataAdapter object, which is more common. (Remember that the Fill() method takes the name of a DataTable object as an argument.) Taking into account that the second way (populating a dataset with the Fill() method) has already been demonstrated in a previous example; we will see how to create a DataTable object using the first way (declaring it explicitly):

```
01 Dim tb As New DataTable("BookStores")
02 ds.Tables.Add(tb)
```

ds may be considered to be the dataset that we saw in the example on dataset creation, and a DataTable object called tb is being added to the dataset's DataTable collection. By the way, you can use this collection to work with a group of datatables rather than a single one in a for each iteration:

```
01 Dim dt as DataTable
02 For Each dt In ds.Tables
03      'Does something here
04 Next
```

However, this DataTable object still does not have a defined schema. To define schema information for a DataTable object, we will need to add DataColumn objects to it—specifically to its DataColumn collection:

```
01 Dim cl1 As DataColumn = tb.Columns.Add("bs_id",Type.GetType("System.Int32"))
02 cl1.AutoIncrement = true
03
04 Dim cl2 As DataColumn = tb.Columns.Add _
05      ("bs_name",Type.GetType("System.String"))
06 cl2.AllowDBNull = false
07
08 tb.Columns.Add("bs_address",Type.GetType("System.String"))
09 tb.Columns.Add("bs_phone",Type.GetType("System.String"))
```

We added four columns (that is, DataColumn objects) to the tb table, and now this table has a defined schema. The two first columns were explicitly created by declaring a variable (c1 and c2, respectively) as instances of the DataColumn class and, subsequently, they were added to the tb table. On the other hand,

the two last columns were implicitly created by adding them to the `tb` table.
The `AutoIncrement` property of `cl1` was set to `true`; this means an incremental
value will be inserted into this column when a new row is inserted into this
datatable. Notice that the `AllowDBNull` property of `cl2` was set to `false`; this
does not allow null values to be inserted into this column.

```
01 Dim arr(1) As DataColumn
02 arr(0) = tb.Columns("bs_id")
03 tb.PrimaryKey = arr
```

The preceding code defines the `bs_id` column as the primary key of the
`tb` table.

> **Note**
>
> You must use the `AcceptChanges()` and `RejectChanges()` methods of the `DataTable` object to commit or
> reject any change to the datatable.

A Few Words About the *DataRelation* Object

The `System.Data` namespace provides a class called `DataRelation`, which
enables you to establish and navigate along column-based relationships
between `DataTable` objects. The following code shows how to create a relationship between two hypothetical datatables called `department` and `employee`,
which are contained within a dataset called `ds`:

```
01 Dim rel As New DataRelation("Dept_Emp", _
02          ds.Tables("department").Columns("id_dept"), _
03          ds.Tables("employee").Columns("id_dept"))
04 ds.Relations.Add(rel)
```

In the preceding sample code, three arguments are passed to the `DataRelation`
class constructor: the name of the relationship being created, the `DataColumn`
object belonging to the parent datatable (`department`), and, finally, the
`DataColumn` object belonging to the child datatable (`employee`). These two
columns, whose names are both `id_dept`, are the base of the relationship
between the `department` and `employee` datatables.

After creating the `DataRelation` object, we need to add it to the
`DataRelation` collection of the `ds` `DataSet` object. By adding a new datarelation to a dataset, two different `Constraint` objects will automatically be
created—in this case, a `UniqueConstraint` object, which will be added to the
`department` datatable, and a `ForeignKeyConstraint` object, which will be added
to the `employee` datatable.

Navigating along our newly created relationship is pretty easy using a
for each:

```
01 Dim parentrow As DataRow
02 Dim childrow As DataRow
03
04 For Each parentrow In ds.Tables("department").Rows
05     'Here you can display the department name, for instance.
06     For Each childrow In parentrow.GetChildRows(rel)
07         'Here you can display the full name of each employee of this
08         'department, for instance.
09     Next
10 Next
```

In the preceding code, you can see that the GetChildRows() method of
the DataRow object is used to obtain the related rows from the child
datatable (employee). The DataRow object is examined further in the
next section.

Using the *DataRow* Object

Because the DataTable object schema is defined and we have a primary key,
we can now perform all the table-related tasks, such as inserting, updating,
and deleting rows. Within a DataTable object, a row is represented by a
DataRow object. Use of the DataRow object to perform data manipulation tasks
will be briefly covered here.

First, let's see how to add a row to the previously created tb DataTable
object:

```
01 Dim row As DataRow = tb.NewRow()
02 row("bs_name") = "Brazilian BookStore"
03 row("bs_address") = "Av. da Esperança, 3001, Belo Horizonte/MG - Brazil"
04 row("bs_phone") = "55-31-34478659"
05 tb.Rows.Add(row)
```

Note

As soon as a new DataRow object is added to the DataRow collection of the DataTable object, the value of the
RowState property is set to Added.

A new row was added to the previous tb DataTable object, specifically to its
DataRow collection (which can be accessed through the Rows property of the
DataTable object). Similarly to the DataTable object, you can use a for each
iteration to work with a group of rows rather than a single row:

```
01 Dim dr as DataRow
02 For Each dr In tb.Rows
03     'Does something here
04 Next
```

Now, suppose you have set a wrong value to the bs_phone column. You will certainly want to change such a value. To edit data in an existing DataRow object, you can use the BeginEdit() method to begin an edit operation and the EndEdit() method to confirm the edits (or the CancelEdit() method to cancel the edits):

```
01 Row.BeginEdit()
02 Row("bs_phone") = "55-31-34538659"
03 Row.EndEdit()
```

Note

As soon as changes are made in a DataRow object, the value of the RowState property of this row is set to Modified.

If you want to delete a row, you must call the Delete() method of the DataRow object:

```
row.Delete()
```

Note

As soon as a DataRow object is removed from the DataTable, the value of the RowState property of this row is set to Deleted.

Note

You must use the AcceptChanges() and RejectChanges() methods of the DataRow object to commit or reject any change in the row.

The following ASP.NET page, shown in Listing 6.5, shows you how to use a DataTable object and a DataRow object to manipulate data into datasets.

Listing 6.5 **Using *DataTable* and *DataRow* to Manipulate Data (605.aspx)**

```
01 <%@ Import Namespace = "System.Data" %>
02 <%@ Import Namespace = "System.Data.SqlClient" %>
03
04 <html>
05 <title>Sample ASP.NET Page</title>
06 <body>
07
08 <script language = "VB" runat = "server">
09
10 Sub Page_Load(sender As Object, e As EventArgs)
11
```

continues ▶

Listing 6.5 **Continued**

```
12    Try
13        Dim ds As New DataSet
14
15        Dim tb As New DataTable("BookStores")
16        ds.Tables.Add(tb)
17
18        Dim cl1 As DataColumn = tb.Columns.Add _
19            ("bs_id",Type.GetType("System.Int32"))
20        cl1.AutoIncrement = true
21
22        Dim cl2 As DataColumn = tb.Columns.Add _
23            ("bs_name",Type.GetType("System.String"))
24        cl2.AllowDBNull = false
25
26        tb.Columns.Add("bs_address",Type.GetType("System.String"))
27        tb.Columns.Add("bs_phone",Type.GetType("System.String"))
28
29
30        Dim arr(1) As DataColumn
31        arr(0) = tb.Columns("bs_id")
32        tb.PrimaryKey = arr
33
34        tb.Acceptchanges()
35
36        Dim row As DataRow = tb.NewRow()
37        row("bs_name") = "Brazilian BookStore"
38        row("bs_address") = _
39            "Av. da Esperança, 3001, Belo Horizonte/MG - Brazil"
40        row("bs_phone") = "55-31-34478659"
41        tb.Rows.Add(row)
42
43        row.AcceptChanges()
44
45        datagrid1.datasource=ds.Tables("BookStores").defaultview
46        datagrid1.databind()
47
48    Catch ex As SqlException
49        Status.Text = ex.Message
50
51    End Try
52
53 End Sub
54
55 </script>
56
57 <h1>Using the DataRow object</h1>
58
59 <asp:label id="Status" runat="server"/>
60 <asp:datagrid id="datagrid1" runat="server" />
61 </body>
62 </html>
```

You can also use the DataRow object to manipulate data in a DataTable object that represents a table that exists in a database. The following ASP.NET page, shown in Listing 6.6, will show it using the Authors table of the Pubs database.

Listing 6.6 **Using the *DataRow* Object to Manipulate Data in a *DataTable* Object (606.aspx)**

```
01 <%@ Import Namespace = "System.Data" %>
02 <%@ Import Namespace = "System.Data.SqlClient" %>
03
04 <html>
05 <title>Sample ASP.NET Page</title>
06 <body>
07
08 <script language = "VB" runat = "server">
09
10 Sub Page_Load(sender As Object, e As EventArgs)
11
12     Dim ConnStr as String
13
14     ConnStr = "Data Source=localhost;Integrated Security=SSPI;"
15     ConnStr = ConnStr + "Initial Catalog=pubs"
16
17     Dim conn As SqlConnection = New SqlConnection(ConnStr)
18
19     Try
20         conn.Open()
21
22         Dim da As New SqlDataAdapter
23         da.SelectCommand = New SqlCommand("SELECT * FROM Authors",conn)
24
25         Dim cb As New SqlCommandBuilder(da)
26
27         Dim ds As New DataSet
28
29         da.Fill(ds,"Authors")
30
31         Dim row As DataRow = ds.Tables("Authors").NewRow()
32         row("au_id") = "999-19-4465"
33         row("au_lname") = "Johnson"
34         row("au_fname") = "Brian"
35         row("phone") = "607 223-4119"
36         row("contract") = true
37         ds.Tables("authors").Rows.Add(row)
38
39         da.Update(ds,"authors")
40
41         row.AcceptChanges()
42
43         datagrid1.datasource=ds.Tables("Authors").defaultview
```

continues ▶

Listing 6.6 **Continued**

```
44         datagrid1.databind()
45
46     Catch ex As SqlException
47         Status.Text = ex.Message
48
49     Finally
50         conn.Close()
51
52     End Try
53
54 End Sub
55
56 </script>
57
58 <h1>Using the DataRow object</h1>
59
60 <asp:label id="Status" runat="server"/>
61 <asp:datagrid id="datagrid1" runat="server" />
62
63 </body>
64 </html>
```

The DataAdapter object called da, through its Update() method, will update
the original Author's table located in the Pubs database on the SQL Server
with updated data from the ds dataset (specifically, from the Author's datatable). Notice that I used a CommandBuilder object there. This object uses the
original table schema returned by the SelectCommand property of the
DataAdapter object to generate automatically the appropriate Command object
(which can be an InsertCommand, an UpdateCommand, or a DeleteCommand) that
will synchronize the original table with the DataTable object.

In the ASP.NET page shown in Listing 6.6, the CommandBuilder object
generated an InsertCommand because the value of the RowState property of the
row DataRow object is "Added," and so this one is a new row that must be
inserted into the original Authors table. If the RowState property was set to
"Modified," an UpdateCommand would be generated, and if it was set to
"Deleted," consequently, a DeleteCommand would be created. (Remember: Do
not call the AcceptChanges() method of the DataRow object before calling the
Update() method of the DataAdapter object. If you do this, then the RowState
property of the DataRow object will be set to Unchanged and no commands
will be generated by the CommandBuilder object.) For further information
about the possible values of the RowState property, see Table 6.3.

Note

Although you can generate the appropriate InsertCommand, UpdateCommand, and DeleteCommand by yourself, it is not necessary if you are working with a single datatable and the original table from which you retrieved the data of that datatable has a primary key. In this case, the CommandBuilder objects (both the SqlCommandBuilder and the OleDbCommandBuilder) are the best choice.

Table 6.3 **Possible Values for the *RowState* Property of the *DataRow* Object**

State	Description
Added	The row was added to the DataTable's DataRow collection and the AcceptChanges() method still was not called.
Deleted	The row was deleted and the AcceptChanges() method still was not called.
Detached	The row was already created but still was not added to the DataRow collection of the DataTable object.
Modified	The row was modified and the AcceptChanges() method still was not called.
Unchanged	The row was not changed since the last call to the AcceptChanges() method.

XML and Datasets

Chapter 8, "XML Web Service Development in ASP.NET," introduced XML Web Services, a revolutionary way of making complex application logic available over the web. The secret behind the .NET XML Web Services is that it is entirely based on the XML language. Walking along the same road, the DataSet object adds more power to the .NET XML Web Services by using XML as its format for transmitting data to and receiving data from XML Web Services consumers.

You can load data from a file, stream, XmlReader object, or string to a dataset, or you can write data from a dataset to a file, stream, or XmlWriter object. In a similar way, you also can load or write the schema information of a dataset.

To write data from a dataset to XML, you can use the WriteXml() method. It takes two arguments: the destination of the XML output, plus the XmlWriteMode, which will be used to define how to write such an output (see Table 6.4).

Table 6.4 *XmlWriteMode* **Options**

XmlWriteMode **Option**	**Description**
IgnoreSchema	The dataset will be written as XML, ignoring the schema information.
WriteSchema	The dataset will be written as XML, as well as the schema information.
DiffGram	The dataset will be written as a DiffGram, which is an XML serialization format that includes both the current and original values of an element.

The following code shows how to write the schema information and the data of the dataset created in the previous sample ASP.NET page to a file called ds.xml:

```
ds.WriteXml("ds.xml", XmlWriteMode.WriteSchema)
```

To load data from XML to a dataset, you may use the ReadXml() method, passing two arguments to it: the source of the XML input and the XmlReadMode, which will be used to determine how such a source will be read. (See Table 6.5.)

Table 6.5 *XmlReadMode* **Options**

XmlReadMode **Option**	**Description**
Auto	It automatically analyzes the XML input and tries to use the appropriate option.
ReadSchema	It reads the schema information and loads it together with data.
IgnoreSchema	It does not take into account any information schema found in the XML input when loading the data into a dataset using its schema.
InferSchema	It does not take into account any information schema found in the XML input when trying to infer the schema using the XML data structure before loading data into a dataset.
DiffGram	It loads data from a DiffGram.
Fragment	It reads fragments of an XML input and loads it to a dataset that matches its schema.

The following code reads and loads the schema information and data from the ds.xml file created previously to a dataset called xmlds:

```
xmlds.ReadXml("ds.xml", XmlReadMode.ReadSchema)
```

The next step is to create an ASP.NET page that will display both data and schema information of the xmlds DataSet object. (Notice that xmlds will be created with the same schema information and data of the original dataset called ds.) To do this, we will use the GetXml() and the GetXmlSchema() methods, respectively, to get the data and the information schema from xmlds and set these values to two string variables, strData and strSchema:

Listing 6.7 **Displaying Data and Schema Information (607.aspx)**

```
01 <%@ Import Namespace = "System.Data" %>
02 <%@ Import Namespace = "System.Data.SqlClient" %>
03
04 <html>
05 <title>Sample ASP.NET Page</title>
06 <body>
07
08 <script language = "VB" runat = "server">
09
10 Sub Page_Load(sender As Object, e As EventArgs)
11
12     Dim ConnStr as String
13
14     ConnStr = "Data Source=localhost;Integrated Security=SSPI;"
15     ConnStr = ConnStr + "Initial Catalog=pubs"
16
17     Dim conn As SqlConnection = New SqlConnection(ConnStr)
18
19     Try
20         conn.Open()
21
22         Dim da As SqlDataAdapter = New SqlDataAdapter _
23             ("SELECT * FROM Authors",conn)
24
25         Dim ds As New DataSet
26
27         da.Fill(ds,"authors")
28
29         ds.WriteXml("ds.xml", XmlWriteMode.WriteSchema)
30
31         Dim xmlds As New DataSet
32
33         xmlds.ReadXml("ds.xml", XmlReadMode.ReadSchema)
34
35         Dim strData, strSchema As String
36
37         strData = xmlds.GetXml()
38         strSchema = xmlds.GetXmlSchema()
39
40         Data.Text = strData
41         Schema.Text = strSchema
```

continues ▶

Listing 6.7 **Continued**

```
42
43    Catch ex As SqlException
44        Status.Text = ex.Message
45
46    Finally
47        conn.Close()
48
49    End Try
50
51 End Sub
52
53 </script>
54
55 <h1>XML and datasets</h1>
56
57 <asp:label id="Status" runat="server"/>
58 <h2>Data:</h2>
59 <asp:textbox id="Data"
60     textmode="multiline" wrap="true"
61     readonly="true" width=700 rows=15
62     runat="server"
63 />
64 <br /><br />
65 <h2>Schema:</h2>
66 <asp:textbox id="Schema"
67     textmode="multiline" wrap="true"
68     readonly="true" width=700 rows=15
69     runat="server"
70 />
71 </body>
```

Figure 6.6 shows the resulting page.

Note

Additionally, you can use an XSD schema to create a strongly typed dataset. A strongly typed dataset is a class that inherits from the original DataSet object and offers a friendly way for accessing tables and columns by name. However, this issue is beyond the scope of this book.

DataView Object and Data Binding

The following section presents three examples that use web controls to display and modify data. Before we go into this, however, we must look at another important ADO.NET object called DataView.

The DataView object is a customized view of the data contained within a DataTable object and is essential to the process known as data binding.

In fact, the `DataTable` object has a default `DataView` object that can be accessed through its `DefaultView` property (we have done this in previous examples). Using a `DataView` you can sort, filter, search, and edit data.

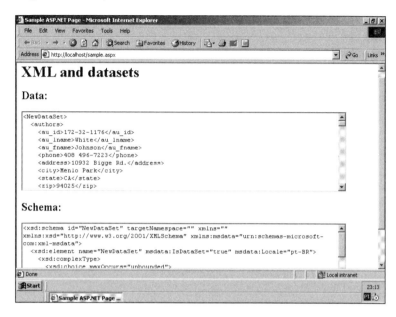

Figure 6.6   An ASP.NET page that displays data and schema information of the `xmlns` dataset.

The following sample ASP.NET page, shown in Listing 6.8, shows how to use a `DataView` to do basic data binding using the Authors datatable.

Listing 6.8   **Using a *DataView* (608.aspx)**

```
01 <%@ Import Namespace = "System.Data" %>
02 <%@ Import Namespace = "System.Data.SqlClient" %>
03
04 <html>
05 <title>Sample ASP.NET Page</title>
06 <body>
07
08 <script language = "VB" runat = "server">
09
10 Sub Page_Load(sender As Object, e As EventArgs)
11
12         Dim ConnStr as String
13
14         ConnStr = "Data Source=localhost;Integrated Security=SSPI;"
15         ConnStr = ConnStr + "Initial Catalog=pubs"
```

continues ▶

Listing 6.8 **Continued**

```
16
17          Dim conn As SqlConnection = New SqlConnection(ConnStr)
18
19     Try
20          conn.Open()
21
22          Dim da As SqlDataAdapter = New SqlDataAdapter _
23              ("SELECT * FROM Authors",conn)
24
25          Dim ds As New DataSet
26
27          da.Fill(ds,"authors")
28
29          Dim dv1 As New DataView(ds.Tables("authors"))
30          dv1.Sort = "au_id DESC"
31
32          Dim dv2 As New DataView(ds.Tables("authors"))
33          dv2.RowFilter = "city='Palo Alto'"
34
35          DataGrid1.DataSource=dv1
36          DataGrid1.DataBind()
37
38          DataGrid2.DataSource=dv2
39          DataGrid2.DataBind()
40
41     Catch ex As SqlException
42          Status.Text = ex.Message
43
44     Finally
45          conn.Close()
46
47     End Try
48
49 End Sub
50
51 </script>
52
53 <h1>DataView object and data binding</h1>
54
55 <asp:label id="Status" runat="server"/>
56 <h2>Sorted rows:</h2>
57 <asp:datagrid id="DataGrid1" runat="server" />
58 <h2>Filtered rows:</h2>
59 <asp:datagrid id="DataGrid2" runat="server" />
60 </body>
61 </html>
```

The preceding code uses two important properties of the DataView object:
Sort and RowFilter. The first DataView uses Sort to sort the data into

descending order based on the au_id column. (By default, the data is sorted in ascending order based on the first column.) The second dataview uses the RowFilter property to limit the data displayed by the corresponding DataGrid to that which has a value in the city column equal to "Palo Alto" (in fact, only two rows are displayed).

Note

Two DataGrid controls are used for demonstration purposes only. It is perfectly fine to use a single DataGrid control and bind it to a dataview that uses both Sort and RowFilter properties at the same time.

Building Data-Oriented Web Forms

ASP.NET emphasizes the use of advanced web controls for building user interfaces. Three main advanced-focused data web controls come with ASP.NET:

- DataGrid
- Repeater
- DataList

This section briefly analyzes three examples of how to use these three controls to display and modify data.

The DataGrid Control

In the previous section, we saw many examples that used the DataGrid control to display data. However, the appearance of the generated ASP.NET pages is not very attractive, even for non-designers, so something needs to change. The DataGrid control enables a lot of customization, and we will see it now in Listing 6.9.

Listing 6.9   **DataGrid Control (609.aspx)**

```
01 <%@ Import Namespace = "System.Data" %>
02 <%@ Import Namespace = "System.Data.SqlClient" %>
03
04 <html>
05 <title>Sample ASP.NET Page</title>
06 <body>
07
08 <script language = "VB" runat = "server">
09
10 Sub Page_Load(sender As Object, e As EventArgs)
```

continues ▶

Listing 6.9 **Continued**

```
11
12    Dim ConnStr as String
13
14    ConnStr = "Data Source=localhost;Integrated Security=SSPI;"
15    ConnStr = ConnStr + "Initial Catalog=pubs"
16
17    Dim conn As SqlConnection = New SqlConnection(ConnStr)
18
19    Try
20        conn.Open()
21
22        Dim da As SqlDataAdapter = New SqlDataAdapter _
23            ("SELECT * FROM Authors",conn)
24
25        Dim ds As New DataSet
26
27        da.Fill(ds,"authors")
28
29        Dim dv1 As New DataView(ds.Tables("authors"))
30        dv1.Sort = "au_fname, au_lname DESC"
31        dv1.RowFilter = "state <= 'KS'"
32
33        DataGrid1.DataSource=dv1
34        DataGrid1.DataBind()
35
36    Catch ex As SqlException
37        Status.Text = ex.Message
38
39    Finally
40        conn.Close()
41
42    End Try
43
44 End Sub
45
46 </script>
47
48 <asp:label id="Status" runat="server"/>
49 <asp:datagrid id="DataGrid1" runat="server"
50     BackColor="lightgreen"
51     BorderColor="gray"
52     Font-Name="Arial"
53     Font-Size="10pt"
54     HeaderStyle-BackColor="gray"
55     MaintainState="false"
56     ShowFooter="false"
57 />
58 </body>
59 </html>
60
```

Pay attention to the highlighted code. In it, several properties that govern the DataGrid control appearance are set, so that you have a more interesting grid for exhibiting the selected data (see Table 6.6).

Table 6.6 **Main Design Properties of a *DataGrid* Object**

AllowPaging	Indicates whether data paging is enabled.
AllowSorting	Indicates whether sorting is enabled.
AlternatingItemStyle	Defines different styles for alternating items in a grid.
AutoGenerateColumns	Defines whether columns automatically generate into a datagrid.
BackColor	Defines the background color of a datagrid.
BackImageUrl	Defines the URL of an image as the background of a datagrid.
BorderColor	Defines the border color of a datagrid.
BorderStyle	Defines the style for borders of a datagrid.
BorderWidth	Defines the width for borders of a datagrid.
CellPadding	Defines how much space must be between the cell content and the cell border.
CellSpacing	Defines how much space must be between cells in a datagrid.
CssClass	Defines the CSS class used by a datagrid.
Enabled	Indicates whether the datagrid is enabled.
EnableViewState	Indicates whether the DataGrid control on the server maintains its view state when the request to this page ends.
Font	Defines the font to be primarily used by a datagrid.
FooterStyle	Defines the style of the footer section of a datagrid.
ForeColor	Defines text color.
GridLines	Defines the style of the grid lines.
HeaderStyle	Defines the style of the header section of a datagrid.
Height	Defines the height of a datagrid.
ItemStyle	Defines the style of the items in a datagrid.
PageSize	Defines how many items are displayed by a single page in a datagrid.
ShowFooter	Indicates whether a footer section will be displayed.
ShowHeader	Indicates whether a header section will be displayed.
Width	Defines the width of a datagrid.

Nevertheless, our datagrid only displays data. You probably want a datagrid that offers a way to manipulate data as well, and you will have it. Necessary code, however, is a bit more complex (and long), so I will show only those parts that are interesting to us now. (You can add the following code into the appropriate places in the previous example. The resulting page is shown in Figure 6.7.)

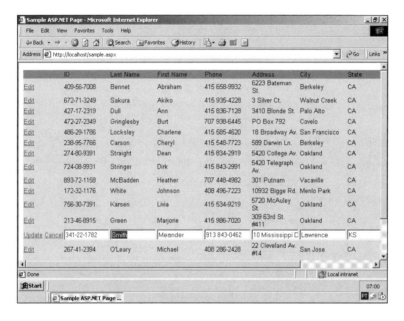

Figure 6.7   Example of a datagrid.

First, we will see how to define a `DataGrid` object, so that it becomes an editable datagrid. See the (long) code shown in Listing 6.10.

Listing 6.10   **Defining a *DataGrid* Object (610.aspx)**

```
001 <form runat="server">
002 <asp:datagrid id="DataGrid1" runat="server"
003      AutoGenerateColumns="false"
004      DatakeyFiled="au_id"
005      OnEditCommand="Edit_Grid"
006      OnCancelCommand="Cancel_Grid"
007      OnUpdateCommand="Update_Grid"
008
009      BackColor="lightgreen"
010      GridLines="none"
011      Font-Name="Arial"
012      Font-Size="10pt"
```

```
013        HeaderStyle·BackColor="gray"
014        ShowFooter="true"
015        MaintainState="false"
016        >
017        <Columns>
018        <asp:EditCommandColumn
019            EditText="Edit"
020            CancelText="Cancel"
021            UpdateText="Update"
022        />
023        <asp:TemplateColumn HeaderText="ID">
024            <ItemTemplate>
025                <asp:label
026                    Text='<%# Container.DataItem("au_id") %>'
027                    runat="server"
028                />
029            </ItemTemplate>
030
031            <EditItemTemplate>
032                <asp:TextBox width=100 id="au_id"
033                    ReadOnly="True"
034                    Text='<%# Container.DataItem("au_id") %>'
035                    runat="server"
036                />
037            </EditItemTemplate>
038        </asp:TemplateColumn>
039        <asp:TemplateColumn HeaderText="Last Name">
040            <ItemTemplate>
041                <asp:label
042                    Text='<%# Container.DataItem("au_lname") %>'
043                    runat="server"
044                />
045            </ItemTemplate>
046
047            <EditItemTemplate>
048                <asp:TextBox width=100 id="au_lname"
049                    Text='<%# Container.DataItem("au_lname") %>'
050                    runat="server"
051                />
052            </EditItemTemplate>
053        </asp:TemplateColumn>
054        <asp:TemplateColumn HeaderText="First Name">
055            <ItemTemplate>
056                <asp:label
057                    Text='<%# Container.DataItem("au_fname") %>'
058                    runat="server"
059                />
060            </ItemTemplate>
061
062            <EditItemTemplate>
063                <asp:TextBox width=100 id="au_fname"
064                    Text='<%# Container.DataItem("au_fname") %>'
```

continues ▶

Listing 6.10 **Continued**

```
065                     runat="server"
066                 />
067             </EditItemTemplate>
068         </asp:TemplateColumn>
069         <asp:TemplateColumn HeaderText="Phone">
070             <ItemTemplate>
071                 <asp:label
072                     Text='<%# Container.DataItem("phone") %>'0
073                     runat="server"
074                 />
075             </ItemTemplate>
076
077             <EditItemTemplate>
078                 <asp:TextBox width=100 id="phone"
079                     Text='<%# Container.DataItem("phone") %>'
080                     runat="server"
081                 />
082             </EditItemTemplate>
083         </asp:TemplateColumn>
084         <asp:TemplateColumn HeaderText="Address">
085             <ItemTemplate>
086                 <asp:label
087                     Text='<%# Container.DataItem("address") %>'
088                     runat="server"
089                 />
090             </ItemTemplate>
091
092             <EditItemTemplate>
093                 <asp:TextBox width=100 id="address"
094                     Text='<%# Container.DataItem("address") %>'
095                     runat="server"
096                 />
097             </EditItemTemplate>
098         </asp:TemplateColumn>
099         <asp:TemplateColumn HeaderText="City">
100             <ItemTemplate>
101                 <asp:label
102                     Text='<%# Container.DataItem("city") %>'
103                     runat="server"
104                 />
105             </ItemTemplate>
106
107             <EditItemTemplate>
108                 <asp:TextBox width=100 id="city"
109                     Text='<%# Container.DataItem("city") %>'
110                     runat="server"
111                 />
112             </EditItemTemplate>
113         </asp:TemplateColumn>
114         <asp:TemplateColumn HeaderText="State">
115             <ItemTemplate>
```

```
116                 <asp:label
117                     Text='<%# Container.DataItem("state") %>'
118                     runat="server"
119                 />
120             </ItemTemplate>
121
122         <EditItemTemplate>
123             <asp:TextBox width=100 id="state"
124                 Text='<%# Container.DataItem("state") %>'
125                 runat="server"
126             />
127         </EditItemTemplate>
128     </asp:TemplateColumn>
129     <asp:TemplateColumn HeaderText="Zip">
130         <ItemTemplate>
131             <asp:label
132                 Text='<%# Container.DataItem("zip") %>'
133                 runat="server"
134             />
135         </ItemTemplate>
136
137         <EditItemTemplate>
138             <asp:TextBox width=100 id="zip"
139                 Text='<%# Container.DataItem("zip") %>'
140                 runat="server"
141             />
142         </EditItemTemplate>
143     </asp:TemplateColumn>
144     <asp:TemplateColumn HeaderText="Contract?">
145         <ItemTemplate>
146             <asp:CheckBox
147                 Enabled="False"
148                 Checked='<%# Container.DataItem("contract") %>'
149                 runat="server"
150             />
151         </ItemTemplate>
152
153         <EditItemTemplate>
154             <asp:CheckBox id="contract"
155                 Enabled="true"
156                 Checked='<%# Container.DataItem("contract") %>'
157                 runat="server"
158             />
159         </EditItemTemplate>
160     </asp:TemplateColumn>
161     </Columns>
162 </asp:DataGrid>
163 </form>
```

Pay attention to the following while you are (carefully) analyzing the preceding code:

- The `EditCommandColumn` object, which creates a column that contains hyperlinks to the procedures that enable you to edit the data through a `DataGrid` object.
- The `Columns` tag, which contains, of course, all the columns that will be displayed on the page.
- See how I used the `TemplateColumn` object to customize the style of each column within our datagrid?
- As you can see, within each `TemplateColumn` there are two tags called `ItemTemplate` and `EditItemTemplate`, respectively. These two tags are the fourth and more important thing to notice, because they govern the style of the non-editable rows and of the editable rows within the datagrid. (By the way, notice that I used Label controls with the non-editable columns and TextBox controls with the editable ones. The exception is the Contract column, with which I used a CheckBox control for both of them because this column represents a bit value.)

Now we will see the procedures passed to the `On...Command` properties of the `DataGrid` object. Such procedures will do the hard work.

The following is the `Edit_Grid()` procedure. When you click the Edit hyperlink in front of a row, you will be calling this procedure, which in turn, makes it editable:

```
01 Sub Edit_Grid(Sender As Object, e as DataGridCommandEventArgs)
02      DataGrid1.EditItemIndex = e.Item.ItemIndex
03      DataGrid1.DataBind()
04 End Sub
```

What the `Edit_Grid()` procedure does is update the value of the `EditItemIndex` property of the `DataGrid` object, so that it corresponds to the index of the row that you want to make editable. Then the DataGrid control is bound again to update the data exhibition.

Subsequently, we have the `Update_Grid()` procedure, which is responsible for updating a changed row in the datagrid to its corresponding row in a table of a data source. Notice in Listing 6.11 that I used the Forms collection of the `Request` object to get the parameters that are passed to the server when the Update hyperlink is clicked.

Listing 6.11 **Using the Forms Collection to Get Parameters (611.aspx)**

```
01 Sub Update_Grid(Sender As Object, e as DataGridCommandEventArgs)
02
03        Dim ConnStr as String
04
05        ConnStr = "Data Source=localhost;Integrated Security=SSPI;"
06        ConnStr = ConnStr + "Initial Catalog=pubs"
07
08        Dim conn As SqlConnection = New SqlConnection(ConnStr)
09
10        conn.Open()
11
12        Dim i as Byte
13
14        if Request.Form(9) = "on" then
15            chkboxContract =1
16        else
17            chkboxContract =0
18 end if
19
20        Dim CmdStr As String
21        CmdStr="UPDATE Authors SET au_lname = '" + Request.Form(2) + "',"
22        CmdStr=CmdStr +"au_fname = " + "'" + Request.Form(3) + "',"
23        CmdStr=CmdStr +"phone = " + "'" + Request.Form(4) + "',"
24        CmdStr=CmdStr +"address = " + "'" + Request.Form(5) + "',"
25        CmdStr=CmdStr +"city = " + "'" + Request.Form(6) + "',"
26        CmdStr=CmdStr +"state = " + "'" + Request.Form(7) + "',"
27        CmdStr=CmdStr +"zip = " + "'" + Request.Form(8) + "',"
28        CmdStr=CmdStr +"contract = " + chkboxContract.ToString() + " "
29        CmdStr=CmdStr +"WHERE au_id = " + "'" + Request.Form(1) + "'"
30
31        Dim cmd As New SqlCommand(CmdStr,conn)
32
33
34        cmd.ExecuteNonQuery()
35
36        DataGrid1.EditItemIndex = -1
37        DataGrid1.DataBind()
38
39 End Sub
```

Finally, the `Cancel_Grid()` procedure sets the `EditItemIndex` property of the `DataGrid` object to -1, which takes the datagrid to its original state without any editable row:

```
01 Sub Cancel_Grid(Sender As Object, e as DataGridCommandEventArgs)
02     DataGrid1.EditItemIndex = -1
03     DataGrid1.DataBind()
04 End Sub
```

This is a simple example of how the `DataGrid` object can be used to edit data. You could easily add new features to this datagrid, such as deleting data, for instance.

The Repeater Control

The Repeater control does not provide any visual output by itself. To display this control, you will have to use templates. Listing 6.12 demonstrates the Repeater control (see also Figure 6.8).

Listing 6.12 **The Repeater Control (612.aspx)**

```
01 <%@ Import Namespace = "System.Data" %>
02 <%@ Import Namespace = "System.Data.SqlClient" %>
03
04 <html>
05 <title>Sample ASP.NET Page</title>
06 <body>
07
08 <script language = "VB" runat = "server">
09
10 Sub Page_Load(sender As Object, e As EventArgs)
11
12     Dim ConnStr as String
13
14     ConnStr = "Data Source=localhost;Integrated Security=SSPI;"
15     ConnStr = ConnStr + "Initial Catalog=pubs"
16
17     Dim conn As SqlConnection = New SqlConnection(ConnStr)
18
19     Try
20         conn.Open()
21
22         Dim da As SqlDataAdapter = New SqlDataAdapter _
23             ("SELECT * FROM Authors",conn)
24
25         Dim ds As New DataSet
26
27         da.Fill(ds,"authors")
28
29         Dim dv1 As New DataView(ds.Tables("authors"))
30         dv1.Sort = "au_fname, au_lname DESC"
31         dv1.RowFilter = "state <- 'KS'"
32
33         Repeater1.DataSource=dv1
34         Repeater1.DataBind()
35
36     Catch ex As SqlException
37         Status.Text = ex.Message
38
39     Finally
40         conn.Close()
41
```

```
42      End Try
043
44 End Sub
45
46 </script>
47
48 <asp:label id="Status" runat="server"/>
49 <asp:Repeater id="Repeater1" runat="server">
50     <HeaderTemplate>
51         <table borders=0 width= "100%"><tr bgcolor="gray">
52         <td>ID</td><td>Last Name</td><td>First Name</td>
53         <td>Phone</td><td>Address</td><td>City</td>
54         <td>State</td><td>Zip</td><td>Contract?</td></tr>
55     </HeaderTemplate>
56     <ItemTemplate>
57         <tr>
58         <td>
59             <%# DataBinder.Eval(Container.DataItem,"au_id") %>
60         </td>
61         <td>
62             <%# DataBinder.Eval(Container.DataItem,"au_lname") %>
63         </td>
64         <td>
65             <%# DataBinder.Eval(Container.DataItem,"au_fname") %>
66         </td>
67         <td>
68             <%# DataBinder.Eval(Container.DataItem,"phone") %>
69         </td>
70         <td>
71             <%# DataBinder.Eval(Container.DataItem,"address") %>
72         </td>
73         <td>
74             <%# DataBinder.Eval(Container.DataItem,"city") %>
75         </td>
76         <td>
77             <%# DataBinder.Eval(Container.DataItem,"state") %>
78         </td>
79         <td>
80             <%# DataBinder.Eval(Container.DataItem,"zip") %>
81         </td>
82         <td>
83             <asp:CheckBox
84
85 Checked=<%#DataBinder.Eval(Container.DataItem,"contract")%>
86                 Enabled="False"
87         </td>
88         </tr>
89     </ItemTemplate>
90     <FooterTemplate>
91         </table>
92     </FooterTemplate>
93 </asp:Repeater>
94 </body>
95 </html>
```

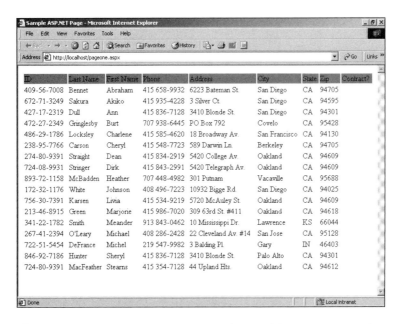

Figure 6.8 Sample page that demonstrates the use of the Repeater control.

This example is self-explanatory, but let's go through and see how things work. First, the `HeaderTemplate` tag is used to display the header of our repeater. Subsequently, `ItemTemplate` is used to define how to display the selected data—in this case, as cells within a table. The `FooterTemplate` only closes the HTML table tag, which was previously opened in the `HeaderTemplate`.

The Repeater control is useful for displaying data in a fully customized way (the DataGrid, on the other hand, always displays data within an HTML table); however, the Repeater control does not offer any support by itself for editing such data.

The DataList Control

The last ADO.NET data-focused control that we will deal with in this section is the DataList control. This control offers many alternatives for customization through its intrinsic properties and templates. For instance, it enables data to flow both horizontally and vertically, a feature that is not available to the Repeater control. Listing 6.13 shows the DataList control.

Listing 6.13 **DataList Control (613.aspx)**

```
01 <%@ Import Namespace = "System.Data" %>
02 <%@ Import Namespace = "System.Data.SqlClient" %>
03
04 <html>
05 <title>Sample ASP.NET Page</title>
06 <body>
07
08 <script language = "VB" runat = "server">
09
10 Sub Page_Load(sender As Object, e As EventArgs)
11
12     Dim ConnStr as String
13
14     ConnStr = "Data Source=localhost;Integrated Security=SSPI;"
15     ConnStr = ConnStr + "Initial Catalog=pubs"
16
17     Dim conn As SqlConnection = New SqlConnection(ConnStr)
18     Try
19         conn.Open()
20
21         Dim da As SqlDataAdapter = New SqlDataAdapter _
22             ("SELECT * FROM Authors",conn)
23
24         Dim ds As New DataSet
25
26         da.Fill(ds,"authors")
27
28         Dim dv1 As New DataView(ds.Tables("authors"))
29         dv1.Sort = "au_fname, au_lname DESC"
30         dv1.RowFilter = "state <= 'KS'"
31
32         datalist1.DataSource=dv1
33         datalist1.DataBind()
34
35     Catch ex As SqlException
36         Status.Text = ex.Message
37
38     Finally
39         conn.Close()
40
41
42     End Try
43
44 End Sub
45
46 </script>
47
48 <asp:label id="Status" runat="server"/>
49 <asp:DataList id="datalist1" runat="server">
50 <HeaderTemplate>
```

continues ▶

Listing 6.13 **Continued**

```
51          <table borders=0 width= "100%"><tr bgcolor="gray">
52          <td>ID</td><td>Last Name</td><td>First Name</td>
53          <td>Phone</td><td>Address</td><td>City</td>
54          <td>State</td><td>Zip</td><td>Contract?</td></tr>
55      </HeaderTemplate>
56      <ItemTemplate>
57          <tr>
58          <td>
59              <%# DataBinder.Eval(Container.DataItem,"au_id") %>
60          </td>
61          <td>
62              <%# DataBinder.Eval(Container.DataItem,"au_lname") %>
63          </td>
64          <td>
65              <%# DataBinder.Eval(Container.DataItem,"au_fname") %>
66          </td>
67          <td>
68              <%# DataBinder.Eval(Container.DataItem,"phone") %>
69          </td>
70          <td>
71              <%# DataBinder.Eval(Container.DataItem,"address") %>
72          </td>
73          <td>
74              <%# DataBinder.Eval(Container.DataItem,"city") %>
75          </td>
76          <td>
77              <%# DataBinder.Eval(Container.DataItem,"state") %>
78          </td>
79          <td>
80              <%# DataBinder.Eval(Container.DataItem,"zip") %>
81          </td>
82          <td>
83            <asp:CheckBox
84              Checked=<% #DataBinder.Eval(Container.DataItem,"contract") %>
85              Enabled="False"
86          </td>
87          </tr>
88      </ItemTemplate>
89      <FooterTemplate>
90          </table>
91      </FooterTemplate>
92 </asp:DataList>
93 </form>
94
95 </body>
96 </html>
```

As you can see, the DataList control in the preceding ASP.NET page displays data using the same layout as the Repeater control in the previous example.

On the other hand, the `DataList` control, similar to the `DataGrid` object, also supports intrinsic features for editing data, including the `EditItemTemplate` tag (or property, whichever you prefer), so that you could perfectly add such a tag and the procedures for manipulating data to the previous page.

Note

We certainly can say that the `DataList` control brings together the better of the two worlds: It is highly customizable, like the `Repeater` control (more than it, in fact), and the `DataList` control offers the same data manipulation features as the `DataGrid` object.

Transaction-Enabled ASP.NET Applications

A *transaction* is a group of operations that need to be successfully executed as a whole. If a single operation within a transaction fails, all the previous operations that were successfully executed will have to be rolled back, and the subsequent operations will never be executed.

ADO.NET provides three methods that, together, enable you to use the power of transactions within your ASP.NET application. The first method is `BeginTransaction()` of the `Connection` object. It is used to instantiate a `Transaction` object, as you can see in the following:

```
Dim trans As SqlTransaction = conn.BeginTransaction()
```

The other two methods belong to the `Transaction` object. Before using them, you will need to use a `Command` object to perform the actions within the transaction. To do this, set the value of the Transaction property of the `Command` object to the newly created `Transaction` object:

```
cmd.Transaction = trans
```

Now you can execute transaction-based commands on tables of the database specified by the `Connection` object. The `Commit()` method of the `Transaction` object will affect the actions performed by the `Command` object in the case that all these actions are successful. On the other hand, if an exception occurs (which indicates that an operation failed), the `RollBack()` method of the `Transaction` object will undo the actions executed before the error.

```
01 Try
02     cmd.CommandText = 'Insert a SQL DML statement here
03     cmd.ExecuteNonQuery()
04     cmd.CommandText = 'Insert another SQL DML statement here
05     cmd.ExecuteNonQuery()
06     trans.Commit()
07 Catch e As Exception
08     trans.RollBack()
09 End Try
```

Note

As well as with most provider-specific objects, there is also an `OleDbTransaction` class.

Listing 6.14 shows a simple transaction-enabled ASP.NET page.

Listing 6.14   **Transaction-Enabled ASP.NET Page (614.aspx)**

```
01 <%@ Import Namespace = "System.Data.SqlClient" %>
02
03 <html>
04 <title>Sample ASP.NET Page</title>
05 <body>
06
07 <script language = "VB" runat = "server">
08
09 Sub Page_Load(sender As Object, e As EventArgs)
10
11    Dim ConnStr as String
12
13    ConnStr = "Data Source=localhost; Integrated Security=SSPI;"
14    ConnStr = ConnStr + "Initial Catalog=pubs"
15
16    Dim conn As SqlConnection = New SqlConnection(ConnStr)
17
18    conn.Open()
19
20    Dim cmd As New SqlCommand()
21    cmd.Connection = conn
22
23    Dim trans As SqlTransaction = conn.BeginTransaction()
24
25    cmd.Transaction = trans
26
27    Try
28        cmd.CommandText = "UPDATE authors SET city='Menlo Park' " & _
29                          "WHERE au_fname='Johnson'"
30         cmd.ExecuteNonQuery()
31        cmd.CommandText = "UPDATE authors SET city='New Orleans' " & _
32                          "WHERE au_fname='Brian'"
33        cmd.ExecuteNonQuery()
34        cmd.CommandText = "UPDATE authors SET country='Japan' " & _
35                          "WHERE au_fname='Akiko'"
36        cmd.ExecuteNonQuery()
37        trans.Commit()
38
39        Status.Text = "All the commands were performed successfully!"
40
41    Catch ex As Exception
42        trans.RollBack()
43
44        Status.Text = ex.Message
```

```
45
46     Finally
47           conn.close()
48
49     End Try
50
51 End Sub
52
53 </script>
54
55 <h1>Transaction-enabled ASP.NET applications</h1>
56
57 <asp:label id="Status" runat="server"/>
58 </body>
59 </html>
```

In the preceding example, the sentence "Invalid column name 'country'" will be returned from the SQL Server by the browser because we tried to update the value of a column called "country," which does not exist in the Authors table. Consequently, taking into account that such an action is part of a transaction, the previous two actions that also are part of that transaction will not be affected (in this case, the RollBack() method of the Transaction object is called and undoes those actions). On the other hand, in the case that the third action was valid, the Commit() method of the Transaction object would affect all the actions.

Note

Transactions are essential for maintaining the consistency of a database whenever actions that are dependent among themselves (such as a transfer of funds between accounts, which involves a credit action in an account and a debit action in another) need to be accomplished.

Summary

In this chapter, you have gained the necessary knowledge for performing the essential data-related tasks in ASP.NET applications using Microsoft's new data access technology, which is being called ADO.NET.

ADO.NET is much more than a simple ADO evolution (in the same way that ASP.NET is not simply a new version of ASP). Keeping with the .NET philosophy, ADO.NET is an entirely new technology that exposes a new way for working with data over the web. This chapter introduced the main ADO.NET objects, as well as the three controls commonly used to build data-oriented Web Forms.

7

Using XML in
ASP.NET Applications

DEVELOPED BY THE WORLD WIDE WEB CONSORTIUM (www.w3.org) in
1996, the eXtensible Markup Language (XML) has been embraced as a
flexible means of communicating and storing data across computing platforms. Originally designed as a subset of the Standard Generalized Markup
Language (SGML), XML was created to be highly structured, as well as easy
to use and implement. Because of its highly adaptable nature, XML is used
in many applications to store relational data without the use of database
software.

   Due to the widespread use of XML throughout the information technol-
ogy industry, new standards based on the language seem to appear every day.
The XML Stylesheet Language (XSL), XML Schema Definition Language
(XSD), and Simple Object Access Protocol (SOAP) all derive from XML.
ASP.NET even uses XML at a foundational level; server-side controls are
written using XML syntax, application configuration files are well-formed
XML documents, and many of the objects in the ASP.NET framework use
XML internally. To fully understand each of these technologies you must
first understand the basics of XML.

Important Considerations

Please note that much of what will be presented in this chapter is only a subset of the tools and technologies available for use with XML. The complete specifications for the W3C technologies in this chapter can be found at:

- Extensible Markup Language (XML)—http://www.w3.org/XML

- Extensible Stylesheet Language (XSL)—http://www.w3.org/Style/XSL

- XML Path Language (XPath)—http://www.w3.org/TR/xpath

- XML Schema—http://www.w3.org/XML/Schema

- Extensible HyperText Markup Language (XHTML)—http://www.w3.org/TR/xhtml1

- HyperText Transfer Protocol (HTTP)—http://www.w3.org/Protocols

- HyperText Markup Language (HTML)—http://www.w3.org/TR/html4

- Document Object Model (DOM)—http://www.w3.org/DOM

- Simple Object Access Protocol (SOAP) 1.1—http://www.w3.org/TR/soap

- XML Web Services Description Language (WSDL) 1.1—http://www.w3.org/wsdl

In addition, WSDL and SOAP are still under development and might change in the future. Make sure to visit the W3C website to see how these specifications mature.

The classes in the ASP.NET system.xml namespace maintain many similarities with the Microsoft XML (MSXML) Parser. However, these objects are not interchangeable. The ASP.NET XMLDocument object does not support XSL transformations directly in the object, as well as other discrepancies. In addition, the MSXML parser works with Internet Explorer 5.0 and Pocket Explorer for Windows CE. In any environment where the browser cannot be guaranteed to support MSXML, you should implement an up-level version of your page, which uses the parser on the client. A down-level version that uses the parser on the server can be used for older browsers or browsers that do not support ActiveX objects.

XML Document Structure

XML is syntactically similar to its cousin, HyperText Markup Language (HTML), and supports a derivative of its cousin, known as XHTML. The guidelines for constructing an XML document are relatively basic, due to the simple structure of the language. Similarities between HTML and XML are compared in this brief introduction to the XML document structure. There is more to XML than can be covered here; you might find it worthwhile to read more on the subject.

More Information on XML

For more information on XML, check out New Riders' *Inside XML* (0-7357-1020-1) by Steve Holzner.

XML Elements

XML and HTML both define document structure using tags and attributes. In both languages, a tag begins and ends with the delimiters < and > respectively, creating a new element of the type named inside the delimiters. As in HTML, an XML element is completed when an end tag is encountered, which begins with `</` and ends with `>`. In HTML, quite a few elements do not require an ending tag. The `<br>` tag performs a carriage return, and has no closing `</br>` tag. XML, however, requires that all elements be completed. Nodes, such as `<br>`, would not constitute a valid element under the XML rule set. Instead, single tag elements have a special delimiter `/>` that appears at the end, changing `<br>` into `</br>`. This notation assures that the document is nested properly.

Immediately following the < delimiter of a tag is the name of the element. In the case of our previous `<br/>` example, the element name would be `"br"`. It is important to note that element names in XML are case sensitive—unlike its HTML counterpart. Elements that begin with the tag `<p>` must end with a `</p>` tag, using a tag such as `</P>` results in an unmatched element.

Every XML document must begin with a single element that marks the root of the document hierarchy. Often called the *document* or *root*, this element forms the highest level of the document. There can be only one document element in any XML document in which all other elements must be contained. Elements within the document element are referred to as *children*; however, a document element need not have any children to create a well-formed XML document.

XML Attributes

When defining the properties of an element in HTML, you use a name-value pair called an *attribute*. Attributes in XML work roughly in the same way as their HTML counterpart; the name of an attribute is placed after the element name and before the end of the tag. Values for attributes must be enclosed in matching single or double quotes, and must follow some basic XML character escaping rules.

The XML specification reserves certain characters that cannot be used inside an attribute or as the text content of an element. There is, however, a means of placing reserved characters, such as `"<"`, `">"`, `"&"`, `"'"`, and `"""` in the value of an attribute or element using escape sequences. Table 7.1 lists some of the commonly used escape sequences in XML.

Table 7.1 **Common XML Escape Sequences**

Character	Escape Sequence
< (Less-than symbol)	&lt;
> (Greater-than symbol)	&gt;
' (Apostrophe)	&apos;
" (Double Quote)	&quot;
& (Ampersand)	&amp;
Carriage Return	&#013;
Line Feed	&#010;
Tab	&#009;

Text and Character Data

Any element can contain text—character data that has been escaped following Table 7.1. Only character data without XML markup will be listed as the text part of an XML element. The following example shows how escaped text can be placed inside an element:

```
01 <parent>
02   This is the text node for the &lt;parent&gt; node.
03   <child>
04     This is the text node for the &lt;child/&gt; node.
05   </child>
06 </parent>
```

You can also use the Character Data (CDATA) tag to place reserved characters inside an element. To use CDATA you must begin the text with <![CDATA[and end it with]]>. The following XML document would contain the same data as the preceding example:

```
01 <parent>
02   <![CDATA[This is the text node for the <parent/> node.]]>
03   <child>
04     <![CDATA[This is the text node for the <child/> node.]]>
05   </child>
06 </parent>
```

Character Data tags allow you to place complex strings as the text of an element—without the need to manually escape the string. The XML parser should be able to handle all necessary input and output escaping.

Comments

Both HTML and XML support comments in the same manner. Any section beginning with <!– and ending with –> in an XML document, is a comment. Any character data including reserved characters, can be placed inside a comment and will be ignored by the XML parser. The following is an example of a comment:

```
01 <parent>
02   <!– the following element is a child of <parent/> –>
03   <child/>
04 </parent>
```

Namespaces and Schemas

A schema is a set of rules that define what types of elements and attributes are allowed in an XML document. Due to the highly extensible nature of XML, it is easy to build documents that do not conform to the requirements of an application. For example, you might want to have a <shoppingCart/> element that only contains <parcel/> elements. You might not want a <person/> to appear within a <shoppingCart/>. Common schemas include the XML Stylesheet Language (XSL) and the XML Schema Definition Language (XSD). To apply a schema to an XML document, it has to be referenced using a namespace. The xmlns reserved attribute defines a namespace that refers to a schema. The following example shows how to include the XSL namespace for a stylesheet:

```
01 <xsl:stylesheet version="1.0"
02   xmlns:xsl="http://www.w3.org/1999/XSL/Transform">
03
04   <xsl:template match="/">
05     Hello World
06   </xsl:template>
07
08 </xsl:stylesheet>
```

In the preceding example, notice that a colon and the name of the namespace, in this case xsl, follow the xmlns attribute. The value of the attribute is a URL that points to a schema. Once the namespace has been declared, prefixing each XML element name with the name of the declared namespace you can use elements from within the namespace. The stylesheet and template elements in the preceding example are defined as the xsl namespace; they have strict requirements as to what attributes must be present.

A default namespace for a document can be assigned by leaving off the name of the namespace in the declaration. For example, the preceding document using the default namespace would look like this:

```
01 <stylesheet version="1.0"
02   xmlns="http://www.w3.org/1999/XSL/Transform">
03
04   <template match="/">
05     Hello World
06   </template>
07
08 </stylesheet>
```

In this case, the standard non-prefixed elements in the document must conform to the imported schema.

How XML Is Used in ASP.NET

Early on, Microsoft realized the extensive range of capabilities that XML provided and based much of the .NET framework around the XML document structure. ASP.NET uses XML in almost every aspect, from application configuration files to the internal data of ADO.NET datasets; the prevailing use of this technology makes it almost a necessity to know how it is used inside the ASP.NET framework.

Application Configuration with Web.config

One of the first places you'll see XML at work is in the application configuration file. The Web.config file stores application specific settings using XML, allowing you to tailor an application to your needs through a simple text editor. Through the use of this configuration file, you can store complex configuration settings, such as configuration sections and serialized objects. This gives you more power through the use of the XML Path and Query language (xPath)—allowing you to quickly search through the XML document. More details on the Web.config file and application configuration can be found in Chapter 3, "Configuring ASP.NET Applications."

Serialization

Another of the myriad uses of XML in the ASP.NET framework comes with the use of the serialization libraries available in the System.Xml.Serialization namespace. Any class written in ASP.NET can be serialized into XML providing the proper class-level and procedure-level attributes have been set. Using the XmlSerializer on classes that are able to be serialized provides you a means to convert your object into an XML document for purposes, such as caching or transmitting through SOAP. Some of the class-level and procedure-level attributes for XML serialization are listed in Table 7.2.

Table 7.2 **Serialization Attributes**

Attribute	Description
XmlArrayAttribute	Informs the XmlSerializer to serialize the member as an array of XML nodes.
XmlAttributeAttribute	Informs the XmlSerializer to serialize the member as an attribute of the current XML node.
XmlElementAttribute	Informs the XmlSerializer to serialize the member as an XML node that is a child of the current XML node.
XmlIgnoreAttribute	Informs the XmlSerializer to ignore the member during serialization.
XmlTextAttribute	Informs the XmlSerializer to serialize the member as the text content of the current XML node.

The XmlSerializer examines an object at runtime and looks for these attributes on the class and its properties and methods. Each attribute informs the serializer how to represent it inside the resulting XML document. When the XmlSerializer completes, it returns the serialized object in the form of a string, which can at some later time be deserialized back into the original object. Quite a bit of the ASP.NET framework relies on serialization, including ADO.NET and XML Web Services.

ADO.NET

Microsoft's new object model for data access and manipulation also uses XML. Earlier versions of the ActiveX Data Object's libraries used a proprietary format for the structure of recordsets. Although it was adaptable, ADO did not scale well in many applications due to the nature in which data was transmitted between servers. ADO used Distributed COM to communicate data between a client and a server. The problem with DCOM was the overhead involved in transmitting the ADO proprietary format. This format also pinned it to a single platform; only clients running the Windows operating system could consume XML Web Services and business objects that exposed ADO recordsets.

To solve these issues, ADO.NET switched away from its proprietary format and moved to using XML for its internal data structures. The ADO.NET DataSet class was the end result. It stores data as XML and serializes easily into an XML document for XML Web Services. The information inside of a DataSet also does not maintain connection information; recordsets retrieved from a database in ADO.NET are truly disconnected. Without the overhead incurred by maintaining connection-specific information, DataSets are more portable and communicate more efficiently.

One of the more interesting features of this change, however, comes with the use of the XmlDataDocument class, a member of the System.Xml namespace. The XmlDataDocument binds to an ADO.NET DataSet, allowing access to the DataSet's internal data. You can then work with the relational data using technologies, such as XPath Queries and the XML Stylesheet Language (XSL). Figure 7.1 depicts the general structure of an ADO.NET DataSet.

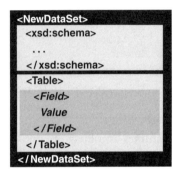

Figure 7.1 Structure of an ADO.NET *DataSet.*

The NewDataSet element wraps the XML representation of the ADO.NET dataset. It serves as the document element and a mnemonic as to what the XML document contains. The first section, xsd:schema, contains information necessary to interpret each field value as a data type. The schema is not always part of the resulting XML document and is shown only when using the WriteXML method of the DataSet with a write mode of XmlWriteMode.WriteSchema. Each Table element in this Dataset represents a row in the resulting recordset, where each field for the row is then listed.

ADO.NET dataset Schema

ADO.NET uses XSD to define the valid schema for the data represented inside of a DataSet. When using the XmlDataDocument, however, you will be unable to see this schema information. Standard manipulation of a DataSet, both through the DataSet object and an XmlDataDocument, affects only the data itself, not the schema and is hidden from the XmlDataDocment. To see the schema used inside of a DataSet, you have to use the DataSet object's WriteXML method. This method serializes the DataSet into an XML document, writing out the internal data to a string. By default WriteXML will not display the schema either. However, an optional argument of XmlWriteMode.WriteSchema includes the schema in the result.

Other XML Technologies

Several other XML technologies are used in the ASP.NET framework besides those that Microsoft has written. The framework also uses several other standards written by the W3C, such as the Web Service Description Language (WSDL), and the Simple Object Access Protocol (SOAP). These languages are often found when building and consuming XML Web Services for your application.

The Web Service Description Language (WSDL)

In many web applications, the information you want to use for one server is available only on another server. For example, a database server contains information, such as an inventory, and a farm of web servers wants to use that information to present it to a client. Before .NET, this was accomplished using the Component Object Model (COM), Distributed COM (DCOM), and the Windows Distributed Networking Architecture (DNA). Developers would expose multiple application tiers in the form of business objects, which were designed for database access—the business logic that defines how the data can be used, and the presentation of the data to the client.

The downside to using DCOM for this model is the need for a specific platform to expose and consume these business objects—namely Microsoft Windows. Applications built using DCOM could not expose their business objects to applications built using other standards—a means of communicating information between applications hosted by different sites is impossible. Imagine you run a site that sells plastics for industrial use. You might have a client who wants to automate the process of purchasing materials from you, rather than making a purchase manually every time they are in need. A developer for your client would have to be able to build a series of objects to consume the business objects of your web site. This is not impossible if you and your client are both running the same platform. However, in many businesses this is not the case.

To solve this issue, Microsoft adopted several technologies of the W3C and added a few of their own to create XML Web Services. XML Web Services are new to the ASP.NET framework and provide application logic to a variety of systems across the Internet, such as servers and client machines. The *Web Service Description Language* (WSDL) is an XML schema used to describe a service, the ports it can use to communicate, the possible messages that can be exchanged, the simple and complex data types involved, and the operations that can be performed. XML Web Services uses WSDL to create a contract. An agreement between the host and the client as to how data sent to and received from the XML Web Service should be interpreted. Due to the use of WSDL in .NET XML Web Services, the output of the service is platform-independent. Your industrial client could easily build an application to consume the service without the need to support the platform you use for your server.

Listing 7.1 shows the basic structure of a WSDL contract. This example does not contain all the elements available in WSDL. For more information on elements not mentioned, visit `http://www.w3.org/TR/wsdl`.

The `<definitions/>` element is the root of our WSDL contract. This tag commonly contains the namespaces to be used inside the contract, including a reference to itself to resolve the complex data types written in an internal XSD schema.

Listing 7.1 **WSDL Contract Outline**

```
01 <?xml version="1.0" encoding="UTF-8"?>
02            <definitions xmlns:s="http://ww.w3.org/2001/XMLSchema"
03            xmlns:http="http://schemas.xmlsoap.org/wsdl/http/"
04            xmlns:mime="http://schemas.xmlsoap.org/wsdl/mime/"
05            xmlns:tm="http://microsoft.com/wsdl/mime/textMatching/"
06            xmlns:soap="http://schemas.xmlsoap.org/wsdl/soap/"
07            xmlns:soapenc="http://schemas.xmlsoap.org/soap/encoding/"
08            xmlns:s0="http://tempuri.org/"
09            targetNamespace="http://tempuri.org/"
10            xmlns="http://schemas.xmlsoap.org/wsdl/">
```

The `<types/>` element contains an XSD schema that is used to define the data types publicly exposed by this service. A WSDL contract can contain only one `<types/>` element.

```
01 <types>
02   <!— Within here you would place a <s:schema/> element and build your XSD schema. —>
03 </types>
```

Following `<types/>` are a series of `<message/>` elements that define the public interfaces with which to request a method implementation and gather the response. Each `<message/>` has a name attribute that is used to reference its parts later in the contract. A `<message/>` element can contain only `<part/>` elements, which are used to define each piece of the content of the request or response message.

The `<part/>` element has a name attribute that defines the name of that part of the message, and a type attribute that defines the data type contained in the part. A WSDL contract can have zero or more `<message/>` elements, and a `<message/>` can have zero or more `<part/>` elements.

In the following lines, a messages for web method `GetBooks` is exposed:

```
01 <!— SOAP Message Exchange for GetBooks —>
02 <message name="GetBooksSoapIn">
03   <part name="parameters" type="s0:GetBooks"/>
04 </message>
```

```
05    <message name="GetBooksSoapOut">
06      <part name="parameters" type="s0:GetBooksResponse"/>
07    </message>
08
09    <!— HTTP GET Message Exchange for GetBooks —>
10    <message name="GetBooksHttpGetIn" />
11    <message name="GetBooksHttpGetOut">
12      <part name="Body" type="s0:DataSet"/>
13    </message>
14
15    <!— HTTP POST Message Exchange For GetBooks —>
16    <message name="GetBooksHttpPostIn" />
17    <message name="GetBooksHttpPostOut">
18      <part name="Body" type="s0:DataSet"/>
19    </message>
```

The preceding `<message/>` elements define the request/response message exchange for the `GetBooks` method of SOAP, HTTP GET, and HTTP POST communication transports. SOAP uses a more complex message format than HTTP GET and POST and refers to the entire message as a set of SOAP parameters in the form of a complex element, which is defined in the schema previously listed in `<types/>`.

In the next portion of the contract, a series of `<portType/>` elements define what `<message/>` elements belong to what communication transports. Request and Response messages that belong to SOAP are grouped together, as are HTTP GET and HTTP POST messages.

```
01    <portType name="LibrarySoap">
02      <operation name="GetBooks">
03        <input message="s0:GetBooksSoapIn"/>
04        <output message="s0:GetBooksSoapOut"/>
05      </operation>
06    </portType>
```

Each `<portType/>` has a `name` attribute that specifies a unique name for the communication transport. Within this element are zero or more `<operation/>` elements for each public method on the XML Web Service. Each `<operation/>` has a `name` that refers to the name of the method it represents. To define what `<message/>` elements correspond with the request and response messages of the method, the elements `<input/>` and `<output/>` are used. The message to which they refer is set in the `message` attribute.

Following `<portType/>` is a list of zero or more `<binding/>` elements that define the communication transport to use for each `<portType/>`. Each `<binding/>` has a `name` attribute that describes the name of the binding and a `type` attribute that points to a `<portType/>` element.

```
01  <binding name="LibrarySoap" type="s0:LibrarySoap">
02    <soap:binding transport="http://schemas.xmlsoap.org/soap/http" style="document"/>
03    <operation name="GetBooks">
04      <soap:operation soapAction="http://tempuri.org/GetBooks" style="document"/>
05      <input>
06        <soap:body use="literal"/>
07      </input>
08      <output>
09        <soap:body use="literal"/>
10      </output>
11    </soap:operation>
12  </binding>
13  <binding name="LibraryHttpGet" type="s0:LibraryHttpGet">
14    <http:binding verb="GET"/>
15    <operation name="GetBooks">
16      <http:operation location="/GetBooks" />
17      <input>
18        <http:urlEncoded />
19      </input>
20      <output>
21        <mime:mimeXml part="Body" />
22      </output>
23    </operation>
24  </binding>
25  <binding name="LibraryHttpPost" type="s0:LibraryHttpPost">
26    <http:binding verb="POST"/>
27    <operation name="GetBooks">
28      <http:operation location="/GetBooks" />
29      <input>
30        <mime:content type="application/x-www-form-urlencoded" />
31      </input>
32      <output>
33        <mime:mimeXml part="Body" />
34      </output>
35    </operation>
36  </binding>
```

Immediately inside the `<binding/>` tag is an element that specifies what kind of transport binding to use in the form of a `<protocol:binding/>` element. After the transport binding comes an `<operation/>` element that defines the entry point for the method. Within the `<operation/>` element are the `<input/>` and `<output/>` elements that specify the format by which the request and response messages are received and sent.

Finally, a WSDL contract contains a single `<service/>` element that enumerates the available communication transports to this service. The `<service/>` element contains zero or more `<port/>` elements who's `name` and `binding` attributes point to an available `<binding/>`. Within each `<port/>` element is a single element that contains a reference to the location of the XML Web Service on the Internet. This element, in the form of `<protocol:address/>`, contains a `location` attribute containing a URL.

Simple Object Access Protocol (SOAP)

Created as a cross-platform protocol for exchanging structured information, *SOAP* has evolved from a simple Remote Procedure Call Service into a more complex but highly extensible object-messaging protocol. Unlike proprietary technologies, such as DCOM, SOAP relies on XML for the data structure and a standardized communication protocol, such as HTTP, to transmit information. Listing 7.2 contains the structure of a SOAP request message for the GetBooks method from the previous section; Listing 7.3 contains the response. These examples do not contain all the capabilities of a SOAP message. For more information on SOAP elements not covered here, visit http://www.w3.org/TR/soap.

Listing 7.2 *GetBooks* **SOAP Request**

```
01 <?xml version="1.0" encoding="utf-8"?>
02 <soap:Envelope xmlns:xsi="http://www.w3.org/2001/XMLSchema-instance"
03              xmlns:xsd="http://www.w3.org/2001/XMLSchema"
04              xmlns:soap="http://schemas.xmlsoap.org/soap/envelope/">
05 <soap:Body>
06   <GetBooks xmlns="http://tempuri.org" />
07 </soap:Body>
08 </soap:Envelope>
```

Listing 7.3 *GetBooks* **SOAP Response**

```
01 <?xml version="1.0" encoding="utf-8"?>
02 <soap:Envelope xmlns:xsi="http://www.w3.org/2001/XMLSchema-instance"
03              xmlns:xsd="http://www.w3.org/2001/XMLSchema"
04              xmlns:soap="http://schemas.xmlsoap.org/soap/envelope/">
05 <soap:Body>
06   <GetBooksResponse xmlns="http://tempuri.org">
07     <GetBooksResult>
08       <xsd:schema>
09         <!-- The XSD schema definition for the data types in the returned result
➥would go here -->
10       </xsd:schema>
11       <!-- The XML content of the DataSet being returned -->
12     </GetBooksResult>
13   </GetBooksResponse>
14 </soap:Body>
15 </soap:Envelope>
```

The *SOAP envelope* is the root element of the XML document and is expressed as the `<soap:Envelope/>` element. The mandatory `<soap:Body/>` element contains the information needed by the message recipient. The contents of this element are defined by the message parts of the WSDL contract.

Using XML in Your Application

Besides the internal use of XML in the ASP.NET framework, application developers can choose to harness XML in their own way. Microsoft has provided several ways of working with XML documents directly in an application. Microsoft originally moved forward with the use of XML inside the Windows Distributed Networking Architecture (DNA) for data exchange between the workflow tier and presentation tier of a multi-tier web application. This concept has moved forward into the ASP.NET framework, and more powerful technologies have been added.

XML, XSL, and XPath

You can use several classes to work directly with the XML-DOM. The `XmlDocument`, `XPathDocument`, and `XmlDataDocument` objects provide you with a means to programmatically build, manipulate, and navigate an XML document. Applications that utilize any of these objects can work with XML for their own purposes—from the storage of relational data to authorized credentials for security.

XML documents loaded into the robust `XmlDocument` object can be built, modified, and validated. Although the `XmlDocument` class provides built-in XPath searching directly on the object, faster `XPath` queries can be performed on an `XPathDocument` object. The `XmlDocument` object validates any XML loaded in, checking for proper syntax. The XML document is also checked against any schemas imported into the document to assure that only valid XML elements and attributes are present—thus validating the contents of the document.

The `XPathDocument` is a slimmed-down version of the `XmlDocument` and is optimized for speedy searching without schema validation.

The `XmlDataDocument` is specifically designed for work with ADO.NET `DataSets`, binding to them in such a way that updating either the original `DataSet` or the `XmlDataDocument` affects both objects. Any of the XML Document classes can be transformed through the use of the `XSLTransform` object that provides the functionality necessary to parse and apply an XSL template to an XML document.

Reading and Writing XML

The ASP.NET framework provides several stream objects for reading and writing XML documents. The XmlTextReader object provides a means to read through a stream that contains XML quickly from beginning to end without cumbersome XML schema validation. The XmlValidatingReader performs the same function as the XmlTextReader, but validates schemas and as a result, is somewhat slower. To quickly read through the contents of an XmlDocument object you would use the XmlNodeReader, which also performs no validation.

The XmlTextWriter class creates an output stream that can be quickly written in a fast forward-only manner. Strongly typed values, such as floating points and dates, can be written quickly to the output stream using the XmlConvert class. The XmlTextWriter can also place binary values into the output stream by using the WriteBase64 method and encoding the binary values into Base64.

XML on the Browser

In addition to its use on the server, XML can also be extremely useful on the client. Browsers, such as Internet Explorer 5.0 and higher, can use the Microsoft XML parser (MSXML) available at http://www.microsoft.com/xml, which provides access to the XML Document Object Model through the MSXML2.DOMDocument class. In addition to the capability to load and parse an XML document, you can also perform XPath queries and XSLT transformations within the object.

In addition, the MSXML parser ships with the XMLHTTP object, which allows you to get and post XML documents over HTTP. This protocol is the foundation of using technologies, such as SOAP, on the client side.

Microsoft has released a Web Service Dynamic HTML (DHTML) scriptlet at http://msdn.microsoft.com/workshop/author/webservice/webservice.asp that adds SOAP functionality to your client-side application. This scriptlet encapsulates all the needed functionality to access an XML Web Service, read its WSDL contract, and communicate using SOAP.

What Is Dynamic HTML?

Many browsers today allow you to change the content and position of HTML elements without reloading the page from the server. This practice is called *Dynamic HTML* or *DHTML*. Microsoft extended the capabilities of Internet Explorer 5.0 to support HTML Components (HTC)—which are files that contain the code used to render the dynamic elements on the screen.

Real-World Examples

Some of the examples in this section deal with topics covered in other chapters in this book. They are meant to show how XML can be leveraged inside an ASP.NET application.

Working with an *XmlDocument*

Listings 7.4 and 7.5 show the basics of how to open an XML document on the server, load XML from a string, perform some basic navigation, and manipulate the nodes of multiple XmlDocument objects.

The library.xml file shown in Listing 7.4 describes the possible "book" elements in the document. The "uri" attribute of each "book" element points to another XML file that contains more data to be loaded at a later time. When dealing with large amounts of data, such as a library card catalog, a single XML document containing all relevant information would be much too cumbersome to work with. Instead, only some of the data for books is directly displayed as members of the document. Extended information on each "book" element is contained in its own XML file. The insideaspnet.xml file presented in Listing 7.5 provides more content as to what appears in the book, including additional "chapter" sub-elements.

Listing 7.4 **library.xml**

```
01  <?xml version="1.0" encoding="UTF-8"?>
02  <library>
03    <book id="1" uri="insideaspnet.xml" title="Inside ASP.NET" />
04  </library>
```

Listing 7.5 **insideaspnet.xml**

```
01  <?xml version="1.0" encoding="UTF-8"?>
02  <book id="1"
03        title="Inside ASP.NET">
04    <chapter uri="chapter1.html" title="Chapter 1" />
05    <chapter uri="chapter2.html" title="Chapter 2" />
06  </book>
```

The code listing in Listing 7.6 shows several functions of the XmlDocument object:

1. First the library.xml file is loaded into the xmlLibrary object, which validates the document against the library.xsd schema file.

2. The `selectSingleNode` method of the `XmlDocument` is used to execute an XPath query against the document, which returns the first valid node or the Visual Basic null object reference, `Nothing`. (`Nothing` is returned if a matching node does not exist.)

3. If a node has been found matching the `XPath` query, the `"uri"` of that node is loaded into the `xmlBook` object, which also validates the document against the `library.xsd` file.

4. A copy of the `xmlBook`'s document element is imported into the `xmlLibrary`'s document context, allowing us to use the copy inside the `xmlLibrary`. By replacing the old `"book"` element with the extended information in the new `"book"` element retrieved from `xmlBook`, we can provide advanced navigation against a more complex document.

Listing 7.6 **default.aspx**

```
01  <html>
02    <script runat="Server" language="VB">
03      Sub Page_Load(Sender As Object, E As EventArgs)
04
05        ' Declarations
06        Dim xmlLibrary As New System.Xml.XmlDocument
07        Dim xmlBook As New System.Xml.XmlDocument
08        Dim nodeBook As System.Xml.XmlElement
09        Dim nodeBookAndChapters As System.Xml.XmlElement
10
11        ' Load the library xml file.
12        xmlLibrary.load(Server.MapPath("library.xml"))
13
14        ' Print out the contents of the current xml file
15        Response.Write("Xml Document before importing a sub-element:<br>")
16        WriteXml(xmlLibrary.OuterXml)
17
18        ' Get the node
19        nodeBook = xmlLibrary.documentElement.selectSingleNode("//book[@id=1]")
20
21        ' If the node was found then...
22        If Not nodeBook Is Nothing Then
23
24          ' Load the uri listed by that node into the xmlBook object
25          xmlBook.load(Server.MapPath(nodeBook.getAttribute("uri")))
26
27          ' Write out the sub-element to be imported
28          Response.Write("Xml Document after importing a sub-element:<br>")
29          WriteXml(xmlBook.OuterXml)
30
31          ' Import the document element from xmlBook into the
32          ' xmlLibrary's document context
```

continues ▶

Listing 7.6 **Continued**

```
33          nodeBookAndChapters = _
34            xmlLibrary.ImportNode(xmlBook.documentElement, true)
35
36          ' Replace the old book node with the new book
37          ' node and chapters
38          xmlLibrary.documentElement.replaceChild(nodeBookAndChapters, nodeBook)
39
40          ' Write out the modified document
41          Response.Write("Xml Document after importing a sub-element:<br>")
42          WriteXml(xmlLibrary.OuterXml)
43
44        End If
45
46      End Sub
47
48      Public Sub WriteXml(ByVal s As String)
49        s = Server.HtmlEncode(s)
50        s = Replace(s, "&gt;&lt;", "&gt;" & "<BR>" & "&lt;")
51        s = "<pre>" & s & "</pre>"
52
53        Response.Write(s)
54
55      End Sub
56
57    </script>
58  </html>
```

Figure 7.2 shows the output of this sample. This example describes a situation that can come up quite often in web applications that use a Table of Contents (TOC) for their web site. Larger sites can break up the navigation path for their TOC into smaller, more manageable chunks that are loaded at runtime invisibly to the client.

XmlDataDocument and *DataSets*

Listing 7.7 shows some basic features of the XmlDataDocument and how they modify a simple DataSet.

Figure 7.2 Output for default.aspx.

Listing 7.7 **default.aspx**

```
01 <html>
02   <script runat="server" language="VB">
03
04     Sub Page_Load(Sender As Object, E As EventArgs)
05       ' Declarations
06       Dim xmlDocument As System.Xml.XmlDataDocument
07       Dim Conn As New System.Data.SqlClient.SqlConnection()
08       Dim Adapter As New System.Data.SqlClient.SqlDataAdapter()
09       Dim Results As New System.Data.DataSet()
10       Dim nodeFirstName As System.Xml.XmlElement
11
12       ' Open a connection to a Data Source
13       Conn.ConnectionString = "Initial Catalog=Northwind;
➥Data Source=localhost;User ID=sa;Password=;"
14       Conn.Open()
15
16       ' Fill a Dataset with the results of a SQL query
17       Adapter.SelectCommand = New System.Data.SqlClient.SqlCommand
➥("SELECT FirstName FROM Employees", Conn)
```

continues ▶

Listing 7.7 **Continued**

```
18      Adapter.Fill(Results)
19
20      ' Returns a Dataset with the values:
21      '
22      '   Name
23      '   _____
24      '   Nancy
25      '   Andrew
26      '   Janet
27      '   ...
28      '   Anne
29
30      ' Bind the Results Dataset to an XmlDataDocument
31      xmlDocument = New System.Xml.XmlDataDocument(Results)
32
33      ' Write out the contents of the XmlDataDocument
34      Response.Write("Xml structure of ADO.Net DataSet:<br>")
35      WriteXml(xmlDocument.outerXml)
36
37      ' Remove constraint enforcement so we can modify this recordset with the
➡XmlDataDocument
38      Results.EnforceConstraints = False
39
40      ' Get the first field
41      nodeFirstName = xmlDocument.selectSingleNode("//FirstName")
42
43      ' Change a value of the field
44      nodeFirstName.InnerText = "Ron"
45
46      ' Change the second value
47      Results.Tables(0).Rows(1).Item("FirstName") = "Bob"
48
49      ' The Dataset now looks like this:
50      '
51      '   Name
52      '   _____
53      '   Ron
54      '   Bob
55      '   Janet
56      '   ...
57      '   Anne
58
59      ' Write out the current ADO.Net dataset
60      Response.Write("Xml structure of ADO.Net DataSet after changes:<br>")
61        WriteXml(xmlDocument.outerXml)
62
63    End Sub
64
65    Public Sub WriteXml(ByVal s As String)
66      s = Server.HtmlEncode(s)
```

```
67        s = Replace(s, "&gt;&lt;", "&gt;" & "<BR>" & "&lt;")
68        s = "<pre>" & s & "</pre>"
69
70        Response.Write(s)
71
72    End Sub
73
74  </script>
75
76 </html>
```

In this listing, a DataSet is created containing the results of a SQL query. After binding the XmlDataDocument to the DataSet, both objects can then work on the same data. As shown in the example, changing the value of a field through either the DataSet or the XmlDataDocument affects the contents of the other object.

Figure 7.3 displays the initial contents of the ADO.NET dataset after it is retrieved from the database.

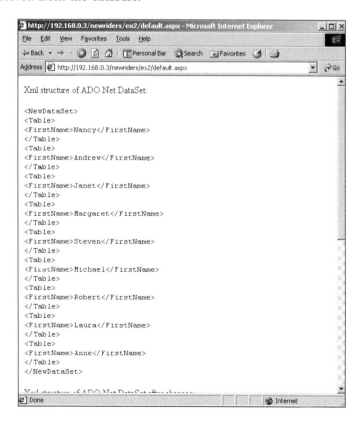

Figure 7.3 Initial contents of a *DataSet.*

Figure 7.4 contains the results of changing the ADO.NET DataSet from both the DataSet object and the XmlDataDocument.

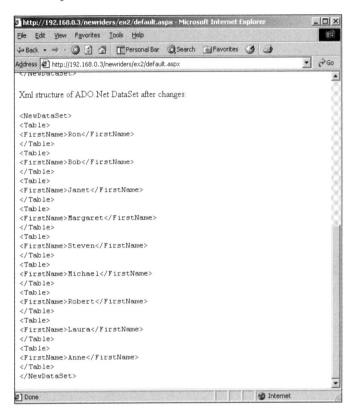

Figure 7.4   *After changing the DataSet.*

Performing an XSL Style Sheet Transformaton

Commonly when working with XML in a DNA style application, data transmitted to the client in the form of XML needs to be changed into a more pleasant presentation format. XSL, the XML Stylesheet Language, is used to process an XML document and transform it into another XML document. One of the common uses of XSL is to convert an XML document into an XHTML document, which can be read the same as normal HTML in almost all browsers. Listings 7.8 and 7.9 show examples of how to do this.

To perform an XSL transformation, you must first load the data to be parsed into an XmlDocument, or an object that implements IXPathNavigable (such as XmlDataDocument or XpathDocument). The XslTransform is then created and set to the parsed document—as well as informed as to what XSL transformation file to use for the operation. The resulting output can be written to the output stream for presentation. Besides being used to output XHTML, XSL can transform an XML document into almost any markup language.

Listing 7.8 again depicts the single book file insideaspnet.xml, which contains the data we want to transform. To perform this transformation, load the XSL stylesheet in Listing 7.9. XML stylesheets work on the concept of *templates*. Each template element matches a node in the input document. Whenever the node in the input document is encountered, its output is processed by the stylesheet. The book.xslt stylesheet contains two templates: one that matches book nodes and one that matches chapter nodes. The book template simply prints out the title of the current book using the `"value-of"` element and selecting the `"title"` attribute by using the attribute symbol `"@"`. To continue processing below the book element, place an `"apply-templates"` element, which in this case is between two XHTML `"blockquote"` tags.

Listing 7.8 **insideaspnet.xml**

```
01  <?xml version="1.0" encoding="UTF-8"?>
02  <book id="1"
03       title="Inside ASP.Net">
04    <chapter uri="chapter1.html" title="Chapter 1" />
05    <chapter uri="chapter2.html" title="Chapter 2" />
06  </book>
```

Listing 7.9 **book.xslt**

```
01  <?xml version="1.0" encoding="UTF-8"?>
02  <xsl:stylesheet
03    version="1.0"
04    xmlns:xsl="http://www.w3.org/1999/XSL/Transform">
05
06    <xsl:template match="book">
07      <p>
08        Book Title: <xsl:value-of select="@title"/> <br />
09        Chapters:
10        <blockquote>
11          <xsl:apply-templates />
12        </blockquote>
13      </p>
14    </xsl:template>
15
16    <xsl:template match="chapter">
17      <div>
18        Chapter:
```

continues ▶

Listing 7.9 **Continued**

```
19    <a href="{@uri}"><xsl:value-of select="@title"/></a>
20    </div>
21  </xsl:template>
22
23 </xsl:stylesheet>
```

The chapter template contains two ways to use `"value-of"`: both the direct implementation of the chapter's `"title"` attribute, and the inclusion of the `"uri"` attribute as the value of the XHTML `"a"` tag. Using the `"{"` and `"}"` symbols inside an attribute in XSL is synonymous with using a combination of `"attribute"` and `"value-of"` tags. The extended version of line 19 in Listing 7.9.

```
<a href="{@uri}"><xsl:value-of select="@title"/></a>
```

Would look like this:

```
01 <a>
02    <xsl:attribute name="href" select="@uri">
03    <xsl:value-of select="@title"/>
04 </a>
```

Listing 7.10 depicts the cardcatalog.aspx file that shows the basic means of performing a simple XML transformation using XSL. The `XslTransform` class can take in the `XmlDocument` and the path to an XSL stylesheet. The result of the `Transform` method can then be written to the response stream. This can be seen in Figure 7.5.

Listing 7.10 **cardcatalog.aspx**

```
01 <html>
02   <script runat="server" language="VB">
03     Sub Page_Load(Sender As Object, E As EventArgs)
04       ' Declarations
05       Dim xmlDocument As New System.Xml.XmlDocument
06       Dim xslTransform As System.Xml.Xsl.XslTransform
07       Dim xmlReader As System.Xml.XmlReader
08       Dim xmlOutput As New System.Xml.XmlDocument
09
10       ' Load the xml document
11       xmlDocument.Load(Server.MapPath("insideaspnet.xml"))
12
13       ' Transform the xml document into parsed output
14       xslTransform = new System.Xml.Xsl.XslTransform()
15       xslTransform.load(Server.MapPath("book.xslt"))
16
17       ' Transform the document with no arguments
```

```
18        xmlReader = xslTransform.Transform(xmlDocument, Nothing)
19        xmlOutput.Load(xmlReader)
20
21        ' Do something with xmlReader
22        Response.Write("Xsl transformation of <i>insideaspnet.xml</i>:<br>")
23        WriteXml(xmlOutput.OuterXml)
24
25      End Sub
26
27      Public Sub WriteXml(ByVal s As String)
28        s = Server.HtmlEncode(s)
29        s = Replace(s, "&gt;&lt;", "&gt;" & "<BR>" & "&lt;")
30        s = "<pre>" & s & "</pre>"
31
32        Response.Write(s)
33
34      End Sub
35
36    </script>
37  </html>
```

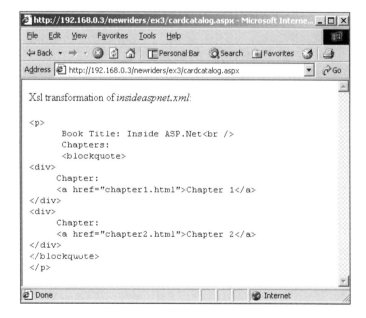

Figure 7.5 The cardcatalog.aspx file in action.

Using MSXML in Internet Explorer 5.0

Listing 7.11–7.16 focuses on using XML on the client side. Internet Explorer 5.0 and higher support the use of the Microsoft XML Parser (MSXML) in the VBScript and JScript client-side languages. Through the use of XML on the browser, you can create effective and dynamic web pages that allow for a more interactive experience through DHTML.

There is quite a bit to the code listings in this sample, so let's start at the beginning. The library.xml and book.xml files are similar to the ones used earlier in this chapter. However, the chapter.xml file has been added as well. Although it is not shown, expect that the library.xsd file has changed accordingly. Whenever the document is loaded, the OnLoad function is called, which performs the first transformation. The library.xml file is loaded into a DOMDocument object, and then transformed with the library.xslt file loaded into the xslLibrary object.

Listing 7.11 **library.xml**

```
01 <?xml version="1.0" encoding="UTF-8"?>
02 <library>
03   <book id="1" uri="insideaspnet/book.xml" title="Inside ASP.Net" />
04   <book id="2" uri="insidexml/book.xml" title="Inside XML"/>
05   <book id="3" uri="insidexslt/book.xml" title="Inside XSLT" />
06 </library>
```

Listing 7.12 **insideaspnet/book.xml**

```
01 <?xml version="1.0" encoding="UTF-8"?>
02 <book id="1"
03       uri="insideaspnet/book.xml"
04       title="Inside ASP.Net">
05   <chapter
06     uri="insideaspnet/chapter1.xml"
07     title="An Overview of ASP.NET"/>
08   <chapter
09     uri="insideaspnet/chapter2.xml"
10     title="Developing Applications with ASP.NET"/>
11   <chapter
12     uri="insideaspnet/chapter3.xml"
13     title="Configuring ASP.NET Applications"/>
14
15   <!— Other nodes follow... —>
16
17   <chapter
18     uri="insideaspnet/chapter7.xml"
19     title=" Using XML in ASP.Net Applications"/>
20
21   <!— Other nodes follow... —>
22
23 </book>
```

Listing 7.13   **insideaspnet/chapter7.xml**

```
01  <?xml version="1.0" encoding="UTF-8"?>
02  <chapter
03    uri="insideaspnet/chapter7.xml"
04    title="Using XML in ASP.Net Applications">
05    <![CDATA[
06      Developed by the World Wide Web Consortium (w3.org) in 1996,
07      the eXtensible Markup Language has been embraced as a
08      flexible means of...
09    ]]>
10  </chapter>
```

Our XSL stylesheet, library.xslt, encapsulates all the presentation logic we need for this application. Whenever the stylesheet is applied to any of our different XML documents, the templates match certain criteria. The first template matches any "library" element that is a document element, as the "/" symbol appears before the element name. Within the "library" element, we apply templates that match any "book" element. The selected template will be the one that matches "book".

Listing 7.14   **library.xslt**

```
01  <?xml version="1.0" encoding="UTF-8"?>
02  <xsl:stylesheet
03    version="1.0"
04    xmlns:xsl="http://www.w3.org/1999/XSL/Transform">
05
06    <!— Library Header, shown in divLibrary —>
07    <xsl:template match="/library">
08      <b>Library:</b>
09      <ul>
10        <xsl:apply-templates select="book"/>
11      </ul>
12    </xsl:template>
13
14    <!— Book Listing, shown in divLibrary —>
15    <xsl:template match="book">
16      <li>
17        <a href="javascript:BookClick('{@uri}');">
18          <xsl:value-of select="@title"/>
19        </a>
20      </li>
21    </xsl:template>
22
23    <!— Book Header, shown in divBook —>
24    <xsl:template match="/book">
25      <b>Book:</b> "<xsl:value-of select="@title"/>"
26      <ul>
```

continues ▶

Listing 7.14 **Continued**

```
27      <xsl:apply-templates select="chapter"/>
28    </ul>
29  </xsl:template>
30
31  <!— Chapter Listing, shown in divBook —>
32  <xsl:template match="chapter">
33    <li>
34      <a href="javascript:ChapterClick('{@uri}');">
35        <xsl:value-of select="@title"/>
36      </a>
37    </li>
38  </xsl:template>
39
40  <!— Chapter Content, shown in divChapter —>
41  <xsl:template match="/chapter">
42    <h3><xsl:value-of select="@title"/></h3>
43    <xsl:value-of select="text()"/>
44  </xsl:template>
45
46  </xsl:stylesheet>
```

As each "book" element in the library.xml file is processed, it appears down the list like this:

```
01  <b>Library:</b>
02  <ul>
03    <li>
04      <a href="javascript:BookClick('insideaspnet/book.xml');">
05        Inside ASP.Net
06      </a>
07    </li>
08
09    ...
10
11  </ul>
```

Whenever a book is clicked in the resulting list, the BookClick function is fired, passing the URI of the book acquired from the transformation. BookClick loads the XML document passed as an argument into the xmlBook object and transforms it again using the library.xslt file. In this instance, the stylesheet matches the "book" element as a document element via the XPath query "/book". This template then parses the "book" element and its children, "chapter" elements.

Listing 7.15 **library.js**

```
01 var xslLibrary = new ActiveXObject('MSXML2.DOMDocument');
02 xslLibrary.async = false;
03 xslLibrary.load('library.xslt');
04
05 function OnLoad() {
06   var xmlLibrary = new ActiveXObject('MSXML2.DOMDocument');
07   xmlLibrary.async = false;
08   xmlLibrary.load('library.xml');
09
10   divLibrary.innerHTML = xmlLibrary.transformNode(xslLibrary);
11   divBook.innerHTML = '';
12   divChapter.innerHTML = '';
13 }
14
15 function BookClick(uri) {
16   var xmlBook = new ActiveXObject('MSXML2.DOMDocument');
17   xmlBook.async = false;
18   xmlBook.load(uri);
19
20   divBook.innerHTML = xmlBook.transformNode(xslLibrary);
21   divChapter.innerHTML = '';
22 }
23
24 function ChapterClick(uri) {
25   var xmlChapter = new ActiveXObject('MSXML2.DOMDocument');
26   xmlChapter.async = false;
27   xmlChapter.load(uri);
28
29   divChapter.innerHTML = xmlChapter.transformNode(xslLibrary);
30 }
31
32 window.attachEvent('onload', OnLoad);
```

Listing 7.16 **library.html**

```
01 <html>
02   <head>
03     <script language="JScript" src="library.js"></script>
04     <style type="text/css">
05       body {
06         overflow:hidden;
07         border:0px;
08         margin:5px;
09       }
10       #divLibrary {
11         width:200px;
12         height:100%;
```

continues ▶

Listing 7.16 **Continued**

```
13        border:1px outset;
14        background-color:menu;
15        font-family:verdana;
16        font-size:12px;
17        padding:5px;
18      }
19      #divBook {
20        height:150px;
21        width:100%;
22        border:1px outset;
23        background-color:#e9e9e9;
24        font-family:verdana;
25        font-size:12px;
26        padding:5px;
27        overflow:auto;
28      }
29      #divChapter {
30        height:100%;
31        width:100%;
32        overflow:scroll;
33        font-family:arial;
34        font-size:12px;
35        padding:5px;
36        border:2px inset;
37      }
38    </style>
39  </head>
40  <body>
41    <table border="0" cellpadding="0" cellspacing="5" height="100%" width="100%">
42      <tr>
43        <td height="100%" width="200" rowspan="2">
44          <div id="divLibrary"></div>
45        </td>
46        <td width="100%" height="150">
47          <div id="divBook"></div>
48        </td>
49      </tr>
50      <tr>
51        <td width="100%" height="100%">
52          <div id="divChapter"></div>
53        </td>
64      </tr>
55    </table>
56  </body>
57 </html>
```

The resulting XHTML would look something like this:

```
01   <b>Book:</b> "Inside ASP.Net"
02   <ul style="height:150px;width:100%;overflow:auto;">
03    <li>
04
05     ...
06
07    <a href="javascript:ChapterClick('insideaspnet/chapter7.xml');">
08       Using XML in ASP.Net Applications
09    </a>
10
11     ...
12
13    </li>
14   </ul>
```

The string result of the transformation is then assigned to the `innerHTML` property `divBook`, displaying the list in the browser.

Finally, whenever a user clicks a chapter in the list, the `ChapterClick` function is called with the location of that chapter's XML file. `ChapterClick` does the same thing as `BookClick`, loading the specified XML file into a `DOMDocument` object and parsing it. The result of this transformation is placed in the `divChapter` DIV tag, and the chapter is then visible to read. The final result should look like Figure 7.6.

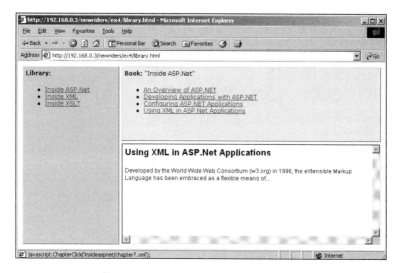

Figure 7.6   Results of selecting a chapter.

Using the XML Web Service HTML Component

In addition to reading from static XML files on the server, a browser can request data from an XML Web Service using SOAP. Listing 7.17–7.19 shows how to do this easily using Microsoft's XML Web Service HTML Component (HTC).

Using the MSXML component on the browser is fine for simple manipulation of XML, but more complex issues arise when creating DHTML applications. The missing piece in client-side application development on the web is the capability to call business objects on a server from the client machine and interpret the results. The answer to this problem is XML Web Services. The WebService.htc file, available at http://msdn.microsoft.com/workshop/ author/ webservice/webservice.htc, contains all the client-side codes needed to bind to an XML Web Service and use its public methods from an Internet Explorer 5.0 browser.

This example is similar to the previous one. However, several distinct changes have been made. Instead of having static XML files for library, book, and chapter, we have an ASP.NET WebService that accesses a data source to retrieve the necessary results as a DataSet. We have left out the XSLT files, which in this case have been separated into three different stylesheets as all DataSets maintain the same internal XML structure. The scripts needed to generate the database for this sample are in the file library.sql, which is included in the downloadable zip file from the New Riders web site for the book.

Listing 7.17 **library.asmx**

```
01 <%@ WebService Language="vb" Class="library" %>
02
03   Imports System.Web.Services
04
05   Public Class library
06
07     Inherits System.Web.Services.WebService
08
09     <WebMethod()> Public Function GetBooks() As System.Data.DataSet
10
11       Dim Conn As New System.Data.SqlClient.SqlConnection()
12       Dim Adapter As New System.Data.SqlClient.SqlDataAdapter()
13       Dim Results As New System.Data.DataSet()
14
15       ' Open a connection to a Data Source
16       Conn.ConnectionString = "Initial Catalog=library;Data Source=localhost;
➥User ID=sa;Password=;"
17       Conn.Open()
18
19       ' Fill a Dataset with the results of a SQL query
20       Adapter.SelectCommand = New System.Data.SqlClient.SqlCommand
```

```
➥("SELECT book_id, title FROM book", Conn)
21        Adapter.Fill(Results)
22
23        Return Results
24
25    End Function
26
27    <WebMethod()> Public Function GetChapters(ByVal BookId As Integer) As
➥System.Data.DataSet
28
29        Dim Conn As New System.Data.SqlClient.SqlConnection()
30        Dim Adapter As New System.Data.SqlClient.SqlDataAdapter()
31        Dim Results As New System.Data.DataSet()
32
33        ' Open a connection to a Data Source
34        Conn.ConnectionString = "Initial Catalog=library;Data Source=localhost;
➥User ID=sa;Password=;"
35        Conn.Open()
36
37        ' Fill a Dataset with the results of a SQL query
38        Adapter.SelectCommand = New System.Data.SqlClient.SqlCommand( _
39          "SELECT chapter_id, title FROM chapter where 39
➥book_id = @book_id", Conn)
40        Adapter.SelectCommand.Parameters.Add("@book_id",
➥System.Data.SqlDbType.Int).Value = BookId
41        Adapter.Fill(Results)
42
43        Return Results
44
45    End Function
46
47    <WebMethod()> Public Function GetChapter(ByVal ChapterId As Integer) As
➥System.Data.DataSet
48
49        Dim Conn As New System.Data.SqlClient.SqlConnection()
50        Dim Adapter As New System.Data.SqlClient.SqlDataAdapter()
51        Dim Results As New System.Data.DataSet()
52
53        ' Open a connection to a Data Source
54        Conn.ConnectionString = "Initial Catalog=library;Data Source=localhost;
➥User ID=sa;Password-;"
55        Conn.Open()
56
57        ' Fill a Dataset with the results of a SQL query
58        Adapter.SelectCommand = New System.Data.SqlClient.SqlCommand( _
59          "SELECT contents FROM chapter where chapter_id = @chapter_id", Conn)
60        Adapter.SelectCommand.Parameters.Add("@chapter_id",
➥System.Data.SqlDbType.Int).Value = ChapterId
61        Adapter.Fill(Results)
62
63        Return Results
64
65    End Function
66
67  End Class
```

When the library.js file is loaded, it makes the first call through libService, the connector to the server-side XML Web Service. Because the client-side object uses callbacks, a function pointer is passed as the first parameter to the callService method.

Listing 7.18   **library.js**

```
01 var bookTitle = '';
02 var chapterTitle = '';
03
04 function OnLoad() {
05   libService.useService("library.asmx?WSDL","library");
06   var iCallId =
07     libService['library'].callService(GetBooksResponse, "GetBooks")
08 }
09
10 function GetBooksResponse(result) {
11   if(result.error) {
12     var errorCode = result.errorDetail.code;
13     var errorDescription = result.errorDetail.string;
14     var errorSOAP = result.errorDetail.raw;
15     // Handle error
16   } else {
17
18     var xslDoc = new ActiveXObject('MSXML2.DOMDocument');
19     xslDoc.async = false;
20     xslDoc.load('books.xslt');
21
22     divLibrary.innerHTML = result.value.transformNode(xslDoc)
23
24   }
25
26 }
27
28 function BookClick(id, title) {
29   bookTitle = title;
30   chapterTitle = '';
31   divChapter.innerHTML = '';
32   var iCallId =
33     libService['library'].callService(GetChaptersResponse,
34       "GetChapters", id)
35 }
36
37 function GetChaptersResponse(result) {
38   if(result.error) {
39     var errorCode = result.errorDetail.code;
40     var errorDescription = result.errorDetail.string;
41     var errorSOAP = result.errorDetail.raw;
42     // Handle error
43   } else {
44     var xslDoc = new ActiveXObject('MSXML2.DOMDocument');
```

```
45    xslDoc.async = false;
46    xslDoc.load('chapters.xslt');
47
48    divBook.innerHTML = '<b>Book:</b> "' + bookTitle + '"<br>' +
49      result.value.transformNode(xslDoc);
50  }
51 }
52
53 function ChapterClick(id, title) {
54   chapterTitle = title;
55   var iCallId =
56     libService['library'].callService(GetChapterResponse,
57       "GetChapter", id)
58 }
59
60 function GetChapterResponse(result) {
61   if(result.error) {
62     var errorCode = result.errorDetail.code;
63     var errorDescription = result.errorDetail.string;
64     var errorSOAP = result.errorDetail.raw;
65     // Handle error
66   } else {
67     var xslDoc = new ActiveXObject('MSXML2.DOMDocument');
68     xslDoc.async = false;
69     xslDoc.load('chapter.xslt');
70
71     divChapter.innerHTML = '<h3>' + chapterTitle + '</h3>' +
72       result.value.transformNode(xslDoc);
73   }
74 }
75
76 window.attachEvent('onload', OnLoad);
```

To handle the change between the earlier XML format and the ADO.NET
`DataSet`'s internal format, a few changes were made to the stylesheets.
Listings 7.19, 7.20, and 7.21 show the new stylesheets broken down by
section.

Listing 7.19 **books.xslt**

```
01 <?xml version="1.0" encoding="UTF-8"?>
02 <xsl:stylesheet
03   version="1.0"
04   xmlns:xsl="http://www.w3.org/1999/XSL/Transform">
05
06   <!-- Library Header, shown in divLibrary -->
07   <xsl:template match="NewDataSet">
08     <b>Library:</b>
09     <ul>
10       <xsl:apply-templates/>
```

continues ▶

Listing 7.19 **Continued**

```
11     </ul>
12   </xsl:template>
13
14   <!— Book Listing, shown in divLibrary —>
15   <xsl:template match="Table">
16     <li>
17       <a href="javascript:BookClick('{book_id}', '{title}');">
18         <xsl:value-of select="title"/>
19       </a>
20     </li>
21   </xsl:template>
22
23 </xsl:stylesheet>
```

Listing 7.20 **chapters.xslt**

```
01 <?xml version="1.0" encoding="UTF-8"?>
02 <xsl:stylesheet
03   version="1.0"
04   xmlns:xsl="http://www.w3.org/1999/XSL/Transform">
05
06   <!— Book Header, shown in divBook —>
07   <xsl:template match="NewDataSet">
08     <ul>
09       <xsl:apply-templates/>
10     </ul>
11   </xsl:template>
12
13   <!— Chapter Listing, shown in divBook —>
14   <xsl:template match="Table">
15     <li>
16       <a href="javascript:ChapterClick('{chapter_id}', '{title}');">
17         <xsl:value-of select="title"/>
18       </a>
19     </li>
20   </xsl:template>
21
22 </xsl:stylesheet>
```

Listing 7.21 **chapter.xslt**

```
01 <?xml version="1.0" encoding="UTF-8"?>
02 <xsl:stylesheet
03   version="1.0"
04   xmlns:xsl="http://www.w3.org/1999/XSL/Transform">
05
```

```
06  <!—Chapter Contents, shown in divChapter —>
07  <xsl:template match="NewDataSet">
08    <xsl:value-of select="//contents/text()"/>
19  </xsl:template>
20
21  </xsl:stylesheet>
```

The library.html file (see Listing 7.22) now includes a div tag that references the webservice.htc HTML Component file.

Listing 7.22 **library.html**

```
01  <html>
02    <head>
03      <script language="JScript" src="library.js"></script>
04      <style type="text/css">
05        body {
06          overflow:hidden;
07          border:0px;
08          margin:5px;
09        }
10        #divLibrary {
11          width:200px;
12          height:100%;
13          border:1px outset;
14          background-color:menu;
15          font-family:verdana;
16          font-size:12px;
17          padding:5px;
18        }
19        #divBook {
20          height:150px;
21          width:100%;
22          border:1px outset;
23          background-color:#e9e9e9;
24          font-family:verdana;
25          font-size:12px;
26          padding:5px;
27          overflow:auto;
28        }
29        #divChapter {
30          height:100%;
31          width:100%;
32          overflow:scroll;
33          font-family:arial;
34          font-size:12px;
35          padding:5px;
36          border:2px inset;
37        }
38      </style>
39    </head>
40    <body>
```

continues ▶

Listing 7.22 **Continued**

```
41    <div id="libService" style="behavior:url(webservice.htc);"></div>
42    <table border="0" cellpadding="0" cellspacing="5" height="100%" width="100%">
43      <tr>
44        <td height="100%" width="200" rowspan="2">
45          <div id="divLibrary"></div>
46        </td>
47        <td width="100%" height="150">
48          <div id="divBook"></div>
49        </td>
50      </tr>
51      <tr>
52        <td width="100%" height="100%">
53          <div id="divChapter"></div>
54        </td>
55      </tr>
56    </table>
57  </body>
58 </html>
```

Using the WebService component might be somewhat difficult for some
developers. Function callbacks are not common in classic ASP or Visual Basic
programming. However, Java and C++ programmers will find themselves at
home. Despite its complexity, using the WebService component on the
browser eliminates the need to maintain a set of static XML files on the
server—allowing you to create a more scaleable web application. Figure 7.7
contains the output for this sample. Note that as far as the presentation is
concerned, this sample and the previous sample are identical.

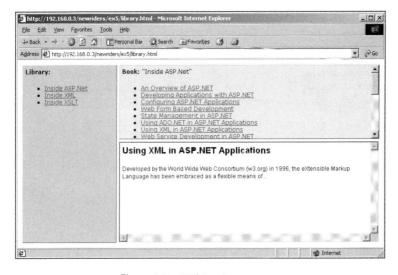

Figure 7.7   WebService output.

Summary

Even as the technology is still in its infancy, XML has shown great promise for a variety of applications. The W3C has gone to great lengths to extend XML into every arena possible and has had much success. Data storage and communication are only the beginning as XML moves into other areas replacing technologies, such as PDF with PGML (Portable Graphics Markup Language), XHTML—the XML variant of the HyperText Markup Language that is making its way into modern day web browsers. The World Wide Web Consortium has many more working drafts of new technologies based on XML at their web site, `http://www.w3.org`. Throughout the ASP.NET framework, many objects expose or implement XML in some way—allowing for greater extensibility and compatibility with many platforms. Due to the open nature of XML and the ease with which it can be added to any ASP.NET application, it is a tool that any programmer will welcome.

IV

Advanced Technologies

8

XML Web Service Development in ASP.NET

THIS CHAPTER DELVES INTO XML WEB SERVICES—an innovative and cross-platform technology for exposing Application Program Interfaces (APIs) over the web. This chapter begins with an explanation of the concepts. It walks you through the creation of a simple XML Web Service and shows you how to build a client that uses the service. Along the way, we investigate the tools and technologies that support XML Web Services and their development in the Windows environment. Near the end of the chapter, you learn how to advertise your XML Web Service on the Internet and query others' services.

This is a very practical chapter with little theory and less product documentation. The goal is to get you using XML Web Services on your system right away. When you are ready to develop more sophisticated services, be sure to look up the reference documentation that Microsoft provides with ASP.NET and the .NET framework.

Note

Many of the tasks covered here are automated in Visual Studio .NET. Although Microsoft's high-end tool increases your efficiency (assuming you have it), it hides most of the process from you. I take the approach that by methodically creating and analyzing the various parts of an XML Web Service, you get a real understanding of the technology. By learning hands-on, you can take the knowledge to any development tool that supports ASP.NET.

Introduction to XML Web Services

XML Web Services are fully supported for the first time in ASP.NET and the .NET framework. When you create an XML Web Service and install it on an *Internet Information Server* (IIS), you make your program's logic and processing power available to many consumer programs, not just web browsers. This technology is just a further refinement of other forms of distributed computing. For example, *Distributed Component Object Model* (DCOM) enables multiple computers to call on a remote server for processing services. The remote server carries out the function and sends back the requested data or computation. This approach worked, but it imposed proprietary technology on the clients, it wasn't cross-platform, it didn't pass easily through firewalls, and it didn't take advantage of open standards.

XML Web Services use technologies that are readily available on non-Microsoft platforms: HTTP and XML. HTTP acts as the highway to pass the data from computer to computer. Extensible Markup Language (XML) wraps the data in a package that other platforms (and even humans) can read and digest. The client party in an XML Web Service contract doesn't need to know or care about the details of the data processing. What matters is that it is accurate, in the correct format, and timely. (You can read more about contracts later in the section, "Making a WSDL File with the SOAP Toolkit.")

An XML Web Service Analogy

To understand the elements of an XML Web Service, let's compare it with ordering food in a restaurant. The acronyms and words in parentheses are teasers to the corresponding technologies that we encounter in this chapter.

I enter the restaurant seeking a service—prepared food. To discover what's available, I consult the menu of the available services (DISCO, Microsoft's Discovery tool, and Universal Description, Discovery, and Integration [UDDI]). The server transmits my order to the kitchen (XML) where the cook calls on the services of others for supporting services, such as providing clean dishes.

While the sandwich is being prepared (XML Web Service), I carry on with other activities, such as browsing a newspaper (ASP.NET page). When the food is ready, the server brings it to me all at once, making as few trips to the kitchen as possible (SOAP).

As a customer, the preparation of the meal is hidden from me (platform independence). What matters is that the end product matches what I requested (WSDL).

Creating a Simple XML Web Service

If you are creating sophisticated XML Web Services for ASP.NET, you will probably work in Visual Studio .NET. However, to grasp what goes into the mix, we're going to code our XML Web Service manually and do our own chores. The tasks include compiling and creating support files.

We are developing a trivial, proof-of-concept service. All it does is accept two numbers and passes back the total. Despite its simplicity, you'll find that it includes the key elements that a complex XML Web Service requires.

Preparing Your Web Server

Before creating our little XML Web Service, you need to prepare your web server (I'm assuming that you have already installed the .NET framework on IIS):

1. Using Windows Explorer, navigate to c:\inetpub\wwwroot (assuming you use the c: drive for IIS) and create a subdirectory called "webservice."

2. Exit Windows Explorer.

3. In Internet Services Manager, expand the web site nodes to locate the webservice subdirectory that you just created.

4. Right-click, and from the context menu, click Properties.

5. On the Directory tab, in the Application Settings area, click the Create button. IIS turns your subdirectory into an Application. The property page should now resemble Figure 8.1.

6. Click OK and then exit Internet Services Manager.

Your server is now ready for you to add a file that delivers an XML Web Service.

Writing the .ASMX File

In ASP.NET, pages that provide XML Web Services use the .ASMX extension. Using Notepad, start a new file called "firstservice.asmx" and add the contents of Listing 8.1.

Listing 8.1 **firstservice.asmx**

```
01 <%@ WebService Language="vb" Class="firstservice"%>
02
03 Imports System.Web.Services
04
05 Class firstservice
06
07     Inherits System.Web.Services.WebService
08
09     <WebMethod()> Public Function Add(ByVal firstnumber As Integer, _
10                    ByVal secondnumber As Integer) As Integer
11         Return firstnumber + secondnumber
12     End Function
13
14 End Class
```

Figure 8.1 Creation of the web application called "webservice" in Internet Services Manager.

Copy firstservice.asmx into the webservice directory that you created earlier.

Before we dissect the lines of code, let's do a little exploration. Open the page in Internet Explorer by navigating to the XML Web Service URL. (In the code and sample URLs in this chapter, I've used my server name, p450. Substitute your server name or IP address.)

```
http://p450/webservice/firstservice.asmx
```

The resulting page, shown in Figure 8.2, may surprise you. The page is not your service, but rather ASP.NET's test base that helps you manipulate your service. Click the Add hyperlink to drill down into the Add method.

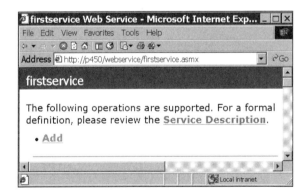

Figure 8.2 ASP.NET displays a web page instead of a service.

Now you see a page like the one shown in Figure 8.3. It enables you to test your XML Web Service. To try the service, type 5 as the value for firstnumber and 7 as the value for secondnumber. Click Invoke.

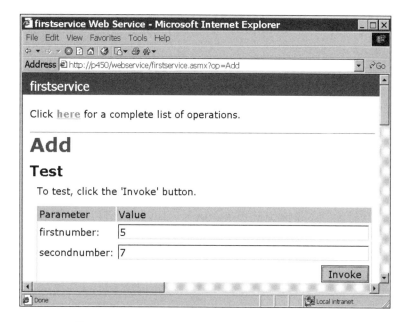

Figure 8.3   ASP.NET enables you to test your service.

The result is an XML file as rendered by your browser. In Figure 8.4, notice the 12 contained within the <int></int> tags. That's the service you have rendered, which accepted the two numbers, added them, and delivered the result.

Figure 8.4   The output of an XML Web Service is data in XML format.

Analyzing the .ASMX File

Now that we've shown that firstservice.asmx works, let's walk through the code in Listing 8.1 to see how it worked.

```
<%@ WebService Language="vb" Class="firstservice"%>
```

The preceding line's @ directive declares this .asmx file as an XML Web Service. The rest of the line tells ASP.NET to use the Visual Basic language interpreter and identifies the class that implements the XML Web Service. All this is wrapped in the familiar inline script tags.

```
Imports System.Web.Services
```

As you might expect, we need to import the ASP.NET namespace that provides the XML Web Service functionality. The preceding line of code does just that.

```
Class firstservice
```

The preceding code gives a name to the class that we are creating (firstservice) and encloses the method that follows.

```
Inherits System.Web.Services.WebService
```

The Inherits keyword specifies that this class acquires all the methods and properties of the base WebService class. Microsoft provides the base class as part of the .NET framework.

```
01 <WebMethod()> Public Function Add(ByVal firstnumber As Integer, _
02     ByVal secondnumber As Integer) As Integer
```

We're now into the activity center of our service. The odd looking <WebMethod()> identifier declares that the following function, Add, is to be exposed as a service. It makes the method a remotely callable function. The Add function accepts two integers, firstnumber and secondnumber, and treats the result as an integer.

```
Return firstnumber + secondnumber
```

Here we reach the core of the service—adding the two values and returning the result. The rest of the file, shown following, wraps up the function and the class declarations.

```
01     End Function
02
03 End Class
```

There's a lot more to offering an XML Web Service. We'll come back to exposing services in the sections "Our Goal: Reusing an Old COM Component" and "Including Security in a SOAP Exchange."

Consuming the XML Web Service

Although we have shown that our XML Web Service can accept values from a browser and return a result in XML, browsing an XML page with Internet

Explorer isn't the normal way for a program to connect to a service. Let's create a tiny client for our tiny service. Again, this is barebones stuff, but the technique applies to real applications.

Scripting an XML Web Service Client

You don't need ASP.NET to consume an XML Web Service. In fact, almost any program that can parse an XML file will do just fine. Our example is in VBScript using *Windows Scripting Host* (WSH).

Note

The small client script requires WSH and the XML Parser version 3.0 or higher. If you have the latest updates to your operating system and to Internet Explorer, you probably have these components. If not, you can download WSH from http://www.microsoft.com/msdownload/vbscript/scripting.asp. The MSXML Parser 3.0 Service Pack 1 XML component is available at http://msdn.microsoft.com/xml. If you encounter unexplained parser errors as you run the scripts provided here, you might need to use the xmlinst.exe utility from Microsoft. You can find it fast with the phrase "Xmlinst.exe Replace Mode Tool".

Open Notepad and start a new file called client.vbs. Add the code from Listing 8.2, and save the file to a computer running Windows 95 or higher.

Listing 8.2 **client.vbs**

```
01 fn=inputbox("Type the value for firstnumber",_
02     "WebService Client",5)
03 sn=inputbox("Type the value for secondnumber",_
04     "WebService Client",7)
05 URL=inputbox("Location of service","WebService Client",_
06     "http://p450/webservice/firstservice.asmx")
07 set doc=CreateObject("MSXML2.DOMDocument")
08 doc.async = False
09 completeURL=URL & "/Add?firstnumber=" & _
10     fn & "&secondnumber=" & sn
11
12 if not doc.Load(completeURL) then
13  msg="Failed to load "
14  msg=msg & "the XML file"
15  msgbox(msg)
16 else
17  doc.setProperty "SelectionLanguage", "XPath"
18  sel="/*"
19  set selectednode = doc.selectSingleNode(sel)
20  txt=selectednode.text
21  msgbox "Here's the result: " & txt,0,"WebService Client"
22 end if
```

The preceding code can be executed in two ways. The easier way is to double-click the filename from Windows Explorer. If that doesn't work, you can use the command prompt to execute the following line:

```
wscript client.vbs
```

The script prompts you for two values and the location of the service (shown in Figure 8.5). The output box from Figure 8.4 (which can take a moment to appear if the service hasn't already been running) displays the returned result of adding the two numbers that you provided.

Figure 8.5 Using Windows Scripting Host as a client.

Analyzing the Mini–XML Web Service Client

Now that you've seen what the tiny client does with the data from the XML Web Service, let's take a brief look at how it works.

After accepting the input values for firstnumber, secondnumber, and the location of your XML Web Service, the script builds all the elements of an HTTP GET statement. For example, the URL might look like this:

```
http://p450/webservice/firstservice.asmx/Add?firstnumber=5&secondnumber=7
```

The part of the code up to firstservice.asmx is easy. That's the address of our service. You might guess that /Add is the name of the function that we created as the core of our service. The question mark (?) is just a signal to the web server that the following data is part of a GET request. Next is the name of the first value that our Add function wants to see, firstnumber. Here, its value is 5. The ampersand (&) separates the first value from the name of the second variable, secondnumber. We round out the request with 7, which is the value of the second variable.

Recall that when we used the browser to navigate to the service, the service returned XML (see Figure 8.4). Our script uses the Load method of the XML parser to fetch and load the XML as sent by the service. From there, the script uses an XPath query to select the first node and the text that it contains.

Figuring Out How to Fetch the Data

The XML Web Service only responds with a calculation when we send it the right data. Although this sample is so easy you could guess the parameters, guesswork is not required. Using your browser, navigate to

```
http://p450/webservice/firstservice.asmx?op=Add
```

Scroll down the page, past the text boxes, until you reach the HTTP GET heading (see Figure 8.6). The documentation you need for using the Add function includes the host (server) name and parameters. On the same page, you'll also find the syntax for POST and SOAP requests. I cover SOAP in the next section.

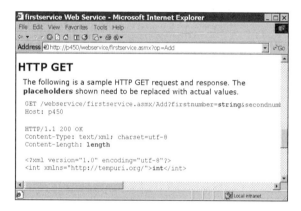

Figure 8.6   Finding the documentation for an HTTP GET request.

Using the SOAP Protocol

Simple Object Access Protocol (SOAP) is an XML-based protocol for exchanging structured information over the Internet. The goal is to enable you to automate data services using standard protocols, such as HTTP.

In this section, we create another mini-client for our XML Web Service, but this time sending and receiving SOAP messages. In essence, it involves submitting a tightly formatted XML document to the service. The XML Web Service parses the XML, extracts the data it needs, and returns a response.

Understanding a SOAP Request

ASP.NET generates the basic XML that constitutes a SOAP call to a service. Unfortunately, it isn't clear what you need to do with the XML and other information to get a response from the service.

The fastest way to get the SOAP data is to navigate to your XML Web Services, as we did before, and click the name of the method. As shown in Figure 8.7, there's more than just XML. Let's analyze the header information and the XML content (see listing 8.3). After that, we can build another mini-client to use it.

Figure 8.7   A SOAP request format provided by ASP.NET.

Listing 8.3   **Header Information for SOAP**

```
01 POST /webservice/firstservice.asmx HTTP/1.1
02 Host: p450
03 Content-Type: text/xml; charset=utf-8
04 Content-Length: length
05 SOAPAction: "http://tempuri.org/Add"
```

Listing 8.3 includes the data that needs to be part of the header when you make a SOAP call. SOAP is picky about what it wants. A syntax error, even a missing quotation mark, can stop the call from working.

The first two lines of Listing 8.3 tell you that you need to generate an HTTP POST (not a GET) request to the server named p450 using the HTTP 1.1 protocol. When put together as a URL, the address becomes:

```
http://p450/webservice/firstservice.asmx
```

The third line indicates that you need to tell the web server that it is getting its content as the text/xml type using the utf-8 character set.

Content-Length is the number of characters in the body of the POST. The word length must be replaced with the actual number of characters.

The SOAPAction value is the HTTP request header field that identifies the namespace of the intended resource. In this case, the URL http://tempuri.org/Add matches the default namespace plus the function name.

Listing 8.4 contains the template XML code that passes two numbers to the Add function, which we built back in Listing 8.1 as part of the Web Service. This is a well-formed XML file that uses the SOAP namespace as defined in the proposal at http://www.w3.org/TR/SOAP/ and the XML Schemas namespace as defined at http://www.w3.org/TR/xmlschema-0/.

Listing 8.4 **XML Content of the SOAP Call**

```
01 <?xml version="1.0" encoding="utf-8"?>
02 <soap:Envelope xmlns:xsi="http://www.w3.org/2001/XMLSchema-instance"
➥xmlns:xsd="http://www.w3.org/2001/XMLSchema"
➥xmlns:soap="http://schemas.xmlsoap.org/soap/envelope/">
03   <soap:Body>
04     <Add xmlns="http://tempuri.org/">
05       <firstnumber>int</firstnumber>
06       <secondnumber>int</secondnumber>
07     </Add>
08   </soap:Body>
09 </soap:Envelope>
```

We need to zero in on the <soap:Envelope> element. A SOAP message must have an Envelope tag as the top element of the XML portion. The Envelope tag, as you might expect, is a container for other data. As we move deeper into the XML hierarchy, we find the mandatory Body tag, <soap:Body>, and then the function name, <Add>. As you recall, our Add function takes two values. This is reflected in the following XML code within the SOAP envelope:

```
01 <firstnumber>int</firstnumber>
02 <secondnumber>int</secondnumber>
```

The int text is just a placeholder waiting for you to insert real integers in each instance. For example, your real code might look like the following:

```
01 <firstnumber>51</firstnumber>
02 <secondnumber>8</secondnumber>
```

Apart from closing the XML tags, that covers the XML content of the SOAP message. Now, we need to build a client that assembles the headers and message content and sends the packaged request to the XML Web Service.

Sending a SOAP Request

Now that we know what must go into a SOAP request, we can build a mini–client that provides everything the XML Web Service needs. This client, like the previous, uses VBScript in Windows Scripting Host. However, the technique is somewhat different because our SOAP data travels with the POST protocol instead of GET as we used before.

In Notepad, start a new file called clientsoap.vbs. Insert the code from Listing 8.5.

Listing 8.5 **clientsoap.vbs**

```
01 fn=inputbox("Type the value for firstnumber",_
02    "WebService Client",51)
03 sn=inputbox("Type the value for secondnumber",_
04    "WebService Client",8)
05 url=inputbox("Location of service","WebService Client",_
06    "http://p450/webservice/firstservice.asmx")
07
08 if (not isNumeric(fn)) OR (not isNumeric(sn)) OR (isEmpty(url)) then
09   msgbox "There's a problem with the input.",0,"WebService Client"
10 else
11
12   soapstring="<?xml version=""1.0"" encoding=""utf-8""?>"
13   soapstring=soapstring & "<soap:Envelope "
14   soapstring=soapstring & "xmlns:soap='http://schemas.xmlsoap.org"
15   soapstring=soapstring & "/soap/envelope/'>"
16   soapstring=soapstring & "<soap:Body>"
17   soapstring=soapstring & "<Add xmlns='http://tempuri.org/'>"
18   soapstring=soapstring & "<firstnumber>" & fn & "</firstnumber>"
19   soapstring=soapstring & "<secondnumber>" & sn & "</secondnumber>"
20   soapstring=soapstring & "</Add>"
21   soapstring=soapstring & "</soap:Body>"
22   soapstring=soapstring & "</soap:Envelope>"
23   msgbox soapstring,0,"WebService Client"
24
25   Set http =   CreateObject("Microsoft.XmlHttp")
26   http.open "POST", url, false
27   http.SetRequestHeader "Content-Type", "text/xml"
28   http.SetRequestHeader "Content-Length", CStr(Len(soapstring))
29   http.SetRequestHeader "SOAPAction", """http://tempuri.org/Add"""
30   http.send   soapstring
31
32   msgbox http.responseText,0,"WebService Client"
33
34   set doc=CreateObject("MSXML2.DOMDocument")
35   doc.async = False
36   if not doc.LoadXML(http.responseText) then
37     msgbox "Failed to load the XML file",0,"WebService Client"
38   else
```

```
39    doc.setProperty "SelectionLanguage", "XPath"
40    sel="/*"
41    set selectednode = doc.selectSingleNode(sel)
42    txt=selectednode.text
43    msgbox "Here's the result: " & txt,0,"WebService Client"
44  end if
45 end if
```

Before getting into the hows and whys of the SOAP mini–client code, let's give the program a try. Don't forget to substitute the URL of your Web Service. Execute clientsoap.vbs from the command line or by double-clicking the filename. See Figure 8.8.

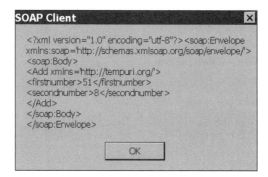

Figure 8.8 The XML content of the SOAP request.

As you can see, when running clientsoap.vbs, I inserted message boxes in the code to track what is being passed back and forth. Figure 8.8 shows how the two values (51 and 8) are wrapped in <firstnumber> and <secondnumber> tags, respectively. The <Add> element acts as the name of the function being called as well as the container for the variable names. The remainder includes the SOAP Body and Envelope tags that we've already discussed. This XML, plus the hidden headers, are sent to the web server.

Figure 8.9 shows the response from the XML Web Service. It is also XML wrapped in its own Envelope tag.

The result value that we are seeking, in this case 59, is embedded in its own tag as shown in the following line.

```
<AddResult>59</AddResult>
```

Although SOAP is called a lightweight protocol, the amount of data in the response may seem like a lot of overhead. By my count, there are 358 characters in the reply, of which we are only interested in two. Of course in a Distributed Component Object Model (DCOM) transaction, the binary data is hidden, so you don't realize how much traffic there is.

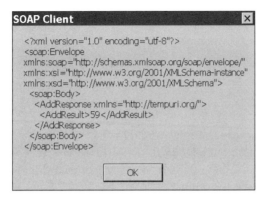

Figure 8.9   The SOAP response from the XML Web Service.

Inside the Mini-Client Code

As you look at Listing 8.5, you see that it starts by accepting the required parameters and does some minor error checking. The next portion of code concatenates the contents of the XML payload. Notice that the values of attributes must be surrounded by quotation marks when they get to the destination; otherwise, the XML is not valid. The code shows two ways of dealing with this: Either use two double quotes where you want one double quote to arrive at the destination server, or substitute a single quote instead of a double quote.

The key part of this code is adding the required HTTP POST headers to keep the XML Web Service happy. This example uses the Microsoft XML-HTTP component to handle the data transfer. After instantiating the object into the variable http, use the Open method to initialize the MSXML2.XMLHTTP request, and specify the method (in this case, POST) and the URL, and set the call to asynchronous mode. Next, use the SetRequestHeader method to pass a Content-Type header with text/xml as the value.

Recall that the XML Web Service wants to know how many characters to expect. Having concatenated everything into the variable soapstring, you can measure the length with the VBScript Len() function and insert the value as a character using CStr() as follows:

```
http.SetRequestHeader "Content-Length", CStr(Len(soapstring))
```

The final header is crucial for ensuring that the XML Web Service acts on this package as a SOAP call.

```
http.SetRequestHeader "SOAPAction", """http://tempuri.org/Add"""
```

In our example, the XML Web Service will return an error if it doesn't recognize the value assigned to the SOAPAction header (http://tempuri.org/Add).

Including Security in a SOAP Exchange

If you don't want the whole world to consume your XML Web Service, you need to implement some form of security. For example, you could use the capabilities that are built in to IIS to allow requests only from a given IP address. Along the same lines, your site could require Windows NT authentication for each access. To stay within the range of SOAP, let's look at a simple application-level method that restricts access.

We've previously used the SOAP body tag to wrap a call to a function and pass the appropriate parameters. SOAP also includes a header element in which you can pass data. We can use this header to send user and password information to the XML Web Service. The XML Web Service reviews the login information contained in the header and, if it is acceptable, carries out the requested function.

Listing 8.6 shows the contents of an XML Web Service file called authservice.asmx.

Listing 8.6 **authservice.asmx**

```
01 <%@ WebService Language="VB" Class="WService" %>
02 Imports System.Web.Services
03 Imports System.Web.Services.Protocols
04
05 Public Class headercontent : Inherits SoapHeader
06     Public Username As String
07     Public Password As String
08 End Class
09
10 <WebService(Namespace:="http://tempuri.org")> _
11 Public Class WService
12 Public HeaderVars As headercontent
13
14 <WebMethod(), SoapHeader("HeaderVars")> _
15 Public Function Add(ByVal firstnumber As Integer, _
16     ByVal secondnumber As Integer) As Integer
17 ' Do a database lookup or other check
18 If HeaderVars.Username = "Administrator" AND _
19     HeaderVars.Password ="mysecret" then
20     Return firstnumber + secondnumber
21 End if
22 End Function
23
24 End Class
```

You access the header content of a SOAP message by deriving your own class from `SoapHeader`, which is found in the `System.Web.Services.Protocols` namespace. Our `headercontent` class declares two string variables, `Username` and `Password`. Those variables represent the header data that the XML Web Service recognizes.

What you should notice about the `Add` function declaration in Listing 8.6 is the addition of the following attribute to the `WebMethod`:

```
SoapHeader("HeaderVars")>
```

This addition ensures that the XML Web Service accepts a header called `HeaderVars`. Using `HeaderVars`, you can reference the `Username` and `Password` variables from within the `Add` function. The validation of the name and password is hardcoded in this trivial example, but your custom authentication routine would probably check the values against a data source. If the name and password check out, the function adds the submitted values and sends the result as before.

Including a SOAP header in the function call requires only a few additional lines of code. Listing 8.7 shows the core content of the SOAP message with attention to the added content that creates and fills the SOAP header.

Listing 8.7   SOAP message content in clientsoapauth.vbs

```
01 soapstring="<?xml version=""1.0"" encoding=""utf-8""?>"
02 soapstring=soapstring & "<soap:Envelope "
03 soapstring=soapstring & "xmlns:soap='http://schemas.xmlsoap.org"
04 soapstring=soapstring & "/soap/envelope/'>"  & vbcrlf
05 soapstring=soapstring & "<soap:Header>"
06 soapstring=soapstring & "<headercontent xmlns='http://tempuri.org'>"
07 soapstring=soapstring & "<Username>Administrator</Username>"
08 soapstring=soapstring & "<Password>mysecret</Password>"
09 soapstring=soapstring & "</headercontent>"
10 soapstring=soapstring & "</soap:Header>"
11 soapstring=soapstring & "<soap:Body>"  & vbcrlf
12 soapstring=soapstring & "<Add xmlns='http://tempuri.org'>"
13 soapstring=soapstring & "<firstnumber>" & fn & "</firstnumber>"
14 soapstring=soapstring & "<secondnumber>" & sn & "</secondnumber>"
15 soapstring=soapstring & "</Add>"  & vbcrlf
16 soapstring=soapstring & "</soap:Body>"  & vbcrlf
17 soapstring=soapstring & "</soap:Envelope>"
```

Unfortunately, the user name and password in the preceding code pass as clear text across the Internet. This makes it possible for an Internet snooper to capture the details. Where security is really important to your XML Web Service, you would want to implement encryption, as provided by the *Secure Sockets Layer* (SSL) protocol.

You can expect to see better security as SOAP and XML standards evolve. For example, the SOAP Security Extensions and Digital Signature proposal submitted to the W3C paves the way for adding security features to the SOAP header. You can read the document at `http://www.w3.org/TR/SOAP-dsig/`.

Using the SOAP Toolkit with XML Web Services

You've already seen how you can use SOAP to get data into and out of a XML Web Service. In this section, we walk through wrapping a COM object into a SOAP call. This isn't a task that you would want to code by hand because it is quite complex. It involves peering into the innards of a COM DLL in much the way Object Browser or the TypeLib component would do. Further, the relevant parts, such as methods and properties, must be converted into an XML file. Instead of a manual operation, we use the Microsoft SOAP Toolkit Version 2.0 or later. You can get a copy from `http://msdn.microsoft.com/soap`. If you haven't already done so, install the SOAP toolkit on the web server.

Our Goal: Reusing an Old COM Component

Even while moving new projects to ASP.NET, there's a good chance that you have existing components that you can't or don't want to rebuild. Perhaps you don't own the source code, or you don't have the time to reconfigure the code for a new platform. Likewise, ASP.NET opens the road to getting some extra mileage out of components by offering them as XML Web Services.

As a starting point, I've built a tiny VB6 component called ProvNames.dll (available by download from this book's support site). It has two functions. The first function accepts the Canada Post two-letter code for a Canadian province or territory and returns the full name. The second function reverses the process—it accepts the whole name and returns the province or territory's initials.

Our goal is to make this component available as an XML Web Service with SOAP. Keep in mind that this DLL knows nothing about ASP.NET or the .NET framework because it was built before they existed. We have to jump through several hoops to expose its functionality on our site, but the tools do a lot of the work.

Installing the COM Component on the Web Server

Before we can get into SOAP and services, we need to install the COM component on the web server and check that it is working. Copy ProvNames.dll and default.asp, which you have downloaded into the webservice folder you created previously. If necessary, skip back to the section, "Prepare Your Web Server," in this chapter for instructions. You need administrator access to the machine for these tasks.

In the webservice directory, use the following statement from the command prompt to register the dynamic library link (DLL):

```
regsvr32 ProvNames.dll
```

You should get the message "DllRegisterServer in ProvNames.dll succeeded." If not, make sure that you have the VB6 runtime component installed on the computer. You can get the runtime from `http://www.microsoft.com/downloads/release.asp?ReleaseID=12704`. The filename is vbrun60sp3.EXE.

Next, test that the component is working with Classic ASP. Using Internet Explorer, navigate to the test ASP page. For example, on my system the URL is `http://p450/webservice/default.asp`, however you need to substitute your server name. Figure 8.10 shows the content of the page that should appear in Internet Explorer. If you get an error, make sure that the Anonymous account (IUSR_<machinename>) has sufficient permissions to execute the DLL and VB6 runtime.

Figure 8.10   Check that the component is working in Classic ASP.

Making a WSDL File with the SOAP Toolkit

You are now ready to build an ASP.NET front end to the COM component. This ASP.NET facade is what makes an ordinary old DLL look like an XML Web Service to the outside world.

The technology behind this is the *Web Services Description Language* (WSDL). WSDL is an XML format that describes services offered by the web server, such as functions and Application Programming Interface (API) calls. WSDL is a rulebook and contract that tells the client the exact format for acceptable requests. Like a contract, it also assures that if the client provides the request correctly, the service responds with the data in the promised format. The SOAP Toolkit generates the WSDL file for us by reading the COM object.

1. On your web server, run the SOAP Toolkit wizard (Start, Programs, Microsoft SOAP Toolkit, WSDL Generator).

2. On the Welcome page, click Next.

3. In the upper textbox, type provname, as shown in Figure 8.11. This will be the base name for the generated files.

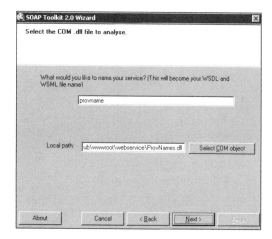

Figure 8.11 The SOAP Toolkit wizard generates the WSDL file.

4. Click the Select COM object button and locate ProvNames.dll. If you are using the same directories used in this chapter, it should be C:\Inetpub\wwwroot\webservice\ProvNames.dll.

5. Click Next. The wizard displays the methods in the COM object that you can expose. See Figure 8.12.

6. Make sure that all the checkboxes are checked. We are exposing the entire component.

7. Click Next. The wizard requests the SOAP Listener information.

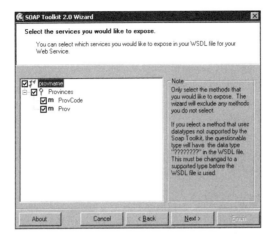

Figure 8.12 Expose both of the methods as XML Web Services.

8. In the Listener URI box, type the address of the website. In my example, this address is `http://p450/webservice/`.

9. Set the Listener type radio button to ISAPI and the XSD Schema Namespace to 2001.

10. Click Next. The wizard requests the location for the files.

11. Set the WSDL file character set to UTF-8.

12. For the file location, select the directory where the XML Web Service files are stored, for example, c:\inetpub\wwwroot\webservice.

13. Click Next, and after the files are created, click Finish.

The wizard has generated two files, provname.wsml and provname.wsdl. To see the contract, use Internet Explorer to navigate to the WSDL file. For example, `http://p450/webservice/provname.wsdl`.

Figure 8.13 shows some of the contract details in the WSDL file. These include names of the messages and the type of values (for example, string) that the client can expect. We need to take a closer look at some parts of the file if we want a client to interact with it.

Deciphering the WSDL File

There's a lot going on in the WSDL file, even for a tiny COM component that only offers two functions. Much of the WSDL content deals with name-spaces which, although necessary, aren't the parts we need to focus on when creating a client call to our XML Web Services. What we want to discover is this: What SOAP message we send to the server to get back the value from a function.

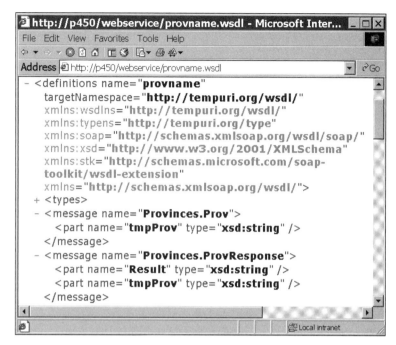

Figure 8.13   The WSDL contract describes the messages and objects.

To make the analysis somewhat easier, let's cheat. Look at Listing 8.8, a snippet from the Visual Basic source code for the ProvCode function. This way, we can compare it with the service description and figure out what the SOAP call needs to do if it is going to match what the component is expecting.

Listing 8.8   **Visual Basic Code for the *ProvCode* Function**

```
01 Public Function ProvCode(tmpProv As String) As String
02          tmpProv = Trim(tmpProv)
03          Select Case tmpProv
04           Case "Alberta"
05           ProvCode = "AB"
06
07           ' Others provinces go here
08
09           Case "Yukon"
10           ProvCode = "YT"
11           Case Else
12           ProvCode = "Error"
13          End Select
14 End Function
```

Listing 8.8 shows that `ProvCode` (a member of the `Provinces` class) accepts `tmpProv` as a string and returns a result as a string. Compare those names and attributes to Listing 8.9, a snippet from our WSDL file.

Listing 8.9   **Snippet of ProvCode Message in WSDL**

```
01 <message name='Provinces.ProvCode'>
02    <part name='tmpProv' type='xsd:string'/>
03 </message>
04 <message name='Provinces.ProvCodeResponse'>
05    <part name='Result' type='xsd:string'/>
06    <part name='tmpProv' type='xsd:string'/>
07 </message>
```

Suddenly, things start to fall in line. The `<message>` element's name attribute points directly to the `Province.ProvCode` function. Its `<part>` child element carries the name `tmpProv` and the type `xsd:string`.

On the return, the `<message>` element with the name `Provinces.ProvCodeResponse` has two `<part>` child elements. One is named `Result` and the other is `tmpProv`. Both are strings.

The significance for our SOAP message is now clear. It needs to create an XML envelope and include data that has a `<tmpProv>` element with a string. That could look like the following:

```
<tmpProv>Ontario</tmpProv>
```

On the receiving end of the contract, we can expect the XML Web Service to return a SOAP envelope that bears two elements, `<Result>` and `<tmpProv>`, with appropriate string values. Therefore, the server should be sending some XML that looks like the following:

```
01 <Result>ON</Result>
02 <tmpProv>Ontario</tmpProv>
```

In short, the XML Web Service is saying, "If you send me a properly packaged `<tmpProv>` tag with 'Ontario' in it, I'll send you back the value you wanted (that is 'ON') wrapped inside a `<Result>` tag. I'll also echo your original request, which you can use or throw away." What constitutes a "proper" package is our next topic.

Using the SOAP Toolkit's Trace Utility

If you think that there must be an easier way to figure out the syntax of a SOAP message, you're right. Hand coding is difficult, especially when you get into all the namespaces. Microsoft provides a tool and some techniques that automate much of this effort.

The Trace tool captures SOAP requests and responses on your web server, so you can eavesdrop on the conversation that has taken place behind the scenes. Before you run Trace, make a little adjustment to your WSDL file. In Notepad, open the file provname.WSDL from your c:\inetpub\wwwroot\webservice directory (or wherever you stored it). Scroll to the bottom of the file, and locate the following line (your server name will be different):

```
<soap:address location='http://p450/webservice/provname.WSDL' />
```

The Trace tool monitors port 8080, so add the port information, so the line looks like the following:

```
<soap:address location='http://p450:8080/webservice/provname.WSDL' />
```

Save the file and close Notepad.

Next, we need to generate some traffic for Trace to trap. We can do this with a small WSH file that uses the SoapClient object. SoapClient is automatically installed with the SOAP Toolkit. This component sends SOAP requests to the server without a lot of fuss. Using Notepad, add the code, change the URL to reflect your server name, and save the file as soapprovclient.vbs (see listing 8.10).

Listing 8.10 **soapprovclient.vbs**

```
01 Dim Provinces
02 set Provinces= CreateObject("MSSOAP.SoapClient")
03 On Error Resume Next
04 Call Provinces.mssoapinit("http://p450/webservice/provname.wsdl",_
05    "provname", "ProvincesSoapPort")
06 if err <> 0 then
07   wscript.echo "initialization failed " + err.description
08 end if
09
10 wscript.echo  Provinces.ProvCode("Ontario")
11 if err <> 0 then
12   wscript.echo    err.description
13   wscript.echo    "faultcode=" + Provinces.faultcode
14   wscript.echo    "faultstring=" + Provinces.faultstring
15   wscript.echo    "faultactor=" + Provinces.faultactor
16   wscript.echo    "detail=" + Provinces.detail
17 end if
18
19 From the command line, run the WSH script using the following syntax:
20 wscript soapprovclient.vbs
```

If all goes well, you see a message box with the letters "ON" on it. The script has sent the value "Ontario" to the ProvCode function and received "ON" as the province's initials. If you got an error, make sure that the SOAP Toolkit is installed on the machine. The toolkit provides the required component that appears in the second line of Listing 8.10.

You are now ready to monitor the XML Web Service traffic using Trace.

1. Start the Trace utility (Start, Programs, Microsoft SOAP Toolkit, Trace utility).

2. From the File menu, click New, Formatted Trace.

3. On the Trace Setup dialogue box, set the Listen port to 8080 (the default).

4. In the Destination Host box, type the name of the web server that is hosting the service, as shown in Figure 8.14.

5. Click OK. A tri-pane window appears indicating that Trace is listening on port 8080.

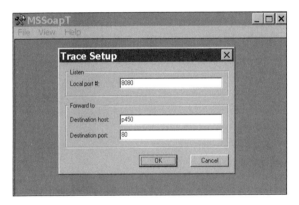

Figure 8.14 Configure the Trace utility to monitor SOAP traffic.

Now we need to generate the traffic. Leaving Trace running, open a command session, and from the command line, run the soapprovclient.vbs script again:

```
wscript soapprovclient.vbs
```

In the left pane of Trace, you should see the IP address of the computer that is being monitored. Expand the node to find Message # 1. Click the message to view the contents. As shown in Figure 8.15, the right panes fill with the complete SOAP transaction. The top pane shows what the client, soapprovclient.vbs, sent in its envelope. You can see that the XML includes the `<tmpProv>Ontario</tmpProv>` code that we predicted earlier. In the bottom pane, the XML Web Service responded with the result value enclosed in tags, as in `<Result>ON</Result>`.

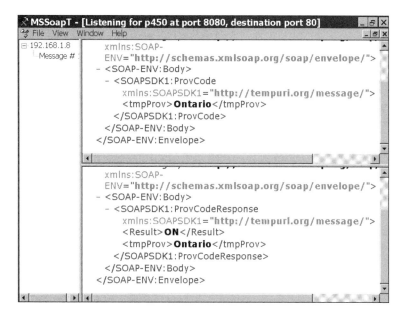

```
xmlns:SOAP-
ENV="http://schemas.xmlsoap.org/soap/envelope/">
- <SOAP-ENV:Body>
  - <SOAPSDK1:ProvCode
      xmlns:SOAPSDK1="http://tempuri.org/message/">
      <tmpProv>Ontario</tmpProv>
    </SOAPSDK1:ProvCode>
  </SOAP-ENV:Body>
</SOAP-ENV:Envelope>
```

```
xmlns:SOAP-
ENV="http://schemas.xmlsoap.org/soap/envelope/">
- <SOAP-ENV:Body>
  - <SOAPSDK1:ProvCodeResponse
      xmlns:SOAPSDK1="http://tempuri.org/message/">
      <Result>ON</Result>
      <tmpProv>Ontario</tmpProv>
    </SOAPSDK1:ProvCodeResponse>
  </SOAP-ENV:Body>
</SOAP-ENV:Envelope>
```

Figure 8.15   The Trace utility shows both SOAP messages.

Here's where Trace saves you hours of frustration. You now have a complete, well-formed and working SOAP transaction on which to build your own client. In fact, you can capture the entire contents of a SOAP message by right-clicking inside the upper pane. Click copy, and then paste the clipboard contents into Notepad. Save that XML code to a file because you'll need it later.

That completes our first session with Trace. You can use it any time to debug SOAP messages. Before you forget, go back into the WSDL file and remove the 8080 port designation so as not to interfere with examples that come later. Let's move on to building a mini-client that talks through SOAP and an XML Web Service to our COM component.

Building a Mini-Client to Query the COM Component

One final piece needs to be in place to get data into and out of our old COM DLL. We need a client that talks SOAP. Actually, we already used a SOAP-aware client in Listing 8.8. However, that was cheating because we used the proprietary SoapClient component from Microsoft. If the goal is to access an XML Web Service from anywhere on the Internet, it wouldn't work to require everyone to install the SoapClient object on a Windows computer.

Instead, we can develop another WSH script that manually prepares the SOAP envelope. Using Notepad, enter the contents of Listing 8.11, updating the URL value to reflect your XML Web Service location. Save the file as clientsoapprov.vbs.

Listing 8.11 **clientsoapprov.vbs—A SOAP to COM Client**

```
01 url=inputbox("Location of WSDL","SOAP Client to COM",_
02     "http://p450/webservice/provname.wsdl")
03 prompt="Type a Canadian Province/Territory Name (Try Newfoundland)"
04
05 province=inputbox(prompt,"SOAP Client to COM", "Alberta")
06 if isEmpty(url) OR isEmpty(prompt) then
07   msgbox "There's a problem with the input.",0,"SOAP Client to COM"
08 else
09   soapstring="<?xml version=""1.0"" encoding=""UTF-8"" "
10   soapstring=soapstring & "standalone=""no""?>"
11   soapstring=soapstring & "<SOAP-ENV:Envelope SOAP-ENV:encodingStyle="
12   soapstring=soapstring & "'http://schemas.xmlsoap.org/soap/encoding/' "
13   soapstring=soapstring & "xmlns:SOAP-ENV="
14   soapstring=soapstring & "'http://schemas.xmlsoap.org/soap/envelope/'>"
15   soapstring=soapstring & "<SOAP-ENV:Body>"
16   soapstring=soapstring & "<SOAPSDK1:ProvCode xmlns:SOAPSDK1='"
17   soapstring=soapstring & "http://tempuri.org/message/'>"
18   soapstring=soapstring & "<tmpProv>" & trim(province) & "</tmpProv>"
19   soapstring=soapstring & "</SOAPSDK1:ProvCode>"
20   soapstring=soapstring & "</SOAP-ENV:Body>"
21   soapstring=soapstring & "</SOAP-ENV:Envelope>"
22
23   msgbox soapstring,0,"SOAP Client to COM"
24
25   Set http =   CreateObject("Microsoft.XmlHttp")
26   http.open "POST", url, false
27   http.SetRequestHeader "Content-Type", "text/xml"
28   http.SetRequestHeader "Content-Length", CStr(Len(soapstring))
29   http.SetRequestHeader "SOAPAction", _
30       """http://tempuri.org/action/Provinces.ProvCode"""
31   http.send   soapstring
32
33   msgbox http.responseText,0,"SOAP Client to COM"
34
35   set doc=CreateObject("MSXML2.DOMDocument")
36   doc.async = False
37   if not doc.LoadXML(http.responseText) then
38     msgbox "Failed to load the XML file",0,"SOAP Client to COM"
39   else
40     doc.setProperty "SelectionLanguage", "XPath"
41     sel="//Result"
42     set selectednode = doc.selectSingleNode(sel)
43     txt=selectednode.text
44     msgbox "Here's the abbreviation: " & txt,0,"SOAP Client to COM"
45   end if
46 end if
```

Run the WHS script from the command line as follows:

```
wscript clientsoapprov.vbs
```

Figure 8.16 shows the client in action. You type the URL of the WSDL file and provide the name of the Canadian province or territory. The message, packaged in a SOAP envelope, goes to the web server. The server detects that this is a SOAP message as opposed to a GET request. It processes the input, calls the COM component (ProvNames.dll), and relays the component's output back to the client. In this case, the output is AB, the Canada Post initials for Alberta.

You've seen that by sending the correct XML-formatted data to the XML Web Service, you fulfill the contract and get the correct response.

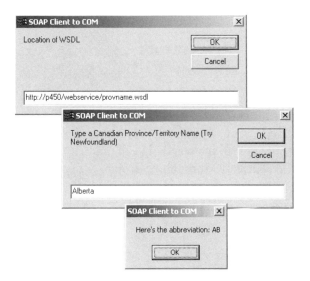

Figure 8.16   The input and output sequence of the SOAP exchange.

Analyzing the SOAP Query of a COM Component

Listing 8.11 is fairly straightforward. It accepts the user input, concatenates the XML content, and inserts the user-provided value into the SOAP envelope. As we saw in the GET client (Listing 8.5), the XML Web Service expects specific headers. Note the following line from Listing 8.9.

```
http.SetRequestHeader "SOAPAction", _
    """http://tempuri.org/action/Provinces.ProvCode"""
```

The Web Service will balk if it doesn't recognize the namespace for the SOAPAction header. Compare the preceding namespace with the following line of code from provname.wsdl. Note that the namespace, especially the last part containing `Provinces.ProvCode`, corresponds exactly to the value of the `soapAction` attribute inside the `operation` element.

```
<soap:operation soapAction='http://tempuri.org/action/Provinces.ProvCode' />
```

It is the client's responsibility to put the returned message into a suitable format. For a machine process, that format may be left as XML. For human consumption, the mini-client uses an XPath query (//Result) to select only the required node—separating the wheat from the chaff, so to speak. Finally, the script reads the text content of the `<Result>` tag and displays the value in a message box as shown in the following code.

```
01 doc.setProperty "SelectionLanguage", "XPath"
02 sel="//Result"
03 set selectednode = doc.selectSingleNode(sel)
04 txt=selectednode.text
05 msgbox "Here's the abbreviation: " & txt,0,"SOAP Client to COM"
```

That completes our analysis of the mini-client and exchanging SOAP messages with a legacy COM object. Although the component's service was trivial, it isn't hard to apply the same techniques to a component that does extensive database lookups on the server side and returns several values packed in the same SOAP envelope through ASP.NET.

XML Web Service Discovery—Advertising Your Service

If you are making an XML Web Service available for public consumption, it makes sense that you have to tell the world about it. Potential users need to know where to find the service (the URL) and precise details of the contract as contained in the WDSL file. With that information, they can query the site and write their own client to consume the service. This section shows how to advertise our tiny COM component service on the Internet.

Using the DISCO Tool

As part of the .NET framework Software Development Kit, Microsoft publishes the XML Web Service Discovery tool. Disco.exe parses a WSDL file and generates an XML file with the extension .discomap. This map file acts as a directory panel in your site's "lobby" to assist visitors who want to discover the services that you offer.

Let's generate a .discomap file for our service and then analyze the contents. First, locate a copy of disco.exe. (It may be in C:\Program Files\Microsoft.NET\FrameworkSDK\Bin.) After updating the URL to reflect your server's name, execute the following from the command line:

```
disco http://p450/webservice/provname.wsdl
```

The discovery process can take a few seconds while the DISCO tool contacts the XML Web Service and reads through the WSDL file. Figure 8.17 shows the command line feedback. It shows that the tool parsed provname.wsdl and generated a file called results.discomap, shown in Listing 8.12.

Figure 8.17 The DISCO tool generates a map to services.

Listing 8.12 **results.discomap**

```
01 <?xml version="1.0" encoding="utf-8"?>
02 <DiscoveryClientResultsFile xmlns:xsi="http://www.w3.org/2001/XMLSchema-instance"
➥xmlns:xsd="http://www.w3.org/2001/XMLSchema">
03   <Results>
04     <DiscoveryClientResult
➥referenceType="System.Web.Services.Discovery.ContractReference"
➥url="http://p450/webservice/provname.wsdl" filename="provname.wsdl" />
05   </Results>
06 </DiscoveryClientResultsFile>
```

The `<DiscoveryClientResult/>` element's attributes include the URL of the service and the filename. What's important is that the tags are being standardized as an XML schema. Humans or machines can look through the discomap and determine exactly where your site keeps its service. Actually, they can't do that until you make the discomap available to them. Rename the file to results.disco, and copy it to the web where its WSDL file is stored (for example, c:\inetpub\wwwroot\webservice\results.disco). As shown in Figure 8.18, processes and browsers can now navigate to your site and discover the services that you offer. As you add services, generate a new discomap.

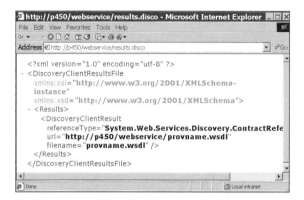

Figure 8.18   A Disco file points to public XML Web Services.

Using UDDI

Although you've learned how to reveal the XML Web Services that you offer to those who come to your site, directing them to the site in the first place is another issue. The web is a big place and it is hard to know where to find anything without a search mechanism. What you need is a type of Yellow Pages directory out on the Internet. You list your service and let potential clients, including their software, search the listings to see who you are and what you offer. That's the role of the *Universal Description, Discovery, and Integration* (UDDI) project on the web at `http://www.uddi.org`.

With UDDI, you publish your business and services at a centralized registry on the web. Your public registry entry includes the company name, contacts, and technical details about the XML Web Service. People who are looking for a service can look up the URL and the contracts that you offer.

Microsoft, a partner with IBM in the UDDI project, has created the UDDI Software Development Kit (see `http://uddi.microsoft.com/developer/default.aspx`) that includes components for exchanging data with the UDDI registry. UDDI registration is beyond the scope of this book, but let's look at how to query the registry for a service.

In reality, UDDI is a service for services that respond to SOAP messages. After you are registered with a UDDI registry, you can send SOAP-compliant XML regarding your offerings and receive stored information back.

Even without becoming a registered user, you can query a registry. Listing 8.13 shows the contents of udditest.vbs, a WSH script that queries IBM's registry for a business called IBM. The UDDI format for a search requires a <find_business> element that contains a <name> element with the search word.

Listing 8.13 **udditest.vbs**

```
01 url=inputbox("Location of WSDL","UDDI Query",_
02    "http://www-3.ibm.com/services/uddi/inquiryapi")
03
04 sstr="<?xml version='1.0' encoding='UTF-8'?>"
05 sstr=sstr & "<Envelope xmlns='http://schemas."
06 sstr=sstr & "xmlsoap.org/soap/envelope/'>"
07 sstr=sstr & "<Body>"
08 sstr=sstr & "<find_business xmlns='urn:uddi-org:api' "
09 sstr=sstr & " generic='1.0' maxRows='100'>"
10 sstr=sstr & "<name>IBM</name>"
11 sstr=sstr & "</find_business>"
12 sstr=sstr & "</Body>"
13 sstr=sstr & "</Envelope>"
14
15 Set http =   CreateObject("Microsoft.XmlHttp")
16 http.open "POST", url, false
17 http.SetRequestHeader "Content-Type", "text/xml"
18 http.SetRequestHeader "Content-Length", CStr(Len(sstr))
19 http.SetRequestHeader "SOAPAction", """"""
20 http.send  sstr
21
22 set doc=CreateObject("MSXML2.DOMDocument")
23 doc.async = False
24 if not doc.LoadXML(http.responseText) then
25    msgbox "Failed to load the XML file",0,"UDDI Query"
26 else
27    'doc.setProperty "SelectionLanguage", "XPath"
28    sel="/Envelope/Body/businessList/businessInfos/"
29    sel=sel & "businessInfo[@businessKey"
30    sel=sel & "=""C843C4F0-3AAF-11D5-80DC-002035229C64""]/name"
31    set selectednode = doc.selectSingleNode(sel)
32    txt=selectednode.text
33    msgbox "Here's the name: " & txt,0,"UDDI Query"
34    sel="/Envelope/Body/businessList/businessInfos/"
35    sel=sel & "businessInfo[@businessKey"
36    sel=sel & "=""C843C4F0-3AAF-11D5-80DC-002035229C64""]"
37    sel=sel & "/description"
38    set selectednode = doc.selectSingleNode(sel)
39    txt=selectednode.text
40    msgbox "Here's the description: " & txt,0,"UDDI Query"
41 end if
```

Note

If you get an error message or unexpected results when your run udditest.vbs, check the URL (http://www.3.ibm.com/services/uddi/inquiryapi) in Internet Explorer to confirm that the service is working.

When you execute udditest.vbs, the IBM site returns a SOAP-compliant XML message with the results. Rather than display all the matching data, I've used an XPath query to return information from a specific node used for testing, as shown in Figures 8.19 and 8.20.

Figure 8.19 An XPath query filters service information.

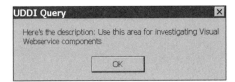

Figure 8.20 IBM has a UDDI registry for testing XML Web Services.

It remains to be seen whether the UDDI project will take off. It holds the promise of making it easy to programatically locate XML Web Services in a standards-based environment.

Using an XML Web Service in ASP.NET Pages

In this section, you build an ASP.NET page that interacts with one of the XML Web Services that you created earlier. The goal is to build an HTML page that enables you to select a province or territory name and ask the remote Web Service to return the corresponding initials from the VB6 COM component. Figure 8.21 shows the working page running on a different computer from the service. Again, the project is trivial, but the techniques apply to complex scenarios.

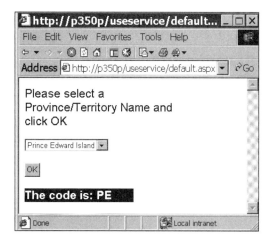

Figure 8.21   The ASP.NET page calls a remote service.

Developing an ASP.NET Consumer in Visual Studio .NET

Until now, all the development work in this chapter has been in Notepad, at the command line, or using free, downloadable tools from Microsoft. This section departs from that approach and moves the development into Visual Studio .NET. There's a practical reason for this: VisualStudio .NET automates many complicated tasks and files that are required to integrate an XML Web Service into an ASP.NET page. Technically, you could do it by hand, but the tool makes it easy. If you don't have Visual Studio .NET, check out the complete source code, which is available from the download site. You can copy the files (maintaining the directory structure) to your ASP.NET server to analyze the code and view the client in action.

Prepare the Web Form Interface

Before connecting to a Web Service, you need to build a project and web page. These steps are the bare minimum required—there's no attention to cosmetics or style.

1. In Visual Studio .NET, start a new Visual Basic web application project. Name the project useservice.

2. Rename Webform1.aspx to default.aspx.

3. From the Web Forms section of the Toolbox, drag and drop a Label control, a DropDownList control, a Button control, and another Label control onto the form. Leave the default names.

4. Select the dropdown List Box (DropDownList1) and, on the Properties page, locate the Items property.

5. Click the Ellipsis button to open the List Item Collection Editor window.

6. Click Add, and in the right pane, enter Alberta for both the Text and Value properties. See Figure 8.22.

7. Click OK to close the Collection Editor.

8. Save your work.

That's all we'll do on the interface. You can clean it up and add more list items later. Next, we connect to the XML Web Service.

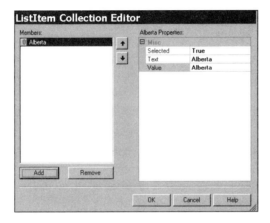

Figure 8.22   Add an item to the dropdown list.

Connecting the XML Web Service to the Project

The basic need for our web page is to know where to find the service it wants to use. Although it appears as though you are only pointing Visual Studio to the service, the reality is that behind the scenes, the environment is generating a great deal of infrastructure.

1. From the Project menu, click Add Web Reference.

2. On the Add Web Reference window, in the Address box, enter the URL of the XML Web Service's WSDL file. For example, on my setup the address is http://p450/webservice/provname.wsdl. See Figure 8.23. Assuming you have network connectivity to the service, the left pane displays the contract details as it discovers them.

3. Click Add Reference. Notice that in the Solution Explorer, Visual Studio .NET has added a Web Reference node that includes the server name and the name of the WSDL file. See Figure 8.24.

4. Save your work.

Figure 8.23 Add the address of the WSDL page as a reference.

Figure 8.24 The remote service appears in Solution Explorer.

Hook up the Web Form to the Service

Now that the project has a reference to the remote service, you can treat the remote method just as if it were part of your local code. The final task before testing is to hook up the button's click event to an XML Web Service method.

1. Double-click the Button control to create an event handler.

2. Add the following code to the `Button1_Click` event, changing the name of the server to reflect your setup:

```
01 Dim cService As New p450.provname()
02 Label2.Text = "The code is: " _
03 & cService.ProvCode(DropDownList1.SelectedItem.Value)
```

3. Save all files.

4. From the Build menu, click Rebuild all.

Unless there are compiler or syntax errors, the project is complete and ready for testing.

Accessing the XML Web Service from the ASP.NET Page

To check the functionality of the XML Web Service, we need to view the page that we just completed.

1. Return to the design view of default.aspx.

2. In the design area, right-click and, from the context menu, click View in Browser.

3. Be patient. The .NET framework may need to compile your files the first time they are run and even start some services.

4. Select the Alberta entry from the listbox. (It may be the only one there if you didn't revisit the page.)

5. Click the button and watch the bottom Label control. The XML Web Service should provide the two-letter code for Alberta, which is AB.

When you analyze it, quite a lot has happened at the click of a button. The ASP.NET page has called a remote object, passed a value to it, returned the response from the remote server, and displayed the text on the web page.

That completes our look at integrating an XML Web Service into an ASP.NET page using Visual Studio .NET.

Summary

In this chapter, you've seen how to create an XML Web Service in pure ASP.NET and a second service using a legacy COM component hosted by the .NET framework. You have created several types of consumers for the XML Web Services, including Windows Scripting Host scripts and an ASP.NET page. Along the way, we've covered the techniques and technologies of XML Web Services, such as WSDL, SOAP messages, the Microsoft SOAP Toolkit, the service discovery utility (DISCO), and UDDI project. Although we've covered a lot of ground, XML Web Services are so flexible, universal, and complex that whole chapters or books could be devoted to the individual technologies.

9

Securing ASP.NET Applications

ASP.NET PROVIDES DEVELOPERS WITH A VARIETY of technologies that can be used to increase the security of their application and protect sensitive materials from prying eyes. The framework covers a wide range of topics, such as client authentication, user and role based permissions, and encryption services. Developers can utilize the authentication services made available by the framework to gather credentials provided by a client, such as username and password. Using internal mechanisms or even custom applications, you can match those credentials to an authority, such as a domain server, database, or XML file.

In addition to the benefit of client authentication, ASP.NET includes built-in resources for testing role membership and determining what authenticated users belong to what groups. You can secure applications based on the type of user, allowing some access for guests, members of the marketing department, and even full access for administrators.

Determining who has the right to access applications is only one concern when it comes to security; you must also protect the data from those who do not have adequate privileges. Using Cryptographic Services, important data such as documents, configuration files, and even web pages themselves can be protected.

Overview of ASP.NET Security Features

Among the major concerns of application developers are the risks involved in protecting private data and restricting access to code. Most applications developed today have some need of authentication, authorization, impersonation, and Encryption Services. Microsoft has provided these features in their core framework, enabling developers to create highly secure software.

Authentication

The first piece of ASP.NET application security is authentication.

Authentication covers the validation of a client's credentials against an authority that can be in an XML file, SQL database, or some other user-defined information store. Beginner developers can easily use the built-in authentication modules available in the System.Web.Security namespace to limit access to files and objects. Advanced developers can control almost every aspect of the authentication system providing a more robust and secure environment.

Authentication in .NET comes in one of three forms:

- Windows authentication
- Forms authentication
- Microsoft Passport Service

Windows Authentication

Windows authentication is the easiest system to use for security, but does not provide the flexibility of Forms or Passport Authentication Services. In this case, the authority used for authentication can be the local server users and groups, a set of users belonging to a domain, or a membership directory, such as the Lightweight Directory Access Protocol (LDAP) or Active Directory. To set up IIS to use Windows authentication, please read the sidebar entitled "IIS and Windows Authentication."

IIS and Windows Authentication

Windows authentication in ASP.NET relies on IIS's built-in directory security (see Figure 9.1). Valid options for directory security require any one of the following:

- Basic authentication (clear-text)
- Digest authentication
- Integrated Windows Authentication (NTLM or Kerberos)

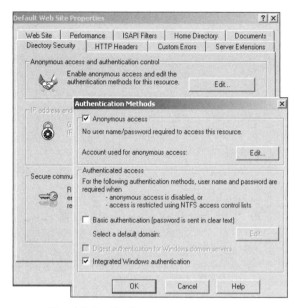

Figure 9.1 IIS directory security settings.

In addition, anonymous access can be enabled for pages that anyone can view.

Any file that requires a valid login should be secured with NTFS permissions (see Figure 9.2). Simply disable Read for both the Everyone account and the IUSR_*MachineName* account, and add Read access to the secured user account.

When an unauthenticated client accesses a page secured through NTFS, the IIS web server returns a `403.2-Forbidden` header in the response. The web browser then prompts the client for a username and password, which is submitted via either Basic (clear-text), Digest, or Integrated Windows authentication (NTLM or Kerberos) back to the server. IIS compares these credentials against the user database of the web server or domain and, if valid, allows the client to access the resource. This process is described in Figure 9.3.

As you can see in Figure 9.3, the following events are occurring:

1. Client requests "`/secure.aspx`".

2. IIS checks current impersonation context (IUSR_*MachineName* if Anonymous) against NTFS permissions.

3. If the impersonation context does not have access, NTFS returns "`Access denied`", or the browser receives "`/secure.aspx`" and the request ends.

4. The browser receives `403.2 error` and asks for credentials.

5. Credentials and requests are posted to IIS.

6. New impersonation context is granted access to "`/secure.aspx`".

7. Browser receives "`/secure.aspx`".

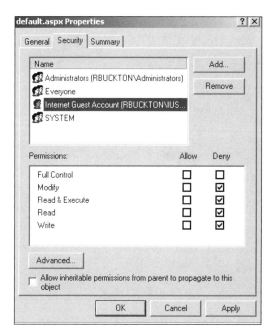

Figure 9.2   NTFS permissions.

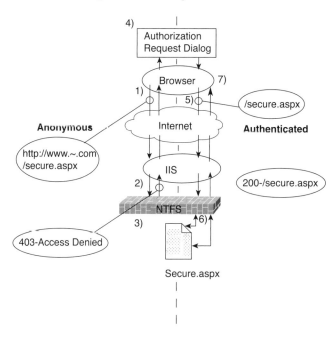

Figure 9.3   Windows authentication process.

After the credentials are validated, the `WindowsAuthenticationModule` provider creates `WindowsPrincipal` and `WindowsIdentity` objects and assigns them to the current `HttpContext`. The `WindowsPrincipal` object maps the identity of the client to a user and its role, and IIS handles all authorization to files on the server.

In addition to securing files, the `WindowsAuthenticationModule` can implement impersonation allowing secure access to system resources. Any process started by a user with a valid system account runs in that user's security context rather than the IUSR_*MachineName* account assigned by IIS. More on impersonation can be found later in this chapter.

To use Windows authentication in your web application, make sure Basic, Digest, Integrated Windows Authentication, or any combination of the three are set under Directory Security in IIS. Set the following directive in your Web.config file:

```
01 <configuration>
02   <system.web>
03
04 ...
05
06 <authentication mode="Windows"/>
07
08     ...
09   </system.web>
10 </configuration>
```

Forms Authentication

An application can define its own set of credentials rather than using the server's domain accounts, thus giving a developer control over application security without the need for access to the server's user database. This is most-commonly accomplished using *Forms authentication*, by which a user submits credentials via a Web Form. These credentials are then matched against a user-defined authority, such as an XML file or SQL database. In the case of Forms authentication, the server needs to be set to allow only Anonymous access rather than Basic, Digest, or Integrated authentication. When authenticated, an authentication ticket in the form of a cookie is stored on the browser and is used to restore the security context on subsequent pages. The following example directive shows how to use Forms authentication in your web application:

```
01 <configuration>
02   <system.web>
03
04   ...
```

```
05    <authentication mode="Forms">
06      <forms name=".ASPXAUTH"
07         loginUrl="/login.aspx"
08          protection="Encryption"/>
09    </authentication>
10
11    ...
12
13   </system.web>
14 <configuration>
```

More information on the `<forms>` tag and its subtags can be found in the section, "Web.config," at the end of the chapter.

When an application is using Forms authentication and the client's credentials have been validated, a `FormsIdentity` object is created and assigned to
a `GenericPrincipal` object in the current `HttpContext`. Developers can code
against the `HttpContext.User` object and perform more complex authorization
techniques by handling the `FormsAuthentication_OnAuthenticate` event in the
global.asax file. This enables them to add information to the current user's
Principal, such as role membership.

Microsoft Passport

Alongside ASP.NET, Microsoft has updated their Passport authentication service for the .NET framework. Passport allows the developer to create a rich
web application with strong application security, adding in Member Profile
Services and the Passport single sign-on. By using the single sign-on capabilities of Passport, a client can maintain one account for a variety of web
applications and share member profile information, thus easing the process of
creating new accounts.

You need more than the ASP.NET framework to use Passport. You
must download and install the Passport SDK that can be found at
`http://www.passport.com/business`. The SDK includes the actual runtimes
needed to communicate with the Passport Service. Finally, you have to sub-
scribe to the Passport network, registering your site on the service. To enable
the Passport Authentication Service in your application, place the following
lines in your Web.config file:

```
01 <configuration>
02   <system.web>
03
04     ...
05
06     <authentication mode="Passport"/>
07
08     ...
```

```
09   </system.web>
10 </configuration>
```

Microsoft Passport exposes the Passport Manager to .NET in the form of the `PassportIdentity` class. Passport Manager facilitates the sign-in, sign-out, and member profile functions exposed to a user. In addition to its other benefits, e-commerce web sites might choose to implement the *Passport Express Purchase Service*, allowing clients to create an online wallet to store credit card information for purchases. Passport also supports mobile devices in the form of WAP and other wireless web technologies.

Authorization

After a client has been authenticated, the next piece of the security puzzle is File and Code Authorization. When working with the Windows Authentication Service, the ASP.NET framework loads a `FileAuthorizationModule` that internally performs user and role checks against files secured with NTFS permissions.

When using Forms or Passport Authentication Services, the framework loads a `UrlAuthorizationModule` into the application that performs security checks when IIS maps the virtual URL to a physical file. The `UrlAuthorizationModule` checks the `<authorization>` section of the Web.config file for file access policies. More on the `<authorization>` node can be found in the section, "Web.config," later in this chapter.

File permissions are only the beginning of the .NET authorization system. Developers can also restrict access to object libraries and the specific methods and properties of an object through code-based access permissions. The `PrincipalPermissionAttribute` class defines code access permissions for user-based and role-based security. Setting the attribute on a class, property, or method allows the developer to restrict access to that portion of the code. Other types of authorization can be achieved directly in a Web Form or class by accessing the `HttpContext.User` object. Through the `User` object, you can access the identity of the current user, as well as test for role membership by using `User.IsInRole`.

Impersonation

Disabled by default for backward-compatibility reasons, *impersonation support* in ASP.NET allows your application to access system resources in the context of a local system or domain account. When a client connects to the web server for the first time, IIS acquires a thread to handle the request. This thread is initially created in the context of the IUSR_MachineName account on the web server. When using impersonation, IIS attempts to change the security context of the thread to a local system user. Impersonation allows the web application to perform actions in the context of the user for accessing system resources, running secured code, monitoring performance counters, and more.

Whenever a client has authenticated, the authentication token IIS creates is then used for impersonation. An entire application can be set to impersonate a specified user when authenticated, as in the case of Passport and Forms authentication where the authentication token might not match a local system account. To enable impersonation in your application, add the following node to your Web.config file:

```
01 <configuration>
02   <system.web>
03
04     ...
05
06     <identity impersonate="true" username="username" password="password"/>
07
08     ...
09
10   </system.web>
11 </configuration>
```

More on the `<identity>` node can be found in the section, "Web.config," at the end of this chapter.

Cryptography

Cryptographic Services provide a means of securing information stored on the server. Using these services, you can encrypt strings and files using some of the more widely used and powerful encryption algorithms.

Microsoft has provided a .NET version of their CryptoAPI library in the `System.Security.Cryptography` namespace. Included in this new library are various implementations of common symmetric (single key) and asymmetric (public and private key) encryption algorithms. Instead of using variables and files for encryption, Microsoft uses a `CryptoStream` object that encrypts data passing through any object that inherits from the `CryptoStream` stream. More on `CryptoStream` and the different Cryptographic Service Providers (CSPs) can be found at the end of this chapter in the section, "Encryption."

Applying Security in ASP.NET Applications

The following sections demonstrate the basic principals behind security in ASP.NET.

Authentication

The following examples detail the use of the different authentication methods of ASP.NET. Please refer to Chapter 3, "Configuring ASP.NET Applications," for more detail on the Web.config file.

Windows Authentication

The `<authentication>` tag in the Web.config file (see Listing 9.1) sets your web application to use Windows authentication. This setting can be placed only in the web application's root Web.config file and propagates across all folders in the application. Please be sure to refer to the sidebar entitled "IIS and Windows Authentication" in the beginning of this chapter to make sure your application is set to work correctly. IIS attempts to authorize a client's credentials against the user database on the server. You can then access that information through code. Listing 9.2 shows a Windows authentication example.

Listing 9.1 **Web.config**

```
01   <configuration>
02     <system.web>
03
04       ...
05
06       <authentication mode="Windows"/>
07
08       <authorization>
09         <allow users="?"/>
10         <deny users="*"/>
11       </authorization>
12
13       ...
14
15     </system.web>
16   </configuration>
```

Listing 9.2 **admin.aspx**

```
01   <%@ Import Namespace="System.Web" %>
02   <%@ Import Namespace="System.Web.UI.WebControls" %>
03   <%@ Import Namespace="System.Web.Security" %>
04
05   <html>
06     <head>
07       <title>
08         Server Administration
```

continues ▶

Listing 9.2 **Continued**

```
09        </title>
10        <script runat="server" language="VB">
11          Public Sub Page_Load(Sender As Object, E As EventArgs)
12
13            If Request.IsAuthenticated Then
14              UserName.Text = HttpContext.Current.User.Identity.Name
15              If HttpContext.Current.User.IsInRole("Administrators") Then
16                manageAllButton.Visible = True
17              End If
18            End If
19          End Sub
20
21          Public Sub manageAllButton_OnClick(Sender As Object, _
22                                             E As EventArgs)
23            Response.Redirect("manageall.aspx")
24          End Sub
25
26        </script>
27      </head>
28      <body>
29        <p>
30          <b>Username:</b> <asp:label runat="server" id="UserName"/>
31        </p>
32        <hr>
33        <p>
34          Available options:
35          <br>
36          <a href="manage.aspx">Manage my Account</a>
37          <br>
38          <asp:linkButton runat="server"
39                          id="manageAllButton"
40                          onclick="manageAllButton_OnClick"
41                          text-"Manage All Accounts"
42                          visible="False"/>
43        </ul>
44        </p>
45      </body>
46  </html>
```

First, examine the <authorization> section of Web.config. The <allow> and
<deny> rules inside of an <authorization> section perform validation in order
of placement. As soon as a rule has been met, the authorization fitting that
rule is used. In this example, a global policy is set that allows only authenticated users; thus, denying everyone else. The asterisk (*) in the users attribute
specifies all users, and the question mark (?) specifies authenticated users. If
an authenticated user is validated against this authorization scheme, it stops
checking as soon as it hits the <allow> tag. In addition to the "?" and "*"

symbols used in the "users" attribute, you can specify a list of users separated by commas.

When a client attempts to access admin.aspx, they are prompted with a username or password dialog box—depending on what browser they are using. That authorization information is processed by IIS, and their credentials are matched against the server user database. After validating their credentials, IIS serves back the secure.aspx page with the options available based upon the user's role-membership.

Forms Authentication

To use Forms authentication, you must set up the Web.config file to use the service. Listing 9.3 shows a basic setup for Forms authentication, Listing 9.4 demonstrates a basic login script, and Listing 9.5 is the default.aspx web page used to test the example.

Listing 9.3 **Web.config**

```
01  <configuration>
02    <system.web>
03
04      ...
05
06      <authentication mode="Forms">
07        <forms name=".ASPXAUTH"
08               loginurl="/login.aspx"
09               protection="Encryption">
10          <credentials passwordformat="SHA1">
11            <user name="Ron" password="AB54B7H109AE41F0"/>
12            <user name="Scott" password="0F14AE901H7B45BA"/>
13          </credentials>
14        </forms>
15      </authentication>
16
17      <authorization>
18        <allow users="Ron,Scott"/>
19        <deny users="*"/>
20      </authorization>
21
22      ...
23
24    </system.web>
25  </configuration>
```

Listing 9.4 **login.aspx**

```
01   <%@ Import Namespace="System.Web" %>
02   <%@ Import Namespace="System.Web.UI.WebControls" %>
03   <%@ Import Namespace="System.Web.Security" %>
04
05   <html>
06     <head>
07       <title>Login Page</title>
08       <script runat="server" language="VB">
09         Public Sub loginButton_OnClick(Sender As Object, _
10                                        E As EventArgs)
11
12           If FormsAuthentication.Authenticate(UserName.Text, _
13                                                Password.Text) Then
14
15             FormsAuthentication.RedirectFromLoginPage(UserName.Text, _
16                                                       Persist.Checked)
17           Else
18
19             ErrorLabel.Text = "Invalid Username/Password combination"
20
21           End If
22
23         End Sub
24
25       </script>
26     </head>
27     <body>
28       <form runat="server">
29         <p>
30           <b>Please Log in</b>
31         </p>
32         <hr>
33         <p>
34           The resource you have requested requires a valid login.
35           Please provide your username and password below.
36         </p>
37         <p>
38           <asp:label runat="server"
39                      id="ErrorLabel"/>
40         </p>
41         <p>
42           <table>
43             <tr>
44               <td>Username:</td>
45               <td>
46                 <asp:textbox runat="server"
47                              id="UserName"
48                              TextMode="SingleLine"/>
49               </td>
50             </tr>
```

```
51              <tr>
52               <td>Password:</td>
53               <td>
54                <asp:textbox runat="server"
55                             id="Password"
56                             TextMode="Password"/>
57               </td>
58              </tr>
59              <tr>
60               <td colspan="2">
61                 <asp:checkbox runat="server"
62                             id="Persist"
63                             Text="Keep me logged in between
64                                 browser restarts"/>
65               </td>
66              </tr>
67              <tr>
68               <td colspan="2">
69                 <asp:linkButton runat="server"
70                             id="loginButton"
71                             text="Log In"
72                             onclick="loginButton_OnClick"/>
73               </td>
74              </tr>
75            </table>
76          </p>
77        </form>
78      </body>
79    </html>
```

Listing 9.5 **default.aspx**

```
01    <%@ Import Namespace="System.Web" %>
02    <%@ Import Namespace="System.Web.UI.WebControls" %>
03    <%@ Import Namespace="System.Web.Security" %>
04
05    <html>
06      <head>
07        <title>Secure Page</title>
08        <script runat="server" language="VB">
09          Public Sub signoutButton_OnClick(Sender As Object, _
10                                          E As EventArgs)
11          FormsAuthentication.SignOut()
12
13          Response.Redirect("/login.aspx")
14
15        End Sub
16        </script>
17      </head>
```

continues ▶

Listing 9.5 **Continued**

```
18    <body>
19      <p>
20        <b>Welcome</b>
21      </p>
22      <p>
23        This is a secure page.
24        <br>
25        <asp:linkButton runat="server"
26                        id="signoutButton"
27                        text="Sign out"
28                        onclick="signoutButton_OnClick"/>
29      </p>
30    </body>
31  </html>
```

When using Forms authentication, you must add some additional configuration options to your Web.config file. The <forms> node specifies values, such as the authentication cookie, the URL of the login script, and the method with which to protect the authentication ticket.

In this example, the <credentials> configuration key is also used, allowing access to the built-in FormsAuthentication.Authenticate method. When this method is called, it validates the client's clear-text username and a SHA1 hash of the client's password against the credentials stored in the Web.config file.

A client who accesses a restricted resource is redirected to the page specified by the "loginUrl" attribute of the <forms> configuration key. The login page is available to all users—regardless of settings specified in the <authorization> node of Web.config— and normally takes in the value ReturnURL in the query string.

Inside the login.aspx file, the client types in his clear-text username and password that they are then sent through a form submission to the server. Because this information is submitted without encryption, it is necessary to use SSL to communicate the password securely. When the server receives the authentication request from the client, the password is hashed using the configured authority's hashing format (SHA1) and is compared against the encrypted password for that user. If the credentials match, FormsAuthentication.Authenticate returns true. FormsAuthentication.RedirectFromLoginPage is called to create an authentication ticket and redirect the client back to the page they previously attempted to access.

Optionally, the client can decide to persist his connection. The authentication ticket is normally scoped to the lifetime of the browser. When the client closes the browser, the cookie removes itself from memory and disk. A persisted authentication ticket remains between restarts of the browser, and maintains a security context until the client signs off manually.

Passport Authentication

Microsoft has included Passport, their Web-Based Authentication Service, in the ASP.NET framework. Through the use of the Passport Service, you can provide users with a very secure single sign-in for all their web applications. To use Microsoft Passport, you must first download and install the Passport SDK, and apply for a Passport site ID. After you have completed Microsoft's implementation steps, you can move on to building Passport authentication into your web application.

Microsoft exposes the Passport API through the `System.Web.Security` namespace in the form of the `PassportIdentity` class. Listing 9.6 describes how Passport Services are included in your Web.config file. Listing 9.7 shows how you can use the basic facilities of the `PassportIdentity` class to sign in using the Passport Authentication Service.

Listing 9.6 **Web.config**

```
01   <configuration>
02     <system.web>
03
04       ...
05
06       <authentication mode="Passport">
07       </authentication>
08
09       ...
10
11     </system.web>
12   </configuration>
```

Listing 9.7 **default.aspx**

```
01   <%@ Import Namespace="System.Web.Security" %>
02   <html>
03     <head>
04       <script runat="server" language="vb">
05         Private Sub Page_Load(ByVal Sender As Object, _
06                                ByVal e As EventArgs)
```

continues ▶

Listing 9.7 **Continued**

```
07
08          Dim lUseDefault As Integer = -1
09          Dim lTimeWindow As Integer = 7200 ' Two hours
10        Dim fForceLogin As Boolean = False ' No manual sign-in
11        Dim SelfURL As String = "http://" & Request.Url.Host & _
12            Request.Url.AbsolutePath
13        Dim PassportMgr As PassportIdentity = _
14            CType(Context.Current.User.Identity, PassportIdentity)
15
16        If PassportMgr.GetFromNetworkServer() Then
17          Response.Redirect(SelfURL)
18        End If
19
20        If PassportMgr.GetIsAuthenticated(lTimeWindow, fForceLogin, _
21            False) Then
22
23          lblMessage.Text = "Welcome to the site!"
24
25        ElseIf PassportMgr.HasTicket Then
26          PassportMgr.LoginUser(HttpUtility.UrlEncode(SelfURL), _
27                                lTimeWindow, _
28                                fForceLogin, _
29                                vbNullString, _
30                                lUseDefault, _
31                                vbNullString, _
32                                lUseDefault, _
33                                False, _
34                                vbNullString)
35
36        Else
37
38          lblMessage.Text = "Please Sign In."
39
40        End If
41
42        lblLogoTag.Text = _
43          PassportMgr.LogoTag2(HttpUtility.UrlEncode(SelfURL), _
44                               lTimeWindow, _
45                               fForceLogin, _
46                               vbNullString, _
47                               lUseDefault, _
48                               False, _
49                               vbNullString, _
50                               lUseDefault, _
51                               False)
52
53      End Sub
54    </script>
55  </head>
56  <body>
```

```
57      <asp:label runat="server" id="lblMessage"/>
58      <br>
59      <asp:label runat="server" id="lblLogoTag"/>
60    </body>
61  </html>
```

To use the `PassportIdentity` object, you need a little more information on what each of the functions in the example does. The `GetFromNetworkServer` property returns a Boolean value that is true if the page was just accessed when returning from the Passport authentication server. In that case, it might be useful to rid your client of the unnecessary `querystring` data that is now stored in a cookie on the client's browser. This can be done by redirecting back to the current page.

`LoginUser` and `LogoTag2` both share three common properties important to this example. The first is the return `url` property, which—when UrlEncoded—is passed to the Passport authentication server as a means of returning the user to the page after authentication. The second parameter is a time window, which specifies the time in minutes since either the user last manually signed in, or since the passport ticket was silently or manually refreshed. The third parameter is a Boolean value that determines whether to apply the time window to the last manual login if true, or the last manual or silent refresh of the passport ticket if false.

`LoginUser` writes a `302-Redirect` status header to the browser, which causes the client to redirect to the Passport authentication server. The client's ticket, if it exists, is refreshed and rewritten to the browser. The Passport authentication server would then redirect the user back to the page specified as the return URL.

`LogoTag2` returns a string that contains an image tag for Passport, and a link to the Passport authentication server. When clients do not have a Passport authentication ticket, they can click the image to sign in. When the link on the image is clicked, it performs the same steps as previously mentioned for LoginUser—forwarding clients to the Passport authentication server and returning them to the specified return URL. When clients have a Passport authentication ticket stored on their browser, `LogoTag2` outputs a link and image enabling the client to sign out.

Most of the other parameters listed are not used and can be left to their default values (`vbNullString` for strings and `-1` for integers). More information on their use can be found in the Passport SDK.

Handle Authentication Events in global.asax

Each of the authentication modules raises an event in the global.asax file that can be handled at runtime and scripted against (see Listing 9.8). The `OnAuthenticate` method is called whenever a client requests an authenticated resource on the web server. It is at this point that you as the developer can assign roles to a user and perform system-wide checks against an authenticated client.

Listing 9.8 **global.asax**

```
01    <%@ Import Namespace="System.Data" %>
02    <%@ Import Namespace="System.Data.SqlClient" %>
03    <%@ Import Namespace="System.Security" %>
04    <%@ Import Namespace="System.Security.Principal" %>
05
06    <script language="VB" runat="server">
07
08      Public Sub FormsAuthentication_OnAuthenticate(Sender As Object, _
09                                                     E As EventArgs)
10
11        ' If the current request is authenticated...
12        If Request.IsAuthenticated = True Then
13
14          ' Create SQL Connection
15          Dim sqlConn As New SqlConnection("DSN=UsersDb,UID=sa,PWD=")
16
17          ' Initialize the SQL Statement and UserName parameter
18          Dim sSqlCmd As String = "Select [Role] From UserRoles Where UserName = ?"
19          Dim sqlPrmUserName As New SqlParameter("@UserName", _
20            HttpContext.Current.User.Identity.Name)
21
22          ' Initialize the other SQL components
23          Dim sqlDataAdapter As New SqlDataAdapter()
24          Dim sqlDataSetRoles As DataSet
25          Dim sqlDataView As DataView
26
27          ' Set up the data adapter to get our role information from the database
28          sqlDataAdapter.SelectCommand = New SqlCommand(sSqlCmd, sqlConn)
29          sqlDataAdapter.SelectCommand.Parameters.Add(sqlPrmUserName)
30
31          ' Connect and fill the DataSet with the results of the query
32          sqlDataAdapter.Fill(sqlDataSetRoles)
33
34          ' Create a view of the results
35          sqlDataView = new DataView(sqlDataSetRoles.Tables(0))
36
37          ' Initialize the Roles array
38          Dim Roles As String()
39
40          ReDim Roles(sqlDataView.Count)
```

```
41
42        ' Fill Roles with values from the view
43        For I = 0 To sqlDataView.Count - 1
44          Roles(I) = sqlDataView.Item(I).Item(0)
45        Next I
46
47        ' Create a new principal to hold the identity and roles
48        Dim prncGeneric As New GenericPrincipal( _
49          HttpContext.Current.User.Identity, _
50          Roles)
51        ' Assign the new principal to the current user
52        HttpContext.Current.User = prncGeneric
53
54      End If
55
56    End Sub
57
58  </script>
```

In this example, the `FormsAuthentication_OnAuthenticate` event is used to add role information to the current user, based on the identity stored in the authentication ticket. In this case, the authority is a SQL Server database, so a connection must be made to gather the role information.

To assign the roles, simply place them into a string array and pass them to the constructor for a `GenericPrincipal` object. Then, replace the current principal assigned to the `User` property of the current `HttpContext`. Any page that uses `User.IsInRole`(*role*) now matches the role specified against one in the array passed.

Code-Based Permissions

Simple code-based permissions can be assigned as an attribute of a class, property, or method. During instantiation of the class or execution of the object, permissions are checked against the current client's principal and only then can the process continue. Listing 9.9 demonstrates a basic use of the `PrincipalPermissionAttribute`.

Listing 9.9   **BusinessLogic.vb**

```
01  Imports System.Security.Permissions
02  ...
03
04  Public Class BusinessLogic
05
06    Public Overloads Function GetAccountInfo(ByVal Username as String, _
```

continues ▶

Listing 9.9 **Continued**

```
07                                                    ByVal Password as String) _
08                                                    As DataView
09      ...
10      ' Data Access Call
11      ...
12   End Function
13
14   <PrincipalPermissionAttribute(SecurityAction.Demand, _
15                             Role="AccountManagers")> _
16   Public Overloads Function GetAccountInfo(ByVal Username as String) _
17                                       As DataView
18      ...
19      ' Permission protected version of GetAccountInfo that does
20      ' not require password access
21      ...
22   End Function
23
24 End Class
```

Multiple users and roles for built-in permissions can be specified by adding
more `PrincipalPermissionAttributes` to the attribute definition.

Encryption

The following examples detail the use of Cryptographic Services in the
ASP.NET framework. The basic implementations of the SHA1 hashing algorithm and the DES block encryption cipher should start you on your way to
robust encryption.

Create a Password Hash Using SHA1

Listing 9.10 shows an example of computing a SHA1 hash on a key for use
with other cryptographic algorithms.

Listing 9.10 **crypto.vb**

```
01   Imports System.Text
02   Imports System.Security.Cryptography
03
04   Public Module MyCryptoLib
05
06   ...
30
31    Public Sub GenerateKey( _
32              ByVal Password As String, _
33              ByVal BlockSize As Integer, _
```

```
34                      ByRef Key() As Byte, _
35                      ByRef IV() As Byte)
36
37        Dim I As Integer
38
39        ' data() holds the ascii representation of the password
40        Dim data() As Byte = Encoding.ASCII.GetBytes(Password)
41
42        ' hash() will hold the temporary result of the hash
43        Dim hash() As Byte
44
45        ' sha is the implementation of the SHA1 CSP
46        Dim sha As New SHA1CryptoServiceProvider()
47
48        ' We must compute an accurate Key and Initialization Vector (IV) for the
49        ' block size of the encryption Algorithm we wish to use.  The BlockSize in
50        ' bits is divided by 8 to convert it into the size of the byte array
51        Dim len As Integer = BlockSize / 8
52
53        ' We must dimension the sizes of the key and IV to hold the resulting hash
54        ReDim Key(len - 1)
55        ReDim IV(len - 1)
56
57        ' Compute the Hash from the ASCII key
58        hash = sha.ComputeHash(data)
59
60        ' Get a portion of the resulting hash to use for the key
61        For I = 0 To len - 1
62          Key(I) = hash(I)
63        Next
64
65        ' Get a portion of the resulting hash to use for the IV
66        For I = len To (2 * len) - 1
67          IV(I - len) = hash(I)
68        Next
69
70      End Sub
71
72      ...
73
74 End Module
```

In the preceding example, the function GenerateKey takes in a string that designates the password or key that needs to be hashed for some other cryptographic algorithm. The Password is converted into a byte array using the GetBytes method of the Encoding class. This byte array is passed to the SHA1 Cryptographic Service Provider (CSP) and a hash is computed using the ComputeHash method. From the resulting hash, a correct size key for the algorithm is gathered and uses the rest of the resulting hash for the Initialization

Vector (IV). Both of these byte arrays are used in later functions to perform encryption and decryption.

Encrypt/Decrypt a String Using a Symmetric Algorithm

Symmetric algorithms, such as DES, are used to encrypt a file or string with a single private key. With a key created using GenerateKey, you can apply ciphers, such as DES, to an open stream. Listing 9.11 shows this in practice using a MemoryStream object to store the values in memory rather than in a file on the filesystem.

Listing 9.11   **crypto.vb**

```
001   Imports System.Text
002   Imports System.Security.Cryptography
003
004   Public Module MyCryptoLib
005
006   ...
007
008    Public Function Encrypt( _
009                   ByVal s As String, _
010                   ByVal Password As String _
011                 ) As String
012
013      ' Get a Byte array of the data to be encrypted
014      Dim data() As Byte = Encoding.ASCII.GetBytes(s)
015
016      ' Get an instance of the CSP
017      Dim des As New DESCryptoServiceProvider()
018
019      ' Create arrays to hold the key and IV for this cipher
020      Dim key() As Byte
021      Dim iv() As Byte
022
023      ' Generate a compatible key and IV for the DES cipher
024      GenerateKey(Password, des.BlockSize, key, iv)
025      des.Key = key
026      des.IV = iv
027
028      ' Create a safe in-memory IO stream to remove the reliance on temporary files
029      Dim mout As New MemoryStream()
030
031      ' Create an encryption stream
032      Dim encStream As New CryptoStream(mout, des.CreateEncryptor(),
➥CryptoStreamMode.Write)
033
034      Dim i As Long
035
036      ' Write the contents of the string to the stream in chunks
```

```
037    For i = 0 To data.Length - 1 Step 4096
038      encStream.Write(data, i * 4096, data.Length - (i * 4096))
039    Next
040
041    ' Flush the output to get accurate results
042    encStream.FlushFinalBlock()
043
044    ' Create a storage array to hold the result of the encryption
045    Dim result(mout.Length - 1) As Byte
046
047    ' Seek to the beginning of the Memory Stream
048    mout.Seek(0, SeekOrigin.Begin)
049
050    ' Read the stream into result()
051    mout.Read(result, 0, result.Length)
052
053    ' Tidy up our open streams
054    encStream.Close()
055    mout.Close()
056
057    ' Convert the result into a Base64 encoded string to preserve the
058    ' binary integrity of the encrypted result and return the value
059    Return Convert.ToBase64String(result)
060
061  End Function
062
063  Public Function Decrypt( _
064                    ByVal s As String, _
065                    ByVal Password As String _
066                  ) As String
067
068    ' Get a Byte array of the data to be decrypted
069    Dim data() As Byte = Convert.FromBase64String(s)
070
071    ' Get an instance of the CSP
072    Dim des As New DESCryptoServiceProvider()
073
074    ' Create arrays to hold the key and IV for this cipher
075    Dim key() As Byte
076    Dim iv() As Byte
077
078    ' Generate a compatible key and IV for the DES cipher
079    GenerateKey(Password, des.BlockSize, key, iv)
080    des.Key = key
081    des.IV = iv
082
083    ' Create a safe in-memory IO stream to remove the reliance on temporary files
084    Dim mout As New MemoryStream()
085
086    ' Create an decryption stream
087    Dim decStream As New CryptoStream(mout, des.CreateDecryptor(),
➥CryptoStreamMode.Write)
```

continues ▶

Listing 9.11 **Continued**

```
088
089    Dim i As Long
090
091    ' Write the contents of the string to the stream in chunks
092    For i = 0 To data.Length - 1 Step 4096
093      decStream.Write(data, i * 4096, data.Length - (i * 4096))
094    Next
095
096    ' Flush the output to get accurate results
097    decStream.FlushFinalBlock()
098
099    ' Create a storage array to hold the result of the decryption
100    Dim result(mout.Length - 1) As Byte
101
102    ' Seek to the beginning of the Memory Stream
103    mout.Seek(0, SeekOrigin.Begin)
104
105    ' Read the stream into result()
106    mout.Read(result, 0, result.Length)
107
108    ' Tidy up our open streams
109    encStream.Close()
110    mout.Close()
111
112    ' Convert the result back to ASCII text
113    Return Encoding.ASCII.GetString(result)
114
115  End Function
116
117 ...
118
119 End Module
```

In this example, two functions are provided for encrypting and decrypting a string using the DES Cryptographic Service Provider. To perform this encryption, you need to perform several basic steps. First, you must convert the string data into a useable array of bytes. The ASP.NET framework facilitates this by providing you with the Encoding class— enabling you to perform a quick conversion from ASCII text to a byte array.

Next, a hash for the key and initialization vectors (IV) is needed. The key is a block of 8 bytes, or 64 bits, which is used to determine how the encryption affects the string. The IV is a length of bytes that are appended to the encrypted array to increase the strength of the encryption. Using the key and the IV, a unique cipher is created that can be reversed only by providing the same key and IV.

To perform encryption, an IO Stream from which to work is needed. In this case, the `MemoryStream` object is used, providing a safe means of reading and writing buffered data to a block of memory—without the use of an intermediary temporary file. This `MemoryStream` can be used as the container for data written to the cryptographic stream.

To perform the actual encryption, an instance of the `CryptoStream` class is needed. The `CryptoStream` performs the actual encryption, ciphering data sent to the input buffer—using an encryptor or decryptor created by our current CSP. DES is a block cipher; data inside each block is encrypted in a single operation. Due to this fact, the input data is cycled through incrementally until the entire string has been fed to the `CryptoStream`.

The results of this operation are stored in the `MemoryStream` created earlier. To access the data in this operation, the `"FlushFinalBlock"` method of `CryptoStream` is called to be sure that all cipher operations have completed. Next, a container is created to store the information inside of the `MemoryStream`. The contents of the `MemoryStream` are read into the container. This array is then converted into a Base64 string to preserve binary integrity, allowing decryption at a later time.

Decryption follows the same basic steps, except the DES decryptor is used rather than the DES encryptor. The encrypted data is converted from the Base64 string back into a byte array and passed through the decryptor. The result can be converted back into ASCII and is then readable.

Encrypt or Decrypt a File Using a Symmetric Algorithm

Encrypting a `MemoryStream` and a `FileStream` are not entirely different. The example in Listing 9.12 shows how file Encryption Services can be added to the application.

Listing 9.12 **crypto.vb**

```
001    Imports System.Text
002    Imports System.Security.Cryptography
003
004    Public Module MyCryptoLib
005
006    ...
007
008    Public Sub EncryptFile( _
009              ByVal File1 As String, _
010              ByVal File2 As String, _
011              ByVal Password As String _
012          )
013
```

continues ▶

Listing 9.12 **Continued**

```
014     ' Get an instance of the CSP
015     Dim des As New DESCryptoServiceProvider()
016
017     ' Create arrays to hold the key and IV for this cipher
018     Dim key() As Byte
019     Dim iv() As Byte
020
021     ' Generate a compatible key and IV for the DES cipher
022     GenerateKey(Password, des.BlockSize, key, iv)
023     des.Key = key
024     des.IV = iv
025
026     ' Create FileStreams for input and output
027     Dim filIn As New FileStream(File1, FileMode.Open , FileAccess.Read)
028     Dim filOut As New FileStream(File2, FileMode.OpenOrCreate, FileAccess.Write)
029
030     ' Create an encryption stream
031     Dim encStream As New CryptoStream(filOut, des.CreateEncryptor(),
➥CryptoStreamMode.Write)
032
033     ' Create a container to hold blocks for our cipher
034     Dim data(4096) As Byte
035
036     ' Variables to hold position information for the FileStream
037     Dim len As Integer
038     Dim readLen As Integer
039     Dim fileLen As Integer = filIn.Length
040
041     Do While readLen < fileLen
042       ' Get block and actual block size
043       len = filIn.Read(data, 0, 4096)
044
045       ' Write block to cipher
046       encStream.Write(data, 0, len)
047
048       ' increment size of read characters
049       readLen += len
050     Loop
051
052     ' Close streams to flush the buffer and write our file
053     encStream.Close()
054     filIn.Close()
055     filOut.Close()
056
057   End Sub
058
059   Public Sub DecryptFile( _
060                   ByVal File1 As String, _
061                   ByVal File2 As String, _
062                   ByVal Password As String _
```

```
063                    )
064
065     ' Get an instance of the CSP
066     Dim des As New DESCryptoServiceProvider()
067
068     ' Create arrays to hold the key and IV for this cipher
069     Dim key() As Byte
070     Dim iv() As Byte
071
072     ' Generate a compatible key and IV for the DES cipher
073     GenerateKey(Password, des.BlockSize, key, iv)
074     des.Key = key
075     des.IV = iv
076
077     ' Create FileStreams for input and output
078     Dim filIn As New FileStream(File1, FileMode.Open , FileAccess.Read)
079     Dim filOut As New FileStream(File2, FileMode.OpenOrCreate, FileAccess.Write)
080
081     ' Create an decryption stream
082     Dim decStream As New CryptoStream(filOut, des.CreateDecryptor(),
➥CryptoStreamMode.Write)
083
084     ' Create a container to hold blocks for our cipher
085     Dim data(4096) As Byte
086
087     ' Variables to hold position information for the FileStream
088     Dim len As Integer
089     Dim readLen As Integer
090     Dim fileLen As Integer = filIn.Length
091
092     Do While readLen < fileLen
093       ' Get block and actual block size
094       len = filIn.Read(data, 0, 4096)
095
096       ' Write block to cipher
097       decStream.Write(data, 0, len)
098
099       ' increment size of read characters
100       readLen += len
101     Loop
102
103     ' Close streams to flush the buffer and write our file
104     decStream.Close()
105     filIn.Close()
106     filOut.Close()
107
108   End Sub
109
110 End Module
```

This example is almost the same as Listing 9.11, with the exception of the input and output `FileStream` objects. In Listing 9.12, a container array is used to store the blocks of data for the cipher as the file is read. The resulting output is encrypted or decrypted, depending on the function call. For more details on this process, refer to the previous example on encrypting a string.

Inside ASP.NET Security

Security in ASP.NET covers quite a few fronts and not all could be mentioned here. The following sections include a description of many of the key pieces needed for the different types of security available.

Web.config

The Web.config file stores much of the necessary information for security services, such as authentication, authorization, and impersonation. It can also serve as a user authority for authorized users. Listing 9.13 lists the valid settings for security in the Web.config file.

Listing 9.13 **Valid Settings for Web.config**

```
01 <configuration>
02   <system.web>
03     ...
04     <authentication mode="{Windows|Forms|Passport|None}">
05       <forms name="CookieName"
06              loginUrl="PathToLoginScript"
07              timeout="minutes"
08              protection="{None|All|Encryption|Validation}"
09              path="pathForCookie">
10 <credentials passwordformat="{Clear|MD5|SHA1}">
11 <user name="UserName" password="Password"/>
12       </credentials>
13       </forms>
14       <passport redirectUrl="internalUrl"/>
15</authentication>
16     ...
17     <authorization>
18       <allow users="UserList" roles="RoleList"/>
19       <deny users="UserList" roles="RoleList"/>
20     </authorization>
21...
22     <identity impersonate="{True|False}"
23              userName="Domain\AccountToImpersonate"
24              password="Password"/>
25...
26   </system.web>
```

```
27
28  <location path="UrlOfResource">
29<system.web>
30      <authorization>
31         ...
32      </authorization>
33    </system.web>
34  </location>
35
36</configuration>
```

When using Windows authentication, the <forms> and <passport> entities are ignored as IIS manages authentication. Forms authentication uses only the <forms> configuration tag and its subtags, whereas Passport authentication uses the <passport> tag. If the authentication mode is set to none, it is assumed the application uses only anonymous users or a custom authentication system is in place.

The <forms> tag contains several key attributes, such as the forms attribute that specifies the name of the cookie or form element used to pass the authentication ticket to subsequent pages. The loginUrl attribute specifies the location of the login page for unauthorized requests. Any file specified here has full access privileges by any user. The protection attribute specifies the method used to protect authentication tickets in the form or cookie and can be set to one of the following:

- **"None"**—Perform no encryption or validation on the ticket.

- **"Encryption"**—Ticket is encrypted using Triple-DES or DES encryption, but no data validation is performed.

- **"Validation"**—Uses a validation scheme that implements a Message Authentication Code (MAC) and is used to verify that the ticket has not been altered in transit.

- **"All"**—Uses both encryption and validation schemes.

The timeout attribute sets the time as an integer of minutes that the ticket should last before expiring. A ticket expires after a period of time specified in timeout, following the last time a client request was received. The path attribute is used to specify the valid virtual path for a cookie used for the authentication ticket.

Below the <forms> tag is the optional <credentials> tag that acts as an internal authority for authentic users. The passwordFormat attribute specifies what cryptographic hashing algorithm to use when creating the encrypted password.

Multiple `<user>` tags can appear inside `<credentials>`, each specifying a clear-text username and password dependent on the `passwordFormat` attribute of the `<credentials>` section. When `FormsAuthentication.Authenticate` is called, it compares the username and password passed as arguments to this authority for validation.

The `<passport>` tag is used only when the authentication mode is set to `"Passport"` and contains only one attribute. The `redirectUrl` attribute specifies a local URL to use to begin the Passport login.

The `<authorization>` tag specifies the policy that grants access to a resource. When the `<authorization>` tag is present in the first `<system.web>` tag, it is applied globally to every resource. If the tag is present below a `<location>` tag, the authorization policy applies only to the path listed in the `path` attribute of the location. In addition to using the `<location>` tag, folder-specific configuration options can be specified by placing a Web.config file in the subfolder of the application that you want to change. This approach is more modular. However, it is easier to loose track of configuration settings. The `<location>` tag lets you specify settings for `<authentication>` on a per URL basis. The `path` attribute can be any folder or file underneath the web application root.

The policies specified in the `<authorization>` tag are set to either allow or deny access. The `<allow>` and `<deny>` tags have only two attributes—users and roles. The users attribute contains either a comma-delimited list of usernames, the question mark (?) for any authenticated user, or the asterisk (*) for any client. When a client attempts to access a resource that has `<authorization>` permissions set, the `FileAuthorizationModule` looks at each `<allow>` and `<deny>` tag in the order it is placed in the Web.config file. Whenever one of these policies matches the request, that policy is used first. If an `<allow users="*"/>` tag appears before a `<deny users="Ron"/>` tag, the user `"Ron"` can still access the site because the `<deny>` tag is never reached.

Impersonation is disabled by default but can be enabled in the application by setting the `impersonate` property of the `<identity>` tag. When `impersonate` is set to `true`, IIS attempts to map the credentials supplied when authorizing the request against a local system account. In lieu of this, you can also force any authorized user to impersonate a specific user account specified by the `userName` and `password` attributes.

The right combination of these settings can enrich the security of your web application and provide tighter control over access to information. More information on the Web.config file can be found in Chapter 3, "Configuring ASP.NET Applications."

System. Web. Security

The System.Web.Security namespace contains the different authentication modules used in the ASP.NET framework. The various modules allow you to interact with the Authentication Services built in to IIS and ASP.NET.

FormsAuthentication

The FormsAuthentication class contains several static methods and properties that can be used to work with the FormsAuthentication Service. When your application is configured to authenticate with forms, the ASP.NET framework creates what is known as a FormsAuthenticationTicket. This contains the necessary information to restore your security context on subsequent requests to application resources. This ticket is encrypted and stored either in a cookie on a cookies-enabled browser, or in a form variable or query string parameter when server-side forms are used.

Authentication is done by either using the FormsAuthentication.Authenticate method, which matches a username and password against the credentials stored in your Web.config file, or through a custom authentication system, such as comparing values stored in a SQL Server database. Once authenticated you can use any of the various forms of ticket persistence. The RedirectFromLoginPage method takes a value, such as a username, and persist it in an authentication ticket. Once the ticket has been created and stored, the method posts the user back to the resource they had attempted to access.

In addition, you could use the Encrypt, Decrypt, SetAuthCookie, and GetAuthCookie static methods of the FormsAuthentication class to perform custom manipulation of the FormsAuthenticationTicket. This kind of control enables you to insert additional information into the ticket and persist it as you see fit.

FormsAuthenticationTicket

A FormsAuthenticationTicket contains information necessary to maintain your security context between subsequent requests for a resource. The ticket contains a variety of information, including username, IssueDate, and the user-defined UserData fields. The ticket can be encrypted into a string using the FormsAuthentication class and then stored, either in a server form or a cookie for re-authentication.

By creating the ticket yourself, you can have more control over parameters, such as persistence, expiration, and additional information, that are not provided in the base FormsAuthentication class. The FormsAuthenticationTicket has a variety of overloaded constructors that allow you to specify as little or as much information as you need for your application.

FormsIdentity

After a client has been authenticated, the `HttpContext.User.Identity` object contains an instance of a `FormsIdentity` class. Through the `FormsIdentity` class, you can access the authentication ticket used to re-establish the security context, the name of the user, and a flag indicating whether authentication has taken place.

In a custom authentication system, you could construct your own `FormsIdentity` object by passing a decrypted authentication ticket to the constructor. The `FormsIdentity` object is then assigned in the constructor to a `GenericPrincipal` object that would replace the `HttpContext.Current.User`.

PassportIdentity

In Microsoft Passport, the `HttpContext.Current.User.Identity` object is instead an instance of the `PassportIdentity` class. This class provides access to functionality needed to interface with the Passport Authentication Service. Through the `PassportIdentity` class, you can access the client's Passport member profile, encrypt and decrypt data through passport for your site, and sign on and off the client from their passport account. For more details on the `PassportIdentity` object, please review the `PassportManager` object in the Microsoft Passport SDK.

System.Security.Principal

The `System.Security.Principal` namespace contains several built-in classes for other `Identity` and `Principal` objects, as well as the interfaces necessary to define your own.

WindowsIdentity

The `WindowsIdentity` class represents the identity of the currently logged-in windows user. Through this class, you can impersonate a local system account and access system resources in the context of the user. The `WindowsIdentity` class works in tandem with the `WindowsPrincipal` class to provide complete support for the users and roles of the operating system.

WindowsPrincipal

Through an instance of the `WindowsPrincipal` class, you can check the role membership of a valid `WindowsIdentity`. A `WindowsPrincipal` object is assigned to the `HttpContext.User` object whenever you have configured your application to use Windows authentication.

GenericIdentity, GenericPrincipal, IIdentity, IPrincipal

The `GenericIdentity` and `GenericPrincipal` classes are simple implementations of the `IIdentity` and `IPrincipal` interfaces. You can use these classes in a custom authentication system to store valid credentials to maintain a security context. The `IIdentity` and `IPrincipal` interfaces can be implemented in custom classes to also define your own authentication system.

System.Security.Permissions

The `System.Security.Permissions` namespace contains a large set of permissions classes and attributes that can be used for code-based and role-based security. In this chapter, we have covered the `PrincipalPermission` object due to its ease of use and relative power. However, many more permissions can be set and validated than what is mentioned here.

PrincipalPermissionAttribute

The `PrincipalPermissionAttribute` can be set as an attribute on any class, method, or property and can define the permissions a user or role has on that element.

   The attribute supports one of several security actions, such as `SecurityAction.Demandm`, which requires that the user has been granted permission to all calls higher in the call stack before accessing this object. `SecurityAction.Deny` specifies that the user or role be denied access to this object despite any other permissions granted the user.

   Specifying the `Name` property of the attribute sets the permissions to the element to validate the name listed; whereas a value in the `Role` property validates against that role. Both, one, or neither of the properties can be specified as having either property empty is the same as listing all users or all roles. Placing values in both `Name` and `Role` requires that a user with the specified name must also be in the specified role to have access. Only one name or role can be specified per attribute, so multiple `PrincipalPermissionAttributes` would have to be defined on an element to list multiple names or roles.

System.Security.Cryptography

Through cryptographic streams, private data can be secured and kept away from prying eyes. The `System.Security.Cryptography` namespace contains various implementations of highly used and highly secure ciphers.

CryptoStream

Cryptography in .NET uses streams to perform encryption. Encrypting `FileStreams` and other objects that inherit from the `System.IO.Stream` class can be done without leaving unwanted access to values in memory. The `CryptoStream` class wraps a stream and either encrypts or decrypts the stream as it is written or read, using one of the Cryptographic Service Providers.

SHA1CryptoServiceProvider

The `SHA1CryptoServiceProvider` class is an example of a hash algorithm. A fixed-length binary string is mapped to a single arbitrary-length key, creating a unique fixed-length hash value. SHA1 hashes are commonly used for password hashing and digital signatures.

TripleDESCryptoServiceProvider

The `TripleDESCryptoServiceProvider` is a symmetric algorithm that encrypts streams, such as files. Like any symmetric algorithm, it uses a single key to perform encryption and decryption.

Other Security Considerations

Many more issues are involved in security beyond the software. Proper configuration of the web server, operating system, and network hardware are needed to reinforce the policies set in your application. Applying the latest service packs and security patches is a necessity, as well as a well-defined firewall. High traffic web sites should also take note of user load and monitor any errors or faults in software, as these can lead to unforeseen security issues.

It is also important to understand the differences between single server and server farm scenarios. Some settings are designed for only one or the other and must be carefully tested. The choice of a user authority is also an important decision in these situations. This is because an XML user's file would have to be carefully replicated, whereas a centralized database server could perform much more reliable functionality.

Summary

Microsoft's path to secure web applications starts with .NET. Application security has become a necessity for developers, and the ease of use of the ASP.NET framework has made working with such security implementations easier. The built-in security features in the Common Language Runtime prevent memory leaks and buffer overflows that are often the major causes of application insecurity—leaving only the entry points to the application as a source for concern. With the security model in ASP.NET, however, developers have a larger set of tools to combat this problem.

10

Using Component Services with ASP.NET

IN THIS CHAPTER YOU ARE INTRODUCED TO component service development with ASP.NET. You will be introduced to business objects and their use in distributed development, how to create business objects, and how to convert a business object into a .NET component that can be re-used by another .NET application. After this is an explanation of serviced components. Finally, we look at interoperability between .NET components, covering the capability to use another .NET component coded and compiled in a different .NET Compliant Language, how to use a COM+ component in a .NET application, and how to use a NET serviced component in a non-.NET language.

Basic knowledge of business objects and knowledge of creating classes with Visual Basic .NET is assumed. For some introductory information on both of these topics, see Chapter 2, "Developing Applications with ASP.NET."

This chapter is only an introduction to Component Services. However, you gain enough knowledge to create and use components in your web-based applications. Components are also used heavily in the sample application in Chapter 17, "Putting It All Together."

What Are Component Services?

Component Services is the name given to the component-based API provided by the .NET framework. It is used to implement components in .NET.

In the world of software development, a component is usually defined as a program, class, or object that performs a specific task or function, and does not need to know anything about either the program, which called or used it, or the environment in which it is operating. Basically, a component is a self-contained part of a system, which relies only on itself to perform tasks.

Now you might be thinking, "Wait a second. Isn't the definition given for Component Services the definition of a business object?" You would be right. However, they are distinctly different. Business objects are generally created from classes and are language-dependent, whereas components are always compiled code, which makes them independent from the language that created them. Components also have a predefined interface that is used to access and manipulate the functionality inside of them. This provides the capability of theoretically using the components from different languages—because the component is easily packaged and deployed, which is not the case with a business object. Business objects are code-based.

A *component* is technically any class or a collection of classes that have been compiled into a separate entity (component), which can be used by other developers without internal knowledge of the component—the need to re-create the classes functionality, or the need to use the same language as the one used to create the component.

The Component Services provided by .NET are virtually an upgraded version of COM+, and have the same key benefits. However, Component Services also have a few new tricks. The new features are the following:

- *Deployment* (easy deployment in most cases)—The component is self-registering and available for use. This is a big advantage of COM+.

- *Versioning*—You can now run multiple versions of the same component concurrently. When you create a new version of a component, all new requests for that component are serviced by the new version. If a user is using the older version, it is still available to them up until the point when they finish with it, which means you can upgrade a system in real-time with limited effect on the running applications. (This is only if the interfaces to the component have not changed too much.)

- *Language interoperability*—.NET components can be used by any .NET supported language. In fact, it is quite possible for a class in a component written in Visual Basic .NET to be used as an inherited class for a C# component or class. This enables developers with different language disciplines to work with the same code base, and is one of the more powerful features of .NET.

- *COM+ interoperability*—Besides the capability to use .NET component with different languages supported by .NET, it is also possible to integrate a .NET component with COM+ Services. This enables a .NET application to work with existing legacy COM+ applications and for .NET components to be used by any languages that can develop COM+ applications. For example, a VB6 application can conceivably use a .NET component for its business logic.

In the .NET framework you can create two main types of components:

- *Standard .NET component*—This is the default type of component and, quite likely, the most common. These components allow code or classes to be easily reused and distributed among .NET applications— irrespective of the .NET language used.

- *Serviced .NET component*—.NET-serviced components are essentially the same as the standard .NET components—with one difference. The serviced .NET component is registered as a COM+ component and can be used by any language that facilitates the use of COM+. This is covered in more detail later on in this chapter.

Two other components can be created, but are not covered in this chapter. They are as follows:

- *Remote components*—Remote components allow a component to be used remotely, either through using HTTP or TCP/IP.

- *Windows Service components*—Windows Service components allow the developer to create a program that runs as a windows service. This enables you to have an application that is always running and processing data in the background.

Applying Component Services in an ASP.NET Application

Throughout the rest of this chapter, the use of business objects used in conjunction with ASP.NET Web Forms is discussed. To this end, the same web page example is used throughout the rest of this chapter. The Web Form is pretty simplistic, but it provides enough scope to demonstrate the various ways of creating business objects, .NET components, and .NET serviced components. The Web Form is shown in Figure 10.1.

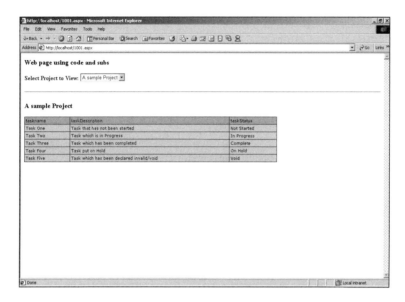

Figure 10.1   ASP.NET Web Form.

The purpose of this form is to allow a user to select a project from a database via the displayed combo box, and then subsequently display all tasks assigned to the project. The source code for this simple application appears in Listing 10.1.

Listing 10.1   **1001.aspx**

```vb
01 <%@ page language="vb"  %>
02
03 <%@ import namespace="system.data" %>
04 <%@ import namespace="system.data.sqlclient" %>
05
06
07 <script runat="server">
08
09 Sub Page_Load(Src As Object, E As EventArgs)
10
11 if not ispostback() then
12   'first time page loaded, so setup all form controls
13   setupCombo
14   setupDataGrid(comboProject.selecteditem.value)
15 end if
16
17 end sub
18
19
20
```

```
21 sub setupcombo()
22
23 'Create Data Connection and Assign resulting dataset to combo box - comboProject
24
25 dim myConn as new SQLConnection("server=localhost;uid=sa;pwd=;database=ProjectPal")
26 dim myAdapter as new SQLDataAdapter("SELECT id, name FROM dbProjects", myConn)
27 dim myDataSet as new DataSet()
28 myAdapter.Fill(myDataSet, "dbProjects")
29
30 'Bind Projects data to Combo Box
31 comboProject.DataSource = myDataSet
32 comboProject.DataTextField = "name"
33 comboProject.DataValueField = "id"
34 comboProject.databind()
35
36 end sub
37
38
39 sub setupDataGrid(projectid as integer)
40
41 'Create Data Connection and Assign resulting dataset to DataGrid - projectTasks
42 dim myConn as new SQLConnection("server=localhost;uid=sa;pwd=;database=ProjectPal")
43 dim myAdapter as new SQLDataAdapter("SELECT taskname, taskDescription, taskStatus FROM
➥vwTasksByProject WHERE ProjID = '"  + ctype(projectid, string) + "'" , myConn)
44 dim myDataSet as new DataSet()
45 myAdapter.Fill(myDataSet, "dbProjects")
46
47 'Bind Project Task data to Datagrid
48 ProjectTasks.datasource = myDataSet
49 ProjectTasks.databind()
50
51 'display Selected Project Name
52 lblProject.text = comboProject.selectedItem.text
53
54 end Sub
55
56
57 Sub getProjectTasks(sender As Object, e As EventArgs)
58
59 'Get Project Tasks for selected Project
60 setupdatagrid(sender.selecteditem.value)
61
62 end sub
63
64 </script>
65
66
67 <html>
68 <body>
69 <form runat="server">
70 <h3>Web page using embedded code and subs</h3>
71 <b>Select Project to View:</b>
72 <asp:DropDownList id="comboProject" runat="server"
```

continues ▶

Listing 10.1 **Continued**

```
73                                    onselectedindexchanged="getProjectTasks"
74                                             autopostback="True">
75 </asp:DropDownList>
76
77 <br><br><hr>
78
79 <h3><asp:label id="lblProject" runat="server"/></h3>
80
81 <ASP:DataGrid id="projectTasks" runat="server"
82              Width="700"
83              BackColor="#ccccff"
84              BorderColor="black"
85              ShowFooter="false"
86              CellPadding=3
87              CellSpacing="0"
88              Font-Name="Verdana"
89              Font-Size="8pt"
90              HeaderStyle-BackColor="#aaaadd"
91              MaintainState="false" />
92
93  </form>
94 </body>
95 </html>
```

The code in Listing 10.1, is pretty straightforward, but for clarity each section of code is explained. First, at the top of the code are the following lines:

```
<%@ page language="vb"  %>

<%@ import namespace="system.data" %>
<%@ import namespace="system.data.sqlclient" %>
```

These lines define the Web Forms default scripting language and import two
required namespaces for the Web Form. In this example, a SQL Server database is used, which does not come with SQL Server—but can be downloaded from this book's companion web site.

Script Block

Next, comes the script block. In this section of code, four subs exist, which
are explained in detail.

```
Sub Page_Load(Src As Object, E As EventArgs)

if not ispostback() then
  'first time page loaded, so setup all form controls
```

```
    setupCombo
    setupDataGrid(comboProject.selecteditem.value)
end if

end sub
```

This is a fairly standard Page_Load event handler, which checks to see if the page is a postback or not. If it is not, it calls two other subs to set up the data of both controls on the Web Form. These subs are as follows:

- SetupCombo

- SetupDataGrid

SetupCombo connects to the database and populates a DropDownList server control. The code is as follows:

```
sub setupcombo()

'Create Data Connection and Assign resulting dataset to combo box - comboProject

dim myConn as new SQLConnection("server=localhost;uid=sa;pwd=;database=ProjectPal")
dim myAdapter as new SQLDataAdapter("SELECT id, name FROM dbProjects", myConn)
dim myDataSet as new DataSet()
myAdapter.Fill(myDataSet, "dbProjects")

'Bind Projects data to Combo Box
comboProject.DataSource = myDataSet
comboProject.DataTextField = "name"
comboProject.DataValueField = "id"
comboProject.databind()

end sub
```

The first five lines of code create a connection to SQL Server, access the 'ProjectPal' database, and subsequently retrieve all the rows of data from the 'dbProjects' table. After this has been done, the results are stored in a DataSet object.

In the final section of code, the DataSet is assigned as the datasource for a DropDownList box called 'comboProject', tells the DropDownList box to use the 'Name' field as the display text, and uses the 'id' as the value of the selected item. The data is then bound.

setupDataGrid connects to Database and populates a DataGrid server control. The code is as follows:

```
sub setupDataGrid(projectid as integer)

'Create Data Connection and Assign resulting dataset to DataGrid - projectTasks
dim myConn as new SQLConnection("server=localhost;uid=sa;pwd=;database=ProjectPal")
dim myAdapter as new SQLDataAdapter("SELECT taskname, taskDescription, taskStatus FROM
➥vwTasksByProject WHERE ProjID = '"  + ctype(projectid, string) + "'" , myConn)
```

```
dim myDataSet as new DataSet()
myAdapter.Fill(myDataSet, "dbProjects")

'Bind Project Task data to Datagrid
ProjectTasks.datasource = myDataSet
ProjectTasks.databind()

'display Selected Project Name
lblProject.text = comboProject.selectedItem.text

end Sub
```

Unsurprisingly, code in this example is almost the same as the 'getProjects' sub, except that this time one parameter is taken into the sub—this being the actual 'id' of the project, for which you want to retrieve tasks. This 'id' is used in the SQL statement's WHERE clause.

The code at the end of the sub again serves the same purpose of the 'getProjects' sub, except that you are binding to two controls:

- First, you are binding the returned data from the preceding query to a DataGrid server control.

- Second, you are binding the text value of a label control to the project's name.

The final sub in this script block is another event handler. This time the event handler is for the 'OnSelectedIndexChanged' event of the 'comboProject' DropDownList control. The code for this is as follows:

```
Sub getProjectTasks(sender As Object, e As EventArgs)

'Get Porject Tasks for selected Project
setupdatagrid(sender.selecteditem.value)

end sub
```

When a user selects a new value in the 'comboProject' control, the event is handled by the getProjectTasks sub. This sub refreshes the displayed DataGrid control with new data by calling the 'setupdataGrid' sub, which has been explained earlier. The parameter passed to this sub is the 'value' property of the DropDownList's control selected item property, which in this case, corresponds to the 'id' of the selected project.

That's the entire script block. Now, let's move on to the Web Form definition. This code is not complex at all. The only three web controls are explained in the following sections.

Web Form Definition

ComboProject is a DropDownList control whose sole purpose is to allow the selection of a single project from the database. After an item is selected, the datagrid 'projectTasks' needs to be updated with new information.

```
<asp:DropDownList id="comboProject"  runat="server"
               onselectedindexchanged="getProjectTasks"
                              autopostback="True">
</asp:DropDownList>
```

There is not much to notice about the control declaration, except that the named event handler defined for the OnSelectedIndexChanged event, and that we have also set the control to automatically postback its state to the Web Form. This ensures that the event handler is processed immediately as an event happens.

LblProject is simply a label web control that is used to display the currently selected project's name above the project's task list.

ProjectTasks is a datagrid web control that is used to display all of a selected project's tasks.

```
<ASP:DataGrid id="projectTasks" runat="server"
             Width="700"
           BackColor="#ccccff"
           BorderColor="black"
           ShowFooter="false"
           CellPadding=3
           CellSpacing="0"
           Font-Name="Verdana"
           Font-Size="8pt"
           HeaderStyle-BackColor="#aaaadd"
           MaintainState="false" />
```

Again, not much to note in this example, except that the maintainstate flag is disabled, which prevents the storage of the entire datagrid's state, and thus reduces the amount of data persisted in the form's __ViewState variable.

The *business* Object

You now have an initial application. We are going to convert the previous example, so instead of having code in the pageload event to access the data we want to present, we will use a component to connect to a datasource and return the data to be used on the Web Form. This object will have the following class structure:

- **Class Name**—boProjectView
- **Attribute**—DSN as String—Holds a DSN string used by the class.

- **Methods:**

  - **GetProjects() as DataSet**—Returns a DataSet containing all projects in the database.

  - **GetTasks(projid as integer) as DataSet**—Returns all tasks that belong to a project whose primary key matches the passed parameter.

Because we are going to convert the initial Web Form code to use a class with the preceding structure, we are going to show only the replacement code for the <script> section of Listing 10.2. A full version of the code is available on this book's web site.

Listing 10.2   **1002.aspx**

```
001 <script runat="server">
002
003 '
004 'Global variables if any
005 '
006 dim myProject as new boProject
007
008
009 '
010 ' Class decalrations if required
011 '
012 Class boProject
013
014 Private _DSN as String
015
016 Public Property DSN as String
017  Set
018   _DSN = Value
019  end Set
020  Get
021       Return _DSN
022  End Get
023 End Property
024
025 Public Function getProjects() as DataSet
026
027    'Create Data Connection and return results
028     dim myConn as new SQLConnection(_DSN)
029     dim myAdapter as new SQLDataAdapter("SELECT id, name FROM dbProjects", myConn)
030     dim myDataSet as new DataSet()
031     myAdapter.Fill(myDataSet, "dbProjects")
032
033     return (myDataSet)
034
```

```
035 end function
036
037
038 Public Function getTasks(projid as integer) as DataSet
039
040     'Create Data Connection and return results
041         dim myConn as new SQLConnection(_DSN)
042         dim myAdapter as new SQLDataAdapter("SELECT taskname, taskDescription, taskStatus
➡FROM vwTasksByProject WHERE ProjID = '"  + ctype(projid, string) + "'" , myConn)
043         dim myDataSet as new DataSet()
044         myAdapter.Fill(myDataSet, "dbProjects")
045
046         Return(myDataSet)
047
048 end function
049
050 End Class
051
052
053 '
054 ' Web Form based code
055 '
056
057
058 Sub Page_Load(Src As Object, E As EventArgs)
059
060     myProject.DSN =
➡"server=localhost;uid=sa;pwd=tong1lou;database=ProjectPal"
061
062         if not ispostback() then
063                 'if first time this page has been accessed setup all form controls
064                 setupCombo
065                 ]setupDataGrid(comboProject.selecteditem.value)
066         end if
067
068 end sub
069
070
071
072 sub SetupCombo
073
074         'Bind Projects data to Combo Box
075         comboProject.DataSource = myProject.getProjects()
076         comboProject.DataTextField = "name"
077         comboProject.DataValueField = "id"
078         comboProject.databind()
079
080 end sub
081
082
083 sub setupDataGrid(projectid as integer)
084
```

continues ▶

Listing 10.2 **Continued**

```
085        'Bind Project Task data to Datagrid
086        ProjectTasks.datasource =
➥myProject.getTasks(comboProject.SelectedItem.Value)
087        ProjectTasks.databind()
088
089        'display Selected Project Name
090        lblProject.text = comboProject.selectedItem.text
091
092 end Sub
093
094
095 Sub getProjectTasks(sender As Object, e As EventArgs)
096   'Get Project Tasks for selected Project
097   setupdatagrid(sender.selecteditem.value)
98 end sub
99
100 </script>
```

As you can see, there are a few changes, which are explained on a section-by-section basis, starting with the first few lines at the top of the script block:

```
'
'Global variables if any
'
dim myProject as new boProject
```

This variable declaration declares and initializes an instance of the boProject business object class. It has been declared with global script scope.

Next, we move onto the actual Class definition. You can immediately see the similarity between the methods in the class and the subs in Listing 10.1. The class has a single attribute defined as follows:

```
Private _DSN as String
```

The DSN attribute holds the DSN string for the datasource we are using. The next few lines set up the Get and Set properties of the DSN attribute

```
Public Property DSN as String
Set
_DSN = Value
end Set
Get
      Return _DSN
End Get
End Property
```

After the Class attribute has been defined, we move onto the real functionality of the Class and the methods. We are creating two methods. The code and explanation of these methods are explained in the following sections.

getProjects Method

This method is used to open a connection with a datasource, and retrieve a DataSet with all the rows from the 'dbProjects' table:

```
Public Function getProjects() as DataSet

'Create Data Connection and return results
dim myConn as new SQLConnection(_DSN)
dim myAdapter as new SQLDataAdapter("SELECT id, name FROM dbProjects",myConn)
dim myDataSet as new DataSet()
myAdapter.Fill(myDataSet, "dbProjects")

return (myDataSet)

end function
```

The preceding code does exactly the same as the top section of the code presented in the sub 'setupCombo' of Listing 10.1. The one noticeable change is that instead of binding to a data control, we return the DataSet to the calling program. This enables us to use this business object to return a datasource, which can be bound to any web control. We no longer need to worry about how to access the data because it is encapsulated inside the class.

GetTasks Method

This method is exactly the same as the preceding method, but it has connection and query code for the project tasks table 'dbTasks'. This method also provides exactly the same reuse benefits. The code for the method is as follows:

```
Public Function getTasks(projid as integer) as DataSet

Data Connection and return results
dim myConn as new SQLConnection(_DSN)
dim myAdapter as new SQLDataAdapter("SELECT taskname, taskDescription, taskStatus FROM
➥vwTasksByProject WHERE ProjID = '"  + ctype(projid, string) + "'" , myConn)
dim myDataSet as new DataSet()
myAdapter.Fill(myDataSet, "dbProjects")

Return(myDataSet)

end function
```

Using the *business* Object

Now that the business object has been defined, all we have to do is see how it is used in the code. If you remember, we created a global instance of the business object at the top of the script. This instance is used in the remaining subs.

The Page_Load is exactly the same as before except that we have a new line of code at the top. This assigns the datasource's DSN to the DSN property of the business object.

```
Sub Page_Load(Src As Object, E As EventArgs)

    myProject.DSN = "server=localhost;uid=sa;pwd=;database=ProjectPal"
```

Now you can see a change. The code in the SetupCombo sub is no longer concerned with accessing the data. Instead, it requests and binds the return value from the business object's getProjects method, which returns a DataSet containing the projects in the database. The method setupCombo does exactly that—no need to worry about the database implementation and code, which is less complex.

```
sub SetupCombo

    'Bind Projects data to Combo Box
    comboProject.DataSource = myProject.getProjects()
    comboProject.DataTextField = "name"
    comboProject.DataValueField = "id"
    comboProject.databind()

end sub
```

The code for the 'SetupData' grid method has changed in exactly the same way as the 'SetupCombo' sub. Again, all the database access code has been effectively moved, making the code more elegant and readable (see Figure 10.2).

```
sub setupDataGrid(projectid as integer)

'Bind Project Task data to Datagrid
ProjectTasks.datasource = myProject.getTasks(comboProject.SelectedItem.Value)
ProjectTasks.databind()

'display Selected Project Name
lblProject.text = comboProject.selectedItem.text

end Sub
```

Figure 10.2   ASP.NET Web Form using a code-based *business* object.

Making the *business* Object a .NET Component

Now that we have a fully functional business object, it would be nice if we could encapsulate its functionality so that other developers writing other applications could utilize its functionality. Rather than creating code themselves to do this task, .NET provides a few ways in which to do this, such as the following:

- The business object can be made into a .NET component. This means that the object is accessible for use by any .NET client.

- The business object can be made into a serviced component. This enables you to use the component in a distributed fashion similar to COM+ and it provides the capability to interoperate with COM+.

As previously stated, one way to make a business object reusable by other .NET developers is to make it a .NET component. We already have created a .NET object that does what we need, so all we have to do is place the class into a separate source file. In this case, it is a .vb file because we are using Visual Basic .NET as the language. Next, we change the code so that it defines the namespace in which the component resides. This namespace is used to reference the component when we want to use it. Before we can use the component, we need to compile it into a .DLL. An explanation for compiling a component is explained after Listing 10.3.

Listing 10.3 **1003.vb**

```vb
01 'setup VB.NET code environment
02 option explicit
03 option strict
04
05 'import all relavent namesapces
06 imports System
07 imports System.Data
08 imports System.Data.SqlClient
09
10
11 'Define Namespace - IAN = Inside ASP.NET, in case you were curious
12 Namespace IAN
13
14
15 '
16 ' Class declarations if required
17 '
18 Public Class boProject
19
20 Public Function getProjects(DSN as String) as DataSet
21
22 'Create Data Connection and return results
23 dim myConn as new SQLConnection(DSN)
24 dim myAdapter as new SQLDataAdapter("SELECT id, name FROM dbProjects", myConn)
25 dim myDataSet as new DataSet()
26 myAdapter.Fill(myDataSet, "dbProjects")
27
28 return (myDataSet)
29
30 end function
31
32
33 Public Function getTasks(DSN as String, projid as integer) as DataSet
34
35 'Create Data Connection and return results
36 dim myConn as new SQLConnection(DSN)
➥dim myAdapter as new SQLDataAdapter("SELECT taskname, taskDescription, taskStatus FROM
➥vwTasksByProject WHERE ProjID = '"  + ctype(projid, string) + "'" , myConn)
37 dim myDataSet as new DataSet()
38 myAdapter.Fill(myDataSet, "dbProjects")
39
40 return(myDataSet)
41
42 end function
43
44 End Class
45
46
47 End NameSpace
```

As previously stated, the only changes we made to the business object class is to move it into a .vb file. The following declarations need to be added, which affects the coding environment of the Visual Basic .NET compiler. Both of these declarations are discussed in Chapter 2.

```
'setup VB.NET code environment
option explicit
option strict
```

Next, we import the namespaces used by the business object:

```
'import all relevant namesapces
imports System
imports System.Data
imports System.Data.SqlClient
```

After the namespaces have been imported, a namespace is declared in which to store the business object. The namespace—for all components in this book—is 'IAN'.

```
Namespace IAN
```

This next minor change is declaring the class to have a public scope. If the class does not have public scope, it cannot be accessed externally. The class is declared as follows:

```
Public Class boProject
```

The final changes in the class are not due to the component being a component, but rather to the component being completely stateless, and thus, more scalable. This has been done by removing the previously defined property 'DSN', and adding a 'DSN' parameter to both of the methods.

The changes required in the code to convert your business object into a component are surprisingly quick and easy. However, before we get too excited, we have yet to compile the Visual Basic .NET code for the component and use it in a Web Form. These topics are covered in the following sections.

Compiling and Registering a .NET Component

As stated in the preceding section, before a .NET component can be used in a .NET-based application, we need to compile the class into a .DLL file. It should be noted that a .NET DLL is not the same kind of file as a windows DLL. It has the only DLL extension for COM+ interoperability. This is described in more detail in "ASP.NET Migration Issues," in Chapter 2.

To compile a .vb source code file called '1003.vb' into a .NET DLL called 'ian.dll', we would use the following command:

```
vbc /out:ian.dll /t:library 1003.vb /r:System.dll /r:System.Data.dll/r:System.XML.dll
```

The command is made up of these separate parts:

- **Vbc**—This command line compiler is used to compile Visual Basic .NET code.

- **/out:ian.dll**—The /out: section defines the output file to be created.

- **1003.vb**—The source file that is being turned into a .NET component.

- **/r:…**—Used to reference any namespaces that are required for the component.

To compile the component from the preceding section, use the command line as is. After the required DLL has been created from the command-line prompt, it needs to be copied into a bin directory, which should be located in the root directory of your web site. ASP.NET looks for this directory when resolving calls for components.

Using a .NET Component in an ASP.NET Web Form

Because we have a compiled .NET component (ian.dll), we can use it in a Web Form—again using the same example, but with noticeably less code. The script section of the code is shown in Listing 10.4.

Listing 10.4 **1004.aspx**

```
01 <%@ page language="vb"  %>
02
03 <%@ import namespace="system.data" %>
04 <%@ import namespace="system.data.sqlclient" %>
05
06 'Import .NET component
07 <%@ import namespace="IAN" %>
08
09
10<script runat="server">
11
12 '
13 'Global variables if any
14 '
15 dim myDSN as String
16 dim myProject as new IAN.boProject
17
18 '
19 ' Web Form based code
20 '
21 Sub Page_Load(Src As Object, E As EventArgs)
22
```

```
23      myDSN = "server=localhost;uid=sa;pwd=;database=ProjectPal"
24
25      if not ispostback() then
26              'if first time used setup all form controls
27              setupCombo
28              setupDataGrid(comboProject.selecteditem.value)
29      end if
30
31 end sub
32
33
34
35 sub SetupCombo
36
37      'Bind Projects data to Combo Box
38      comboProject.DataSource = myProject.getProjects(myDSN)
39      comboProject.DataTextField = "name"
40      comboProject.DataValueField = "id"
41      comboProject.databind()
42
43 end sub
44
45
46 sub setupDataGrid(projectid as integer)
47
48      'Bind Project Task data to Datagrid
49      ProjectTasks.datasource = myProject.getTasks(myDSN,comboProject.SelectedItem.Value)
50      ProjectTasks.databind()
51
52      'display Selected Project Name
53      lblProject.text = comboProject.selectedItem.text
54      end Sub
55
56
57 Sub getProjectTasks(sender As Object, e As EventArgs)
58   'Get Project Tasks for selected Project
59   setupdatagrid(sender.selecteditem.value)
60 end sub
61
62 </script>
63
64 <html>
65 <body>
66 <form runat="server">
67 <h3>Web page using Code based Business object</h3>
68 <b>Select Project to View:</b>
69 <asp:DropDownList id="comboProject" runat="server"
70                                     onselectedindexchanged="getProjectTasks"
71                                             autopostback="True">
```

continues ▶

Listing 10.4 **Continued**

```
72 </asp:DropDownList>
73
74 <br><br><hr>
75
76 <h3><asp:label id="lblProject" runat="server"/></h3>
77
78 <ASP:DataGrid id="projectTasks" runat="server"
79              Width="700"
80           BackColor="#ccccff"
81           BorderColor="black"
82           ShowFooter="false"
83           CellPadding=3
84           CellSpacing="0"
85           Font-Name="Verdana"
86           Font-Size="8pt"
87           HeaderStyle-BackColor="#aaaadd"
88           MaintainState="false" />
89
90  </form>
91 </body>
92 </html>
```

In the preceding code, the change we have is a new `import` statement:

```
<%@ import namespace="IAN" %>
```

This `import` statement imports the new namespace we defined in Listing 10.4 and makes the classes defined therein available to our Web Form. Also the previously defined class code has been removed. Because it is no longer needed, this gives the immediate effect of making the entire source of the Web Form more readable. The only other change is the first two lines inside the script block:

```
dim myDSN as String
dim myProject as new IAN.boProject
```

The first line declares a page-wide–scoped variable for storing the data-source's DSN, and the second creates a new instance of the business object, by referencing the namespace that was previously imported.

That's all it takes to make a .NET component and test it. A screenshot of this working code is shown in Figure 10.3.

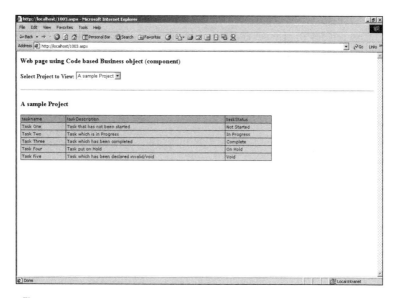

Figure 10.3   ASP.NET Web Form using a component-based *business* object.

Serviced Components

At the beginning of this chapter, another kind of component was mentioned—the serviced component. The serviced component is used to integrate with existing COM+ Service. This provides the capability for .NET components to be used in COM+ transactions and also by any COM+ capable tool.

A *serviced component* is a component managed by Windows Component Services (COM+). This enables a component to share the same context as other managed components and to take part in transactions that take place in this context. This is run-of-the-mill for a regular COM+ component. However, the architecture of a .NET component is somewhat different. It is possible for a .NET component to make itself available to be managed by a Windows COM+ Service manager. Read the following sections to learn how to do this.

Creating a Serviced Component

A component class as declared in the previous chapters is fine for a regular component. However, for a serviced component the class you create has to do the following:

- Inherit the properties and methods from the `ServicedComponent` class. This class resides in the `System.EnterpriseServices` namespace.

- Add a `'transaction'` attribute to the class definition and place any relevant transaction context methods so that it is available to participate in COM+ Services.

After these changes have been made, you have to create what is called a *strong name* for the component. Finally, some assembly attributes are added to the class file.

As you can see from the previous sequence of events, there is quite a bit to do to make your component serviced. Do not worry—using the component that was created earlier as a base, each task in a working example of the class is described a step at a time.

Listing 10.5 is a complete example of a serviced class, which includes all changes. After the listing is an explanation of the exact changes and why they are implemented.

Listing 10.5   **1005.vb—A serviced component class**

```
01 'setup VB.NET code environment
02 option explicit
03 option strict
04
05 'import all relevant namesapces
06 imports System
07 imports System.Data
08 imports System.Data.SqlClient
09 imports System.EnterpriseServices
10 imports System.Reflection
11
12
13 'Assembly Attributes
14 <assembly:AssemblyKeyfileAttribute ("boProjectServiced.snk")>
15 <assembly:ApplicationName("boProjectServiced")>
16 <assembly:Description("Serviced component example for Inside ASP.NET")>
17
18
19 'Define Namespace
20
21 Namespace IAN
22
23
24 '
25 ' Class declarations if required
26 '
27 <Transaction(TransactionOption.RequiresNew)> Public Class boProjectServiced
        Inherits ServicedComponent
```

```
28
29 Public Function getProjects(DSN as String) as DataSet
30
31 'Create Data Connection and return results
32 dim myConn as new SQLConnection(DSN)
33 dim myAdapter as new SQLDataAdapter("SELECT id, name FROM dbProjects", myConn)
34 dim myDataSet as new DataSet()
35 myAdapter.Fill(myDataSet, "dbProjects")
36
37 ContextUtil.SetComplete()
38
39 return (myDataSet)
40
41 end function
42
43
44 Public Function getTasks(DSN as String, projid as integer) as DataSet
45
46 'Create Data Connection and return results
47 dim myConn as new SQLConnection(DSN)
48 dim myAdapter as new SQLDataAdapter("SELECT taskname, taskDescription, taskStatus FROM
➥vwTasksByProject WHERE ProjID = '"  + ctype(projid, string) + "'" , myConn)
49 dim myDataSet as new DataSet()
50 myAdapter.Fill(myDataSet, "dbProjects")
51
52 ContextUtil.SetComplete()
53
54 return(myDataSet)
55
56 end function
57
58 End Class
59
60
61 End NameSpace
```

Listing 10.5 contains the changes required to make the previously used component into a Windows serviced component. A detailed explanation starting with the new namespace declarations at the top of the code follows:

```
imports System.EnterpriseServices
imports System.Reflection
```

These two namespaces are required to provide access to the assembly attributes and the transaction services provided by COM+. The next few lines show some of the possible assembly attributes you can declare in a serviced component:

```
<assembly:AssemblyKeyfileAttribute("boProjectServiced.snk")>
<assembly:ApplicationName("boProjectServiced")>
<assembly:Description("Serviced component example for Inside ASP.NET")>
```

These attributes and their descriptions are shown in Table 10.1.

Table 10.1 **Attributes for a Serviced Component**

Attribute	Description
Assemblykeyfile	This is used to get and set a strong name for the serviced component. The file to which it points is a strong name keyfile, and it holds details on both the public and private keys used by the assemblies strong name. A strong name enables the serviced component to have multiple versions, running concurrently on a server—because each version of a serviced component will have its own strong name. You create a components strong name keyfile by using the following command line: `SN -k boProjectServices.snk` The preceding command line creates a string name keyfile with the filename `boProjectServices.snk`.
ApplicationName	The name of the application.
Description	The description of the application.

After the assembly attributes have been assigned, we move on to the actual class declaration syntax:

```
<Transaction(TransactionOption.RequiresNew)>
Public Class boProjectServiced Inherits ServicedComponent
```

This becomes a little complex. The first part of the declaration sets a 'Transaction' attribute for the serviced component. In this example, we have specified 'RequiresNew' a list of the possible values as shown in Table 10.2.

Table 10.2 **Possible Values of the Transaction Attribute**

Value	Description
Disabled	This is the default transaction mode for a serviced class and means that the transactions will be ignored by the component.
NotSupported	This setting enables the transaction context. However, it also disables the components interaction in any transactions.
Supported	This component runs in transaction scope if one is available. If not, it runs without a transaction.

Value	Description
Required	This component requires that it is in a transaction. If there is not a transaction active, the component creates its own transaction.
RequiresNew	This component always creates a new transaction whenever it is run.

The other change to the class is that it now inherits attributes, methods, and events from the ServicedComponent class. This class provides the functionality to enable your component to interoperate with the Windows Component Services (COM+).

The final change made to the class is the line added to both of its methods, before returning a DataSet:

```
ContextUtil.SetComplete()
```

This line tells the transaction manager that the methods have completed their tasks safely. If an error occurs and was trapped, the following statement could be used to notify the transaction manager that something went wrong:

```
ContextUtil.SetAbort()
```

Registering and Using a Serviced Component

The class is now complete and needs to be compiled, registered, and used like before. Except, it now operates as a services component. The compilation and registration process is explained here.

Before we can use a serviced component, we have to compile the component. This is done in the same way as before, except you need to reference the System.EnterpriseServices.dll. We now have a component with a strong name created. We can register the component with COM+ Services. This is done by using the 'regsrvcs' command-line tool. An example of its use follows:

```
Regsrvcs ian.dll
```

The preceding command line registers the component stored in ian.dll with the Windows Component Services.

Summary

.NET components provide powerful and flexible code re-usability features, which—although possible in ASP—were somewhat of a specialist area. In this chapter you have seen how easy it is to convert a code-intensive web page into a business object—subsequently turn that business object into a component, and finally to adapting the final component so that it can be recognized by a COM+ system. However, only the fundamentals of this technology have been covered. Two other component types that can be created were mentioned, but we have not gone into detail on serviced components. This chapter's intention was to enlighten you on the use and general application of components in .NET applications. For more advanced component development, see Chapter 17, "Putting It All Together." Almost all of the business logic and data access is done through Component Services in the sample application that is presented.

11

Using Messaging Services with ASP.NET

THIS CHAPTER TAKES A LOOK AT the messaging services provided by the .NET framework and how they can be used in ASP.NET-based web applications. The following topics are covered in this chapter.

- **Messaging systems**—A brief overview of the messaging paradigm
- **Microsoft Message Queue (MSMQ) Messaging System**—An overview of MSMQ, what it is, what it can do, and instructions on how to use the Microsoft Management Console to manage MSMQ.
- **The .NET Messaging Services**—An overview of the .NET Messaging Services, classes, and objects.

By the end of this chapter, you should be able to integrate messaging into your web-based application and understand the fundamental concepts behind messaging.

Introduction to Messaging Systems

Most developed applications are generally centralized in nature. The business logic and the data services are all managed by one or more servers processing the workload and only the application's clients are distributed. However, after you move out of a centralized server-based application environment and move into the more expansive, distributed-server application model, things become more complex to manage.

In contrast to a centralized environment where you need to worry only about the server going down, a distributed environment requires that you be concerned with two main issues. The first issue is the server going down, just like in the centralized environment; however, another issue is that the server might not be local, and because of this, it might be harder to maintain.

The second issue is the reliability and availability of the network between the distributed servers and their clients. Communication links by remote servers are significantly less reliable than a local network, which is typically used to connect a centralized model.

Enter the MSMQ messaging service. This technology has the capability to send requests for processing or data to a distributed server, and should the server not be available for any reason, the processing or data request is stored locally until the distributed server becomes available again. Hence, client users can still process some of their work; however, it must be noted that if the processing or data request requires immediate feedback, MSMQ will not help. It only comes into its own domain when asynchronous fire and forget processing are required.

MSMQ enables application developers to communicate with other applications in a reliable and efficient manner by sending messages to each other—pretty much the same way we communicate with others through email by sending messages.

MSMQ enables you to design your applications with fault tolerance in mind, thus providing a more robust and stable environment for carrying out business processes across a distributed system.

Messaging System Concepts

In a messaging system, there are three major components:

- Messages
- Message queues
- Message servers or managers

Messages are somewhat similar in architecture to emails, insofar as both of the message constructs have various properties that hold information about the message and the actual message itself. This is where the similarities end. The only common property between a messaging system message and an email message is that they both store the content of a message in a property called the *body*.

The messages themselves are sent to *message queues*. These queues are a container for messages, and a message server manages these message queues. The server acts as a coordinator of the message sent from its source to its new destination. The main purpose of the message server is to ensure that a message gets to its destination. If for some reason the message cannot be sent to its destination, it is stored until it can be successfully sent to its destination.

The purpose of the *message server* is to transmit messages in a reliable way to the destination as soon as possible.

There are two main types of message queues available in MSMQ; both of these have two subtypes each, as shown in Table 11.1.

Table 11.1 **Message Queue Types**

Type of Message	QueueSubtype	Description
User Generated	Public Queue	A public queue is available to all MSMQ servers and clients.
	Private Queue	A private queue is available only on a client machine, and is not available to all users or the message queue system.
System Generated	Journal Queue	Journal queues normally are used to store copies of messages that are being sent because after a message has been sent to another computer, it is removed from the local machine. Should you need to resend the message, you can get all the message's information from the journal queue.
	Dead Letter Queue	The dead letter queue is used by the system to store undeliverable messages or expired messages. (Messages can have an expiry property set, so that the system does not keep trying to send a failed message forever.) Dead letter messages are stored on the MSMQ server where the message expired; this may be different than the original server from which the message was sent.

MSMQ Application Process Types

In MSMQ applications, you normally have two types of processing patterns. The first pattern is the *sender process*. All this process does is create and send a message to a message queue for later processing. The second type of process is the *receiver process*; this process retrieves a message from a message queue.

Figure 11.1, shows a sample application structure with both senders and receivers in an application.

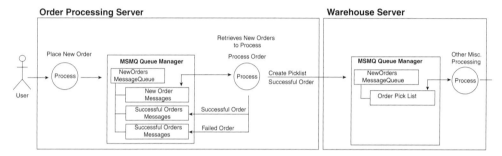

Figure 11.1   Simple Messaging System Architecture.

In Figure 11.1, you can see that when a user places an order through the CreateNewOrder process, a NewOrder message is generated, and subsequently forwarded to the NewOrder's public message queue on the Order Processing server. The user can, in many systems, place orders without concern for the status of the previous orders. In such systems, it is not important for the order entry person to know whether the order can be filled immediately from inventory.

The ProcessOrders proccss on the orders server retrieves any messages (orders) waiting to be processed. The ProcessOrders process reads the next available message and then performs some processing on the order. If the order is successfully processed, a message is sent to the SuccessfulOrders queue (this could be sent to a journal), and another message is sent through to the GoodstoPick message queue on the warehouse server. However, if the order processing fails, a message is sent to the FailedOrders message queue.

Message System Security

The contents of a message can be made secure using the following security methods built into Windows 2000:

- **Authentication**—*Authentication* is normally implemented using certificate, Windows NTLM (NT LAN Manager), and Kerberos V5 Security.

The certificates are used for message authentication (verifying the sender of the message). Kerberos and NTLM are used for server side authentication of the message. Authentication provides a reasonable assurance of the identity of the application or user requesting access to a resource.

- **Encryption**—*Encryption* is used to encode the message body before it is sent and again to decrypt the message on receipt.

- **Access Control Rights**—*Access control* is the process of restricting user access to message queue objects. Access control is implemented by adding descriptors to objects. The message queue objects that can have access control set are MSMQ servers and queues. A descriptor lists the users and groups that are granted and denied access to an object; it also details the available permissions given to users and groups for the object as well. Access control rights control the access allowed to an authenticated application or user.

Managing MSMQ Message Queues with Windows 2000

One of the most useful applications or tools that comes with Windows 2000 is the *Microsoft Management Console* (MMC). This application enables the user to monitor and configure most Windows 2000 components and many additional applications installed on Windows 2000.

The following sections show you how to use the MMC to perform basic configuration and management of MSMQ queues.

Creating a New Queue

To create a new public or private message queue, just follow the steps below:

1. On the left side of the MMC window, the message queues set up on your server are displayed. Right-click the queue type you want, either public or private, and from the pop-up menu, select the New option, and then select Public queue or Private queue, depending on which type of queue you need to create. Figure 11.2 shows the process for creating a public queue.

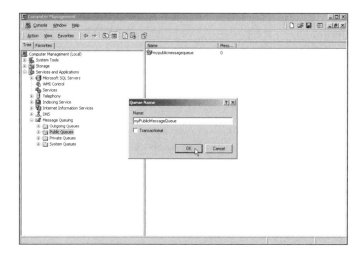

Figure 11.2   Creating a Public Queue—Step 1.

2. You should be presented with a dialog box, as shown in Figure 11.2. Here you type the name of the queue you are creating. You also have the option of setting the message queue's transactional management ability, which is unchecked by default.

3. After clicking OK, you see that the MSMQ service section of the MMC now has the new public queue you just created. Also note that there are two subelements or folders below the public queue you created, which are Queue messages and Journal messages. This is shown in Figure 11.3.

Deleting a Queue

In the normal use of a message queue, it is unlikely that you will have to delete a message queue; however, there might be good reason for deleting a message queue in an application. To delete an existing public or private message queue, just right-click the queue, and select delete.

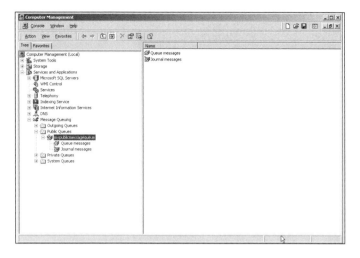

Figure 11.3 Creating a Public Queue—Step 2.

Purging Messages from a Queue

Sometimes you might need to purge (remove all messages) from a message queue. This task is done quite regularly for the journal message queues because they just grow. To purge all the messages from a message queue, follow the directions in the following paragraph.

Right-click the message queue from which you want to purge messages. From the pop-up menu, select the Purge option. You will be presented with a confirmation dialog box. After the purge has been confirmed, all the messages in the selected message queue are permanently deleted from the message queue.

Architecture of the .NET Messaging Services

The preceding sections discussed what MSMQ is, and went through the basic procedures, including adding a message queue. This section talks about the objects and classes used to implement MSMQ in web applications.

The messaging services are in the `System.Messaging` namespace. This namespace includes the following key objects and classes, shown in Table 11.2.

Table 11.2 *System.Messaging* **Namespace Objects and Classes**

`MessageQueue`	The `MessageQueue` is used to provide a reference to an MSMQ queue. This reference can then be used to manipulate the queue. In essence, the `MessageQueue` object is used to interact with a message queue on the server.
`Message`	The `message` object is a message in the message queue, and contains all of its associated properties and actions.
`MessageQueueCriteria`	This is used to control which queues are returned from a search of message queues.
`MessageEnumerator`	`MessageEnumerator` allows forward-only access to the message queue.
`MessageQueueException`	This is the Exception object used to handle a message queue error.

There are other objects in the `System.Messaging` namespace, which I am not going to cover in this chapter because we are only looking at how to create and manipulate message queues and messages.

The `MessageQueue` object enables you to create new queues, delete existing queues, send simple and complex messages, purge messages from a queue, and also retrieve or peek at existing messages.

The `Message` object is the object you'll use the most in the .NET messaging services framework. Although you do not need it to send a simple message (just a body), you do need to use it when manipulating messages received, or for sending a complex message that takes advantage of the advanced features of MSMQ.

Referencing a Message Queue

Before you can use a message queue, you must get its reference. `MessageQueue` objects can reference a queue in three different ways; these are outlined in Table 11.3.

Table 11.3   **Referencing a Queue**

Method	Description
Path	The `Path` is a unique identifier made up of two parts: the first is the name of the machine where the queue is hosted, and the second is the name of the queue you want to use.
FormatName	The `FormatName` is a unique identifier (GUID) generated by MSMQ as part of the message queue creation process.
LabelName	The `LabelName` is descriptive text assigned to the queue after the message queue's creator has created it.
	It should be noted that it is quite possible to have duplicate labels on an MSMQ server, so because of this, you should not really use it to locate a message queue.

Path Reference Type

The `Path` reference type must be used when creating queues because the `FormatName` and the `Label` of a message queue are assigned after the message queue has been created.

Using a *Path* Reference

The most common way of referencing a message queue is through its path. Because it is also the reference type, you must use it when creating a message queue.

The format of a `Path` reference is pretty much like a regular directory path. At the beginning of the `Path` statement, you put the name of the machine that hosts the message queue. After this, you put a backslash "\" followed by the queue you want to access. Some of the most common queues accessed are listed here:

Public Queues	MachineName\QueueName
Private Queues	MachineName**private$**\QueueName
Journal Queue	MachineName\QueueName**journal$**

Using the Path Reference Format

If you are trying to reference a message queue that may not be online, you cannot use the Path reference format; you can only use the FormatName reference format.

Also, with the Path reference format, it should be noted that its performance is slower than the FormatName reference format. This is because when a message queue server receives a Path format reference, it must then locate the message queue's FormatName (or GUID) before any process is applied to the queue.

In short, the Path reference is a nice, easy way to reference a message queue; however, it does come at the price of performance.

Using a *FormatName* Reference

The FormatName reference type is also made up of two parts, the first being a unique identifier, which is generated by MSMQ as part of the queue creation process; this unique identifier is actually a GUID.

The FormatName reference type is also made up of two parts. The first a unique identifier (FORMATNAME:), which is generated by MSMQ as part of the queue creation process; the second part is the actual ID of the queue. Listed here are the most commonly used format names:

Public Queues	`FORMATNAME:PUBLIC = QueueGUID`
Private Queues	`FORMATNAME:PRIVATE = MachineGUID/QueueGUID`
Journal Queue	`FORMATNAME:PUBLIC = QueueGUID;JOURNAL`

The FormatName reference type is the fastest way to access a message queue because it is the most direct method—the MSMQ server does not have to find the GUID as it must with the Path and Label reference formats.

Sending Messages to a Disconnected Message Queue

Should you want to send messages to a disconnected message queue, you have to reference the queue by its FormatName because the Path will not be available, and as such, it is impossible to resolve against the unavailable server.

Also worthy of note is the fact that if you should delete and recreate the queue, it is very likely that the queue's GUID will be different. Should this be the case, you should try to use Path references instead, even though they are slower. Speed is not an issue when deleting and recreating queues because the GUID is resolved at runtime from the server that hosts the queue.

Using a *Label* Reference

The Label reference type is just a piece of descriptive text that is assigned to the queue after it has been created. This label is assigned by the queue creator. The label itself, therefore, is just a text string.

You should be aware that labels are not unique, and duplicates are quite possible. The `Label` reference type is generally used for switching machines that host the queue. To do this, you would just change the queue label on the replacement queue to that of the queue you want to replace, and then remove the original label.

Manipulating a *MessageQueue*

After you have a reference to a message queue, you can start to manipulate the queue. The following sections list the most common tasks that can be done with MSMQ:

Accomplishing Tasks Using MSMQ and .NET

This section shows code snippets that accomplish the following tasks with MSMQ and .NET.

Creating Message Queues

Creating a message queue programmatically in ASP.NET is pretty straight forward; however, the most common practice for creating message queues is to use the MMC and create the queues through the MSMQ snap-in.

To create a public message queue:

```
01 Dim myMQ as New Messaging.MessageQueue
02 MyMQ.Create ("inspiration\myPublicMessageQueue")
```

To create a public message queue that is transactional:

```
01 Dim myMQ as New Messaging.MessageQueue
02 MyMQ.Create ("inspiration\myPublicMessageQueue", True)
```

To create a private message queue:

```
01 Dim myMQ as New Messaging.MessageQueue
02 MyMQ.Create ("inspiration\private$\myPublicMessageQueue")
```

To create a public queue that is transactional:

```
01 Dim myMQ as New Messaging.MessageQueue
02 MyMQ.Create ("inspiration\private$\myPublicMessageQueue", True)
```

As you can see from the preceding code, the method of creating message queues—whether they are public or private—is pretty much straightforward. In line 1, we create a `MessageQueue` object from the `System.Messaging` namespace; then in line 2, we simply call the `Create` method of the `MessageQueue` object to create the required queue. After the queue is created, a reference to the queue is maintained by the instantiated `MessageQueue` object.

Deleting Message Queues

Sometimes you may have to delete a `MessageQueue` programmatically. You can do this by calling the `Delete` method of the `MessageQueue` object as shown here:

```
01 Dim myMQ as New Messaging.MessageQueue
02 MyMQ.Delete ("inspiration\myPublicMessageQueue")
```

In line 1, we create the `MessageQueue` object; then we simply delete the queue we want to remove.

Removing All Messages from a Message Queue

Sometimes you may need to purge all messages in a `MessageQueue` programmatically. You can do this by calling the `Purge` method of the `MessageQueue` object as shown here:

```
01 Dim myMQ as New Messaging.MessageQueue
02 myMQ.Path = "inspiration\myPublicMessageQueue"
03 MyMQ.Purge ()
```

In line 1, we create the `MessageQueue` object; then we set the `MessageQueue` Path to the path of the `MessageQueue` we want to purge in line 02. Finally, we call the `Purge` method of the `MessageQueue` object to delete all messages therein.

Retrieving a List of *MessageQueues*

Sometimes you may need to purge all messages in a `MessageQueue` programmatically. You can do this by calling the `Purge` method of the `MessageQueue` object, as shown here.

To retrieve all private message queues:

```
01 Dim myMQArray () as New Messaging.MessageQueue
02 MyMQArray.GetPrivateQueuesByMachine ("inspiration")
```

To retrieve all public message queues:

```
01 Dim myMQArray () as Messaging.MessageQueue
02 MyMQArray.GetPublicQueues ()
```

To retrieve all public message queues by machine:

```
01 Dim myMQArray () as Messaging.MessageQueue
03 MyMQArray.GetPublicQueuesByMachine ("inspiration")
```

To retrieve all public message queues by label:

```
01 Dim myMQArray () as Messaging.MessageQueue
03 MyMQArray.GetPublicQueuesByLabel ("myPublicMessageQueue")
```

To retrieve all public message queues by category:

```
01 Dim myMQArray () as Messaging.MessageQueue
03 MyMQArray.GetPublicQueuesByCategory (New Guid("{5A5F7535-AE9A-41d4-935C-
➥845C2AFF7112}"))
```

In all these examples, an array of MessageQueue objects is returned. The code required to retrieve an array of queues is very similar to that used to retrieve a specific queue—the only difference is the method being called and the parameter being passed. However, the following code shows a more flexible and complex way of retrieving public message queues by means of a criteria-based filter.

To retrieve all public message queues by user-defined criteria:

```
01 Dim myMQ as Messaging.MessageQueue
02 Dim myMQArray() as New Messaging.MessageQueue
03 Dim myCriteria as New MessageQueueCriteria
04
05 myCriteria.Category = New Guid("{5A5F7535-AE9A-41d4-935C-845C2AFF7112}")
06 myCriteria.CreatedAfter = DateTime.Now.Subtract(new TimeSpan(1, 0, 0, 0))
07 myCriteria.CreatedBefore = DateTime.Now.Subtract(new TimeSpan(1,0,0,0))
08 myCriteria.Label = "Inspiration"
09 myCriteria.MachineName = "Inspiration"
10 myCriteria.ModifiedAfter = DateTime.Now.Subtract(new TimeSpan(1,0,0,0))
11 myCriteria.ModifiedBefore = DateTime.Now.Subtract(new TimeSpan(1,0,0,0))
12
13 MyMQArray.GetPublicQueues(myCriteria)
14
15 For Each myMQ in myMQArray
16   Response.write(myMQ.Category  + "<BR>")
17   Response.write(myMQ.CreatedAfter  + "<BR>")
18   Response.write(myMQ.CreatedBefore + "<BR>")
19   Response.write(myMQ.Label + "<BR>")
20   Response.write(myMQ.MachineName + "<BR>")
21   Response.write(myMQ.ModifiedAfter  + "<BR>")
22   Response.write(myMQ.ModifiedBefore + "<BR>")
23   Response.write("<BR><BR>")
24 Next
```

Lines 1–3 create instances of a MessageQueue, an array of MessageQueue objects, and MessageQueueCriteria objects. Lines 5–10 demonstrate all the possible values that can be set on a MessageQueueCriteria object. Line 13 retrieves the array of MessageQueue objects that match the criteria. Lines 14–24 iterate through the returned array and output some message queue properties to the browser.

Properties Used by a MessageQueueCriteria Object

The possible properties that can be used by a `MessageQueueCriteria` object are as follows:

- Category—GUID category used for grouping `MessageQueue` objects

- CreatedAfter—Date/time after which the `MessageQueue` was created

- CreatedBefore—Date/time before which the `MessageQueue` was created

- Label—Text Label assigned to the `MessageQueue`

- MachineName—Path of the `MessageQueue` machine

- ModifiedAfter—Date/time after which the `MessageQueue` was modified

- ModifiedBefore—Date/time before which the `MessageQueue` was modified

Using an Enumerator to Iterate Through the Queues

You can also create an `enumeration` object to iterate through the public queues of the MSMQ server. The following is an example of the enumerator creation:

```
01 Dim myEnum as MessageQueuesEnumerator
02 myEnum = MessageQueue.GetMessageQueuesEnumerator
```

Line 1 creates a `MessageQueueEnumerator` object, and then line 2 subsequently initializes it with the public queues from the MSMQ server.

Sending Messages to a Message Queue

At the core of the messaging services functionality is the capability to send, receive, and process sent messages in the order in which they are received. In this example, we will be focusing on sending messages.

You can send two types of messages to a message queue: the first is a simple message, and the second is a complex message. Both of these are illustrated in the following sections.

Creating/Sending a Simple Message

You can send a simple message to an MSMQ message queue by simply passing a variable, string, or object as a parameter to the `MessageQueue` objects Send method, as shown in the following code:

```
01 Dim myMQ as new MessageQueue ("Inspiration\myPublicMessageQueue")
02 myMQ.Send (100)
03 myMQ.Send ("A simple Text Message")
```

Line 1 declares a `MessageQueue` object and sets it to reference the `myPublicMessageQueue` message queue on the Inspiration server. Line 2 sends an integer value as the message, and line 3 does the same with a string.

You can send any object to the `MessageQueue` as a message body because the object gets serialized into XML before being sent to a message queue. (The object will be de-serialized at the other end when the message is received.)

Sending a Simple Message

It should be noted that when you send a simple message, the message body is made up of the passed parameter of the send method, and all other properties of the sent message are set to default values.

Creating/Sending Complex Messages

Besides sending a simple message by sending an object through the `MessageQueue`'s `Send` method, you can send a complex message.

A complex message only means that you have more control over how the message is sent through the messaging services framework, and as such, it is more complex than just sending an object.

An example of a complex message is in the following code:

```
01 Dim myMQ as new MessageQueue ("Inspiration\myPublicMessageQueue")
02 Dim myMsg as Message
03
04 myMsg = new Message("A More Complex Message")
05 myMsg.Label = "This is the label"
06 myMsg.Priority = MessagePriority.High
07 myMsg.UseAuthentication = True
09
09 myMQ.Send(myMsg)
```

Lines 1 and 2 declare and initialize a `MessageQueue` object and a `Message` object. Line 4 initializes the `Message` object and sets the `Message` object's body property to the passed string. Lines 5–7 set some message-specific properties—the first is the label attached to a message, and the second is the priority rating of the message. Then line 7 sets the authentication mode of the message, so that it is authenticated at the messaging server. Line 9 sends the message.

Retrieving the Next Available Message in a Message Queue

At the core of the messaging services functionality is the capability to send, receive, and process sent messages in the order in which they are received. In this example, we will be focusing on retrieving messages.

To retrieve a message from a message queue, we use the Receive method of the `MessageQueue` object. This method takes a single parameter, which ids the number of milliseconds to wait for a message if there are messages waiting to be processed. This value is normally set to `0`, so that the calling application regains control.

```
01 Dim myMQ as new MessageQueue("inspiration\myPublicMessageQueue")
02 Dim myMsg as Message
03 myMsg = myMQ.Receive(0)
```

Lines 1 and 2 set up and initialize both the `MessageQueue` object and the `Message` object. In Line 3, we call the `MessageQueue` Receive method and store the resulting value.

Retrieved Messages Are Gone

When you retrieve a message from a queue, it is removed from that queue permanently.

Peeking at the Next Available Message in a *MessageQueue*

Sometimes when working with message queues, it can be useful to know information about the next available message on a queue without actually receiving it. This is done using the Peek method of the `MessageQueue` object, as shown in the following code:

```
01 Dim myMQ as new MessageQueue("inspiration\myPublicMessageQueue")
02 Dim myMsg as Message
03 myMsg = myMQ.Peek(0)
```

As you can see, the code is almost exactly the same as it is for retrieving a message, with the only difference being that you call the Peek method instead of the Retrieve method.

Retrieving a Collection of Messages in a *MessageQueue*

It may be necessary for you to retrieve a list of all the messages in a queue; this can be done by either returning a static array of all messages in a queue or by creating an enumerator and iterating through the messages in a queue.

You can retrieve a static list of messages in a queue by using the `MessageQueue` method `GetAllMessages`; this returns an array of message objects, which represent all the messages in a specified message queue, as shown in the following code:

```
01 Dim myMQ as New MessageQueue ("Inspiration\myPublicMessageQueue")
02 Dim myMsgs() as Message
03 myMsgs = myMQ.GetAllMessages()
```

Lines 1–2 declare and initialize the MessageQueue and Message objects respectively. In line 3, we call the GetAllMessages method of the MessageQueue object, and we assign the returned array of message objects to the myMsgs variable.

You can also access a MessageEnumerator object that enables you to iterate through the messages in a specified queue sequentially one at a time, as shown in the following code:

```
01 Dim myMQ as New MessageQueue ("Inspiration\myPublicMessageQueue")
02 Dim myMsgEnum as MessageEnumerator
03 myMsgs = myMQ.GetMessageEnumerator
```

Summary

The .NET messaging services are a powerful way to implement disconnected processing in enterprise servers. You should now have the knowledge required to implement MSMQ messaging in your applications. However, this is only an introduction to MSMQ and the .NET messaging services. For further information on MSMQ, you can go to the Microsoft MSMQ resource site: www.microsoft.com/msmq.

12

Using Directory Services with ASP.NET

THE DIRECTORY SERVICES PROVIDED BY THE .NET framework are a set of classes that encapsulate and expose Microsoft's Active Directory Service Interfaces (ADSI) for use in .NET-based applications. ADSI enable programmers to make use of not only Active Directory but also directory service providers.

By using directory services, you can create applications that can perform common administration tasks, some of which are listed below:

- Use a single application-programming interface to perform tasks on multiple directory systems by offering the user a variety of protocols.
- Perform queries on directory systems. Active Directory allows you to search for an object by specifying query information. The two different query models available are Structured Query Language (SQL) and Lightweight Directory Access Protocol (LDAP).
- Access and use a single, hierarchical structure for administering and maintaining diverse and complicated network configurations through the Active Directory tree.
- Maintain users and provide system authentication against resources listed in directory services.

In this chapter, a brief overview of ADSI is given including the two main classes used to access and manipulate Active Directory, and examples of using Active Directory from an ASP.NET web page. Active Directory is a large and complex technology, and if this chapter whets your appetite, more information can be found in Appendix G, ".NET Resource List."

Introducing Directory Services

The Active Directory service is a key component of Windows 2000. In this section, concepts and technologies behind Active Directory Services are introduced. This is by no means a detailed account, but enough information is presented to understand the fundamentals behind directory service. An overview of how Active Directory works is presented, as well as an outline of the key technical benefits it offers to ASP.NET applications.

Modern operating systems require mechanisms for managing the identities and relationships of the resources, which make up the networked environments in which they operate. A directory service provides a central place to store information about network-based entities. These entities can be

- Applications
- Files
- Printers
- Users

Directory services also provide a way to name, describe, locate, access, manage, and secure information about these resources. A directory service also can act as the main switchboard to a network-based operating system. It is through this service that an operating system or an application can manage the identities and relationships between networked resources, thus enabling interoperability between resources.

Because a directory service can supply this network system functionality, it must be tightly coupled with the management and security mechanisms of the operating system to ensure the integrity of the network. The directory service also plays a key role in an organization's ability to maintain the network infrastructure, perform system administration, and control the company's information systems from a central repository of resources.

What Is an Active Directory?

As previously stated, Active Directory is an essential part of the Windows 2000 architecture, which is an improvement over the domain architecture of Windows NT. It is designed to provide a directory service that was specifically optimized for distributed networking environments, such as the Internet and large organizations. Active Directory enables companies and developers to share and maintain network resources and users. Active Directory also acts as the central authority for network security handling the authentication and authorization of user's access to resources accessible by the network. Active Directory also can be used as an integration tool between differing operating systems and tools. Because Active Directory is based on the LDAP industry standard application program interface (API) for directory services, this means you can share resources between two different operating systems that have an LDAP compliant directory service running on them.

In short, Active Directory Services provide a single point of management for Windows-based user accounts, clients, servers, and applications. It also can help companies integrate disparate systems that are not Windows-based or using Windows-based applications.

Why Use Directory Services?

In most companies, there are various pieces of software, most of which may contain sensitive data. As such, they require password access. In addition to the systems inside the company, the software might have an intranet or a web site that might require password access. Finally, consider the company staff member's desktop, which also needs a password to access it. The problem is now apparent. In the previous scenario, we have multiple passwords for multiple systems. From an administrator's point of view, that's a lot of passwords to track, considering every person in a company accesses these applications. From a user's standpoint, it is an irritating chore. A brief recap of these issues follows:

- End users must employ multiple user accounts and passwords to log in to different systems, and they must know the exact locations of information on the network.

- Administrators must understand how to manage each directory within the network and must duplicate many steps when procedures, such as adding a new employee to a company, involve many different directories and/or applications.

- Application developers must write different logic for every directory that their applications need to access, and also take into account the network security issues of which they might have little or no knowledge.

If all of the applications support Active Directory, it can be of immediate use. After the user logs in, he is authenticated for all of the resources used by these applications. The developers, therefore, use one API for authenticating users and network resources, and the network administrators update and maintain one user account for that user/employee, no matter how many applications they use.

In the real world, it is unlikely all applications will support directory services; however, it is becoming more and more common. Even if new applications only use this functionality, it still saves development and administration effort and time.

How Does Active Directory Work?

Active Directory lets developers store information in a hierarchical, object-oriented fashion.

Active Directory uses objects to represent network resources, such as users, groups, machines, devices, and applications. It also uses containers to represent organizational data, such as departments, or collections of related objects, such as printers or users. The information is organized in a tree-like structure made up of containers and objects, similar to the way the Windows operating system uses folders and files to organize data.

Active Directory also manages the relationships between containers and objects, which provides a centralized view of the company and its resources. This makes it easier to find, manage, and use resources in a distributed network environment.

The Active Directory hierarchy structure is flexible and configurable enough to allow developers to use resources in a way that optimizes their usability and manageability.

Containers are used to represent collections of users, machines, devices, and applications. Containers can be nested inside each other to show an accurate organizational structure.

As mentioned earlier, Active Directory stores information about its environment as objects. These objects are assigned attributes, which describe specific characteristics about the object. This enables developers to store a wide range of information in a directory and tightly control access to it, or use this managed information for specific tasks in their applications.

Active Directory implements object and attribute-level security that enables both developers and administrators to control the access of information stored in the directory. Developers and administrators can also assign access privileges for each attribute of an object, as well as for the entire object.

The Benefits of Active Directory

Active Directory is integrated at a very low level with Windows 2000 Server and gives network administrators, developers, and users access to a directory service that

- Simplifies most administration tasks.
- Strengthens network security by providing a single point of access and authentication.

Simplifying Administration Tasks

As companies add applications to their infrastructure and hire more personnel, they need to distribute more software to the desktop, intranet, Internet, and manage multiple application directories. Active Directory enables administrators to significantly reduce administration time by providing a centralized place to manage users, groups, network resources, and applications; distribute software; and manage desktop/application configuration. Here are two examples:

- Provides centralized management for Windows user accounts, clients, servers, and applications as well as the ability to synchronize with existing directory services.
- Simplifies the management and use of file and print services by making network resources easier to find, configure, and use.

Because users and network resources are hierarchically organized, Active Directory allows administrators and developers to have centralized management for user accounts, clients, servers, and applications. This reduces the time and effort required to create, maintain, and support multiple users with multiple user accounts. It also reduces the complexity of the network security model and resource usage.

In addition to making network management easier for administrators, Active Directory also makes it easier for everyone to use the network; users have fewer logins to contend with and they do not need to know where network resources are located. Active Directory does this for them. Life is made easier for developers because centralized authentication and authorization is provided for their applications. Also provided is the ability to store application-specific data in an efficient hierarchal manner, as well as the ability to store user-based information.

Strengthening Network Security

Active Directory provides robust security services that are used to manage user authentication and authorize access to network resources, applications, and application-specific data stored in the active server. Security is a complex topic and is prone to errors. It can also take a considerable amount of development time to implement. Luckily, Active Directory centralizes resource management and forces a role-based security model for all of its stored resources. The following list mentions some of the security features provided by Active Directory:

- **Password Security and User Management**—Provides single sign-on to network resources with integrated, security services that are transparent to users.

- **Locked Application Configuration**—Ensures that application configuration data is tamper-proof by configuring desktop and web application configuration settings and preventing access to administration operations.

- **More Scaleable Deployment**—Increases the flexibility in which an application can be deployed and makes said applications more scalable and secure.

- **Strict Security Access**—Tightly controls security by setting access control privileges on directory objects and their attributes.

Many companies have a diverse collection of technologies that need to work together. As a direct result of this, the companies' networks also have an equally diverse collection of directories to work with, such as those used for email servers, applications, network devices, and e-commerce applications. Active Directory provides a standard interface for application integration to ensure that Windows can interoperate with a wide variety of applications and devices for the following reasons:

- Flexibility for all future applications' features and network infrastructure.

- Consolidated management of application directories.

- Development and deployment of directory-enabled applications.

Active Directory, as mentioned previously, can become a centralized integration point for distributed systems and for consolidating directory and administration tasks. By exposing all of the Windows 2000 directory features through standard-based interfaces such as LDAP, ADSI, and a few others, developers and companies can consolidate existing directories and develop directory-enabled applications and network infrastructure.

Active Directory also provides a development platform for directory-enabled applications, enabling application developers to control the behavior of an application based on the user's role in the company. A directory-enabled application can store additional application-specific data in a user's profile in the directory, and use it to provide user-specific information and access rights in the application.

Beyond Windows

Active Directory ensures interoperability of the Windows platform with a wide variety of applications and devices. By supporting the LDAP API standard, this enables Active Directory to integrate, share, and manipulate data/information stored in other systems using an LDAP-compatible directory service.

Active Directory Technology Summary

In this section of the chapter is a detailed explanation of the two main classes used by the .NET framework that access and manipulate data stored in the Windows 2000 Active directory.

The Directory Services API, which is part of the .NET framework through this API, enables accessing, reading, and manipulating Active Directories. The Directory Services API consists of two main classes:

- `DirectoryEntry`—Used to retrieve and manipulate Active Directory objects and properties.

- `DirectorySearcher`—Used to search through the active directory for objects to retrieve and manipulate.

These classes are in the `System.DirectoryServices` namespace and must be included in ASP.NET web pages that use directory services.

```
<%@ Imports namespace="System.DirectoryServices" %>
```

After this has been done, the `DirectoryEntry` and the `DirectorySearcher` classes will become available.

The *DirectoryEntry* Class

This class is used to directly retrieve and then subsequently manipulate an Active Directory object. An example would be retrieving a user profile and displaying some of the user's profile information.

The common properties and methods of the `DirectoryEntry` class along with some syntax examples are explained in the following examples.

DirectoryEntry Class Properties

The `DirectoryEntry` class properties are as follows:

- `AuthenticationType`—Gets or sets the type of authentication to use. It can be any of the following values: `Anonymous`, `Delegation`, `Encryption`, `FastBind`, `None`, `ReadonlyServer`, `Sealing`, `Secure`, `SecureSocketsLayer`, `ServerBind`, `Signing`.

Syntax example:
```
Dim myDirectoryEntry as New DirectoryServices("WinNT://BOA-SERVER/Users/Worleys")
```

Syntax example:
```
MyDirectoryEntry.AuthenticationType = AuthenticationTypes.None
```

- **Children**—Returns a DirectoryEntries collection containing the child entries of this node in the Active Directory hierarchy.

Syntax example:
```
01 Dim myDirectoryEntry as New DirectoryServices("WinNT://BOA-SERVER/Users/Worleys")
02 Dim myDirChildren as System.DirectoryServices.DirectoryEntries
03 MyDirChikldren = MyDirectoryEntry.Children
```

- **Exists**—Searches Active Directory at the specified path to see whether an entry exists.

Syntax example:
```
01 If MyDirectoryEntry.Exists("WinNT://BOA-SERVER/Users/worleys") then
02      'User worleys exists on the BOA-SERVER, so now we can do
03      'some processing
04 Else
05      'Do some kind of error processing
06      'User worleys does not exist in the users domain of BOA-SERVER
07 End if
```

- **Name**—Returns the name of the object as named with the underlying directory service.

Syntax example:
```
01 Dim myDirectoryEntry as New DirectoryServices("WinNT://BOA-SERVER/Users/Worleys")
02 Response.write(MyDirectoryEntry.Name)
```

- **Parent**—Returns a directory entry's parent in the Active Directory hierarchy.

Syntax example:
```
01 Dim myParentEntry as DirectoryServices.DirectoryEntry
02 MyParentEntry = MyDirectoryEntry.Parent
```

- **Password**—Gets and sets the password to use when authenticating a client.

Syntax example:
```
01 Dim myDirectoryEntry as New DirectoryServices("WinNT://BOA-SERVER/Users/Worleys")
02 MyDirectoryEntry.Password = "LetMeIn"
```

- **Path**—Gets and sets the path for this `DirectoryEntry`.

Syntax example:
```
01 Dim myDirectoryEntry as New DirectoryServices("WinNT://BOA-SERVER/Users/Worleys")
02 Reponse.write(MyDirectoryEntry.Path)
```

- **Properties**—Returns a `PropertyCollection` of properties set on this object and enables direct access to property values.

Syntax example: Returning a properties collection.
```
01 Dim myDirectoryEntry as New DirectoryServices("WinNT://BOA-SERVER/Users/Worleys")
02 Dim myEntryProperties as propertyCollection
03 myEntryProperties = MyDirectoryEntry.Properties
```

Syntax example: Modifying a property value.
```
01 Dim myDirectoryEntry as New DirectoryServices("WinNT://BOA-SERVER/Users/Worleys")
02 Response.write("Name: "+myDirectoryEntry.properties("Name")(0))
```

The preceding example returns the `name` property of the user `worleys` in the user's container of the `BOA-SERVER` domain.

- **SchemaClassName**—Returns name of the schema used for this `DirectoryEntry`.

Syntax example:
```
01 Dim myDirectoryEntry as New DirectoryServices("WinNT://BOA-SERVER/Users/Worleys")
02 Response.write(MyDirectoryEntry.SchemaClassName)
```

- **SchemaEntry**—Returns `DirectoryEntry` that holds schema information for this entry. An entry's `SchemaClassName` determines what properties are valid for it.

Syntax example:
```
01 Dim myDirectoryEntry as New DirectoryServices("WinNT://BOA-SERVER/Users/Worleys")
02 Dim mySchema as DirectoryEntry
03 mySchema = MyDirectoryEntry.SchemaEntry
```

- **UsePropertyCache**—Returns a value indicating whether the cache should be committed after each operation.

Syntax example:
```
01 Dim myDirectoryEntry as New DirectoryServices("WinNT://BOA-SERVER/Users/Worleys")
02 MyDirectoryEntry.UsePropertyCache = False
```

- **Username**—Returns which username to use when authenticating the client.

Syntax example:
```
01 Dim myDirectoryEntry as New DirectoryServices("WinNT://BOA-SERVER/Users/Worleys")
02 Response.write(MyDirectoryEntry.UserName)
```

DirectoryEntry Class Methods

The DirectoryEntry class methods are as follows:

- **Close**—Closes the DirectoryEntry.

Syntax example:
```
01 Dim myDirectoryEntry as New DirectoryServices("WinNT://BOA-SERVER/Users/Worleys")
02 MyDirectoryEntry.Close()
```

- **CommitChanges**—Saves any changes to a directory entry in Active Directory.

Syntax example:
```
01 Dim myDirectoryEntry as New DirectoryServices("WinNT://BOA-SERVER/Users/Worleys")
02 MyDirectoryEntry.Properties("Name")(0) = "A new name for me"
03 MyDirectoryEntry.CommitChanges
```

- **DeleteTree**—Deletes a directory entry and its subtree from Active Directory.

Syntax example:
```
01 Dim myDirectoryEntry as New DirectoryServices("WinNT://BOA-SERVER/Custom")
02 MyDirectoryEntry.DeleteTree()
```

The preceding example binds to a user's defined schema in Active Directory called *Custom*, and then promptly deletes the schema and any objects within it.

- **RefreshCache**—Loads property values for a directory entry into the property cache.

Syntax example:

```
01 Dim myDirectoryEntry as New DirectoryServices("WinNT://BOA-SERVER/Users/Worleys")
02 MyDirectoryEntry.RefreshCache()
```

- `Rename`—Changes the name of a directory entry to another name.

Syntax example:

```
01 Dim myDirectoryEntry as New DirectoryServices("WinNT://BOA-SERVER/Users/Worleys")
02 MyDirectoryEntry.Rename("NewObjectName")
```

The *DirectorySearcher* Class

The `DirectorySearcher` class is used to define and apply criteria for a search against any Active Directory entries.

The common properties and methods of the `DirectorySearcher` class along with some syntax examples are explained in the following examples.

DirectorySearcher Properties

The `DirectorySearcher` class properties are as follows:

- **CacheResults**—Gets or sets a value indicating whether the result is cached on the client's machine.

Syntax example:

```
01 Dim myDirectoryEntry as
02 New DirectoryServices.DirectoryEntry("WinNT://BOA-SERVER/Users")
03 Dim myDirectorySearcher as New DirectoryServices.DirectorySearcher(myDirectoryEntry)
04 myDirectorySearcher.CacheResults = True
```

- **ClientTimeout**—Gets and sets the maximum amount of time that the client waits for the server to return results. If the server does not respond within this time, the search is aborted and no results are returned.

Syntax example:

```
01 Dim myDirectoryEntry as New
02 DirectoryServices.DirectoryEntry("WinNT://BOA-SERVER/Users")
03 Dim myDirectorySearcher as New DirectoryServices.DirectorySearcher(myDirectoryEntry)
04 MyDirectorySearcher.ClientTimeOut = 30
```

- **Filter**—Gets and sets LDAP filter string.

Syntax example:
```
01 Dim myDirectoryEntry as New DirectoryServices("LDAP://CN=users DC=BOA-
02 SERVER DC=com")
03 Dim myDirectorySearcher as New DirectoryServices.DirectorySearcher(myDirectoryEntry)
04 Dim myDirectorySearcher as New DirectorySearcher(myDirectoryEntry)
05 MyDirectorySearcher.Filter = "(Name=Worleys)"
```

The preceding example sets an LDAP search filter to search the user's area of the domain BOA-SERVER for users with a Name attribute equal to worleys. This does not perform the search, but instead sets up the query string to be used.

- **PropertiesToLoad**—Returns DirectoryEntry properties retrieved during the search. By default, the Path and Name properties are retrieved.

Syntax example:
```
01 Dim myDirectoryEntry as New
02 DirectoryServices.DirectoryEntry("WinNT://BOA-SERVER/Users")
03 Dim myDirectorySearcher as New DirectoryServices.DirectorySearcher(myDirectoryEntry)
04 MyDirectorySearcher.PropertiesToLoad.Add("Name")
05 MyDirectorySearcher.PropertiesToLoad.Add("Address")
06 MyDirectorySearcher.PropertiesToLoad.Add("HomeNumber")
```

- **PropertyNamesOnly**—Gets and sets a value indicating whether the search retrieves only the names of attributes to which values have been assigned.

Syntax example:
```
01 Dim myDirectoryEntry as New
02 DirectoryServices.DirectoryEntry("WinNT://BOA-SERVER/Users")
03 Dim myDirectorySearcher as New
04 DirectoryServices.DirectorySearcher(myDirectoryEntry)
05 MyDirectorySearcher.PropertyNamesOnly = True
```

- **SearchRoot**—Gets and sets the node in the Active Directory hierarchy where the search starts.

Syntax example:
```
01 Dim myDirectoryEntry as New
02 DirectoryServices.DirectoryEntry("WinNT://BOA-SERVER/Users")
03 Dim myDirectorySearcher as New
04 DirectoryServices.DirectorySearcher(myDirectoryEntry)
05 MyDirectorySearcher.SearchRoot(new
06 DirectoryServices.DirectoryEntry("WinNT://BOA-SERVER"))
```

- **SearchScope**—Gets and sets the scope of the search that is observed by the server.

The scope can be defined as any one of the following:

- **Base**—Limits the search to the `base` object. The result contains a maximum of one object.
- **OneLevel**—Searches one level of the current `children`, excluding the `base` object.
- **Subtree**—Searches the whole subtree.

Syntax example:

```
01 Dim myDirectoryEntry as New
02 DirectoryServices.DirectoryEntry("WinNT://BOA-SERVER/Users")
03 Dim myDirectorySearcher as New
04 DirectoryServices.DirectorySearcher(myDirectoryEntry)
05 MyDirectorySearcher.SearchScope = Base
```

- **ServerTimeLimit**—Gets and sets the maximum amount of time the server spends searching. If the time limit is reached, only entries found up to that point are returned.

Syntax example:

```
01 Dim myDirectoryEntry as New
02 DirectoryServices.DirectoryEntry("WinNT://BOA-SERVER/Users")
03 Dim myDirectorySearcher as New
04 DirectoryServices.DirectorySearcher(myDirectoryEntry)
05 MyDirectorySearcher.ServerTimeLimit = 60
```

- **SizeLimit**—Gets or sets the maximum number of objects the server returns in a search.

Syntax example:

```
01 Dim myDirectoryEntry as New
02 DirectoryServices.DirectoryEntry("WinNT://BOA-SERVER/Users")
03 Dim myDirectorySearcher as New
04 DirectoryServices.DirectorySearcher(myDirectoryEntry)
05 MyDirectorySearcher.SizeLimit = 100
```

- **Sort**—Gets and sets the `DirectoryEntry` property on which the results are sorted.

Syntax example:
```
01 Dim myDirectoryEntry as New
02 DirectoryServices.DirectoryEntry("WinNT://BOA-SERVER/Users")
03 Dim myDirectorySearcher as New DirectoryServices.DirectorySearcher(myDirectoryEntry)
04 Dim mySort as DirectoryServices.SortOption
05 mySort.Direction = sortDirection.ascending
06 mySort.Property = "Name"
07 MyDirectorySearcher.Sort = mySort
```

DirectorySearcher Methods

The `DirectorySearcher` class methods are as follows:

- **FindAll**—Executes the search and returns a collection of entries that are found.

Syntax example:
```
01 Dim myDirectoryEntry as New
02 DirectoryServices.DirectoryEntry("WinNT://BOA-SERVER/Users")
03 Dim myDirectorySearcher as New DirectoryServices.DirectorySearcher(myDirectoryEntry)
04 Dim myResults as DirectoryServices.SearchResultCollection
05 MyResults = MyDirectorySearcher.FindAll()
```

- **FindOne**—Executes the search and returns only the first entry found.

Syntax example:
```
01 Dim myDirectoryEntry as New DirectoryServices.DirectoryEntry("WinNT://BOA-SERVER/Users")
02 Dim myDirectorySearcher as New DirectoryServices.DirectorySearcher(myDirectoryEntry)
03 Dim myResult as DirectoryServices.SearchResult
04 MyResult = MyDirectorySearcher.FindOne()
```

Summary

Active Directory Services within Windows 2000 provides a centralized point for managing and securing Windows user accounts, clients, servers, and applications. Active directory support through .NET Directory Services can be a powerful tool in Internet development when you need a fast directory-based information source with a very structured and robust security system.

13

Localizing and Globalizing ASP.NET Applications

T HIS CHAPTER INTRODUCES LOCALIZATION and globalization with ASP.NET. It introduces the concepts of localization and gives a brief overview of what is involved. It also explains the differences between localization and globalization, and then looks at the localization features supported by ASP.NET. By the end of this chapter, you should have an understanding of how to localize and globalize an ASP.NET application.

Terms You Need to Know

The following lists various terms and technologies that are used in this chapter:

- **Localization**—This is the process that translates information from its base or initial language and culture settings to another culture's language.

- **Globalization**—This is the same as localization, however the information is localized for a group of cultures rather than just one, therefore, it is global in scope.

- **Culture**—This term is used to describe the cultural settings for a country.

- **Language**—The term *language* is known by everyone, and it is used to define a group of sounds and symbols for communication.

- **Locale**—A locale is a specific classification for an international area where a user might be working. Generally, locale is referred to as opposed to a language because languages by themselves do not necessarily indicate locale. For instance, in both the United States and the United Kingdom, English is the spoken language; however, the date format and currency symbols are quite different.

What Is Localization?

Since the advent of the Internet, it has never been easier to communicate information to a worldwide audience. In fact, the web is ideally suited for this purpose. However, before taking advantage of this audience, you must be aware that having a worldwide audience for a web application does not necessarily mean that the audience can use it. In fact, most web sites and web applications on the Internet are only written in one language—American English. However, if the customer does not understand American English, the site or application is useless to them, and you are missing out on a very large audience for your products and services. This chapter looks at how to make your web applications global. This is done by creating a localized version of the site for each country and culture to which you want to make your web site accessible.

Fortunately, ASP.NET comes with a strong set of tools to enable the creation of multilanguage- and multiculture-based web applications. The following is a list of tools provided:

- **Cultural Information**—Sets culture-based information for the current user of the application through their browser or by programmed code.

- **Regional Information**—Sets region-based information for the current user of the application.

- **Resource Management and Usage**—Used to load and retrieve string resources from external files for use in localized applications.

Cultural Information

When you localize a web application, you are making the application conform to a specific language of a country locale; you have to take many issues into account, which generally fall into the following areas:

- **Language Translation**—The process of translating from one language, to another (for instance, from English to French.)

- **UI Conformity**—User interface conformity is one area that seems to cause the most problems for web developers. This is mainly because a lot of web sites are designed with only one language in mind and when you apply cultural changes to that interface, the whole web site's look and feel changes. For example, even if we take a simple text-only web site with tables, some pretty big layout issues still exist due to the differing lengths of words and the grammar used in various languages. One way around this is to have multiple user interfaces for each language that are specifically localized and designed for the culture in which it is to be used. While this is the perfect solution, it is not necessarily realistic because of the sheer amount of work and maintenance involved.

White Space

Generally, most web sites use a "one-design-fits-all" approach, which means the web site design takes into account the various language issues involved by making the user interface more open in appearance. White space around the elements that make up the page provides space for elements, which when translated to another language, can be longer than the original elements for which the application was designed to support.

- **Number formats**—Another set of localization issues regards number formats, which are noticeable mostly in the currency number formats where the symbol of currency changes, as does the usage and placement of ',' and '.' in large decimal-based numbers.

- **Date and time formats**—The next set of issues to deal with are those regarding time and date formats. These too can be quite different depending on the culture. Personally, this is the one area where I have had the most issues because I am British, live in Canada, and do a lot of business with the United States. I always forget to swap the days and months around in the standard date format from dd/mm/yyyy to mm/dd/yyyy.

- **Calendars**—Some cultures use different calendars than in the West. For example, in Japan, the calendar can be different from the western calendar in terms of months, days in a month, weeks in a month, and months in a year.

- **String collation (sorting) and manipulation**—When translating from one language to another, simply replacing the text and fixing the grammar might not be enough. In some languages, the collation (sort) order of text can be different from what you are used to. This has an even greater impact than most people realize when they work with data-driven web sites because most of these sites present data logically grouped and sorted, but when translated, these groupings tend to get messed up and should be addressed. Fortunately, most large database suppliers allow you to change the collation orders used on tables of data, or you can create your own data access routines that deal with this issue.

- **Culture-specific taboos**—In some countries, certain words have other meanings, as do colors and objects. Some of these meanings can be quite different from the base language's meaning and could be offensive to some web users. Unfortunately, this is a very hard issue to deal with.

All the items mentioned could be dealt with using software solutions except for the last one, culture-specific taboos, which is one of the trickiest to deal with. For example, take a relatively trivial thing, such as using the color blue in a lot of areas of your web site. In most cultures, this is not an issue. However, in some areas of the world, the color blue is associated with death—it is used in the same way black is used for funerals in western society. Another example could quite simply have to do with the way a phrase was translated and might be offensive.

Problems with Translation

Consider the following: A Chinese, e-commerce web site is fully translated into English using a western layout. However, the translators have done a direct translation. At first glance this does not seem so bad until you realize that the Chinese language is very direct and simplistic in nature, which when directly converted into English, can come across as arrogant or offensive.

To further this example, I have a Chinese friend in England who, when learning to speak English, had difficulties because of language and grammar issues. One notable example was when my friend needed some change, so he could make a phone call. He would ask quite literally, "Give money now, need for phone." As you can see, while accurate to his needs, this comes across as quite rude and some people could be offended.

Regional Information

Regional information is a more limited set of cultural information available to developers for their web sites.

Unlike cultural information, regional information in ASP.NET is not tied to any settings. The regional information available is just that—information of the localization specifics of a region. ASP.NET provides access to regional information through the `RegionInfo` object.

Resource Management and Usage

One of the ways to support more than one language on a site is to use the *external string resource files*. These files contain all the displayed text in text-based files. A *resource manager* is used to get text-based data from a resource file by using its key value, and then returning the text for that key in the language of choice.

Localizing an ASP.NET Web Application

This section explains the main objects used when globalizing an ASP.NET web application and provides examples of their use. The topics covered are as follows:

- web.config globalization section and its application
- `@Page` directive and localization
- The `CultureInfo` object
- The string resource manager

By the end of this section, you will understand how to localize and globalize your web applications using ASP.NET and the tools it provides.

web.config Globalization Section and Its Application

The web.config file has a section in it specifically designed for use in localized and globalized applications. This section is the *globalization section*. An example of this section is shown in the following:

```
01 <configuration>
02
03   <system.web>
04
05     <globalization
06           fileEncoding="utf-8"
07           requestEncoding="utf-8"
08           responseEncoding="utf-8"
09           culture="en-US"
10           uiCulture="en-US"
11       />
12
13   </system.web>
14
15 </configuration>
```

The globalization section has five attributes, all of which can be set through the @Page directive on a Web Form, with the exception of the fileEncoding attribute, which can only be set in the web.config file. The globalization section should be used to setup the base locale of your application.

fileEncoding

fileEncoding is used to define the encoding type for .aspx, .asmx, and .asax file parsing. It can accept any of the following encoding types:

- **UTF-7**—Represents the Unicode UTF-7 byte encoding.
- **UTF-8**—Represents the Unicode UTF-8 byte encoding. This is also the most common web-based Unicode format.
- **UTF-16**—Represents the Unicode UTF-16 byte encoding.
- **ASCII**—Represents the Standard ASCII.

The following is an example of the use of the fileEncoding attribute:

```
fileEncoding="utf-8"
```

requestEncoding

requestEncoding specifies the encoding type of each incoming request that is processed by ASP.NET. It accepts the same encoding types as the fileEncoding attribute.

The following is an example of the use of the requestEncoding attribute:

```
requestEncoding="utf-8"
```

responseEncoding

responseEncoding specifies the encoding type of each outgoing response that is produced by ASP.NET. It accepts the same encoding types as the fileEncoding attribute.

The following is an example of the use of the responseEncoding attribute:

```
responseEncoding="utf-8"
```

culture

culture specifies the default culture that ASP.NET uses when processing incoming web requests.

uiCulture

uiCulture specifies the culture that ASP.NET uses to search for resources to use when processing a Web Form. A list of possible culture values is shown in Table 13.1.

Table 13.1   **Common Culture Codes**

Culture Code	Language/Country/Region	Culture Code	Language/Country/Region
af	Afrikaans	bg-BG	Bulgarian/Bulgaria
af-ZA	Afrikaans/South Africa	ca	Catalan
sq	Albanian	ca-ES	Catalan/Spain
sq-AL	Albanian/Albania	zh-HK	Chinese/Hong Kong S.A.R.
ar	Arabic	zh-MO	Chinese/Macau S.A.R.
ar-DZ	Arabic/Algeria	zh-CN	Chinese/China
ar-BH	Arabic/Bahrain	zh-CHS	Chinese (Simplified)
ar-EG	Arabic/Egypt	zh-SG	Chinese/Singapore
ar-IQ	Arabic/Iraq	zh-TW	Chinese/Taiwan
ar-JO	Arabic/Jordan	zh-CHT	Chinese (Traditional)
ar-KW	Arabic/Kuwait	hr	Croatian
ar-LB	Arabic/Lebanon	hr-HR	Croatian/Croatia
ar-LY	Arabic/Libya	cs	Czech
ar-MA	Arabic/Morocco	cs-CZ	Czech/Czech Republic
ar-OM	Arabic/Oman	da	Danish
ar-QA	Arabic/Qatar	da-DK	Danish/Denmark
ar-SA	Arabic/Saudi Arabia	div	Dhivehi
ar-SY	Arabic/Syria	div-MV	Dhivehi/Maldives
ar-TN	Arabic/Tunisia	nl	Dutch
ar-AE	Arabic/United Arab Emirates	nl-BE	Dutch/Belgium
ar-YE	Arabic/Yemen	nl-NL	Dutch/The Netherlands
hy	Armenian	en	English
hy-AM	Armenian/Armenia	en-AU	English/Australia
az	Azeri	en-BZ	English/Belize
Cy-az-AZ	Azeri (Cyrillic)/Azerbaijan	en-CA	English/Canada
Lt-az-AZ	Azeri (Latin)/Azerbaijan	en-CB	English/Caribbean
eu	Basque	en-IE	English/Ireland
eu-ES	Basque/Spain	en-JM	English/Jamaica
be	Belarusian	en-NZ	English/New Zealand
be-BY	Belarusian/Belarus	en-PH	English/Philippines
bg	Bulgarian	en-ZA	English/South Africa
		en-TT	English/Trinidad and Tobago

continues ▶

Table 13.1 **Continued**

Culture Code	Language/Country/ Region	Culture Code	Language/Country/ Region
en-GB	English/United Kingdom	he-IL	Hebrew/Israel
en-US	English/United States	hi	Hindi
en-ZW	English/Zimbabwe	hi-IN	Hindi/India
et	Estonian	hu	Hungarian
et-EE	Estonian/Estonia	hu-HU	Hungarian/Hungary
fo	Faroese	is	Icelandic
fo-FO	Faroese/Faroe Islands	is-IS	Icelandic/Iceland
fa	Farsi	id	Indonesian
fa-IR	Farsi/Iran	id-ID	Indonesian/Indonesia
fi	Finnish	it	Italian
fi-FI	Finnish/Finland	it-IT	Italian/Italy
fr	French	it-CH	Italian/Switzerland
fr-BE	French/Belgium	ja	Japanese
fr-CA	French/Canada	ja-JP	Japanese/Japan
fr-FR	French/France	kn	Kannada
fr-LU	French/Luxembourg	kn-IN	Kannada/India
fr-MC	French/Monaco	kk	Kazakh
fr-CH	French/Switzerland	kk-KZ	Kazakh/Kazakhstan
gl	Galician	kok	Konkani
gl-ES	Galician/Spain	kok-IN	Konkani/India
ka	Georgian	ko	Korean
ka-GE	Georgian/Georgia	ko-KR	Korean/Korea
de	German	ky	Kyrgyz
de-AT	German/Austria	ky-KZ	Kyrgyz/Kazakhstan
de-DE	German/Germany	lv	Latvian
de-LI	German/Liechtenstein	lv-LV	Latvian/Latvia
de-LU	German/Luxembourg	lt	Lithuanian
de-CH	German/Switzerland	lt-LT	Lithuanian/Lithuania
el	Greek	mk	FYRO Macedonian
el-GR	Greek/Greece	mk-MK	FYRO Macedonian/Former Yugoslav Republic of Macedonia
gu	Gujarati		
gu-IN	Gujarati/India		
he	Hebrew	ms	Malay

Culture Code	Language/Country/Region	Culture Code	Language/Country/Region
ms-BN	Malay/Brunei	es-CL	Spanish/Chile
ms-MY	Malay/Malaysia	es-CO	Spanish/Colombia
mr	Marathi	es-CR	Spanish/Costa Rica
mr-IN	Marathi/India	es-DO	Spanish/Dominican Republic
mn	Mongolian	es-EC	Spanish/Ecuador
mn-MN	Mongolian/Mongolia	es-SV	Spanish/El Salvador
no	Norwegian	es-GT	Spanish/Guatemala
nb-NO	Norwegian (Bokmål)/Norway	es-HN	Spanish/Honduras
		es-MX	Spanish/Mexico
nn-NO	Norwegian (Nynorsk)/Norway	es-NI	Spanish/Nicaragua
pl	Polish	es-PA	Spanish/Panama
pl-PL	Polish/Poland	es-PY	Spanish/Paraguay
pt	Portuguese	es-PE	Spanish/Peru
pt-BR	Portuguese/Brazil	es-PR	Spanish/Puerto Rico
pt-PT	Portuguese/Portugal	es-ES	Spanish/Spain
pa	Punjabi	es-UY	Spanish/Uruguay
pa-IN	Punjabi/India	es-VE	Spanish/Venezuela
ro	Romanian	sw	Swahili
ro-RO	Romanian/Romania	sw-KE	Swahili/Kenya
ru	Russian	sv	Swedish
ru-RU	Russian/Russia	sv-FI	Swedish/Finland
sa	Sanskrit	sv-SE	Swedish/Sweden
sa-IN	Sanskrit/India	syr	Syriac
Cy-sr-SP	Serbian (Cyrillic)/Serbia	syr-SY	Syriac/Syria
Lt-sr-SP	Serbian (Latin)/Serbia	ta	Tamil
sk	Slovak	ta-IN	Tamil/India
sk-SK	Slovak/Slovakia	tt	Tatar
sl	Slovenian	tt-TA	Tatar/Tatarstan
sl-SI	Slovenian/Slovenia	te	Telugu
es	Spanish	te-IN	Telugu/India
es-AR	Spanish/Argentina	th	Thai
es-BO	Spanish/Bolivia	th-TH	Thai/Thailand

continues ▶

Table 13.1 **Continued**

Culture Code	Language/Country/ Region	Culture Code	Language/Country/ Region
tr	Turkish		
tr-TR	Turkish/Turkey	uz	Uzbek
uk	Ukrainian	Cy-uz-UZ	Uzbek (Cyrillic)/Uzbekistan
uk-UA	Ukrainian/Ukraine	Lt-uz-UZ	Uzbek (Latin)/Uzbekistan
ur	Urdu	vi	Vietnamese
ur-PK	Urdu/Pakistan	vi-VN	Vietnamese/Vietnam

@Page Directive and Localization

As well as being able to define default culture settings in the web.config page, you can also configure each Web Form to change or use any of the attributes supported by the web.config configuration file, with the exception of the fileEncoding type because it is needed to read the Web Form's source file. The following lists the four main localization settings supported by the @Page directive:

- responseEncoding
- requestEncoding
- culture
- uiCulture

These attributes take the same values as those previously discussed in the section "web.config Globalization Section and Its Application."

The following is an example of syntax:

```
01 <%@ Page responseEncoding="utf-8"
02 requestEncoding="utf-8"
03 culture="en-US"
04 uiCulture="en-US" %>
```

The *CultureInfo* Object

The CultureInfo object lies at the core of the ASP.NET globalization API. By using this object's properties, we can make our applications act in a localized manner. The CultureInfo is used to setup culture environmental settings, and the uiCulture object holds the information used by the resource manager and by the internal presentation objects of ASP.NET when rendering Web Forms. For this reason, I am only going to describe the culture object and its most common properties and methods, which are listed in Table 13.2 and 13.3.

Table 13.2   **The *CultureInfo* Object Properties**

Property	Description
CurrentCulture	Returns a CultureInfo object for the current culture.
CurrentUICulture	Returns a CultureInfo object for the current UI culture.
DateTimeFormat	Returns a DateTimeFormatInfo object.
Name	Returns the culture name in the format "<languagefull> (<country/regionfull>)" in English.
LCID	Returns the culture identifier for the current culture.
NativeName	Returns the culture name in the format "<languagefull> (<country/regionfull>)" in the language of the current culture.
NumberFormat	Returns a NumberFormatInfo object.
OptionalCalendars	Returns a list of optional calendars that can be used by the current culture.
ThreeLetterISOLanguageName	Returns the ISO 639-2 three-letter code for the current language of the current culture.
ThreeLetterWindowsLanguageName	Returns the three-letter code for the current language as defined in the Windows API.
TwoLetterISOLanguageName	Returns the ISO 639-1 two-letter code for the language of the current culture.

Table 13.3   **The *CultureInfo* Object Methods**

Method	Description
CreateSpecificCulture	Creates a new CultureInfo object for a specific culture.
GetCultures	Returns a collection of supported cultures.

Now that you have some idea of what culture information you have access to, it is time to look at a working example. In Listing 13.1, I have created a simple application that first accepts a culture code through a DropDownList control; after it has been selected, some of its properties are displayed.

Listing 13.1   **(1301.aspx)** *CultureInfo* **Demonstration**

```
001 <%@Page Language="VB" ResponseEncoding="UTF-8"%>
002
003 <%@Import Namespace="System.Threading"%>
004 <%@Import Namespace="System.Globalization"%>
005
006
007 <html>
008 <head>
009
010 <script runat="server" Language="VB">
011
012 dim _culture as cultureinfo = cultureinfo.currentculture()
013
014 Sub Page_Load(sender As Object, args As EventArgs)
015
016 If not IsPostBack() Then
017
018  dim allCultures() as CultureInfo
019
020  allcultures = CultureInfo.GetCultures(CultureTypes.InstalledWin32Cultures)
021
022   'Bind all cultures to Combo Box
023   comboCultures.DataSource = allCultures
024   comboCultures.DataTextField = "englishname"
025   comboCultures.DataValueField = "name"
026   comboCultures.databind()
027
028 else
029
030   _culture = CultureInfo.createspecificculture(ctype(comboCultures.selecteditem.Value,
➥string))
031
032 End If
033
034 End Sub
035
036
037
038 sub showoptionalcalendars ()
039
040    dim colCal() as System.Globalization.Calendar
041    dim myCal as System.Globalization.Calendar
042
043    colCal = _culture.OptionalCalendars
044
045        for each myCal in colCal
046             if not myCal.tostring = _culture.calendar.tostring then
047                  response.write(ctype(mycal.tostring, string) + "<br>")
048             end if
049        next
050
051
```

```
052 end sub
053
054
055 sub showtextinfo ()
056
057     response.write("ANSI Code Page: " + ctype(_culture.textinfo.ANSICodePage, string) +
↵"<br>")
058     response.write("EBCDIC Code Page: " + ctype(_culture.textinfo.EBCDICCodePage, string)
+ "<br>")
059     response.write("MAC Code Page: " + ctype(_culture.textinfo.MacCodePage, string) +
↵"<br>")
060     response.write("OEM Code Page: " + ctype(_culture.textinfo.OemCodePage, string) +
↵"<br>")
061     response.write("ANSI Code Page: " + ctype(_culture.textinfo.ANSICodePage, string) +
↵"<br>")
062     response.write("List Separator: " + ctype(_culture.textinfo.ListSeparator, string) +
↵"<br>")
063
064 end sub
065
066 </script>
067
068 </head>
069
070 <body>
071
072
073 <h3>Culture Settings</h3>
074
075 <form runat="server">
076 Select Culture
077
078 <asp:DropDownList id="comboCultures" runat="server" autopostback="True" />
079
080 <hr>
081
082 <table colspacing="3">
083
084 <tr>
085 <td><b>English Name</b> </td>
086 <td><%= _culture.EnglishName %></td>
087 </tr>
088
089 <tr>
090 <td><b>Display Name</b></td>
091 <td><%=_culture.DisplayName%></td>
092 </tr>
093
094 <tr>
095 <td><b>Is Neutral Culture</b></td>
096 <td> <%= _culture.IsNeutralCulture %></td>
097 </tr>
```

continues ▶

Listing 13.1 **Continued**

```
098
099 <tr>
100 <td><b>Is Read Only</b></td>
101 <td> <%= _culture.IsReadOnly %></td>
102 </tr>
103
104 <tr>
105 <td><b>LCID</b></td>
106 <td> <%= _culture.LCID %></td>
107 </tr>
108
109 <tr>
110 <td><b>Name</b></td>
111 <td> <%= _culture.name %></td>
112 </tr>
113
114 <tr>
115 <td><b>Native Name</b></td>
116 <td> <%= _culture.nativename %></td>
117 </tr>
118
119 <tr>
120 <td><b>Calendar</b></td>
121 <td> <%= _culture.calendar.tostring %></td>
122 </tr>
123
124 <tr>
125 <td><b>Optional Calendars</b></td>
126 <td> <% showoptionalcalendars() %></td>
127 </tr>
128
129 <tr>
130 <td valign="top"><b>Text Information</b></td>
131 <td> <% showtextinfo() %></td>
132 </tr>
133
134 </table>
135 </form>
136
137 </body>
138
139 </html>
```

The easiest way to explain this code is to walk through the process as the user uses the interface.

When the user first uses the application, the following page is presented (see Figure 13.1).

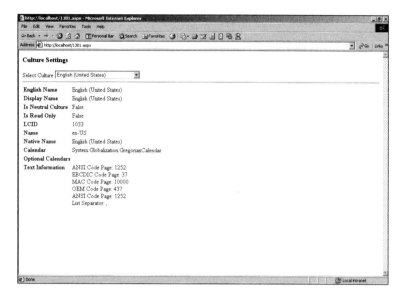

Figure 13.1 `CultureInfo` demo when first used.

After a selection is made, the same page is displayed with differing information (see Figure 13.2). Also note that you only see cultures supported by your system in the list.

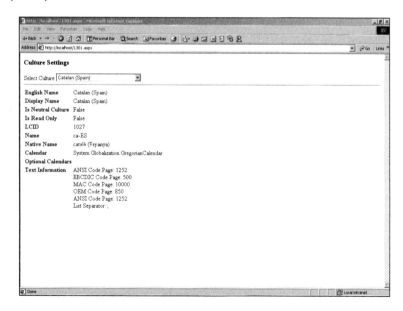

Figure 13.2 `CultureInfo` demo after selecting a new culture.

The first thing to look at is the combo box. The combo box has a list of all the supported cultures available on the user's machine. This is accomplished by using the code in the following form_load event:

```
01 If not IsPostBack() Then
02
03  dim allCultures() as CultureInfo
04
05  allcultures = CultureInfo.GetCultures(CultureTypes.InstalledWin32Cultures)
06
07  'Bind all cultures to Combo Box
08  comboCultures.DataSource = allCultures
09  comboCultures.DataTextField = "englishname"
10  comboCultures.DataValueField = "name"
11  comboCultures.databind()
12
13 else
14
15   _culture = CultureInfo.createspecificculture(ctype(comboCultures.selecteditem.Value,
➡string))
16
17 End If
18
19 End Sub
```

Line 3 simply declares a new array of objects of CultureInfo type, which is subsequently updated with an array of cultures installed on the system (server side). The next few lines bind the combo box data source to the array, bind the combo box DataTextField property to the englishname property of the passed objects, and sets the DataValueField to the name property of the passed objects.

At the bottom of the page, is a list of properties that pertain to the selected culture in the combo box. When a new item is selected, the new culture information is displayed. The code for this is almost always in the Web Form and consists of accessing the CultureInfo object's properties directly. The exception to this is the optionalCalendars property, where I have created a separate sub to enumerate through the returned values and output any items. The other exception is the textinfo property. The subs that do these are as follows:

```
01 sub showoptionalcalendars ()
02
03 dim colCal() as System.Globalization.Calendar
04 dim myCal as System.Globalization.Calendar
05
06 colCal = _culture.OptionalCalendars
07
08 for each myCal in colCal
```

```
09    if not myCal.tostring = _culture.calendar.tostring then
10          Response.write(ctype(mycal.tostring, string) + "<br>")
11    end if
12 next
13
14 end sub
```

The `showoptionalcalendars` sub first creates an array of `calendar` objects (line 1), which are then filled with an array of `calendar` objects from the `culture.OptionalCalendars` property. Lines 8 through 12 simply iterate through the array and write the name of the `calendar` objects that have been passed out.

```
01 sub showtextinfo ()
02
03    response.write("ANSI Code Page: " + ctype(_culture.textinfo.ANSICodePage, string) +
↪"<br>")
04    response.write("EBCDIC Code Page: " + ctype(_culture.textinfo.EBCDICCodePage, string)
↪+ "<br>")
05    response.write("MAC Code Page: " + ctype(_culture.textinfo.MacCodePage, string) +
↪"<br>")
06    response.write("OEM Code Page: " + ctype(_culture.textinfo.OemCodePage, string) +
↪"<br>")
07    response.write("ANSI Code Page: " + ctype(_culture.textinfo.ANSICodePage, string) +
↪"<br>")
08    response.write("List Separator: " + ctype(_culture.textinfo.ListSeparator, string) +
↪"<br>")
09
10 end sub
```

The `showtextinfo()` sub simply writes out each `textinfo` object property to the web browser. I have put in a separate sub to enhance the readability of the web page.

The String Resource Manager

ASP.NET provides the capability to use string resource files as a basis for displayed text on a web site. This enables the developer to have one Web Form, which can support more than one language. This section shows you how to create a resource file and use it in a Web Form through the resource manager class.

Creating Resource Files for Localization

Creating string resource files is pretty straightforward. An example text-based resource file is shown in Listing 13.2.

Listing 13.2 **(en-US.txt) English-US String Resource File**

```
01 ;String resource file for US - English localization
02
03 ;user interface Labels and text
04 UI_label_01_name = Language Translation Using Resource Files
05 UI_label_02_name = Select Language
06
07 UI_Select_01_item_01 = English
08 UI_Select_02_item_02 = French
09 UI_Select_03_item_03 = Simplified Chinese
10
11 UI_response_text_01_01 = This web page is now in English
12 UI_response_text_01_02 = The current date is:
13 UI_response_text_01_03 = The current time is:
```

The first line in Listing 13.2 is a comment. This is denoted by the ; character at the beginning of the file. You can use comments anywhere in the file. The rest of the file contains simple name value pairs, where the value is the text you want to display in the language of the culture of the file.

Now that you know the format for resource files, it is necessary to create one for the base language of the web application and additional ones for each new language. Please note that it is important to observe the following naming conventions:

- The base resource file can be any name with an extension of .txt.

- Any additional resource files need to use the initial base filename plus the culture ID of the resource file.

An example of these files are as follows:

- **myApp.en-US.txt**—English American
- **myApp.fr-FR.txt**——French
- **myApp.zh-CN.txt**—Simple Chinese

Compiling a Resource File

Now that a resource file has been created for each culture you want to support, the resources must be compiled into .NET resource files. This is done using the command-line tool resgen. This utility converts a text file to a .NET resource file. The resgen utility takes two parameters, the first being the file you want to convert and the second being the name of the file you want to create. An example of using the resgen utility is shown in the following:

```
01 resgen mytext.en-US.txt mytext.en-US.resources
02 resgen mytext.fr-FR.txt mytext.fr-FR.resources
03 resgen mytext.zh-CN.txt mytext.zh-CN.resources
```

After these resource files have been generated, you need to copy the resource file to the directory on your server where you want to store the resource files.

Using Resources in an ASP.NET Web Form

Now that you have compiled resources located in the bin directory, create a Web Form that uses these resources. Listing 13.3 shows a global.asax file, which creates an instance of the ResourceManager class, and assigns it an initial resource file to use.

Listing 13.3   **(global.asax) Configuring ASP.NET Applications to Use a *ResourceManager* Object**

```
01 <%@Import namespace="System.Globalization"%>
02 <%@Import namespace="System.Resources"%>
03 <%@Import namespace="System.Threading"%>
04 <%@Import Namespace="System.IO"%>
05
06
07 <script runat="server" language="VB">
08
09 Sub Application_OnStart()
10    Application("RM") = ResourceManager.CreateFileBasedResourceManager("1302", _
11              ➥Server.MapPath("."), Nothing)
12 End Sub
13
14
15
16 Sub Application_BeginRequest(sender As Object, args As EventArgs)
17 try
18       Thread.CurrentThread.CurrentCulture =
➥CultureInfo.CreateSpecificCulture(Request.UserLanguages(0))
19    Catch
20       Thread.CurrentThread.CurrentCulture = new CultureInfo("en-US")
21    End Try
22
23    Thread.CurrentThread.CurrentUICulture = Thread.CurrentThread.CurrentCulture
24 End Sub
25
26 </script>
```

In the Application_OnStart sub, a new application variable called "RM" is created which is used to hold a reference to a resource manager. A new instance of a `ResourceManager` is assigned to the application variable and the initial source file to be used is set. This is the base resource file created earlier:

```
01 Application("RM") = ResourceManager.CreateFileBasedResourceManager("myApp", _
02              Server.MapPath("."), Nothing)
```

The next sub in the global.asax file is a handler for the `Application_BeginRequest` event. This event is processed whenever a new web request is received. The code in this sub sets the current culture of the session to that of the first user language defined on the browser. If for some reason an error occurs, default the culture to `en-US`.

The end result of this processing in the global.asax is to set the culture of the displayed Web Forms to match that of the user's browser.

Next, create a web page to use the resource files. A sample Web Form is shown in Listing 13.4.

Listing 13.4 (1304.aspx) Web Page Using Resources from a Resource File

```
01 <%@Page Description="Localized Page" %>
02 <%@ OutputCache Duration="1" VaryByParam="none" %>
03
04 <%@Import Namespace="System.Globalization"%>
05 <%@Import Namespace="System.Resources"%>
06 <%@ Import Namespace="System.Threading"%>
07
08
09 <script runat="Server" Language="VB">
10
11 Dim rm as ResourceManager
12 Dim culture as CultureInfo
13
14 Sub Page_Load(sender As Object, args As EventArgs)
15
16   If not isPostback then
17
18     MyCulture.Items.Add("en-US")
19     MyCulture.Items.Add("fr-FR")
20     MyCulture.Items.Add("zh-CN")
21     MyCulture.AutoPostBack = True
22
23   End if
24
25   Thread.CurrentThread.CurrentCulture =
➥CultureInfo.CreateSpecificCulture(myCUlture.selecteditem.text)
26   Thread.CurrentThread.CurrentUICulture = Thread.CurrentThread.CurrentCulture
27   _culture = cultureinfo.currentculture()
28
29 End Sub
```

```
30
31 </script>
32
33
34 <body>
35
36 <form runat="server">
37
38 <h3><%=rm.GetString("UI_label_01")%></h3>
39
40 <%=rm.GetString("UI_label_02")%>: 
41
42 <asp:DropDownList id="myCulture" runat="server"/>
43
44 <hr>
45
46 <B><%=rm.GetString("UI_response_01") %></B> <%=_culture.nativename %><br>
47 <B><%=rm.GetString("UI_response_02") %></B> <%=datetime.today.ToLongDateString
➥%><br>
48 <B><%=rm.GetString("UI_response_03") %></B> <%=datetime.now.ToShortTimeString %><br>
49
50 </form>
51
52 </body>
```

The preceding code starts by making sure all required namespaces are referenced. The following code is a script block, which holds a declaration for a ResourceManagement object and a Page_Load sub. The code is repeated in the following:

```
01 Sub Page_Load(sender As Object, args As EventArgs)
02
03   If not isPostback then
04
05     MyCulture.Items.Add("en-US")
06     MyCulture.Items.Add("fr-FR")
07     MyCulture.Items.Add("zh-CN")
08     MyCulture.AutoPostBack = True
09
10   End if
11
12   rm = ResourceManager.CreateFileBasedResourceManager("1302", Server.MapPath("."),
➥Nothing)
13
14   Thread.CurrentThread.CurrentCulture =
➥CultureInfo.CreateSpecificCulture(myCUlture.selecteditem.text)
15   Thread.CurrentThread.CurrentUICulture = Thread.CurrentThread.CurrentCulture
16   _culture = cultureinfo.currentculture()
17
18   End Sub
```

To begin, check for a `PostBack` event. If this is the first time the page runs, initialize and bind the culture selection combobox. This is used to change the displayed culture settings dynamically. The section of code after the post-back check simply sets the current session culture to match the one selected in the combobox. It also creates a new instance of the `ResourceManager` object, which is to be used for retrieving string resources for the interface.

After the script block, is a simple Web Form with a combobox on it to select a culture. However, note the rendering tags and their contents before the combobox control and the ones after it. The code is shown in the following:

```
01 <body>
02
03 <form runat="server">
04
05 <h3><%=rm.GetString("UI_label_01")%></h3>
06
07 <%=rm.GetString("UI_label_02")%>: 
08
09 <asp:DropDownList id="myCulture" runat="server"/>
10
11 <hr><BR>
12
13 <B><%=rm.GetString("UI_response_01") %></B> 
14 <%=_culture.nativename %><br>
15 <B><%=rm.GetString("UI_response_02") %></B> 
16 <%=datetime.today.ToLongDateString %><br>
17 <B><%=rm.GetString("UI_response_03") %>
18 </B> <%=datetime.now.ToShortTimeString %><br>
19
20 </form>
21
22 </body>
```

Line 5 calls the resource manager and requests a string resource with the name of (`"UI_label_01"`) it renders the returned string, which in English is

Select Language

Lines 5,7,9,11, and 17 return the following strings. In English these are

```
Language Translation Using Resource Files
Select Language
This web page is now in
The current date is:
The current time is:
```

However, as soon as you change the culture, the values are retrieved automatically from the respective culture resource file and displayed appropriately. Figure 13.3 shows the application when it's first run, and figures 13.4 and 13.5 show the application in French and Chinese, respectively.

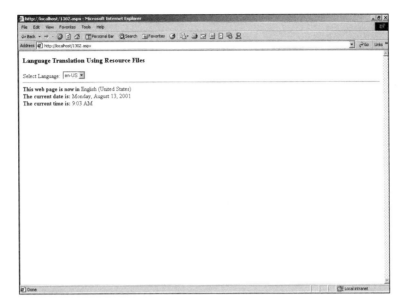

Figure 13.3   The application when first run.

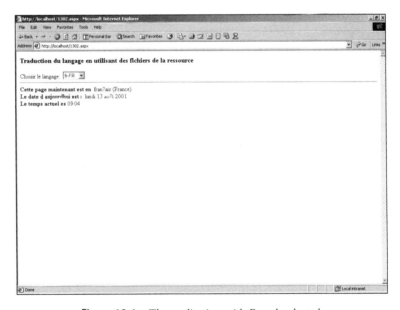

Figure 13.4   The application with French selected.

Figure 13.5 The application with Chinese selected.

Summary

This chapter introduced the basics of localization. You now can create functional, multilingual, localized web sites. However, there is a lot more to globalization than covered here, such as right-to-left formatting for languages that read in a different direction, using localized images, and localizing database information. You can get more information on these topics from the ASP.NET's online help system, by searching for "globalization."

V

Advanced Web Forms

14

Cache Control in ASP.NET

THIS CHAPTER INTRODUCES THE CACHING FEATURES of ASP.NET, and is structured as follows:

- **ASP.NET cache management**—Looks at what cache management is and how it can be used.
- **Page output caching**—Looks at ASP.NET Web Form output caching.
- **Fragment caching**—Looks at ASP.NET fragment caching, which has the capability of caching only sections of a page through the use of user controls.
- **Request caching**—Looks at request caching in an ASP.NET application and demonstrates its use.

By the end of this chapter, you should be able to integrate cache management into your web-based applications and understand the concepts behind cache management.

ASP.NET Cache Management

Cache management is one of the more interesting features in ASP.NET. Cache management enables you to store application data in a memory cache, which in turn enables you to create better performing scalable web applications.

So what exactly does cache management mean? It is a term used to describe the development pattern and process of storing frequently used data in memory.

By caching data in an ASP.NET application, you can gain substantial boosts to a web application's performance. Any processing needed to create the data or object you want to cache is only created or processed once, then it is stored in the cache. All further access of this data or object uses the cached version without the overhead of processing, and as such, it is far more efficient.

Page Output Caching

Page output caching enables the Web Form content to be cached. This means that the processing required to create an ASP.NET Web Form or control only happens before it is first put into the cache or when the cache expires. It needs to be updated with new data; otherwise, the page is loaded from the cache and very little processing is required.

After all the web page processing has been completed, what is left is a web page that has a lot of processing used in its creation (for example, heavy database access or business logic processing). The only processing that needs to be done is when the page is initially requested. The requested page is then stored in memory on the web server that handles the web page requests. If this cached version of the web page becomes invalid due to a predefined event (this could be an expired date or time or because some of the data being displayed has changed), the page would be processed again, and subsequently, stored in the memory cache.

This process gives the web developer a way of optimizing his application's performance.

Figure 14.1 outlines the process that occurs after a web server receives a Web Form request.

As you can see, when using page output cache management for data being used on a Web Form, the following order of events occurs. (The events listed are for illustrative purposes only, and are not the exact low-level mechanics involved in ASP.NET):

1. The user requests a web page.

2. ASP.NET checks to see if the page has been flagged as cacheable. If it is not cacheable, the web page is processed, and the results are sent to the user.

3. If the page is flagged as cacheable, ASP.NET checks to see if the page has been cached. If the page has not been cached, the page is processed and the results are stored in the cache prior to sending it to the user. However, if there is a cached version, ASP.NET checks the validity of the cached data.

4. If the cached page is valid, it is sent to the user. Otherwise, the page is processed, stored in the cache, and sent to the user.

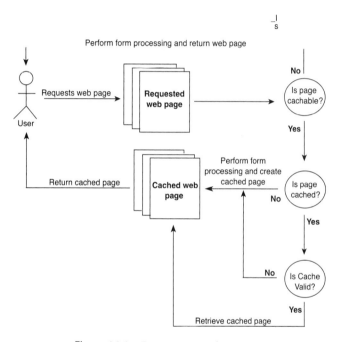

Figure 14.1   Page output caching process.

The @ *OutputCache* Web Form Directive

The OutputCache directive is used to enable cache control for a Web Form or for a user control.

You can cache the whole web page or part of a web page (see the section, "Fragment Caching [Partical Page Caching]"). The cache can have dependencies set up, which are used to determine how and when a cached version of a web page is invalidated and when it will need to be rebuilt.

To cache an ASP.NET Web Form, you must make the following modification to a Web Form:

```
<%@ OutputCache Duration="15" VaryByParam="None" %>
```

The preceding directive tells ASP.NET that the current page is now visible to the Cache Manager and also that the cache will expire after 15 seconds. The directive also states that the cache has a VaryByParam cache dependency requirement. An example of this is shown in Listing 14.1.

Listing 14.1 **Use of the @*Output Page* Directive**

```
01 <%@ Page Language="vb" %>
02 <%@ OutputCache Duration="15" VaryByParam="None" %>
03
04 <html>
05
06   <script language="VB" runat="server">
07   Sub Page_Load(Src As Object, E As EventArgs)
08       myLabel.Text = DateTime.Now.ToLongDateString + " - "
➥+datetime.now.tolongtimestring
09   End Sub
10   </script>
11
12   <body>
13   <form id="myForm" runat="server">
14     <b>Page OutputCache Demo</b><br><br>
15     Last Cached: <asp:label id="myLabel" runat="server"/><br>
16   </form>
17   </body>
18
19 </html>
```

This is the creation of a web page that has its output cached the first time it is run (line 2). The output of the page is simply the date and time the page was last run or cached. The duration of the cache is set for 15 seconds. During this time, any subsequent access to the page results in the cached page output being displayed to the user.

Figure 14.2 shows the page when it is initially run. The cached version of this page expires exactly 15 seconds after it was initially created. After the web page cache has expired, and the page is reloaded, a new cached version is created, and the date time on the page changes to the time the cache was created.

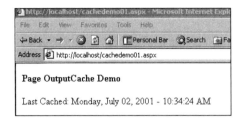

Figure 14.2 Simple page OutputCache example.

To do the same without the @ OutputCache directive, use the following two lines of code in the page load event of a Web Form:

```
Response.Cache.SetCacheability(HttpCacheability.Public)

Response.Cache.SetExpires(DateTime.Now.AddSeconds(15))
```

The first line tells ASP.NET that this web page is now visible to the Cache Manager with a public visibility. The second line tells the Cache Manager that this web page's cache expires 15 seconds after the current execution of the web page.

ASP.NET and the OutputCache Directive

When the @ OutputCache directive is used, ASP.NET actually calls the InitOutPutCache method of the page objects used to translate the Cache directive into the correct HTTPCachePolicy method calls.

The Output Cache Process

After a web page has been enabled for caching, the Cache Manager caches it the next time a web page response is generated from the page. From then on, any new requests for that page will be serviced by the cached version of the page.

All requests for the page uses the cached version of the page until the cache expires, based upon the expiration or dependency rules defined for the cache.

Set the Cache Visibility/Location for a Web Page

As mentioned earlier, when enabling a web page for caching, you have to set the page's *cache visibility*.

The cache visibility is set by using the location attribute in an ASP.NET declaration or by using the HttpResponse.Cache object. Both of these techniques are shown in the following:

```
<%@ OutputCache Duration="15" Location="Client" VaryByParam="none" %>
```

The format for the `HttpResponse.Cache` object is

```
01 Response.Cache.SetExpires(DateTime.Now.AddSeconds(15))
02 Response.Cache.SetCacheability(HttpCacheability.Private)
```

As you might have noticed, the @ `OutputCache` directive uses a different value for the `location` attribute to that of the `Response.Cache.SetCacheability` parameter. This can sometimes be a little confusing. These are covered in the next section.

Enable Page Output Caching by Any Device

The default setting for a cached page is the value of `Any`. This enables caching on all cache-capable devices that are involved in fulfilling the user's requests. These devices could be any of the following: the client browser, the responding server, or a proxy server through which the response passes. An example of the @ `OutputCache` directive for this is

```
<%@ OutputCache Duration="15" Location="Any" VaryByParam="None" %>
```

The previous directive generates the following code when compiled:

```
01 Response.Cache.SetExpires(DateTime.Now.AddSeconds(15))
02 Response.Cache.SetCacheability(HttpCacheability.Public)
```

Disabling Page Output Caching

To disable cache management for a Web Form or user control, you can set the @ `OutputCache` directive to

```
<%@ OutputCache Location="None" VaryByParam="None" %>
```

The previous directive generates the following code when compiled:

```
Response.Cache.SetCacheability(HttpCacheability.NoCache)
```

Enable Page Output Caching to be Server-Side Only

The page output cache is stored and processed server-side only. An example of the @ `OutputCache` directive for server-side caching is

```
<%@ OutputCache Duration="15" Location="Server" VaryByParam="None" %>
```

The previous directive generates the following code when compiled:

```
01 Response.Cache.SetExpires(DateTime.Now.AddSeconds(15))
02 Response.Cache.SetCacheability(HttpCacheability.Server)
```

Enable Page Output Caching to be Client-Side Only

In some circumstances, the default output cache might not be what is required. For example, you might have some secure pages on your site that require the client to be authenticated and some, if not all, of the page to be cached. An example of the @ OutputCache directive for client-side caching is

```
<%@ OutputCache Duration="15" Location="Any" VaryByParam="Client" %>
```

The preceding directive generates the following code when compiled:

```
01 Response.Cache.SetExpires(DateTime.Now.AddSeconds(15))
02 Response.Cache.SetCacheability(HttpCacheability.Private)
```

Enable DownStream Page Output Caching

All caching for the page is dealt with by devices between the client and the server. For example, on a proxy server, this setting would generally be used when operating a web site or service from a web farm that uses a single proxy to communicate with the World Wide Web. In this case, it is best that the proxy manages the cache because it cannot be guaranteed that the same server will process all client request and response interactions.

An example of the @ OutputCache directive downstream caching is

```
<%@ OutputCache Duration="15" Location="Location" VaryByParam="None" %>
```

The previous directive generates the following code when compiled:

```
01 Response.Cache.SetExpires(DateTime.Now.AddSeconds(15))
02 Response.Cache.SetCacheability(HttpCacheability.Public)
03 Response.Cache.SetNoServerCaching()
```

The location Attribute

Using the location attribute on a web page does not mean that the specified location will be used for any user controls on the page; the same applies for disabling a web page. This also does not mean that any user controls on the page have their caching disabled as well.

Multiple Caches for the Same Web Form

It is quite rare these days for a web page to return the same response or data to a client time after time. Of course, there is some repetition. However, depending on various environmental issues, such as web pages based on dynamic content, a web page's response can be different. This poses an interesting problem for the web page developer—we obviously want to benefit from the performance benefits of caching, yet, how do we ensure that the cached version of a web page contains up-to-date information?

Thankfully, when designing the cache management system in ASPNET, Microsoft has taken this issue into account and has provided a mechanism to deal with it. The first of these solutions is setting an expiration policy for a cached page, and the second, more flexible, solution is to set up a cache dependency rule.

Cache Expiration Policies

You can set up a cache expiration policy for a cached page by using the duration element in the @ `OutputCache` directive or by using the `Response.Cache.SetExpires` methods, both of which have been demonstrated earlier in this chapter.

Cache Dependencies

When a web page is processed, it is likely that it might generate multiple versions of the same page that are slightly different. This can be because of the use of a `querystring` or a difference in the request header sent to the web page. The Cache Manager in ASP.NET enables you to create separate cached versions of each different instance of a Web Form's response, if required. This is made possible by using one or more of the following @ `OutputCache` directives described in the following sections.

VaryByParam

`VaryByParam` is used to create a separate cache for GET- and POST-based form responses by specifying the parameters from GET and POST operations.

Each request for a page that has a different value stored in the variable, specified in the `VaryByParam` attribute, has its page output cached separately.

```
<%@ OutputCache Duration="15" Location="Server" VaryByParam="Topic" %>
```

The preceding line shows the @ `OutputCache` declaration that is used in one of the Web Forms used in Chapter 17, "Putting It All Together." As you can see the `OutputCache` is set up to use the `VaryByParam` attribute. The `OutputCache` is instructed to create different caches based on the passed variable which, in the case of the following Http requests, have been sent to the server for that page.

Varying the Output Caches

Should you need to vary the output caches for more than one parameter, you can list them with a semicolon between the passed name value pairs name, as shown:

```
<%@ OutputCache Duration="15" VaryByParam="Project;Topic" %>
```

VaryByHeader

This attribute is used to vary the cache pages created and used based on the page request header. For example, you could have a page that generates different versions of output based on the Accept-Language HTTP Header variable, which would produce language-specific web page content.

The @ OutputCache directive for this scenario would be:

```
<%@ OutputCache Duration="15" VaryByHeader="Accept-Language" VaryByParam="None" %>
```

If the page was requested from various clients with differing accept-language header values as shown below,

- en-us
- fr
- ch-cn
- en-us

Only three different output caches are created.

VaryByCustom

This attribute uses either the browser type or a custom value generated by your web application to vary the page caches generated and used by your web page. An example of the browser-based use of the VaryByCustom attribute is shown:

```
<%@ OutputCache Duration="60" VaryByCustom="Browser" VaryByParam="None" %>
```

The preceding line generates different output caches for each specific browser type that accesses the page; this information is retrieved from the page's Request.Browser.Type property.

Also, as stated previously, you can define application-specific values that define whether a page should have varying cached versions. This is done by placing an overridden method in the Global.asax file, which is used for this purpose. The method in question is the GetVaryByCustomString method. Its use is demonstrated in Listing 14.2.

Listing 14.2 **Caching a Page Based on a Custom Value**

```
01 (code in ProjectHome.aspx)
02 <%@ OutputCache Duration="60" VaryByCustom="SystemAccess" VaryByParam="None"%>
03
04
05 (Global.asax File in web application root)
06
07 Public Overrides Function GetVaryByCustomString(HttpContext context, string custom)
08   Return Ctype(Session("SystemAccess"), string)
09 End Function
```

The directive in the ProjectHome.aspx file tells ASP.NET to cache the output of pages based on a custom cache variable called SystemAccess. This cache variable has been defined in the overridden method GetVaryByCustomString method. This method simply returns a string value when a page request is made with the defined dependency. The page is cached based on differing versions of this string, which in this case, happens to be the current value of a session variable used by the application.

Fragment Caching (Partial Page Caching)

Although caching a whole web page is desirable sometimes, it is likely that you might only want to cache a specific portion of the web page. (For example, if you have a data-intensive or processing-intensive process used to generate a section of a page, which is dynamic in nature, but the rest of the page was not).

In this scenario, you want to cache only the resource-intensive sections of the page. This can be done by creating user controls for each area that needs to be cached.

After you create user controls for the cached fragments of the web page, you can set their @ OutputCache attributes as if they were a regular web page. This process is referred to as *fragment* or *partial page caching*. Fragment caching enables sections of a Web Form's content to be cached. This is achieved through the use of user controls. It is important to set these controls so that they are cached independently of the page to which they are bound. See Chapter 15, "Creating User and Custom Controls for ASP.NET."

When using cached user controls on a Web Form, the controls are treated independently from the form. This means that the cache directives used on the web page are independent of the cache directives on the user controls, so that if the web page has been made visible to the Cache Manager, it does not mean that the user controls are cached unless they too have been made visible to the Cache Manager. A simple example of this is shown in Listings 14.3, 14.4, and 14.5.

Listing 14.3 **Fragment Caching a Page Based on a Custom Control (Cachedemo2.ascx)**

```
01 <%@ OutputCache Duration="5" VaryByParam="None" %>
02
03 <table border=1 >
04   <tr>
05     <td>
06     <%
07     response.write("<b>User Control One - 5 Second Duration</b><br><br>")
08     response.write("<b>Last Cached:</b> " + DateTime.Now.ToLongDateString + " - "
→+datetime.now.tolongtimestring  +"<br>")
```

```
09        %>
10      </td>
11    </tr>
12  </table>
```

Listing 14.4 **Fragment Caching a Page Based on a Custom Control (Cachedemo21.ascx)**

```
01  <%@ OutputCache Duration="15" VaryByParam="None" %>
02
03  <table border=1 >
04    <tr>
05      <td>
06      <%
07      response.write("<b>User Control Two - 15 Second duration</b><br><br>")
08      response.write("<b>Last Cached:</b> " + DateTime.Now.ToLongDateString + " -
➥" +datetime.now.tolongtimestring  +"<br>")
09      %>
10      </td>
11    </tr>
12  </table>
```

Listing 14.5 **Web Form (Cachedemo2.aspx)**

```
01  <%@ OutputCache Location="None" VaryByParam="none" %>
02
03  <%@ Register TagPrefix="frag1" TagName="fragmentcache" Src="Cachedemo2.ascx" %>
04  <%@ Register TagPrefix="frag2" TagName="fragmentcache" Src="Cachedemo21.ascx" %>
05
06  <html>
07
08    <script language="VB" runat="server">
09
10      Sub Page_Load(Src As Object, E As EventArgs)
11          myLabel.Text = DateTime.Now.ToLongDateString + " - "
➥+datetime.now.tolongtimestring
12      End Sub
13
14    </script>
15
16  <body>
17    <form id="myForm" runat="server">
18        <b>Page OutputCache Demo</b><br><br>
19      Last Cached: <asp:label id="myLabel" runat="server"/><br>
20        <br><br>
21        <frag1:fragmentcache id="fragment1" runat="server" />
22        <br>
```

continues ▶

Listing 14.5 **Continued**

```
23          <frag2:fragmentcache id="fragment2" runat="server" />
24        </form>
25
26    </body>
27
28  </html>
```

I have created two different web controls for the fragment cache example. The first control is set to a cache duration of 5 seconds, and the second control is set to a 15 second duration; both of these controls are placed on an uncached Web Form. When this example is run, the date time stamp on the Web Form changes every time the page is refreshed and the two controls are cached separately so that every 5 seconds the first control updates its output cache, and only every 15 seconds the second user control gets its output cached. Figure 14.3 shows an example of how this code will appear.

Figure 14.3 Fragment cache demo.

Manipulating a Cached User Control

If you have code in your web page that explicitly tries to programmatically manipulate a cached user control, an error will occur. This is because the user control is cached on its first use and all subsequent calls are using the cached output version. All programmatic manipulation of a cached user control can only occur inside that control.

Caching Multiple Versions of a Fragment Cached Page

Just as you can cache varying versions of a web page, you can do the same for a user control. The directives that are available in a user control are described in the following sections.

VaryByParam

This directive operates the same way as the attribute of the same name in a standard web page.

VaryByControl

This attribute is used to cache varying cache control responses based on a user control ID. When doing this, you have to explicitly check for the existence of a cached user control before you can program against it.

The @ OutputCache declaration for this feature is pretty simple:

```
<%@ OutputCache Duration="15" VaryByControl="myCustomControlID" VaryByParam="None"%>
```

You also can have the situation where a user control generates data based on attributes passed to it—when it is placed on a Web Form—by using a fully qualified identifier, which uniquely names a user control. Basically, this means that when you declare a user control on a page and include an ID property in its tag, ASP.NET can distinguish it from other user controls on the page.

Request Caching

Request caching enables you to cache any object or data across multiple requests. The cached items have the same scope as application state variables. This powerful and easy-to-use caching technology provides the capability of storing expensive objects in memory across HTTP requests. (Note that expensive means a heavy processing load or time-intensive processes.)

The request caching mechanism is implemented by the Cache class, which creates instances of itself that are private to each running application on a web server. As such, the cache has a lifetime equal to the time the application is running, which is exactly what application state variables do.

Each time an ASP.NET web application is restarted, the cache is cleared and then subsequently re-created.

The request class has been designed with ease of use at its core. In fact, Microsoft has made request caching as simple as setting a session or application variable (the syntax is almost identical).

You can simply use the request cache by using key values paired with the data you want to store in the cache. Although the request cache has a simplistic interface, it also has some other very powerful features for managing the expiration of the data in the cache.

Scavenging Server Resources

One of the issues with request caching is the sheer amount of server resources that can be used. To protect against this as much as possible, the ASP.NET request cache system invokes a process called *resource scavenging*. This generally means that the cache management system removes less important cache data when the server resources become low.

Prioritization

You can tell the request cache to give certain cached data items priority over other data items when resource scavenging is performed. Indicating that a cached data item is of a higher or lower priority than another does this.

Expiration

It is also possible to establish an expiration policy for a data item when you put it in the request cache. This enables you to specify the time and the date are item will expire based on the time it is accessed. After a data item expires, it is removed from the cache. If you should make an attempt to retrieve its data, it will return a null value unless the item has been added to the request cache after it was removed.

Volatile Data

For data items stored in the request cache that have consistent updates—or those whose data is only valid for a fixed timeframe, and as such is termed volatile—you should set an expiration policy that keeps those items in the cache as long as their data remains current.

Validity

Request caching also has the capability of defining the validity of a cached data item based on external files, directories, or even another cached data items. This technique is referred to as file dependencies and key dependencies. If these dependencies should changes, the cached data item is invalidated and, subsequently, removed from the request cache.

It should be noted that the request cache has no information about the contents of the data items in it; the request cache only stores the raw data and dependency information, nothing else.

Adding Data Items to a Request Cache

There are three ways to can add data to the request cache object.

The first way is to add an item to the cache specifying its key and value. The following code demonstrates this:

```
Cache("myData") = "This is some data to Cache"
```

The ways to add data to a request cache, (illustrated in the previous line of code is very simple) but it does not take advantage of the scavenging, expiration, or dependency support offered by the request cache system. To take advantage of these features you must use either the `Cache.Insert` method or the `Cache.Add` methods. These methods have the same syntax, however, the `Add` method returns an object that represents the cached item and the insert method does not.

To add items to the request cache, see the examples shown:

```
01 MyDataVariable = Cache.Add("MyData", "")
02
03 Cache.Insert("MyData",
04              "Sample Data to Cache",
05              Nothing,
06              DateTime.Now.AddMinutes(30),
07              TimeSpan.Zero)
```

Both the `Add` and the `Insert` methods of the `Cache` class offer a great amount of control over the cache conditions, in which the cached data item remains. They support the capability of making the cached data item dependent on external files or directories.

When you add an item to the cache with a cache dependency, the `Cache` class creates an instance of the `CacheDependency` class, which is used to track changes to any of the dependencies you defined in the `Add` or `Insert` methods. Should any of these dependencies change, the data item they are attached to will be removed from the request cache.

Adding Data to a Request Cache with a Dependency Rule

When adding data to the request cache, you use the dependencies parameter in the `Add` or `Insert` methods. See the following example:

```
01 Cache.Insert("MyData", "Sample data to cache",
02              new CacheDependency(Server.MapPath("\file.txt")))
03
04 [Visual Basic]
```

A data item was added to the preceeding code to the request cache using the `Insert` method. The cached data item has a file dependency attached to it based on the file.txt file. If this file is moved or updated in any way, the cached data expires and removed from the request cache.

Setting the Expiration Dependency for Data in a Request Cache

You also can use the Add and Insert methods to fix expiration policies for a data item in the request cache. This is done by adding an item to the cache with expiration policies passed through the Add and Insert methods. Both of these methods have an absoluteExpiration parameter and a slidingExpiration parameter.

The following code shows an example Add method call with an expiration time set to 30 minutes after the data item has been inserted into the request cache. After it has expired, the data is removed.

```
01 Cache.Insert("MyData",
02            "Sample Data to Cache",
03            Nothing,
04            DateTime.Now.AddMinutes(30),
05            TimeSpan.Zero)

01 Cache.Insert("MyData", Source, null,
02            DateTime.Now.AddHours(1), TimeSpan.Zero);
```

The next example shows a sliding time expiration policy set to 15 minutes after the cache was last accessed:

```
01 Cache.Insert("MyData",
02            "sample Data to Cache",
03            Nothing,
04            System.Web.Caching.Cache.NoAbsoluteExpiration, _
05             TimeSpan.FromMinutes(15))
```

It should be noted that you only can use either an absolute expiration duration or a sliding time expiration dependency. This is because sliding expiration is converted into an absolute expiration internally.

Setting the Priority of a Cached Item in the Request Cache

You also can use the Add or Insert method to define the prioritization of a cached data item by using the CacheItemPriority and CacheItemPriorityDecay when you create a cached data item. These priority settings assist the web server when it needs to scavenge resources to free up used memory. The scavenger removes lower priority items from the cache before the higher priority items. An example of using the priority parameters is shown below:

```
01 Cache.Insert("MyData",
02            "Sample Data to Cache",
03            None,
04 System.Web.Caching.Cache.NoAbsoluteExpiration,
►TimeSpan.FromMinutes(15),
05            CacheItemPriority.High,
06            CacheItemPriorityDecay.Never, Nothing)
```

The preceeding code creates a cached data item with a sliding expiration policy of 15 minutes. It also is set to high priority, with the priority decay set to Never, which means that the priority setting does not denote over time.

Retrieving Data Items from the Request Cache

Retrieving data from the cache is pretty straightforward; you only have to specify the key that represents the data item in the request cache. Here is an example:

```
myCachedData = CType(Cache("MyData"), String)
```

When retrieving data from a cache, it is necessary to check that the items exist this way you can create the data and cache it if needed. (That is if it is not already cached.) A sample of this process is shown below:

```
01 'Get Data from RequestCache
02
03 <%@ Page Language="vb" Trace="true" %>
04 <%
05 'Get Data from RequestCache
06 Dim myData
07 myData=CType(Cache("MyData"), String)
08
09 'If Cached version does not exist create data and cache it
10 If myData Is Nothing Then
11  myData = "New Sample Data String."
12  Cache.Insert("myData", myData)
13 End if
14
15 Response.write("Cached data is: " & mydata)
16 %>
```

Deleting Items from a Request Cache

On occasion, you might need to remove an item from the request cache programmatically. This is done explicitly by removing items from the request cache using the Cache.Remove method. This method only takes one parameter, which is the key of the cache item you want to delete. A sample method call is shown:

```
01  'Remove the myData Request Cache element if it exists
02 Cache.Remove("MyData")
```

Summary

As you can see, ASP.NET provides easy-to-use and powerful caching capabilities, whether you want to cache data requests for dynamic data or sections of Web Forms. By using these caching capabilities, you can create better-performing web applications.

15

Creating User and Custom Controls for ASP.NET

Asp.net comes with a rich array of pre-fabricated HTML and web server controls. These will meet most of your needs, but for demanding developers, ASP.NET features a mechanism through which you can create your own controls. Based on how they are created, they are differentiated as user controls or custom controls.

The first half of this chapter deals with understanding the concept, architecture, and the use of user controls, while the second half of the chapter explains the why, how, and when of custom controls.

User Controls

A *user control* allows you to package frequently used user interface and the processing logic in such a way that it can be used as a pluggable component. This helps you attain the following two objectives:

- This increases reusability of your code. The next time you need to add a similar functionality in your ASP.NET pages, just plug in this user control instead of rewrite similar code.

- User controls help in encapsulating part of page user interface and logic, which in turn makes your pages easier to understand and maintain.

After you have created a user control, you can use it on your Web Forms just like any built-in server control. User controls can also expose a set of properties that you can customize to alter the behavior of the control.

Developing a Simple User Control

Listing 15.1 shows a very simple user control and demonstrates how it actually works. Let us call this `MyTime` user control; it fetches current time from the server. This user control is written in a file named "MyTime.ascx." Note that the file extension for this user control is always ".ascx."

Listing 15.1 **ch1501.ascx** *MyTime* **User Control**

```
01 <%@ Control ClassName="MyTime" %>
02 <table width="40%" bgcolor="beige">
03    <tr>
04       <td><h3>Current Time is:</h3></td>
05    </tr>
06    <tr>
07       <td><h4><%=Now.ToString("hh:mm:ss tt")%></h4></td>
08    </tr>
09 </table>
```

Listing 15.1 shows a pretty straightforward code displaying time formatted in a table. The only new piece of code is in line 1 in the form of a `Control` directive. It encapsulates the contents of this file as a control and identifies it using the value specified in the `ClassName` attribute. The `Control` directive is especially helpful when creating user controls programmatically. This example even works without using the `Control` directive, but it is good practice to have the `Control` directive in the user controls at all times. (This directive is discussed later in this chapter.) The server does not allow you to load the ".ascx" file directly within the browser. A user control can only be requested from within a Web Form. Listing 15.2 shows a simple web page in which this control is placed.

Listing 15.2 **ch1502.aspx** **Demonstrating the *MyTime* User Control**

```
01 <%@Register TagPrefix="NewRiders" TagName="MyTime" Src="ch1501.ascx"%>
02 <html>
03    <head>
04       <Title>MyTime User Control Demonstration</Title>
05    </head>
06    <body>
07       <NewRiders:MyTime id="MyTime1" runat="Server"/>
08    </body>
09 </html>
```

In this example, two important lines to look at are lines 1 and 7. In line 1, a `Register` directive is used. As the name says, this directive registers the user control. It takes the following three parameters:

- **TagPrefix** — This is the namespace to which the user control belongs. This is used to differentiate the user controls from those written by other people.

- **TagName** — This is the name by which the user control is recognized in this `aspx` page. Any name can be used, irrespective of the physical filename in which the user control is stored.

- **Src** — Specifies the virtual path to the source code file of user control.

We can now use this user control in our page.

In line 7 we are inserting the `MyTime` user control using the `TagPrefix` and `TagName` we just registered. Just like any other server control, we use a `runat="server"` attribute. The ID parameter is required if you want to create more than one `MyTime` control on the same page. In that case, ASP.NET differentiates them by their ID.

When you load the Web Form ch1502.aspx in the browser, it looks similar to Figure 15.1.

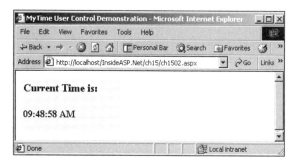

Figure 15.1 *MyTime* user control.

User Controls Can Be Written in Different Languages

Because .NET framework supports multiple languages, it is possible to write user controls in any language supported by the Common Language Runtime. You can host many user controls, each written in different language on the same Web Form.

Architecture of User Control

After you see how this simple user control works, we can talk about the architecture of user control before delving into detailed examples.

User controls are based on the same programming model as Web Forms, so the execution life cycle of user control is much like that of a Web Form.

User control is of the type `System.Web.UI.UserControl`, which inherits directly from `System.Web.UI.Control`. This base class belongs to the `System.Web.UI` namespace, which contains the elements common to all ASP.NET server controls.

User controls can be composed of HTML controls, ASP.NET server controls, client-side scripts, and other user controls.

Just like any ASP.NET page, a user control has its own set of events available. You can understand how the different events are fired when a user control is loaded with the code shown in Listings 15.3 and 15.4.

Listing 15.3   **ch1503.ascx**   **Event Ordering in a User Control**

```
01 <%@ Control ClassName="MyUserControl" %>
02 <script runat="server" language="vb">
03   Sub Page_Init(Source As Object, E as EventArgs)
04     Response.Write("<font color='red'>Message from Init Event of User
➥Control<BR><font>")
05   End Sub
06   Sub Page_Load(Source As Object, E As EventArgs)
07     Response.Write("<font color='red'>Message from Load Event of User
➥Control<BR><font>")
08   End Sub
09   Sub Page_PreRender(Source As Object, E As EventArgs)
10     Response.Write("<font color='red'>Message from PreRender Event of User
➥Control<BR><font>")
11   End Sub
12 </script>
```

Listing 15.4   **ch1504.aspx**   **Event Firing in a User Control**

```
01 <%@ Register TagPrefix="NewRiders" TagName="MyUserControl" src="ch1503.ascx" %>
02 <script runat="server" language="vb">
03   Sub Page_Init(Source As Object, E as EventArgs)
04    Response.Write("<font color='blue'>Message from Init Event of Web Form<BR></font>")
05   End Sub
06  Sub Page_Load(Source As Object, E As EventArgs)
07    Response.Write("<font color='blue'>Message from Load Event of Web Form<BR></font>")
08  End Sub
09  Sub Page_PreRender(Source As Object, E As EventArgs)
10    Response.Write("<font color='blue'>Message from PreRender Event of
➥WebForm.aspx<BR></font>")
11   End Sub
12 </script>
13 <NewRiders:MyUserControl id="uc1" runat="server"/>
```

If you load ch1504.aspx in your browser, the result looks similar to Figure 15.2.

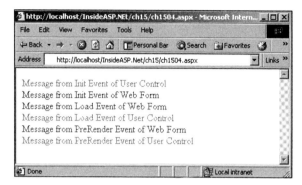

Figure 15.2 User control events.

Writing user controls is similar to writing a regular ASP.NET Web Form. In fact, with few modifications any Web Form can be converted to a user control. The following are a few differences you need to be aware of:

- User controls are always identified by the file extension ".ascx," as opposed to the ".aspx" of Web Forms.

- User controls cannot be directly requested from the server. They must be embedded within some Web Form. If you try loading ch1503.ascx directly in your browser, the server responds with a server error saying "This type of page is not served.".

- Because user controls are always embedded inside some Web Form, you should not use tags, such as <html>, <body> and <form>, within a user control as these tags belong to the container Web Form and cause nesting problems.

- If the Web Form that you are converting into a user control contains a @Page directive, change it to a @Control directive.

Usage Patterns

This section gives you a few ideas about where you can use user controls. This list is by no means complete and is provided to give you a basic idea:

- You can increase the performance of the web site by making use of features, such as partial output caching.

- You can use user controls to provide a consistent user interface throughout the web site by encapsulating your web site banners, sidebars, headers, and footers in the user controls. This not only increases consistency, but if later you are requested to change the UI or code inside a header, you need only to change it at one place and it is immediately reflected everywhere.

- You can store parts of your pages that you find yourself re-using in other pages into a user control. A good example might be a Login user control that encapsulates authentication user interface and code.

Scope of User Control's Reusability

User controls supports reusability, but this reusability is limited only to the web application to which the user control belongs.

User controls are not accessible to other web applications residing on the same web server.

Partial Output Caching

User controls are compiled before use. You can use partial page-caching techniques to cache the output of the user controls to increase efficiency of the web site. Take a scenario of a web page that has sections that are dynamically generated every time the page is accessed. One of these sections is *Top Searches*, which fetches the top 10 search strings from the database. Because this data does not change very frequently, we should choose to cache the contents of just this section leaving the rest of the page as it is. This can be achieved by encapsulating the section of Top Searches in a user control and caching the output of this user control so that successive database hits can be saved. (This ensures faster page delivery.)

It doesn't take much effort to enable partial output caching. In fact, you only need to modify your user control to add a directive. This is demonstrated by modifying the MyTime user control shown previously in Listing 15.1. The only modification is adding the following code before line 1:

```
<%@ OutputCache Duration="10" VaryByParam="None" %>
```

When you access ch1502.aspx from your browser, the page and the user control are run on the first request, and the result of the user control is cached for 10 seconds. On subsequent requests, the page is executed, and the cached result of the user control is added to the page's output until the cache duration expires. This is the time when the user control is generated again. The second attribute to the OutputCache directive (VaryByParam) is used to control caching based on the parameters supplied to the web page through HTTP GET/POST. This is a required attribute, although we are not caching based on any parameter passed to the web page; rather, we need to specify it so that in our example its value is being set to "None". Note that partial output caching is a feature of ASP.NET Premium Edition. If you do not have Premium Edition installed on your computer, then caching will not work. There is more information about caching in Chapter 14, "Cache Control in ASP.NET."

User Control Customization

User controls are customizable. Just like a typical server control, a user control can expose properties that you can set to change its behavior or appearance.

Let's look at a relatively detailed example of user control. Note that the basic design pattern still remains the same. In Listing 15.5 a list of products from the Northwind sample database is retrieved. The list of products is displayed in a user control that exposes two properties, Category and ColorScheme. In the container Web Form, these properties can be changed to alter the behavior of the user control.

Listing 15.5   **ch1505.ascx   User Control Customization**

```
01 <%@ Control ClassName="ProductList" %>
02 <%@ Import Namespace=System.Data %>
03 <%@ Import Namespace=System.Data.SqlClient%>
04 <script language="VB" runat="server">
05   Public Category as String = "Beverages"
06   Public ColorScheme as String = "Blue"
07   Dim darkShade as String, lightShade as String
08   Sub Page_Load(Src as Object, E as EventArgs)
09     ProductList_DataBinder(Category, ColorScheme)
10   End Sub
11   Sub ProductList_DataBinder(strCategory as String,
12                 strColorScheme as String)
13     Dim ds as DataSet
14     Dim MyConn as SqlConnection
15     Dim MyAdapter as SqlDataAdapter
16     Dim SqlPrdLst as String
17     MyConn = new SqlConnection("server=(local)\netsdk;" & _
18             "database=northwind;Trusted_Connection=yes")
19     SqlPrdLst="SELECT ProductName, QuantityPerUnit,UnitPrice, "& _
20             "UnitsInStock, UnitsOnOrder FROM Products WHERE "& _
21             "CategoryID=(Select categoryID from Categories " & _
22             "where CategoryName='" & strCategory & "') "
23     MyAdapter = new SqlDataAdapter(SqlPrdLst, MyConn)
```

continues ▶

Listing 15.5 **Continued**

```
24      MyAdapter.SelectCommand.Connection.Open()
25      ds = new DataSet()
26      MyAdapter.Fill(ds, "ProductList")
27      MyRepeater.DataSource = ds.Tables("ProductList").DefaultView()
28      Select Case strColorScheme.ToLower()
29        Case "green"
30          darkShade = "#879966"
31          lightShade = "#c5e095"
32        Case "red"
33          darkShade = "#9c0001"
34          lightShade = "#dfa894"
35        Case "purple"
36          darkShade = "#91619b"
37          lightShade = "be9cc5"
38        Case else 'blue
39          darkShade = "#6699cc"
40          lightShade = "#b6cbeb"
41      End Select
42      MyRepeater.DataBind()
43 End Sub
44 </script>
45 <asp:Repeater id="MyRepeater" runat="server">
46   <HeaderTemplate>
47      <table width="100%" style="font: 8pt verdana">
48        <tr>
49          <td colspan="5" style="height:20"
50              bgcolor="<%#DarkShade%>" cellspacing="0"
51              cellpadding="0" width="100%">
52          </td>
53        </tr>
54        <tr>
55          <td colspan="5" align="right"
56            style="height:70;font-family:Arial;
57              font-weight:bold;font-size:32pt;color:white"
58            width="100%"
59            bgcolor="<%#lightShade%>"><%#Category%>
60          </td>
61        </tr>
62        <tr style="color:white;background-color:<%#DarkShade%>">
63          <td>Product Name     </td>
64          <td>Quantity Per Unit</td>
65          <td>Unit Price       </td>
66          <td>Unit In Stock    </td>
67          <td>Units On Order   </td>
68        </tr>
69   </HeaderTemplate>
70   <ItemTemplate>
71      <tr style="background-color:<%#lightShade%>">
72          <td><%# DataBinder.Eval(Container.DataItem, "ProductName")%></td>
73          <td><%# DataBinder.Eval(Container.DataItem, "QuantityPerUnit")%></td>
```

```
74        <td><%# DataBinder.Eval(Container.DataItem, "UnitPrice", "$ {0}")%></td>
75        <td><%# DataBinder.Eval(Container.DataItem, "UnitsInStock")%></td>
76        <td><%# DataBinder.Eval(Container.DataItem, "UnitsOnOrder") %></td>
77      </tr>
78   </ItemTemplate>
79   <FooterTemplate>
80      </table>
81   </FooterTemplate>
82 </asp:Repeater>
```

Listing 15.5 fetches a list of products from a given category. The database connection string in lines 17 and 18 is given for a typical ASP.NET installation. You might need to change it, depending on your installation settings. Apart from the usual database access and databinding logic, there is just one thing on which to focus in this listing: if you look at lines 5 and 6 of this listing, two public variables are declared. Public variables of a user control are exposed as properties of the user control on the container web page. You could have also used the Property syntax to explicitly create a property in the user control as opposed to public variables. These public variables have been initialized. The initial values set the default behavior of user control.

The plumbing logic in the container web page is shown in Listing 15.6.

Listing 15.6   ch1506.aspx   User Control Customization Container Page

```
01 <%@ Register TagPrefix="NewRiders"
02          TagName="ProductList"
03          Src="ch1505.ascx" %>
04 <html>
05 <head>
06   <title>User Control Customization</title>
07 </head>
08 <Body>
09   <form runat="server">
10     <NewRiders:ProductList id="ProductList1"
11             Category="Produce" runat="server"/><hr>
12     <NewRiders:ProductList id="ProductList2"
13             Category="Confections"
14             ColorScheme="Red" runat="server"/><hr>
15     <NewRiders:ProductList id="ProductList3"
16             Category="Beverages"
17             ColorScheme="Purple" runat="server"/>
18   </form>
19 </Body>
20 </html>
```

Lines 1 through 3 have the usual `Register` directive that provides all basic information to refer to our user control inside this Web Form. In lines 10 and 11, I am adding a user control to this page. Only one of its properties (`Category`) is customized, so the other properties should be displayed with their default values specified in the user control (`ColorScheme="Blue"`). Later, in lines 12 through 17, two more instances of this user control with different values to its properties are created. When you run this Web Form in the browser, your screen looks like the one shown in Figure 15.3.

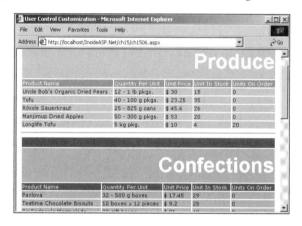

Figure 15.3 Customizing user controls.

Handling User Control Events

Writing event-handling methods for user controls is quite similar to that of the Web Form. The event handlers for user control events needs to be written in the user control itself and not in the container Web Form.

Listing 15.7 shows a modification of the `ProductList` example so that it allows the selection of `Category` and `ColorScheme` from a drop-down list.

Listing 15.7 ch1507.ascx User Control Event Handling

```
001 <%@ Control ClassName="ProductList" %>
002 <%@ Import Namespace=System.Data %>
003 <%@ Import Namespace=System.Data.SqlClient%>
004 <script language="VB" runat="server">
005   Dim darkShade as String, lightShade as String
006   Sub Page_Load(Src as Object, E as EventArgs)
007     If Not IsPostBack()
008       ProductList_DataBinder(Cat.SelectedItem.Text, _
009         Clr.SelectedItem.Text)
```

```
010     End If
011  End Sub
012  Sub Cat_Select(Src as Object, E as EventArgs)
013     ProductList_DataBinder(Cat.SelectedItem.Text, _
014        Clr.SelectedItem.Text)
015  End Sub
016  Sub Clr_Select(Src as Object, E as EventArgs)
017     ProductList_DataBinder(Cat.SelectedItem.Text, _
018        Clr.SelectedItem.Text)
019  End Sub
020  Sub ProductList_DataBinder(strCat as String, strClr as String)
021     Dim ds as DataSet
022     Dim MyConn as SqlConnection
023     Dim MyAdapter as SqlDataAdapter
024     Dim SqlPrdLst as String
025     MyConn = new SqlConnection("server=(local)\netsdk; " & _
026              "database=northwind;Trusted_Connection=yes")
027     SqlPrdLst = "SELECT ProductName, QuantityPerUnit, " & _
028:                 "UnitPrice, UnitsInStock, UnitsOnOrder " & _
029                 "FROM Products WHERE CategoryID = " & _
030                 "(Select CategoryID from Categories where " & _
031                 " CategoryName='" & strCat & "') "
032     MyAdapter = new SqlDataAdapter(SqlPrdLst, MyConn)
033     MyAdapter.SelectCommand.Connection.Open()
034     ds = new DataSet()
035     MyAdapter.Fill(ds, "ProductList")
036     MyRepeater.DataSource = ds.Tables("ProductList").DefaultView()
037     Select Case strClr.ToLower()
038        Case "green"
039           darkShade = "#879966"
040           lightShade = "#c5e095"
041        Case "red"
042           darkShade = "#9c0001"
043           lightShade = "#dfa894"
044        Case "purple"
045           darkShade = "#91619b"
046           lightShade = "be9cc5"
047        Case else 'blue
048           darkShade = "#6699cc"
049           lightShade = "#b6cbeb"
050     End Select
051     MyRepeater.DataBind()
052  End Sub
053  </script>
054  <h4>
055  Select Cat:
056  <asp:DropDownList id="Cat" runat="server" AutoPostBack="true"
057                   OnSelectedIndexChanged="Cat_Select">
058    <asp:ListItem value="Beverages" />
059:   <asp:ListItem value="Confections" />
060:   <asp:ListItem value="Produce" />
```

continues ▶

Listing 15.7 **Continued**

```
061:    <asp:ListItem value="Seafood" />
062: </asp:DropDownList>
063 Select Color Scheme :
064 <asp:DropDownList id="Clr" runat="server" AutoPostBack="true"
065                 OnSelectedIndexChanged="Clr_Select">
066    <asp:ListItem value="Blue" />
067    <asp:ListItem value="Green" />
068:    <asp:ListItem value="Red" />
069    <asp:ListItem value="Purple" />
070: </asp:DropDownList>
071 </h4>
072 <asp:Repeater id="MyRepeater" runat="server">
073    <HeaderTemplate>
074       <table width="100%" style="font: 8pt verdana">
075          <tr>
076             <td colspan="5" style="height:20"
077                 bgcolor="<%#DarkShade%>" cellspacing="0"
078                 cellpadding="0" width="100%"></td>
079          </tr>
080          <tr>
081             <td colspan="5" align="right"
082                 style="height:70;font-family:Arial;
083                     font-weight:bold;font-size:32pt;color:white"
084                 width="100%" bgcolor="<%#lightShade%>">
085                 <%#Cat.SelectedItem.Text%></td>
086          </tr>
087          <tr style="color:white;background-color:<%#DarkShade%>">
088             <td>Product Name      </td><td>Quantity Per Unit</td>
089             <td>Unit Price        </td><td>Unit In Stock    </td>
090             <td>Units On Order    </td>
091          </tr>
092    </HeaderTemplate>
093    <ItemTemplate>
094       <tr style="background-color:<%#lightShade%>">
095          <td><%# DataBinder.Eval(Container.DataItem, "ProductName")%></td>
096          <td><%# DataBinder.Eval(Container.DataItem, "QuantityPerUnit")%></td>
097          <td><%# DataBinder.Eval(Container.DataItem, "UnitPrice", "$ {0}")%></td>
098          <td><%# DataBinder.Eval(Container.DataItem, "UnitsInStock")%></td>
099          <td><%# DataBinder.Eval(Container.DataItem, "UnitsOnOrder") %></td>
100       </tr>
101    </ItemTemplate>
102    <FooterTemplate>
103       </table>
104    </FooterTemplate>
105 </asp:Repeater>
```

This user control features three event handlers:

- Page_Load
- Cat_Select (for category selection)
- Clr_Select (for color scheme selection)

In lines 56 and 57 and in lines 64 and 65, we have associated the respective drop-down list with their event handlers. In lines 6 through 19, we are calling the DataBinder method whenever we get into each of these event handlers, except for Page_Load, where we are calling the DataBinder method only if the page is loaded fresh (for example, is not a postback) to save some of the DataBinder calls.

Notice that the way these event handlers work is not at all different from the Web Form event handling. The Web Form that hosts this user control is pretty clean—as apparent from Listing 15.8.

Listing 15.8 **ch1508.aspx   User Control Event Handling**

```
01 <%@ Register TagPrefix="NewRiders" TagName="ProductList"
02          Src="ch1507.ascx" %>
03 <html>
04 <head>
05   <title>User Control Event Handling</title>
06 </head>
07 <Body>
08    <form runat="server">
09       <NewRiders:ProductList id="ProductList1"
10                runat="server"/>
11    </form>
12 </Body>
13 </html>
```

If you load the ch1508.aspx in your browser, a page similar to Figure 15.4 displays.

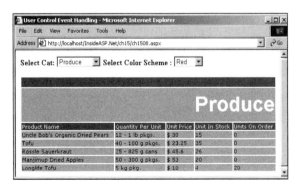

Figure 15.4 User control events.

Using *CodeBehind* with User Controls

CodeBehind gives us a powerful way to separate code from the user interface. You can take complete advantage of CodeBehind—even in writing user controls. When we use CodeBehind with user controls, the user interface part of the user control goes to the ".ascx" file, while the code goes to a ".vb" file. This way when a graphic designer works with the ".ascx" file to enhance it, she is not distracted by the code and cannot accidentally modify it.

Let's see how our product list example works with CodeBehind. The code listing for user control's ascx file is shown in Listing 15.9.

Listing 15.9   **ch1509.ascx   Demonstrating User Control with *CodeBehind***

```
01 <%@ Control ClassName="ProductList"
02           Inherits="MyCodeBehind" Src="ch1510.vb" %>
03 <h4>Select Category:
04 <asp:DropDownList id="Category" runat="server" AutoPostBack="true"
05                 OnSelectedIndexChanged="Category_Select">
06    <asp:ListItem value="Beverages" />
07:    <asp:ListItem value="Confections" />
08:    <asp:ListItem value="Produce" />
09:    <asp:ListItem value="Seafood" />
10: </asp:DropDownList>
11 Select Color Scheme :
12 <asp:DropDownList id="ColorScheme" runat="server" AutoPostBack="true"
13                 OnSelectedIndexChanged="ColorScheme_Select">
14    <asp:ListItem value="Blue" />
15:    <asp:ListItem value="Green" />
16:    <asp:ListItem value="Red" />
17:    <asp:ListItem value="Purple" />
18: </asp:DropDownList>
19 </h4>
20 <asp:Repeater id="MyRepeater" runat="server">
21    <HeaderTemplate>
22       <table width="100%" style="font: 8pt verdana">
23          <tr>
24             <td colspan="5" style="height:20
25                bgcolor="<%#DarkShade%>" cellspacing="0"
26                cellpadding="0" width="100%"></td>
27          </tr>
28          <tr>
29             <td colspan="5" align="right" width="100%"
30                bgcolor="<%#lightShade%>"
31                style="height:70;font-family:Arial;
32                   font-weight:bold;font-size:32pt;color:white" >
33                <%#Category.SelectedItem.Text%></td>
34          </tr>
35          <tr style="color:white;background-color:<%#DarkShade%>">
```

```
36                      <td>Product Name     </td><td>Quantity Per Unit</td>
37                      <td>Unit Price       </td><td>Unit In Stock    </td>
38                      <td>Units On Order   </td>
39              </tr>
40          </HeaderTemplate>
41          <ItemTemplate>
42              <tr style="background-color:<%#lightShade%>">
43                  <td><%# DataBinder.Eval(Container.DataItem, "ProductName")%></td>
44                  <td><%# DataBinder.Eval(Container.DataItem, "QuantityPerUnit")%></td>
45                  <td><%# DataBinder.Eval(Container.DataItem, "UnitPrice", "$ {0}")%></td>
46                  <td><%# DataBinder.Eval(Container.DataItem, "UnitsInStock")%></td>
47                  <td><%# DataBinder.Eval(Container.DataItem, "UnitsOnOrder") %></td>
48              </tr>
49          </ItemTemplate>
50          <FooterTemplate>
51              </table>
52          </FooterTemplate>
53  </asp:Repeater>
```

In this example, all the code from the user control has been pruned out, while keeping the user interface part. The code goes to a separate file named ch1510.vb. Again, you can choose any filename, caring only about the extension ".vb"—as that instructs the runtime to invoke a Visual Basic compiler on it. Lines 1 and 2 provide the linkage between the user control and the code file by using the Control directive.

The Control directive has the following three attributes:

- ClassName—Specifies the class name for the user control that identifies this user control by a string name. Though it is not required to have a ClassName in this example, it's a good practice to include it, as you might require it at a later stage.

- Inherits—Specifies the class from which this user control inherits. This class exists in the ".vb" code file.

- Src—Specifies the file that contains the CodeBehind source.

The code in ".vb" files is shown in Listing 15.10.

Listing 15.10 **ch1510.vb** Demonstrating User Control with *CodeBehind*

```
01  Imports System
02  Imports System.Data
03  Imports System.Data.SqlClient
04  Imports System.Web.UI
05  Imports System.Web.UI.WebControls
06  Imports System.Web.UI.HtmlControls
```

continues ▶

Listing 15.10 **Continued**

```
07 Public Class MyCodeBehind : Inherits UserControl
08   Protected MyRepeater as Repeater
09   Protected Category as DropDownList
10   Protected ColorScheme as DropDownList
11   Protected darkShade as String, lightShade as String
12   Protected Sub Page_Load(Src as Object, E as EventArgs)
13     If Not IsPostBack()
14       ProductList_DataBinder(Category.SelectedItem.Text, _
15               ColorScheme.SelectedItem.Text)
16     End If
17   End Sub
18   Protected Sub Category_Select(Src as Object, E as EventArgs)
19     ProductList_DataBinder(Category.SelectedItem.Text, _
20             ColorScheme.SelectedItem.Text)
21   End Sub
22   Protected Sub ColorScheme_Select(Src as Object, E as EventArgs)
23     ProductList_DataBinder(Category.SelectedItem.Text, _
24             ColorScheme.SelectedItem.Text)
25   End Sub
26   Protected Sub ProductList_DataBinder(strCategory as String, _
27             strColorScheme as String)
28     Dim ds as DataSet
29     Dim MyConnection as SqlConnection
30     Dim MyAdapter as SqlDataAdapter
31     Dim SqlPrdLst as String
32     MyConnection = new SqlConnection("server=(local)\netsdk;" & _
33                 "database=northwind;Trusted_Connection=yes")
34     SqlPrdLst = "SELECT ProductName, QuantityPerUnit, UnitPrice, " & _
35                 "UnitsInStock, UnitsOnOrder FROM Products WHERE " & _
36                 "CategoryID = (Select categoryID from Categories " & _
37                 "where CategoryName='" & strCategory & "') "
38     MyAdapter = new SqlDataAdapter(SqlPrdLst, MyConnection)
39     MyAdapter.SelectCommand.Connection.Open()
40     ds = new DataSet()
41     MyAdapter.Fill(ds, "ProductList")
42     MyRepeater.DataSource = ds.Tables("ProductList").DefaultView()
43     Select Case strColorScheme.ToLower()
44       Case "green"
45         darkShade = "#879966"
46         lightShade = "#c5e095"
47       Case "red"
48         darkShade = "#9c0001"
49         lightShade = "#dfa894"
50       Case "purple"
51         darkShade = "#91619b"
52         lightShade = "be9cc5"
53       Case else 'blue
54         darkShade = "#6699cc"
```

```
55           lightShade = "#b6cbeb"
56      End Select
57      MyRepeater.DataBind()
58   End Sub
59 End Class
```

When you run this sample, you should run it from the Web Form. The code of the Web Form has not changed from its non-code behind version, except for the reference to the source file in line 2. The new version is shown in Listing 15.11.

Listing 15.11   **ch1511.aspx**   **Demonstrating User Control with** *CodeBehind*

```
01 <%@ Register TagPrefix="NewRiders" TagName="ProductList"
02              Src="ch1509.ascx" %>
03 <html>
04 <head>
05   <title>Code Behind in User Control</title>
06 </head>
07 <Body>
08    <form runat="server">
09       <NewRiders:ProductList id="ProductList1"
10                 runat="server"/>
11    </form>
12 </Body>
13 </html>
```

In this example, we restructured the code for better maintainability while keeping the functionality and user interface intact. If you load the Web Form ch1511.aspx in your browser, you will still see the results shown in Figure 15.4.

Creating User Controls Programmatically

User controls can be created programmatically in its containing Web Form by using the Page object's LoadControl method. However, you need to take care of a few things. This is explained in context to the code shown in Listing 15.12.

Listing 15.12   **ch1512.aspx**   **Demonstrating Programmatic Creation of User Controls**

```
01 <%@ Register TagPrefix="NewRiders" TagName="ProductList"
02              Src="ch1505.ascx" %>
```

continues ▶

Listing 15.12 **Continued**

```
03 <html>
04 <head>
05     <title>Programmatic Creation of User Control</title>
06     <script language="VB" runat="server">
07         Sub Page_Load(Sender As Object, E As EventArgs)
08             Dim plCtrl as Control
09             plCtrl = LoadControl("ch1505.ascx")
10             CType(plCtrl, ProductList).Category  = "Beverages"
11             Page.Controls.Add(plCtrl)
12             Page.Controls.Add(New HtmlGenericControl("hr"))
13             plCtrl = LoadControl("ch1505.ascx")
14             CType(plCtrl, ProductList).Category  = "Confections"
15             CType(plCtrl, ProductList).ColorScheme = "Red"
16             Page.Controls.Add(plCtrl)
17             Page.Controls.Add(New HtmlGenericControl("hr"))
18             plCtrl = LoadControl("ch1505.ascx")
19             CType(plCtrl, ProductList).Category  = "Produce"
20             CType(plCtrl, ProductList).ColorScheme = "Green"
21             Page.Controls.Add(plCtrl)
22             Page.Controls.Add(New HtmlGenericControl("hr"))
23             plCtrl = LoadControl("ch1505.ascx")
24             CType(plCtrl, ProductList).Category  = "Seafood"
25             CType(plCtrl, ProductList).ColorScheme = "Purple"
26             Page.Controls.Add(plCtrl)
27         End Sub
28     </script>
29 </head>
30     <Body></Body>
31 </html>
```

Everything else being the same, let us focus on line 9. In this example, we are using the Page object's LoadControl method to create an instance of the user control stored in ch1505.ascx file.

The LoadControl returns a Control type that is a more generic type and does not have properties of our user control. If you need to access the properties of our user control, you first need to convert this object to the type of the user control. If you look back to the code in ch1505.ascx, line 1 is a Control directive:

```
<%@ Control ClassName="ProductList" %>
```

With the use of Control directive, the user control is available to us as of type ProductList.

Back in the Web Form, we are converting the control type to ProductList type in line 10.

After we have the ProductList type of object, we can access its Category and ColorScheme properties to customize this control. Later in line 11, the newly created control is added to the current page controls for proper rendering.

The code in line 12 shows how we can create instances of
`HtmlGenericControl` to programmatically insert HTML elements in the
Web Form. The output of this Web Form looks similar to the one shown
in Figure 15.3.

Programmatic Manipulation and Partial Output Caching

You should take care if you are programmatically manipulating a user control that contains an @ `OutputCache`
directive. In the case of output caching the page is dynamically generated only for the first request, and later
requests are satisfied from the output cache until the control expires. So, any programmatic manipulation that
must occur to create the content of the user control must be included in the control. You can include this logic in
the `Page_Load` event or `Page_PreRender` event. Otherwise, you will get an error.

Introduction to Custom Controls

ASP.NET provides us a facility to encapsulate our custom user interface and
functionality in a reusable form that is known as *custom controls*. This approach
of writing controls is quite different from the approach of writing user controls. You would write custom controls when you want to extend the functionality of an existing control (for example, extending the `Calendar` control
to work as an appointment diary), or when you want to create a new functionality that did not exist before (for example, creating a specialized tab
control for your product catalog). In this section, we delve into understanding and using custom controls.

The major differences between custom controls and user controls are
listed in Table 15.1.

Table 15.1 **Custom Controls Versus User Controls**

Custom Controls	User Controls
Custom controls are written in separate program files that are compiled explicitly and are persisted as an assembly (.dll).	User controls are authored using the ASP.NET page syntax, either in the script block or in `CodeBehind` pages and are implicitly just-in-time compiled by the ASP.NET runtime system.
They are nicely suited for general re-use as they are easy to package and redistribute as third-party controls.	They are best suited for reuse within a web application. Because they are persisted as source files, less chances exist that third parties would like to distribute them.

continues ▶

Table 15.1 **Continued**

Custom Controls	User Controls
Once created, a custom control can be added to the toolbox of a visual designer, such as Visual Studio .NET, and dragged and dropped onto a page—just like any built-in server control. The visual designer can also support visual manipulation of custom control's various properties.	User controls provide minimal support for use with a visual designer toolbox.
A custom control provides minimal support for design-time authoring in a visual designer.	A user control provides design-time support for authoring in a visual designer—just like an ASP.NET page.

Creating a Custom Control

Now, let's discuss the steps to create a simple custom control by designing a Converter custom control. The Converter control is intended to convert quantities from one unit to another unit.

Custom controls are written in a separate program file and must be compiled before use. This custom control is written in the file named ch1513.vb (see Listing 15.13).

File Extension Does Not Matter with Custom Controls

Custom controls are not required to be stored in a file with a specific extension, such as ".vb" for Visual Basic or ".cs" for C#. A file named ch1513.cls is as good as a file named ch1513.vb.

This is because we compile the code into a DLL before it is executed. At runtime, the source file is not required and unlike user controls, the runtime does not determine what language compiler to call. The code in a DLL file is ready for execution by runtime.

Compilation is done by using commands, such as vbc to call Visual Basic compiler and csc to call C# compiler. These compilers do not force use of specific file extensions, and once the code is compiled into a DLL, it has nothing to do with its original source file.

Listing 15.13 **ch1513.vb   Creating a Custom Control**

```
01 Imports System
02 Imports System.Web.UI
03 NameSpace NewRiders
04    Public Class Converter : Inherits Control
05       Overrides Protected Sub Render(Output as HtmlTextWriter)
```

```
06          Output.WriteLine("<table>")
07          Output.WriteLine("<tr><td>")
08          Output.WriteLine("<input size='5'> &deg F to &deg C")
09          Output.WriteLine("</td></tr>")
10          Output.WriteLine("</table>")
11      End Sub
12   End Class
13 End NameSpace
```

The first two lines import the namespaces that any typical custom control uses. The namespace System contains the core system classes and the namespace System.Web.UI contains ASP.NET control classes, such as Control and HtmlTextWriter.

Line 3 marks the beginning of the namespace NewRiders. This namespace uniquely identifies the control class defined in line 4. We will be calling our control as Converter and it inherits from the Control class, which belongs to System.Web.UI namespace. All the custom controls inherit from the Control class—as it defines the properties, methods, and events that are shared by all server controls in the Web Forms page framework. Further, we have defined our control as Public so that it remains accessible from ASP.NET Web Forms.

In line 5, we are overriding the Render method provided by the Control class to gain control over the default rendering logic of the control. This method makes an HtmlTextWriter object accessible to us, through which we can send our own HTML to the page output stream.

After you have written your custom control class, you need to compile it into a DLL using the Visual Basic compiler. Issuing the following command to the compiler can do this:

```
vbc /t:library /out:bin\converter.dll /r:System.dll,System.Web.dll ch1513.vb
```

In the preceding command, the /t switch tells the compiler to create output as a library. The /r switch specify the compiler to include references for System.dll and System.Web.dll classes. The last argument is the name of the source file.

/out specifies the location of the output file. You need to take care as to where you store the DLL file. The runtime checks for it at two places: either in the Global Assembly Cache (GAC) or in the bin directory of the web application in question. How and when to put assemblies in GAC is explained later in this chapter. For now, you need to store it in the bin directory of your web application. For example, if your compilation directory is: c:\inetpub\wwwroot\InsideASP.Net\ch15 and your web application is also pointing to it, then the previous command works fine. But, if your web application has been set up in c:\inetpub\wwwroot\InsideASP.Net, then you need to change your command to:

```
vbc /t:library /out:..\bin\converter.dll /r:System.dll,System.Web.dll ch1513.vb
```

You also need to make sure that you have a bin directory created in your web application. If it's not there, then go ahead and create it.

Setting Environment Variables for Compilation

If you have Visual Studio .NET installed, you can open up a command prompt with all environment variables properly set for you by navigating this path: Start, Programs, Microsoft Visual Studio .NET 7.0, Visual Studio .NET Tools, Visual Studio .NET Command Prompt.

Otherwise, if you are just using the .NET framework SDK, then you can set the environment variable by invoking the command prompt and running the corvars.bat file located in c:\Program_Files\Microsoft.NET\ FrameworkSDK\Bin directory. You might need to change the drive, depending on where you have installed the .NET framework SDK on your computer.

After you have set the environment, you can compile your program from the command line.

Figure 15.5 shows you what a typical compile session looks like.

Figure 15.5 Compiling a custom control.

After the compilation is done, the control is created and is ready to use. You can use this control in ASP.NET pages like any other server control. Listing 15.14 shows an ASP.NET file that hosts our custom control.

Listing 15.14 **ch1514.aspx Using Custom Control**

```
01 <%@ Register TagPrefix="MyCustomControl" NameSpace="NewRiders"
02              Assembly="Converter" %>
03 <html>
04    <head>
05      <Title>Using Custom Control</Title>
```

```
06   </head>
07 <body>
08   <form runat="server">
09      <h4><asp:Label Text="Converter Custom Control:"
10              Runat="server" /> </h4>
11      <MyCustomControl:Converter Runat="server" /><br>
12      <asp:Button Text="Convert" Runat="server" />
13   </form>
14 </body>
15 </html>
```

Lines 1 and 2 contain a `Register` directive. It tells the ASP.NET runtime system that whenever it finds any tag name prefixed with the tag prefix `MyCustomControl`, it should look for the code of the associated custom control in the assembly named `Converter` in the namespace `NewRiders`. In this case, tag prefix differentiates between controls written by us and the controls written by other people or the inbuilt controls. The namespace and assembly establishes a link with the compiled code of custom controls.

Aside from the usual ASP and HTML code in line 11, the custom control is included. The system finds the code in the web application's bin directory—from where it renders the control in the ASP.NET page. The output should look like Figure 15.6. The control is good to see, but it doesn't do anything at this stage because no conversion logic exists in the control. You still need to work out certain things before you are finished.

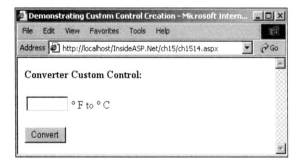

Figure 15.6   Using a custom control.

Assigning Properties to a Custom Control

Custom controls expose their public variables so that their value can be customized in the Web Form containing them. A nice way of exposing public fields is through the use of property syntax, because it is much more powerful and is also supported by visual designers.

If the property being exposed is the object of a class that has further properties inside it, these inner properties are exposed as sub-properties and can be accessed from the ASP.NET pages by using the `PropertyName-SubProperty` syntax.

Listing 15.15 extends the `Converter` custom control to show the use of properties and sub-properties. Let us first see the modifications to the custom control code.

Listing 15.15 ch1515.vb Customizing a Custom Control

```
01 Imports System
02 Imports System.Web.UI
03 NameSpace NewRiders
04  Public Class ConverterFormat
05     Private _bgcolor as String
06     Public Property BgColor as String
07        Get
08           return _bgcolor
09        End Get
10        Set
11           bgcolor = Value
12        End Set
13     End Property
14     Private _width as String
15     Public Property Width as String
16        Get
17           return _width
18        End Get
19        Set
20           width = Value
21        End Set
22     End Property
23     Private _height as String
24     Public Property Height as String
25        Get
26           return _height
27        End Get
28        Set
29           height = Value
30        End Set
31     End Property
32  End Class
33  Public Class Converter : Inherits Control
34     Private _format as ConverterFormat = new ConverterFormat()
35     Public ReadOnly Property Format as ConverterFormat
36        Get
37           return _format
38        End Get
```

```
39    End Property
40    Private _type as String, _label1 as String, _label2 as String
41    Public Property Type as String
42      Get
43         return _type
44      End Get
45      Set
46         _type = Value.ToLower()
47         Select Case _type
48            Case "distance"
49               _label1 = "Miles"
50               _label2 = "Kilometers"
51            Case Else 'temperature
52               _label1 = "&deg F"
53               _label2 = "&deg C"
54         End Select
55      End Set
56    End Property
57    Overrides Protected Sub Render(Output as HtmlTextWriter)
58      Output.Write("<Table bgcolor='" & Format.BgColor & "'")
59      Output.Write(" Height='" & Format.Height & "'")
60      Output.WriteLine(" Width='" & Format.Width & "'>")
61      Output.WriteLine("<tr><td>")
62      Output.Write("<input name=" & Me.UniqueID & " size='5'> ")
63      Output.WriteLine(_label1 & " to " & _label2)
64      Output.WriteLine("</td></tr>")
65      Output.WriteLine("</table>")
66    End Sub
67  End Class
68 End NameSpace
```

Lines 4 through 32 contain a newly added class that maintains format-related information. It has exposed three format properties, namely BgColor, Width, and Height. Inside the Converter custom control class in line 34, you are creating an instance of the ConverterFormat class, and in lines 35 through 39, we write a property accessor for it. This code enables us to access sub-properties of ConverterFormat. In line 41, we are creating a property named Type. We use this to set the type of the control (whether we need to convert temperature or distance) and also set labels appropriately in the control.

In line 62, I am using Me.UniqueID. This gets a unique name for this control every time it is accessed. This is helpful because the name of the control will not collide with other controls and its own instances. This source file can be compiled by the same command discussed before. You need to change only the name of the source file.

Listing 15.16 shows how to customize this control by modifying these properties from inside an ASP.NET Web Form.

Listing 15.16 **ch1516.aspx**   **Customizing a Custom Control**

```
01 <%@ Register TagPrefix="MyCustomControl" NameSpace="NewRiders"
02              Assembly="Converter" %>
03 <html>
04 <head>
05     <Title>Demonstrating Custom Control Properties</Title>
06 </head>
07 <body>
08    <form runat="server">
09        <h4><asp:Label Text="Converter Custom Control:"
10                     Runat="server" /> </h4>
11        <MyCustomControl:Converter
12                Type="distance"
13                Format-Height="50"
14                Format-Width="200"
15                Format-BgColor="#CCCCCC"
16                Runat="server" />
17        <MyCustomControl:Converter
18                Type="temperature"
19                Format-Height="50"
20                Format-Width="200"
21                Format-BgColor="#CCCCCC"
22                Runat="server" /><br>
23        <asp:Button Text="Convert" Runat="server" />
24    </form>
25 </body>
26 </html>
```

Everything else being the same, let's analyze lines 11 through 16. In this case, we have inserted the Converter custom control and set its various properties. As you can see, the properties can be directly accessed as well as sub-properties using the Property-SubProperty syntax. In lines 17 through 22, we have instantiated one more Converter custom control with a different set of properties. When you load this page in the browser, it renders output similar to Figure 15.7. It is a nice learning exercise to see the HTML generated by the ASPX pages. You can see this in Internet Explorer by selecting the Source option from the View menu.

Handling Postback in Custom Controls

So far we have developed a simple custom control that can render HTML, but it does not do anything with the input provided by the user. Our next step is to make our control responsive to user input (also called *postback*). All controls that want to handle postback data processing must implement the System.Web.UI.IPostBackDataHandler interface.

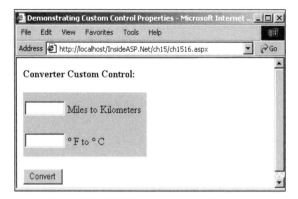

Figure 15.7 Using custom control properties.

The `IpostBackDataHandler` interface has the following two methods:

- **LoadPostData**—The `LoadPostData` is invoked when the postback occurs and the control has postback data. It has the following signature:

```
Function LoadPostPostData(ByVal postDataKey as String, _
ByVal postCollection as NameValueCollection) As Boolean
```

In this case, `postCollection` has access to all the postback data that was submitted. You could use a `postDataKey` variable as a key to get data from this collection. The value of `postDataKey` is the unique name of the control. You would return a true value from this method if you wanted to raise an event after the postback. You would otherwise return a false value.

- **RaisePostDataChangedEvent**—The `RaisePostDataChangedEvent` method is called when the `LoadPostData` method is executed for all server controls on a page. It is called only for those controls where the `LoadPostData` method returns true. The `RaisePostDataChanged` method is used to raise events. It has the following signatures:

```
Sub RaisePostDataChangedEvent()
```

Let us see how this mechanism can be used in the `Converter` custom control to respond to postback. The modified source code is shown in Listing 15.17.

Listing 15.17   ch1517.vb   Using Postback in Custom Control

```
01 Imports System
02 Imports System.Web.UI
03 Imports System.Collections.Specialized
04 NameSpace NewRiders
```

continues ▶

Listing 15.17 **Continued**

```
05 Public Class Converter : Inherits Control : Implements IPostBackDataHandler
06 Private _type as String, _label1 as String, _label2 as String
07 Public Property Type as String
08     Get
09         return _type
10     End Get
11     Set
12       _type = Value.ToLower()
13         Select Case _type
14           Case "distance"
15             _label1 = "Miles"
16             _label2 = "Kilometers"
17           Case Else 'temperature
18             _label1 = "&deg F"
19             _label2 = "&deg C"
20         End Select
21     End Set
22   End Property
23   Private _convertedValue as Integer
24   Private _value as Integer
25   Public Property Value as Integer
26     Get
27         return _value
28     End Get
29     Set
30       value = Value
31         Select Case Type
32           Case "distance"
33             _convertedValue =  CType((value * 1.609), Integer)
34           Case Else 'temperature
35             _convertedValue = CType((5.0/9.0) * (Value - 32), Integer)
36         End Select
37     End Set
38   End Property
39   Public ReadOnly Property ConvertedValue as Integer
40     Get
41         return _convertedValue
42     End Get
43   End Property
44   Public Function LoadPostData(PostDataKey as String, _
45                   Values as NameValueCollection) As Boolean _
46                 Implements IPostBackDataHandler.LoadPostData
47       Me.Value = Int32.Parse(Values(Me.UniqueID))
48       Return false
49   End Function
50   Public Sub RaisePostDataChangedEvent() _
51             Implements IPostbackDataHandler.RaisePostDataChangedEvent
52   End Sub
53   Overrides Protected Sub Render(Output as HtmlTextWriter)
54     Output.Write("<input name=" & Me.UniqueID & " size='5' Value='" & Me.Value & "'>")
55     Output.WriteLine(_label1 & " to " & _label2)
```

```
56    End Sub
57 End Class
58 End NameSpace
```

In line 5, we are setting up our class to implement `IPostBackDataHandler`. To implement this interface, we need to implement both of its methods. As we discussed previously, the `LoadPostData` method has access to the postback data. We program this function to get the postback data and use it in our calculations. In line 47, we accessed the `NameValueCollection` and retrieved the data posted in the text box through its `UniqueID` value. As soon as we set the `Value` property in this line, the `Set` accessor of this property (see lines 29 through 37) does the actual conversion work and stores the converted value in `_convertedValue`. We are then exposing this private variable as a public read-only property named `ConvertedValue` that is accessible to the Web Form hosting custom control.

As a result of this code, whenever the user submits the Web Form containing this custom control, the `LoadPostData` method is invoked server-side as a result of this postback. It analyzes the postback data inside the text box and sets the converted value in the `_convertedValued` variable, which is then available to the Web Form as the `ConvertedValue` property of this control. In line 54, we are generating the HTML input field and setting its value as the value submitted by user. This time when the page is reloaded, the text box remembers its value.

Because we are not raising any events right now, we are returning false from `LoadPostData` method and in turn, we have not written anything inside the `RaisePostDataChangedEvent` as there is nothing to do. It was necessary to write the definition of this function even if it is empty because it is required by the `IPostBackDataHandler` interface.

Now, let us look at the Web Form that hosts this custom control (see Listing 15.18).

Listing 15.18   ch1518.aspx   Using Postback in Custom Control

```
01 <%@ Register TagPrefix="MyCustomControl" NameSpace="NewRiders"
02              Assembly="Converter" %>
03 <html>
04 <head>
05    <Title>Demonstrating Custom Control</Title>
06    <script language="vb" runat="server">
07       Private Sub ConvertBtn_Click(Sender as Object, E as EventArgs)
08          Message.Text = MyCustomControl.ConvertedValue
09       End Sub
10    </script>
```

continues ▶

Listing 15.18 **Continued**

```
11 </head>
12 <body>
13    <form runat="server">
14       <h4><asp:Label Text="Converter Custom Control:"
15                Runat="server" /> </h4>
16       <MyCustomControl:Converter id="MyCustomControl"
17                       Type="distance" runat="server" />
18       <asp:Button Text="Convert" OnClick="ConvertBtn_Click"
19                Runat="server" />
20       <hr>
21       The converted value is:
22       <asp:Label ID="Message" Runat="server" />
23    </form>
24.</body>
25 </html>
```

In lines 7 through 9, we are defining the event handler of the Convert
button. When we click the Convert button, postback occurs and fires the
LoadPostData method, which in turns set the value of the custom control.
After the postback is done, and we re-create the Web Form, the text of label
Message is being changed inside the event handler of Convert button by setting it with the current value of the Converter custom control. When you
load the Web Form in the browser, it looks like Figure 15.8.

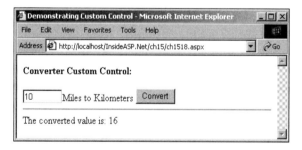

Figure 15.8   Handling postback in custom controls.

Raising Custom Events in Custom Controls

When we define custom controls, we can also raise our own custom events.
For example, we can raise a change event in response to the data changed by
the user. These events can be then exposed so that they can be handled in
Web Form. Let's modify the previous example to introduce a Change event in
our custom control.

This requires us to make three changes to the code in Listing 15.17. Because the changes are minor, the full code listing is not included here, but the modified lines of code are indicated.

First, we declare an event by making the following change to Converter class:

```
01 Public Class Converter : Inherits Control
02     Implements IPostBackDataHandler
03   Public Event Change as Eventhandler  '<— new line added
04   Private _type as String
```

We have made the event public so that it is accessible inside the Web Form, where we can add the event handler to it.

For the second change, we need to return true from LoadPostData. Returning true causes RaisePostDataChangedEvent to be invoked, which is the place where we actually raise events. The modified LoadPostData function looks like this:

```
01 Public Function LoadPostData(PostDataKey as String, _
02           Values as NameValueCollection) As Boolean _
03           Implements IPostBackDataHandler.LoadPostData
04   Me.Value = Int32.Parse(Values(Me.UniqueID))
05   Return true   '<— return value changed from false to true
06 End Function
```

The third and final change is inside the RaisePostDataChangedEvent, which is modified as shown:

```
01 Public Sub RaisePostDataChangedEvent() _
02           Implements IPostbackDataHandler.RaisePostDataChangedEvent
03   RaiseEvent Change(Me, EventArgs.Empty)  '<— New line added
04 End Sub
```

Change takes two arguments. The first is the object on which this event is raised. We are passing references to the custom control itself. The second is the object of EventArgs type that holds additional information that we would likc to supply in context to this event. In this example, we want to raise the event and not supply any other information, thus we are using EventArgs.Empty.

We need to compile ch1517.vb after we have entered these changes. The code inside the Web Form is found in Listing 15.19.

Listing 15.19 **ch1519.aspx Raising Events in Custom Control**

```
01 <%@ Register TagPrefix="MyCustomControl" NameSpace="NewRiders"
02           Assembly="Converter" %>
03 <html>
```

continues ▶

Listing 15.19 **Continued**

```
04    <head>
05        <Title>Demonstrating Custom Control</Title>
06        <script language="vb" runat="server">
07           Private Sub OnControlChange(Sender as Object, E as EventArgs)
08              Message.Text = MyCustomControl.ConvertedValue
09           End Sub
10        </script>
11    </head>
12    <body>
13      <form runat="server">
14          <h4><asp:Label Text="Converter Custom Control:"
15                 Runat="server" /> </h4>
16          <b>Enter a value and press enter key:</b><BR>
17          <MyCustomControl:Converter id="MyCustomControl"
18               Type="temperature" OnChange="OnControlChange"
19               runat="server" />
20           <hr>The converted value is:
21           <asp:Label ID="Message" Runat="server" />
22        </form>
23    </body>
24 </html>
```

Lines 17 through 19 include the custom control. In line 18, we are using the attribute OnChange to add an event handler to the Change event of the custom control. Prefixing an "On" to event names is a convention in ASP.NET. In this case, a custom event handler—OnControlChange—is attached to our event handler and is called whenever postback occurs and the Change event is raised.

Using Client-Side JavaScript for Custom Postback

In this section, you will learn to use client-side JavaScript code for raising custom postback. Normally, a postback is caused only by controls, such as Button or ImageButton, but in certain situations you might prefer other HTML elements, such as hyperlinks, to cause postback. We can use client-side JavaScript code to cause postback to occur from most HTML tags.

To do this, we need to do a few changes to code in Listing 15.17. For brevity, only the modified portions are shown. The first change is in the definition of class.

In the following example, postback is invoked from the click of a button. If you would rather work with hyperlinks, then you need to modify the code a little. The code listing of our custom control goes like this:

```
01 05: NameSpace NewRiders
02 Public Class Converter : Inherits Control
03          Implements IPostBackDataHandler
04          Implements IPostBackEventHandler '<— New line added
```

In this sample, for client-side postback we need to implement one more interface—IPostBackEventhandler.

IPostBackEventHandler requires the definition of the RaisePostBackEvent method. We define it after we define RaisePostBackDataChangedEvent. Though we are not doing anything in this method, it is required by the interface.

```
01 Public Sub RaisePostBackEvent(EventArgument As String) Implements _
02          IPostBackEventHandler.RaisePostBackEvent
03 End Sub
```

The final change is inside the Render method. The modified method is as follows:

```
01 Protected Overrides Sub Render(Output as HtmlTextWriter)
02    Output.Write("<input name=" & Me.UniqueID & _
03              " size='5' Value='" & Me.Value & "'>")
04    Output.Write(_label1 & " to " & _label2)
05    Output.Write("<input type=button value=Compute OnClick=""jscript:")
06    Output.Write(Page.GetPostBackEventReference(Me, "Compute") & _
07              """"><hr>")
08    Output.Write("The converted value is: " & ConvertedValue)
09 End Sub
```

In this example, in the third and fourth Output.Write method, we have rendered an HTML button and on its OnClick event, we are writing Page.GetPostBackEventReference(Me, "Compute"). This piece of code obtains a reference to a client-side script function, which causes the server to postback to the form. The first argument, Me, is a reference to server control that processes the postback. The second argument, "Compute", is a message we are passing back to the Web Form on postback. We are not doing anything with this message, so it just goes unnoticed. In other cases, we could have used it to influence our processing logic.

The code of the container Web Form is as shown in Listing 15.20.

Listing 15.20   **ch1520.aspx   Client-Side JavaScript for Custom PostBack**

```
01 <%@ Register TagPrefix="MyCustomControl" NameSpace="NewRiders"
02          Assembly="Converter" %>
03 <html>
04   <head>
05     <Title>Demonstrating Custom Control</Title>
06   </head>
```

continues ▶

Listing 15.20 **Continued**

```
07   <body>
08     <form runat="server">
09       <h4><asp:Label Text="Converter Custom Control:"
10                 Runat="server" /> </h4>
11       <MyCustomControl:Converter id="MyCustomControl"
12                 Type="distance" runat="server" />
13     </form>
14   </body>
15 </html>
```

When you load this Web Form into your browser, it still looks like the one shown in Figure 15.8, but the way the postback is internally working is different. It would be interesting to view the HTML code sent to the browser to see how this postback is actually implemented.

Creating Composite Controls

We can also create a custom control by combining existing controls. In this case, our control is a composition of one or more existing controls, which we refer to as ChildControls. The child controls render their own user interface, so we do not need to render the user interface from the scratch.

When you are designing a composite control, you must take care of two things:

- **Override the protected CreateChildControl method**—This method is a member of the Control class. It is used to create the instances of child control and add them to the controls collection.

- **Implement INamingContainer interface**—This is an interface with no methods, but when you implement it, ASP.NET creates a new naming scope under this control. As a result of this, the child controls that you create in this control belong to a unique namespace and avoid any name collision problems that might arise.

In Listing 15.21, I have modified the Converter custom control such that the text box, button, horizontal ruler, and the result label now render their own user interface.

Listing 15.21 **ch1521.vb Composite Custom Control**

```
01 Option Strict Off
02 Imports System
03 Imports System.Web
04 Imports System.Web.UI
```

```
05 Imports System.Web.UI.WebControls
06 NameSpace NewRiders
07     Public Class Converter : Inherits Control
08                 Implements INamingContainer
09        Private _type as String, _label1 as String, _label2 as String
10        Public Property Type as String
11           Get
12               return _type
13           End Get
14           Set
15               _type = Value.ToLower()
16               Select Case _type
17                  Case "distance"
18                     _label1 = "Miles"
19                     _label2 = "Kilometers"
20                  Case Else 'temperature
21                     _label1 = "&deg F"
22                     _label2 = "&deg C"
23               End Select
24           End Set
25        End Property
26        Private _convertedValue as Integer
27        Public ReadOnly Property ConvertedValue as Integer
28           Get
29              Dim Ctrl As TextBox = Controls(0)
30              Dim SourceValue as Integer
31              SourceValue =  Int32.Parse(Ctrl.Text)
32              Select Case Type
33                 Case "distance"
34                    _convertedValue =  CType((SourceValue * 1.609), Integer)
35                 Case Else 'temperature
36                    _convertedValue = CType((5.0/9.0) * _
37                             (SourceValue - 32), Integer)
38              End Select
39              return _convertedValue
40           End Get
41        End Property
42        Protected Overrides Sub CreateChildControls()
43           Dim Box as New TextBox
44           Box.Text = "0"
45           Box.Columns = 5
46           Me.Controls.Add(Box)
47           Me.Controls.Add(New LiteralControl(" " & _label1 & _
48                       " to " & _label2 & "<BR>"))
49           Dim ConvertButton as new Button
50           ConvertButton.Text = "Convert"
51           AddHandler ConvertButton.Click, AddressOf ConvertBtn_Click
52           Me.Controls.Add(ConvertButton)
53           Me.Controls.Add(New LiteralControl("<HR>The converted value is: "))
54           Dim Result as New Label
55           Me.Controls.Add(Result)
56        End Sub
```

continues ▶

Listing 15.21 **Continued**

```
57        Private Sub ConvertBtn_Click(Sender as Object, E as EventArgs)
58            Dim Ctrl As Label = Controls(4)
59            Ctrl.Text = ConvertedValue
60      End Sub
61    End Class
62 End NameSpace
```

In line 5, we are importing System.Web.UI.WebControls, as we are making use of controls, such as TextBox, which belong to it. Lines 7 and 8 start the definition of the Converter custom control where we are implementing the INamingContainer interface. Major changes in our code come by the introduction of the CreateChildControls method. Instead of using Output.Write to render the control's user interface, we will create instances of child controls and they will render their own user interface. In lines 43 through 46, we are instantiating a TextBox that sets its properties and adds it to custom control. In line 47, we are creating objects of the LiteralControl class. This is used to add HTML elements and text strings in our control. In line 51, AddHandler is used to attach ConvertBtn_Click method with the Click event of ConvertButton child control.

You can compile this code and invoke it using the old ch1520.aspx Web Form, as there is nothing that changes. The result still looks similar to Figure 15.8 shown previously in this chapter.

Developing Templated Controls

Some of the ASP.NET server controls support templates. With this feature you can separate the data inside the control with its presentation. You can also design your own templated custom controls. However, you need to be aware of the following requirements:

- The templated custom control is required to implement the System.Web.UI.INamingContainer interface. It creates a new namespace under our control so that all its child controls are uniquely identified. (Refer to lines 6 and 22 in Listing 15.22.)

- You will apply the ParseChildren attribute to your control and pass a value true to it. This indicates ASP.NET will parse the control's declaration in the Web Form and read its template property tags. (Refer to line 20 of Listing 15.22.)

- You will create a template container class (lines 5 through 19 of Listing 15.22). In our control example, this class is not doing much, but it is holding a string.

- Define at least one property of type `System.Web.UI.ITemplate`. This property must have an attribute of type `System.Web.UI.TemplateContainerAttribute`. In line 37, it is indicating the use of the `ConverterItem` type as a template container. The `ITemplate` interface provides us a method `InstantiateIn` that creates the controls using the template in the Web Form (see line 54 of Listing 15.22).

- Override the `CreateChildControls` method to create the child controls in the template (lines 50 through 59 of Listing 15.22). In these lines, you do three things: Firstly, instantiate the template container (line 53); secondly, invoke the `InstantiateIn` method on the property declared as `ITemplate` and pass the newly created template container to it (line 54); finally, add the instance of the template container to the controls collection of our templated control (line 55).

- Override the `DataBind` method of the `Control` class and invoke the `EnsureChildControls` method to make sure that the child controls in the template are created before any databinding expression is evaluated (line 47 of Listing 15.22).

Listing 15.22 **ch1522.vb** **A Templated Custom Control**

```
01 Imports System
02 Imports System.Web
03 Imports System.Web.UI
04 Namespace NewRiders
05 Public Class ConverterItem : Inherits Control
06             Implements INamingContainer
07    Private _type As String = Nothing
08    Public Sub New(Type As String)
09      _type = Type
10    End Sub
11    Public Property Type As String
12       Get
13          return _type
14       End Get
15       Set
16         _type = Value
17       End Set
18    End Property
19 End Class
20 <ParseChildren(true)> Public Class Converter
21                     Inherits Control
22                     Implements INamingContainer
23    Private _converterTemplate As ITemplate = Nothing
24    Private _type As String = Nothing
25    Public Property Type As String
```

continues ▶

Listing 15.22 **Continued**

```
26      Get
27        If (_type = "temperature") Then
28          Return "Converts &deg F to &deg C"
29        Else
30          Return "Converts Miles to Kilometers"
31        End If
32      End Get
33      Set
34        _type = Value.ToLower()
35      End Set
36    End Property
37    <TemplateContainer(GetType(ConverterItem))> _
38        Public Property ConverterTemplate As ITemplate
39        Get
40          Return _converterTemplate
41        End Get
42        Set
43          _converterTemplate = Value
44        End Set
45    End Property
46    Public Overrides Sub DataBind()
47      EnsureChildControls()
48      MyBase.DataBind()
49    End Sub
50    Protected Overrides Sub CreateChildControls()
51      If Not (ConverterTemplate Is Nothing)
52        Controls.Clear()
53        Dim I As New ConverterItem(Me.Type)
54        ConverterTemplate.InstantiateIn(I)
55        Controls.Add(I)
56      Else
57        Me.Controls.Add(New LiteralControl(Me.Type))
58      End If
59    End Sub
60  End Class
61 End Namespace
```

If we create a non-templated instance of this control, the condition in line 51 evaluates to false and hence, a plain literal control is added to the output. In the case of templated controls, the condition evaluates to true, and the output is formatted according to the formatting specified inside the template container.

We will now place the custom control in a Web Form. If you look into its code shown in Listing 15.23, we have created two instances of our custom control. Lines 17 through 19 show the non-templated version, and lines 22 through 29 show the templated version.

Listing 15.23 **ch1523.aspx   A Templated Custom Control**

```
01 <%@ Register TagPrefix="MyCustomControl"
02              Namespace="NewRiders"
03              Assembly="Converter" %>
04 <html>
05    <head>
06      <title>Templated Custom Control</title>
07      <script runat=server language=VB>
08        Sub Page_Load()
09          DataBind()
10        End Sub
11      </script>
12    </head>
13    <body>
14      <form method="POST" runat="server">
15        This is non-templated version of
16                       converter control:<br>
17        <MyCustomControl:Converter
18              Type="Temperature"
19              runat=server/>
20        <hr>
21        This is templated version of custom control:<br>
22        <MyCustomControl:Converter
23              Type="distance" runat=server>
24          <ConverterTemplate>
25            <b><i>
26              <%# Container.Type%>
27            </i></b>
28          </ConverterTemplate>
29        </MyCustomControl:Converter>
30      </form>
31  </body>
32 </html>
```

The output of this Web Form looks like Figure 15.9.

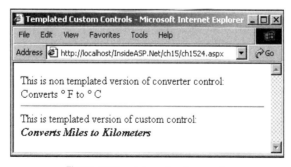

Figure 15.9   A templated control.

Developing a Templated Databound Control

The previous example demonstrated how to bind a control with a single data item. In the next example, you learn how to write a custom control that binds to a data source of collection type. In Listing 15.24, the template container exposes properties that will be evaluated for each item in the data collection. In this case, the main logic is in lines 37 through 50—where we have defined the OnDataBinding method. For each item in a data collection, we instantiate a template container and set its properties.

Listing 15.24   **ch1524.vb   A Templated Databound Control**

```
01 Imports System
02 Imports System.Collections
03 Imports System.Web
04 Imports System.Web.UI
05 Namespace NewRiders
06     <ParseChildren(true)> _
07     Public Class Converter : Inherits Control
08                 Implements INamingContainer
09        Private _itemTemplate As ITemplate = Nothing
10        <TemplateContainer(GetType(ConverterItem))> _
11        Public Property ItemTemplate As ITemplate
12           Get
13               return _itemTemplate
14           End Get
15           Set
16               _itemTemplate = value
17           End Set
18        End Property
19        Private _dataSource As ICollection = Nothing
20        Public Property DataSource As ICollection
21           Get
22               Return _dataSource
23           End Get
24           Set
25             _dataSource = Value
26           End Set
27        End Property
28        Private _type as String = "temperature"
29        Public Property Type as String
30           Get
31               Return _type
32           End Get
33           Set
34               _type = Value
35           End Set
36        End Property
37        Protected Overrides Sub OnDataBinding(E As EventArgs)
38           If Not DataSource Is Nothing
39               Dim DataEnum As IEnumerator = _
```

```
40                            DataSource.GetEnumerator()
41                 Dim I As Integer = 0
42                 Do While (DataEnum.MoveNext())
43                     Dim Item As ConverterItem = _
44                         New ConverterItem(I, DataEnum.Current,Type)
45                     ItemTemplate.InstantiateIn(Item)
46                     Controls.Add(Item)
47                     I = I + 1
48                 Loop
49             End If
50         End Sub
51  End Class
52  Public Class ConverterItem : Inherits Control
53               Implements INamingContainer
54     Private _sourceValue as Integer, _targetValue as Integer
55     Private _sourceUnit as String, _targetUnit as String
56     Private _ItemIndex As Integer
57     Public ReadOnly Property ItemIndex As Integer
58         Get
59             return _ItemIndex
60         End Get
61     End Property
62     Public Sub New(ItemIndex As Integer, SourceData As Object, Type as String)
63         MyBase.New()
64       _ItemIndex = ItemIndex
65       Select Case Type.ToLower()
66         Case "distance"
67             _sourceUnit = "Miles"
68             _targetUnit = "Kilometers"
69             _sourceValue = CType(SourceData, Integer)
70             _targetValue = CType((_sourceValue * 1.609), Integer)
71         Case Else 'temprature
72             _sourceUnit = "&deg F"
73             _targetUnit = "&deg C"
74             _sourceValue = CType(SourceData, Integer)
75             _targetValue = CType((5.0/9.0) * (_sourceValue - 32), Integer)
76       End Select
77     End Sub
78     Public ReadOnly Property SourceUnit as String
79         Get
80             return _sourceUnit
81         End Get
82     End Property
83     Public ReadOnly Property TargetUnit as String
84         Get
85                 return _targetUnit
86         End Get
87   End Property
88     Public ReadOnly Property SourceValue As Object
89         Get
90             return _sourceValue
```

continues ▶

Listing 15.24 **Continued**

```
91        End Get
92      End Property
93      Public ReadOnly Property TargetValue As Object
94        Get
95          return _targetValue
96        End Get
97      End Property
98   End Class
99 End Namespace
```

Inside the Web Form hosting this custom control, we are initially creating a data source inside the Page_Load method. Later in the custom control, we are creating a few label controls and assigning them with the properties of the template container. Because these labels are inside ItemTemplate, they will be created for each item in data collection (see Listing 15.25). The output looks like Figure 15.10.

Listing 15.25 **ch1525.aspx   A Templated Databound Control**

```
01 <%@ Register TagPrefix="MyCustomControl"
02            Namespace="NewRiders"
03            Assembly="Converter"%>
04 <html>
05 <head>
06   <title>Templated Databound Custom Control</title>
07   <script language="VB" runat=server>
08     Sub Page_Load(Sender As Object, E As EventArgs)
09        If Not (IsPostBack)
10          Dim Values As New ArrayList
11          Values.Add("50")
12          Values.Add("60")
13          Values.Add("70")
14          Values.Add("80")
15          Values.Add("90")
16          MyList.DataSource = Values
17          MyList.DataBind()
18        End If
19     End Sub
20   </script>
21 </head>
22 <body>
23   <MyCustomControl:Converter id="MyList"
24                  type="distance" runat=server>
25      <ItemTemplate>
26          <asp:label id="SourceValue"
27              Text="<%#Container.SourceValue%>"
28              runat=server/>
```

```
29              <asp:label id="SourceUnit"
30                  Text="<%#Container.SourceUnit%>"
31                  runat=server/>
32          equals
33          <I><B><asp:label id="TargetValue"
34                  Text="<%#Container.TargetValue%>"
35                  runat=server/>
36          <asp:label id="TargetUnit"
37                  Text="<%#Container.TargetUnit%>"
38                  runat=server/>
39          </B></I><hr align=left width=200>
40      </ItemTemplate>
41  </MyCustomControl:Converter>
42 </body>
43 </html>
```

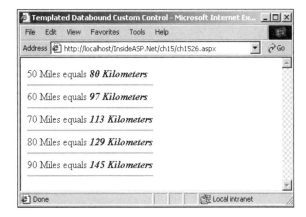

Figure 15.10   A templated databound control.

Global Assembly Cache

So far in the previous examples, you have been keeping your custom controls (.dll files) in the bin directory of your web application. This way you can use custom controls only in one web application. If instead you would prefer that your custom controls are globally available throughout all the web applications on a machine, you need to install these components in the GAC (see Figure 15.11).

Each computer that is installed with ASP.NET runtime also maintains a GAC as a place to keep shared assemblies. Typically, it is located at c:\WINNT\assembly. The exact path can vary depending on your installation.

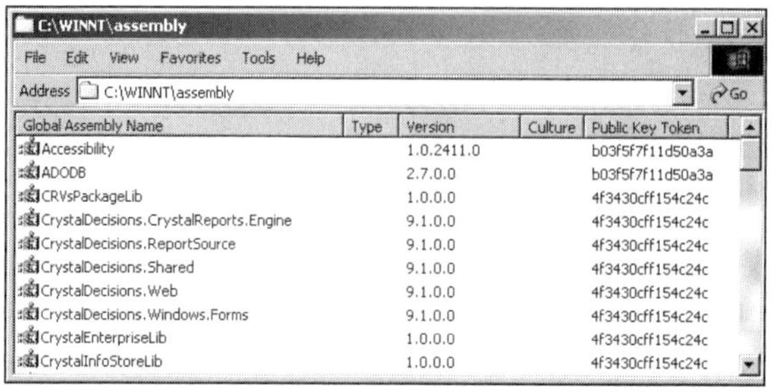

Figure 15.11   Global Assembly Cache.

Besides acting as central repository of compiled code, the GAC also supports side-by-side existence of assemblies with the same name but different versions. This is a great feature that ends all DLL-related confusion, which is created when you release an upgrade or patch for your software. To support these features, the assemblies installed in GAC must have a strong name. The strong name consists of a name, version, culture info, a public key, and a digital signature. Strong names can be created either directly from Visual Studio .NET or from a command line using the Strong Name Tool (sn.exe) and the Assembly Generation Tool (al.exe).

Three ways you can install your components in the GAC are as follows:

- Dragging and dropping using Windows Explorer
- Using GACUtil.exe
- Using an installer designed for the GAC

For more information on creating strong name assemblies and deploying them in the GAC, search for "Global Assembly Cache" in the MSDN Library Online at `http://msdn.microsoft.com/library/default.asp` or in the .NET framework documentation installed on your system.

Summary

This chapter discussed user-control and custom-control development. It talked about different ways of creating both user controls and custom controls, and supported them with extensive examples. These are powerful techniques for code reusability and maintenance. You will see yourself when using them often while developing with ASP.NET.

16

Mobile Device Development with ASP.NET

MOBILE DEVICES ARE BECOMING INCREASINGLY popular. Over the past few years, mobile phones have become so common that it is more of a rarity to see someone without one. *Personal Digital Assistants* (PDAs), such as Palm Pilots, also are popular. Combine this with the fact that the Internet is everywhere. It goes without saying that tremendous opportunity exists for the savvy web developer to take advantage of this current state of accessibility.

So, how can a developer take advantage of this? Consider the following: Most people use the Internet as a means of finding information. Ironically, it is not always possible to get to an Internet PC or Mac; however, most people have more convenient access to a mobile phone or PDA. This means that there is an enormous, untapped market for mobile Internet services. After all, imagine being able to use your mobile device not only for sending and receiving your email, but also for receiving information from the sports and news feeds or the company you work for, or being able to book and purchase tickets through online services. The possibilities are limitless!

This chapter introduces the mobile device types you can develop, and provides a brief overview of the underlying technology used for writing applications for mobile devices:

- Covering Wireless Application Protocol (WAP)
- Wireless Markup Language (WML)
- WMLScript (the script language for WML)

This chapter provides an overview of the ASP.NET Mobile Internet Toolkit (SDK designed for developing Mobile Device applications). It also explains some issues dealing with mobile device development and some key differences between ASP.NET forms and controls, and ASP.NET Mobile forms and Controls. From here, it describes each Mobile control and gives examples of their uses. Finally, a brief overview of the mobile device support in the application presented in Chapter 17, "Putting It All Together" is provided.

Software You Need for This Chapter

To use the examples in this chapter, your development machine has to have the following software installed as well as ASP.NET:

- **Mobile Internet Toolkit**—This can be downloaded from http://www.asp.netwww.asp.net.

- **A WAP-enabled Microbrowser or emulator**—this book uses Openwave UP Simulator 4.1. For the examples in this book, you can download this emulator from http://www.phone.com.

Wireless Application Protocol (WAP)

The *WAP* architecture is not that different from the WWW architecture. In fact, the WAP architecture is based on the existing WWW architecture, which means if you understand the WWW architecture, you can understand the WAP architecture.

Most of the technology developed for the Internet has been designed with the desktop user in mind, which in itself presents some rather interesting issues when developing Mobile Internet Device applications. For instance, a desktop user has a large display with which to view, a keyboard for data entry, and a fast Internet connection. Compare this to the mobile device user who has a limited display area and limited data entry ability.

The WAP architecture, although based on existing web technology, has numerous optimizations for wireless data transfer. Most of these optimizations deal with the fact that the wireless data communications technology available to the public has a small bandwidth capacity. In most cases, the bandwidth capacity is less than 15Kbps, which is considerably less when compared to conventional web browsing technology, which runs at an average minimum of 56Kbps.

When a mobile device user requests a web page, the following request and response process occurs:

1. The user requests a URL from his Microbrowser.

2. The WAP browser encodes the request into WML format and then sends the request to a WAP gateway.

3. The WAP gateway receives the WAP request, converts the WAP request into an HTTP request, and then sends it to a web server.

4. The web server receives the HTTP request, performs whatever processing is required, and then sends back an HTTP response to the WAP gateway.

5. The WAP gateway receives the HTTP response, converts the HTTP response into a WAP response, and then sends it to the WAP device that requested it.

6. The WAP Microbrowser software receives a WAP response and renders it to the mobile device display.

WAP Forum

The *WAP Forum* is an association that developed the WAP standard. It is made up of more than 500 members worldwide. It has the sole objective of promoting the WAP standard and assisting companies in the adoption of the standard.

For more detailed information on the WAP architecture, go to the WAP Forum web site at www.wapforum.org.

Wireless Markup Language (WML)

The WAP architecture also includes a markup language that is similar to HTML in structure; this is called *WML*. This markup language is used to render information back to the user of a mobile device through a Microbrowser.

WML is not an overly complex language, and it benefits from being based on HTML; however, the similarity is only in the structure of the syntax. In Listing 16.1, you can see a simple WML application.

Listing 16.1   **(1601.wml) Simple WML Application**

```
01 <?xml version="1.0"?>
02 <!DOCTYPE wml PUBLIC "-//WAPFORUM//DTD WML 1.1//EN"
03                      "http://www.wapforum.org/DTD/wml_1.1.xml">
04 <wml>
05   <card id="main" title="Hello Mobile Device World Example">
06     <p>
07        Hello Mobile Device User
08     </p>
09   </card>
10 </wml>
```

In line 4, you can see the `<wml>` element. This element outlines what is referred to as a *deck*, a collection of cards and forms for a mobile device application. In line 5, we encounter the first `<card>` element. A `<card>` element is used like a page. It contains all the rendering commands for a single screen of data on a mobile device. The WML file can have more than one card nested inside the `<wml>` elements. After the card definition, we use a `<p>` tag to surround any content we need to display. The `<p>` is not optional—it has to be used or the mobile device will not render any of the content for the card. Line 7 contains text to display on the device.

Figure 16.1 shows the screen after the mobile device receives the WML file.

Figure 16.1   WML example.

Enter ASP.NET

So, now you have had a brief look at WAP and WML. It's time to see how this all relates to the Mobile Device SDK for ASP.NET. Table 16.1 outlines some key elements used in WAP/WML development and explains the equivalent elements in ASP.NET:

Table 16.1   Comparing WAP/WML to ASP.NET

WAP Element	Mobile Internet Control
Deck, `<wml>`	This is the name of the file sent to a mobile device; the deck can be made up of one or more cards.
MobilePage	The `MobilePage` class is similar to the Web Form page class, but it is specifically for the creation of mobile Web Forms.

WAP Element	Mobile Internet Control
<card>	The <card> is the term given to a chunk of presentation logic for a mobile device page. You can have more than one card to a deck. The first card in the deck file is the first card to be displayed or processed by the mobile device.
Mobile:Form	The Mobile:Form control encapsulates the functionality of the WML <card> element. You can have many forms to a MobilePage. The first form is the form that is initially displayed by the mobile device.
<do>, <go>	When a user interface event occurs, the device performs the associated <do> task.
Mobile:Command	The Mobile:Command control provides a mechanism that enables the user to call an ASP.NET event handler for a task.
<fieldset>	The <fieldset> element enables you to group multiple text or input items on a card.
Mobile:Panel	The Mobile:Panel control enables the user to group controls on a form together, so that they can be rendered on one screen (if the mobile device supports that feature).
<a>, <anchor>	These elements instruct the device to display another card from the current card.
Mobile:Link	Mobile:Link provides a hyperlink to another file or to another form in the current file.
<input>	The <input> element provides the user with data entry functionality.
Mobile:TextBox	The Mobile:TextBox control provides data entry support for text data for the user.
<select>	This element renders a list of options from which the user can choose.
Mobile:List	The Mobile:List control enables the user to select an item from a list of possible values.

Note

You can use <wml> elements inside ASP.NET mobile forms without any problems. However, it is better to use ASP.NET controls because the mobile control's toolkit can generate either WML or HTML depending on the capabilities of the device to which it is rendering.

Creating a Mobile Device Application

ASP.NET Mobile controls are defined as elements in exactly the same manner as regular ASP.NET controls. The only thing you have to do with Mobile controls is make sure that at the top of your web page, you register the Mobile Internet Toolkit controls and namespace as shown:

```
01 <%@ Page Inherits="System.Web.UI.MobileControls.MobilePage" Language="vb" %>
02 <%@ Register TagPrefix="mobile" Namespace="System.Web.UI.MobileControls"
03            Assembly="System.Web.Mobile" %>
```

On the first line, the Web Form properties are inherited from the `System.Web.UI.MobileControls.MobilePage` class. This class provides the core functionality of a mobile device web page. Also, the language is set for any script on the web page to use Visual Basic .NET. The second line registers the `TagPrefix` to `mobile` for the namespace `System.Web.Mobile.UI.MobileControls`. This enables access to a Mobile control without having to type in the long namespace first. For more on this, see Chapter 2, "Developing Applications with ASP.NET."

After this has been done, you are ready to start using the Mobile Internet Toolkit controls to build your application.

The *Form* Element

The `Form` element is required for every single mobile device web page without exception. You can have more than one form to a Web Form source file; however, only one form at a time will be rendered on the mobile device. The first form definition in your source file is the initial form that will be displayed on the mobile device. The syntax for the form control follows:

```
01 Mobile:Form runat=server
02           id="id-of-control"
03           StyleReference="StyleReference"
04           OnActivate="OnActivateHandler"
05           OnDeactivate="OnDeactivateHandler">
```

The `id` attribute is used to create a unique identifier for the `Form` in the source file. This is important because you can have many forms in a file, and you will need to reference each form for navigational purposes if nothing else. The `StyleReference` attribute is used to apply a style sheet to any controls inside the `Form` elements. More on this attribute in the "Presentation Controls" section later in this chapter. The `OnActivate` and `OnDeactivate` attributes are used to call a function after these events happen. The `OnActivate` event occurs when the form is first displayed, and the `OnDeactivate` event occurs when the form is replaced by another form.

An example of the `Form` control with an `OnActivate` event handler is defined in Listing 16.2.

Listing 16.2 **An Example of a Simple Mobile Form–Based Application**

```
01 <%@ Page Inherits="System.Web.UI.MobileControls.MobilePage" Language="vb"
02    %>
03 <%@ Register TagPrefix="mobile" Namespace="System.Web.UI.MobileControls"
04             Assembly="System.Web.Mobile" %>
05 <script language="vb" runat=server>
06   sub One_OnActivate (Source as Object, E as EventArgs)
07     ActiveForm = Two
08   End Sub
09 </script>
10 <Mobile:Form id="One" runat=server OnActivate="One_OnActivate">
11   <Mobile:Label runat=server>Form One</Mobile:Label>
12 </Mobile:Form>
13 <Mobile:Form id="Two" runat=server>
14   <Mobile:Label runat=server>Form Two</Mobile:Label>
15 </Mobile:Form>
```

Do not be daunted by the amount of code in Listing 16.2. Most of it is straightforward. Lines 1 and 3 set up the Web Form as a mobile Web Form. In line 10, the definition of form `"One"` begins. Notice that the form has an event handler defined for the `OnActivate` event. The handler itself is defined in the script block (lines 5–9); all the handler does is get the mobile device to display another form, in this case `"Two"`, which is defined in line 13.

When this code is run, the screen (shown in Figure 16.2) displays form `"Two"`, not form `"One"`.

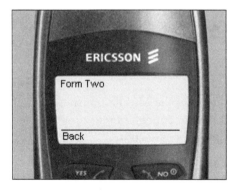

Figure 16.2   `Mobile:Form` example.

Developing Applications for Mobile Devices

The Mobile Internet Toolkit comes with its own collection of web controls, which can be used to create the user interface of a mobile device application. These controls can be separated into three main areas of functionality:

- **Presentation**—Controls used to present content or data to the mobile device display

- **Navigation**—Controls used to navigate from one mobile form to another

- **Data Entry**—Controls used to get input from the user

All the mobile device controls have some default attributes. These are outlined in the following list and apply to all mobile device controls unless otherwise stated:

- `Id`—The `Id` attribute is used to create a unique identifier for the control. This is important because you can have many controls on a form, and you may need to reference the label to programmatically change its value.

- `StyleReference`—The `StyleReference` attribute is used to apply a stylesheet style to the control.

- `Runat`—The `Runat` attribute is required for all mobile device controls, and its value should be set to `Server`, otherwise, the web controls will not be processed and the mobile application will not run.

> **Note**
>
> All the examples in this section are based on mobile device development for mobile phones and have been tested with the Openwave UP SDK. All the examples work on any WAP 1.1-capable device; however, the rendered results can be different because of the different capabilities of each device.

Presentation Controls

As mentioned previously, the Mobile Internet Toolkit has a collection of controls designed for presenting content on a mobile device. These controls are outlined in the next few sections.

The *Mobile:Label* Control

The `Mobile:Label` control is used to display some static text on the mobile device display area, or it is used as a placeholder for some display text.

The syntax of the `Mobile:Label` control is as follows:

```
01 <mobile:Label runat="server"
02              id="id"
03              StyleReference="StyleRef"
04              Text="Text">
05 Text
06 </mobile:Label>
```

A specific attribute of the `Mobile:Label` control is the `Text` attribute, which is the text to display on the Web Form.

An example of `Mobile:Label` control use is shown in Listing 16.3.

Listing 16.3   *Mobile:Label* **Example**

```
01 <%@ Page Inherits="System.Web.UI.MobileControls.MobilePage" Language="vb"
02       %>
03 <%@ Register TagPrefix="mobile" Namespace="System.Web.UI.MobileControls"
04             Assembly="System.Web.Mobile" %>
05 <script language="vb" runat=server>
06   sub One_OnActivate (Source as Object, E as EventArgs)
07     DynamicLabel.text = "Dynamic text"
08   End Sub
09 </script>
10 <Mobile:Form id="One" runat=server OnActivate="One_OnActivate">
11  <Mobile:Label runat=server Text ="Simple Text" />
12  <Mobile:Label runat=server>
13  More Text
14  </Mobile:Label>
15  <Mobile:Label runat=server id="DynamicLabel" text="static text" />
16 </Mobile:Form>
```

The preceding code demonstrates three different uses of the `Mobile:Label` control. Line 11 uses the `Text` attribute to set the value of the text to display on the device. The second control in line 12 uses both opening and closing elements and enables free text to be typed between them. The final `Label` control in line 15 sets its text value to one value, then has it changed by the form's `OnActivate` event to another value. The script block references the `Label` control by its id of `DynamicLabel`, and then set its `Text` attribute to a new value.

Figure 16.3 shows the resulting screenshot of the preceding code on a mobile device.

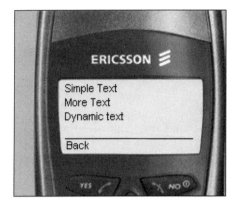

Figure 16.3   `mobile:Label` example.

The *Mobile:TextView* Control

The `Mobile:TextView` control is used to display multi-line static text on the mobile device display area.

```
01 <mobile:TextView
02     runat="server"
03     id="id"
04     StyleReference="styleReference"
05     Wrapping={NotSet|Wrap|NoWrap}
06     Text="Text">
07 Text
08 </mobile:TextView>
```

The specific attributes of the `Mobile:TextView` control include

- **Wrapping**—The `Wrapping` attribute is used to define how the text in the control is wrapped across the device display.

- **Text**—The `Text` attribute is the text displayed on the Web Form.

An example of the `Mobile:TextView` control is shown in Listing 16.4.

Listing 16.4   *Mobile:TextView* Example

```
01 <%@ Page Inherits="System.Web.UI.MobileControls.MobilePage" Language="C#" %>
02 <%@ Register TagPrefix="mobile" Namespace="System.Web.UI.MobileControls"
➥Assembly="System.Web.Mobile" %>
03 <mobile:Form runat="server">
04   <mobile:TextView runat="server" id="TV" Alignment="Center"
➥Font-Bold="true">
05   This is an example of a mobile:TextView control!
06   </mobile:TextView>
07 </mobile:Form>
```

The preceding code line demonstrates the use of the `Mobile:TextView` control in lines 4–6. Figure 16.4 shows a resulting screenshot of the code on a mobile device.

Figure 16.4 `mobile:TextView` example.

The *Mobile:Image* Control

The `Mobile:Image` control is used to display images on the mobile device. These images can be from an internal list of symbols on the mobile device, or they can be external graphic files. One additional feature of the `Mobile:Image` control is that you can assign a URL to the image, so it works like a `Mobile:Link` control. (`Mobile:Link` controls are covered later in this chapter in the "Navigation Controls" section.

The syntax of the `Mobile:Image` control is as follows:

```
01 <mobile:Image
02     runat="server"
03     id="id"
04     Alignment={NotSet | Left | Center | Right}
05     StylcReference="styleReference"
06     Wrapping={NotSet | Wrap | NoWrap}
07     AlternateText="AltText"
08     ImageURL="masterImageSource"
09     NavigateURL="targetURL">
10 </mobile:Image>
```

The specific attributes of the `Mobile:Image` control include

- **Alignment** The `Alignment` attribute is used to set the physical alignment of the image on the mobile device display area. The `Mobile:Image` can be displayed on the left, right, and center of the screen.

- **Wrapping**—The Wrapping attribute is used to define how the text in the control is wrapped across the device display.

- **AlternateText**—This attribute is used to describe the image. It is rendered to the mobile device as a Mobile:Label control, if the mobile device does not support the use of images.

- **ImageURL**—The ImageURL attribute is a URL of an image file displayed to the user. It can also be an internal symbol name for an internal image on the mobile device. To use a symbol name, you have to prefix the mobile device's internal symbol identifier with symbol. An example of the Mobile:Image control is in Listing 16.5.

- **NavigateURL**—If this attribute is used, the image becomes a link to another Mobile Web Form. The value used with this attribute is the same as the one for the Mobile:Link control, which is described in more detail later in the "Navigation Controls" section of this chapter.

In Listing 16.5, we have a more complex sample application.

Listing 16.5 *Mobile:Image* **Example**

```
01 <%@ Page Inherits="System.Web.UI.MobileControls.MobilePage" Language="C#" %>
02 <%@ Register TagPrefix="mobile" Namespace="System.Web.UI.MobileControls"
➥Assembly="System.Web.Mobile" %>
03 <mobile:Form runat="server">
04 <mobile:label runat="server" text="Image Control Example" />
05 <br>
06 Open Folder
07 <mobile:Image runat="server" id="myImage3" ImageURL="symbol:folder2"
08             NavigateURL="#form2" />
09 Closed Folder
10 <mobile:Image runat="server" id="myImage2" ImageURL="symbol:folder1"
11             NavigateURL="#form3" />
12 </mobile:Form>
13
14 <mobile:Form id="form2" runat="server">
15 <mobile:TextView runat="server"  font-bold="True"
16                 text="You Selected the open Folder" />
17 </mobile:Form>
18 <mobile:Form id="form3" runat="server">
19 <mobile:TextView runat="server" font-bold="True"
20                 text="You Selected the Closed Folder" />
21 </mobile:Form>
```

In this application, I have added a Mobile:Label control (line 4) to be used as the title of the application. Then two image controls follow (lines 7–8), which are using the mobile device's internal symbol library and have been assigned an internal form URL to jump to once they have been selected. The output of these lines is shown in Figures 16.5 and 16.6.

Figure 16.5 Mobile:Image example, first page.

Figure 16.6 Mobile:Image example, after selection.

The *Mobile:Panel* Control

Mobile:Panel controls are used to group controls together and also to apply styles to a group of controls. Listing 16.6 uses a panel control to apply a style to nested controls in two different panels.

The syntax of a Mobile:Panel control is as follows:

```
01 <mobile:Panel
02    runat="server"
03    id="id"
04    Alignment={NotSet|Left|Center|Right}
05    StyleReference="styleReference" >
06 … Controls inside Panel Control go here
07 </mobile:Panel>
```

The specific attributes of the Mobile:Panel control include the alignment attribute, which is used to set the physical alignment of the controls inside the panel on the mobile device display area. The Mobile:Image can be displayed on the left, right, or center of the screen.

Listing 16.6 shows a simple example of using the Mobile:Panel control to apply group formatting.

Listing 16.6 *Mobile:Panel* **Example**

```
01 <%@ Page Inherits="System.Web.UI.MobileControls.MobilePage" Language="c#" %>
02 <%@ Register TagPrefix="mobile" Namespace="System.Web.UI.MobileControls"
➥Assembly="System.Web.Mobile"  %>
03 <mobile:Form runat="server">
04 <mobile:Panel runat="server" Font-Italic="true" Alignment="left">
05   <mobile:Label runat="server">First Panel</mobile:Label>
06   <mobile:Label runat="server">is up here</mobile:Label>
07 </mobile:Panel>
08 <mobile:Panel runat="server" Font-Bold="true" Alignment="right">
09   <mobile:Label runat="server">Second Panel here</mobile:Label>
10 </mobile:Panel>
11 </mobile:Form>
```

The first Mobile:Panel control (lines 4–7) sets the font to italic and also fixes the alignment to the left side. For all controls in the panel, the second Mobile:Panel control (lines 8–10) has only one control, which is right-aligned and set to bold. Figure 16.7 shows the output.

Figure 16.7   Mobile:Panel example.

The *Mobile:StyleSheet* Control

This control is used to create user-defined style sheets to apply to mobile device controls.

The syntax of the `Mobile:StyleSheet` control is as follows:

```
01 <mobile:Stylesheet
02     runat="server"
03     id="id"
04     Font-Name="fontName"
05     Font-Size={NotSet | Normal | Small | Large}
06     Font-Bold={NotSet | False | True}
07     Font-Italic="{NotSet | False | True}
08     ForeColor="foregroundColor"
09     BackColor="backgroundColor"
10     Alignment={NotSet | Left | Center | Right}
11     StyleReference="styleReference"
12     Wrapping={NotSet | Wrap | NoWrap}
13     ReferencePath="externalReferencePath" >
14 </mobile:Stylesheet>
```

The specific attributes of the `Mobile:StyleSheet` control include the following:

- **Font-Name**—This attribute enables you to select the name of the font you want to use. For most mobile phones, this attribute does nothing because it generally only supports one font.

- **Font-Size**—This attribute enables you to select the size of the font used on the mobile device. Again, this has very little use on mobile phones because the display area is so small.

- **Font-Bold**, **Font-Italic**—These two attributes act like switches. They should be set to either `true` or `false`.

- **ForeColor**, **BackColor**—These are used to set the foreground and background colors for text display on a mobile device, for mobile phone development, they are not very useful but because most mobile devices are monochrome in nature.

- **StyleReference**—The `StyleReference` control can be used to inherit the style settings from another stylesheet control.

- **ReferencePath**—This attribute holds a relative path to a user control (.ascx file), which contains a set of style elements. These style controls can then be used in the current mobile application file.

In Listing 16.7, we declare a style sheet at the beginning of the code (lines 3–6), which has two styles defined—`Style1` and `Style2`, respectively. These styles only apply font-bold and font-italic style properties, but the styles can use any combination of styles shown in the control's syntax. After the styles have been defined, simply apply them to any control we want by using the `StyleReference` attribute of the control. Listing 16.7 uses `Mobile:Label` controls.

Listing 16.7 *Mobile:StyleSheet* **Example**

```
01 <%@ Page Inherits="System.Web.UI.MobileControls.MobilePage" Language="C#" %>
02 <%@ Register TagPrefix="mobile" Namespace="System.Web.UI.MobileControls"
➥Assembly="System.Web.Mobile" %>
03 <mobile:StyleSheet runat="server">
04    <Style Name="Style1" font-bold="true"/>
05    <Style Name="Style2" font-italic="true"/>
06 </mobile:StyleSheet>
07 <mobile:Form runat="server">
08 <mobile:Label runat="server" StyleReference="Style1">
09               This is Style 1</mobile:Label>
10 <mobile:Label runat="server"  StyleReference="STyle2">
11               This is Style 2</mobile:Label>
12 </mobile:Form>
```

The output is shown in Figure 16.8.

Figure 16.8 `Mobile:StyleSheet` example.

Navigation Controls

There are two types of navigation controls in a mobile web application:

- **Internal navigation**—This is used to change the currently displayed form to another form in the same .aspx file.

- **External navigation**—This is how you navigate to the first form in another .aspx file.

To use internal navigation, you must prefix the form that you want to navigate with a "#" symbol, and to navigate to an external form, just supply the filename:

- **#Form1**—Navigates to the form with the ID `form1`.
- **File1.aspx**—Navigates to the first available form in the File1.aspx file.

The *Mobile:Link* Control

The `Mobile:Link` control is used to display a text label that operates as a hyperlink to another form in the same file or external document.

The syntax of the `Mobile:Link` control is as follows:

```
01 <mobile:Link
02     runat="server"
03     id="id"
04     Text="Text"
05     NavigateURL="relativeLink"
06     SoftkeyLabel="softkeyLabel">
07 </mobile:Link>
```

The specific attributes and properties of the `Mobile:Link` control include

- **Text**—Sets the text to display the link on the mobile device.
- **NavigateURL**—Holds the URL of the form that you want to render. If the value of the NavigateURL property begins with a (#), the remainder of the value is assumed to be the identifier of a form on the current `Mobile:Page` control. Otherwise, the value of the NavigateURL property is treated as a standard URL.
- **SoftKey**—Holds the text that is displayed above the softkey of a softkey-capable mobile device.

Listing 16.8 shows a single link control that, when selected, will navigate to the 123 Jump news and finance WAP portal. See Figures 16.9 and 16.10 to see how this appears on your mobile device.

Listing 16.8 *Mobile:Link* **Example**

```
01 <%@ Page Inherits="System.Web.UI.MobileControls.MobilePage" Language="C#" %>
02 <%@ Register TagPrefix="mobile" Namespace="System.Web.UI.MobileControls"
➥Assembly="System.Web.Mobile" %>
03 <mobile:Form runat="server">
04 <mobile:Link runat="server"
05    NavigateURL="http://www.123jump.com">123 Jump WAP Portal</mobile:Link>
06 </mobile:Form>
```

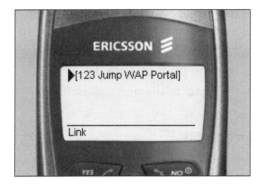

Figure 16.9 Mobile:Link example, link page.

Figure 16.10 Mobile:Link example, www.123Jump.com.

The *Mobile:Command* Control

The Mobile:Command control is used to display a text label that operates as a hyperlink to another form in the same file or an external document.

The syntax of the Mobile:Command control is as follows:

```
01 <mobile:Command
02    runat="server"
03    id="id"
04    Text="text"
05    CommandArgument="commandArgument"
06    CommandName="commandName"
07    OnClick="clickEventHandler"
08    OnItemCommand="commandEventHandler"
09    SoftkeyLabel="softkeyLabel">
10 </mobile:Command>
```

The specific attributes and properties of the `Mobile:Command` control include

- **Text**—This attribute sets the text to display as the command on a mobile device.
- **OnClick**—Holds the name of a sub, which is to be called when the user selects a `Mobile:Command` control.
- **SoftKey**—Holds the text that is displayed above the softkey of a softkey-capable mobile device.

Listing 16.9 shows an example of the `Mobile:Command` control, which basically requests both the user's first and last names (lines 11 and 13), and then when the command button is selected (line 14), the procedure `myCmd_OnClick` (lines 03–07) is called, and a second form is subsequently displayed with values entered by the user (lines 17–19). See Figures 16.11, 16.12, and 16.13.

Listing 16.9 *Mobile:Command* **Example**

```
01 <%@ Page Inherits="System.Web.UI.MobileControls.MobilePage" Language="vb" %>
02 <%@ Register TagPrefix="mobile" Namespace="System.Web.UI.MobileControls"
➥Assembly="System.Web.Mobile" %>
03 <script language="vb" runat="server">
04 Protected Sub myCmd_OnClick(sender As Object, e As EventArgs)
05     myLabel.Text = "Hello: " + FNEdit.Text + " " + LNEdit.Text
06     ActiveForm = form2
07 end sub
08 </script>
09 <mobile:Form runat="server">
10     <mobile:Label runat="server" font-bold="True">Enter First Name</mobile:Label>
11     <mobile:TextBox runat="server" id="FNEdit" />
12     <mobile:Label runat="server" font-bold="True">Enter Last Name</mobile:Label>
13     <mobile:TextBox runat="server" id="LNEdit" />
14     <mobile:Command runat="server" id="myCmd" OnClick="myCmd_OnClick">
15         OK
16     </mobile:Command>

17 </mobile:Form>
18 <mobile:Form runat="server" id="form2">
19     <mobile:Label runat="server" id="myLabel" />
20 </mobile:Form>
```

The *Mobile:Image* Control

This control has already been covered earlier in this chapter, but you can use the `NavigateURL` attribute to assign a link to which a page can navigate.

The *Mobile:List* Control

You can also use the `Mobile:List` control to navigate to other pages. This is covered in the "*Data Entry* Controls" section of this chapter.

Figure 16.11   Mobile:Command example, first name.

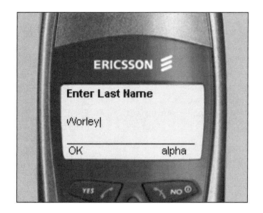

Figure 16.12   Mobile:Command example, last name.

Figure 16.13   Mobile:Command example, hello message.

The Code-Based Alternative

You also can navigate to another form within the current mobile page by setting the `ActiveForm` property of the `mobilePage` class. This property takes the name of a form to navigate to as its value. After the property is assigned, the new form is displayed on the device screen. An example call is shown by the following:

```
ActiveForm = Form1
```

The preceding code tells the mobile device to display a form with the ID of Form1.

Data Entry Controls

The Mobile Internet Toolkit supports data entry through two data entry controls:

- `Mobile:TextBox`
- `Mobile:List`

Although this seems to be a very limited set of controls, you must not forget that the browser display is limited in display area size, and mobile devices also generally have limited processing power and memory. However, with some ingenuity, you can create an intuitive user interface for data entry.

The *Mobile:TextBox* Control

The `Mobile:TextBox` control is used to get information from the user of a mobile device. It supports only two types of data entry: general text and password formats. The control enables you to specify formatting rules for the text entered, and you can also limit the amount of text entered in the control as well as the physical size of the control in characters.

The syntax of the `Mobile:TextBox` control is as follows:

```
01 <mobile:TextBox
02     runat="server"
03     id="id"
04     MaxLength="maxLength"
05     Numeric="{true, false}"
06     Password="{true, false}"
07     Size="textBoxLength"
08     Text="Text">
09 </mobile:TextBox>
```

The specific attributes of the `Mobile:Textbox` control include

- **Text**—This attribute sets the text to display as the mobile device.
- **MaxLength**—This attribute is used to define how much text can be entered into the `Mobile:TextBox` control. A value of 0 means there is no length restriction for the textbox.

- **Numeric**—This attribute tells the textbox to only accept numeric input. It can be set to either `true` or `false`.

- **Password**—This attribute tells the textbox to `mask all data entry` as though a password were being entered. (The characters typed are echoed back to the display as `*` characters.)

Listing 16.10 demonstrates three different uses of the `Mobile:TextBox` control. These are normal data entry, password data entry, and numeric-only data entry. Figures 16.14, 16.15, 16.16, and 16.17 show the output for this code.

Listing 16.10   *Mobile:TextBox* **Example**

```
01 <%@ Page Inherits="System.Web.UI.MobileControls.MobilePage" Language="vb" %>
02 <%@ Register TagPrefix="mobile" Namespace="System.Web.UI.MobileControls"
➥Assembly="System.Web.Mobile" %>
03 <script language="vb" runat="server">
04
05 protected sub Button_OnClick(o as Object, e as EventArgs)
06    ActiveForm=form2
07    lblName.Text = "Name: " + txtName.Text
08    lblPassword.Text = "Password: " + txtPassword.Text
09    lblBalance.Text = "Bank Balance: " + txtBalance.Text
10 end sub
11 </script>
12 <mobile:Form runat="server">
13    <mobile:Label runat="server" font-Bold="True">
14 Enter your name</mobile:Label>
15    <mobile:TextBox runat="server" id="txtName" />
16
17    <mobile:Label runat="server" font-Bold="True">Enter your password</mobile:Label>
18    <mobile:TextBox runat="server" id="txtPassword" password="true"/>
19
20    <mobile:Label runat="server" font-Bold="True">Enter your Bank Balance</mobile:Label>
21    <mobile:TextBox runat="server" id="txtBalance" numeric="true" />
22
23    <mobile:Command runat="server" id="Button" OnClick="Button_OnClick">
24       OK
25    </mobile:Command>
26 </mobile:Form>
27 <mobile:Form id="form2" runat="server">
28    <mobile:Label runat="Server" font-bold="True" Text="You entered" />
29    <mobile:Label runat="server" id="lblName" />
30    <mobile:Label runat="server" id="lblPassword" />
31    <mobile:Label runat="server" id="lblBalance" />
32 </mobile:Form>
```

Figure 16.14 Mobile:TextBox example, name.

Figure 16.15 Mobile:TextBox example, password.

Figure 16.16 Mobile:TextBox example, bank balance.

Figure 16.17 Mobile:TextBox example, display all entered text.

The *Mobile:List* Control

The Mobile:List control can be used to render a list of items to the mobile device user. These are either static or loaded into the control from a data source.

The syntax of the Mobile:List control is as follows:

```
01 <mobile:List
02     runat="server"
03     id="id"
04     DataTextField="dataTextField"
05     DataValueField="dataValueField"
06     OnItemCommand="onItemCommandHandler"
07 …Mobile item controls that make up the list control
08 </mobile:List>
```

The specific attributes and property of the Mobile:List control include:

- **DataTextField**—Specifies which property of a data bound item to use when determining an item's text property.

- **DataValueField**—Specifies which property of a data bound item to use when determining an item's value property.

- **OnItemCommand**—Holds the name of the event handler to be called when an individual list item generates an event.

- **Datasource**—Holds the data source to which the control is bound.

Listing 16.11 uses a Mobile:List control to display a list of books. After an item is selected, the selected book title and the author who wrote it are displayed.

Listing 16.11 *Mobile:List* **Example**

```
01 <%@ Page Inherits="System.Web.UI.MobileControls.MobilePage" Language="vb" %>
02 <%@ Register TagPrefix="mobile" Namespace="System.Web.UI.MobileControls"
➥Assembly="System.Web.Mobile" %>
03 <script runat="server" language="vb">
04 protected sub List_EventHandler(o as Object, e as ListCommandEventArgs)
05    lblBook.Text = e.ListItem.Text
06    lblAuthor.Text = e.ListItem.Value
07    ActiveForm = form2
08
09 end sub
10 </script>
11 <mobile:Form id="myList" runat="server">
12 <mobile:Label runat="server" id="label1" text="Select Book"/>
13 <mobile:List runat="server" id="ListProduce" OnItemCommand="List_EventHandler" >
14 <item Text="Inside ASP.NET" Value="Scott Worley" />
15 <item Text="Inside XSLT" Value="Steven Holzner" />
16 <item Text="Inside XML" Value="Steven Holzner" />
17 </mobile:List>
18 </mobile:Form>
19 <mobile:Form id="form2" runat = "server">
20    <mobile:Label runat="server" font-bold="True" Text="Book Selected"/>
21    <mobile:Label runat="server" id="lblBook"/>
22    <mobile:Label runat="server" font-bold="True" Text="Author"/>
23    <mobile:Label runat="server" id="lblAuthor"/>
24 </mobile:Form>
```

On line 13, I have created a simple Mobile:List control and assigned the
event handler sub List_EventHandler to process any selection made from the
list. On lines 14–16, I have assigned items to the list. When the form is run,
the list is displayed, and when an item has been selected, the eventhandler
will call the List_EventHandler sub at the beginning of the code listing. This
sub reads information from the Mobile:List control and assigns its value to a
Mobile:Label control on the form form2. Figures 16.18 and 16.19 show the
output to this code.

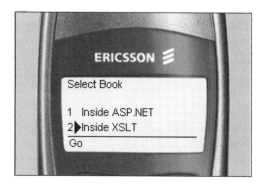

Figure 16.18   Mobile:List example, book selection list.

Figure 16.19 `Mobile:List` example, display selection details.

You also can bind the `Mobile:List` control to a data source. Listing 16.12 demonstrates this technique.

Listing 16.12 **Databound *Mobile:List* Example**

```
01 <%@ Page Inherits="System.Web.UI.MobileControls.MobilePage" Language="vb" %>
02 <%@ Register TagPrefix="mobile" Namespace="System.Web.UI.MobileControls"
➥Assembly="System.Web.Mobile" %>
03 <%@ import namespace="System.Data.SqlClient" %>
04 <script runat="server" language="VB">
05
06 Protected Sub Page_Load(sender As Object, e As EventArgs)
07  If (Not IsPostBack)
08    Dim connString as String
09    Dim sqlString as String
10    Dim myConn as SQLConnection
11    Dim myCmd as SQLCommand
12    Dim myReader as SQLDataReader
13
14    connString = "Initial Catalog=Pubs;Data Source=p450;uid=sa;pwd=;"
15    sqlString = "SELECT fname+' '+lname as name, hire_date FROM employee"
16    myConn = new SqlConnection(connString)
17    myCmd = new SqlCommand(sqlString, myConn)
18    myConn.Open()
19
20    myReader = myCmd.ExecuteReader()
21    MenuList.DataSource = myReader
22    MenuList.DataBind()
23    myReader.Close()
24
25    End If
26 End Sub
27 Protected Sub Menu_OnItemCommand(sender As Object, e As ListCommandEventArgs)
28    lblEmployee.Text = e.ListItem.Text
```

```
29    lblHireDate.Text = Ctype(e.ListItem.Value, String)
30    ActiveForm = form2
31 End Sub
32 </script>
33 <mobile:Form runat="server">
34    <mobile:Label runat="server" StyleReference="title">Select Employee</mobile:Label>
35    <mobile:List runat="server" id="MenuList" OnItemCommand="Menu_OnItemCommand"
36        DataTextField="name" DataValueField="hire_date" />
37 </mobile:Form>
38 <mobile:Form id="form2" runat="server">
39    <mobile:Label runat="server" font-bold="True" Text="Employee:" />
40    <mobile:Label runat="server" id="lblEmployee" />
41    <mobile:Label runat="server" font-bold="True" Text="Date Hired:" />
42    <mobile:Label runat="server" id="lblHireDate" />
43 </mobile:Form>
```

The preceding listing uses a Page_Load event handler to connect to a SQL Server database—in this case, the pubs database, which is supplied with SQLServer. A SQLDataReader is used to get data from the Employees table, and then subsequently is bound to the Mobile:List control defined on line 47. The data binding process used with mobile controls is the same as that used by regular ASP.NET forms. One thing to note are lines 47 and 48.

Of special interest here are the last two attributes, DataTextField and DataValueField. These attributes are the column names from the SQL query with which the Mobile:List control is bound. For the binding to work, you must have these two attributes. See Figures 16.20 and 16.21.

Figure 16.20 Databound Mobile:List example, employee selection.

Figure 16.21 Databound Mobile:List example, display selection details.

Data binding is covered in a lot more detail in Chapter 6, "Using ADO.NET in ASP.NET Applications."

Summary

As you have seen, the Mobile Internet Toolkit enables you to create very functional mobile applications very quickly and without the need to understand the inner workings of the devices you develop. However, in this chapter, I have only scratched the surface of what is possible with the toolkit. You can get further information from the online documentation.

VI

Putting It All Together

17

Putting It All Together

WELCOME TO THE FINAL CHAPTER OF THIS BOOK. This is where you create a simple web-based application to demonstrate not only the power and flexibility of ASP.NET and the .NET framework, but also how to create a web application using fairly simplistic code. I have avoided using complex components and code where possible throughout this chapter. The end result is a functional application, which although not as optimized or scalable as it could be, is a good example of ASP.NET development that uses many of the technologies covered in this book.

An online version of the ProjectPal Application is available at `www.project-inspiration.com/ProjectPal`.

The full source code also is available from the New Riders Publishing web site `www.newriders.com` and is contained in the CH17.zip file. Instructions for installing this application are covered later in this chapter.

What Is ProjectPal?

The ProjectPal application is a project task manager. By using ProjectPal, you can create a project, define the stages of a project, and then assign tasks to a stage. The ProjectPal application has been designed to be scalable from the ground up, and it has the ability to support three main user interfaces:

- **Browser**—Two main interface sets for web browser-based clients.
- **Mobile Device**—A mobile phone-based interface for the system, which provides up-to-date information on select areas of the system.
- **XML Web Service**—An XML Web Service interface used to expose business object functionality of the ProjectPal system to SOAP-enabled clients.

Overviews of these interfaces can be found in the section, "ProjectPal Client Interfaces."

The ProjectPal application makes good use of Components and User controls for implementing almost all the interface requirements and business logic used by the system.

Business Profile

ProjectPal has been created to fulfill the fundamental business need of task management. When creating the ProjectPal application, I followed a list of high-level business requirements, which are described in the next sections.

As you can see, there are quite a few high-level requirements, most of which are pretty straightforward. However, creating this type of scalable application with Classic ASP would take weeks of work.

General System Use

The system must allow for the creation, deletion, and maintenance of Project-related information across the following areas:

- **Project Details**—High-level project information, such as project name, description, start date, expected end date, project manager, and project status.
- **Project Stages**—Capability of defining the stages of a project, designating which tasks will be assigned, must be dynamic in nature. Not all projects will have the same amount of stages. (In ProjectPal you can define the names of stages 1–4 of a project. This is done through the project registration process discussed later in this chapter in the section, "Registering a New Project.")

- **Staff Maintenance**—Capability of maintaining staff-related data for use in the system.
- **Tasks per Stage**—Capability of creating tasks and assigning members of staff to fulfill the task.

User Profiles

The system must support two different types of users and alter the available functionality or features of the system to match that user. The two types of user are

- **Project Manager**—The project manager is responsible for creating a project and stages, assigning tasks to staff members, and tracking the use of the system.
- **Staff Member**—The staff member can only see project information related to his assigned tasks and can only alter task information in a limited way by progressing the status of a task and its completion date.

Technology Profile

The system must support the following technologies:

- **Web Browser Interfaces**—The system must run from inside a web browser. This is the main interface used by project managers and staff.
- **Mobile Devices**—The capability to get or read the messages and tasks of a project through a mobile phone is required. The capability to get basic information on projects is also required.
- **SOAP-Based XML Web Services**—These are used to enable maximum accessibility of the ProjectPal system because we need to implement a way of sending project information to a SOAP-based client.

Installing the ProjectPal Application

Before I start talking about the application architecture and elaborate on the parts of the system and how and why they have been created, you must install the ProjectPal application. This section provides a brief walkthrough of its functionality.

The requirements for the ProjectPal system are

- **The Premium Edition of the ASP.NET Development Framework**
- **Windows 2000 Server or Windows XP**

- **Internet Information Server 5+ (IIS)**
- **SQL Server 2000**
- **10 Mb of Storage Space**
- **CH17.zip**—This is available from the New Riders web site (www.newriders.com) and also from www.project-inspiration.com/projectpal/source.

The installation process noted in the following sections assumes that you have administrative rights to the system you are using, that all the aforementioned requirements have been met, and all requirements have been installed with the exception of the CH17.exe file.

Step 1: Installing the Application Files

The first thing to do is execute the CH17.exe file. After you have executed the file, you will be presented with the screen shown in Figure 17.1.

From this screen, you either select Install to copy all contents of the archive to your machine in the default directory C:\ProjectPal, or you can choose another location on your machine. Note that all examples and references in this chapter are based on the default installation directory.

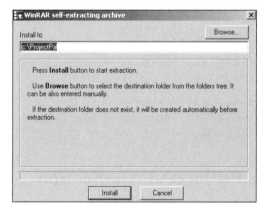

Figure 17.1   Installing the ProjectPal source code.

After the files have been extracted, you should have the following directory structure setup on your machine:

C:\ProjectPal	Root directory for the web application
C:\ProjectPal\Bin:	Contains the compiled components and resource files used by the web application

`C:\ProjectPal\Images:`	Contains all images used by the web application
`C:\ProjectPal\Browser:`	Contains all secure Web Forms (browser version)
`C:\ProjectPal\Source:`	Contains all source code for the application except for the Web Forms
`C:\ProjectPal\Source\Data:`	Contains an SQL Server backup file that holds the ProjectPal system data schema and sample data
`C:\ProjectPal\Uploads:`	File upload directory used by the ProjectPal system

Step 2: Creating a Virtual Directory

Now that we have the files set up, we need to create a virtual directory for the web site. To do this, you need to run the Internet Services Manager application, which is part of Windows 2000. It can be found by selecting the Start menu, and then choosing Settings, Control Panel, Administrative Tools, and finally the icon for the Internet Services Manager. After the Internet Services Manager application has been loaded, you should see the screen shown in Figure 17.2.

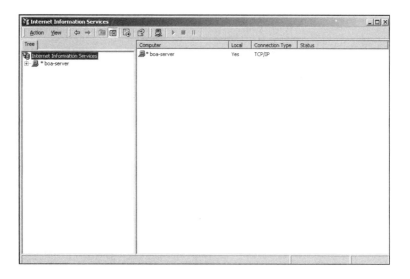

Figure 17.2 Creating a virtual directory for the web site.

From here, expand the first node on the left side of the screen. The text is your server name. Next, you need to expand the Default Web Site item. You should now be presented with the screen shown in Figure 17.3.

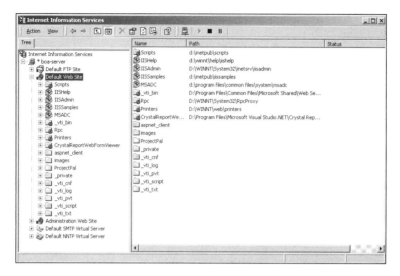

Figure 17.3   The virtual directory setup.

Now you can see the virtual directory's setup on your machine. Select the Action Menu item followed by New, and then select Virtual Directory. You are presented with the Virtual Directory Creation Wizard, as shown in Figure 17.4.

Figure 17.4   The Virtual Directory Creation Wizard.

Click Next to get the next page of the wizard. On this page, you are asked for the name of the virtual directory alias to create. For this application, I use the name ProjectPal, as shown in Figure 17.5.

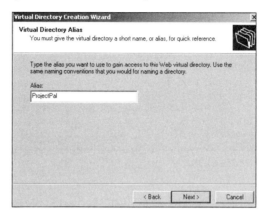

Figure 17.5   Assigning a web site alias.

After entering a virtual directory alias and selecting Next, you are asked to provide the directory where all the web site content is stored. This should be set to the directory where you installed the application, which in my case is the C:\ProjectPal directory. The screen for this is shown in Figure 17.6.

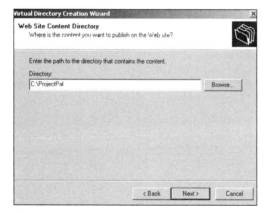

Figure 17.6   Web Site Content Directory Dialog.

After you have entered the content directory's location (in this case C:\ProjectPal), you are asked to set access permissions for the virtual directory (see Figure 17.7). For this purpose, just use the default values.

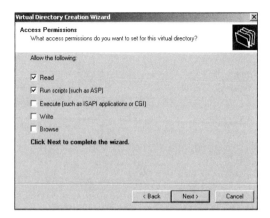

Figure 17.7   Access Permissions dialog.

After selecting Next, the last page of the wizard is presented. Click Finish, and look at the default directory's folder. A virtual directory is setup under the alias name you have chosen. Figure 17.8 shows the virtual directory highlighted.

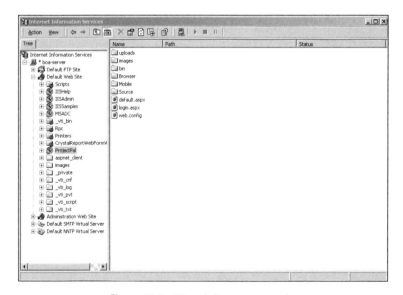

Figure 17.8   Virtual directory created.

Step 3: Compiling the Components

Now that the virtual directory is set up, it is necessary to compile all the components used by the system. As you might remember, the components are stored in the C:\projectpal\source\components directory. A batch file called Makeitall.bat is also in this directory, which is used to create all the required components in the order required because some components depend on others.

To run the batch file, simply double-click it in the Explorer window; it will set up all environment variables required for the compilation process. The process should take no longer than a few minutes.

After you complete the setup, a collection of .dll files are in the C:\ProjectPal\Bin directory, and are all ready for use in the ProjectPal web application.

Step 4: Setting Up SQL Server

Setting up the ProjectPal application is almost completed. The final task is to create the database and data used by the ProjectPal system. To do this, it is necessary to restore a SQL Server 2000 backup file. The backup file is called ProjectPal.dat and is located in the C:\ProjectPal\Source\ Data directory. However, before you can restore the backup file, you must create a database in SQL Server. To do this, load the SQL Server Enterprise Manager application. This is normally loaded by clicking the Start button, and then Programs, Microsoft SQL Server, and finally by selecting Enterprise Manager. After a few seconds, the screen shown in Figure 17.9 appears.

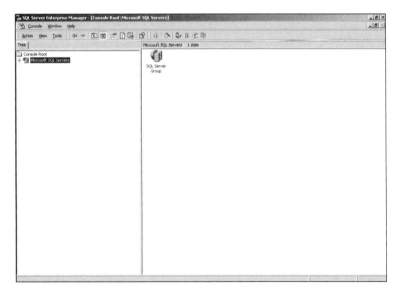

Figure 17.9   SQL Server Enterprise Manager main screen.

From here, expand the Microsoft SQL Servers option and the SQL Server group (Local)(Windows NT). After you select Databases, the screen shown in Figure 17.10 appears.

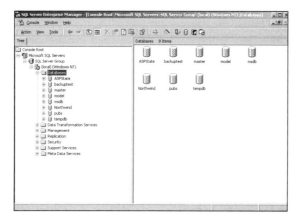

Figure 17.10   Selecting Databases in the SQL Server Enterprise Manager.

From here, click Action followed by New Database and then Database. The dialog shown in Figure 17.11 is presented.

Figure 17.11   Enter the name of the new database.

Enter the name of the database, which must be called ProjectPal. If it is not, the backup does not restore properly. After this is done, you are sent back to the preceding window. However, now you see a database called ProjectPal in the list.

Highlight the ProjectPal database, right-click it to bring up the Context menu, and then select All Tasks followed by Restore Database. After you have done this, a new dialog appears. Select the From Device radio button, and the dialog changes to what is shown in Figure 17.12.

From this dialog, select the Select Devices button halfway down the page, and a new dialog appears. From this dialog, select the Add button and another dialog appears. Enter the following into the filename textbox:

```
C:\ProjectPal\Source\Data\ProjectPal.dat
```

After this is done, select OK, which takes you back to the previous dialog. From here, select OK again to go back to the first dialog, and then click OK a last time to restore the database.

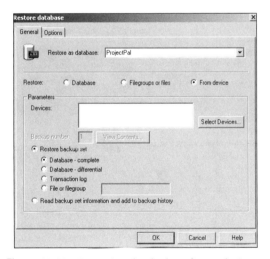

Figure 17.12   Restoring the database from a device.

A Brief Application Walkthrough

Now that we have an installed version of the ProjectPal web application, it's only fair that we walk through some of its functionality. To start with, I look at the ProjectPal application from the viewpoint of a project manager, and then look at it from the viewpoint of a staff member.

The Project Manager's Viewpoint

The project manager's view of the system is that of an administrator. The project manager has complete access to the whole ProjectPal application and is the only user who can create projects, stages, and tasks.

When a project manager logs into the ProjectPal system, the login area can be found just below the ProjectPal logo at the top of the page in the toolbar area, as shown in Figure 17.13.

After you have logged in, you are presented with the Project Management Desktop; this is a user control, which is used to maintain projects in the system. This page is loaded automatically for project managers in the system. This is a secure form and can be viewed only after logging into the system. If the person who logs in is not a project manager, he sees the *Project Management Workplace*, which is a large user control that enables the viewing of project information and limited editing facilities. This is covered in the section, "The Staff Member's Viewpoint."

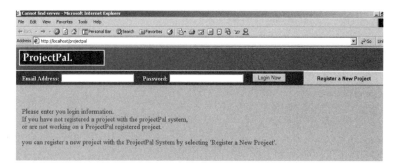

Figure 17.13   ProjectPal homepage.

The Project Management Desktop

As previously stated, this is the main interface from which the project manager administers the projects under his control.

A screen shot of the Project Management Desktop is shown in Figure 17.14.

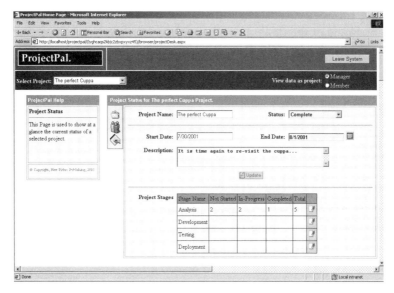

Figure 17.14   Project Management Desktop—The project manager's view.

The top of the page is the ProjectPal title bar. Below this, a user control (project bar) operates as a project toolbar. By using this toolbar, the project manager can select any of the projects he is working on; he can also change the desktop's mode of operation on projects from project manager to staff member. Two windows are beneath the toolbar. The one on the left is an information window, which is used to give help information to the user. The window on the right is the core of the ProjectPal system and is used to view information on projects. This window is made up of two parts; on the left is a list of icons that are used to change the type of data being displayed (shown in Figure 17.14), and on the right is an area of the screen used to display various types of project information.

All this functionality is explained in more detail in the "ProjectPal Client Interface" section of this chapter.

The Staff Member's Viewpoint

When using the system as a regular staff member, you are redirected to the restricted version of the Project Management Desktop after you have logged in. This has the same layout, but with the following exceptions:

- The toolbar beneath the title area does not have the option of changing the mode of the desktop. Staff members can only view the project desktop as a staff member. The Project list on the toolbar only shows projects for which the staff member has tasks.

- It is impossible for a staff member user to create project, stages, tasks, or assign tasks to other staff.

- The staff member can only change the status and completion dates for a task.

Application Architecture

This section outlines the architecture used by the ProjectPal system. The architecture is a slightly re-worked version of the Microsoft DNA architecture with the features of scalable web-based applications, taking into account a few minor observations and modifications.

The Tiers of DNA and ASP.NET

In a traditional Distributed interNet Applications architecture (DNA) n'Tier application, you split up the application into three main areas of operation commonly referred to as *layers* (see Figure 17.15). DNA defines these areas as

- **User Services**—The User Services layer is responsible for providing client applications with information needed for rendering. It is also capable of performing tasks against that data, taking into account any business rules for the task.

  This is generally a client user interface made up of windows, data entry controls, images, and buttons.

- **Business Services**—The Business Services layer acts as an intelligent interface between the User Services layer and the Data Services layer and also can apply some business logic for a task. The Business layer normally contains functionality and restricts data access to a fixed scope; for example, an Invoicing Business object would only have access to invoice-related data and processes.

- **Data Services**—The Data Services layer simply acts as an interface to a data store of some kind, normally a database, but it can be any kind of data. The Data Services layer is also referred to as the *Data Access Layer* or DAL for short.

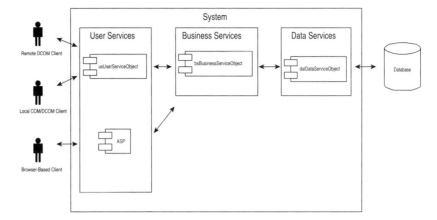

Figure 17.15 Traditional DNA architecture.

The high-level architecture of a DNA system is shown in Figure 17.15. We can see from Figure 17.15 that we have three main types of clients:

- Web-based client
- Local COM client
- Remote COM/DCOM client

Each of these clients has different requirements of the system:

- **The web-based client**—The web-based client is accessed through ASP, which in turn uses COM-/DCOM-based business objects in the Data Services layer, which interfaces with a database.
- **Local COM and Remote DCOM clients**—Both of these clients use an intermediate Business Service's object to access a COM-/DCOM-based business object. This Business Service's object basically wraps the business objects as a DCOM-capable class. The only difference lies in the transport mechanism from the business object to the Web Client.

Now that the DNA architecture is covered, I will outline the differences between the DNA architecture and the ASP.NET Distributed Application Framework architecture; but before going any further, take a look at Figure 17.16.

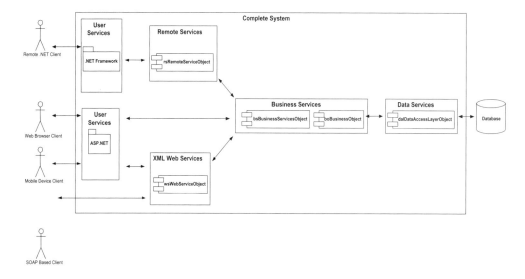

Figure 17.16 ASP.NET Distributed Application Framework.

As you may have noticed, User Services still exists. Business Services, Data Services, and their functions are the same as previously mentioned, with a few minor differences. However, two new services exist that make up a new tier of development.

These two service-based components have come into existence because of the amazing success of Internet technology and the need to develop highly distributed and scalable systems.

- **XML Web Services**—These are web-based services that provide access to business object functionality through the use of SOAP and XML. The biggest benefit of XML Web Services is the potential interoperability between one SOAP-based system and another. The SOAP format enables a Machine/Language/Operating system way of independently transporting data, objects, and processing requests. Now that's fine, but you no doubt know that this can be done using DCOM (in a limited way) or .NET Remote Services. However, the one area where SOAP really can be put to use is in its capability to be used through firewall security. Because of its XML-based nature, all SOAP data is sent as a text stream across HTTP/HTTPS and not as binary data.

- **Remote Services**—Remote Services are an upgraded and more scalable version of COM+, and in the DNA architecture they are used the same way—to provide a remote interface to existing business objects. The benefit they have over SOAP is raw performance, however. Because Remote Services sends data in a binary format, you need to take special consideration with firewall security. (Firewalls generally block all binary data sources, unless access has been explicitly approved. Also Remote Services will only work with other .NET- or DCOM-based systems.)

The ASP.NET architecture has a more scalable nature than the DNA architecture by virtue of its use of Remote Services, and XML Web Service support is better able to integrate and interoperate with legacy systems as well as with other web-based technologies and products.

ProjectPal Service Layers

The ProjectPal web application makes extensive use of components. Each of these components provides a service in the nature of information, processing, or both.

This section outlines the various Service layers and how they are applied in the ProjectPal application. I begin in the order of right to left because it is easier to explain the architecture from a ground up perspective. From here, I go on to explain some details of the Client Interface layers in the section "ProjectPal Client Interfaces."

Throughout this section is overview of how each component-based service is used in the ProjectPal application.

Data Services

The Data Services in the ProjectPal application are used to interface with an SQL Server 2000 database; all data services are implemented as SQL Server Stored Procedures. More on the Data Services components can be found in this chapter in the section "The ProjectPal Components."

Business Service

The Business Services used in the ProjectPal application are a collection of business objects, which provide various services to a client application. In our case, this is an ASP.NET application.

An example of this is the `boProject` business object, which is used to manipulate and manage project-related data in the dbProjects table.

XML Web Services

The Project Pal system as it stands at the moment, does not support XML Web Services; however, these can be easily implemented by creating a component that exposes the functionality of the *business* object via an XML Web Service interface. More on this technique can be found in Chapter 8, "XML Web Service Development in ASP.NET."

Remote Services

The ProjectPal system does not actually make use of Remote Services, however, I decided to leave a reference regarding how they could be used to provide remote access to ProjectPal `Business Service`'s objects for other .NET- and DCOM-based applications. Again, the process is simply creating a facade object that is based on the `Business Service`'s object, but it also adds the necessary functionality to enable remote use of the ProjectPal system.

ProjectPal Client Interfaces

The ProjectPal system supports three main types of client interfaces—the browser interface, the mobile interface, and the XML Web Service interface; each of these interfaces has two different versions.

(It should be noted that I am discussing the browser interface in this chapter.)

Web Browser-Based Client

This client is the main client for the ProjectPal application; it is a web browser-based environment, which is rendered by ASP.NET. This interface comes in two flavors—the first interface is what the project manager uses, and the second interface is what the team member uses.

The ProjectPal Database

Let's get our hands a little dirtier by looking at the data, code, and techniques used to create the ProjectPal system.

Not all the code in the ProjectPal system is here because of space constraints and the fact that some of the code is quite repetitive. However, you can download the full source code, as mentioned at the beginning of this chapter, or play with it online at `www.project-inspiration.com/projectpal`.

The ProjectPal system uses SQL Server 2000 as its main datasource. The system is made up of various tables, views, and stored procedures. Throughout this section, I assume you have knowledge of SQL Server, SQL Queries, and basic Transact SQL.

Database Schema

The Database schema used by the ProjectPal system is not too complex; however, there are a few tables involved, so I show you the whole database schema in Figure 17.17. Figure 17.17 is taken directly from SQL Server, and it shows some of the relations and Primary Keys used in the ProjectPal System.

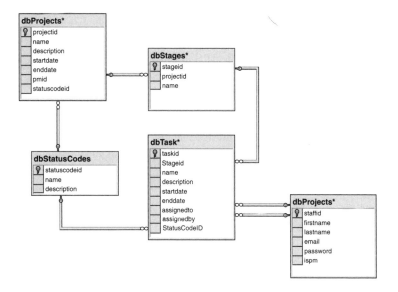

Figure 17.17 ProjectPal Entity Relationship (ER) diagram.

Let's look at this schema in more detail. First, I give an overview of the tables one at a time, showing their structures and relationships.

Tables

The dbProjects table holds the high-level information of the projects inside the ProjectPal application (see Table 17.1).

Table 17.1 **The dbProject Table**

Field	Data Type	Description
projectid	Int	Internal project ID number that's auto-generated.
Name	varchar	Name of the project.
description	varchar	A more detailed description of the project.
StartDate	Datetime	Start date of the project.
Enddate	Datetime	Planned completion date of the project.
statuscodeid	Int	The current status of the project.

The dbProject table has the following relationships:

dbProjects.id	1 to Many	dbStages.projid
dbProjects.statusid	1 to Many	dbStatusCode.id

The dbStages table holds the high-level information of each project stage for a specified project in the ProjectPal application (see Table 17.2).

Table 17.2 **The dbStages Table**

Field	Data Type	Description
stageid	Int	Internal stage ID number that's auto-generated.
projectid	int	Project ID number to which this stage belongs.
Name	varchar	The name of the project stage.

The dbStages table is the key table in the ProjectPal system; it is the main link to all project data.

dbStages.projid	Many to 1	dbProjects.id
dbStages.id	1 to Many	dbTasks.stageid

The dbTasks table is used to hold information on tasks assigned to staff members (see Table 17.3).

Table 17.3 **The dbTasks Table**

Field	Data Type	Description
taskId	int	Internal TaskID number that's auto-generated.
Stageid	int	Stage ID number to which this task belongs.
Name	varchar	Name of task.
description	varchar	Detailed description of the task.
Startdate	Datetime	Date task starts.
EndDate	Datetime	Actual end date of the task.
assignedto	int	Staff member assigned to the task.
Statuscodeid	int	Current status of the task.

The dbTask's table has the following relations:

dbTasks.projectid	Many to 1	dbProjects.id
dbTasks.id	1 to Many	dbStages.taskid
dbTasks.statuscodeid	1 to Many	dbStatusCodes.statuscodeid

The dbStaff table holds information on the users of the ProjectPal system (see Table 17.4).

Table 17.4 **The dbStaff Table**

Field	Data Type	Description
staffId	int	Internal StaffID number that's auto-generated.
firstname	varchar	First name of staff member.
surname	varchar	Last name of staff member.
Ispm	bit	Boolean value denoting whether the staff member is a project manager.
Email	varchar	Email address of the staff member.
password	varchar	Password of the staff member.

The dbStaff table has the following relations:

dbStaff.staffid	1 to Many	dbTasks.assignedTo

Views

The ProjectPal system makes use of SQL views for all queries against data. There are views for each table as well as views used to gather statistical information. The following list outlines the views used in the ProjectPal system:

- **vwProjectsPM**—All projects in the system for a project manager.
- **vwProjectsStaff**—All projects in the system for a member of a project.
- **vwProjectDetail**—All details of a specific project.
- **vwStages**—All stages in the system for a project.
- **vwStaffByStages**—All staff members who have been assigned a task in a project.
- **vwStaffDetail**—All details of a specific member of staff.
- **vwTasksByProject**—All tasks in a project.
- **vwTasksByStage**—All tasks in a projects stage.
- **vwTasksTotalByStage**—Returns the total tasks, tasks-in-progress, and tasks not started totals for tasks in a single stage of a project.

SQL Views

A SQL view is a way of organizing reusable sets of data on which to perform queries against. It is also used to provide a level of abstraction from the underlying tables of data from which they are based. This provides the capability to change the data structure of a table without affecting an external application.

The ProjectPal Components

As previously mentioned, the ProjectPal system makes very heavy use of components. What follows in this section is a brief overview of some of the components used in the application. A walkthrough of each kind of component is given here.

The Data Access Layer

The *Data Access Layer* (DAL) components in the ProjectPal are actually SQL Server stored procedures. These are used to send and receive SQL Server data.

Each table has a set of stored procedures that mirror the views used for data retrieval; the only difference is that the stored procedures take a parameter or two for querying purposes.

Stored procedures also are defined for creating, deleting, and updating each of the tables in the system; and finally, there are some utility-stored procedures used for tasks, such as collecting statistics.

A complete list of the stored procedures used by the ProjectPal system is as follow:

- Project–Based Data:
  - `spCreateProject`
  - `spUpdateProject`
  - `spGetProjectsAsPM`
  - `spGetProjectsAsStaff`
  - `spGetProjectDetail`
- Project Stage-Based Data:
  - `spCreateStage`
  - `spUpdateStage`
  - `spgetStagesByProject`
  - `spGetStagesByProjectWithTasks`
- Project Staff–Based Data:
  - `spCreateStaff`
  - `spUpdateStaff`
  - `spGetStaff`
  - `spGetStaffByStage`
  - `spGetStaffByDetail`
- Project Task–Based Data:
  - `spCreateTask`
  - `spUpdateTask`
  - `spGetTasksByProject`
  - `spGetTasksByStage`

The Business Services Layer

In the ProjectPal system, there are business objects defined for DAL components. Most of these services just act as an interface to a DAL; however, some of these business services also provide data validation and formatting services for communication between the DAL and user interface layers.

There are four main business objects used by the ProjectPal system presented in this chapter:

- boProject
- boStage
- boStaff
- boTask

Inside the ProjectPal Code

This section explains the physical architecture and source of the ProjectPal web application. I am not detailing all areas of the system because of space constraints and the fact that a fair amount of the code is somewhat repetitive.

Configuration

The ProjectPal system uses two web.config files for various settings. The first file is in the application's root directory, and it sets up the ASP.NET environment. The second file is in the browser directory and is used to apply authorization rules to any files in its directory. The web.config file from the root directory is shown in Listing 17.1.

Listing 17.1 **ProjectPal web.config**

```
01 <?xml version="1.0" encoding="utf-8" ?>
02 <configuration>
03
04  <appSettings>
05 <add  key="projectPalDSN"
06 value="server=localhost;uid=sa;pwd=;database=projectpal" />
07  </appSettings>
08
09  <system.web>
10
```

```
11    <trace  enabled="true"
12          requestLimit="20"
13          pageOutput="false"
14           traceMode="SortByTime"
15           localOnly="true" />
16
17    <sessionState
18            mode="InProc"
19            cookieless="true"
20            timeout="60"
21    />
22
23  <authentication mode="Forms">
24    <forms name="projectpal" loginUrl="default.aspx" />
25  </authentication>
26
27  </system.web>
28
29 </configuration>
```

<appSettings> Section

The <appSettings> section sets up one custom application setting
"projectPalDSN". This setting is used by the ProjectPal system to connect to a
data source, and it is used in all the business objects extensively, as the following code snippet from the boProject business object shows:

```
...
dim myDSN as String =
ConfigurationSettings.AppSettings("ProjectPalDSN")
dim myConn As new SqlConnection(myDSN)
...
```

The first line assigns the value of the AppSettings setting to the string variable myDSN, and the second line uses myDSN to create an SqlConnection object.

<trace> Section

The <trace> section is used to set up the tracing used in the application, and
in the case of ProjectPal, the tracing functionality has been enabled, but only
on the web server on which it is running. No trace data will be shown to
the client unless a web page has a trace attribute enabled. To see any trace
results, you have to use the trace.axd application. This is covered in more
detail in Chapter 3, "Configuring ASP.NET Applications."

<sessionState> Section

The `<sessionState>` section enables cookieless, in-process, session management with a session timeout set to 60 seconds.

<authentication> Section

The `<authentication>` section enables forms-based authentication for the application and sets the default web page as default.aspx, which the user should be redirected to when a failed authentication occurs. This page is covered in the next section "Security in ProjectPal."

These settings are used in conjunction with those of the second web.config file in the application root directory mentioned earlier, as shown in Listing 17.2.

Listing 17.2 **ProjectPal web.config in the \browser Directory**

```
01 <?xml version="1.0" encoding="utf-8" ?>
02 <configuration>
03  <system.web>
04
05      <authorization>
06          <deny users="?" />
07      </authorization>
08
09  </system.web>
10
11 </configuration>
```

In this file, we have stated that any access to this directory requires authorization.

Security in ProjectPal

Security is enforced in the ProjectPal system through forms authentication. This was briefly mentioned in the previous section.

When a user first tries to access any part of the ProjectPal system, he will be redirected to the default.aspx web page. This is a login screen for the ProjectPal system, and a screen shot is shown in Figure 17.18.

In this screen shot, you can see that the page is broken up into two main parts: a title bar and a login tool bar (loginbar.ascx).

The login toolbar is an ASP.NET user control, and it is used to authenticate a user's access to the ProjectPal system. It also enables the user to register a new project with the ProjectPal system as a project manager. If the user is not already a member of a project he needs to use the registration form, which is discussed in the next section.

Before explaining more on how the login bar works, let's look at the code in Listing 17.3.

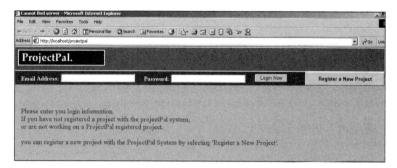

Figure 17.18   default.aspx—Login screen for the ProjectPal system.

Listing 17.3   **Source Code for loginbar.ascx**

```
01 <%@ import namespace="system.data" %>
02 <%@ import namespace="system.data.SqlClient" %>
03 <%@ Import Namespace="System.Web.Security " %>
04
05 <%@ import namespace="projectpal.bo" %>
06
07
08 <script language="VB" runat="server">
09
10 Sub loginLink_Click(sender As Object, e As EventArgs)
11
12    dim myStaff as new ProjectPal.bo.boStaff()
13
14    if myStaff.authenticate(txtEmail.text, txtPassword.text) then
15         formsauthentication.SetAuthCookie(txtEmail.text, false)
16         response.redirect("browser/projectDesk.aspx")
17    else
18         lblMessageBar.text="Login failed, you have entered invalid credentials, try
➥again or register a new project."
19    end if
20
21 end sub
22
23
24 Sub RegisterLink_Click(sender As Object, e As EventArgs)
25
26    response.redirect("registerProject.aspx")
27
28 end sub
29
30
```

continues ▶

Listing 17.3 **Continued**

```
31 </script>
32
33
34
35 <table width="100%" cellspacing="0" cellpadding="0" border="0">
36     <tr bgcolor="#191970">
37         <td colspan="2"  height="36" valign="center">
38
39         <font color="#FFFFFF">    <b>Email Address:</b> </font>
40
41         <asp:textbox id="txtEmail" width="200" runat="server" />
42
43             
44
45         <font color="#FFFFFF"><b>Password:</b> </font>
46
47         <asp:textbox id="txtPassword" textMode="password" width="200" runat="server" />
48
49             
50
51         <asp:Button id="loginLink"
52                           Text="Login Now"
53                     OnClick="loginLink_Click"
54                       runat="server" />
55         </td>
56         <td align="right" valign="center">
57         <asp:Button id="RegisterLink"
58                           height="36"
59                           font-bold="true"
60                           Text="Register a New Project"
61                     OnClick="RegisterLink_Click"
62                       runat="server" />
63     </td>
64     </tr>
65
66     <tr bgcolor="#b0c4de" >
67         <td >    </td>
68         <td width="100%">
69             <br>
70             <asp:Label id="lblMessageBar" text="" forecolor="#dc143c" font-size="16"
➥font-bold="true" runat="server" />
71             <font size="4">
72             <br><br>
73             <font color="#483d8b">
74             Please enter your login information.
75             <br>
76             If you have not registered a project with the ProjectPal system, <br>
77             or are not working on a ProjectPal registered project.
78             <br><br>
79              you can register a new project with the ProjectPal System by selecting
➥'Register a New Project'.
```

```
80                  </font>
81                  <br><br><br>
82          </td>
83          <td>
84          </td>
85      </tr>
86
87 </table>
88 <%@ Control language="vb" debug="true"%>
```

The login bar control is relatively straightforward; it has only two subs for processing "loginLink_click" and "RegisterLink_Click", which are called when the relevant button controls are pressed.

The "loginLink_Click" sub first creates a staff business object (boStaff), which is then used to authenticate a user through its authenticate method. This method returns true if the user's email and password exist in the dbStaff table. The code for this method of the boStaff business object is shown in Listing 17.4.

Listing 17.4 *Authenticate* **Method of the** *boStaff* **Business Object**

```
01 public function Authenticate (email as string, password as string) as boolean
02
03 dim myDSN as String = ConfigurationSettings.AppSettings("ProjectPalDSN")
04 dim mySQL as String = "Select count(*) from dbStaff where email = '" + email + "' and
➥password = '" + password + "'"
05 dim mySQLReader as SqlDataReader
06 dim myConn As new SQLConnection(myDSN)
07 dim mySQLCommand as new SqlCommand(mySQL, myConn)
08
09 myConn.Open()
10 mySQLReader = mySQLCommand.ExecuteReader()
11
12 while (mySQLReader.Read())
13 return( not (mySQLReader.GetInt32(0) = 0) )
14 end while
15
16 mySQLReader.Close
17 myConn.Close
18
19 Return ( False )
```

If the user is successfully authenticated, he is redirected to the \browser\projectDesk.aspx web page via the RegisterLink_Click subroutine as shown below.

```
20 Sub RegisterLink_Click(sender As Object, e As EventArgs)
21    response.redirect("registerProject.aspx")
22 end sub
```

If the user authentication procedure fails, an authentication message is displayed, and he can try to login again, or he can register a new project in his name.

Registering a New Project

When you first start the ProjectPal system, it is likely that you are not a member of an existing project, in which case, you can create a project of your own by clicking the New Project Registration button on the login page. The registration page should then appear on your screen, as shown in Figure 17.19.

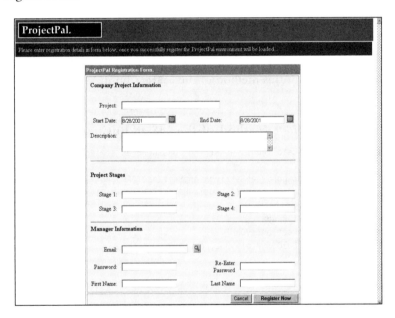

Figure 17.19   ProjectPal registration screen.

This form is split into the following four sections listed top to bottom:

- Project information
- Project stages
- Project manager information
- Control area

The project information area is where you enter project details. This area also makes use of two pop-up calendars for entering the start and end dates of a project. The code for this section of the page follows.

From the script block:

```
01 Sub Page_Load(Sender As Object, E As EventArgs)
02
03 if not page.ispostback() then
04 txtStartDate.text = datetime.today()
05 txtEndDate.text = datetime.today()
06 end if
07
08 End Sub
09
10 Sub btnCalStartDate_Click(sender As Object, e As ImageClickEventArgs)
11
12 calStartDate.SelectedDate = ctype(txtStartDate.text, datetime)
13 calStartDate.visible = not calStartDate.visible
14
15 End Sub
16
17
18 Sub btnCalEndDate_Click(sender As Object, e As ImageClickEventArgs)
19
20 calEndDate.SelectedDate = ctype(txtEndDate.text, datetime)
21 calEndDate.visible = not calEndDate.visible
22
23 End Sub
24
25
26 Sub calStartDate_Changed (sender as Object, e As EventArgs)
27
28 txtStartDate.text = calStartDate.SelectedDate.ToShortDateString
29
30 end Sub
31
32
33 Sub calEndDate_Changed (sender as Object, e As EventArgs)
34
35 txtEndDate.text = calEndDate.SelectedDate.ToShortDateString
36
37 end Sub
```

From page layout:

```
01 <tr>
02 <td colspan="45"><h4>Project Information</h4></td>
03 </tr>
04
05 <tr>
06 <td align="right">Project: </td>
07 <td colspan="3"><asp:textbox id="txtProject"  columns="40" runat="server" /></td>
08 </tr>
09
10 <tr>
11 <td align="right">Start Date: </td>
```

```
12 <td>
13 <asp:textbox id="txtStartDate"
14 columns="15"
15 readonly="true"
16 runat="server" />
17
18 <asp:ImageButton        id="btnCalStartDate"
19 imageurl="images/calendar.gif"
20 OnClick="btnCalStartDate_Click"
21 causesValidation="false"
22 runat="server" />
23 </td>
24
25 <td align="right" width="80">End Date: </td>
26 <td>
27 <asp:textbox id="txtEndDate"
28 columns="15"
29 readonly="true"
30 runat="server" />
31
32 <asp:ImageButton        id="btnCalEndDate"
33 imageurl="images/calendar.gif"
34 OnClick="btnCalEndDate_Click"
35 causesValidation="false"
36 runat="server" />
37 </td>
38 </tr>
39
40 <tr>
41 <td colspan="2" align="right">
42 <asp:calendar  id="calStartDate"
43 visible="false"
44 OnSelectionChanged="calStartDate_Changed"
45 runat="server" />
46 </td>
47 <td colspan="2" align="right">
48 <asp:calendar  id="calEndDate"
49 visible="false"
50 OnSelectionChanged="calEndDate_Changed"
51 runat="server" />
52 </td>
53 </tr>
54
55 <tr >
56 <td align="right" valign="top">Description: </td>
57 <td colspan="3"><asp:textbox id="txtDescription" textMode="MultiLine" columns="50"
58 rows="3" runat="server" /></td>
59 </tr>
```

In the script block code, we have a standard `Page_Load` event that simply sets the values of the date range controls to the current date.

The next two subs, `btncalStartDate_Click` and `btncalEndDate_click`, are used to toggle the display of the two Calendar controls, `calStartDate` and `calEndDate`. These two controls are not visible when the page is first loaded, and they have their visibility toggled by the following lines of code in these subs (the following example is from the `btncalEndDate_Click` sub):

```
01 calEndDate.SelectedDate = ctype(txtEndDate.text, datetime)
02 calEndDate.visible = not calEndDate.visible
```

The first line ensures that the Calendar control is looking at the correct date (in this code example, from the `txtEndDate` textbox control on the form), and the second line toggles the `visible` attribute of the Calendar control.

The next two subs in the script block simply update the relevant text controls with the values selected in the Calendar controls. The following example shows the subroutine for the `calStartDate_Changed` and the `calEndDate_Changed` events:

```
01 Sub calStartDate_Changed (sender as Object, e As EventArgs)
02      txtStartDate.text = calStartDate.SelectedDate.ToShortDateString
03 end Sub
04
05
06 Sub calEndDate_Changed (sender as Object, e As EventArgs)
07      txtEndDate.text = calEndDate.SelectedDate.ToShortDateString
08 end Sub
```

That completes the coverage of the registration process. Next, we look at the stages section.

Reader Exercise

I have disabled the textbox controls for both the start and enddate textbox controls; however, as an exercise, you could enable both textboxes and create compare validators to ensure that a valid date range is entered. If the date is not valid, the system will crash when it tries to assign a non-date value to the `SelectedDate` property of a Calendar control. You can find information on how to do this in the last section of Chapter 4, "Web Form-Based Development."

The Stages Section

This section is used to define stages 1–4 for your project. Any areas with values when a project is registered will become the name of a stage of the project.

The User Details Section

The next section of the registration page deals with your user details and requires you to enter an email address. (This is used for authentication throughout the application.) You must enter a password and confirm it, and enter your first and last names again because no validation was in place on this section of the form. However, there is a button with a spy glass image, which is used to get your first name and last name from the ProjectPal system. If you are already a registered user on another project, you must have entered your email address and password for this to work. The code that does this is shown in Listing 17.5.

Listing 17.5 **Finding a user's details by their email address**

```
01 Sub btnFindByEmail_Click(sender As Object, e As ImageClickEventArgs)
02
03    dim myStaff as new projectpal.bo.bostaff
04    dim staffData as new projectpal.bo.structStaff
05
06    if myStaff.Authenticate(txtEmail.text, txtPassword1.text) then
07
08         staffData = myStaff.Detail(txtEmail.text)
09
10         txtFirstName.text = staffData.firstname
11         txtLastName.text = staffData.lastname
12
13    end if
14
15
16 End Sub
```

This function basically does the same as the loginbar control such that it creates a boStaff object and then authenticates the user's details against the dbStaff table. If authenticated, we call a new boStaff business object method, Detail. This object is used to retrieve the details of a staff member from the system and pass them to the calling program as a custom object staffData.

If authenticated, the txtFirstname and txtLastName fields are updated with the returned data. See Listing 17.6.

Listing 17.6   *Detail* **Method of the** *bo.staff* **Object**

```
01  public function Detail (email as string) as structStaff
02
03    dim myDSN as String = _ ConfigurationSettings.AppSettings("ProjectPalDSN")
04    dim mySQLReader as SqlDataReader
05    dim myConn As new SQLConnection(myDSN)
06    dim mySQLCommand as new SQLCommand("spGetStaffDetail", myConn)
07    dim myStruct as new structStaff()
08
09    mySQLCommand.CommandType = CommandType.StoredProcedure
10    mySQLCommand.Parameters.Add(New _ SqlParameter("@email", SqlDbType.varchar))
11    mySQLCommand.Parameters("@email").Value = email
12
13    myConn.Open()
14    mySQLReader = mySQLCommand.ExecuteReader()
15
16    while (mySQLReader.Read())
17      myStruct.id = mySQLReader.GetInt32(0)
18      myStruct.firstname = mySQLReader.GetString(1)
19      myStruct.lastname = mySQLReader.GetString(2)
20      myStruct.email = mySQLReader.GetString(3)
21      myStruct.password = mySQLReader.GetString(4)
22      myStruct.isPM = mySQLReader.GetInt32(5)
23    end while
24
25    mySQLReader.Close
26    myConn.Close
27
28    Return ( myStruct )
29
30  end function
```

The code in the Detail object is again relatively straightforward. Note that we are returning a structStaff object. This is a custom object used by the ProjectPal system for marshaling record-like data. Also notice that we are getting the DSN for the database connection from the web.config configuration file.

In this code, I am calling the stored procedure spGetStaffDetail (line 05). This procedure returns a row of data for a specified staff member through his email address. This row of data is then copied into a structStaff object from a datareader, and then the structStaff object is returned to the calling application.

The staffData Object

The staffData object is an object that has properties for each field in a database table. It is used by the business objects and interfaces of ProjectPal to share record information. Each business object defines a data structure for the data they work with. This object is normally used to get received information from a database record or to create or insert data from a database table. This object also calls a single method, toInsertString, which simply creates a string of fields used in the update stored procedures in this system. More on information on the staffData object can be found in the section "The User Details Section." See Listing 17.7.

Listing 17.7 *structStaff* Class Used to Create the *staffData* Object

```
01 public class structStaff
02
03 Public id as Integer            ' id of staff member (internal)
04 Public firstName As String      ' First Name
05 Public lastName As String       ' Last Name
06 Public email As String          ' email address
07 Public password AS String    ' password
08 Public isPM As integer       ' Is Project Manager?
09
10 Public function toInsertString () as string
11
12 return(   "'" + ctype(firstname, string) +"', '" + _
13           ctype(lastname, string) +"', '" + _
14           ctype(email, string) +"', '" + _
15           ctype(password, string) +"', " + _
16           ctype(ispm, string) )
17
18 end function
```

The Control Area

The control area of the form holds two buttons:

- Cancel
- Register

The Cancel button simply ignores any edits and redirects you back to the login form.

The Register button, however, does a lot more. The first thing the Register button's click event does is package up all the page's information into three main data structures. These are

- **StaffData**—structStaff object
- **ProjectData**—structProject object
- **StageData**—arrayList object

After this has been done, another new method is called. This time it is the create method of the boProject business object that is called, and it is used to create a new staff member as a project manager. If project does not exist already within the same email and password, create a new project and assign the project manager to be the user who registered the project; and finally, create all required stages for the project. If the data is created successfully, the user is authenticated to the system through the formsauthentication.SetAuthCookie method and is redirected to the ProjectPal project desk.

The code for the registration click is shown in Listing 17.8 followed by the code for the boProject.Create method, which is shown in Listing 17.9.

Listing 17.8 *btnRegister_Click* **Sub of the registerproject.aspx Web Page**

```
01 Sub btnRegister_Click(sender As Object, e As EventArgs)
02
03    dim myProject as new ProjectPal.bo.boProject
04    dim projectData as new projectpal.bo.structProject()
05    dim staffData as new projectpal.bo.structStaff()
06    dim stageData as new arraylist()
07
08    'populate staff Data structure
09    staffData.id = 0
10    staffData.firstname = txtfirstname.Text
11    staffData.lastname = txtlastname.Text
12    staffData.email = txtemail.Text
13    staffData.password = txtpassword1.Text
14    staffData.isPM = 1
15
16
17    'populate Project Data structure
18    projectData.id = 0
19    projectData.name = txtProject.text
20    projectData.description = txtDescription.text
21    projectData.startDate = txtStartDate.text
22    projectData.endDate = txtEndDate.text
23    projectData.PMID = 0
24
25    'populate Stages Array
26    stageData.add(txtStage1.text)
27    stageData.add(txtStage2.text)
28    stageData.add(txtStage3.text)
29    stageData.add(txtStage4.text)
30
31    if myproject.Create(staffData, projectData, stageData) then
32        formsauthentication.SetAuthCookie(txtemail.text, false)
33        response.redirect("browser/projectDesk.aspx")
34    end if
35
36
37 end sub
```

Listing 17.9   *Create* **Method of the** *boProject* **Business Object**

```
01 function Create(staffData as structStaff, projectdata as structProject, stageData as
➥ArrayList) as boolean
02
03    dim myDSN As String = ConfigurationSettings.AppSettings("ProjectPalDSN")
04    dim myConn As new SqlConnection(myDSN)
05    dim myCommand As SqlCommand
06    dim myParm As SqlParameter
07    dim myStaff AS new projectpal.bo.boStaff()
08    dim myTran As SqlTransaction
09
10 try
11    myConn.Open()
12    myTran = myConnection.BeginTransaction()
13
14
15    'before we create a PM need to make sure PM does not already exist
16    if myStaff.Authenticate (staffData.email, staffData.password) then
17         'PM in Database, get his details
18         staffData = myStaff.Detail(staffData.email)
19         projectData.pmid = ctype(staffData.id, integer)
20    else
21         'PM not in database create him
22         myCommand = New SqlCommand("spCreateStaff", myConn)
23         myCommand.CommandType = CommandType.StoredProcedure
24         myCommand.Transaction = myTran
25         myParm = myCommand.Parameters.Add("@staffdata", _ SqlDbType.varchar, 250)
26         myParm.Value =  staffData.toinsertstring()
27
28         myParm  = myCommand.Parameters.Add("@staffid", SqlDbType.int)
29         myParm.Direction = ParameterDirection.Output
30
31         myCommand.ExecuteNonQuery()
32
33         projectData.pmid=ctype(myCommand.Parameters("@staffid").Value, _ integer)
34    end if
35
36    'Project Creation
37    myCommand = New SqlCommand("spCreateProject", myConn)
38    myCommand.CommandType = CommandType.StoredProcedure
39    myCommand.Transaction = myTran
40    myParm = myCommand.Parameters.Add("@projectdata", SqlDbType.varchar, _ 2048)
41    myParm.Value =  projectData.toinsertstring()
42
43    myParm  = myCommand.Parameters.Add("@projectid", SqlDbType.int)
44    myParm.Direction = ParameterDirection.Output
45
46    myCommand.ExecuteNonQuery()
47
48
49    'Stage creation
```

```
50    Dim myEnum As System.Collections.IEnumerator = _ stageData.GetEnumerator()
51    Dim myProjectid as integer = _ ctype(myCommand.Parameters("@projectid").Value,
→integer)
52
53    While myEnum.MoveNext()
54
55        if ctype(myEnum.Current(), string).length > 0 then
56
57            myCommand = New SqlCommand("spCreateStage", myConn)
58            myCommand.CommandType = CommandType.StoredProcedure
59            myCommand.Transaction = myTran
60            myParm = myCommand.Parameters.Add("@projectid", _ SqlDbType.int)
61            myParm.Value = myProjectid
62
63            myParm = myCommand.Parameters.Add("@stageData", _SqlDbType.varchar, 50)
64            myParm.Value = ctype(myEnum.Current(), string)
65            myCommand.ExecuteNonQuery()
66
67        end if
68
69    End While
70
71    myTrans.commit()
72
73
74 catch e as SqlException
75    myTrans.rollback()
76    throw e
77
78 finally
79    myConn.Close
80
81 end try
82
83
84 return(t
```

The boProject.Create method is split into four parts:

- Variable declaration
- Creating the staff data
- Creating project data
- Creating stage data

In the variable declaration section, we see very little that's new with the exception of the declaration of an SQLTransaction object. Because we are doing a multiple transaction process, and by using transaction processing here, we have the ability to rollback and restore any changes made to the database if a stage is not created because of a database error, thus ensuring corrupt data is not generated. The transaction object must be assigned to each SQLCommand object operating on the database. This is done with the following statement from the previous code:

```
myCommand.Transaction = myTran
```

Apart from the transaction management side of things, we are introduced to three new data creation stored procedures. These are

- SpCreateProject

- spCreateStage

- SpCreateStaff

Each of these stored procedures works exactly the same way; they all take a single inbound parameter of a varchar/string datatype. This variable represents a list of values formatted for SQL Server to use in an SQL statement. This list is created by the struct…objects of each business object, and in the case of the spCReateProject and spCreateStaff objects, have a single outbound parameter indicating the identity column value for the newly created item. The spCreateProject Stored procedure is shown in Listing 17.10.

Listing 17.10 *spCreateProject* **Stored Procedure**

```
01 CREATE PROCEDURE spCreateProject
02 @projectdata as varchar (2048),
03 @projectid int OUTPUT
04 AS
05 EXEC ('INSERT dbprojects  VALUES ( '+@projectData+' )')
06 select @projectid = @@IDENTITY
```

The preceding code looks a little different from regular SQL insert because of a technique used. This technique enables the user to avoid creating screens full of parameter objects in ASP.NET at the cost of a little performance. To do this, a complete value list of data is sent to insert into a table as a single parameter, and an insert string is created inside the stored procedure for the whole insert required. After this is done, I simply call the EXEC function to execute the insert statement. Again, this is one of the reasons to use the struct... objects in each business object, so this string can be generated when needed. For all operations in ProjectPal where inserts are required, this technique was used.

This technique also has the nice side effect of making code more readable in both SQL Server and ASP.NET.

The Project Desktop

The most used part of the ProjectPal system is the project desktop. From here, project managers can view and edit project-based information for their projects or can view and change task status for their projects.

After registration, the ProjectPal desktop should look similar to Figure 17.20 when you are logged in as a project manager.

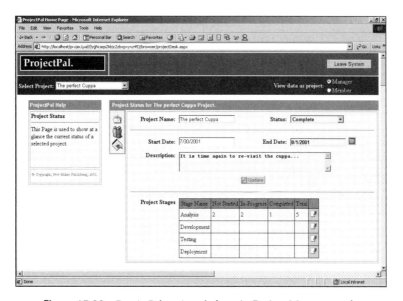

Figure 17.20   ProejctPal project desktop in Project Manager mode.

The interface is made up of four main parts:

- Title bar
- Project toolbar
- Help window
- Project control panel

The Title Bar

The title bar of the project desk is unremarkable; its only feature, apart from a stunning logo, is a Leave system button. This button logs the user out of the system and returns him to the login screen when it is clicked.

The following code is self-explanatory:

```
01 private Sub LogOut_Click(sender As Object, e As EventArgs)
02
03        formsAuthentication.signOut()
04        response.redirect("..\default.aspx")
05
06 end sub
```

The Project Toolbar

The ProjectPal toolbar serves various purposes. First and foremost, it enables you to select any projects for which you are a project manager, or of which you are a member.

If you are a project manager, the toolbar enables you to switch between the projects you manage and those of which you are a member.

It should be noted that a project manager using the system has the ability to:

- Create new staff members for the system
- Edit existing staff member details
- Create new tasks and assign them to a user
- Edit existing tasks
- Edit the current project's end date, description, and status

This switching of abilities is only possible when a project manager has been assigned a task in another project.

When the project desk is loaded, a session variable called isPM is created and is used to denote whether or not a user is a project manager. This is done in the web page's Page_Load sub shown in Listing 17.11.

Listing 17.11 *Page_Load* **Sub of projectDesk.aspx (Project Desktop)**

```
01 Sub Page_Load(Sender As Object, E As EventArgs)
02
03   if not ispostback() then
04        dim staffData as new projectpal.bo.structStaff()
05        dim myStaff as new projectpal.bo.boStaff()
06        staffData = myStaff.detail(request.servervariables("AUTH_USER"))
07
08            session("isPM") = staffData.isPM
09
10        end if
11
12   End Sub
```

This code is quite interesting. First, only update the data if it is the first time the page is loaded. Next, create a `structStaff` object, which you are getting quite used to by now, and then create an instance of the staff business object, `boStaff`. Next call the `boStaff.Detail` method, which again you have seen before, however, this time send the value of the server variable `AUTH_USER`. This variable holds the email of the user. After the system has authenticated the user, it is available to be used for the rest of the user's session. After receiving the staff data, create or assign the isPM property of the `staffData` object to the session variable `isPM`.

The project bar changes its display based on the session variable `isPM`; the project bar's `Page_Load` event handles this logic. See Listing 17.12:

Listing 17.12 **_Page_Load_ Sub for projectbar.ascx**

```
01 Sub Page_Load(Sender As Object, E As EventArgs)
02
03  If not page.IsPostback() Then
04
05    dim myStaff as new projectpal.bo.boStaff
06
07
08 session("pmMode") = session("isPM")
09
10
11    if ctype(session("pmMode"), integer) = 1 and
➥myStaff.isProjectStaff(request.servervariables("AUTH_USER")) then
12              lblMode.visible = true
13              radpmMode.visible = true
14              radpmMode.selectedindex = 0
15    else
16          lblMode.visible = false
17          radpmMode.visible = false
18    end if
19
20    bindData()
21
22  end if
23
24 end sub
```

In this `Page_Load` sub, you create a staff object for use in the sub again, only it is not a `postback` event. You also create and assign a new session variable, which is used to denote the current mode of the project desktop. A value of 1 indicates a PM. A value of 0 is used if the user is not a PM.

Next, check to see if the logged in user is a project manager by calling a new method of the `boStaff` object, `isProjectStaff`. This method checks to see if the logged in project manager is also a member of any projects (that is, has been assigned any tasks). If the project manager has been assigned tasks, a radio list control is displayed, enabling the user to toggle between the functionality of the project manager's view of data and the staff member's view of data.

The final part of the `Page_Load` sub is the call to another sub, `bindData()`. This sub is used to bind data to the project list box. The following is the code for this:

```
01 sub binddata()
02
03      dim myProjects as new ProjectPal.bo.boProject
04
05      if ctype(session("pmMode"), integer) = 1 then
06          ddlProjectList.DataSource = myProjects.getProjectsAsPM(
07 request.servervariables("AUTH_USER") )
08      else
09          ddlProjectList.DataSource = myProjects.getProjectsAsStaff(
10 request.servervariables("AUTH_USER") )
11      end if
12
13      ddlProjectList.DataTextField="name"
14      ddlProjectList.DataValueFIeld="projectID"
15      ddlProjectList.DataBind
16
17      if ddlProjectList.items.count > 0 then
18          session("projectID") = ddlProjectList.selecteditem.value
19          session("projectName") = ddlProjectList.selecteditem.text
20      end if
21
22 end sub
```

The `bindData()` method creates an instance of the `boProject` business object, which is used later to retrieve projects to which the user has access; but before that, we check to see whether or not the user is in project manager mode. If the user is, we call the `boProject.getProjectsAsPM()` method to retrieve project data and then to populate the dropdownlist control's datasource. If the user is not in project manager mode, we call the `boProject.GetProjectsAsStaff()` method.

Both of these methods return the same kind of information; however, the views of the data are quite different. The `getProjectsAsPM()` method simply uses the dbProjects file. However, the `getProjectsAsStaff()` method is far more involved because we have to find any tasks assigned to the user and then the projects to which the tasks belong.

Finally, we create and assign two new and very important session variables, `projectID` and `ProjectName`. These are used by the project control panel, so it knows what project to display.

This is great. However, just changing the session variable used to define what project data is displayed on the control panel does not automatically ensure that the control panel is updated when a new project has been selected. To do this, you have to get the project panel user control to update its data and do any data binding based on the new setting. This is achieved by creating a reference to the project control panel control (projectInfo.ascx), and then calling its data binding method as soon as a new project is selected in the project's DropDownList box.

This is achieved by using the following code:

```
01 sub ddlProjectListIndexChanged(sender As Object, e As EventArgs)
02
03        session("projectID") = sender.selecteditem.value
04        session("projectName") = sender.selecteditem.text
05
06        dim mycontrol = page.findcontrol("projectInfo")
07        ctype(mycontrol, ASP.projectInfo_ASCX).UpdateInfo(session("currentPage"))
08
09 end sub
```

This sub routine is called when a `ListIndexChanged` event occurs on the project dropdownlist control. First, store the ever-important `projectID` and `projectname` session variables, and then create and locate the projectInfo control on the processed web page that is holding all the controls. After you have the control, you have to cast its type as the `ASP.projectInfo_ASCX` class. This class is the file name of the imported user control. The user control must be registered for this page. After this control is cast, we call the `UpdateInfo()` method of the project control panel to force it to update its display appropriately for the selected project.

The Help Window

The Help Window user control is somewhat less complex than the loginbar control. The Help Window is a support control for the project control panel; it is used to display help messages regarding the selected page of the control panel. It is forced to update itself with the login bar in the same manner as the project panel.

The code for this control is shown in Listing 17.13.

Listing 17.13 **Help Window User Control**

```
01 <%@ Control language="vb" debug="true"%>
02
03 <script language="VB" runat="server">
04
05 Sub Page_Load(Sender As Object, E As EventArgs)
06     if not page.ispostback() then
07          update()
08     end if
09 End Sub
10
11
12 sub update()
13     Select Case session("currentPage")
14          Case 0
15               phtitle.text = "Project Status"
16               phdesc.text = "This Page is used to show at a glance the current status of
➥a selected project."
17
18          Case 1
19               phtitle.text="Staff Information"
20               phdesc.text="This Page is used to show at a glance all of the staff
➥allocated to a single stage or all stages of a selected project."
21
22          Case 2
23               phtitle.text="Task Information"
24               phdesc.text="This Page is used to show at a glance all of the tasks
➥allocated to a single stage or all stages of a selected project."
25
26
27     End Select
28 end sub
29
30 </script>
31
32
33 <table width="200" cellspacing="0" cellpadding="0" border="0">
34 <tr>
35 <td colspan="2" bgcolor="#6495ed" height="26">
36 <font face="Arial" size="-1" color="#FFFFFF"> <b>ProjectPal Help</b></font>
37 </td>
38 </tr>
39 <tr>
```

```
40 <td valign="top">
41 <table width="200" height="200" cellpadding="2" cellspacing="3"  border="1"
➥bordercolor="#6495ed" >
42 <tr>
43 <td align="left" valign="top" bgcolor="#f5f5f5">
44 <asp:label id="phtitle"    runat="server" text="" font-bold="true"/>
45 <hr>
46 <asp:label id="phdesc"      runat="server" text="" />
47 </td>
48 </tr>
49 <tr>
50 <td height="60" align="center" valign="top" bgcolor="#f5f5f5" >
51 <font size="-3" color="#808080">&copy Copyright, New Riders Publishing, 2001.</font>
52 </td>
53 </tr>
54 </table>
55 </td>
56 </tr>
57 </table>
```

As you can see, the Help Window control simply looks for a session variable called currentPage, which it uses in a select statement to update two label controls with the text for the displayed page of information in the project control panel.

The Project Control Panel (projectInfo.asc)

The project control panel is at the core of the ProjectPal interface. It is made up of two main parts, the icon menu on the left side and the content panel on the right.

The projectInfo object manages all interactions between the menu and the data displayed in the content area. The code for the layout of the project desk is shown in Listing 17.14.

Listing 17.14 **projectInfo.ascx—Layout Code**

```
01 <table width="700" align="center" cellspacing="0" cellpadding="0" border="0">
02 <tr>
03 <td colspan="2" bgcolor="#6495ed" height="26">
04 <font face="Arial" size="-1" color="#FFFFFF"> <b><%= GetTitleText() %></b></font>
05 </td>
06 </tr>
07
08 <tr>
09 <td valign="top">
10 <table align="center" cellspacing="0" cellpadding="6" border="1" bordercolor="#6495ed"
➥bgcolor="#f0e8f8" >
11 <tr>
```

continues ▶

Listing 17.14 **Continued**

```
12 <td align="Center">
13 <asp:DataList  id="ControlPanel" runat="server"
14                      CellPadding="0"
15                      CellSpacing="0"
16                          OnItemCommand="DataList_ItemCommand">
17
18         <ItemTemplate>
19                 <asp:ImageButton id="commands"
20                     ImageAlign="Middle"
21                     width="28" Height="34"
22                     CommandName="select"
23                     ImageUrl= <%# DataBinder.Eval(Container.DataItem, "key",
➥"../images/lm{0}.gif")%>
24                     Alt= <%# DataBinder.Eval(Container.DataItem, "value", "{0}")%>
25                     runat="server" />
26
27         </ItemTemplate>
28
29          <SelectedItemTemplate>
30                 <img align="Middle" width="28" height="34" border="0" src="<%#
➥DataBinder.Eval(Container.DataItem, "key", "../images/lc{0}.gif")%>" alt= <%#
➥DataBinder.Eval(Container.DataItem, "value", "{0}")%>          >
31          </SelectedItemTemplate>
32
33     </asp:DataList>
34 </td>
35
36 </tr>
37 </table>
38 </td>
39          <td>
40          <table width="700" align="center" Height="350" cellpadding="2" cellspacing="3"
➥border="1" bordercolor="#6495ed" >
41 <tr>
42                  <td align="left" valign="top" bgcolor="#f5f5f5">
43                      <asp:placeholder id="phList" runat="server" />
44                      <asp:placeholder id="phCreate" runat="server"/>
45                      </td>
46                  </tr>
47          </table>
48      </td>
49   </tr>
50 </table>
```

There is quite a lot there, but it's not as bad as it seems. The first row of the
table displays the title of the display window. To do this, it calls a TitleText()
sub. This sub returns a string of text to display in its place:

```
01 Private function GetTitleText() as string
02 return(" "+session("pageMode")+" for "+ _
03 session("ProjectName")+" Project.")
04 end function
```

Again, you should notice that the same session variables are used for the project name and the current `pageMode` of the system. (The `pageMode` is actually the name of the page being displayed in the content area of this Web Form, and it directly corresponds to the icon menu.)

The next area of interest to look at is the `<datalist>` control declaration. In this interface, I am using a datalist for the icon menu. This list is populated in the `Page_Load` method of the web control as follows:

```
01 private Sub Page_Load(Sender As Object, E As EventArgs)
02       if controlpanel.selectedindex < 0 then
03       controlpanel.selectedindex = 0
04       end if
05
06    If Not IsPostBack Then
07          BindControlPanel()
08       End If
09
10       UpdateInfo(ControlPanel.SelectedIndex)
11 end sub
```

First, it is necessary to ensure that the current index position of the icon menu is non-negative. One item must always be selected, and you should default to the top item if ever in any doubt. Next, if it is the first time the page is loaded, call the `bindControlPanel()` sub, which binds an arraylist of image names and descriptions to the datalist. The code for this is shown in Listing 17.15. Next, call the `UpdateInfo` sub for this web page. This is covered in more detail in Listing 17.16, but in short, it ensures that the content pane of the project control panel displays the correct information.

Listing 17.15   *bindControlPanel()* **Sub**

```
01 Private Sub BindControlPanel()
02    dim imageList as sortedlist = new sortedlist()
03
04    imageList.add("Info1", "Project Status")
05    imageList.add("Info2", "Staff")
06    imageList.add("Info3", "Tasks")
07
08    ControlPanel.DataSource = imageList
09 ControlPanel.DataBind()
10
11 End Sub
```

All the `bindControlPanel()` sub does is create an arraylist object and populate it with three elements in the format of:

`<IconName>, <Name of Page>`

This arraylist is then bound to the DataList control.

The DataList control uses the bound arraylist's key values to provide the name of the images to use.

The content area of the web control is simply a placeholder control, which is used to hold web pages loaded into it by the `UpdateInfo` sub, shown in Listing 17.16:

Listing 17.16 **The *UpdateInfo* Sub-Routine**

```
01 public sub UpdateInfo (pageMode as string)
02
03 Dim myControl As Control
04
05 select case     pageMode
06    Case 0
07           myControl = LoadControl("..\browser\projectStatus.ascx")
08           ctype(myControl, ASP.projectStatus_ASCX).ID =  "projectStatus"
09           phList.Controls.clear()
10           phList.Controls.Add(myControl)
11
12           phList.visible = true
13           phCreate.visible=false
14
15           Session("pageMode") = "Project Status"
16
17    Case 1
18           myControl = LoadControl("..\browser\StaffList.ascx")
19           ctype(myControl, ASP.stafflist_ASCX).ID =  "stafflist"
20           phList.controls.clear()
21           phList.Controls.Add(myControl)
22
23           myControl = LoadControl("..\browser\StaffCreate.ascx")
24           ctype(myControl, ASP.staffCreate_ASCX).ID =  "staffCreate"
25           phCreate.controls.clear()
26           phCreate.Controls.Add(myControl)
27
28           if session("subMode") = "List" then
29                 phList.visible = true
30                 phCreate.visible=false
31           else
32                 phList.visible = true
33                 phCreate.visible=false
34           end if
35
36           Session("pageMode") = "Staff"
37
```

```
38    Case 2
39          myControl = LoadControl("..\browser\TaskList.ascx")
40          ctype(myControl, ASP.tasklist_ASCX).ID =  "tasklist"
41          phList.controls.clear()
42          phList.Controls.Add(myControl)
43
44          myControl = LoadControl("..\browser\TaskCreate.ascx")
45          ctype(myControl, ASP.taskCreate_ASCX).ID =  "taskCreate"
46          phCreate.controls.clear()
47          phCreate.Controls.Add(myControl)
48
49          if session("subMode") = "List" then
50                phList.visible = true
51                phCreate.visible=false
52          else
53                phList.visible = true
54                phCreate.visible=false
55          end if
56
57          Session("pageMode") = "Tasks"
58
59 end select
60
61 session("CurrentPage")=pageMode
62
63 mycontrol = page.findcontrol("helpWindow")
64 ctype(mycontrol, ASP.helpWindow_ASCX).update()
65
66 end sub
```

The preceding code is not as daunting as it looks; in fact, what is going on here is quite simple. To start with, it creates an instance of a control object used to hold a web control you want to display in the place holder control that was previously mentioned. Next, enter a select case structure based on the current pageMode variable (this value is the index of the currently selected item in the icon menu).

After you get to the case statement, it is necessary to simply load a web control into the defined control:

```
myControl = LoadControl("..\browser\TaskList.ascx")
```

and assign it an ID value:

```
ctype(myControl, ASP.tasklist_ASCX).ID =  "tasklist"
```

Clear the previous contents of the placeholder control we are using:

```
phList.controls.clear()
```

Add the new user control to the control's collection of the placeholder control:

```
phList.Controls.Add(myControl)
```

If you are dealing with the staff of task's content, you also store a second control. The process is exactly the same except that the control and place-holder names are different.

After the placeholders have been updated with new page contents, display one of the placeholders and hide the other one. This is only used on the staff and project pages:

```
01 if session("subMode") = "List" then
02                 phList.visible = "true"
03                 phCreate.visible="false"
04         else
05                 phList.visible = "false"
06                 phCreate.visible="true"
07             end if
```

Finally, set the `pageMode` Session variable to the page we are viewing:

```
Session("pageMode") = "Tasks"
```

Project Status

The Project Status web control is used as the main content of the `projectInfo` object. Its main function is to display the details of the selected project in the project toolbar and to give a summary report on the tasks and stages of a project. See Figure 17.21.

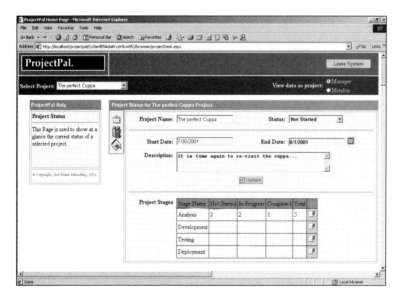

Figure 17.21 Project Status web control in action.

This web control is made up of two main sections:

- Projects details
- Stage summary

The project details section of the page is pretty straightforward, however, the initial set up of the web control is interesting because if you are a project manager, you can edit the project and stage data displayed. However, if you are not a project manager, you can only view the data. So without further ado, let's look at the Page_Load sub code in Listing 17.17:

Listing 17.17   *Page_Load* **Sub of the Project Status Web Control**

```
01 Sub Page_Load(Sender As Object, E As EventArgs)
02
03    dim myProject as new projectpal.bo.boProject
04    dim projectData as new projectpal.bo.structProject
05
06    projectData = myProject.Detail(session("projectID"))
07
08    'setup screen for PM edit mode
09    if session("ISPM") = 1 then
10            'setup status field (if PM show combo with edit functionality
11            ddlStatus.visible = true
12            txtStatus.visible = false
13
14            ddlStatus.datasource = myProject.GetStatusCodes(0)
15            ddlStatus.DataTextField="name"
16            ddlStatus.DataValueField="statuscodeid"
17            ddlStatus.SelectedIndex = projectData.status
18            ddlStatus.DataBind()
19
20            ddlStatus.backcolor = color.Linen
21            ddlStatus.font.bold=true
22
23            'setup enddate field
24            txtEndDate.backcolor = color.Linen
25            txtEndDate.font.bold=true
26            txtEndDate.readonly=true
27            btnEndDate.visible=true
28
29            'setup Description field
30            txtDescription.readonly=false
31            txtDescription.backcolor = color.linen
32            txtDescription.font.bold = true
33
34            'Setup Save Changes button
35            btnSaveData.visible=true
36
37            'setup STage grid Edit
```

continues ▶

Listing 17.17 **Continued**

```
38          dgStage.Columns(6).visible=true
39
40    else
41          ddlStatus.visible = false
42          txtStatus.visible = true
43....end if
44
45
46    txtProjectName.text = projectData.name
47    txtStartDate.text = ctype(projectData.startdate, string)
48    txtEndDate.text = ctype(projectData.enddate, string)
49    txtDescription.text = projectData.description
50
51    BindGrid()
52
53
54 end Sub
```

Okay, first things first. We declare instances of both the boProject business object, and then we create a structProject data structure to hold project information. Next, we come across an if statement that sets up the controls on the screen for data entry mode if the user is a project manager, and as usual, this is done by checking the value of the isPM session variable.

If a project manager is using the system, we display a combo box of status codes that is editable, so the user can change a project's status. We enable editing on the description field and we display a pop-up calendar button, so that the end date of a project can be edited. All these controls also have the background color set to a different color, so that editable fields are noticeable. Next, we show an image button used to save changes to the database. After these changes have been made, we enable the edit column of the datagrid used to display the stages of the project, so that they can be edited.

After the editable controls have been set up, we then set up the non-editable controls, and then we bind the datagrid to its data source through the bindGrid() method, as shown in Listing 17.18:

Listing 17.18 *bindData()* **Method**

```
01 sub bindGrid()
02
03    dim myStage as new projectpal.bo.boStage
04    dgStage.datasource=myStage.GetStagesByProject(session("projectID"))
05    dgStage.databind()
06
07 end sub
```

All this routine does is create a boStage business object, call its getStagesByProject method, and then binds its returned data to the datagrid.

The Stages DataGrid

The second main area on the screen is the Stages DataGrid. The DataGrid is used to display the stages of the selected project. The DataGrid is made editable and uses editing in place of data entry if a project manager is using the application. The layout and source code for the DataGrid is outlined in Listing 17.19.

Listing 17.19 **Layout of DataGrid**

```
01 <asp:DataGrid id="dgStage" runat="server"
02      BorderColor="black"
03      BorderWidth="1"
04      CellPadding="3"
05      HeaderStyle-BackColor="#00aaaa"
06      AutoGenerateColumns="false"
07      OnEditCommand="dgStage_Edit"
08      OnCancelCommand="dgStage_Cancel"
09      OnUpdateCommand="dgStage_Update"
10 >
11
12 <Columns>
13      <asp:BoundColumn
14      HeaderText="Stage Id"
15      DataField="stageid"
16      visible="false">
17      </asp:BoundColumn>
18
19      <asp:BoundColumn
20      HeaderText="Stage Name"
21      DataField="name">
22      </asp:BoundColumn>
23
24      <asp:BoundColumn
25      HeaderText="Not Started"
26      DataField="Tasks Not Started"
27      ReadOnly="true">
28      </asp:BoundColumn>
29
30      <asp:BoundColumn
31      HeaderText="In-Progress"
32      DataField="Tasks In-Progress"
33      ReadOnly="true">
34      </asp:BoundColumn>
35
36     <asp:BoundColumn
37      HeaderText="Completed"
38      DataField="Tasks Completed"
```

continues ▸

Listing 17.19 **Continued**

```
39          ReadOnly="true">
40          </asp:BoundColumn>
41
42          <asp:BoundColumn
43          HeaderText="Total"
44          DataField="Total Tasks"
45          ReadOnly="true">
46          </asp:BoundColumn>
47
48          <asp:EditCommandColumn
49          EditText="<img src='../images/edit.gif' alt='Edit' border='0'>"
50          CancelText="<img src='../images/remove.gif' alt='Cancel' border='0'>"
51          UpdateText="<img src='../images/add.gif' alt='Update' border='0'>"
52          ItemStyle-Wrap="false"
53          ItemStyle-BackColor="#d3d3d3"
54          HeaderText=""
55          HeaderStyle-Wrap="false"
56          Visible="false" />
57
58  </Columns>
59
60  </asp:datagrid>
```

This DataGrid defines seven columns of data of which only five are initially displayed. Also, the EditCommandColumn uses images for its edit, cancel, and update text values. This is achievable by using single quotes around the attribute values within the string, which generally gives it a more attractive user interface.

LIsting 17.20 **Source of DataGrid**

```
01 Sub dgStage_Edit(sender As Object, e As DataGridCommandEventArgs)
02          dgStage.EditItemIndex = e.Item.ItemIndex
03          BindGrid()
04 End Sub
05
06 Sub dgStage_Update(sender As Object, e As DataGridCommandEventArgs)
07
08      dim stageData as new structStage
09      dim myStage as new projectpal.bo.boStage
10         dim mycontrol as control
11
12      stageData.id = ctype(ctype(e.item.cells(0).controls(0), textbox).text, integer)
13      stageData.name = ctype(e.item.cells(1).controls(0), textbox).text
14
15      'update data
16      myStage.Update(stageData)
17
18      dgStage.EditItemIndex = - 1
```

```
19     BindGrid()
20
21 end sub
22
23 Sub dgStage_Cancel(sender As Object, e As DataGridCommandEventArgs)
24     dgStage.EditItemIndex = - 1
25     BindGrid()
26 End Sub
```

The subs used to maintain the DataGrid are straightforward. First, we will look at the Edit command sub:

```
01 Sub dgStage_Edit(sender As Object, e As DataGridCommandEventArgs)
02     dgStage.EditItemIndex = e.Item.ItemIndex
03     BindGrid()
04 End Sub
```

All this sub does is assign the EditItemIndex of the DataGrid to match the selection, and then we bind the grid. The reason that the EditItemIndex is not automatically updated is so we can do any processing before the last item is deselected and a new item is selected. But for our needs, we just assign the index values and then re-bind the data, so the changed selection is shown.

The next sub to look at is equally as simple; it's the Cancel command sub:

```
01 Sub dgStage_Cancel(sender As Object, e As DataGridCommandEventArgs)
02     dgStage.EditItemIndex = - 1
03     BindGrid()
04 End Sub
```

This time, because you are editing data, just assign the EditItemIndex to -1; this ensures that the edit mode is cancelled because there is no index -1. Re-bind the data to re-display the grid.

Finally, we have the Update command, as shown in the following code:

```
01 Sub dgStage_Update(sender As Object, e As DataGridCommandEventArgs)
02
03     dim stageData as new structStage
04     dim myStage as new projectpal.bo.boStage
05     dim mycontrol as control
06
07     stageData.id = ctype(ctype(e.item.cells(0).controls(0), textbox).text, integer)
08     stageData.name = ctype(e.item.cells(1).controls(0), textbox).text
09
10     'update data
11     myStage.Update(stageData)
12
13     dgStage.EditItemIndex = - 1
14     BindGrid()
15
16 end sub
```

This code first creates a `structStage` object and then a `boStage` business object with which to update data. After this, we assign values from the DataGrid's edited item to those of the `structStage` object. You will see that the method of accessing this data is somewhat messy; take the following line for example:

```
stageData.id = ctype(ctype(e.item.cells(0).controls(0), textbox).text, integer)
```

Read the following pseudo code to determine more clearly what's going on:

```
01 get control 0 in Cell 0 of currently selected datagrid row
02 e.item.cells(0).controls(0)
03
04 same as above but cast it as a textbox object and retrieve its text property
05 ctype(e.item.cells(0).controls(0), textbox).text
06
07 now this is great for text properties however stageid is an integer so I have to do the
➥above plus
08 ctype(ctype(e.item.cells(0).controls(0), textbox).text, integer)
09
10 A before but after getting text value re-cast text as an integer
11
12 Phew! that's a lot of work for one value, however after a while
13
14 it is not that bad.
```

After this is done and we have the values we want in our data structure, we call the `boStage.Update` method with the structure as its parameter and the business object updates the database. Finally, we re-bind the data once again to ensure we have the latest data displayed.

The staff pages and task pages all operate in a similar manner to the project status page, the only main differenece being the data, and that there is only a DataGrid used in the information area.

Summary

By now you have a good understanding of how to create a distributed web application that can take advantage of many of the features in ASP.NET.

Due to space and time constraints, I could not cover all the source code in this application here. However, the full source is available at the New Riders web site. You can also play with this application at `www.project-inspiration.com/ProjectPal`.

VII

Appendixes

An Overview of .NET

NOW IT'S TIME TO LOOK AT the .NET framework architecture in more detail. This chapter contains a list of some features that the .NET framework has brought to the table. This appendix is only a brief overview. For more information on the .NET framework, see the list of information sources at the end of this appendix.

As you can see from the server software listed in this appendix, .NET is not restricted to a development technology. Microsoft has made a big commitment to the .NET technology and architecture. In fact, almost all the planned technologies being released from Microsoft over the next few years will use and enhance the .NET technology.

Multiple Development Platforms

No longer is Microsoft making you develop only for the mighty Windows platform. The .NET framework has been designed so that you can port it to other operating systems. It is available only for the Microsoft platforms. However, Microsoft has implied that the .NET framework can be easily ported to other platforms by other companies. There are rumors of Corel possibly doing a port of the .NET platform to Linux, but as of yet, this has not been publicly announced.

Multiple Development Languages

The .NET framework enables the developer to use a preferred language syntax to develop applications. This is good for the developer because the learning curve for developing a new technology should be substantially smaller. However, in reality, this might not be the case because the syntax of a language is only a small part of what is required to develop with it.

To elaborate a little more, if you know C++ and have been developing applications that deal with File Import and Export filters, does that mean that your experience is of use for developing a graphical information system? Probably not.

The ability to learn the syntax of a new language is potentially less taxing than learning a new Application Program Interface (API) or object library, which is where the real learning curve exists. Unfortunately for .NET, this can be quite large, depending on what kind of development experience the programmer has. However, the good news is that after a programmer has a good understanding of the .NET framework Base Class Libraries, developing in other .NET languages becomes simply a matter of understanding the languages syntax. This is possible because all the classes and their uses are identical.

The languages currently supported by .NET are as follows:

- C#
- Visual Basics .Net
- JScript.NET

Languages currently under development include the following:

- Perl.NET
- Python.NET
- COBOL.NET

One language that currently is not under development for .NET is Java. This is not surprising if you know about the industry fight between Sun and Microsoft over the past year or so. However, .NET will have a conversion utility called *JUMP* that will enable code to be converted to C# code from Java. Expect this to be a rough conversion, and expect to make a lot of manual changes to the code to get it to run as it would in Java.

As a final note, there has been a lot of concern over the differences between VB6 and Visual Basic .NET. This concern is due to the fact that the programming model of Visual Basic has changed, and so has the basic language syntax. They were changed so that Visual Basic .NET could utilize the .NET Base Class Libraries and share its code and classes with the other .NET languages.

You should expect other languages that are ported to .NET to have issues similar to those of Visual Basic. The issues are similar because the languages need additions to take advantage of the new technologies made available by the .NET framework.

.NET Base Class Libraries

This section provides brief overview of most of the Base Class Libraries in the .NET framework. Table A.1 does not show a brief overview.

Table A.1   **.NET Base Class Library Overview**

Namespace	Description
`System`	Provides fundamental classes and base classes that define commonly used value and reference data types, events and event handlers, interfaces, attributes, and processing exceptions.
`System.CodeDom`	Provides classes that can be used to represent the elements and structure of a source code document.
`System.CodeDom.Compiler`	Provides classes that can be used to manage the generation and compilation of source code in supported programming languages based on the structure of Code Document Object Model (CodeDOM) source code models.
`System.Collections`	Provides interfaces and classes that define various collections of objects, such as lists, queues, arrays, hash tables, and dictionaries.
`System.Collections.Specialized`	Provides specialized and strongly typed collections (for example, a linked list dictionary, a bit vector and collections that contain only strings).
`System.Data`	Provides classes that constitute the ADO.NET architecture. The ADO.NET architecture enables you to build components that efficiently manage data from multiple data sources.

continues ▶

Table A.1 **Continued**

Namespace	Description
System.Data.Common	Provides classes shared by the .NET data providers. A .NET data provider describes a collection of classes used to access a data source, such as a database, in the managed space.
System.Data.OleDb	Provides classes that support the OLE DB .NET data provider.
System.Data.SqlClient	Provides classes that support the SQL Server .NET data provider.
System.Data.SqlTypes	Provides classes for native data types within a SQL Server. These classes provide a safer, faster alternative to other data types.
System.Diagnostics	Provides classes that allow you to debug your application and to trace the execution of your code, as well as start system processes, read and write to event logs, and monitor system performance using performance counters.
System.DirectoryService	Provides easy access to the Active Directory from managed code.
System.Globalization	Provides classes that define culture-related information, including the language, the country/region, the calendars in use, the format patterns for dates, currency and numbers, and the sort order for strings.
System.IO	Provides types that allow synchronous and asynchronous reading from and writing to data streams and files.
System.IO.IsolatedStorage	Provides types that allow the creation and use of isolated stores. These stores allow the reading and writing of data in a way that is separated from the standard file system. Data is stored in compartments that are isolated by the current user and by the assembly the saving code exists in.
System.Messaging	Provides classes that allow you to connect to message queues on the network, send messages to queues, and receive or peek (read without removing) messages from queues.
System.Net	Provides a simple programming interface to many of the protocols found on the network today. The WebRequest and WebResponse classes form the basis of

Namespace	Description
	pluggable protocols—an implementation of network services that enable you to develop applications that use Internet resources without worrying about the specific details of the protocol used.
System.Net.Sockets	Provides a managed implementation of the Windows Sockets interface for developers that need to tightly control access to the network. Developers familiar with the Winsock API should have no problems developing applications using the Socket class.
System.Reflection	Provides classes and interfaces that provide a managed view of loaded types, methods, and fields, with the capability to dynamically create and invoke types.
System.Runtime.InteropServices	Provides a collection of classes useful for accessing COM objects, and native APIs from .NET. The types in the InteropServices namespace fall into the following areas of functionality: attributes, exceptions, managed definitions of COM types, wrappers, type converters, and the Marshal class.
System.Runtime.Remoting	Provides classes and interfaces that allow developers to create and configure tightly or loosely coupled distributed applications. Some of the more important classes of the System.Runtime.Remoting namespace are the RemotingConfiguration class, the RemotingServices class, and the ObjRef class.
System.Runtime.Serialization	Provides classes that can be used for serializing and deserializing objects. Serialization is the process of converting an object or a graph of objects into a linear sequence of bytes for either storage or transmission to another location. Deserialization is the process of taking in stored information and recreating objects from it.
System.Security	Provides the underlying structure of the common language runtime security system, including base classes for permissions.
System.Security.Cryptography	Provides cryptographic services, including secure encoding and decoding of data, as well as many other operations, such as hashing, random number generation, message authentication, and formation of digital signatures.

continues ▶

Table A.1 **Continued**

Namespace	Description
System.Security.Permissions	Defines classes that control access to operations and resources based on policy.
System.Security.Policy	Defines classes that use a configurable set of rules to determine what permissions to grant to code, based on the code's domain, user, and assembly.
System.Security.Principal	Defines a principal object that represents the security context under which code is running.
System.ServiceProcess	Provides classes that allow you to install and run services. Services are long-running executables that run without a user interface. They can be installed to run under a system account, which enables them to be started at computer reboot.
System.Text	Provides classes representing ASCII, Unicode, UTF-7, and UTF-8 character encodings; abstract base classes for converting blocks of characters to and from blocks of bytes; and a helper class that manipulates and formats String objects without creating intermediate instances of String.
System.Text.RegularExpressions	Provides classes that provide access to the .NET framework regular expression engine. The namespace provides regular expression functionality that can be used from any platform or language that runs within the Microsoft .NET framework.
System.Threading	Provides classes and interfaces that enable multi-threaded programming. This namespace includes a ThreadPool class that manages groups of threads, a Timer class that enables a delegate to be called after a specified amount of time, and a Mutex class for synchronizing mutually exclusive threads. System.Threading also provides classes for thread scheduling, wait notification, and deadlock resolution.
System.Timers	Provides the Timer component, which allows you to raise an event on a specified interval.
System.Web	Provides classes and interfaces that enable browser/server communication. This namespace includes the HTTPRequest class that provides extensive information about the current HTTP request, the HTTPResponse class that manages HTTP output to the client, and the HTTPServerUtility class that provides access to server-side utilities and processes. System.Web

Namespace	Description
	also includes classes for cookie manipulation, file transfer, exception information, and output cache control.
System.Web.Caching	Provides classes for caching frequently used resources on the server. This includes ASP.NET pages, XML Web Services, and user controls. Additionally, a cache dictionary is available for you to store frequently used resources, such as hash tables and other data structures.
System.Web.Configuration	Provides classes that are used to set up ASP.NET configuration.
System.Web.Security	Provides classes that are used to implement ASP.NET security in web server applications.
System.Web.Services	Provides classes that enable you to build and use XML Web Services. An *XML Web Service* is a programmable entity residing on a web server exposed using standard Internet protocols.
System.Web.Services.Description	Provides classes that enable you to publicly describe a web service using Service Description Language (WSDL).
System.Web.Services.Discovery	Provides classes that allow XML Web Service consumers to locate the available XML Web Services on a web server through a process called *discovery*.
System.Web.Services.Protocols	Provides classes that define the protocols used to transmit data across the wire during the communication between ASP.NET XML Web Service clients and XML Web Services.
System.Web.UI	Provides classes and interfaces that allow you to create controls and pages that will appear in your web applications as user interface on a web page. This namespace includes the Control class, which provides all controls, whether HTML, web, or user controls, with a common set of functionality. It also includes the Page control, which is generated automatically whenever a request is made for a page in your web application. Also provided are classes that provide the Web Forms Server Controls Data-Binding functionality, the capability to save the view state of a given control or page, as well as parsing functionality for both programmable and literal controls.

continues ▶

Table A.1 **Continued**

Namespace	Description
System.Web.UI.HtmlControls	Provides classes that allow you to create HTML server controls on a web page. HTML server controls run on the server and map directly to standard HTML tags supported by all browsers. This allows you to programmatically control the HTML elements on the web page.
System.Web.UI.WebControls	Provides classes that allow you to create web server controls on a web page. Web controls run on the server and include form controls, such as buttons and text boxes, as well as special purpose controls, such as a calendar. This allows you to programmatically control these elements on a web page. Web controls are more abstract than HTML controls. Their object model does not necessarily reflect HTML syntax.
System.Xml	Provides classes that provide standards-based support for processing XML.
System.Xml.Serialization	Provides classes that are used to serialize objects into XML format documents or streams.
System.Xml.Xpath	Provides the XPath parser and evaluation engine.
System.Xml.Xsl	Provides support for XSLT transformations.

Common Language Runtime (CLR)

The CLR is a core part of the .NET framework. The CLR makes it easy to design components and applications across multiple languages.

Components written in different languages can integrate and communicate with each other. This cross-language integration is possible because the individual language compilers follow the runtime rules and conditions for creating, persisting, and binding new data types.

The CLR can provide the following benefits:

- Performance increases
- A comprehensive set of standard language features
- Development language integration, especially cross-language inheritance
- Automatic memory management
- The capability to compile once and then run the compiled code on any computing platform that supports the runtime

Language Interoperability

The CLR can and is used by multiple languages. A few of these languages are listed in the following sections.

C#

C# is the new programming language developed by Microsoft specifically for the .NET framework. C# is very similar to both C++ and Java in syntax.

Visual Basic .NET

Visual Basic .NET is the new version of Visual Basic. Microsoft has made Visual Basic a more robust development language; however, this does have a slight negative impact because the language structure and syntax has changed. The changes occurred because of the new functionality and power provided by the .NET development framework.

JSCRIPT.NET

JSCRIPT.NET is a newer version of JScript that has language extensions for the .NET development framework.

ASP.NET

ASP.NET is a development framework that is designed for web development, and is covered in more detail throughout this book.

Common Type System (CTS)

As stated, the CLR enables multiple languages to use the same base functionality provided by the Base Class Libraries of the .NET framework. This is possible due to another technology inside the framework. This technology is CTS and it is responsible for providing development languages with a base collection of data types to ensure that all .NET-based languages can use and manipulate the same types of data.

.NET Server Products

Microsoft has a wide range of server products that are designed to support the use of the .NET framework for developing enterprise-wide distributed applications. The following sections describe these products.

Application Center 2000

Application Center 2000 is a deployment and management tool for managing groups of servers that are running a distributed application.

BizTalk Server 2000

BizTalk Server 2000 provides structure and tools for building successful e-commerce sites and communities. It provides tools that enable you to quickly build dynamic business processes by easily integrating applications.

Commerce Server 2000

Commerce Server 2000 is a complete e-commerce solution that provides extensive e-commerce, personalization, and decision support functionality for sites and communities. It enables you to target content to users based on profile information, to provide sophisticated reports on site visitors, and to create business-to-consumer (B2C) and business-to-business (B2B) sites.

Exchange Server 2000

Microsoft Exchange Server 2000 has been designed to meet the messaging and collaboration needs of businesses of all sizes.

Host Integration Server 2000

Host Integration Server 2000 integrates intranet/Internet and client/server technologies by utilizing legacy applications.

Internet Security and Acceleration Server 2000

Internet Security and Acceleration Server 2000 provides secure, fast, and manageable Internet services by integrating an extensible enterprise firewall and a high-performance web cache.

SQL Server 2000

SQL Server 2000 provides enterprise database management and analysis functionality with strong support for web standards solutions.

B

ASP.NET Common Object Reference

THIS APPENDIX IS A QUICK METHOD and property reference for the following commonly used ASP.NET classes and intrinsic objects:

- HttpContext
- HttpApplication
- HttpApplicationState
- HttpSessionState
- HttpRequest
- HttpResponse
- HttpServerUtility
- SMTPMail

HttpContext Object (Context Intrinsic Control)

The HttpContext provides access to the HTTP-specific context used by the web server to process web requests. See Table B.1 and B.2 for the HttpContext class properties and methods.

Table B.1   *HttpContext* **Class Properties**

Property	Description
AllErrors	An array (collection) of errors accumulated while processing a request.
Application	Retrieves a reference to the application object for the current HTTP request.
ApplicationInstance	Retrieves a reference to the application object for the current HTTP request.
Cache	Gets a reference to the Cache object for the current request.
Error	Gets the first error during request processing.
Handler	Retrieves or assigns a reference to the HttpHandler object for the current request.
IsCustomErrorEnabled	Are custom errors enabled for this request.
IsDebuggingEnabled	Is debugging enabled for this request.
Items	Retrieves a key-value collection that can be used to build up and share data between an HttpModule and an HttpHandler during a request.
Request	Retrieves a reference to the HttpResponse object for the current response.
Response	Retrieves a reference to the HttpResponse object for the current response.
Server	Gets a reference to the HttpServerUtility for the current request.
Session	Gets a reference to the HttpSessionState instance for the current request.
Timestamp	Gets the initial timestamp of the current request.
Trace	Retrieves a reference to the TraceContext object for the current response.
User	Gets or sets security information for the current HTTP request.

Table B.2   *HttpContext* **Class Methods**

Method	Description
AddError	Registers an error for the current request.
ClearError	Clears all errors for the current request.
GetConfig	Provides access to the settings in the Config.web configuration file.

The *HttpApplication* Class

The HttpApplication class is used to access application wide information within an ASP.NET web application or site. Table B.3 shows the HttpApplication class properties.

Table B.3   *Application* **Class Properties**

Property	Description
Application	Returns a reference to an HttpApplicationState bag instance. This is the object that is used in the global.asax and any ASP.NET Web Form; it is this collection that holds the Application scoped variables/objects/components.
Context	Provides access to an HttpContext object for the current instance of HttpApplication, which provides access to HTTP pipeline-module exposed objects (Request/Response, for example).
Modules	Provides access to a collection of all HttpModules configured for the current web application or site. You can find further information on HttpModules in Chapter 3, "Configuring ASP.NET Applications."
Request	Provides access to the HttpRequest object, which provides access to incoming HTTP request data. (You can find more information on this object later in this chapter.)
Response	Provides access to the HttpResponse, which allows transmission of HTTP response data to a client.
Server	Provides access to an ASP-compatible web server intrinsic object (HttpServerUtility class).
Session	Provides access to an HttpSessionState object.

Table B.4 shows the application methods for the HttpApplication class.

Table B.4   *HttpApplication* **Methods**

Method	Description
CompleteRequest()	Forces the current processing request to complete early.
Init()	Used to initialize HttpModule instance variables, and to set up event handlers in the current HttpApplication instance.
Dispose()	Used to clean up HttpModule instance variables.

Table B.5 shows the Application events for the HttpApplication class.

Table B.5 **Application Events**

Error()	Fires when the application encounters an error. It can be used to create or re-assign a new error handler for the web application.
BeginRequest()	Fires when the application receives a new request.
EndRequest()	Fires when the application completes a new request.
AuthenticateRequest()	Fires when the application receives a new request and it is ready for authentication.
AuthorizeRequest()	Fires when the application receives a new request and it is ready for authorization.

The *HttpApplicationState* Class (*Application Intrinsic* Object)

An instance of the HttpApplicationState class is created for each ASP.NET web application or site on the web server. This instance is then exposed via the Application property on the Context object, which is provided to all HttpModules of a web application or site during a web request. See Table B.6 for a description of the class properties. Table B.7 describes the HttpApplicationState class methods.

Table B.6 *HttpApplicationState* Class Properties

Property	Description
AllKeys	Provides access to the keys in the HttpApplicationState collection.
Contents	Provides a reference to the HttpApplicationState object.
Count	Overridden—Gets the number of objects in the HttpApplicationState collection.
Item	Gets access to an object in an HttpApplicationState collection. This property is overloaded to allow access to an object by name or numerical index.
Keys	Returns a NameObjectCollectionBase. KeysCollection instance in the HttpApplicationState collection.
StaticObjects	Returns objects declared via an <object runat=server></object> tag within the ASP.NET application.

Table B.7 *HttpApplicationState* **Class Methods**

Method	Description
Add	Adds a new object to the `HttpApplicationState` collection.
Clear	Removes all objects from an `HttpApplicationState` collection.
Get	Gets an `HttpApplicationState` object by name or index.
GetEnumerator	Returns an enumerator that can iterate through the `NameObjectCollectionBase`.
GetKey	Gets an `HttpApplicationState` object name/key by index.
Lock	Locks access to an `HttpApplicationState` variable to access synchronization.
Remove	Removes an object from the `HttpApplicationState` collection.
RemoveAll	Removes all objects from an `HttpApplicationState` collection.
Set	Updates the value of an object in an `HttpApplicationState` collection.
UnLock	Unlocks access to an `HttpApplicationState` variable for access synchronization.

The *HttpSessionState* **Class** (*Session Intrinsic* **Object**)

An instance of the `HttpSessionState` class is created for each ASP.NET web application or site user. This instance is then exposed via the `Session` property on the `Context` object provided to all `HttpModules` of a web application or site during a web request. Table B.8 describes the `HttpSessionState` class properties.

Table B.8 *HttpSessionState* **Class Properties**

Method	Description
CodePage	Gets or sets the code page identifier for the current session.
Contents	Gets a reference to the current session state object.
Count	Gets the number of items in the session state collection.
IsCookieless	Gets a value indicating whether the session is managed using a cookieless session.
IsNewSession	Gets a value indicating whether the session has been created with the current request.
IsReadOnly	Gets a value indicating whether the session is read-only.
Item	Gets or sets individual session values.
Keys	Gets a collection of all session keys.

continues ▶

Table B.8 **Continued**

Method	Description
LCID	Gets or sets the locale identifier (LCID) of the current session.
Mode	Gets the current session state mode.
SessionID	Gets the unique session ID used to identify a session.
StaticObjects	Gets a collection of objects declared by <object runat=server> tags within the ASPX application file global.asax.
Timeout	Gets and sets the timeout period (in minutes) allowed between requests before the session state provider terminates the session.

Table B.9 shows the HttpSessionState class methods.

Table B.9 *HttpSessionState* **Class Methods**

Method	Description
Abandon	Cancels the current session.
Add	Adds a new item to the session state.
Clear	Clears all values from session state.
CopyTo	Copies the collection of session state values to a one-dimensional array, starting at the specified index of the array.
GetEnumerator	Gets an enumerator of all session state values in the current session.
Remove	Deletes an item from the session state collection.
RemoveAll	Clears all session state values.

The *HttpRequest* Class (*Request Intrinsic* Object)

When a client navigates to a web page on a web server, it is called a *request* because the user is technically requesting that the web server send the page to their browser for consumption. The Request object is used to get information from a web server and the client browser. Table B.10 describes the HttpRequest class properties.

Table B.10 *HttpRequest* **Class Properties**

Property	Description
AcceptTypes	Returns a string array of client-supported Multipurpose Internet Mail Extensions (MIME) accept types. This property is read-only.
ApplicationPath	Returns the current application's virtual directory path on the server.
Browser	Provides information about incoming client's browser capabilities.
ClientCertificate	Returns information on the current request's client-security certificate.
ContentEncoding	Indicates the character set of data supplied by the client. This property is read-only.
ContentType	Indicates the MIME content type of the incoming request. This property is read-only.
Cookies	Returns a collection of client's cookie variables.
FilePath	Indicates the virtual path of the current request. This property is read-only.
Files	Returns the collection of client-uploaded files.
Form	Returns a collection of Form variables.
HttpMethod	Indicates the HTTP data transfer method used by the client (GET, POST). This property is read-only.
InputStream	Provides access to the raw contents of the incoming HTTP entity body.
IsAuthenticated	Indicates whether the HTTP connection is authenticated.
IsSecureConnection	Indicates whether the HTTP connection is secure (that is, HTTP). This property is read-only.
Path	Indicates the virtual path of the current request. This property is read-only.
QueryString	Gets the collection of QueryString variables.
RequestType	Indicates the HTTP data transfer method used by client (GET, POST).
ServerVariables	Returns a collection of web server variables.
TotalBytes	Returns the number of bytes in the current input stream.
Url	Returns information regarding the URL of the current request.
UrlReferrer	Returns information regarding the URL of the client's previous request, which is linked to the current URL.
UserAgent	Returns the client browser's raw User Agent string.
UserHostAddress	Returns the IP host address of the remote client.
UserHostName	Returns the DNS name of the remote client.
UserLanguages	Returns a sorted array of client-language preferences.

Table B.11 shows the `HttpRequest` class methods.

Table B.11 *HttpRequest* **Class Methods**

Method	Description
`BinaryRead(int32 numBytes)`	Performs a binary read of a specified number of bytes from the current input stream.
`MapImageCoordinates(String imageFieldName)`	Maps an incoming image field form parameter into x/y coordinate values.
`MapPath(String VirtualPath)`	Maps a virtual path (in requested URL) to physical path on a server for the current request.
`SaveAs(String filename, Boolean incHeaders)`	Saves an HTTP request to disk.

The *HttpResponse* Class (Response *Intrinsic* Object)

The `Request` object is used to send information from web server to the client browser. Table B.12 describes the `HttpResponse` class properties. Table B.13 describes the `HttpResponse` class methods.

Table B.12 *Response* **Class Properties**

Property	Description
`Buffer`	Gets or sets a boolean that switches buffering on or off.
`BufferOutput`	Gets or sets a value indicating whether HTTP output is buffered.
`Cache`	Returns the caching semantics of the web page (expiration time, privacy, and vary clauses).
`CacheControl`	Sets the `CacheControl` HTTP header to Public or Private.
`Charset`	Gets or sets the output character set for HTTP output.
`ContentEncoding`	Gets or sets the HTTP character set of output.
`ContentType`	Gets or sets the HTTP MIME type of output.
`Cookies`	Gets the HttpCookie collection sent by the current response.
`Expires`	Gets or sets the Expires setting on the client.
`IsClientConnected`	Gets a value indicating whether the client is still connected to the server.
`Output`	Enables custom output to the outgoing HTTP content body.
`OutputStream`	Enables binary output to the outgoing HTTP content body.

Property	Description
StatusCode	Gets or sets the HTTP status code of output returned to client.
StatusDescription	Gets or sets the HTTP status string of output returned to the client.
SuppressContent	Gets or sets a value indicating that HTTP content will not be sent to client.

Table B.13 *HttpRequest* **Class Methods**

Method	Description
AppendToLog(String logEntry)	Adds custom log information to the IIS log file.
BinaryWrite(byte[] byteArray)	Writes a string of binary characters to the HTTP output stream.
Clear()	Clears all headers and content output from the buffer stream.
ClearContent()	Clears all the content from the buffer stream.
ClearHeaders()	Clears all headers from the buffer stream.
Close()	Closes the socket connection to a client.
End()	Sends all currently buffered output to the client, and then closes the socket connection.
Flush()	Sends all currently buffered output to the client.
Pics(String PicsValue)	Appends a Platform for Internet Content Selection (PICS) label HTTP header to the output stream.
Redirect(String newUrl)	Redirects a client to a new URL.
SetCookie(HttpCookie)	Sets the value of a cookie in the cookie collection.
Write(String outputString)	Writes values to an HTTP output content stream.
WriteFile(Filename)	Writes a file directly to an HTTP content output stream.

The *Server* Class (*HttpServerUtility*)

The HttpServerUtility object is pretty much the same as the ASP server object. It provides access to useful server-side tools for use in an ASP.NET application. A brief class overview is shown in Tables B.14 and B.15.

Table B.14   *HttpServerUtility* **Class Properties**

Property	Description
MachineName	Returns the web server's name.
ScriptTimeout	Requests timeout for server-side scripts in seconds.

Table B.15   *HttpServerUtility* **Class Methods**

Method	Description
CreateObject(String progid)	Instantiates a COM object identified via a progid.
Execute	Executes another web page on the server and holds execution of the current page until the server has finished processing a new page on the server.
GetLastError	Returns the last recorded exception in the current web application or site.
HtmlEncode	HTML encodes a string and returns the encoded string.
HtmlDecode	HTML decodes a string and returns the decoded string.
Mappath	Maps a virtual path to a physical path.
Transfer	Terminates execution of the current page and begins execution of a new request using the supplied URL path.
UrlEncode	URL decodes a string.
UrlDecode	URL decodes a string.
UrlPathEncode	URL encodes a path portion of a URL string and returns the encoded string.

SMTPMail API

This API is made up of three classes:

- **SMTPMail class**—Used to send the email.
- **SMTPMessage class**—Used to create an email message.
- **SMTPAttachement class**—Used to represent a file-based attachment to a message.

The *SMTPMail* Class

The SMTPMail class provides the capability to send email and email attachments using the SMTPMail service built into Microsoft Windows 2000.

The SMTPMail class property is SmtpServer, which gets or sets the name of the local SMTP server being used.

The SMTPMail class method is Send, which is used to send a MailMessage object to a previously defined SMTPmail server.

The *MailMessage* Class

This class is used to construct and configure email messages for use with the SMTPMail class. Table B.16 shows the MailMessage class properties.

Table B.16   *MailMessage* **Class Properties**

Property	Description
Attachments	Specifies the list of attachments, which is transmitted with the message.
Bcc	Gets or sets a semicolon-delimited list of email addresses that receive a Blind Carbon Copy (BCC) of the email message.
Body	Gets or sets the body of the email message.
BodyEncoding	Gets or sets the encoding type of the email body.
BodyFormat	Gets or sets the content type of the email body.
Cc	Gets or sets a semicolon-delimited list of email addresses that receive a Carbon Copy (CC) of the email message.
From	Gets or sets the email address of the sender.
Headers	Specifies the custom headers that are transmitted with the email message.
Priority	Gets or sets the priority of the email message.
Subject	Gets or sets the subject line of the email message.
To	Gets or sets the email address of the recipient.
UrlContentBase	Gets or sets the URL base of all relative URL's used within the HTML encoded body.

The *MailAttachment* Class

This class provides the capability to construct an email attachment for use with a MailMessage object. Table B.17 shows the MailAttachment class properties.

Table B.17 *MailAttachment* **Class Properties**

Property	Description
Encoding	Indicates the type of encoding used to encode the email attachment.
Filename	Indicates the name of the file to attach to the email.

C

ADO Common Object Reference

T HE FOLLOWING SECTIONS DETAIL THE SYNTAX of ADO.NET common. I am showing only the most commonly used properties and methods of each class. For more information on the use of these objects, see Chapter 6, "Using ADO.NET in ASP.NET Applications."

DataSet Object

This object represents an in-memory collection of data. This data is generally in the form of one or more tables of information from a database (see Tables C.1, C.2, and C.3).

Table C.1 **Properties of the *DataSet* Object**

Property	Description
CaseSensitive	The Case Sensitivity flag is used in string comparisons. If set to true, all comparisons take character case into account; otherwise, they do not.
DataSetName	Gets or sets the name of the DataSet.
DefaultViewManager	Gets a default DataView object for the DataSet.
EnforceConstraints	Gets or sets the Enforce Contraints flag.
ExtendedProperties	Gets or sets extended properties for the DataSet. These are developer-provided properties created at runtime.
HasErrors	Returns true if the tables that the DataSet is based on have any errors.

continues ▶

Table C.1 **Continued**

Property	Description
Locale	Gets or sets the locale of the DataSet through a CultureInfo object. (See Chapter 13, "Localizing and Globalizing ASP.NET Applications," for more information on this.)
Namespace	Gets or sets an XML namespace for the DataSet.(See Chapter 7, "Using XML in ASP.NET Applications" for more information on this.)
Prefix	Gets or sets an XML prefix for the DataSet. (See Chapter 7 for more information on this.)
Relations	Returns a collection of Relation objects belonging to the DataSet.
Tables	Returns a collection of tables belonging to the DataSet.

Table C.2 **Methods of the *DataSet* Object**

Method	Description
AcceptChanges	Commits all changes made to the DataSet since it was last loaded or had the AcceptChanges method called.
Clear	Clears all data in all tables of the DataSet.
Clone	Creates a Copy of the existing DataSet object's structure, including all properties and collections.
Copy	Creates a full copy of the DataSet structure by first cloning the structure and then by copying the data into the newly-cloned structure.
GetChanges	Returns a DataSet containing all changes since the last AcceptChanges method call.
GetXML	Returns the DataSet rendered as XML.
GetXMLSchema	Returns the XML schema for the DataSet.
HasChanges	Returns true if changes have been made to the DataSet since the last call to the AcceptChanges method.
Merge	Merges one DataSet with another.
ReadXML	Reads an XML file into a DataSet. (See Chapter 7 for more information on this.)
ReadXMLSchema	Reads an XML schema into the DataSet. (See Chapter 7 for more information on this.)

Method	Description
RejectChanges	Performs a rollback for any changes made to a DataSet since the last call to AcceptChanges.
WriteXML	Writes an XML file with the structure and data from a DataSet.
WriteXMLSchema	Writes an XML schema for the DataSet. (See Chapter 7 for more information on this.)

Table C.3   **Events of the *DataSet* Object**

Event	Description
MergeFailed	Event fired when a MergeProcess fails.
PropertyChanged	Event fired when a property has changed in the DataSet.

DataTable Object

The DataTable object contains all information on a Table, which is contained in a DataSet object (see Tables C.4, C.5, and C.6).

Table C.4   **Properties of the *DataTable* Object**

Property	Description
CaseSensitive	Case Sensitivity flag.
ChildRelations	Returns a collection of Relation objects belonging to the DataTable.
Columns	Returns the Columns collection for the DataTable.
Constraints	Returns the Constraints collection for the DataTable.
DataSet	Returns a reference to the DataSet to which the DataTable belongs.
DefaultView	Gets a default DataView object for the DataTable.
Extended Properties	Gets or sets extended properties for the DataSet. These are developer-provided properties created at runtime.
HasErrors	Returns true if any of the tables in the DataSet on which this DataTable is based have any errors.
Locale	Gets or sets the locale of the DataSet through a CultureInfo object. (See Chapter 13 for more information on this.)
MimimumCapacity	Gets or sets the initial starting capacity of the DataTable in rows.

continues ▶

Table C.4 **Continued**

Property	Description
NameSpace	Gets or sets an XML namespace for the DataSet. (See Chapter 7 for more information on this.)
ParentRelations	Returns a collection of Relation objects belonging to the DataTable.
Prefix	Gets or sets an XML prefix for the DataSet. (See Chapter 7 for more information on this.)
PrimaryKey	Gets or sets an array of columns that make up the primary key of the DataTable.
Rows	Returns a collection of all data rows in the DataTable.
TableName	Gets or sets the name of the DataTable.

Table C.5 **Methods of the *DataTable* Object**

Method	Description
AcceptChanges	Commits all changes made to the DataTable since it was last loaded or had the AcceptChanges method called.
Clear	Clears all data in all tables of the DataTable.
Clone	Creates a clone copy of the DataTable structure, including all properties and collections, but no data.
Compute	Returns the result of an aggregate function applied against the data in the DataTable.
Copy	Creates a full copy of the DataTable structure, including all properties, collections, and data.
GetChanges	Returns a DataTable containing all changes since the last AcceptChanges method call.
GetErrors	Returns an array of DataTable objects containing all errors since the last AcceptChanges method call.
ImportRow	Imports a row from another DataTable
LoadDataRow	Locates and updates a specific row in the DataTable. If a matching row is not located, then a new row is created using the passed values.
NewRow	Creates a new row in the DataTable.
RejectChanges	Performs a rollback for any changes made to a DataTable since the last call to AcceptChanges.
Select	Returns a collection of rows from the DataTable based on the passed Select statement.

Table C.6 **Events of the *DataTable* Object**

Event	Description
ColumnChanged	This event is raised when a column has been changed in the DataTable.
ColumnChanging	This event is raised when a column is being changed in the DataTable.
PropertyChanged	This event is raised when a property has changed in the DataTable.
RowChanged	This event is raised when a row has changed in the DataTable.
RowChanging	This event is raised when a row is being changed in the DataTable.
RowDeleted	This event is raised when a row has been deleted from the DataTable.
RowDeleting	This event is raised when a row is being deleted from the DataTable.

DataColumn Object

The DataColumn object represents the column information of a Table (see Table C.7).

Table C.7 **Properties of the *DataColumn* Object**

Property	Description
AllowDBNull	Gets or sets a value defining whether Null values are allowed in this DataColumn.
AutoIncrement	Gets or sets a value defining whether this DataColumn is to be auto incremented.
AutoIncrementSeed	Gets or sets the AutoIncrement Initial value.
AutoIncrementStep	Gets or sets the AutoIncrement step size. It defaults to 1.
Caption	Gets or sets the caption of the DataColumn used by some web controls.
ColumnMapping	Gets or sets the mapping type for the DataColumn. The values can be: None, Element, Attribute, Text, and Internal.
ColumnName	Gets or sets the name of the DataColumn.
DataType	The type of data to store in the DataColumn.
DefaultValue	The default value for the DataColumn.

continues ▶

Table C.7 **Continued**

Property	Description
Expression	Defines an expression to be evaluated for the DataColumn value.
ExtendedProperties	Gets or sets extended properties for the DataColumn. These are developer-provided properties created at runtime.
Namespace	Gets or sets an XML namespace for the DataColumn. (See Chapter 7 for more information on this.)
Ordinal	Gets the ordinal position of the column in the DataColumnCollection collection.
Prefix	Gets or sets an XML prefix for the DataSet. (See Chapter 7 for more information on this.)
ReadOnly	Gets or sets the ReadOnly flag for DataColumn.
Table	Returns a reference of the DataTable to which the DataColumn belongs.
Unique	Gets or sets the Unique flag for the DataColumn. This is used to set a Unique value constraint on any data stored in this column.

DataRow Class

The DataRow object represents a row of information in a table (see Tables C.8 and C.9).

Table C.8 **Properties of the *DataRow* Object**

Property	Description
HasErrors	Returns true if the DataRow has any errors.
Item	Gets or sets the Data value in a specified DataColumn.
ItemArray	Gets or sets the data for DataRow through an array of values.
RowError	Gets or sets a user-defined error message for the DataRow.
RowState	Returns the current state of the DataRow. The state can have any of the following values: • **Detached**—The DataRow is created but is not part of a DataRowCollection. • **Added**—The DataRow has been added to a DataTable row's collection, but AcceptChanges has not been called yet. • **Deleted**—The DataRow has been deleted from a DataTable row's collection, but AcceptChanges has not been called yet.

Property	Description
	■ **Modified**—Tthe DataRow has been modified or updated, but AcceptChanges has not been called yet.
	■ **Unchanged**—No changes have been made to DataRow since the last time AcceptChanges was called for the DataRow.
Table	Returns a reference of the DataTable to which the DataRow belongs.

Table C.9 **Methods of the *DataRow* Object**

Method	Description
AcceptChanges	Commits all changes made to the DataTable since it was last loaded or had the AcceptChanges method called.
BeginEdit	Puts the DataRow into edit mode, which enables changes to be made.
CancelEdit	Cancels the DataRow's edit mode and rolls back all changes.
ClearErrors	Clears all errors for the DataRow.
Delete	Deletes the DataRow.
EndEdit	Completes the DataRow edit process. It is called implicitly by the AcceptChanges method.
GetChildRows	Gets a collection of DataRows for the child side of a relation for the DataRow if one exists.
GetColumnError	Returns an error message for a DataColumn.
GetColumnsInError	Returns an array of DataColumns that have errors.
GetParentRow	Gets a DataRow for the parent side of a relation for the DataRow if one exists.
GetParentRows	Gets a collection of DataRows for the parent side of a relation for the DataRow if one exists.
HasVersion	Returns the DataRow version used to check for data changes. Possible values are Default, Original, Current, and Proposed.
IsNull	Returns true if the specified DataColumn contains a Null value.
RejectChanges	Performs a rollback for any changes made to a DataRow since the last call to AcceptChanges.
SetColumnError	Sets an error description for a DataColumn.
SetParentRow	Sets a new ParentRow for a DataRow.

DataRelation Object

The DataRelation Object is used to create and maintain relationships between data in a DataSet (see Tables C.10 and C.11).

Table C.10 **Properties of the *DataRelation* Object**

Property	Description
ChildColumns	Returns a collection of child DataColumns in the DataRelation.
ChildKeyConstraint	Returns a foreign key constraint of the DataRelation.
ChildTable	Returns a DataTable for the child of the DataRelation.
DataSet	Returns the DataSet to which the DataRelation belongs.
ExtendedProperties	Gets or sets Extended properties for the DataRelation. These are developer-provided properties that are created at runtime.
Nested	Gets or sets a value defining whether the DataRelation is nested.
ParentColumns	Returns a collection of parent DataColumns in the DataRelation.
ParentKeyConstraint	Returns the (Primary Key or Unique Key) constraint of the DataRelation.
ParentTable	Returns a DataTable for the parent of the DataRelation.
RelationName	Gets or sets the name of the DataRelation.

Table C.11 **Events of the *DataRelation* Object**

Event	Description
PropertyChanged	Event fired when a property has changed in the DataRelation.

DataView Object

The DataView object is used to create a temporary view of data from a DataTable. You need to use a DataView to bind data to most web controls. (See Tables C.12, C.13, and C.14.)

Table C.12 **Properties of the *DataView* Object**

Property	Description
AllowDelete	Gets or sets the Allow Deletion flag for the DataView.
AllowEdit	Gets or sets the Allow Edit flag for the DataView.
AllowNew	Gets or sets the Allow New flag for the DataView.

Property	Description
ApplyDefaultSort	Gets or sets the ApplyDefaultSort flag for the DataView. This is used to apply default sorting to the DataView's data.
Item	Returns a DataRowView from the DataView.
RowFilter	Gets, sets, or clears the filter used to determine what data in the DataTable is shown in the DataView.
RowStateFilter	Applies the passed state filter to the DataView. Possible states on which to filter are None, Unchanged, Added, Deleted, ModifiedCurrent, ModifiedOriginal, OriginalRows, and CurrentRows.
Sort	Gets or sets the sort order of the DataView.
Table	Returns the DataTable that the DataView uses.

Table C.13 **Methods of the *DataView* Object**

Method	Description
AddNew	Adds a new DataRowView to the DataView.
Delete	Deletes a DataRowView from the DataView at the specified index.
Find	Locates a DataRowView in the DataView and then returns its index.
GetEnumerator	Returns an Enumerator object for the DataView.

Table C.14 **Events of the *DataView* Object**

Event	Description
ListChanged	Event fired when the DataRowView collection is changed. (This is accessed through the Item property of the Enumerator object.)
PropertyChanged	Event fired when a property has changed in the DataView.

DataRowView Class

The DataRowView class holds all the row data for a DataView. (See Tables C.15 and C.16.)

Table C.15 **Properties of the *DataRow* Object**

Property	Description
DataView	Returns the DataView to the DataRowView to which it belongs.
IsEdit	Returns true if the DataRowView is in edit mode.

continues ▶

Table C.15 **Continued**

Property	Description
IsNew	Returns true if the DataRow associated with the DataRowView was added and hasn't been committed to the DataSet.
Item	Gets or sets the value in the specified DataColumn.
Row	Returns the DataRow being viewed.
RowVersion	Returns the DataRow version used to check for concurrent data changes. Possible values are Default, Original, Current, and Proposed.

Table C.16 **Methods of the *DataRow* Object**

Method	Description
BeginEdit	Puts the DataRow into edit mode.
CancelEdit	Cancels the DataRow's edit mode and rolls back all changes.
Delete	Deletes the DataRow.
EndEdit	Completes the DataRow edit process. It is called implicitly by the AcceptChanges method.

OLEDBDATA Objects

OLEDB objects are used to interface with OLEDB–compatible data sources.

OLEDBAdapter Object

The OLEDBAdapter class represents a set of OLEDBCommands and a OLEDBConnection, which are used to populate a DataSet. (See Tables C.17, C.18, and C.19.)

Table C.17 **Properties of the *OLEDBAdapter* Object**

Property	Description
DeleteCommand	Gets or sets a SQL statement used to delete rows from a DataSet.
InsertCommand	Gets or sets a SQL statement used to insert new rows into a DataSet.
SelectCommand	Gets or sets a SQL statement used to retrieve rows from a DataSet.
UpdateCommand	Gets or sets a SQL statement used to update rows in a DataSet.

Table C.18 **Methods of the *OLEDBAdapter* Object**

Method	Description
Fill	Updates the DataSet object to reflect the data in the data source.
Update	Updates the data source with the changes made in the DataSet.

Table C.19 **Events of the *OLEDBAdapter* Object**

Event	Description
RowUpdated	Event fired after a row has been updated in the original data source.
RowUpdating	Event fired during a row update in the original data source.

OLEDBDataReader Object

The OLEDBDataReader class is used to sequentially read data from a data source one field at a time. (See Tables C.20 and C.21.)

Table C.20 **Properties of the *OLEDBDataReader* Object**

Property	Description
FieldCount	Returns the number of columns for the current row.
IsClosed	Returns true if the OLEDBDataReader is closed.
Item	Returns the value of a column in its native format.
RecordsAffected	Returns the total number of rows affected by the DataReader.

Table C.21 **Methods of the *OLEDBDataReader* Object**

Method	Description
Close	Closes the OLEDBDataReader.
GetValue	Returns the value of a specified column ordinal.
GetValues	Returns an array of all columns.
IsDBNull	Returns true if the column contains a Null value.
NextResult	Moves the DataReader to the next result set in batch SQL statements.
Read	Moves the OLEDBDataReader onto the next row.

OLEDBConnection Object

The OLEDBConnection object is used to represent a connection to an OLEDB data source. (See Tables C.22, C.23, and C.24.)

Table C.22 **Properties of the *OLEDBConnection* Object**

Property	Description
ConnectionString	Gets or sets the database connection string.
ConnectionTimeout	Gets or sets a connection timeout.
Database	Returns the name of the connection database.
DataSource	Gets or sets the name of the connection data source.
Provider	Gets or sets the name of the database provider.
State	Returns the current state of the connection. Possible values are Broken, Closed, Connecting, Executing, Fetching, and Open.

Table C.23 **Methods of the *OLEDBConnection* Object**

Method	Description
BeginTransaction	Initiates a database transaction and returns an OLEDBTransaction object.
Close	Closes a connection with a data source.
CreateCommand	Creates and returns an OLEDBCommand object.
Open	Opens a connection with a data source.

Table C.24 **Events of the *OLEDBConnection* Object**

Event	Description
InfoMessage	Event fired when the provider sends an error or status message.
StateChange	Event fired when the connection state changes.

OLEDBCommand Object

The OLEDBCommand object is used to represent a SQL statement. (See Tables C.25 and C.26.)

Table C.25 **Properties of the *OLEDBCommand* Object**

Property	Description
CommandText	Gets or sets the SQL statement to use the specific provider-based syntax for execution at the data source.
CommandTimeout	Gets or sets the timeout for the passed OLEDBCommand.
CommandType	Defines how the OLEDBCommand is processed. Possible types are StoredProcedure, CommandText and TableDirect.
Connection	Gets or sets the connection to be used for the OLEDBCommand. This is done through an OLEDBConnection object.
Parameters	Returns the OLEDBParameters collection, which holds a list of parameters used for a stored procedure.
UpdatedRowSource	Gets or sets how command results are applied to the DataRow when used by the Update method of the OLEDBDataAdapter.

Table C.26 **Methods of the *OLEDBCommand* Object**

Method	Description
CreateParameter	Creates a parameter and adds it to the OLEDBParameters collection.
ExecuteNonQuery	Executes an OLEDBCommand that returns the number of rows affected by the query; however, it does not return any rows.
ExecuteReader	Executes the OLEDBCommand and returns an OLEDBDataReader object.
ExecuteScalar	Executes the OLEDBCommand and returns the first column of the first row from the result set returned by the OLEDBCommand.
Prepare	Creates a compiled version of the OLEDBCommand on the data source as a stored procedure.

OLEDBTransaction Object

The OLEDBTransaction object is used to manage database transaction processing functionality for an OLEDB data source. (See Table C.27.)

Table C.27 **Methods of the *OLEDBTransaction* Object**

Methods	Description
Begin	Begins a new transaction.
Commit	Commits the transaction to the data source.
RollBack	Rolls back all changes to the data source since the Begin method.

OLEDBError Object

The OLEDBError object is used to keep track of any errors that occur with the provider and data source of an OLEDBConnection. (See Table C.28.)

Table C.28 **Properties of the *OLEDBError* Object**

Property	Description
Message	Gives a brief description of the error message.
NativeError	A database provider-generated error message.
Source	Returns the name of the OLEDB provider that caused the error.
SQLState	Returns the five-character error code for an ANSI SQL database error.

SQLData... Objects

The SQLData... objects are a collection of optimized data access and manipulation objects designed for working with SQL Server databases.

SQLDataAdapter Object

The SQLDataAdapter object represents a set of SQLDataCommands and a SQLDataConnection, which are used to manipulate data. (See Tables C.29, C.30, and C.31.)

Table C.29 **Properties of the *SQLDataAdapter* Object**

Property	Description
DeleteCommand	Gets or sets a SQL statement used to delete rows from a DataSet.
InsertCommand	Gets or sets a SQL statement used to insert rows of data into a DataSet.
SelectCommand	Gets or sets a SQL statement used to retrieve rows from a DataSet.
UpdateCommand	Gets or sets a SQL statement used to update rows in a DataSet.

Table C.30 **Methods of the *SQLDataAdapter* Object**

Method	Description
Fill	Used to add, update, or fill data in a DataSet from the original data source.
Update	Updates the DataSource with the changes made in the DataSet.

Table C.31 **Events of the *SQLDataAdapter* Object**

Event	Description
RowUpdated	Event fired after a row has been updated in the original data source.
RowUpdating	Event fired during a row update in the original data source.

SQLDataReader Object

The SQLDataReader object is used to sequentially read data from a data source, one field at a time (see Tables C.32 and C.33).

Table C.32 **Properties of the *SQLDataReader* Object**

Property	Description
FieldCount	Returns the number of columns for the current row.
IsClosed	Returns true if the SQLDataReader object is closed.
Item	Returns the value of a column.
RecordsAffected	Returns the total number of rows affected by the SQLDataReader.

Table C.33 **Methods of the *SQLDataReader* Object**

Method	Description
Close	Closes the SQLDataReader.
GetValue	Returns the value of a specified column ordinal.
GetValues	Returns an array of all columns.
IsDBNull	Returns true if the column contains a Null value.
NextResult	Moves the Data Reader to the next result set in batch SQL statements.
Read	Moves the SQLDataReader onto the next row.

SQLDataConnection Object

The SQLDataConnection object class is used to represent a connection to a SQL Server data source (see Tables C.34, C.35, and C.36).

Table C.34 **Properties of the *SQLDataConnection* Object**

Property	Description
ConnectionString	Gets or sets the database connection string.
ConnectionTimeout	Gets or sets a connection timeout.
Database	Returns the name of the database to which the SQLDataConnection object is connected.
DataSource	Gets or sets the name of the connection data source.
ServerVersion	Returns the version of SQL Server being used as a string.
State	Returns the current state of the connection. Possible values are Broken, Closed, Connecting, Executing, Fetching, and Open.

Table C.35 **Methods of the *SQLDataConnection* Object**

Method	Description
BeginTransaction	Initiates a new database transaction and returns a SQLTransaction object.
Close	Closes a connection with a data source.
CreateCommand	Creates and returns a SQLCommand object.
Open	Opens a connection with a data source.

Table C.36 **Events of the *SQLDataConnection* Object**

Event	Description
InfoMessage	Event fired when the provider sends an error or status message.
StateChange	Event fired when the connection state changes.

SQLDataCommand Class

The SQLDataCommand class is used to represent a SQL statement (see Tables C.37, C.38, and C.39).

Table C.37 **Properties of the *SQLDataCommand* Object**

Property	Description
CommandText	Gets or sets the SQL statement to use or the specific provider-based syntax to use for execution at the data source.
CommandTimeout	Gets or sets the timeout for the passed SQL command.

Property	Description
CommandType	Defines how the SQL command is processed. Possible types are StoredProcedure, CommandText, and TableDirect.
Connection	Gets or sets the connection to be used for the SQL that will be processed by the SQLDataCommand object.
Parameters	Returns the SQLDBParameters collection, which holds a list of parameters used for a stored procedure.
UpdatedRowSource	Gets or sets how command results are applied to the DataRow when used by the Update method of the SQLDataAdapter.

Table C.38 **Methods of the *SQLDataCommand* Object**

Method	Description
Cancel	Cancels the execution of the SQL.
CreateParameter	Creates a parameter and adds it to the SQLParameters collection.
ExecuteNonQuery	Executes a SQL that does not return any rows.
ExecuteReader	Executes the SQL and returns a SQLDataReader object.
ExecuteScalar	Executes the SQL and returns the first column of the first row from the result set returned by the SQLDBCommand.
Prepare	Creates a compiled version of the SQL on the data source.

Table C.39 **Properties of the *SQLDataCommand* Object**

Event	Description
InfoMessage	Event fired when the provider sends an error or status message.
StateChange	Event fired when the connection state changes.

SQLTransaction Object

The SQLTransaction object is used to explicitly manage data transaction management (see Table C.40).

Table C.40 **Methods of the *SQLTransaction* Object**

Methods	Description
Commit	Commits the transaction to the data source.
RollBack	Rolls back all changes to the data source since the Begin method or rolls back all changes since a save point.
Save	Saves a point in a transaction to which to rollback.

SQLError Object

The sQLError object is used to retrieve information on an error that has occurred during a process on the data provider. (See Table C.41.)

Table C.41 **Properties of the *SQLError* Object**

Property	Description
Class	Returns the numeric level of error returned from the SQL Server.
LineNumber	Returns the Transact-SQL line number of the stored procedure that caused an error.
Message	Returns the error message as a string value.
Number	Returns the error number.
Procedure	Returns the name of the stored procedure that caused an error.
Server	Returns the name of the database server that caused the error.
Source	Returns the name of the data provider that caused the error.
State	Returns the error state code.

D

HTML Server Control Reference

In the following sections, I detail the syntax of the HTML server-side controls. Note that I am showing only the most commonly used properties and methods of each class. For more information on the use of these controls, see Chapter 4, "Web Form-Based Development," and Chapter 15, "Creating User and Custom Controls for ASP.NET."

An HTML server-side control is created in one of two ways:

- By using the RUNAT="server" attribute/value pair in the control tag in the .aspx and .ascx files
- By creating the control programmatically in a .NET code behind a form file

HtmlForm Object—*<form>* Element

This defines an HTML form. The values of controls within the form are posted to the server when the form is submitted. Table D.1 lists the properties of the HtmlForm object, and Table D.2 lists the methods.

Table D.1 **Properties of the *HtmlForm* Object**

Property	Description
Action	Gets or sets the Action attribute of the form control.
	The Action attribute is the URL of a web page that processes the form's data.
	The Action attribute defaults to the current page.
Enctype	Gets or sets the Enctype attribute of the form.
	The Enctype attribute is the encoding type that browsers use when posting a form's data.
	Possible values include multipart/form-data, text/plain, and image/jpeg.
	The Enctype attribute defaults to application/x-www-form-urlencoded.
Method	Gets or sets the Method attribute of the form control.
	The Method defines the way a browser posts form data for processing.
	The Method attribute defaults to POST.
	You can override the default value to use the GET method instead. However, GET requests have a restriction on how much data can be passed, which can cause the postback and state management capabilities provided by a Web Form page to break.
ID	Gets or sets the ID (identifier) of the form control.
Target	Gets or sets the URI of the frame or window to render the results of a POST request.
Disabled	Gets or sets a value that indicates whether the Disabled attribute is included when an HTML control is rendered on the browser. Including this attribute makes the control read-only.
InnerHtml	Gets or sets the content found between the opening and closing tags of the control.
	The InnerHtml does not provide automatic HTML encoding and decoding.
InnerText	Gets or sets all text between the opening and closing tags of the specified control.
	The InnerText provides automatic HTML encoding and decoding.
MaintainState	Gets or sets a value stating whether the control should maintain its view state and the view states of any child controls it might contain.
Controls	Gets a ControlCollection object that represents the child controls for this control.
Visible	Gets or sets a value that indicates whether a control should be rendered on the page.

Table D.2   **Methods of the *HtmlForm* Object**

Method	Description
AddParsedObject	Adds a parsed control element to the ControlCollection object maintained by the parent control.
Databind	Causes data binding to occur on the invoked control and all its child controls.
FindControl	Searches the current control container for a specified control.
HasControls	Determines whether any child controls exist for this control.

Web Form syntax:

```
01 <FORM RUNAT="server"
02      ID="ID-of-control"
03      [METHOD=POST || GET]
04      [ACTION="URL Action"] >
05 </FORM>
```

Web Form example:

```
01 <FORM ID="myForm" RUNAT="server">
02   <%— Controls that make up the form go here —%>
03 </FORM>
```

HtmlInputText Object—*<input>* Element

This displays an input box control that can be edited. This control also enables you to mask data entry with asterisks (★), so you can conceal password text. Table D.3 lists the properties of the HtmlInputText object, and Table D.4 lists the method.

Table D.3   **Properties of the *HtmlInputText* Object**

Property	Description
ID	Gets or sets the ID (identifier) of the HtmlInputText control.
MaxLength	Gets or sets the maximum number of characters that can be typed by the user into the text box control.
Size	Gets or sets the size of a text box control, in characters.
Value	Gets or sets the contents of a text box control.
Disabled	Gets or sets a value that indicates whether the Disabled attribute is included when an HTML control is rendered on the browser. Including this attribute makes the control read-only.
Visible	Gets or sets a value that indicates whether a control should be rendered on the page.
MaintainState	Gets or sets a value stating whether the control should maintain its view state and the view states of any child controls it might contain.

Table D.4 **Method of the *HtmlInputText* Object**

Method	Description
Databind	Causes data binding to occur on the invoked control and all its child controls.

Web page syntax:

```
01 <input TYPE=text || password
02        RUNAT="server"
03        ID="ID-of-Control"
04        [MAXLENGTH="Maximum-length-of-Characters"]
05        [SIZE="Width-of-Input-Control"]
06        [VALUE="Default-Value"]
07 >
```

Web Form example:

```
Enter Name: <INPUT ID="myText" TYPE="text" SIZE="40" RUNAT="server">
Enter Password: <INPUT ID="myPW" TYPE="password" SIZE="40" RUNAT="server">
```

HtmlInputHidden Object—*<input type="hidden">* Element

This stores state information for a form. State information is information that needs to be available with each round trip to the server. Table D.5 lists the properties of the HtmlInputHidden object, Table D.6 lists the method, and Table D.7 lists the events.

Table D.5 **Properties of the *HtmlInputHidden* Object**

Property	Description
ID	Gets or sets the ID (identifier) of the HtmlInputHidden control.
MaxLength	Gets or sets the maximum number of characters that can be typed by the user into the Hidden box control.
Value	Gets or sets the contents of a Hidden box control.
MaintainState	Gets or sets a value stating whether the control should maintain its view state and the view states of any child controls it might contain.

Table D.6 **Method of the *HtmlHiddenText* Object**

Method	Description
Databind	Causes data binding to occur on the invoked control and all its child controls.

Table D.7 **Event of the *HtmlInputHidden* Object**

Event	Description
ServerChange	Event fired when a server postback process changes the content of the control.

Web Form syntax:

```
01 <INPUT TYPE="hidden"
02      RUNAT="server"
03      ID="ID-of-Control"
04      [VALUE="Default-Value"]
05      [OnServerChange="OnServerChangeEventHandler"] >
```

Web Form example:

```
<INPUT ID="myHiddenValue" TYPE="hidden" VALUE="Default-Value" RUNAT="server">
```

HtmlInputCheckbox Object—*<input type="checkbox">* Element

This creates a box that users can click to turn on and off. Table D.8 lists the properties of the HtmlInputCheckbox object, Table D.9 lists the method, and Table D.10 lists the event.

Table D.8 **Properties of the *HtmlInputCheckbox* Object**

Property	Description
ID	Gets or sets the ID (identifier) of the HtmlInputCheckbox control.
Checked	Gets or sets a value indicating whether the checkbox has been selected (Boolean value).
Disabled	Gets or sets a value that indicates whether the Disabled attribute is included when an HTML control is rendered on the browser. Including this attribute makes the control read-only.
Visible	Gets or sets a value that indicates whether a control should be rendered on the page.
MaintainState	Gets or sets a value stating whether the control should maintain its view state and the view states of any child controls it might contain.

Table D.9 **Method of the *HtmlInputCheckbox* Object**

Method	Description
Databind	Causes data binding to occur on the invoked control and all its child controls.

Table D.10 **Event of the *HtmlInputCheckbox* Object**

Event	Description
ServerChange	Fires when a server postback process changes the content of the control.

Web Form syntax:

```
01 <INPUT TYPE="checkbox"
02      RUNAT="server"
03       ID="ID-of-Control"
04       [CHECKED]
05       [OnServerChange="OnServerChangeEventHandler"] >
```

Web Form example:

```
<INPUT ID="myCheckbox" TYPE="checkbox" RUNAT="server"> put me on mailing list
```

HtmlInputRadioButton Object—*<input type= "radiobutton">* Element

This displays a button that can be turned on or off. Radio buttons are typically used to enable the user to select one item from a short list of fixed options. Table D.11 lists the properties of the `HtmlInputRadioButton` object, and Table D.12 lists the method.

Table D.11 **Properties of the *HtmlInputRadioButton* Object**

Property	Description
ID	Gets or sets the ID (identifier) of the `HtmlInputRadioButton` control.
Name	Gets the value of the HTML `Name` attribute that is rendered to the browser and is used to group radio buttons.
Checked	Gets or sets a value indicating whether the radio button has been selected (Boolean value).
Disabled	Gets or sets a value that indicates whether the `Disabled` attribute is included when an HTML control is rendered on the browser. Including this attribute makes the control read-only.

Property	Description
Visible	Gets or sets a value that indicates whether a control should be rendered on the page.
MaintainState	Gets or sets a value stating whether the control should maintain its view state and the view states of any child controls it might contain.

Table D.12   **Method of the *HtmlInputRadioButton* Object**

Method	Description
Databind	Causes data binding to occur on the invoked control and all its child controls.

Web Form syntax:

```
01 <INPUT TYPE="radio"
02      RUNAT="server"
03      ID="ID-of-Control"
04      [NAME="radio-button-group"]
05      [CHECKED]
06 >
```

Web Form example:

```
01 <INPUT TYPE="radio" ID="rb1" NAME="myGroup" RUNAT="server" />Option 1
02 <br>
03 <INPUT TYPE="radio" ID="rb2" NAME="myGroup" RUNAT="server" CHECKED />Opt 2
04 <br>
05 <INPUT TYPE="radio" ID="rb3" NAME="myGroup" RUNAT="server" />Option 3
```

HtmlInputFile Object—*<input type="file">* Element

This enables users to specify files to be uploaded to a server. The files being uploaded are sent to the uploaded files directory on the web server. Table D.13 lists the properties of the HtmlInputFile object, and Table D.14 lists the method.

Table D.13   **Properties of the *HtmlInputFile* Object**

Property	Description
ID	Gets or sets the ID (identifier) of the HtmlInputFile control.
Accept	Gets or sets a comma-separated list of MIME encoding that can be used to constrain the file types that the browser lets the user select.
Size	Gets or sets the size of a text box control, in characters.

continues ▶

Table D.13 **Continued**

Property	Description
PostedFile	Gets access to the uploaded file.
Value	Gets or sets the contents of the filename text box control.
Disabled	Gets or sets a value that indicates whether the Disabled attribute is included when an HTML control is rendered on the browser. Including this attribute makes the control read-only.
Visible	Gets or sets a value that indicates whether a control should be rendered on the page.
MaintainState	Gets or sets a value stating whether the control should maintain its view state and the view states of any child controls it might contain.

Table D.14 **Methods of the *HtmlInputFile* Object**

Method	Description
Databind	Causes data binding to occur on the invoked control and all its child controls.

Web Form syntax:

```
01 <INPUT TYPE="file"
02  ID="ID-of-Control"
03      RUNAT="server"
04      [ACCEPT="MIMEencodings"]
05      [MAXLENGTH="maximum-filepath-length"]
06      [SIZE="filepath-textbox-width"]
07      [POSTEDFILE="uploaded-filename"]
08 >
```

Web Form example:

```
01 <HTML>
02
03 <BODY>
04 <FORM ENCTYPE="multipart/form-data" RUNAT="server">
05   Select File to Upload: <INPUT ID="MyFile" TYPE="file" RUNAT="server">
06 </FORM>
07 </BODY>
08 </HTML>
```

HtmlTextArea Object—*<textarea>* Element

This displays large quantities of text. It is used for multi-line text entry and display. Table D.15 lists the properties of the HtmlTextArea object, Table D.16 lists the method, and Table D.17 lists the event.

Table D.15 **Properties of the *HtmlTextArea* Object**

Property	Description
ID	Gets or sets the ID (identifier) of the HtmlTextArea control.
Cols	Indicates the display width (in characters) of the text area.
Rows	Indicates the display height (in lines) of the text area.
MaxLength	Gets or sets the maximum length of the file path of the file to upload from the client machine.
Value	Gets or sets the contents of a text box control.
InnerHtml	Gets or sets the content found between the opening and closing tags of the control. The InnerHtml does not provide automatic HTML encoding and decoding.
InnerText	Gets or sets all text between the opening and closing tags of the specified control. The InnerText provides automatic HTML encoding and decoding.
Disabled	Gets or sets a value that indicates whether the Disabled attribute is included when an HTML control is rendered on the browser. Including this attribute makes the control read-only.
Visible	Gets or sets a value that indicates whether a control should be rendered on the page.
MaintainState	Gets or sets a value stating whether the control should maintain its view state and the view states of any child controls it might contain.

Table D.16 **Method of the *HtmlTextArea* Object**

Method	Description
Databind	Causes data binding to occur on the invoked control and all its child controls.

Table D.17 **Event of the *HtmlTextArea* Object**

Event	Description
ServerChange	Fires when a server postback process changes the content of the control.

Web Form syntax:

```
01 <TEXTAREA RUNAT="server"
02         ID="ID-of-Control"
03         [COLS="numberofcolsintextarea"]
04         [NAME="namepassedtobrowser"]
05         [ROWS="numberofrowsintextarea"]
06         [OnServerChange="OnServerChangeEventHandler"] >
07
08 </TEXTAREA>
```

Web Form example:

```
<TEXTAREA ID="myTextArea" cols="60" ROWS="5" RUNAT="server" />
```

HtmlButton Object—*<button>* Element

This performs a task. This control can contain any arbitrary HTML; therefore, it is very flexible in look and feel. However, it is not compatible with all browsers. Table D.18 lists the properties of the HtmlButton object, and Table D.19 lists the event.

Table D.18 **Properties of the *HtmlButton* Object**

Property	Description
ID	Gets or sets the ID (identifier) of the HtmlButton control.
Value	Gets or sets the Caption of the button.
InnerHtml	Gets or sets the content found between the opening and closing tags of the control.
	The InnerHtml does not provide automatic HTML encoding and decoding.
InnerText	Gets or sets all text between the opening and closing tags of the specified control.
	The InnerText provides automatic HTML encoding and decoding.
Disabled	Gets or sets a value that indicates whether the Disabled attribute is included when an HTML control is rendered on the browser. Including this attribute makes the control read-only.
Visible	Gets or sets a value that indicates whether a control should be rendered on the page.
MaintainState	Gets or sets a value stating whether the control should maintain its view state and the view states of any child controls it might contain.

Table D.19 **Events of the *HtmlButton* Object**

Event	Description
ServerClick	Occurs when the control is clicked.

Web Form syntax:

```
01 <button ID="ID-of-Control"
02         RUNAT="server"
03       OnServerClick="OnServerClickEventHandler" >
04
05 </button>
```

Web Form example:

```
01 <button ID="myBtn" OnServerClick="myBtn_Click" RUNAT="server">
02   my button control!
03 </button>
```

No example is available in C#, C++, or JScript. To view a Visual Basic example, click the Language Filter button in the top-left corner of the page.

HtmlInputButton Object—*<input type="button">* Element

This performs a task. This button is supported on all browsers. Table D.20 lists the properties of the HtmlInputButton object, and Table D.21 lists the event.

Table D.20 **Properties of the *HtmlInputButton* Object**

Property	Description
ID	Gets or sets the ID (identifier) of the HtmlInputButton control.
Value	Gets or sets the Caption of the button.
Disabled	Gets or sets a value that indicates whether the Disabled attribute is included when an HTML control is rendered on the browser. Including this attribute makes the control read-only.
Visible	Gets or sets a value that indicates whether a control should be rendered on the page.
MaintainState	Gets or sets a value stating whether the control should maintain its view state and the view states of any child controls it might contain.

Table D.21 **Events of the *HtmlInputButton* Object**

Event	Description
ServerClick	Occurs when the control is clicked.

Web Form syntax:

```
01  <INPUT TYPE="button" || "submit" || "reset"
02      ID="ID-of-Control"
03      RUNAT="server"
04      [VALUE=""]
05      [OnServerClick="OnServerClickEventHandler"] >
```

Web Form example:

```
01  <INPUT TYPE="button" VALUE="MyBtn" OnServerClick="MyBtn_Click"
02          RUNAT="server">
03  <INPUT TYPE="submit" VALUE="Enter" OnServerClick="Submit_Click"
04          RUNAT="server">
05  <INPUT TYPE="reset" OnServerClick="Reset_Click" RUNAT="server">
```

HtmlAnchor Object—*<a>* Element

This creates a web navigation hyperlink. Table D.22 lists the properties of the
HtmlAnchor object, and Table D.23 lists the event.

Table D.22 **Properties of the *HtmlAnchor* Object**

Property	Description
ID	Gets or sets the ID (identifier) of the HtmlAnchor control.
HREF	Gets or sets the URL target of the link specified in the HtmlAnchor server control.
Title	Gets or sets the title that the browser displays when identifying linked content.
Target	The target window or frame into which to load web page content.
InnerHtml	Gets or sets the content found between the opening and closing tags of the control.
	The InnerHtml does not provide automatic HTML encoding and decoding.
InnerText	Gets or sets all text between the opening and closing tags of the specified control.
	The InnerText provides automatic HTML encoding and decoding.
Disabled	Gets or sets a value that indicates whether the Disabled attribute is included when an HTML control is rendered on the browser. Including this attribute makes the control read-only.

Property	Description
Visible	Gets or sets a value that indicates whether a control should be rendered on the page.
MaintainState	Gets or sets a value stating whether the control should maintain its view state and the view states of any child controls it might contain.

Table D.23 **Event of the *HtmlAnchor* Object**

Event	Description
ServerClick	Occurs when the control is clicked.

Web Form syntax:

```
01 <A ID="ID-of-Control"
02    RUNAT="server"
03    HREF="linkurl"
04    [TARGET="target-for-link"]
05    [TITLE="titleforlink"]
06    [OnServerClick="OnServerClickHandler"] >
07
08 </A>
```

Web Form example:

```
<A ID="myAnchor" OnServerClick="Anchor_Click" RUNAT="server">Click Me!</a>
```

HtmlImage Object—*<img>* Element

This displays an image. Table D.24 lists the properties of the HtmlImage object.

Table D.24 **Properties of the *HtmlImage* Object**

Property	Description
ID	Gets or sets the ID (identifier) of the HtmlImage control.
ALT	Gets or sets the caption of the Image control.
SRC	Source file of the image (URI/URL).
Height	Height of the image to be displayed.
Width	Width of the image to be displayed.
Align	Gets or sets the alignment of the image with surrounding text.
Border	Width of the image border, which defaults to 0.
Disabled	Gets or sets a value that indicates whether the Disabled attribute is included when an HTML control is rendered on the browser. Including this attribute makes the control read-only.

continues ▶

Table D.24 **Continued**

Property	Description
Visible	Gets or sets a value that indicates whether a control should be rendered on the page.
MaintainState	Gets or sets a value stating whether the control should maintain its view state and the view states of any child controls it might contain.

Web Form syntax:

```
01 <IMG ID="ID-of-Control"
02     RUNAT="server"
03     [SRC="source-file"]
04     [ALIGN="absbottom||absMiddle||baseline||bottom||middle||left||right"]
05     [BORDER="0"]
06     [ALT="alternate-text-to-display-for-image"]
07     [WIDTH="16"]
08     [HEIGHT="16"]
09 >
```

Web Form example:

```
<IMG ID="MyImage" ALT="This is my Image" SRC="MyImage.gif" RUNAT= "server" />
```

HtmlInputImage Object—*<input type="image">* Element

This is like a button control except that it displays a custom graphic to use as the button. Table D.25 lists the properties of the HtmlInputImage object, and Table D.26 lists the events.

Table D.25 **Properties of the *HtmlInputImage* Object**

Property	Description
ID	Gets or sets the ID (identifier of the HtmlInputImage control.
ALT	Gets or sets the caption of the Image control.
SRC	Source file of the image (URI/URL).
Height	Height of the image to be displayed
Width	Width of the image to be displayed.
Align	Gets or sets the alignment of the image with surrounding text.
Border	Width of the image border, which defaults to 0.
Disabled	Gets or sets a value that indicates whether the Disabled attribute is included when an HTML control is rendered on the browser. Including this attribute makes the control read-only.

Property	Description
Visible	Gets or sets a value that indicates whether a control should be rendered on the page.
MaintenState	Gets or sets a value stating whether the control should maintain its view states of any child controls it might contain.

Table D.26   **Event of the *HtmlInputImage* Object**

Event	Description
ServerClick	Occurs when the control is clicked.

Web Form syntax:

```
01 <INPUT TYPE="image"
02        ID="ID-of-Control"
03        RUNAT="server"
04        SRC="source-file"
05        [ALIGN="absbottom| |absMiddle| |baseline| |bottom| |middle| |left| |right"]
06        [BORDER="0"]
07        [ALT="alternate-text-to-display-for-image"]
08        [WIDTH="16"]
09        [HIEGHT="16"]
10        [OnServerClick="OnServerClickEventHandler"]
```

Web Form example:

```
01 <INPUT ID="myImgBtn" TYPE="image" src="myImage.gif"
02        OnServerClick="myImgBtn_Click" RUNAT="server">
```

HtmlSelect Object—*<select>* and *<option>* Elements

This displays a collection of text elements as a list. Table D.27 lists the properties of the HtmlSelect object, Table D.28 lists the method, and Table D.29 lists the event.

Table D.27   **Properties of the *HtmlSelect* Object**

Property	Description
ID	Gets or sets the ID (identifier) of the HtmlSelect control.
DataSource	Gets or sets the data source to which to bind the control, thus providing data with which to populate the select list.
DataTextField	Gets or sets the field in the data source that provides the text for an option entry in the control.
DataValueField	Gets or sets the field in the data source that provides the option item value for the control.

continues ▶

Table D.27 **Continued**

Property	Description
Items	Gets the list of option items in the control.
Multiple	Gets or sets a value indicating whether the multiple item selection feature is enabled for a selection list.
SelectedIndex	Gets or sets the index of the selected item in the control.
	If multiple items are allowed, this property contains the index of the first item selected in the list.
Size	Gets or sets the number of items visible in the browser at one time. A value greater that 1 causes most browsers to display a scrolling list of items.
Value	Gets or sets the current item selected in the control.
Disabled	Gets or sets a value that indicates whether the Disabled attribute is included when an HTML control is rendered on the browser. Including this attribute makes the control read-only.
Visible	Gets or sets a value that indicates whether a control should be rendered on the page.
MaintainState	Gets or sets a value stating whether the control should maintain its view state and the view states of any child controls it might contain.

Table D.28 **Method of the *HtmlSelect* Object**

Method	Description
Databind	Causes data binding to occur on the invoked control and all its child controls.

Table D.29 **Event of the *HtmlSelect* Object**

Event	Description
ServerChange	Fires when a server postback process changes the content of the control.

Web Form syntax:

```
01 <select RUNAT="server"
02         ID="ID-of-Control"
03         [OnServerChange="OnServerChangeHandler"]
04         [DATASOURCE="bind-source"]
05         [DATATEXTFIELD="field-to-bind- -text"]
```

```
06          [DATAVALUEFIELD="field-to-bind-option-value"]
07          [MULTIPLE]
08          [ITEMS="collection-of-option-elements"]
09          [SELECTEDINDEX="index-of-currently-selected-item"]
10          [SIZE="num-of-visible-items"]
11          [VALUE="current-item-value"]
12 >
13   <OPTION>value1</OPTION>
14   <OPTION>value2</OPTION>
15 </SELECT>
```

Web Form example:

```
01 <SELECT ID="MySelctionList" SIZE="1" RUNAT="server">
02   <option>Option 1</option>
03   <option>Option 2</option>
04 </select>
```

HtmlTable Object—*<table>* Element

This creates a table element on a web page. Table D.30 lists the properties of the HtmlTable object, and Table D.31 lists the method.

Table D.30 **Properties of the *HtmlTable* Object**

Property	Description
ID	Gets or sets the ID (identifier) of the HtmlTable control.
Align	Gets or sets the alignment of content within the control.
BgColor	The background color of the control.
Border	Gets or sets the width of the border of the control.
BorderColor	Gets or sets the color of the control's border.
CellPadding	Gets or sets the cell padding.
CellSpacing	Gets or sets the cell spacing.
Width	Gets or sets the width of the table.
Height	Gets or sets the height of the table.
Rows	The rows collection belonging to the table. They can be programmatically added to or deleted through the code on the server.
Disabled	Gets or sets a value that indicates whether the Disabled attribute is included when an HTML control is rendered on the browser. Including this attribute makes the control read-only.
Visible	Gets or sets a value that indicates whether a control should be rendered on the page.
MaintainState	Gets or sets a value stating whether the control should maintain its view state and the view states of any child controls it might contain.

Table D.31 **Methods of the *HtmlTable* Object**

Method	Description
Databind	Causes data binding to occur on the invoked control and all its child controls.

Web Form syntax:

```
01 <table RUNAT="server"
02       ID="ID-of-Control"
03       [ALIGN="left || center || right]
04       [BGCOLOR="background-color"]
05       [BORDER="border-width-in-pixels"]
06       [BORDERCOLOR="border-color"]
07       [CELLPADDING="spacing-within-cells-in-pixels"]
08       [CELLSPACEING="spacing-between-cells-in-pixels"]
09       [HEIGHT="table-height"]
10       [ROWS="collection-of-rows"]
11       [WIDTH="table-width"]                      >
12
13 </TABLE>
```

Web Form example:

```
<TABLE ID="myTbl" CELLPADDING="5" CELLSPACING="0" BORDER="1" RUNAT="server">
  <TR ID="ROW01">
    <TD>Row 01</TD>
  </TR>
  <TR ID="ROW02">
    <TD>Row 02</TD>
  </TR>
</TABLE>
```

HtmlTableRow Object—*<tr>* Element

This creates an individual row within a table. Table D.32 lists the properties of the HtmlTableRow object, and Table D.33 lists the methods.

Table D.32 **Properties of the *HtmlTableRow* Object**

Property	Description
ID	Gets or sets the ID (identifier) of the HtmlTableRow control.
Align	Gets or sets the alignment of content within the control.
Valign	Gets or sets the vertical alignment of content within the control.
BgColor	The background color of the control.
BorderColor	Gets or sets the color of the controls border.

Property	Description
Width	Gets or sets the width of the row.
Height	Gets or sets the height of the row.
Cells	Gets or sets the table cells contained within the table row.
Disabled	Gets or sets a value that indicates whether the Disabled attribute is included when an HTML control is rendered on the browser. Including this attribute makes the control read-only.
Visible	Gets or sets a value that indicates whether a control should be rendered on the page.
MaintainState	Gets or sets a value stating whether the control should maintain its view state and the view states of any child controls it might contain.

Table D.33 **Method of the *HtmlTableRow* Object**

Method	Description
Databind	Causes data binding to occur on the invoked control and all its child controls.

Web Form syntax:

```
01 <TR RUNAT="server"
02     ID="ID-of-Control"
03     [ALIGN="table-content-alignment"]
04     [BGCOLOR="row-background-color"]
05     [BORDERCOLOR="border-color"]
06     [HEIGHT="height"]
07     [CELLS="collection-of-table-cells"]
08     [VALIGN="vertical-alignment-of-row-content"] >
09
10 </TR>
```

Web Form example:

```
<TABLE ID="myTbl" CELLPADDING="5" CELLSPACING="0" BORDER="1" RUNAT="server">
  <TR ID="ROW01">
    <TD>Row 01</TD>
  </TR>
  <TR ID="ROW02">
    <TD>Row 02</TD>
  </TR>
</TABLE>
```

HtmlTableCell Object—*<td>* Element

This creates an individual cell in a table row. Table D.34 lists the properties of the `HtmlTableCell` object, and Table D.35 lists the method.

Table D.34 **Properties of the *HtmlTableCell* Object**

Property	Description
ID	Gets or sets the ID (identifier) of the `HtmlTableCell` control.
Align	Gets or sets the alignment of content within the control.
VAlign	Gets or sets the vertical alignment of content within the control.
BgColor	Background color of the control.
BorderColor	Gets or sets the color of the control borders.
Width	Gets or sets the width of the cell.
Height	Gets or sets the height of the cell.
ColSpan	Gets or sets the number of columns that the cell spans.
RowSpan	Gets or sets the number of rows that the cell spans.
InnerHtml	Gets or sets the content found between the opening and closing tags of the control. The `InnerHtml` does not provide automatic HTML encoding and decoding.
InnerText	Gets or sets all text between the opening and closing tags of the specified control. The `InnerText` provides automatic HTML encoding and decoding.
Disabled	Gets or sets a value that indicates whether the `Disabled` attribute is included when an HTML control is rendered on the browser. Including this attribute makes the control read-only.
Visible	Gets or sets a value that indicates whether a control should be rendered on the page.
MaintainState	Gets or sets a value stating whether the control should maintain its view state and the view states of any child controls it might contain.

Table D.35 **Method of the *HtmlTableCell* Object**

Method	Description
Databind	Causes data binding to occur on the invoked control and all its child controls.

Web Form syntax:

```
01 <TH RUNAT="server"
02     [ID="ID-of-Control"]
03     [COLSPAN="num-of-cols-to-span"]
04     [ROWSPAN="num-of-rows-to-span"]
05     [NOWRAP="True ¦¦ False"]
06     [ALIGN="table-content-alignment"]
07     [BGCOLOR="row-background-color"]
08     [BORDERCOLOR="border-color"]
09     [HEIGHT="height"]
10     [CELLS="collection-of-table-cells"]
11     [VALIGN="vertical-alignment-of-row-content"] >
12
13 </TH>
```

or

```
01 <TD RUNAT="server"
02     [ID="ID-of-Control"]
03     [COLSPAN="num-of-cols-to-span"]
04     [ROWSPAN="num-of-rows-to-span"]
05     [NOWRAP="True ¦¦ False"]
06     [ALIGN="table-content-alignment"]
07     [BGCOLOR="row-background-color"]
08     [BORDERCOLOR="border-color"]
09     [HEIGHT="height"]
10     [CELLS="collection-of-table-cells"]
11     [VALIGN="vertical-alignment-of-row-content"] >
12
13 </TD>
```

Web Form example:

```
01 <TABLE ID="myTbl" CELLPADDING="5" CELLSPACING="0" BORDER="1" RUNAT="server">
02   <TR ID="ROW01">
03     <TD>Row 01</TD>
04   </TR>
05   <TR ID="ROW02">
06     <TD>Row 02</TD>
07   </TR>
08 </TABLE>
```

E

ASP Server Control Reference

This appendix covers the following controls:

- Static Content Display
    - **Label**—Displays some text that users cannot edit; also acts as a placeholder for dynamic text insertion.
    - **Image**—Displays an image.
- Data Entry
    - **TextBox**—Displays a textbox control that can be edited by users; also supports masked edits.
    - **DropDownList**—Allows users to select an item from a list.
    - **ListBox**—Displays a list of choices; the list also can support multiple selections.
    - **CheckBox**—Displays a box that users can click to turn on and off; generally used for Boolean values (Yes/No, True/False).
    - **CheckBoxList**—Creates a collection of check boxes that are optimized for data binding.
    - **RadioButton**—Displays a single button that can be turned on or off.
    - **RadioButtonList**—Creates a collection of radio buttons; only one button can be selected at a time.

- Navigation and Command
    - **Button**—A button is displayed and when clicked, calls a subroutine to process.
    - **LinkButton**—Same functionality as a Button control, but displays as a hyperlink.
    - **ImageButton**—Same functionality as a Button control, but uses an image instead of a button.
    - **HyperLink**—Creates web navigation links.
- Layout and Formatting
    - **Table**—Creates a table.
    - **TableCell**—Creates an individual cell within a table row.
    - **TableRow**—Creates an individual row within a table.
    - **Panel**—Creates a container on the Web Form, which is rendered as a DIV in HTML.
- List/Browse
    - **Repeater**—Renders data using a set of HTML elements and controls that are developer defined, repeating all the elements and controls once for each item of data.
    - **DataList**—Works like the Repeater control, except the DataList control has more formatting and layout options—allowing DataList control to specify its editing behavior.
    - **DataGrid**—Renders information that is normally bound to data in tabular form with columns; also gives the capability to dynamically edit and sort data.
- Utility
    - **AdRotator**—Displays a sequence of predefined images, such as a web banner advertisement.
    - **Calendar**—Displays an HTML-based calendar that allows users to select a date.

All the web controls inherit the following common properties, methods, and events from the Webcontrol class.

Common Properties of the *Webcontrol* Class

A lot of these properties only apply to certain controls, and as such, might not contain any values when accessed directly in code. Table E.1, E.2, and E.3 list the properties, methods, and events for Webcontrol.

Table E.1 **Common Properties of the *Webcontrol* Class**

Property	Description
AccessKey	Sets or retrieves the keyboard shortcut key (AccessKey) for setting the current focus to the control.
BackColor	Gets or sets the background colors of the web control.
BorderColor	Gets or sets the border colors of the web control.
BorderStyle	Gets or sets the border style of the web control.
BorderWidth	Gets or sets the border width of the web control.
Controls	Gets a ControlCollection object, which represents the child controls for a specified server control in the UI hierarchy.
CssClass	Gets or sets the CSS class rendered by the web control.
Enabled	Gets or sets a value indicating whether the web control is enabled.
EnableViewState	Gets or sets a value indicating whether the server control maintains its view state, and the view state of any child controls it contains when the current page request ends.
Font	Returns the web control font information.
ForeColor	Gets or sets foreground colors of the web control.
Height	Gets or sets height of the web control.
ID	Gets or sets the program identity assigned to the server control.
Page	Returns a reference to the page instance that contains the server control.
Parent	Returns a reference to the server control's parent control in the page UI hierarchy.
Style	Returns a collection of text attributes that will be rendered as a style attribute on the outer tag of the web control.
Visible	Gets or sets a value that indicates whether a server control is rendered as UI on the page.
Width	Gets or sets width of the web controls.

Table E.2 **Common Methods of the *Webcontrol* Class**

Method	Description
DataBind	Binds a data source to the invoked server control and its child controls.
FindControl	Searches the current naming container for the specified server control.
HasControls	Determines if the server control contains any child controls.

Table E.3 **Common Events of the *Webcontrol* Class**

Event	Description
DataBinding	Triggered when the server control binds to a data source.
Init	Triggered when the server control is initialized, which is the first step in its lifecycle.
Load	Triggered when the server control is loaded into the page object.
PreRender	Triggered when the server control is about to render to its containing page object.
Unload	Triggered when the server control is unloaded from memory.

The *Label* Control

The property of the Label control is Text, which gets or sets the text content of the Label control.

The *Image* Control

The properties of the Image control are shown in Table E.4.

Table E.4 **Properties of the *Image* Control**

Property	Description
AlternateText	Returns the alternate text displayed in the Image control when the image is unavailable.
Font	Returns the font properties of the alternate text element.
ImageAlign	Returns the alignment of the Image control in relation to other elements on the web page.
ImageUrl	Returns the location of an image to display in the Image control.

The *TextBox* Control

The properties and events of the TextBox control are shown in Tables E.5 and E.6.

Table E.5   **Properties of the *TextBox* Control**

Property	Description
AutoPostBack	Gets or sets a value indicating whether an automatic postback to the server will occur whenever the user changes the content of the text box.
Columns	Gets or sets the display width of the text box in characters.
MaxLength	Gets or sets the maximum number of characters allowed in the text box.
ReadOnly	Gets or sets a Boolean value denoting whether the text box is read-only.
Rows	Gets or sets the display height of a multi-line text box.
Text	Gets or sets the text content of the text box.
TextMode	Gets or sets the behavior mode of the text box.
Wrap	Gets or sets a Boolean value indicating whether the text content wraps within the text.

Table E.6   **Event of the *TextBox* Control**

Event	Description
TextChanged	Triggered when the content of the text box is changed upon server postback.

The *DropDownList* Control

The properties and events of the DropDownList control are shown in Tables E.7 and E.8.

Table E.7   **Properties of the *DropDownList* Control**

Property	Description
AutoPostBack	Gets or sets a value indicating whether a postback to the server automatically occurs when the user changes the list selection.
DataMember	Gets or sets the specific table in the DataSource to bind to the control.

continues ▶

Table E.7 **Continued**

Property	Description
DataSource	Gets or sets the data source that populates the items of the list control.
DataTextField	Gets or sets the field of the data source that provides the text content of the list items.
DataTextFormatString	Gets or sets the formatting string used to control how data, bound to the list control, is displayed.
DataValueField	Gets or sets the field of the data source that provides the value of each list item.
Items	Gets the collection of items in the list control.
SelectedIndex	Gets or sets the index of the selected item in the DropDownList control.
SelectedItem	Gets the selected item with the lowest index in the list control.
ToolTip	Gets or sets the ToolTip text displayed when the mouse pointer rests over the control.

Table E.8 **Events of the *DropDownList* Control**

Event	Description
SelectedIndexChanged	Triggered when the selection on the list changes and is posted back to the server.

The *ListBox* Control

The properties and events of the ListBox control are shown in Tables E.9 and E.10.

Table E.9 **Properties of the *ListBox* Control**

Property	Description
DataMember	Gets or sets the specific table in the DataSource to bind to the control.
DataSource	Gets or sets the data source that populates the items of the list control.
DataTextField	Gets or sets the field of the data source that provides the text content of the list items.

Property	Description
DataTextFormatString	Gets or sets the formatting string used to control how data, bound to the list control, is displayed.
DataValueField	Gets or sets the field of the data source that provides the value of each list item.
Items	Gets the collection of items in the list control.
Rows	Gets or sets the number of rows displayed in the ListBox control.
SelectedIndex	Gets or sets the lowest ordinal index of the selected items in the list.
SelectedItem	Gets the selected item with the lowest index in the list control.
SelectionMode	Gets or sets the selection mode of the ListBox controls.
ToolTip	Gets or sets the ToolTip text displayed when the mouse pointer is over the control.

Table E.10 **Events of the *ListBox* Control**

Event	Description
SelectedIndexChanged	Triggered when the selection on the list changes and is posted back to the server.

The *CheckBox* Control

The properties and events of the CheckBox control are shown in Tables E.11 and E.12.

Table E.11 **Properties of the *CheckBox* Control**

Property	Description
AutoPostBack	Gets or sets a value indicating whether the CheckBox state automatically posts back to the server when clicked.
Checked	Gets or sets a value indicating whether the CheckBox control is checked.
Text	Gets or sets the text label associated with the CheckBox.
TextAlign	Gets or sets the alignment of the text label associated with the CheckBox control.

Table E.12 **Events of the *CheckBox* Control**

Event	Description
CheckedChanged	Triggered when the Checked property is changed.

The *CheckBoxList* Control

The properties and events of the CheckBoxList control are shown in Table E.13 and the events in Table E.14.

Table E.13 **Properties of the *CheckBoxList* Control**

Property	Description
AutoPostBack	Gets or sets a value indicating whether a postback to the server automatically occurs when the user changes the list selection.
CellPadding	Gets or sets the distance between the border and contents of the cell.
CellSpacing	Gets or sets the distance between cells.
DataMember	Gets or sets the specific table in the DataSource to bind to the control.
DataSource	Gets or sets the data source that populates the items of the list control.
DataTextField	Gets or sets the field of the data source that provides the text content of the list items.
DataTextFormatString	Gets or sets the formatting string used to control how data, bound to the list control, is displayed.
DataValueField	Gets or sets the field of the data source that provides the value of each list item.
Items	Gets the collection of items in the list control.
RepeatColumns	Gets or sets the number of columns to display in the CheckBoxList control.
RepeatDirection	Gets or sets a value that indicates whether the control displays vertically or horizontally.
RepeatLayout	Gets or sets the layout of the check boxes.
SelectedIndex	Gets or sets the lowest ordinal index of the selected items in the list.
SelectedItem	Gets the selected item with the lowest index in the list control.
TextAlign	Gets or sets the text alignment for the check boxes within the group.

Table E.14 **Events of the *CheckBoxList* Control**

Event	Description
SelectedIndexChanged	Triggered when the selection on the list changes and is posted back to the server.

The *RadioButton* Control

The properties and events of the RadioButton control are shown in Table E.15 and E.16.

Table E.15 **Properties of the *RadioButton* Control**

Property	Description
AutoPostBack	Gets or sets a value indicating whether the RadioButton state automatically posts back to the server when clicked.
Checked	Gets or sets a value indicating whether the RadioButton control is checked.
GroupName	Gets or sets the name of the group to which the RadioButton belongs.
Text	Gets or sets the text label associated with the RadioButton.
TextAlign	Gets or sets the alignment of the text label associated with the RadioButton control.

Table E.16 **Events of the *RadioButton* Control**

Event	Description
CheckedChanged	Triggered when the Checked property is changed.

The *RadioButtonList* Control

The RadioButtonList control properties and events are shown in Tables E.17 and E.18.

Table E.17 **Properties of the *RadioButtonList* Control**

Property	Description
AutoPostBack	Gets or sets a value indicating whether a postback to the server automatically occurs when the user changes the list selection.
CellPadding	Gets or sets the distance between the border and the contents of the table cell.
CellSpacing	Gets or sets the distance between adjacent table cells.
DataMember	Gets or sets the specific table in the DataSource to bind to the control.
DataSource	Gets or sets the data source that populates the items of the list control.
DataTextField	Gets or sets the field of the data source that provides the text content of the list items.
DataTextFormatString	Gets or sets the formatting string used to control how data, bound to the list control, is displayed.
DataValueField	Gets or sets the field of the data source that provides the value of each list item.
Items	Gets the collection of items in the list control.
RepeatColumns	Gets or sets the number of columns to display in the RadioButtonList control.
RepeatDirection	Gets or sets the direction the radio buttons within the group are displayed.
RepeatLayout	Gets or sets the layout of radio buttons within the group.
SelectedIndex	Gets or sets the lowest ordinal index of the selected items in the list.
SelectedItem	Gets the selected item with the lowest index in the list control.
TextAlign	Gets or sets the text alignment for the radio buttons within the group.

Table E.18 **Events of the *RadioButtonList* Control**

Event	Description
SelectedIndexChanged	Triggered when the selection on the list changes and is posted back to the server.

The *Button* Control

The Button control properties and events are shown in Tables E.19 and E.20.

Table E.19 **Properties of the *Button* Control**

Properties	Description
CausesValidation	Gets or sets a value indicating whether validation is performed when the Button control is clicked.
CommandArgument	Gets or sets an optional parameter passed to the Command event along with the associated CommandName.
CommandName	Gets or sets the command name associated with the Button control that is passed to the Command event.
Text	Gets or sets the text caption displayed in the Button control.

Table E.20 **Events of the *Button* Control**

Event	Description
Click	Triggered when the Button control is clicked.
Command	Triggered when the Button control is clicked.

The *LinkButton* Control

The properties and events of the LinkButton control are shown in Tables E.21 and E.22.

Table E.21 **Properties of the *LinkButton* Control**

Property	Description
CausesValidation	Gets or sets a value indicating whether validation is performed when the LinkButton control is clicked.
CommandArgument	Gets or sets an optional argument passed to the Command event handler along with the associated CommandName property.
CommandName	Gets or sets the command name associated with the LinkButton control. This value is passed to the Command event handler along with the CommandArgument property.
Text	Gets or sets the text caption displayed on the LinkButton control.

Table E.22 **Events of the *LinkButton* Control**

Event	Description
Click	Triggered when the LinkButton control is clicked.
Command	Triggered when the Button control is clicked.

The *ImageButton* Control

The properties and events of the ImageButton control are shown in Tables E.23 and E.24.

Table E.23 **Properties of the *ImageButton* Control**

Property	Description
AlternateText	Gets or sets the alternate text displayed in the Image control when the image is unavailable.
CausesValidation	Gets or sets a value indicating whether validation is performed when the ImageButton control is clicked.
CommandArgument	Gets or sets an optional argument that provides additional information about the CommandName property.
CommandName	Gets or sets the command name associated with the ImageButton control.
Font	Gets the font properties for the alternate text.
ImageAlign	Gets or sets the alignment of the Image control in relation to other elements on the web page.
ImageUrL	Gets or sets the location of an image to display in the Image control.

Table E.24 **Events of the *ImageButton* Control**

Event	Description
Click	Occurs when the ImageButton is clicked.
Command	Occurs when the ImageButton is clicked.

The *HyperLink* Control

The properties of the Hyperlink control are shown in Table E.25.

Table E.25 **Properties of the *HyperLink* Control**

Property	Description
ImageUrl	Gets or sets the path to an image to display for the HyperLink control.
NavigateUrl	Gets or sets the URL to link to when the HyperLink control is clicked.
Target	Gets or sets the target window or frame to display the web page content linked to when the HyperLink control is clicked.
Text	Gets or sets the text caption for the HyperLink control.

The *Table* Control

The properties of the Table control are shown in Table E.26.

Table E.26 **Properties of the *Table* Control**

Property	Description
BackImageUrl	Indicates the URL of the background image to display behind the table. The image will be tiled if it is smaller than the table.
CellPadding	Gets or sets the distance between the border and the contents of the table cell.
CellSpacing	Gets or sets the distance between table cells.
GridLines	Gets or sets the gridlines property of the Table class.
HorizontalAlign	Gets or sets the horizontal alignment of the table within the page.
Rows	Gets the collection of rows within the table.

The *TableCell* Control

The properties of the TableCell control are shown in Table E.27.

Table E.27 **Properties of the *TableCell* Control**

Property	Description
ColumnSpan	Gets or sets the number of columns in the Table control that the cell spans.
HorizontalAlign	Gets or sets the horizontal alignment of the contents in the cell.
RowSpan	Gets or sets the number of rows in the Table control that the cell spans.
Text	Gets or sets the text contents of the cell.
VerticalAlign	Gets or sets the vertical alignment of the contents in the cell.
Wrap	Gets or sets a value that indicates whether the content of the cell wraps in the cell.

The *TableRow* Control

The properties of the TableRow control are shown in Table E.28.

Table E.28 **Properties of the *TableRow* Control**

Property	Description
Cells	Gets a collection of TableCell objects that represent the cells of a row in a Table control.
HorizontalAlign	Gets or sets the horizontal alignment of the contents in the row.
VerticalAlign	Gets or sets the vertical alignment of the contents in the row.

The *Panel* Control

The properties of the Panel control are found in Table E.29.

Table E.29 **Properties of the *Panel* Control**

Property	Description
BackImageUrl	Gets or sets the URL of the background image for the Panel control.
HorizontalAlign	Gets or sets the horizontal alignment of the contents within the panel.
Wrap	Gets or sets a value indicating whether the content wraps within the panel.

The *Repeater* Control

The properties of the Repeater control are found in Table E.30. The events are shown in Table E.31.

Table E.30 **Properties of the *Repeater* Control**

Property	Description
AlternatingItemTemplate	Gets or sets the template that defines how alternating items are rendered.
DataMember	Gets or sets the specific table in the DataSource to bind to the control.
DataSource	Gets or sets the data source that provides data for populating the list.
FooterTemplate	Gets or sets the template that defines how the control footer is rendered.
HeaderTemplate	Gets or sets the template that defines how the control header is rendered.
Items	Gets a collection of RepeaterItem objects in the Repeater.
ItemTemplate	Gets or sets the template that defines how items are rendered.
SeparatorTemplate	Gets or sets the template that defines how separators between items are rendered.

Table E.31 **Events of the *Repeater* Control**

Event	Description
ItemCommand	Triggered when a button is clicked in the Repeater control.
ItemCreated	Triggered when an item is created in the Repeater control.
ItemDataBound	Triggered after an item in the Repeater is databound, but before it is rendered on the page.

The *DataList* Control

The properties of the DataList control are shown in Table E.32. The events are shown in Table E.33.

Table E.32 **Properties of the *DataList* Control**

Property	Description
AlternatingItemStyle	Gets the style properties for alternating items in the DataList control.
AlternatingItemTemplate	Gets or sets the template for alternating items in the DataList.
CancelCommandName	Represents the Cancel command.
DeleteCommandName	Represents the Delete Command.
EditCommandName	Represents the Edit command.
EditItemIndex	Gets or sets the index number of the selected item in the DataList control to edit.
EditItemStyle	Gets the style properties for the item selected for editing in the DataList control.
EditItemTemplate	Gets or sets the template for the item selected for editing in the DataList control.
ExtractTemplateRows	Gets or sets a value that indicates whether the rows of a Table control, defined in each template of a DataList control, are extracted and displayed.
FooterStyle	Gets the style properties for the footer section of the DataList control.
FooterTemplate	Gets or sets the template for the footer section of the DataList control.
GridLines	Gets or sets the grid line style for the DataList control.
HeaderStyle	Gets the style properties for the heading section of the DataList control.
HeaderTemplate	Gets or sets the template for the heading section of the DataList control.
Items	Gets a collection of DataListItem objects representing the individual items within the control.
ItemStyle	Gets the style properties for the items in the DataList control.
ItemTemplate	Gets or sets the template for the items in the DataList control.
RepeatColumns	Gets or sets the number of columns to display in the DataList control.
RepeatDirection	Gets or sets whether the DataList control displays vertically or horizontally.

Property	Description
RepeatLayout	Gets or sets whether the control is displayed in a table or flow layout.
SelectCommandName	Represents the Select command.
SelectedIndex	Gets or sets the index of the selected item in the DataList control.
SelectedItem	Gets the selected item in the DataList control.
SelectedItemStyle	Gets the style properties for the selected item in the DataList control.
SelectedItemTemplate	Gets or sets the template for the selected item in the DataList control.
SeparatorStyle	Gets the style properties of the separator between each item in the DataList control.
SeparatorTemplate	Gets or sets the template for the separator between the items of the DataList control.
ShowFooter	Gets or sets a value indicating whether the footer section is displayed in the DataList control.
ShowHeader	Gets or sets a value indicating whether the header section is displayed in the DataList control.
UpdateCommandName	Represents the Update Command.

Table E.33 **Events of the *DataList* Control**

Event	Description
CancelCommand	Occurs when the Cancel button is clicked for an item in the DataList control.
DeleteCommand	Occurs when the Delete button is clicked for an item in the DataList control.
EditCommand	Occurs when the Edit button is clicked for an item in the DataList control.
ItemCommand	Occurs when any button is clicked in the DataList control.
ItemCreated	Occurs on the server when an item in the DataList control is created.
ItemDataBound	Occurs when an item is data bound to the DataList control.
SelectedIndexChanged	Occurs when an item on the list is selected.
UpdateCommand	Occurs when the Update button is clicked for an item in the DataList control

The *DataGrid* Control

The properties of the DataGrid control are shown in Table E.34.

Table E.34 **Properties of the *DataGrid* Control**

Property	Description
AllowCustomPaging	Gets or sets a value that indicates whether custom paging is enabled.
AllowPaging	Gets or sets a value that indicates whether paging is enabled.
AllowSorting	Gets or sets a value that indicates whether sorting is enabled.
AlternatingItemStyle	Gets the style properties for alternating items in the DataGrid control.
AutoGenerateColumns	Gets or sets a value that indicates whether BoundColumn objects are automatically created and displayed in the DataGrid control for each field in the data source.
BackImageUrl	Gets or sets the URL of an image to display in the background of the DataGrid control.
CancelCommandName	Represents the Cancel command name.
CellPadding	Gets or sets the amount of space between the contents of a cell and the cell's border.
CellSpacing	Gets or sets the amount of space between cells.
Columns	Gets a collection of objects that represent the columns of the DataGrid control.
CurrentPageIndex	Gets or sets the index of the currently displayed page.
DataKeyField	Gets or sets the primary key field in the data source referenced by DataSource.
DataKeys	Gets a collection of the key fields in the data source.
DataMember_	Gets or sets the specific data member in a multi-member DataSource to bind to the list control.
DataSource	Gets or sets the source to a list of values used to populate the items within the control.
DeleteCommandName	Represents the Delete command name.
EditCommandName	Represents the Edit command name.
EditItemIndex_	Gets or sets the index of an item in the DataGrid control to edit.
EditItemStyle	Gets the style properties of the item selected for editing in the DataGrid control.

Property	Description
GridLines	Gets or sets a value that specifies the grid line style.
HeaderStyle	Gets the style properties of the heading section in the DataGrid control.
Items	Gets a collection of DataGridItem objects that represent the individual items in the DataGrid control.
ItemStyle	Gets the style properties of the items in the DataGrid control.
NextPageCommandArgument	Represents the NextPage command argument.
PageCommandName	Represents the Page command name.
PrevPageCommandArgument	Represents the PrevPage command argument.
PageCount	Gets the total number of pages required to display the items in the DataGrid control.
PagerStyle	Gets the style properties of the paging section of the DataGrid control.
PageSize	Gets or sets the number of items to display on a single page of the DataGrid control.
SelectedIndex	Gets or sets the index of the selected item in the DataGrid control.
SelectCommandName	Represents the Select command name.
SelectedItem	Gets a DataGridItem object that represents the selected item in the DataGrid control.
SelectedItemStyle	Gets the style properties of the currently selected item in the DataGrid control.
ShowFooter	Gets or sets a value that indicates whether the footer is displayed in the DataGrid control.
ShowHeader	Gets or sets a value that indicates whether the header is displayed in the DataGrid control.
SortCommandName	Represents the Sort command name.
UpdateCommandName	Represents the Update command name.
VirtualItemCount	Gets or sets the virtual number of items in the DataGrid control when custom paging is used.

The events of the DataGrid control are shown in Table E.35.

Table E.35 **Events of the *DataGrid* Control**

Event	Description
CancelCommand	Triggered when the Cancel button is clicked for an item in the DataGrid control.
DeleteCommand	Triggered when the Delete button is clicked for an item in the DataGrid control.
EditCommand	Triggered when the Edit button is clicked for an item in the DataGrid control.
ItemCommand	Triggered when any button is clicked in the DataGrid control.
ItemCreated	Triggered on the server when an item in the DataGrid control is created.
ItemDataBound	Triggered when an item is data bound to the DataGrid control.
PageIndexChanged	Triggered when one of the page selection elements is clicked.
SelectedIndexChanged	Triggered when an item on the list is selected.
SortCommand	Triggered when a column is sorted.
UpdateCommand	Triggered when the Update button is clicked for an item in the DataGrid control.

The *AdRotator* Control

The properties of the AdRotator Control are shown in Table E.36. The events for this control are shown in Table E.37.

Table E.36 **Properties of the *AdRotator* Control**

Property	Description
AdvertisementFile	Gets or sets the path to an XML file that contains advertisement information.
KeywordFilter	Gets or sets a category keyword to filter for specific types of advertisements in the XML advertisement file.
Target	Gets or sets the name of the browser window or frame to which the contents of the web page linked are displayed when the AdRotator control is clicked.

Table E.37 **Events of the *AdRotator* Control**

Event	Description
AdCreated	Triggered once per round trip to the server after the creation of the control, but before the page is rendered.

The *Calendar* Control

The properties of the Calendar control are shown in Table E.38.

Table E.38 **Properties of the *Calendar* Control**

Property	Description
CellPadding	Gets or sets the amount of space between the contents of a cell and the cell's border.
CellSpacing	Gets or sets the amount of space between cells.
DayHeaderStyle	Gets the style properties for the section that displays the day of the week.
DayNameFormat	Gets or sets the name format of days of the week.
DayStyle	Gets the style properties for the days in the displayed month.
FirstDayOfWeek	Gets or sets the day of the week to display in the first day column of the Calendar control.
NextMonthText	Gets or sets the text displayed for the next month Navigation control.
NextPrevFormat	Gets or sets the format of the next and previous month's navigation elements in the title section of the Calendar control.
NextPrevStyle	Gets the style properties for the next and previous month's navigation elements.
OtherMonthDayStyle	Gets the style properties for the days on the Calendar control that are not in the displayed month.
PrevMonthText	Gets or sets the text displayed for the previous month's navigation control.
SelectedDate	Gets or sets the selected date.
SelectedDates	Gets a collection of System.DateTime objects that represent the selected dates on the Calendar control.
SelectedDayStyle	Gets the style properties for the selected dates.
SelectionMode	Gets or sets the date selection mode on the Calendar control that specifies whether the user can select a single day, a week, or an entire month.

continues ▶

Table E.38 **Continued**

Property	Description
SelectMonthText	Gets or sets the text displayed for the month selection element in the selector column.
SelectorStyle	Gets the style properties for the week and month selector column.
SelectWeekText	Gets or sets the text displayed for the week selection element in the selector column.
ShowDayHeader	Gets or sets a value indicating whether the heading for the days of the week is displayed.
ShowGridLines	Gets or sets a value indicating whether the days on the Calendar control are separated with grid lines.
ShowNextPrevMonth	Gets or sets a value indicating whether the Calendar control displays the next and previous month's navigation elements in the title section.
ShowTitle	Gets or sets a value indicating whether the title section is displayed.
TitleFormat	Gets or sets the title format for the title section.
TitleStyle	Gets the style properties of the title heading for the Calendar control.
TodayDayStyle	Gets the style properties for today's date on the Calendar control.
TodaysDate	Gets or sets the value for today's date.
VisibleDate	Gets or sets the date that specifies the month to display on the Calendar control.
WeekendDayStyle	Returns the style properties for the weekend dates on the Calendar control.

The events for the Calendar control are shown in Table E.39.

Table E.39 **Events of the *Calendar* Control**

Event	Description
DayRender	Triggered when each day is created in the control hierarchy for the Calendar control.
SelectionChanged	Triggered when the user selects a day, a week, or an entire month by clicking the date selector controls.
VisibleMonthChanged	Triggered when the user clicks the next or previous month's navigation controls on the title heading.

F

Microsoft Mobile Internet Toolkit

IN THE FOLLOWING SECTIONS, I DETAIL the syntax of the controls in the Mobile Device toolkit. (I am showing only the most commonly used properties and methods of each class. For more information on the use of these controls, see Chapter 16, "Mobile Device Development with ASP.NET.")

To use the Mobile Device toolkit, you must have the following lines of code at the top of each page you create:

```
01 <%@ Page Inherits="System.Mobile.UI.MobilePage" Language="vb" %>
02 <%@ Register TagPrefix="mobile" Namespace="System.Mobile.UI" %>
```

The first line makes the web page being created inherit from the MobilePage class, and the second line registers a TagPrefix for the System.Mobile.UI namespace. After this has been done, you can use any of the other Mobile Device controls on the page.

The MobilePage class has an ActiveForm property that is used to set the currently displayed form on a mobile device or to retrieve the ID of a currently displayed form.

Control Groups

Mobile Device controls can be put into six main areas of functionality:

Form and layout:	`<Mobile:Form>`
	`<Mobile:Panel>`
	`<Mobile:StyleSheet>`
Presentation:	`<Mobile:Label>`
	`<Mobile:Image>`
Navigation:	`<Mobile:Link>`
	`<Mobile:Command>`
Data entry:	`<Mobile:TextBox>`
	`<Mobile:List>`
Validation controls:	`<Mobile:RequiredFieldValidator>`
	`<Mobile:RangeValidator>`
	`<Mobile:CompareValidator>`
	`<Mobile:RegularExpressionValidator>`
	`<Mobile:ValidationSummary>`
	`<Mobile:CustomValidator>`
Utility controls:	`<Mobile:Call>`
	`<Mobile:AdRotator>`
	`<Mobile:Calendar>`

Form and Layout Controls

The Form control is used to create a form to display on a mobile device, and the Layout controls (`Form`, `Panel`, and `StyleSheet`) are used to aid in the layout of controls on a mobile device.

<Mobile:Form> Control

The Form control is required for every single mobile device web page, without exception. The Form control acts as a container for other controls. You can have more than one form for a web page source file; however, only one form at a time is rendered on the mobile device. The first form definition in your source file is the initial form that is displayed on the mobile device. Table F.1 lists the properties of the Form control, and Table F.2 lists the events.

Table F.1 **Properties of the Form Control**

Property	Description
ID	ID of the control.
Alignment	Alignment of the control's subcontrols. Possible values are NotSet, Left, Center, and Right.
ForeColor	Foreground color of the control's subcontrols.
BackColor	Background color of the control's subcontrols.
FontName	Font of the control's subcontrols.
FontSize	Font size of the control's subcontrols. Possible values are NotSet, Normal, Small, and Large.
FontStyle	Font style of the control's subcontrols. Possible values are NotSet, Normal, Strong, and Emphasis.
StyleReference	Style reference ID of the control's subcontrols.
Visible	Visibility flag for the control. If true, the control and all its subcontrols are rendered to the mobile device. If false, the control and its subcontrols are not rendered to the mobile device.
Wrapping	Wrapping mode for the form. It can be any one of the following: NotSet, Wrap, NoWrap, and Preformatted.
OnActivate	Subroutine to be called when the event is fired.
OnDeactivate	Subroutine to be called when the event is fired.

Table F.2 **Events of the Form Control**

Event	Description
OnActivate	This event is fired when a form becomes active. This can happen when a page is first requested, when a form is programmatically activated by setting the ActiveForm property of the page, or when a user navigates to a new form.
OnDeactivate	This event is fired when a form gets deactivated. This can happen when a form is programmatically activated. By setting the ActiveForm property of the page, the currently active form becomes inactive and is deactivated. When a user navigates to a form, the currently active form becomes inactive and is deactivated.

<Mobile:Form> control syntax:

```
01 <Mobile:Form runat="server"
02          id="id"
03          StyleReference="StyleRef"
04          FontSize="{NotSet|Normal|Small|Large}"
05          FontName="FontName"
06          FontStyle="{NotSet|Normal|Strong|Emphasis}"
07          ForeColor="Color"
08          BackColor="Color"
09          Alignment="{NotSet|Left|Center|Right}"
10          Wrapping="{NotSet|Normal|NoWrap|Preformatted}"
11          OnActivate="OnActivateHandler"
12          OnDeactivate="OnDeactivateHandler" >
13
14 </Mobile:Form>
```

<Mobile:Panel> Control

The Panel control is used to group controls. It is normally used to ensure that certain controls are kept together on the same mobile sevice screen. The Panel control acts as a container for other controls. Table F.3 lists the properties of the Panel control.

Table F.3 **Properties of the Panel Control**

Property	Description
ID	ID of the control.
Alignment	Alignment of the control's subcontrols. Possible values are NotSet, Left, Center, and Right.
ForeColor	Foreground color of the control's subcontrols.
BackColor	Background color of the control's subcontrols.
FontName	Default font of the control's subcontrols.
FontSize	Font size of the control's subcontrols. Possible values are NotSet, Normal, Small, and Large.
FontStyle	Font style of the control's subcontrols. Possible values are NotSet, Normal, Strong, and Emphasis.
StyleReference	Style reference ID of the control's subcontrols.
Visible	Visibility flag for the control. If true, the control and all its subcontrols are rendered to the mobile device. If false, the control and its subcontrols are not rendered to the mobile device.
Wrapping	Wrapping mode for the form. It can be any one of the following: NotSet, Wrap, NoWrap, and Preformatted.

<Mobile:Panel> control syntax:

```
01 <Mobile:Panel runat="server"
02          id="id"
03          StyleReference="StyleRef"
04          FontSize="{NotSet|Normal|Small|Large}"
05          FontName="FontName"
06          FontStyle="{NotSet|Normal|Strong|Emphasis}"
07          ForeColor="Color"
08          BackColor="Color"
09          Alignment="{NotSet|Left|Center|Right}"
10          Wrapping="{NotSet|Normal|NoWrap|Preformatted"}
11
12 </Mobile:Panel>
```

<Mobile:StyleSheet> **Control**

The StyleSheet control is a container for Style controls. Table F.4 lists the properties of the StyleSheet control.

Table F.4 **Properties of the StyleSheet Control**

Property	Description
ID	ID of the control.
Alignment	Alignment of the control's subcontrols. Possible values are NotSet, Left, Center, and Right.
ForeColor	Foreground color of the control's subcontrols.
BackColor	Background color of the control's subcontrols.
FontName	Font of the control's subcontrols.
FontSize	Font size of the control's subcontrols. Possible values are NotSet, Normal, Small, and Large.
FontStyle	Font style of the control's subcontrols. Possible values are NotSet, Normal, Strong, and Emphasis.
StyleReference	Style reference ID of the control's subcontrols.
Wrapping	Wrapping mode for the applied style. It can be any one of the following: NotSet, Wrap, NoWrap, and Preformatted.

<Mobile:StyleSheet> control syntax:

```
01 <Mobile:Stylesheet runat="server">
02              id="id"
03              StyleReference="StyleRef"
04              Alignment="{NotSet|Left|Center|Right}"
05              FontSize="{NotSet|Normal|Small|Large}"
06              FontName="FontName"
```

```
07                  FontStyle="{NotSet|Normal|Strong|Emphasis}"
08                  ForeColor="Color"
09                  BackColor="Color"
10                  Wrapping="{NotSet|Normal|NoWrap|Preformatted}"
11
12 </Mobile:Stylesheet>
```

<Mobile:Style> Control

The Style control is used to define a set of style formats that can be assigned to a Mobile Device control. This control is always inside a StyleSheet container control. Table F.5 lists the properties of the Style control.

Table F.5 **Properties of the Style Control**

Property	Description
ID	ID of the control.
Alignment	Alignment of the control's subcontrols. Possible values are NotSet, Left, Center, and Right.
ForeColor	Foreground color of the control's subcontrols.
BackColor	Background color of the control's subcontrols.
FontName	Font of the control's subcontrols.
FontSize	Font size of the control's subcontrols. Possible values are NotSet, Normal, Small, and Large.
FontStyle	Font style of the control's subcontrols. Possible values are NotSet, Normal, Strong, and Emphasis.
Wrapping	Wrapping mode for the form. It can be any one of the following: NotSet, Wrap, NoWrap, and Preformatted.

<Mobile:Style> control syntax:

```
01 <Mobile:Style runat="server">
02                  id="id"
03                  StyleReference="StyleRef"
04                  Alignment="{NotSet|Left|Center|Right}"
05                  FontSize="{NotSet|Normal|Small|Large}"
06                  FontName="FontName"
07                  FontStyle="{NotSet|Normal|Strong|Emphasis}"
08                  ForeColor="Color"
09                  BackColor="Color"
10                  Wrapping="{NotSet|Normal|NoWrap|Preformatted}"
11
12 </Mobile:Stylesheet>
```

Presentation Controls

Presentation controls are used to present static content to a mobile device user.

<Mobile:Label> Control

The Label control is used to render text to the mobile device. You can enter the text to be rendered to the mobile device in three different ways:

- Use the Text property of the control.
- Assign a value to the Text property through program code.
- Put the text between the <Mobile:Label> and </Mobile:Label> element tags.

Table F.6 lists the properties of the Label control.

Table F.6 **Properties of the Label Control**

Property	Description
ID	ID of the control.
Text	Text of the label to render to the mobile device.
Alignment	Alignment of the control's subcontrols. Possible values are NotSet, Left, Center, and Right.
ForeColor	Foreground color of the control's subcontrols.
BackColor	Background color of the control's subcontrols.
FontName	Font of the control's subcontrols.
FontSize	Font size of the control's subcontrols. Possible values are NotSet, Normal, Small, and Large.
FontStyle	Font style of the control's subcontrols. Possible values are NotSet, Normal, Strong, and Emphasis.
Wrapping	Wrapping mode for the form. It can be any one of the following: NotSet, Wrap, NoWrap, and Preformatted.

<Mobile:Label> control syntax:

```
01 <Mobile:Label runat="server"
02             id="id"
03             StyleReference="StyleRef"
04             FontSize={NotSet|Normal|Small|Large}
05             FontName="FontName"
06             FontStyle={NotSet|Normal|Bold|Italic}
07             ForeColor="Color"
08             BackColor="Color"
```

```
09                Alignment="{NotSet|Left|Center|Right}"
10                Wrapping="{NotSet|Normal|NoWrap|Preformatted}"
11                Text="Text">
12
13 </Mobile:Label>
```

<Mobile:Image> Control

The Image control is used to display a bitmap image on the device display. You should use only small monochrome images for mobile device development because of bandwidth limitations and the display limitations of mobile devices. Table F.7 lists the properties of the Image control.

Table F.7 **Properties of the Image Control**

Property	Description
ID	ID of the control.
Source	The URL for the image source.
AlternateText	Alternate text to use if the image cannot be displayed.
ImageReference	References another image by its ID attribute.
Alignment	Alignment of the control's subcontrols. Possible values are NotSet, Left, Center, and Right.

<Mobile:Image> control syntax:

```
01 <Mobile:Image  runat="server"
02            id="id"
03            Source="MasterImgSource"
04            AlternateText="AltText"
05            StyleReference="StyleRef"
06            Alignment={NotSet|Left|Center|Right}
07 </Mobile:Image>
```

Navigation Controls

The Navigation controls are used by the mobile device to enable the user to access other mobile device pages of information.

<Mobile:Link> Control

The Link control is used to navigate to another form on a mobile device. You can enter the text to be displayed as the link name on the mobile device in three different ways:

- Use the Text property of the control.
- Assign a value to the Text property through program code.
- Put the text between the `<Mobile:Link>` and `</Mobile:Link>` element tags.

Table F.8 lists the properties of the Link control.

Table F.8 **Properties of the Link Control**

Property	Description
ID	ID of the control.
Text	Text of the label to render to the mobile device.
Target	URI of the form to render. If the value of the Target property begins with a (#), the value is treated as the identifier of another form on the current mobile device page.
Alignment	Alignment of the control's subcontrols. Possible values are NotSet, Left, Center, and Right.
ForeColor	Foreground color of the control's subcontrols.
BackColor	Background color of the control's subcontrols.
FontName	Font of the control's subcontrols.
FontSize	Font size of the control's subcontrols. Possible values are NotSet, Normal, Small, and Large.
FontStyle	Font style of the control's subcontrols. Possible values are NotSet, Normal, Strong, and Emphasis.
Wrapping	Wrapping mode for the form. It can be any one of the following: NotSet, Wrap, NoWrap, and Preformatted.

`<Mobile:Link>` control syntax:

```
01 <Mobile:Link runat="server"
02            id="id"
03            Target="LinkTarget"
04            StyleReference="StyleRef"
05            FontSize={NotSet|Normal|Small|Large}
06            FontName="FontName"
07            FontStyle={NotSet|Normal|Strong|Emphasis}
08            ForeColor="Color"
09            BackColor="Color"
10            Alignment={NotSet|Left|Center|Right}
11            Wrapping={NotSet|Normal|NoWrap|Preformatted}
12            Text="Text">
13
14 </Mobile:Link>
```

<Mobile:Command> Control

The Command control is used to create a command option that runs a specified subroutine when selected. You can enter the text to be displayed as the command name on the mobile device in three different ways:

- Use the Text property of the control.
- Assign a value to the Text property through program code.
- Put the text between the <Mobile:Command> and </Mobile:Command> element tags.

Table F.9 lists the properties of the Command control, and Table F.10 lists the events.

Table F.9 **Properties of the Command Control**

Property	Description
ID	ID of the control.
Text	Text of the Command control to display on the mobile device.
OnClick	URI of a new form to display on the mobile device. If the value of the Target property begins with a (#), the value is treated as the identifier of another form on the current mobile device page.
Alignment	Alignment of the control's subcontrols. Possible values are NotSet, Left, Center, and Right.
ForeColor	Foreground color of the control's subcontrols.
BackColor	Background color of the control's subcontrols.
FontName	Font of the control's subcontrols.
FontSize	Font size of the control's subcontrols. Possible values are NotSet, Normal, Small, and Large.
FontStyle	Font style of the control's subcontrols. Possible values are NotSet, Normal, Strong, and Emphasis.
Wrapping	Wrapping mode for the form. It can be any one of the following: NotSet, Wrap, NoWrap, and Preformatted.

Table F.10 **Event of the Mobile Command Control**

Event	Description
OnClick	This event is fired when a command is selected on the mobile device.

`<Mobile:Command>` control syntax:

```
01 <Mobile:Command runat="server"
02                 id="id"
03                 OnClick="EventHandler"
04                 StyleReference="StyleRef"
05                 FontSize={NotSet|Normal|Small|Large}
06                 FontName="FontName"
07                 FontStyle={NotSet|Normal|Strong|Emphasis}
08                 ForeColor="Color"
09                 BackColor="Color"
10                 Alignment={NotSet|Left|Center|Right}
11                 Wrapping={NotSet|Normal|NoWrap|Preformatted}
12                 Text="Text">
13
14 </Mobile:Command>
```

Data Entry Controls

The Data Entry controls are used to retrieve and store information from the mobile device user. Only two controls for data entry exist because of the limitations of most mobile device displays and input mechanisms.

<Mobile:TextBox> Control

The TextBox control is used to retrieve a text string from the user. The TextBox control comes in three flavors: numeric text, regular text, and password text. Password text is the same as regular text, but all data entry is masked by a (★). Table F.11 lists the properties of the TextBox control, and Table F.12 lists the events.

Table F.11 **Properties of the TextBox Control**

Property	Description
ID	ID of the control.
Text	Text of the TextBox control to display on the mobile device. It can be used to set a default value of the TextBox control.
Type	Type of data entry to perform in the TextBox control. Possible values are Text, Numeric, and Password.
Size	Size of the TextBox by the string length in characters.
OnTextChanged	Subroutine that can be called when the Text property of the control is changed.
Alignment	Alignment of the control's subcontrols. Possible values are NotSet, Left, Center, and Right.

continues ▶

Table F.11 **Continued**

Property	Description
ForeColor	Foreground color of the control's subcontrols.
BackColor	Background color of the control's subcontrols.
FontName	Font of the control's subcontrols.
FontSize	Font size of the control's subcontrols. Possible values are NotSet, Normal, Small, and Large.
FontStyle	Font style of the control's subcontrols. Possible values are NotSet, Normal, Strong, and Emphasis.
Wrapping	Wrapping mode for the form. It can be any one of the following: NotSet, Wrap, NoWrap, and Preformatted.

Table F.12 **Event of the TextBox Control**

Event	Description
OnTextChanged	This event is fired when the text of the control is changed. This event needs a Mobile Command object to be called on the page before it will work. For more information on this, see Chapter 16.

`<Mobile:TextBox>` control syntax:

```
01 <Mobile:TextBox runat="server"
02                 id="id"
03                 text="default value of control"
04                 type={text | numeric | password}
05                 size="length in characters"
06                 OnTextChange="EventHandler"
07                 StyleReference="StyleRef"
08                 FontSize={NotSet | Normal | Small | Large}
09                 FontName="FontName"
10                 FontStyle={NotSet | Normal | Strong | Emphasis}
11                 ForeColor="Color"
12                 BackColor="Color"
13                 Alignment={NotSet | Left | Center | Right}
14                 Wrapping={NotSet | Normal | NoWrap | Preformatted} >
15
16 </Mobile:TextBox>
```

<Mobile:List> **Control**

The List control is used to display a list of items on the mobile device. The List control is a container for `<Item>` elements:

```
<Item Text="Item Value" />
```

As you can see, the Item control is very simple. It has just one attribute of text, which is the label to display on the List control. Table F.13 lists the properties of the List control, and Table F.14 lists the event.

Table F.13 **Properties of the List Control**

Property	Description
ID	ID of the control.
AllowPaging	Value for paging if true internal pagination is allowed.
AllowCustomPaging	CustomPaging value. If true, paging is allowed. Otherwise, it is not.
VirtualItemCount	If the AllowCustomPaging property is set to true, this property is used to determine the total page count.
SelectionMode	Indicates whether the list should be in selection mode. Possible values are true and false.
SelectedIndex	Index of the selected item.
DataTextField	Sets property of a databound item to use when determining an item's Text property.
DataValueField	Sets property of a databound item to use when determining an item's Value property.
OnItemCommand	Event that is fired when an individual list item is selected.
OnPageIndexChanged	Event that is fired when the PageIndex changes for the list.
Alignment	Alignment of the control's subcontrols. Possible values are NotSet, Left, Center, and Right.
ForeColor	Foreground color of the control's subcontrols.
BackColor	Background color of the control's subcontrols.
FontName	Font of the control's subcontrols.
FontSize	Font size of the control's subcontrols. Possible values are NotSet, Normal, Small, and Large.
FontStyle	Font style of the control's subcontrols. Possible values are NotSet, Normal, Strong, and Emphasis.
Wrapping	Wrapping mode for the form. It can be any one of the following: NotSet, Wrap, NoWrap, and Preformatted.

Table F.14 **Event of the List ControlEvent**

Event	Description
OnTextChanged	This event is fired when the text of the control is changed. This event needs a Mobile Command object to be called on the page before it will work. For more information on this, see Chapter 16.

`<Mobile:List>` control syntax:

```
01 <Mobile:List runat="server"
02           id="id"
03           StyleReference="StyleRef"
04           FontSize={NotSet|Normal|Small|Large}
05           FontName="FontName"
06           FontStyle={NotSet|Normal|Strong|Emphasis}
07           ForeColor="Color"
08           BackColor="Color"
09           Alignment={NotSet|Left|Center|Right}
10           Wrapping={NotSet|Normal|NoWrap|Preformatted}
11           AllowPaging="{True|False}"
12           AllowCustomPaging="{True,I}"
13           VirtualItemCount="VirtualItemCount"
14           SelectionMode="{True|False}"
15           SelectedIndex="SelectedIndex"
16           DataTextField="DataTextField"
17           DataValueField="DataValueField"
18           Decoration="{None | Bulleted | Numbered}"
19           SelectType="{Dropdown | Listbox | Radio}"
20           OnItemDataBind="OnItemDataBindHandler"
21           OnItemCommand="OnItemCommandHandler"
22           OnPageIndexChanged="OnPageIndexChangedHandler" >
23
24   <item Text="Item Value" />
25   <item Text="Item Value" />
26
27 </Mobile:List>
```

Validation Controls

The Validation controls are used to test data entry fields for valid data (in the case of mobile device development, the TextBox and List controls). For more information, see Chapter 16.

<Mobile:RequiredFieldValidator> **Control**

The RequiredFieldValidator control checks to make sure that the value of another control is not a null value. Table F.15 lists the properties of the RequiredFieldValidator control.

Table F.15 **Properties of the RequiredFieldValidator Control**

Property	Description
ID	ID of the control.
Text	Text value for a control. The value of this property takes priority over the setting in the validated control.
ControlToValidate	ID of the control to validate.
Display	Display behavior of the Validator control. If true, the validation text is displayed. If false, the validation text is not displayed.
ErrorMessage	Text value that is used for an error message.
InitialValue	Value for the validator. If the values are the same, the validator assumes that the value for the required field has not been filled in, and it reports a validation error.
Alignment	Alignment of the control's subcontrols. Possible values are NotSet, Left, Center, and Right.
ForeColor	Foreground color of the control's subcontrols.
BackColor	Background color of the control's subcontrols.
FontName	Font of the control's subcontrols.
FontSize	Font size of the control's subcontrols. Possible values are NotSet, Normal, Small, and Large.
FontStyle	Font style of the control's subcontrols. Possible values are NotSet, Normal, Strong, and Emphasis.
StyleReference	Style reference ID of the control's subcontrols.
Visible	Visibility flag for the control. If true, the control and all its subcontrols are rendered to the mobile device. If false, the control and its subcontrols are not rendered to the mobile device.
Wrapping	Wrapping mode for the form. It can be any one of the following: NotSet, Wrap, NoWrap, and Preformatted.

<Mobile:RequiredFieldValidator> control syntax:

```
01 <Mobile:RequiredFieldValidator runat="server"
02                     id="id"
03                     StyleReference="StyleRef"
04                     FontSize={NotSet|Normal|Small|Large}
05                     FontName="FontName"
06                     FontStyle={NotSet|Normal|Strong|Emphasis}
07                     ForeColor="Color"
08                     BackColor="Color"
09                     Alignment={NotSet|Left|Center|Right}
10                     Wrapping={NotSet|Normal|NoWrap|Preformatted}
11                     ControlToValidate="IdOfTargetControl"
```

```
12                          Display={True|False}
13                          ErrorMessage="ErrorTextForSummary"
14                          InitialValue="initialValueInTheControl"
15                          Text="Text value of Control">
16
17 </Mobile:RequiredFieldValidator>
```

<Mobile:RangeValidator> Control

The RangeValidator control checks to make sure that the value of another control is in a specified range. Table F.16 lists the properties of the RangeValidator control.

Table F.16   **Properties of the RangeValidator Control**

Property	Description
ID	ID of the control.
Text	Text value for a control. The value of this property takes priority over the setting in the validated control.
ControlToValidate	ID of the control to validate.
Display	Display behavior of the Validator control. If true, the validation text is displayed. If false, the validation text is not displayed.
ErrorMessage	Text value that is used for an error message.
Type	Returns the data type of control to be validated. Possible values are Currency, Date, Double, Integer, and String.
MinimumValue	The value of the control you are validating must be greater than or equal to this value.
MaximumValue	The value of the control you are validating must be less than or equal to this value.
MinimumControl	The value of the control you are validating must be greater than or equal to the value of this control.
Maximum Control	The value of the control you are validating must be less than or equal to the value of this control.
Alignment	Alignment of the control's subcontrols. Possible values are NotSet, Left, Center, and Right.
ForeColor	Foreground color of the control.
BackColor	Background color of the control's subcontrols.
FontName	Font of the control's subcontrols.
FontSize	Font size of the control's subcontrols. Possible values are NotSet, Normal, Small, and Large.

Property	Description
FontStyle	Font style of the control's subcontrols. Possible values are NotSet, Normal, Strong, and Emphasis.
StyleReference	Default style reference ID of the control's subcontrols.
Visible	Visibility flag for the control. If true, the control and all its subcontrols are rendered to the mobile device. If false, the control and its subcontrols are not rendered to the mobile device.
Wrapping	Wrapping mode for the form. It can be any one of the following: NotSet, Wrap, NoWrap, and Preformatted.

<Mobile:RangeValidator> control syntax:

```
01 <Mobile:RangeValidator runat="server"
02                 id="id"
03                 StyleReference="StyleRef"
04                 FontSize={NotSet | Normal | Small | Large}
05                 FontName="FontName"
06                 FontStyle={NotSet | Normal | Strong | Emphasis}
07                 ForeColor="Color"
08                 BackColor="Color"
09                 Alignment={NotSet | Left | Center | Right}
10                 Wrapping={NotSet | Normal | NoWrap | Preformatted}
11               ControlToValidate="IdOfTargetControl"
12                 Display={True | False}
13                 ErrorMessage="ErrorTextForSummary"
14                 Type={Currency | DateTime | Double | Integer | String}
15                 MinimumValue="minValue"
16                 MaximumValue="maxValue"
17                 MinimumControl="IdOfMinimumControl"
18                 MaximumControl="IdOfMaximumControl"
19                 Text="Text value of control">
20
21 </Mobile:RangeValidator>
```

<Mobile:CompareValidator> **Control**

The CompareValidator control checks to make sure that the value of another control is the same as another value. Table F.17 lists the properties of the CompareValidator control.

Table F.17 **Properties of the CompareValidator Control**

Property	Description
ID	ID of the control.
Text	Text value for a control. The value of this property takes priority over the setting in the validated control.
ControlToValidate	ID of the control to validate.
Display	Display behavior of the Validator control. If true, the validation text is displayed. If false, the validation text is not displayed.
ErrorMessage	Text value that is used for an error message.
Type	Returns the data type of control to be validated. Possible values are Currency, Date, Double, Integer, and String.
Operator	Comparison operator to be used in validation. Possible values are DataTypeCheck, Equal, GreaterThan, GreaterThanEqual, LessThan, LessThanEqual, and NotEqual.
ValueToCompare	Value to compare against.
ControlToCompare	The control to compare against.
Alignment	Alignment of the control's subcontrols. Possible values are NotSet, Left, Center, and Right.
ForeColor	Foreground color of the control's subcontrols.
BackColor	Background color of the control's subcontrols.
FontName	Font of the control's subcontrols.
FontSize	Font size of the control's subcontrols. Possible values are NotSet, Normal, Small, and Large.
FontStyle	Font style of the control's subcontrols. Possible values are NotSet, Normal, Strong, and Emphasis.
StyleReference	Style reference ID of the control's subcontrols.
Visible	Visibility flag for the control. If true, the control and all its subcontrols are rendered to the mobile device. If false, the control and its subcontrols are not rendered to the mobile device.
Wrapping	Wrapping mode for the form. It can be any one of the following: NotSet, Wrap, NoWrap, and Preformatted.

<Mobile:CompareValidator> control syntax:

```
01 <Mobile:CompareValidator runat="server"
02                  id="id"
03                  StyleReference="StyleRef"
04                  FontSize={NotSet|Normal|Small|Large}
05                  FontName="FontName"
```

```
06                     FontStyle={NotSet|Normal|Strong|Emphasis}
07                     ForeColor="Color"
08                     BackColor="Color"
09                     Alignment={NotSet|Left|Center|Right}
10                     Wrapping={NotSet|Normal|NoWrap|Preformatted}
11                     ControlToValidate="IdOfTargetControl"
12                     Display={True|False}
13                     ErrorMessage="ErrorTextForSummary"
14                     Type={Currency|DateTime|Double|Integer|String}
15                     Operator={DataTypeCheck|Equal|GreaterThan|
16   GreaterThanEqual|LessThan|LessThanEqual| NotEqual}
17                     ValueToCompare="maxValue"
18                     ControlToCompare="IdOfMinimumControl"
19                     MaximumControl="IdOfMaximumControl"
20                     Text="Text value of control">
21
22 </Mobile:CompareValidator>
```

<Mobile:RegularExpressionValidator> Control

The RegularExpression `Validator` control checks to make sure that the control to validate value matches the passed regular text expression. Table F.18 lists the properties of the RegularExpressionValidator control.

Table F.18   **Properties of the RegularExpressionValidator Control**

Property	Description
ID	ID of the control.
Text	Text value for a control. The value of this property takes priority over the setting in the validated control.
ControlToValidate	ID of the control to validate.
Display	Display behavior of the Validator control. If `true`, the validation text is displayed. If `false`, the validation text is not displayed.
ErrorMessage	Text value that is used for an error message.
ValidationExpression	Regular expression assigned as the validation rule for the control.
Alignment	Alignment of the control's subcontrols. Possible values are `NotSet`, `Left`, `Center`, and `Right`.
ForeColor	Foreground color of the control's subcontrols.
BackColor	Background color of the control's subcontrols.
FontName	Font of the control's subcontrols.
FontSize	Font size of the control's subcontrols. Possible values are `NotSet`, `Normal`, `Small`, and `Large`.

continues ▶

Table F.18 **Continued**

Property	Description
FontStyle	Font style of the control's subcontrols. Possible values are NotSet, Normal, Strong, and Emphasis.
StyleReference	Style reference ID of the control's subcontrols.
Visible	Visibility flag for the control. If true, the control and all its subcontrols are rendered to the mobile device. If false, the control and its subcontrols are not rendered to the mobile device.
Wrapping	Wrapping mode for the form. It can be any one of the following: NotSet, Wrap, NoWrap, and Preformatted.

<Mobile:RegularExpressionValidator> control syntax:

```
01 <Mobile:RegularExpressionValidator runat="server"
02                            id="id"
03                            StyleReference="StyleRef"
04                            FontSize={NotSet | Normal | Small | Large}
05                            FontName="FontName"
06                            FontStyle={NotSet | Normal | Strong | Emphasis}
07                            ForeColor="Color"
08                            BackColor="Color"
09                            Alignment={NotSet | Left | Center | Right}
10                            Wrapping={NotSet | Normal | NoWrap | Preformatted}
11                            ControlToValidate="IdOfTargetControl"
12                            Display={True | False}
13                            ErrorMessage="ErrorTextForSummary"
14                            ValidationExpression="regexp"
15
16 </Mobile:RegularExpressionValidator>
```

<Mobile:ValidationSummary> **Control**

The ValidationSummary control displays a list of validation errors that have occurred during the rendering of a mobile device form. It is used for data entry. Table F.19 lists the properties of the ValidationSummary control.

Table F.19 **Properties of the ValidationSummary Control**

Property	Description
ID	ID of the control.
FormToValidate	ID of the form to validate.
BackLabel	Value used to create a link that is rendered on the Validation Summary page. It enables the user to return to the form after viewing validation error messages.

Property	Description
HeaderText	Header information to show at the top of the Validation Summary page.
Alignment	Alignment of the control's subcontrols. Possible values are NotSet, Left, Center, and Right.
ForeColor	Foreground color of the control's subcontrols.
BackColor	Background color of the control's subcontrols.
FontName	Font of the control's subcontrols.
FontSize	Font size of the control's subcontrols. Possible values are NotSet, Normal, Small, and Large.
FontStyle	Font style of the control's subcontrols. Possible values are NotSet, Normal, Strong, and Emphasis.
StyleReference	Style reference ID of the control's subcontrols.
Visible	Visibility flag for the control. If true, the control and all its subcontrols are rendered to the mobile device. If false, the control and its subcontrols are not rendered to the mobile device.
Wrapping	Wrapping mode for the form. It can be any one of the following: NotSet, Wrap, NoWrap, and Preformatted.

<Mobile:ValidationSummary> control syntax:

```
01 <Mobile:ValidationSummary  runat="server"
02                            id="id"
03                            StyleReference="StyleRef"
04                            fontSize={NotSet|Normal|Small|Large}
05                            fontName="FontName"
06                            fontStyle={NotSet|Normal|Strong|Emphasis}
07                            foreColor="Color"
08                            backColor="Color"
09                            alignment={NotSet|Left|Center|Right}
10                            wrapping={NotSet|Normal|NoWrap|Preformatted}
11                            formToValidate="FormID"
12                            backLabel="BackLabel"
13
14 </Mobile:ValidationSummary>
```

<Mobile:CustomValidator> Control

The CustomValidator control enables the developer to provide a custom mechanism for validating a mobile device control. Table F.20 lists the properties of the CustomValidator control.

Table F.20 **Properties of the CustomValidator Control**

Property	Description
ID	ID of the control.
ControlToValidate	ID of the control to validate.
Display	Display behavior of the Validator control. If true, the validation text is displayed. If false, the validation text is not displayed.
OnServerValidate	Subroutine used to validate contents of control. If this control returns true, the control's contents are valid; otherwise, the data is not valid.
Alignment	Alignment of the control's subcontrols. Possible values are NotSet, Left, Center, and Right.
ForeColor	Foreground color of the control's subcontrols.
BackColor	Background color of the control's subcontrols.
FontName	Font of the control's subcontrols.
FontSize	Font size of the control's subcontrols. Possible values are NotSet, Normal, Small, and Large.
FontStyle	Font style of the control's subcontrols. Possible values are NotSet, Normal, Strong, and Emphasis.
StyleReference	Style reference ID of the control's subcontrols.
Visible	Visibility flag for the control. If true, the control and all its subcontrols are rendered to the mobile device. If false, the control and its subcontrols are not rendered to the mobile device.
Wrapping	Wrapping mode for the form. It can be any one of the following: NotSet, Wrap, NoWrap, and Preformatted.

<Mobile:CustomValidator> control syntax:

```
01 <Mobile:CustomValidator  runat="server"
02                          id="id"
03                          Text="ErrorText"
04                          StyleReference="StyleRef"
05                          FontSize={NotSet|Normal|Small|Large}
06                          FontName="FontName"
07                          FontStyle={NotSet|Normal|Strong|Emphasis}
08                          ForeColor="Color"
09                          BackColor="Color"
10                          Alignment={NotSet|Left|Center|Right}
11                          Wrapping={NotSet|Normal|NoWrap|Preformatted}
12                          ControlToValidate="IdOfTargetControl"
13                          Display={True|False}
14                          ErrorMessage="ErrorTextForSummary"
15                          OnServerValidate="EventHandler" >
16
17 </Mobile:CustomValidator>
```

G

.NET Resource List

ASP.NET Web Hosting Sites

www.ORCSWEB.com

www.BRINKSTER.com

www.ERASERVER.com

ASP.NET Web Sites

http://www.123aspx.com

http://www.411asp.com

http://www.4guysfromrolla.com

http://www.AngryCoder.com

http://www.askasp-plus.com

http://www.ASP101.com

http://www.aspalliance.com

http://www.ASPNextGen.com

http://www.ASPNG.com

http://www.edgequest.com

http://www.superexpert.com

C# Web Sites

http://www.codehound.com

http://www.csharphelp.com

http://www.csharpindex.com

http://www.csharp-corner.com

http://www.csharp-station.com

http://www.learn-c-sharp.com

http://www.mastercsharp.com

Visual Basic .NET Web Sites

http://www.hultqvist.nu/vbnet/

http://www.vb-joker.com

http://www.vbwire.com

.NET Web Sites

http://www.activestate.com/Products/NET/index.html

http://www.angrycoder.com

http://www.codeproject.com/dotnet

http://www.devx.com/dotnet

http://www.dotnet101.com

http://www.dotnetbooks.com

http://www.dotnettoday.com

http://www.dotnetexperts.com

http://www.dotnetwire.com

http://www.worldofdotnet.net

XML Web Services

http://www.devxpert.com/newsletter/

http://www.salcentral.com/salnet/webserviceswsdl.asp

http://www.xmethods.net

Microsoft .NET Websites

http://www.asp.net

http://www.gotdotnet.com

http://www.msdn.Microsoft.com/net

Microsoft .NET Newsgroups

To access the newsgroups, you need to have a news group reader installed on your machine.

```
microsoft.public.dotnet.academic
microsoft.public.dotnet.framework
microsoft.public.dotnet.framework.adonet
microsoft.public.dotnet.framework.aspnet
microsoft.public.dotnet.framework.aspnet.webservices
microsoft.public.dotnet.framework.clr
microsoft.public.dotnet.framework.interop
microsoft.public.dotnet.framework.sdkmicrosoft.public.dotnet.framework.sdk
microsoft.public.dotnet.framework.sdk.setup
microsoft.public.dotnet.framework.windowsforms
microsoft.public.dotnet.general
microsoft.public.dotnet.languages.csharp
microsoft.public.dotnet.languages.jscript
microsoft.public.dotnet.languages.vb
microsoft.public.dotnet.languages.vb.upgrade
microsoft.public.dotnet.languages.vc
microsoft.public.dotnet.xml
microsoft.public.msdn.webservices
microsoft.public.vsnet.enterprise.tools
microsoft.public.vsnet.general
microsoft.public.vsnet.idemicrosoft.public.vsnet.ide
microsoft.public.vsnet.setup
microsoft.public.vsnet.vfp
microsoft.public.vsnet.visual_studio_modeler
microsoft.public.vsnet.vss
```

.NET Mailing Lists

```
http://www.discuss.develop.com/dotnet.html
http://www.dotnet@discuss.develop.com
http://www.asplists.com/asplists/aspngevery.asp
```

Magazines

.NET Magazine—Fawcette Publishing at:
```
http://www.thedotnetmag.com
```
.NET Developer—Pinnicle Publishing at:
```
http://pinnaclepublishing.com/net
```

Index

E

T

U

W

VOICES THAT MATTER

HOW TO CONTACT US

VISIT OUR WEB SITE

WWW.NEWRIDERS.COM

On our web site, you'll find information about our other books, authors, tables of contents, and book errata. You will also find information about book registration and how to purchase our books, both domestically and internationally.

EMAIL US

Contact us at: **nrfeedback@newriders.com**

- If you have comments or questions about this book
- To report errors that you have found in this book
- If you have a book proposal to submit or are interested in writing for New Riders
- If you are an expert in a computer topic or technology and are interested in being a technical editor who reviews manuscripts for technical accuracy

Contact us at: **nreducation@newriders.com**

- If you are an instructor from an educational institution who wants to preview New Riders books for classroom use. Email should include your name, title, school, department, address, phone number, office days/hours, text in use, and enrollment, along with your request for desk/examination copies and/or additional information.

Contact us at: **nrmedia@newriders.com**

- If you are a member of the media who is interested in reviewing copies of New Riders books. Send your name, mailing address, and email address, along with the name of the publication or web site you work for.

BULK PURCHASES/CORPORATE SALES

If you are interested in buying 10 or more copies of a title or want to set up an account for your company to purchase directly from the publisher at a substantial discount, contact us at 800-382-3419 or email your contact information to corpsales@pearsontechgroup.com. A sales representative will contact you with more information.

WRITE TO US

New Riders Publishing
201 W. 103rd St.
Indianapolis, IN 46290-1097

CALL/FAX US

Toll-free (800) 571-5840
If outside U.S. (317) 581-3500
Ask for New Riders
FAX: (317) 581-4663

New Riders

RELATED NEW RIDERS TITLES

Debugging ASP.NET

Jonathan Goodyear, Brian Peek, Brad Fox

This first book to cover debugging for ASP.NET will save you hundreds of hours, dollars, and headaches by providing real-world problems and their real-world coding solutions.

ISBN: 0735711410
375 pages
US$34.99

ISBN: 0735711232
485 pages
US$44.99

SQL Server DTS

Jim Samuelson, et al.

Covering both SQL Server 7 and SQL Server 2000, this book is for developers and database administrators who are faced with the common situation of having to migrate or integrate data from one location into another using DTS, which allows for quick changes to databases that feed into today's mission-critical commerce-oriented web sites.

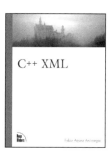

ISBN: 073571052X
330 pages with CD-ROM
US$39.99

C++ XML

Fabio Arciniegas

The demand for robust solutions is at an all-time high. Developers and programmers are asking the question, "How do I get the power performance found with C++ integrated into my web applications?" Fabio Arciniegas knows how. He has created the best way to bring C++ to the web through development with XML. In this book, he shares the secrets developers and programmers worldwide are searching for.

ISBN: 073570970X
768 pages
US$49.99

PHP Functions Essential Reference

Graeme Merrall, Landon Bradshaw, et al.

Co-authored by some of the leading developers in the PHP community, *PHP Functions Essential Reference* is guaranteed to help you write effective code that makes full use of the rich variety of functions available in PHP 4.

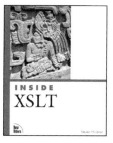

ISBN: 0735711364
640 pages
US$49.99

Inside XSLT

Steven Holzner

To work with XML fully, you need to be up to speed with XSLT and this is the book to get you there. Covering everything from creating Xpath expressions to transforming XML to HTML, *Inside XSLT* will have you heading straight down the road to programming efficiency.

ISBN: 0735710201
1100 pages
US$49.99

Inside XML

Steven Holzner

Inside XML is a foundation book that covers both the Microsoft and non-Microsoft approach to XML programming. It covers in detail the hot aspects of XML, such as, DTD's vs. XML schemas, CSS, XSL, XSLT, Xlinks, Xpointers, XHTML, RDF, CDF, parsing XML in Perl and Java, and much more.

ISBN: 0735711127
360 pages
US$44.99

XML and SQL Server 2000

John Griffin

SQL Server 2000 has added several new features that make working with XML easier for the developer. *XML and SQL Server 2000* helps SQL developers to understand and utilize these new XML capabilities.

Solutions from experts you know and trust.

www.informit.com

OPERATING SYSTEMS

WEB DEVELOPMENT

PROGRAMMING

NETWORKING

CERTIFICATION

AND MORE...

**Expert Access.
Free Content.**

New Riders has partnered with **InformIT.com** to bring technical information to your desktop. Drawing on New Riders authors and reviewers to provide additional information on topics you're interested in, **InformIT.com** has free, in-depth information you won't find anywhere else.

- **Master the skills you need, when you need them**

- **Call on resources from some of the best minds in the industry**

- **Get answers when you need them, using InformIT's comprehensive library or live experts online**

- **Go above and beyond what you find in New Riders books, extending your knowledge**

As an **InformIT** partner, **New Riders** has shared the wisdom and knowledge of our authors with you online. Visit **InformIT.com** to see what you're missing.

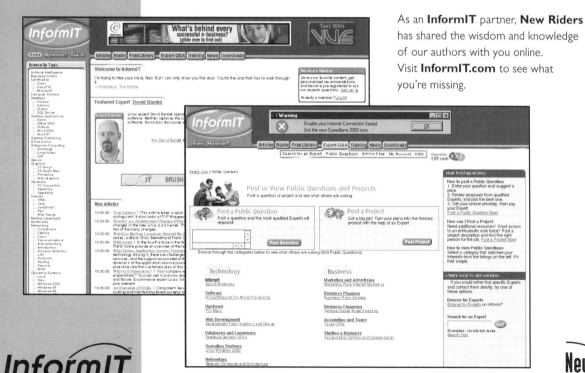

www.informit.com ▪ **www.newriders.com**

Publishing
the Voices
that Matter

| web development | graphics & design | server technology | certification |

You already know that New Riders brings you the Voices that Matter.

But what does that mean? It means that New Riders brings you the

Voices that challenge your assumptions, take your talents to the next

level, or simply help you better understand the complex technical world

we're all navigating.

Visit **www.newriders.com** to find:

▶ Never before published chapters

▶ Sample chapters and excerpts

▶ Author bios

▶ Contests

▶ Up-to-date industry event information

▶ Book reviews

▶ Special offers

▶ Info on how to join our User Group program

▶ Inspirational galleries where you can submit
  your own masterpieces

▶ Ways to have your Voice heard

WWW.NEWRIDERS.COM

Colophon

On the cover is a photograph by Adam Crowley of the Parthenon in Athens, Greece. The Parthenon, built between 454 B.C. and 447 B.C., was a symbol of power for the Athenian empire. The architects of this grand temple, Iktinos and Kallikrates, used Doric and Ionic type columns within the building's construction. Also featured on the Parthenon are metopes of battles and scenes of criminal chaos. The word Parthenon means "apartment of the virgin" and housed a gold and ivory statue of the Greek goddess Athena. Remnants of the Parthenon still remain today even though it has been shaken to its core from various wars and conquests.

This book was written and edited in Microsoft Word, and laid out in QuarkXPress. The fonts used for the body text are Bembo and MCPdigital. It was printed on 50# Husky Offset Smooth paper at R.R. Donnelley & Sons in Crawfordsville, Indiana. Prepress consisted of PostScript computer-to-plate technology (filmless process). The cover was printed at Moore Langen Printing in Terre Haute, Indiana, on 12pt, coated on one side.